The Age of Danger

The Age

MAJOR
SPEECHES
ON AMERICAN
PROBLEMS

of Danger

Edited by

Harold F. Harding

OHIO STATE UNIVERSITY

Random House
New York

Copyright, 1952, by Harold F. Harding

First Printing

All rights reserved under International and Pan-American Copyright Conventions. Published in New York by Random House, Inc., and simultaneously in Toronto, Canada, by Random House of Canada, Limited. Library of Congress Catalog Card Number: 52-5157

Designer: Ernst Reichl   Manufactured in the United States of America

Copyright Acknowledgments

"America and the Atomic Age," "Background of Korea," "The Present Crisis and the American Economy," "Stress and Disease," "National Security and Individual Freedom," Copyright, 1950, 1951, by The University of Chicago.

"What Are the Real Issues in Our Fight Against Communism?" "How Can We Stop Rising Prices?" "How Can Modern Man Find Faith?" "Is Youth Forgetting Religion?" Copyright, 1950, 1951, by The Town Hall, Inc.

"New Problems, New Philosophers," "The Stake of the Arts in the Democratic Way of Life," "The Need for a Spiritual Revival," "Religious Philosophy and Intergroup Progress" (in *Perspectives on a Troubled Decade: Science, Philosophy and Religion, 1939-49*) Copyright, 1950, by Harper & Brothers.

"Scientific Manpower," Copyright, 1951, by American Institute of Physics.

"Weighed in the Balance," Copyright, 1951, by Southern Medical Association.

Preface

WHOEVER IS learning to speak or to write needs to have ideas. He needs also to have examples from those who have achieved proficiency in these arts. *The Age of Danger* aims to give students of communication and of public affairs good materials and good models. The speeches, many of which have not been previously published, should also be of interest to the general reader.

A generation ago Professors A. M. Drummond and Everett L. Hunt of Cornell University launched a book whose purposes were similar to this one. It was called *Persistent Questions in Public Discussion* and it contained a score or more of provocative addresses and essays. They served in an admirable way the students of public speaking and English composition of that day.

The sixty-odd addresses and discussions included here are intended as subject matter for present-day students. More than a thousand speeches were considered—either by the test of reading or listening. Most of those finally selected come within the eventful years 1946-1952. In fact, the six years since Winston Churchill's famous speech at Fulton, Missouri truly comprise an Age of Danger. We can afford to turn back and read what our leaders have been telling us in these years. We need to consider their ideas for our future courses of action. As speakers we can profitably study their persuasive methods for our own improvement.

Timeliness and content rather than literary merit or form have been most frequently the bases for selection. Many of the speeches, however, possess both sets of virtues. And again, a number of the speakers are proof—and this will be painful for teachers to admit—that success often comes to those who disobey the commonly accepted and traditional principles of rhetorical theory. In spite of rules and textbooks and teachers the speeches accomplish the chief end of nearly all speechmaking, the changing of belief.

Indeed, there are selections in this volume which call to mind an observation of Samuel Johnson, recorded by Boswell in his *Journal* for 28 July 1763: "He said that human experience which was constantly contradicting theory, was the great test of truth. He stated that the experience built upon the discoveries of a great many minds was always of greater weight than the mere workings of one mind, which can do little of itself." And so it may also hold that the discoveries of many speakers

Preface

and the orderly bringing together of their speeches are more valuable than the composition of any one person—especially on so wide a range of topics as in this collection.

The task of trying to reproduce in one book *all* the significant addresses in these discursive years is impossible. Doubtless many excellent speeches that deserve to be recognized have been omitted. From a practical point of view, however, a good deal more is included than can adequately be covered in an introductory course. The instructor and the student are therefore free to choose those parts which provide the most appeal. Nevertheless, by spreading assignments it should be possible to discuss and to prepare speeches on most of the eighteen sections.

The speeches nearly all fall within the realm of public affairs. It is evident that the majority are of a persuasive or argumentative nature. But the methods of exposition, description, and narration are illustrated throughout. And so are those special devices of oral presentation—attention-getting and interest-developing, along with others easily recognizable to students.

Except in a few cases the entire text as spoken has been printed. The opportunity is therefore present to analyze the whole speech and thus to criticize fairly and in detail the speaker and his ideas.

Resourceful readers will find additional uses for the speeches of *The Age of Danger*. Besides serving as specimens, as suggesting subjects for classroom speeches, as grist for class discussion, evaluation, and criticism —they can also be the starters and guides for further reading and research. With good leadership a genuine interest in some of the vital problems of our day should result. To assist the process a set of questions, lists of possible topics for development, and ways for stimulating discussion have been included.

To the many persons who have aided in this undertaking the editor expresses his appreciation and gratitude. The names of those who have furnished suggestions are included under Acknowledgments. I extend my special thanks to Mrs. Vera Sayre, secretary in the Department of Speech, Ohio State University, and to my library assistant, Mrs. Virginia Palmer, for their unfailing help in bringing order out of chaos. For errors in judgment and editorial slips I alone am responsible. Letters calling mistakes to attention and giving recommendations for increasing the usefulness of the book will be most welcome.

Harold F. Harding

Columbus, Ohio
April 1952

Acknowledgments

I AM HAPPY to acknowledge below the generous assistance of the several score of persons—college and university professors, editors, directors of public affairs programs, and others, who have contributed valuable suggestions to the making of this book. In fact, they have sent in far more good ideas than could be incorporated in one volume. The copyright holders of the addresses used in *The Age of Danger* are listed separately. To all these kind helpers the editor and the publishers express their grateful appreciation.

Academic titles and departments have been generally omitted:
Carroll C. Arnold, Cornell University
Barnet Baskerville, University of Washington
Batsell Barrett Baxter, David Lipscomb College
William A. Behl, Brooklyn College
W. Norwood Brigance, Wabash College
Lyman Bryson, Teachers College, Columbia University
E. C. Buehler, University of Kansas
Dean John Ely Burchard, Massachusetts Institute of Technology
J. Calvin Callaghan, Syracuse University
Robert R. Carson, Hamilton College
Burr Chase, President, Silver Burdett Company
Giraud Chester, Queens College
H. P. Constans, University of Florida
Allen B. Crow, President, The Economic Club of Detroit
Thomas F. Daly, Jr., President, *Vital Speeches*
President Carter Davidson, Union College
George V. Denny, Jr., Moderator, America's Town Meeting of the Air
G. E. Densmore, University of Michigan
Wallace W. Douglas, Northwestern University
A. M. Drummond, Cornell University
J. Garber Drushal, College of Wooster
Ray Ehrensberger, University of Maryland
Thorrel B. Fest, University of Colorado
John C. Gerber, State University of Iowa
Dorothy Gordon, Moderator, Youth Forums, *The New York Times*
Willis H. Griffin, Teachers College, Columbia University

Acknowledgments

Warren Guthrie, Western Reserve University
Frederick W. Haberman, University of Wisconsin
A. Mason Harlow, McGraw-Hill Book Company
M. C. Harrison, Virginia Polytechnic Institute
Hugo E. Hellman, Marquette University
Benjamin B. Hickok, Michigan State College
Howard T. Hill, Kansas State College
W. Samuel Howell, Princeton University
Raymond F. Howes, American Council on Education
Robert B. Huber, University of Vermont
Dean Everett L. Hunt, Swarthmore College
Catherine D. Johnson, Editor, The University of Chicago Round Table
T. Earle Johnson, University of Alabama
Ray E. Keesey, University of Delaware
John F. Kouwenhoven, Barnard College, Columbia University
Magdalene Kramer, Teachers College, Columbia University
Lou LaBrant, New York University
Colonel G. A. Lincoln, United States Military Academy
Edward Linnehan, University of Pennsylvania
President David A. Lockmiller, University of Chattanooga
Gerald E. Marsh, University of California
Robert E. Mathews, College of Law, Ohio State University
J. E. Michael, Kenyon College
Edd Miller, University of Michigan
Alice W. Mills, Mount Holyoke College
Alan H. Monroe, Purdue University
Richard Murphy, University of Illinois
Helen Newman, Librarian, United States Supreme Court
David C. Phillips, University of Connecticut
Thomas Clark Pollock, New York University
Robert C. Pooley, University of Wisconsin
David Potter, Michigan State College
Benfield Pressey, Dartmouth College
Brooks Quimby, Bates College
Helen Rogers Reid and Whitelaw Reid, *New York Herald Tribune*
Edgar E. Robinson, Stanford University
Noel Sargent, National Association of Manufacturers
Joseph F. Smith, University of Hawaii
Raymond G. Smith, Indiana University
Paul L. Soper, University of Tennessee

Acknowledgments

Robert E. Spiller, University of Pennsylvania
Colonel George R. Stephens, United States Military Academy
Ordway Tead, Editor, Harper and Brothers
William E. Utterback, Ohio State University
Tracy S. Voorhees, Vice-Chairman, Committee on the Present Danger
The late Russell H. Wagner, University of Virginia
Harold Weiss, Southern Methodist University
Kenneth D. Wells, President, Freedoms Foundation, Inc.
Eugene E. White, University of Miami
Herbert A. Wichelns, Cornell University
Francis O. Wilcox, Chief of Staff, Foreign Relations Committee, U. S. Senate
Arleigh B. Williamson, New York University
James A. Winans, Ithaca, New York
Colonel Robert J. Wood, Secretary, Supreme Headquarters Allied Powers Europe
Ernest J. Wrage, Northwestern University
George S. Wykoff, Purdue University
George B. Zehmer, Director, Institute of Public Affairs, University of Virginia

For coöperation in supplying texts and in granting permission to reprint, further acknowledgment is made to the following:

To The University of Chicago Round Table and the National Broadcasting Company, for "America and the Atomic Age," "Background of Korea," "The Present Crisis and the American Economy," "Stress and Disease," and "National Security and Individual Freedom."

To America's Town Meeting of the Air and the American Broadcasting Company, for "What Are the Real Issues Against Communism?" "How Can We Stop Rising Prices?" "How Can Modern Man Find Faith?" and "Is Youth Forgetting Religion?"

To The Chicago Council on Foreign Relations, for "Peace Without Appeasement," by Frederick L. Schuman.

To the *Illinois Law Review,* for "The National Interest of the United States," by George Kennan.

To the Technology Press of the Massachusetts Institute of Technology and to John Wiley & Sons, Inc., for "The State of Science," by Karl T. Compton and "The Twentieth Century—Its Promise and Its Realization," by Winston Churchill; published in *Mid-Century,* ed. John E. Burchard, 1950.

To the *Journal of Higher Education,* for "The Citizen's Stake in Aca-

Acknowledgments

demic Freedom," by Quincy Wright; Vol. XX, No. 7, October 1949, pp. 339-345.

To Harper & Brothers, for four papers published in *Perspectives on a Troubled Decade; Science, Philosophy and Religion, 1939-49*, Lyman Bryson, Louis Finkelstein, R. M. MacIver, editors, New York, 1950.

To *Vital Speeches* for "The Defense of the Free World," by Vannevar Bush; "Peace in the Atomic Era," by Albert Einstein; "Let Us Make Peace," by John Foster Dulles; "The Integration of Europe," by Konrad Adenauer; "The Present Danger," by James B. Conant; "Where Do We Go from Here in Education," by Robert M. Hutchins; "Man Thinking," by Alfred W. Griswold; "The Goals of Education Are Not Sufficient Today," by Millicent C. McIntosh; and "The Challenge of Our Time," by Dwight D. Eisenhower.

To the *Christian Science Monitor*, for "The Fulcrum of Western Civilization," by Arnold Toynbee and for "The Authentic Revolution," by Erwin D. Canham; the *New York Herald Tribune*, for "Mobilizing America's Strength for World Security," by W. Averell Harriman, "Mobilizing and Training a Citizen Army," by Mark W. Clark, "Mobilizing for Defense," by Charles E. Wilson; the National Association of Manufacturers, for "What Road to Labor Peace," by John L. McCaffrey; the Economic Club of Detroit, for "How Communists Make Converts," by Benjamin Gitlow, "The United States, Russia, and the Atomic Bomb," by Frederick Osborn, "Where Do We Go from Here in Education," by Robert M. Hutchins, and "Organized Labor and Current International Developments," by Matthew Woll; the Associated Press, for "Address to the Congress," by Douglas MacArthur; and the *New York Times* and the Associated Press together for "An Interview with a *Pravda* Correspondent" by Joseph Stalin and "A Report from the President of France," by Vincent Auriol.

Finally, grateful acknowledgment is made to the authors of the speeches in this volume, each of whom has readily given permission to reprint here.

Contents

Preface   v

Acknowledgments   vii

Prelude

1. The Twentieth Century—
   Its Promise and Its Realization   3   Winston S. Churchill

Part One   The World Outlook in the Atomic Age

2. Selections from *America and the Atomic Age*, University of Chicago Round Table Discussions   19   Robert M. Hutchins, Reuben Gustavson, William F. Ogburn, and Robert Redfield
3. Peace Without Appeasement   40   Frederick L. Schuman
4. The Defense of the Free World   54   Vannevar Bush
5. Peace in the Atomic Era   58   Albert Einstein
6. The Road to Peace   61   Trygve Lie

Part Two   The United States and Foreign Affairs

General

7. The Fulcrum of Western Civilization   77   Arnold Toynbee
8. The National Interest of the United States   80   George F. Kennan
9. Tensions Between the United States and the Soviet Union   85   Dean Acheson
10. The State of the Union (1952)   95   Harry S. Truman

The War in Korea

11. Background of Korea   109   John M. Chang, Edward Ackerman, Niles Bond, and Arthur C. Bunce
12. The Frank and Candid Light   118   Ben C. Limb

Contents

13.	An Address to the Security Council of the United Nations	126	Wu Hsiu-Chuan
14.	On Assuming Command of the Eighth Army	138	Matthew B. Ridgway
15.	Preventing a New World War	140	Harry S. Truman
16.	Address to the Congress	146	Douglas MacArthur

The Far East

17.	United States Policy Toward Asia	154	Dean Acheson
18.	Chinese-American Friendship	165	Dean Rusk
19.	A World in Revolution	169	William O. Douglas
20.	Let Us Make Peace	175	John Foster Dulles

Russia and Communism

21.	An Interview with a Pravda Correspondent	191	Joseph Stalin Louis Fischer,
22.	What Are the Real Issues in Our Fight Against Communism?	196	Harold H. Velde
23.	How Communists Make Converts	202	Benjamin Gitlow
24.	The United States, Russia, and the Atomic Bomb	211	Frederick Osborn

The Defense of Europe

25.	A Report to the Nation	220	Dwight D. Eisenhower
26.	A Statement before the Senate Armed Services Committee and the Senate Foreign Relations Committee	225	George C. Marshall
27.	A Report from the President of France	230	Vincent Auriol
28.	The Integration of Europe	237	Konrad Adenauer

Part Three The United States and Home Affairs

Problems of Mobilization and Manpower

29.	Mobilizing America's Strength for World Security	245	W. Averell Harriman
30.	The Moral Core of Military Strength	249	Charles T. Lanham
31.	The Present Danger	256	James B. Conant
32.	Mobilizing and Training a Citizen Army	265	Mark W. Clark

Contents

Control of Production

33. The Present Crisis and the American Economy — 271 — Roy Blough, Robert A. Taft, and Richard Weil, Jr.
34. Mobilizing for Defense — 281 — Charles E. Wilson
35. How Can We Stop Rising Prices? — 285 — Michael V. DiSalle, Walter P. Reuther, and Herschel D. Newsom

Science and Research

36. The State of Science — 294 — Karl T. Compton
37. Science, Technology, and National Security — 312 — Louis N. Ridenour
38. Scientific Manpower — 317 — Henry D. Smyth
39. Nuclear Energy Development and Military Technology — 321 — Alvin M. Weinberg

Health and Medicine

40. Stress and Disease — 328 — Jerome Conn, Albert Dorfman, and Hans Selye
41. An American Medical Association Presidential Inaugural Address — 337 — Elmer L. Henderson
42. Weighed in the Balance — 343 — Hamilton W. McKay
43. What Health Insurance Would Mean to You — 350 — Oscar R. Ewing
44. Prepayment Plans — 355 — Paul R. Hawley

Education

45. Where Do We Go from Here in Education? — 359 — Robert M. Hutchins
46. The Citizen's Stake in Academic Freedom — 369 — Quincy Wright
47. Man Thinking — 376 — A. Whitney Griswold
48. The Goals of Education Are Not Sufficient Today — 382 — Millicent C. McIntosh
49. A High School Commencement Address — 386 — E. J. Thomas

Philosophy, Literature, and the Arts

50. New Problems, New Philosophers — 391 — Harry A. Overstreet
51. On Accepting the Nobel Award — 397 — William Faulkner

Contents

52. The Stake of the Arts in the Democratic Way of Life ... 398 ... Walter Pach

Labor and Industry
53. Organized Labor and Current International Developments ... 410 ... Matthew Woll
54. Labor's Role in Higher Education ... 419 ... Philip Murray
55. What Road to Labor Peace? ... 423 ... John L. McCaffrey
56. Business, Government, and Education ... 429 ... Paul G. Hoffman

Civil Rights and Liberties
57. The Rough Road Ahead ... 437 ... Roger N. Baldwin
58. National Security and Individual Freedom ... 440 ... Francis Biddle, Robert Carr, Adlai Stevenson, and Harold Urey

Racial Problems
59. The International Significance of Human Relations ... 452 ... Ralph Bunche
60. The Ideals of American Youth ... 462 ... Harold Taylor
61. Segregation in the Armed Forces ... 469 ... William L. Dawson

Religion
62. Time is Running Out ... 472 ... Edward D. Gates
63. How Can Modern Man Find Faith? ... 480 ... Fulton Oursler, Austin Pardue, and Irwin Edman
64. Is Youth Forgetting Religion? ... 489 ... James Harry Price, Paul Weaver
65. The Need for a Spiritual Revival ... 495 ... Swami Nikhilananda
66. Religious Philosophy and Intergroup Progress ... 506 ... John LaFarge

Postlude
67. The Authentic Revolution ... 517 ... Erwin D. Canham
68. The Challenge of Our Time ... 529 ... Dwight D. Eisenhower

Appendix
Questions and Topics for Discussions ... 535
Methods for Stimulating Discussion ... 556

Index ... 559

The Age of Danger

Prelude

The Twentieth Century—
Its Promise and Its Realization
Winston S. Churchill

This address was delivered before a distinguished audience of nearly fifteen thousand persons in the Boston Garden on 31 March 1949. The occasion was the Massachusetts Institute of Technology Mid-Century Convocation on the Social Implications of Scientific Progress. Mr. Churchill was the principal speaker. He was as eagerly anticipated here as when he spoke at Westminster College, Fulton, Missouri on 5 March 1946. Then, it will be recalled, he proclaimed: "From Stettin in the Baltic to Trieste in the Adriatic, an iron curtain has descended across a continent. Behind that line lie all the capitals of the ancient states of Central and Eastern Europe. . . . The Communist parties, which were very small in these Eastern States of Europe, have been raised to preëminence and power far beyond their numbers and are seeking everywhere to obtain totalitarian control. . . . Whatever conclusions may be drawn from these facts—and facts they are—this is certainly not the liberated Europe which we fought to build up. Nor is it one which contains the essentials of permanent peace."

In the speech below Mr. Churchill reëxamines the effects of Communism in the light of his experiences as a first citizen during the first half of the twentieth century.

Mr. Bernard M. Baruch, adviser to Presidents and elder American statesman, introduced the speaker in brief but fitting remarks and concluded by saying: "Through the thirty years I have known him, in his darkest moments, although always mindful of his country's welfare, I have never known him to make an ignoble proposal. I present the greatest living Englishman, the finest flowering of the leadership and statesmanship that England ever produced, the Right Honorable Winston Churchill."

The text here reproduced admirably serves to introduce a collection of addresses and discussions presented mainly during the post-World War II period. The speaker recognizes the scientific advances of the first half of the twentieth century and analyzes the tensions confronting the world at the opening of the decade 1950-60.

For a scholarly description of the setting of the speech and the reaction in leading newspapers the reader is referred to the detailed footnotes (pp. 50-74) and Appendix C (pp. 470-76) of the book, *Mid-Century, The Social Implications of Scientific Progress,* edited by John Ely Burchard (1950).

On 26 October 1951 Mr. Churchill, the head of the Conservative party which won the British general election, was asked by King George VI to resume his duties as British Prime Minister and to form a new government.

I AM honored by your wish that I should take part in the discussions of the Massachusetts Institute of Technology. We have suffered in Great Britain by the lack of colleges of university rank in which engineering and the allied subjects are taught. Industrial production depends on technology and it is because the Americans, like the prewar Germans, have realized this and created institutions for the advanced training of large numbers of high-grade engineers to translate the advantages of pure science into industrial technique, it is for that reason that their output per head and consequent standard of life are so high. It is surprising that England, which was the first country to be industrialized, has nothing of comparable stature. If tonight I strike other notes than those of material progress, it implies no want of admiration for all the work you have done and are doing. My aim, like yours, is to be guided by balance and proportion.

The outstanding feature of the twentieth century has been the enormous expansion in the numbers who are given the opportunity to share in the larger and more varied life which in previous periods was reserved for the few and for the very few. This process must continue at an increasing rate. If we are to bring the broad masses of the people in every land to the table of abundance, it can only be by the tireless improvement of all our means of technical production, and by the diffusion in every form of education of an improved quality to scores of millions of men and women. Even in this darkling hour I have faith that this process will go on.

I rejoice in Tennyson's celebrated lines:

Men, my brothers, men the workers, ever reaping something new;
That which they have done but earnest of the things that they shall do.

I was, however, a little disquieted, I must admit, that you found it necessary to debate the question, to quote Dr. Burchard's opening address, "of whether the problem of world production yielding at least a minimum living to the whole population can be solved, and whether man has so destroyed the resources of his world that he may be doomed to die of starvation." If, with all the resources of modern science, we find ourselves unable to avert world famine, we shall all be to blame, but a peculiar responsibility would rest upon the scientists. I do not believe they will fail, but if they do, or perhaps were not allowed to succeed, the consequences would be very unpleasant because it is quite certain that mankind would not agree to starve equally, and there might be some very sharp disagreements about how the last crust was to be shared. As our greatest intellectual authorities here will readily admit, that would simplify our problem in an unduly primordial manner.

Ladies and gentlemen, I frankly confess that I feel somewhat overawed in addressing this vast scientific and learned audience on the subjects which your panels are discussing. I have no technical and no university education, and have just had to pick up a few things as I went along. Therefore I speak with a diffidence, which I hope to overcome as I proceed, on these profound scientific, social, and philosophic issues, each of which claims a lifelong study for itself, and are now to be examined, as schoolmen would say, not only in their integrity but in their relationship, meaning thereby not only one by one but all together.

I was so glad that in the first instance you asked me to talk about the past rather than to peer into the future, because I know more about the past than I do about the future, and I was well content that the President of the United States, whose gift of prophecy was so remarkably vindicated by recent electoral results, should have accepted that task. We all regret that his heavy state duties prevent him from being here tonight. I shall therefore have to try to do a little of the peering myself.

Ladies and gentlemen, for us in Britain the nineteenth century ended amid the glories of the Victorian era, and we entered upon the dawn of the twentieth in high hope for our country, our empire and the world. The latter and larger part of the nineteenth century had been the period of liberal advance (liberal with a small "l"). In 1900 a sense of moving hopefully forward to brighter, broader, and easier days was predominant. Little did we guess that what has been called the Century of the Common Man would witness as its outstanding feature more common men killing each other with greater facilities than any other five centuries put together in the history of the world. But we entered this terrible twentieth century with confidence. We thought that with improving transportation nations would get to know each other better. We believed that as they got to know each other better they would like each other more, and that national rivalries would fade in a growing international consciousness. We took it almost for granted that science would confer continual boons and blessings upon us, would give us better meals, better garments, and better dwellings for less trouble, and thus steadily shorten the hours of labor and leave more time for play and culture. In the name of ordered but unceasing progress, we saluted the Age of Democracy, democracy expressing itself ever more widely through parliaments freely and fairly elected on a broad or universal franchise. We saw no reason then why men and women should not shape their own home life and careers without being cramped by the growing complexity of the state, which was to be their servant and the protector of their rights. You had the famous American maxim, "Governments derive their just powers from the consent of the governed," and we both noticed that the world was divided into peoples that owned the governments and governments that owned the peoples. At least I heard all this around that time and liked some of it very much.

I was a Minister in the British Liberal government (with a large "L" please this time), returned by a great majority in 1906. That new Liberal government arrived in power with much of its message already delivered and most of its aims already achieved. The days of hereditary aristocratic privilege were ended or numbered. The path was opened for talent in every field of endeavor. Primary education was compulsory, universal, and free, or was about to become so. New problems arising, as problems do, from former successes, awaited the new administration. The independence of the proletariat from thralldom involved at least a minimum standard of life and labor and security for old age, sickness, and the death of the family breadwinner. It was to these tasks of social reform and social insurance that we addressed ourselves. Ladies and gentlemen, the name of Lloyd George will ever be associated in Great Britain with this new departure. I am proud to have been his lieutenant in this work and also later as a Conservative Chancellor of the Exchequer and later still as head of the wartime National Coalition, to have carried these same themes forward on a magnified scale. That is how we began the century.

Science presently placed novel and dangerous facilities in the hands of the most powerful countries. Humanity was informed that it could make machines that would fly through the air and vessels which could swim beneath the surface of the seas. The conquest of the air and the perfection of the art of flying fulfilled the dream which for thousands of years had glittered in human imagination. Certainly it was a marvelous and romantic event. Whether the bestowal of this gift upon an immature civilization composed of competing nations whose nationalism grew with every advance of democracy and who were as yet devoid of international organization, whether this gift was a blessing or a curse has yet to be proved. On the whole I remain an optimist. For good or for ill, air mastery is today the supreme expression of military power, and fleets and armies, however vital and important, must accept a subordinate rank. This is a memorable milestone in the march of man.

The submarine, to do it justice, has never made any claim to be a blessing or even a convenience. Now, I well remember when it became an accomplished fact of peculiar military significance to the British Isles and to the British Navy, there was a general belief even in the Admiralty where I presided that no nation would ever be so wicked as to use these underwater vessels to sink merchantmen at sea. How could a submarine, it was asked, provide for the safety of the crews of the merchant ships it sunk? And public opinion was shocked when old Admiral Fisher bluntly declared that this would be no bar to the submarines being used by the new and growing German Navy in a most ruthless manner. His prediction was certainly not stultified by what was soon to happen.

Here then we have these two novel and potent weapons placed in the hands of highly nationalized sovereign states in the early part of the twentieth century, and both of them dwell with us today for our future edification.

A third unmeasured sphere opened to us as the years passed, which for the sake of comprehensive brevity I will describe as radar. This radar, with its innumerable variants and possibilities, has so far been the handmaiden of the air, but it has also been the enemy of the submarine and in alliance with the air may well prove its exterminator. Thus we see the changes which were brought upon our society.

In the first half of the twentieth century, fanned by the crimson wings of war, the conquest of the air affected profoundly human affairs. It made the globe seem much bigger to the mind and much smaller to the body. The human biped was able to travel about far more quickly. This greatly reduced the size of his estate, while at the same time creating an even keener sense of its exploitable value. In the nineteenth century Jules Verne wrote *Around the World in Eighty Days*. It seemed a prodigy. Now you can get around it in four; but you do not see much of it on your way. The whole prospect and outlook of mankind grew immeasurably larger, and the multiplication of ideas also proceeded at an incredible rate. This vast expansion was unhappily not accompanied by any noticeable advance in the stature of man, either in his mental faculties, or his moral character. His brain got no better, but it buzzed the more. The scale of events around him assumed gigantic proportions while he remained about the same size.

By comparison therefore he actually became much smaller. We no longer had great men directing manageable affairs. Our need was to discipline an array of gigantic and turbulent facts. To this task we have certainly so far proved unequal. Science bestowed immense new powers on man and at the same time created conditions which were largely beyond his comprehension and still more beyond his control. While he nursed the illusion of growing mastery and exulted in his new trappings, he became the sport and presently the victim of tides and currents, of whirlpools and tornadoes amid which he was far more helpless than he had been for a long time.

Hopeful developments in many directions were proceeding in 1914 on both sides of the Atlantic and they seemed to point to an Age of Peace and Plenty, when suddenly violent events broke in upon them. For more than twenty years there had been no major war in Europe. Indeed, since the Civil War in the United States, there had been no great struggle in the West. A spirit of adventure stirred the minds of men and was by no means allayed by the general advance of prosperity and science. On the contrary, prosperity meant power, and science offered weapons. We read in the Bible, I hope you still read the Bible, ". . . Jeshurun waxed fat, and kicked." For several generations Britannia had ruled the waves—for long periods at less cost annually than that of a single modern battleship.

History, I think, ladies and gentlemen, history will say that this great trust was not abused. American testimony about the early period of the Monroe Doctrine is upon record. There was the suppression of the slave trade and piracy. During our prolonged naval supremacy, undeterred by the rise of foreign tariffs, we kept our ports freely open to the commerce of the world. Our colonial and oriental empire, even our coastal trade, was free to the shipping of all the nations on equal terms. We in no way sought to obstruct the rise of other states or navies. For nearly the whole of the nineteenth century the monopoly of sea power in British hands was a trust discharged faithfully in the general interest. But in the first decade of the twentieth century, with new patterns of warships, naval rivalries became acute and fierce. Civilized governments began to think in dreadnoughts. It was in such a setting very difficult to prevent the First World War, far more difficult than it would have been to have prevented the Second.

There was, of course, one way to prevent it—one way then *as now*—the creation of an international instrument, strong enough to adjust the disputes of nations and enforce its decisions against an aggressor. Much wisdom, eloquence, and earnest effort was devoted to this theme in which the United States took the lead, but we only got as far as the World Court at the Hague and improvements in the Geneva Convention. The impulses towards a trial of strength in Europe were far stronger at this time. Germany, demanding her "place in the sun," was faced by a resolute France with her military honor to regain. England, in accordance with her foreign policy of three hundred years, sustained the weaker side. France found an ally in the Russia of the Czars, and Germany in the crumbling Empire of the Hapsburgs. The United States, for reasons which were natural and traditional, but no longer so valid as in the past, stood aloof and expected to be able to watch as a spectator the thrilling, fearful drama unfold from across what was then called "the broad Atlantic." These expectations, as perhaps you may remember, were not wholly borne out by what happened.

After four years of hideous mechanical slaughter, illuminated by infinite sacrifice, but not remarkably relieved by strategy or generalship, the victorious allies assembled at Versailles. High hopes and spacious opportunities awaited them. War, stripped of every pretension of glamour or romance, had been brought home to the masses of the peoples and brought home in forms never before experienced except by the defeated. To stop another war was the supreme object and duty of the statesmen who met as friends and allies around the peace table. They made great errors. The doctrine of self-determination was not the remedy for Europe, which needed then above all things, unity and larger groupings. The idea that the vanquished could pay the expenses of the victors was a destructive and crazy delusion. The failure to strangle Bolshevism at its birth and to bring Russia, then prostrate, by one means or another into the general democratic system lies heavy upon us today. Nevertheless, the statesmen at Versailles, largely at the inspiration of President Wilson, an inspiration implemented effectively by British thought, created the League of Nations. This is their defense before history, and had the League been resolutely sustained and used, it would have saved us all.

This was not to be. Another ordeal even more appalling than the first lay before us. Even when so much else had failed we could have obtained a prolonged peace, lasting all our lives at least, simply by keeping Germany disarmed in accordance with the Treaty and by treating her with justice and magnanimity. This latter condition was very nearly achieved at Locarno in 1925, but the failure to enforce the disarmament clauses and above all to sustain the League of Nations, both of which purposes could easily have been accomplished, brought upon us the Second World War. Once again the English-speaking world gloriously but narrowly emerged, bleeding and breathless, but united as we never were before. This unity is our present salvation, because after all our victories we are now faced by perils, both grave and near, and by problems more dire than have ever confronted Christian civilization, even in this twentieth century of storm and change.

There remains, however, a key of deliverance. It is the same key which was searched for by those who labored to set up the World Court at the Hague in the early years of the century. It is the same conception which animated President Wilson and his colleagues at Versailles, namely the creation of a world instrument capable at least of giving to all its members security against aggression. The United Nations Organization which has been created under the inspiring leadership of my great wartime friend, President Roosevelt, that organization which took the place of the former League, has so far been rent and distracted by the antagonism of Soviet Russia and by the fundamental schism which has opened between Communism and the rest of mankind. But we must not despair. We must persevere, and if the gulf continues to widen, we must make sure that the cause of freedom is defended by all the resources of combined forethought and superior science. Here lies the best hope of averting a third world struggle, and a sure means of coming through it without being enslaved or destroyed.

One of the questions which you are debating here is defined as "the failure of social and political institutions to keep pace with material and technical change." Scientists should never underrate the deep-seated qualities of human nature and how, repressed in one direction, they will certainly break out in another. The *genus homo*—if I may display my Latin, I have some—not much—the *genus homo* is a tough creature who has traveled here by a very long road. His nature has been shaped and his virtues ingrained by many millions of years of struggle, fear, and pain, and his spirit has, from the earliest dawn of history, shown itself upon occasion capable of mounting to the sublime, far above material conditions or mortal terrors. He still remains, man still remains as Pope described him two hundred years ago:

> *Placed on this isthmus of a middle state,*
> *A being darkly wise, and rudely great . . .*
> *Created half to rise and half to fall,*
> *Great lord of all things, yet a prey to all;*
> *Sole judge of truth, in endless error hurled,*
> *The glory, jest, and riddle of the world.*

In his introductory address, Dr. Burchard, the Dean of Humanities, spoke with awe of "an approaching scientific ability to control men's thoughts with precision." I shall be very content, personally, if my task in this world is done before that happens. Laws just or unjust may govern men's actions. Tyrannies may restrain or regulate their words. The machinery of propaganda may pack their minds with falsehood and deny them truth for many generations of time. But the soul of man thus held in a trance or frozen in a long night can be awakened by a spark coming from God knows where, and in a moment the whole structure of lies and oppression is on trial for its life. Peoples in bondage need never despair. Let them hope and trust in the genius of mankind. Science, no doubt, if sufficiently perverted, could exterminate us all, but it is not in the power of material forces, at present or in any period which the youngest here tonight need take into practical account, to alter permanently the main elements in human nature and restrict the infinite variety of forms in which the soul and genius of the human race can and will express itself.

How right you are, Dr. Compton, in this great institution of technical study and achievement, to keep a Dean of Humanities and give him so commanding a part to play in your discussions! No technical knowledge can outweigh knowledge of the humanities in the gaining of which philosophy and history walk hand in hand. Our inheritance of well-founded slowly conceived codes of honor, morals and manners, the passionate convictions which so many hundreds of millions share together of the principles of freedom and justice, are far more precious to us than anything which scientific discoveries could bestow. Those whose minds are attracted or compelled to rigid and symmetrical systems of government should remember that logic, like science, must be the servant and not the master of man. Human beings and human societies are not structures that are built or machines that are forged. They are plants that grow and must be tended as such. Life is a test and this world a place of trial. Always the problems, or it may be the same problem, will be presented to every generation in different forms. The problems of victory may even be more baffling than those of defeat. However much the conditions change, the supreme question is how we live and grow and bloom and die, and how far each human life conforms to standards which are not wholly related to space or time.

And here I speak not only to those who enjoy the blessings and consolation of revealed religion, but also to those who face the mysteries of human destiny alone. I say that the flame of Christian ethics is still our highest guide. To guard and cherish it is our first interest, both spiritually and materially. The fulfillment of spiritual duty in our daily life is vital to our survival. Only by bringing it into perfect application can we hope to solve for ourselves the problems of this world, and not of this world alone. I, ladies and gentlemen, I cannot speak to you here tonight without expressing to the United States—as I have perhaps some right to do—the thanks of Britain and of Europe for the splendid part America is playing in the world. Many nations have risen to the summit of human affairs, but here is a great example where new-won supremacy has not been used for self-aggrandizement but only for further sacrifice.

Three years ago I made a speech at Fulton, Missouri under the auspices of President Truman. Many people here and in my own country were startled and even shocked by what I said. But events have vindicated and fulfilled in much detail the warnings which I deemed it my duty to give at that time.

Today there is a very different climate of opinion. I am in cordial accord with much that is being done. We have, as dominating facts, the famous Marshall Aid, the new unity in Western Europe, and now the Atlantic Pact. How has this tremendous change in our outlook and policy been accomplished? Let us inquire into that. The responsible Ministers in all the countries concerned deserve high credit. There is credit enough for all. In my own country the Foreign Secretary, Mr. Bevin, who has come here tonight to sign the Atlantic Pact, has shown himself, like many American public men, above mere partisan interest in dealing with these national and world issues. No one could, however, have brought about these immense changes in the feeling of the United States, of Great Britain, and of Europe but for the astounding policy of the Russian Soviet government. We may well ask, "Why have they deliberately acted for three long years so as to unite the free world against them?" It is certainly not because there are not some very able men among them. Why have they done it? I will offer you my own answer to this strange conundrum. It is because they fear the friendship of the West more than its hostility. They cannot, they cannot afford to allow free and friendly intercourse to grow up between the vast areas they control and the civilization of the West. The Russian people must not see what is going on outside, and the world must not see what goes on inside the Soviet domain. Thirteen men in the Kremlin, holding down hundreds of millions of people and aiming at the rule of the world, feel that at all costs they must keep up the barriers. Self-preservation, not for Russia but for themselves, lies at the root and is the explanation of their sinister and malignant policy.

In consequence of the Soviet conduct the relations of Communist Russia with the other great powers of the world are without precedent in history. Measures and counter-measures have been taken on many occasions which in any previous period could only have meant or accompanied armed conflict. The situation has been well described by distinguished Americans as the "cold war." And the question is asked, "Are we winning the cold war?" Well, this cannot be decided by looking at Europe alone. We must also look at Asia. The worst disaster since our victory has been the collapse of China under the Communist attack and intrigue. China, in which the United States have always taken a high interest, comprises an immense part of the population of the world. The absorption of China and of India into the Kremlin-controlled Communist Empire would certainly bring measureless bloodshed and misery to eight or nine hundred million people.

On the other hand, the position in Europe has so far been successfully maintained. The prodigious effort of the Berlin Airlift has carried us through the winter. Time, though dearly bought, has been gained for peace. The efficiency of the American and British Air Forces has been proved and improved. Most of all the spectacle of the British and Americans trying to feed the two million Germans in Berlin, in their zone in Berlin, while the Soviet government was trying to starve them out, has been an object lesson to the German people far beyond anything that words could convey. I trust that small and needless provocations of German sentiment may be avoided by the Western Powers. The revival and union of Europe cannot be achieved without the earnest and freely given aid of the German people.

This has certainly been promoted by the Berlin Airlift which has fully justified itself. Nevertheless, ladies and gentlemen, fear and its shadows brood over Western Europe today. A month ago in Brussels I spoke to a meeting of thirty thousand Belgians. I could feel at once their friendship and their anxiety. They have no Atlantic Ocean, no English Channel, between them and the Russian Communist armored divisions. Yet they bravely and ardently support the cause of United Europe. I admired them. I was also conscious of the hope and faith which they, like the Greek people, place in the United States. I could see the movement of this vast crowd when I spoke of the hand, the strong hand stretched out across the ocean by the great republic. You have great responsibilities there for much faith is placed upon you.

We are now confronted with something quite as wicked but in some ways more formidable than Hitler, because Hitler had only the Herrenvolk pride and anti-Semitic hatred to exploit. He had no fundamental theme. But these thirteen men in the Kremlin have their hierarchy and a church of Communist adepts, whose missionaries are in every country as a fifth column, obscure people but awaiting the day when they hope to be the absolute masters of their fellow-countrymen and pay off old scores. They have their anti-God religion and their Communist doctrine of the entire subjugation of the individual to the state. And behind this stands the largest army in the world, in the hands of a government pursuing imperialist expansion as no Czar or Kaiser had ever done.

I must not conceal from you tonight the truth as I see it. It is certain that Europe would have been communized, like Czechoslovakia, and London under bombardment some time ago but for the deterrent of the atomic bomb in the hands of the United States.

Another question is also asked. Is time on our side? This, ladies and gentlemen, is not a question that can be answered except within strict limits. We have certainly not an unlimited period of time before a settlement should be achieved. The utmost vigilance should be practiced, but I do not think myself that violent or precipitate action should be taken now. War is not inevitable. The Germans have a wise saying, "The trees do not grow up to the sky." Often something happens to turn or mitigate the course of events. Four or five hundred years ago Europe seemed about to be conquered by the Mongols. Two great battles were fought almost on the same day near Vienna and in Poland. In both of these the chivalry and armed power of Europe was completely shattered by the Asiatic hordes of mounted archers. It seemed that nothing could avert the doom of the famous continent from which modern civilization and culture have spread throughout the world. But at the critical moment something happened, the Great Khan died. The succession was vacant and the Mongol armies and their leaders trooped back on their ponies across the seven thousand miles which separated them from their capital in order to choose a successor. They never returned till now.

We need not abandon hope or patience. Many favorable processes are on foot. Under the impact of Communism all the free nations are being welded together as they never have been before and never could be, but for the harsh external pressure to which they are being subjected. We have no hostility to the Russian people and no desire to deny them their legitimate rights and security. I hoped that Russia, after the war, would have access, through unfrozen waters, into every ocean, guaranteed by the world organization of which she would be a leading member; I hoped that she would have the freest access, which indeed she has at the present time, to raw materials of every kind; and that the Russians everywhere would be received as brothers in the human family. That still remains our aim and our ideal. We seek nothing from Russia but goodwill and fair play. If, however, there is to be a war of nerves let us make sure that our nerves are strong and are fortified by the deepest convictions of our hearts. If we persevere steadfastly together, and allow no appeasement of tyranny and wrongdoing in any form, it may not be our nerve or the structure of our civilization which will break; something else will break and peace may yet be preserved.

This is a hard experience in the life of the world. After our great victory, which we believed would decide the struggle for freedom for our time at least, we thought we had deserved better of fortune. But unities and associations are being established by many nations throughout the free world with a speed and reality which would not have been achieved perhaps for generations. Of all these unities the one most precious to me is, to use an expression I first used at Harvard six years ago, the one most precious to me is the fraternal association between the British Commonwealth of Nations and the United States. Do not, my friends, I beg of you, underrate the enduring strength of Britain. As I said at Fulton, "Do not suppose that half a century from now you will not see seventy or eighty millions of Britons spread about the world and united in defense of our traditions, our way of life, and the world causes which you and we espouse." United we stand secure.

Let us then move forward together in discharge of our mission and our duty, fearing God and nothing else.

Part One
The World Outlook in the
Atomic Age

America and the Atomic Age
Robert M. Hutchins, Reuben Gustavson, William F. Ogburn, and Robert Redfield

These discussions were broadcast over the University of Chicago Round Table program during the period 1944-49. They have been brought together in shorter form in the pamphlet entitled *America and the Atomic Age;* the text below is a selection from the pamphlet.

Dr. Robert M. Hutchins, now Associate Director of the Ford Foundation, is the principal speaker. The others are Dr. Reuben Gustavson, atomic physicist and chancellor of the University of Nebraska, Dr. William F. Ogburn, professor of sociology, University of Chicago, and Dr. Robert Redfield, professor of anthropology, University of Chicago.

During his twenty-one years as president and chancellor at Chicago Dr. Hutchins, in the words of the editors of *Life,* "turned the university upside down." He abolished intercollegiate football, instituted the Great Books program, launched the atomic research program under the direction of Enrico Fermi, and assembled one of the most distinguished faculties in the United States or in the world.

The profound questions which atomic fission has raised are brilliantly discussed in the dialogues that follow. They are further developed in the selected addresses from the succeeding speakers included in this section.

The Crisis of Our Time

Broadcast December 24, 1944

MR. HUTCHINS: A theologian, a philosopher, and a scientist have shown that the crisis of our time is a moral crisis. They have shown that, unless we can surmount this crisis, such civilization as we have will fall apart, for civilization is a moral fabric. They have shown that the defeat of our enemies in this war, though it may be an indispensable means to the preservation of our civilization, in no sense guarantees its preservation. Peace without good will cannot be durable, because it cannot be just. And technology is not a substitute for justice. Our machines seem, in fact, on the point of wiping us off the face of the earth.

They are, moreover, so expensive that we cannot afford to let them stand idle. We must fight for the oil to feed them. We must die that our machines may live. So a distinguished educator said before Pearl Harbor that we should have to go to war with Japan to get rubber for our tires.

The speakers who have preceded me on this program have emphasized that the underlying problem is one of ends, goals, and ideals. With the tremendous resources which science has placed in our hands we should be able to reach almost any conceivable human goal. But if we have the wrong ideals, or if we fail to live up to good ones, the great scientific accomplishments of modern man will end in suicide.

The testimony of the educator is the same as that of the theologian, the philosopher, and the scientist. The educational system of a country is a reflection of what the country thinks it wants. What is honored in a country will be cultivated there. If we look at the educational system of the United States, we get the same impression we got from the speeches in the last campaign—what the American people want is not peace and good will, but peace and a good job. The ideal of the full dinner pail and a chicken in every pot and two cars in every garage has been attenuated to the mere possession of a job, any kind of job that will sustain life. It is not surprising, therefore, that although it has never been possible to obtain federal appropriations for education for citizenship, a representative of the United States Office of Education has lately advocated a federal appropriation of three hundred million dollars for vocational training. It is not surprising that every suggestion affecting our youth is considered in terms of the labor market. It has been proposed in high quarters that men ought to be kept in the army if jobs cannot be found for them after the war. One of the current arguments for universal military training is that it would give at least a million young men a year something to do.

Now certainly there is no use talking about the aims of life to those who are starving to death. Mass unemployment is a menace to any society. But are we to work merely to exist? Is a job a good thing just because it is a job, no matter how trivial and degrading the occupation? Jobs are means, not ends; and our problem is: What are we working for and what are we living for? If the answer is that we are living merely to live, the whole process loses its meaning. We are in search of values, and there are no values here.

In so far as we have a definite goal, then, it appears to be a goal of success interpreted in material terms. Though material goods are goods, there are other goods beyond them; for, in the order of goods, material goods do not stand high. The passionate pursuit of material goods disrupts human relations—as when a prominent labor leader was asked whether, now that China was our ally, we should not repeal the Chinese Exclusion Act, and he replied, "A Chinaman is still a Chinaman."

The passionate pursuit of material goods disrupts the common good, for our government is now the sport of pressure groups—each seeking its material advantage. The passionate pursuit of material goods impairs the hope of world organization and necessarily substitutes security for good will. For each country, even if it does not want territory for itself, must grab territory in order to keep other nations from grabbing it.

America is the strongest and richest nation on earth. Since we are not under the material pressure to which other nations are subject, since we are not in danger of starvation or invasion, we have no excuse for failing to offer the world what it needs most—moral leadership and a moral example. For the sake of suffering humanity everywhere the people of this country must rediscover the ends of human life and of organized society; they must base their own lives and their own society upon these foundations. As Santayana said of the United States long ago: "This soil is propitious to every seed, and tares must needs grow in it. But why should it not also breed clear thinking, honest judgment, and rational happiness? These things are indeed not necessary to existence, and without them America might long remain rich and populous, like many a barbarous land in the past. But in that case its existence will be hounded, like theirs, by falsity and remorse. May Heaven avert the omen, and make the new world a better world than the old."

There is a slight trace of selfishness in Santayana's prayer. Let us change it to read, "May the new world help to make the whole world new."

Atomic Force: Its Meaning for Mankind

Broadcast August 12, 1945 (five days after Hiroshima)

MR. HUTCHINS: Gentlemen, is the atomic bomb good or bad for the world?

MR. GUSTAVSON: On the day that the first atomic bomb was dropped, I met the director of the university laboratory which helped to develop it. His first words to me were: "This is a very sad day for us. Let us hope that we've not placed dynamite in the hands of children."

MR. HUTCHINS: Was it wise to use this bomb against Japan?

MR. OGBURN: By ending the war, it saved more lives than were lost at Hiroshima.

MR. HUTCHINS: Was the war not going to end anyway?

MR. OGBURN: But when? The Japanese minister to Sweden has said that the atomic bomb brought the plea for peace. We cannot have peace or progress without paying the costs, as Charles Darwin showed.

MR. HUTCHINS: This is the kind of weapon, I believe, which should be used, if at all, only as a last resort in self-defense. At the time that this bomb was dropped the American authorities knew that Russia was going to enter the war. It was said that Japan was blockaded and that its cities were burned out. All the evidence points to the fact that the use of this bomb was unnecessary. Therefore, the United States has lost its moral prestige.

MR. GUSTAVSON: At the very least we might have used another method. We might have demonstrated the effectiveness of the bomb by calling our shot in advance and by giving the Japanese an opportunity to watch us drop a bomb on an uninhabited part of Japan and then calling upon Japan to surrender.

MR. HUTCHINS: Perhaps the future is more important than the past. Ogburn, as a social forecaster, what seems most important to you about the atomic bomb?

MR. OGBURN: This may well be one of the most important inventions of all time. The explosive energy in the atomic bomb, in my opinion, undoubtedly brightens the prospect for abolishing war, but if, in addition, atomic energy is harnessed, we will usher in the "Atomic Age" and may produce sweeping changes comparable to those of the Industrial Revolution, which was brought in by steam. The Industrial Revolution, we all know, created our cities, made nations bigger, shifted world power, weakened the family, revolutionized agriculture, built an enormous industry, and led to the creation of powerful central government—more powerful than the world had ever known.

MR. HUTCHINS: Gustavson, you are a scientist. What do you say?

MR. GUSTAVSON: I would say that the bomb teaches us the value of fundamental research. The work done by Professor Fermi and others on the effect of the neutron on the uranium atom was research carried on out of curiosity and for the general purpose of increasing human understanding. There was no specific purpose of producing atomic energy—certainly no intention of producing world-shattering bombs. The basic work was an attempt to find out about the universe in which we live. To me that is the important lesson; and that is the way all really important discoveries are made.

MR. HUTCHINS: My own conviction is that the moral burden which this discovery places upon the peoples of the earth and the necessity of a world organization to control this force are most important. Let us take up in order the social and industrial consequences, the implications for research, and the impact of this discovery upon war, peace, and world organization.

MR. OGBURN: Let us first see what we are talking about. If we are talking about the explosive capacities of uranium—which is the only thing that is known definitely and publicly now—that is one thing; if we are talking about harnessing power from uranium and regulating its flow through machines—which is something I have not yet heard whether we can do—then the social consequences, of course, will be much greater; but if we are talking about releasing atomic energy not from uranium alone but from other and more abundant materials— such as, for instance, clay or water—and of this I am skeptical as well as uninformed—then, in my judgment, no human imagination can encompass the consequences.

MR. GUSTAVSON: This is the most important discovery that has been made since the discovery of fire. It is more important than all the inventions since the Industrial Revolution combined. This discovery is the answer to the dream of the alchemist. We are dealing here with the transmutation of elements, the destruction of matter, and the liberation of tremendous quantities of energy—energy the intensity of which defies description. For example, when dynamite explodes, there is an intensity represented by about four volts. We are now talking about something of the order of two hundred million volts.

MR. OGBURN: This is very impressive, but inventions are nearly always overpromised. Ninety-five per cent of them never materialize at all. Take, for instance, the singing wire or the talking book, which were invented in the 1890's. They have not been put to public use yet. Or take another invention—that of gas warfare—which put fear in our hearts and which was certainly overpromised twenty-five years ago at the end of the First World War. It has never materialized up to its promises. My calculations show that it takes, on the average, about thirty-five years for an invention to materialize, and sometimes it takes two or three hundred years or longer. All inventions of the past which I have studied have been resisted. Let us look at the example of prefabricated housing, for instance. We could have had it fifty years ago, but instead it has been resisted by the building trades, certain real estate interests, and, of course, the mortgage companies. They do not want it.

MR. GUSTAVSON: It seems to me that the trend today, however, is away from resistance and toward too-ready acceptance of new things. As a people, we are credulous and volatile rather than skeptical and slow to change. Take vitamins and nylon, for example.

MR. OGBURN: We must not allow ourselves to begin talking like Jules Verne.

MR. HUTCHINS: Maybe this time Jules is justified.

MR. OGBURN: If Jules Verne were sitting around the Round Table this morning, he would be using the atomic bomb for organizing a war on Mars.

But there are many, many forces which slow up change. Civilization is merely a complicated mass of interrelationships, like a huge piece of machinery. We cannot change one part without changing many parts. To bring in a regulated atomic power means, for instance, changing railroads, electric-power systems, banks, factories, and many other types of social organizations. All this takes time. We do not get inventions adopted overnight.

MR. GUSTAVSON: We may not get inventions adopted overnight, but we do know certain things about this discovery. We do know that we get out of it incredible heat, incredible power, incredible radioactivity, and new elements.

MR. OGBURN: But there is a third factor, it seems to me, which slows up the use of inventions. An invention will not be used if it costs too much. President Truman told us that atomic energy cannot compete, in terms of costs, with coal or electricity at this stage. The first two atomic bombs cost, it is reported, one billion dollars apiece. One cannot pick up a piece of U-235 as cheaply as one can pick up a piece of coal and put it in the furnace. The question still is whether it will be brought down cheap enough, and this we certainly do not know yet.

MR. HUTCHINS: Then let us assume that we have a fundamental discovery, but that it is in a very early stage. What are the social consequences, Ogburn, that you as a social scientist can reasonably foresee, even at this stage?

MR. OGBURN: I have been trying to argue that we need not get a case of the jitters and that inventions, though they disturb our sense of security, have a way of developing slowly. They develop against social inertia and in the face of resistances arising from the complicated nature of our society, and they come with the handicap of high costs. But to answer your question. If we cannot abolish war, we can pretty well count on a considerable effect on the layout of our cities and on city planning. The cities have already been dispersed by the automobile and more recently by the bomber. If explosives of this kind can reach them, our cities will be further dispersed and spread outward. Thus, this is a tendency which is already underway.

MR. GUSTAVSON: Can we look forward to more leisure?

MR. OGBURN: Any great new use of energy has the potentialities of reducing and, I may say, even abolishing physical toil. We might, if we look forward into the future, even have factories without any laborers in them at all; but, of course, this will all come slowly.

MR. GUSTAVSON: Could we not have technological unemployment on a scale of which we have never dreamed?

MR. OGBURN: We could, if the inventions came quickly enough, but most inventions produce technological unemployment only temporarily. Unemployment, in the main, is really caused by the business cycle, fluctuations, and by population changes. I have calculated, for instance, that during the depressions of the 1930's only 15 per cent of it was technological.

MR. GUSTAVSON: Remember, this is a fundamental discovery of very fundamental character. It could affect our whole industrial civilization.

MR. HUTCHINS: What about the effect on the standard of living?

MR. OGBURN: It will make the atomic age an age of abundance. I am particularly excited, though, about the possibilities for transportation, which I have been studying recently. If atomic energy could be put in a rocket—and that does not seem to be very difficult—and if these rockets could be kept cool and slowed near their destination, it would be perfectly possible, I think, to travel three thousand miles an hour. This would mean that we could leave New York one day and arrive in China the day before.

MR. HUTCHINS: Who is talking like Jules Verne now?

MR. GUSTAVSON: Let us not forget that the bomb is the end product of a series of discoveries. In all probability the liberation of atomic power, in a fashion that can be controlled for industry, will likely be much simpler than the making of the bomb.

MR. HUTCHINS: I am interested in the suggestion that this discovery will favor the big industries—at least in its present stage where we have relatively rare materials and a relatively expensive process. How do you gentlemen feel about public versus private control of this material and this process?

MR. OGBURN: Let me give some illustrations on this point. Most of our power inventions which we have now have developed big industries of the public utility type—electricity, railroads, aviation. These are certainly not the industries for small businesses. I suspect that the development of atomic energy will be in this class. It will tend to strengthen the big industries. It is very likely, by the way, to speed us further on the "road to serfdom," as the term is now used. It will tend to reinforce movements toward monopoly and toward cartels if, of course, we do not do something about it. But if it can be used in very small packages, then it may, of course, not accentuate this tendency. Most probably, however, it will put tremendous power in the hands of large industrial units. That brings us to the question of what we are going to do about it.

MR. GUSTAVSON: It seems to me that it will go about the way the development of power in general has gone. We have seen the government step into the power problem to control the great water resources for the development of electrical power. We are increasingly coming to the conclusion, I believe, that anything so fundamental to our economic structure as electricity, or power in general, has to be something that is government controlled. The government would logically have a lot to say about the development and distribution of atomic power.

MR. OGBURN: I agree. Military reasons, of course, are added to the economic reasons in this case.

MR. HUTCHINS: You both thus feel that on the military side there is no question but that the government will have to continue in control of this process and the materials used in it. But if large industries are the only ones which are in a position to develop the process or exploit the material at the present time, then we shall have to have governmental regulation of those industries.

What are the implications of this discovery for medicine and for health and for biology?

MR. GUSTAVSON: They are tremendous, of course. The radioactivity associated with all this work has great possibilities for good and for harm—industrial hazards, for example, in the new industries—the exposure of workingmen to dangers which we never suspected before. We are going to use these radioactive materials, too, in the study of disease processes. We are going to use them in attempting to follow the fundamental researches in biology. The implications for public health, as I said, probably cannot be overstated.

MR. HUTCHINS: You think that we may have as great a revolution in medical treatment and in biological investigation as we can see ahead of us in the physical sciences and in technology, is that correct?

MR. GUSTAVSON: There is no question about it!

Peace and the Atom Bomb

Broadcast November 11, 1945

MR. HUTCHINS: This Armistice Day the world is blessed with peace, except in China, Java, Palestine, and a few other places. We are also blessed with the atomic bomb. This is a good time to ask whether America, which gave the world the atomic bomb, has a foreign policy which makes for peace.

It seems to me that the American people now realize that the United States, for the first time, is vulnerable from every quarter of the globe. Americans are striking out in all directions under the impact of the discovery of atomic energy, striving, first of all, for what they think is national security.

MR. REDFIELD: I agree that this is a new and a terrible fear and that we are acting under the influence of that fear. Many of the actions which we are taking are therefore unreasonable actions. It is not surprising, I believe, that we turn first to the new military strength which has just won us victory. But we hide behind it blindly. The question for us to consider here is whether this military strength is really the protection which we like to think it is.

MR. GUSTAVSON: In addition, we are also reorganizing our whole domestic life in the light of this fear which has come over us. We are now talking about putting scientific research in atomic energy in the United States under the cloak of secrecy. This will hamper and delay the developments in the field of biology, in the field of medicine, and in the field of atomic power for industry. The end result of this policy is that we deny ourselves the very things which will make future wars less likely.

MR. HUTCHINS: In short, the official policy of the United States is a policy of force. We find it manifested in all kinds of different ways, in almost everything that comes out of Washington. We hear that we are going to keep the so-called "secret" of the atomic bomb; that we are going to have the largest navy in the world. At the moment when we are the most powerful nation on earth, we are going to introduce the innovation of universal military training. We are going to put atomic energy under a dictatorship. We are going to get island bases to protect us. We are going to have the largest espionage service in the world.

MR. GUSTAVSON: Even when we go about fostering science through a proposed National Research Foundation, we do it in the name of military strength.

MR. HUTCHINS: One of the most distressing aspects of this policy is the air of moral superiority with which we state it. Mr. Truman hints that we are entitled to world domination because we are devoted to the Ten Commandments and the Golden Rule. But it is a little difficult to see how dropping atomic bombs, without warning, upon the men, women, and children of Hiroshima and Nagasaki could have been suggested to us by either the Ten Commandments or the Golden Rule.

But perhaps we have not time to discuss our alleged moral superiority. Let us ask, instead, whether the policy of force which our government is following makes sense.

MR. REDFIELD: It must make only one kind of sense to people in other countries. To them it must seem that we are preparing to dominate the world by force. The policy would at least be one which could be carried out if America were, in fact, determined to dominate the world, but I do not believe that one hundred and thirty million Americans are. So the first thing to be said about the government policy is that it is confused. It threatens while we do not really mean the threat.

MR. GUSTAVSON: Our policy is complete confusion. Let us take, for example, the policy of keeping the secret of the atomic bomb. Every scientist who has said anything about this problem has said that in terms of fundamental principles there is no secret; that our secrets (such as they are) consist in industrial "know-how." We should remember that Germany, even though she was bombed almost continuously, made great progress toward the liberation of atomic energy. This simply means that any country which is capable of making a great industrial effort can have atomic bombs, just as any country which wants automobiles can have them.

MR. HUTCHINS: In addition to England and Canada, scientists at least in France and Denmark are familiar with this whole development.

MR. GUSTAVSON: That is true. We simply have to contemplate a world in which every nation which is capable of making the effort can have atomic bombs in five years; and there are a number of them—some are small, and some are large—who are capable of making that effort.

MR. HUTCHINS: But do I not understand Einstein to say that this atomic bomb is not a very serious weapon after all?

MR. GUSTAVSON: Yes, when asked if all the people would be killed in the next atomic-power war, he said, "No, only two-thirds of them," if that is any consolation.

MR. REDFIELD: In other words as a friend of mine put it, there is nothing to worry about. We have nothing to lose but our lives and our property.

J. R. Oppenheimer, an atom-bomb scientist, who should know something about this, was a little more conservative. He gave his opinion that forty million Americans might be killed in one night.

MR. HUTCHINS: What you gentlemen are saying, I take it, is that the atomic bomb is a new threat to civilization—a threat which will be fatal unless something is done to control it. You are also saying that our effort to control it by preserving the secret is absurd. That policy will fail.

MR. REDFIELD: The evidence of confusion in this policy is also present in other matters. I do not think that the question as to armament, in terms of the ordinary army and navy, has been frankly faced in terms of the atom bomb.

MR. GUSTAVSON: If we are to have a large army, we should know what we are to do with it—if we destroy the cities of our enemy or if the enemy destroys our cities.

MR. REDFIELD: The Secretary of War said last week that universal military training is needed so that trained men will be available to restore public utilities after our cities have been atom-bombed. Perhaps the army will teach them to connect the sewers and the electric-light wires. The Japanese certainly had universal military training, but did they connect the plumbing after Hiroshima? They did not; they gave up. Moreover, I ask, what is to support the army after all the cities have been destroyed?

MR. GUSTAVSON: In spite of all which has been written, the American people still fail to realize the tremendous power, even at its present state of development, in one atomic bomb, to say nothing of what the future might bring.

For comparison, let us look at the Fifth and Eighth Air Forces. They dropped a million tons of bombs on Europe during the war, and we have some faint notion of the terrible destruction which was accomplished. One atomic bomb is equivalent to twenty thousand tons of TNT, which to carry requires five freight trains of eighty cars each. Fifty atomic bombs carried by fifty planes could carry the equivalent of all the TNT bombs dropped on Europe. Obviously, if this is the case, for what do we want a large navy?

MR. REDFIELD: Similar difficulty can be found with the suggestion that naval bases must be maintained and defended. As General Arnold tells us, these bombs can today be carried by nonstop airplanes to any part of the world. We know that even if some of the planes were intercepted, enough are sure to get through to destroy the industrial base of an enemy or of ourselves. Why, then, do you need naval bases? What kind of a navy do you need if one can destroy an enemy's industrial foundations in a few hours from one's own home country?

MR. HUTCHINS: What kind of air force do we need if we are going to fire atomic bombs by rockets, or if we are going to send agents into potential enemy countries who will plant bombs which will be detonated when war is decided upon?

MR. GUSTAVSON: The answer which the professional military people make is that we must have a large army to occupy a defeated country.

MR. HUTCHINS: Yes, we may need a relatively small army of occupation if we insist upon occupying a defeated country after its cities have been devastated. In order to get this small army of occupation to the defeated country, we may need an air force and a navy, not for combat but for transport. But this means a much smaller number of ships and airplanes and an entirely different kind of ship and airplane than is being proposed.

But this policy of force, which is exemplified by a policy of secrecy in regard to the atomic bomb, is not merely confused, is it, gentlemen? It is dangerous, also, because if we claim to have a secret when there is no secret and if we keep telling the people that we are going to protect them by keeping a secret that does not exist, then we lull them into a false sense of security.

MR. REDFIELD: The pretense that we are protected, then, works us a double injury. In the first place, relying upon a protection which is really not a protection in the long run, we fail to take the steps to build international confidence which might save us. In the second place, it greatly enhances the fear and suspicion which are directed against us, and so brings war nearer.

MR. GUSTAVSON: That is very obvious in the recent attitude which Russia has expressed in her failure to attend conferences and in her maintaining an attitude of almost complete silence on the whole problem of the military bomb.

The Russians, for example, recently celebrated the two hundred and twentieth anniversary of the founding of the Russian Academy of Science. As a part of that celebration, they invited scientists from all over the world to join them, including the outstanding scientists in America. Pressure was brought to bear upon our scientists to prevent them from attending, presumably for fear that they might give up some of our so-called secrets. In other words, we have gotten to the place where we do not even trust our own people. We seem headed in the same general direction as Germany was headed when she tried to build a Nazi science. We are trying to build a highly nationalistic American science.

MR. REDFIELD: When scientists want to talk things over with other scientists, they are not traitors. Scientists have to be internationalists, for no nation can go it alone in science and not lag behind in scientific progress.

MR. GUSTAVSON: Let us put ourselves wholeheartedly to the task of feeding the world; to clothing the world; to housing it. Let us pool our resources against disease. We have the know-how; let us go to work. Let us get our mind off the military problem and put it back on the fundamental problem of making a decent world.

MR. HUTCHINS: But all the discussions in the American Congress about atomic energy have been conducted on the assumption that what we are dealing with here is a weapon.

MR. GUSTAVSON: It is interesting, of course, to contrast the attitude of our own government, as reflected in our press, with what we can read in papers such as the *London Times*. In England, industrialists are gathering a fund of something like a half a billion dollars—that is a fourth of the money we spent on the atomic bomb—for the investigation of the peacetime uses of atomic energy. In our own country there has been practically no discussion along that line. In fact, all our legislation is headed in the direction of using this entirely as a military weapon.

MR. HUTCHINS: Take the May-Johnson Bill, for example. The May-Johnson Bill attempts to control all atomic research. It maintains that secrecy is necessary in order that the research may succeed. This can be true only if one is thinking in military terms. The bill places the administration of atomic research in the hands of an independent, practically irresponsible agency, exercising a kind of control which can be justified (if it can be justified at all) only on military grounds. In fact, there is reason to believe that the bill contemplates placing a military officer in charge of atomic research in this country.

MR. REDFIELD: Again in contrast with our own obsession with the control of the discovery for warfare is the tenor of Molotov's speech made last week. You will remember that he promised the Russians an early development of atomic energy in their own country. But all his emphasis was upon the development of that energy in the building-up of the country.

On the other hand, in our own country, the army has tried to hurry through Congress a strait jacket for scientific research—the May-Johnson Bill, which Hutchins just mentioned. If the bill should pass, the development of atomic energy for peaceful purposes will be hampered. Indeed, under such a law, research for military purposes would be hampered.

MR. GUSTAVSON: As I recall it, Molotov scarcely referred to the military use of atomic energy in Russia. It is the United States which seems to be beginning an armament race in atomic armaments. History suggests that any armament race ends in very serious consequences; and an atomic-bomb armament race, as we have learned from the statements of Einstein and Oppenheimer, is something too frightening to contemplate.

MR. HUTCHINS: If we go into an atomic-bomb armament race, can we hope to win it?

MR. REDFIELD: I say that this is a kind of race which nobody can really win. Such an arms race would end in an explosion which would be catastrophe. A victory would mean only that more Americans would be left than citizens of the enemy country. This is a race toward just one goal—world suicide.

MR. HUTCHINS: Suppose that Mr. Truman suddenly decides to reveal the so-called "secrets" of the atomic bomb to all the nations of the world. What kind of policy have we then?

MR. REDFIELD: We have considerable improvement, but essentially we still have the same policy, have we not? We have a policy which emphasizes military domination by our country. If everybody had bombs, nevertheless, the various measures which you have listed, Hutchins, would add up to the same desperate and ultimately suicidal armaments race.

MR. HUTCHINS: In this discussion it becomes clear that the policy of the United States is based on force. It is a policy which will seem to other countries a policy directed toward world domination. The policy is confused, contradictory, and incoherent. It is a bad means to a bad end. The general tendency of the policy, moreover, is to increase enormously the difficulty of developing confidence among peoples; to exaggerate the tensions leading to war; and to create a world which must live in perpetual fear.

MR. GUSTAVSON: In other words, here we are with all the technical skills to produce all the food we need; all the clothing we need; and, what is more wonderful, new tools which grow out of atomic-energy research for fighting disease; all the necessary skills for housing the world. Yet we are chained to the psychology of war.

MR. HUTCHINS: We take the substance of the people and devote it to a fruitless armament race.

MR. REDFIELD: We take the substance, and we corrupt the spirit. The current policy would make exaggerated military power a main basis of national life. This is to make the people accept force as a principle of living. The hope lies in extending common understandings to make a world community, but we now frustrate that hope by accepting force as our principle.

MR. HUTCHINS: This is the doctrine of power politics.

MR. REDFIELD: That doctrine may now become not merely a public policy but also a mode of life.

MR. GUSTAVSON: And it is a question whether any of us want to live under it. I am reminded of Lord Acton, when he said, "Power always corrupts; and absolute power corrupts absolutely."

MR. HUTCHINS: That is, we would say that this policy is suicidal; but, what is much more important, it is degrading. Even if we survive, we ought not to want to.

The situation is all the more menacing because the world which is emerging seems to be a world of two major powers—Russia and the United States. By constantly building up our military strength, we are daily threatening the other major power in the world—namely, Russia.

MR. GUSTAVSON: Suppose that Russia had the atomic bomb and suppose that Russia were building the largest navy in the world and suppose she were keeping her army at its present great strength and suppose she were legislating for her science so that everything would go down a military channel, would we look upon that as a threat to world peace?

MR. REDFIELD: Of course we would. I would answer that argument by saying that I think that we would be seriously mistaken if we should attempt to justify the present policy in this country on the ground that the Russians, if they were in our shoes, would do the same things. Maybe they would; but if they would make the mistake we are making, that is no reason why we should make it.

Here the atom bomb comes in again. Before its advent, people had a chance to dominate the world without destroying themselves. The Nazis had that chance. But, today, although through fear or desperation men may nevertheless make the attempt, the ruin of all will be the result.

MR. HUTCHINS: The Russians are human, and conceivably they might be as stupid if they were in our position. But there is no reason

America and the Atomic Age

why we should be stupid just because we think somebody else might be under the same circumstances.

But I understand that Mr. Truman has telegraphed congratulations to Russia on the anniversary of the Revolution and has expressed hopes for lasting coöperation. So, perhaps, we do not have to worry about the problem of Russian relations.

MR. GUSTAVSON: I know all about that. But when someone holds out his right hand to shake hands with somebody and, at the same time, puts his left hand on his gun, there results a situation where mutual confidence is impossible.

MR. HUTCHINS: What you are saying is that if these policies are calculated to convince the Russians that we are proposing to attack them, what is needed now is not fair words but a repudiation of the policy.

The Third Year of the Atomic Age: What Should We Do Now?

Broadcast August 24, 1947

MR. HUTCHINS: Two years ago, the Sunday after the bomb dropped, the University of Chicago Round Table discussed "Atomic Force—Its Meaning for Mankind."

The University of Chicago had been one of the principal centers of research on the bomb. The first chain reaction took place on its campus on December 2, 1942.

The University, even before the Round Table of two years ago, had determined to do what it could to maintain the leadership of the United States in atomic studies and to hold together some of the members of the group which had produced the bomb. For this purpose it had already created three new research institutes. The University representatives on that Round Table had therefore some qualifications to speak on the subject, and the institution they represented was deeply involved in whatever atomic energy might mean for mankind.

The fundamental facts about the atomic bomb today are those which the Round Table emphasized two years ago. There is no secret. There is no defense. Since there is no secret, other nations will have the bomb almost any day. Since there is no defense, military preparations to defend ourselves against the bomb are a waste of time.

In another war the atomic bomb will be used. International agreements for the control of atomic energy will simply mean that the next war will end with atomic bombs instead of beginning with them. The minute that war breaks out, every nation that knows how will start making atomic bombs.

It is generally thought that another nation will be able to make atomic bombs within five years from the day on which we dropped the first bomb on Japan. If this is so, we have already frittered away 40 per cent of the time we had to organize ourselves to preserve mankind.

The *New York Times,* in its editorial on the second anniversary of the bomb, says that the ultimate protection against it can only be the abolition of war itself. The *Times* suggests that the final success of efforts to abolish war can be realized only in an ultimate world government.

I do not understand the use of the word "ultimate" in this connection. We have now arrived at the ultimate stage in history. We cannot do something intermediate now and ultimately do something ultimate. What is ultimately required of us is required of us now. If what is ultimately required of us is the abolition of war through a world government, then we had better set about trying to get war abolished through world government now.

Any proposal for a world atomic authority is a proposal for world government. Such an authority must have a monopoly of atomic bombs, which means that every nation would be at its mercy, and it must have the right to enter, inspect, and destroy atomic installations anywhere in the world. No nation could call itself sovereign in any usual sense under such conditions.

The major premise of all discussions looking toward agreements for the control of atomic energy has been that the nations retain their sovereignty. Hence, these discussions have not succeeded and cannot succeed. Either we have world federal government and real atomic control, or we have no agreements, or agreements that are meaningless, and eventually atomic war.

It will be said, of course, that if nations will not collaborate in an alliance or debating society like the United Nations, they cannot be expected to come together or stay together in a world state. The American States could not or would not collaborate under the Articles of Confederation before 1787, but they did come together, and, with the exception of one period, they stayed together under the Constitution.

It may be admitted that there were ties which united them which do not unite the nations today. On the other hand, we should not forget that many differences deeply divided the American States, so much so that, three months before the Constitutional Convention, Madison wrote that "he trembled for the issue."

Mr. Hooker has lately shown in the magazine *Common Cause* how serious the divisions among the States in the Confederation were. Virginia had twelve times as many people as Delaware. Georgia claimed a hundred times as many square miles as Rhode Island. There were so many Germans in Pennsylvania that Franklin feared they might make German the language of the State. It was impossible to get along in some sections in New York without knowing Dutch. The trip from Boston to New York, which now takes less than an hour, took four days to a week along the finest road, or longer than it takes now to go around the world.

Gouverneur Morris thought that a federal tax was impossible because of the extent of the country; and one member of the Convention asked, "How can it be supposed that this vast country, including the western territory, will, one hundred and fifty years hence, remain one nation?"

When Washington took charge of the armies surrounding Boston, he wrote that the New Englanders were an exceedingly dirty and nasty people. On the other hand, Ephraim Paine, of Vermont, complained that the southern members of Congress regarded themselves as a superior order of animals. Tithes were levied by New York, Pennsylvania, and Maryland on the goods of other States; and New Jersey taxed the New York lighthouse on Sandy Hook. New York, New Hampshire, and Massachusetts quarreled about Vermont, and Pennsylvanians battled Virginians on the Upper Ohio. It is no wonder that, when the Constitution was completed by the Convention, the principal attack upon it was that it was utopian—a visionary project, an indigestible panacea.

And it barely was accepted. In the conventions in the critical States it just squeaked through. In Massachusetts it carried by twenty-nine votes; in Virginia, by ten; and in New York by only three.

To borrow a phrase from Mr. Borgese, world government is necessary and therefore possible. Of course, the world government can mean much, little, or nothing. An effort to find out what a free and federal world constitution would be like is now proceeding in the Committee To Frame a World Constitution. Whether this effort succeeds or fails, it will at least serve to clarify the issues and to focus the thought of the world on the method of forming a federal union which shall embrace all men.

It is very late. Perhaps nothing can save us. But the handwriting on the wall is plain enough. It says to the peoples of the earth, "Unite or die."

The Problem of World Government

Broadcast April 4, 1948

MR. HUTCHINS: We come now to the practical and immediate bearing upon American foreign policy of the two eloquent statements which you have heard.

The official American policy is to frighten Russia out of her alleged intention to establish world government, on the Russian plan, by force and fraud. According to present indications, the American elections next autumn can make little change in this policy; for each candidate for the Republican nomination is seeking favor on the ground that his principles and personality will frighten the Russians more than those of any of his rivals. Many Americans want to go farther still. They see that a policy of frightening Russia will merely postpone the war which is to decide whether we have world government on the Russian plan or world government on the American plan. Therefore, they want to fight Russia now while we are overwhelmingly stronger than she. They are calling for a preventive war.

Talk of a preventive war is vicious and perverted. If we seriously entertain the idea of a preventive war, we ought first to make our apologies to the Nazis we hanged at Nuremberg. Talk of any war, now or later, is not much better. The best that can be said for it is that it is recklessly frivolous. This is, we often hear, a Christian country; and the message of Christ calls us to good will, to the love of our neighbor, to the renunciation of the goods of this world, to humility, and to the forgiveness, not the slaughter, of our enemies. To say that we must kill Communists because they are atheists and we are Christians is a strange distortion of Christianity.

Those who believe in preventive war have one point on their side. They are correct in holding that a policy of frightening Russia cannot permanently succeed. Some day Russia will have the atomic bomb. Some day Russia will feel strong enough to prefer fighting to being frightened. Then the next war will come, and after it will come world government for such world as we have left. World government will come by conquest, instead of by orderly constitutional procedure.

Have we forgotten what the scientists have told us about the next war? If it comes when both sides have the atomic bomb, the cities of both sides will be destroyed. I do not care about architecture. The men, women, and children in our cities will be blown to bits. The atomic bomb is a weapon directed against civilians. If we go to war before the

Russians have the atomic bomb, we may expect the horrors of bacteriological warfare. We may expect the death of millions of innocent people. We may expect the disruption of our own economy and of our own form of government. We shall lay Europe waste—Europe, our ancestral homeland; Europe, for the sake of which we are now preparing for war. And when the war is over, if it ever is, we shall have the task of imposing our will by force for centuries on the peoples we have defeated. World government by the conquest of the world means perpetual war.

That we can lightheartedly discuss such a program not three years after the death of Hitler suggests that Hitler has triumphed after all. He was the symbol of brute force in our time. He was defeated, but we, his conquerors, are now preparing to bow down before the idol which he worshiped.

There is a good deal of hypocrisy about our attitude toward Russia. We do not believe that Russia is ready to attack us. We cannot seriously think that all Russians are bloodthirsty villains and that all the actions of the American government through history have the pure, angelic quality which we ascribe to them. Have we forgotten how we got the Panama Canal? Have we forgotten our continual interference, often for no better reason than the protection of our investments, in the internal affairs of Latin America? The Russians have behaved stupidly, rudely, tyrannically. Our own consciences cannot be altogether clear. We might ask ourselves how we should feel if the Russian secretary for air were to say of us what our secretary for air said of Russia a week or so ago, when he stated publicly that our planes could now drop bombs on Russian cities and return to their bases in America.

The peoples of the earth want freedom and justice. They do not want to be individuals without duties or automatons without rights. Communism denies them freedom. The critical spirit of man works against Communism. Differences among individuals work against Communism, for it holds that all men are identical. The European tradition of free expression, a free press, and political parties works against Communism. Invention in the arts, discovery in the sciences, carelessness, restlessness, humor, rational skepticism, and religious faith work against it.

What works for it? Nothing but injustice, which appears to millions today in the prospect of endless starvation and exploitation. The people of Europe do not want and will not long tolerate Communist justice at the expense of freedom. But the people of Europe cannot be permanently intimidated, and they cannot be permanently bought. They must have before their eyes some positive idea, some positive program which offers them both freedom and justice.

The "Stop Russia" program does not meet these requirements. The time is one for imagination, invention, for the effort to raise ourselves by our own bootstraps into a different spiritual world. This effort is harder than a policy of vast military preparations and resounding threats. But it has the merit of relieving us from condemnation by our own moral code. It has the merit of offering hope to mankind. Another war will mean the end of all hopes whatever.

We should strain our minds and imaginations to invent a political structure which may unite the world in freedom and justice. The aim is unity, which comes by agreement, not unification, which is imposed by force. The aim is a world state which rests not on the uneasy, impermanent, and unjust foundation of conquest but on the durable basis of the consent of the governed.

Such a world state must be a federal government, for only a federal government can create peace and safeguard liberty while preserving order. Such a world government must be a government, and not, like the United Nations, a league of independent, sovereign states, perpetuating the malady of nationalism. Such a world government must protect freedom; and it must be founded on justice, for men will fight until they get their rights.

Can such a world constitution be invented? I think so, for the Committee To Frame a World Constitution, established at Chicago two and a half years ago at the initiative of G. A. Borgese, has just published a draft of a possible world constitution which contains these elements.

Can such a world constitution be adopted? Nobody knows. But such a world constitution offers a positive idea. Hence it has a chance of gaining the adherence of mankind.

Can such a constitution guarantee that there will never be another war? Of course not. But it offers a *hope* that there will not be another war—and the only hope which we have. If a constitution proposing freedom and justice is accepted by most of the world, with the exception of Russia and her satellites, then there *may* be war. But it will be a war in which we cannot be accused of seeking our own aggrandizement, the submission of others to our will, or the domination of the world. A war, if it comes then, will be one in which the issues will be far plainer, in which our allies will be far more numerous and more loyal, and in which our sense of righteousness and high purpose will be far stronger than they can be today.

But the main point of contrast is this: the foreign policy of the

United States means that war is inevitable. World government founded on freedom and justice means that war, though still possible, is no longer inevitable. If war is inevitable, civilization has no future.

All Americans who hope for a future for their children, all Americans who want one good world, all Americans who believe in the brotherhood of man, should call upon the President and upon Congress to initiate a world constitutional convention.

The mission of America is not to dominate the world but to transform it.

Peace Without Appeasement
Frederick L. Schuman

Frederick L. Schuman was born in Chicago in 1904. He studied at the University of Chicago (Ph.B., 1924; Ph.D., 1927) and taught there from 1927 to 1936, when he went to Williams College. He has been Woodrow Wilson professor of government at Williams since 1938 and has been a visiting professor at Harvard, California, Cornell, and Columbia. His books on United States foreign policy and on Russia include *American Policy toward Russia since 1917* (1928), *International Politics—An Introduction to the Western State System* (4th edition, 1948), and *Soviet Politics* (1946).

This address was given before an audience of members of the Chicago Council on Foreign Relations in Chicago on 15 March 1951. Mr. Schuman spoke under the same auspices before the same group on 21 February 1950 on the subject "Atomic Diplomacy." In the address printed below he brings up to date his views on how to get along with the Russians.

THE IDES of March have come. Great Caesar's ghost does not this day walk visibly among us. Yet the shadow of a new and more sinister Caesarism falls darkly upon us as we painfully deliver up this day our reluctant tribute to the gods of war—whose worship is now enshrined in the Bureau of Internal Revenue. The priests of this shrine, we know, will exact ever heavier tribute year by year until war, called by Heraclitus "the father of all things," may well become the consumer of all things, the destroyer of all things, the subversion of the Republic, and the ruination of us all.

Happily there lie before us in the nearer future St. Patrick's day and the Spring Festival of the Resurrection. Still more happily for the immediate future your speaker of the day, I am advised on highest authority, is to talk not of war, of which you have assuredly heard much, but of peace, of which you have probably heard little of late.

My text for today's sermon is taken not from the words of Lewis Carroll, my favorite authority on world politics, but from the words of Herbert Pell, a distinguished elder statesman who was formerly a member of Congress, New York State Chairman of the Democratic Party, Minister to Portugal and Hungary, and American Member of the UN Commission for the Investigation of War Crimes. In a public letter dated January 10 of this year (*The New York Times*, Jan. 14, 1951), Herbert Pell wrote as follows:

> I am for peace. . . . Peace is the only possible base for our civilization. It was built on peace and without peace it will die. War will, ineluctably, end the customs and the outlook and the way of life, the ideals and the national purposes which we inherited from our fathers to be held as a sacred trust for our children. . . . Today, does any sane person believe that a conflict with Russia will mean anything but mutual destruction and ruin? . . . It is manifest that a war with Russia will end in a collapse of common exhaustion. The representatives of a shattered Russia will meet the emissaries of a worn and exhausted United States and devise a means by which both can survive without continuing mutual slaughter and destruction. Is there any person in the world who imagines any other result possible? . . . Yet, here, there, and everywhere you hear the politicians shouting against compromise. They have the effrontery to attack as cowards all who disagree with anything they shout . . .

> How much courage does anyone think it would take for me, sixty-six years old, living on an ample income quietly in the country, to clamor for gore, to demand the sacrifice of a million men 40 years younger than I am and then end my heroic address with a bitter note of regret that my years or my grapevines prevented me from joining the brave boys whom I envy? . . . Most of the political shouters think that they are backing a winning horse—that's all. I have been in politics for 40 years and I know. Twenty-five years ago thousands of American politicians attacked the Catholics to get the Klan vote. Today they follow McCarthy. Twenty years ago, they said as they drank their bootleg liquor: "There's one more election and prohibition." Today, safe behind desks, they think that war and hatred will keep their snouts in the public trough in 1952. It is as simple as that . . . I am for peace. I am on the side of the Angels of God who sang "Peace on Earth, Good Will To Men." They were not popular

with those who filled the Inn and crowded Mary into the stables, but they were right all the same. Why not negotiate now while the young men are still alive?

I suspect, as I know you do, that the matter is not quite so simple as Mr. Pell would make it. Yet he calls attention to a curious phenomenon of our time, namely the disposition of many publicists to denounce with angry words anyone who speaks for peace. This disposition would be more easily understandable if we were engaged in a war which we expected to win. But this is not the case, despite our fifty thousand casualties and our eight thousand honored dead in Korea—fallen in what we hoped was a crusade for freedom and for peace, now unhappily become the most extravagantly expensive and politically purposeless military operation in the history of the Republic.

This operation is not a war. It is officially represented as a United Nations "police action," whatever that may be. Nobody expects to win it, despite the fall of Seoul for the fourth time yesterday. General MacArthur announced on March 7 that no victory in Korea is possible. Our campaign is currently designated as "Operation Killer." Its only objective is to kill as many of the enemy as possible. Its effect is to turn Korea into a desert. The horror of Korea is the microcosm of what may well become the macrocosm of our world—a war which is not a war, in which there is no objective save death, in which no victory is conceivable, no peace is possible, and no end to slaughter and destruction can be arranged, foreseen, or even hoped for.

Some at least who still dare to speak for peace sincerely believe that it is still possible to avoid converting all the world into one vast and hideous Korea. They may be mistaken. But I still think it permissible to raise with you the question (which is more than a merely interesting question since it is literally a question of life or death) as to why we are so suspicious and frightened of advocates of peace.

A small part of the answer is that those among us who are committed to war are growing in numbers and influence. A larger part of the answer is that Communists advocate peace in their own dishonest and specious way. We as a people have almost brought ourselves to the point of being against anything that Communists say they are for, and for anything Communists say they are against. We now increasingly accept it as part of the American credo, moreover, that people are not to be judged by what they do or say, or even by the company they keep, but by the simpler test of possible similarity between what they say they believe in and what Communists make believe they believe in. Guilt by association is more and more replaced with guilt by coincidence. Therefore, if a Congregationalist advocates peace while Communists advocate peace, the Congregationalist is all but certain to be suspected by someone shortly of being a Communist. Even Quakers are not above suspicion, though we try to preserve the good old American tradition that Quakers who advocate peace are merely amiable and harmless eccentrics.

But the largest part of the answer to the question of why we fear advocates of peace is to be found, I believe, in our folk-memory of the advocates of peace in the 1930's. In the face of the totalitarian despotisms then in power in Rome, Berlin, and Tokyo, the peacemakers of two decades ago led their countries and the world toward disaster. Their very names are now anathema: Chamberlain, Hoare, Halifax, Daladier, Laval, Bonnet, Lindbergh, Wheeler, and the America First Committee. We praised them then but we damn them now, for we say: these were the appeasers, this was appeasement, and here is the road to war and ruin. Therefore, we regard all advocates of peace in the 1950's in the face of the totalitarian despotisms now in power in Moscow and Peiping as, at worst, enemy agents or, at best, architects of catastrophe.

It may be that in our abhorrence of appeasement, we are victims of semantic self-deception. Henry Steele Commager, once my fellow-student at the University of Chicago, has recently argued (*The New York Times Magazine,* February 11, 1951) that "these issues are not to be solved by calling them names. The term appeasement is not a conclusion. It is not even a point of departure. It is an avoidance of thinking." Perhaps so. If so, permit me to invite you to an adventure in thinking about the nature and meaning of appeasement in the 1930's and its relevance to the crisis of the 1950's.

The term appeasement, unhappily popularized by Neville Chamberlain fifteen years ago, originally meant: to make peace, to preserve peace, to negotiate and bargain in the interest of peace. Do we believe in the abstract that such activities are reprehensible? Of course not. Do we believe that appeasement as practiced by the governments of the democratic powers in the 1930's was an evil thing? Of course we do. We judge it to have been wrong because of its results. We are a pragmatic people. We take seriously, sometimes, the biblical injunction: "By their fruits ye shall know them." The fruit of appeasement in the 1930's was not peace but war, World War II, the most monstrous, murderous and destructive war, thus far, in all human experience.

I believed then, and I believe now, that the attitudes and policies called "appeasement" were in truth the most important single factor in making World War II inevitable. I found then that this belief was highly unpopular. I lean now to an even more unpopular belief—namely, the belief that the appeasement analogy between the 1930's and the 1950's is possibly invalid and, if invalid, is so misleading as to be false and potentially tragic in its probable result. But it is precisely this analogy, coupled with our justified horror at Red Sin and Communist aggression, and coupled with a number of delusions about world politics of which I shall speak later, which lies at the very heart of most of our current confusions, anxieties and dangers.

Therefore, I would put to you a very vital current question: Why did appeasement in the 1930's produce not peace, but war? It seems clear to me, from a record which can now be elaborately documented, that there are two general answers to be given to this question.

The first answer is that appeasement as practiced by the democratic powers in the 1930's in dealing with Fascist totalitarianism was an attempt to appease the unappeasable, to satisfy the insatiable, to reason with the irrational, and to bargain with those whose objective was not bargaining but annihilation.

The Fascist Caesars were at one and the same time the spokesmen of middle-class mass madness and the agents of feudal aristocrats and industrial monopolists who felt their privileges threatened by the obvious sickness of unstable and maladjusted societies suffering from economic depression and wholesale unemployment and impoverishment. The Fascist surgeons performed a highly successful operation, the beauty of which was only slightly marred by the fact that, in the end, the patient died. But the operation was highly successful. It consisted in providing emotional outlets for middle-class mass madness and restoring full employment, national productivity and general prosperity through total militarism, armed aggression, and conquest for purposes of exploiting the conquered. The whole society and the whole economy became dependent for ephemeral well-being and transient stability on public spending for armaments, for preparations for war, for the waging of war, and for the systematic robbery or planned extermination of the vanquished. This process was of the essence of the dynamic of the Fascist form of totalitarianism.

Under these circumstances, it proved quite impossible for the Western democracies to appease the Fascist Caesars or to compromise with them or to establish the conditions of peaceful coexistence, because war and conquest were the pre-conditions of the very survival of these totalitarian regimes. Therefore, in the end the issue was starkly simple: either the Western democracies would destroy Fascist totalitarianism or be destroyed by it.

The second answer to our question is that appeasement as practiced by the democratic powers in the 1930's was an attempt, once it came to be realized that Fascist aggression was inevitable, not to deter aggression but to deflect aggression against others. Appeasement in the 1930's was not merely a policy based upon a misconception of the nature of Fascist totalitarianism. It was also, after 1935 at least, a policy which took belated cognizance of the inevitability of Fascist aggression and sought to direct that aggression away from the Atlantic democracies and against Communist totalitarianism as embodied in the Soviet Union. This was the inner logic and meaning in terms of Realpolitik of Western acquiescence, and even connivance, in the Fascist conquests of Manchuria, Ethiopia, Spain, the Rhineland, the China coast, Austria, and Czechoslovakia. The practical premise of appeasement, looked at in these terms, was that the fanatically anti-Communist war-lords of Rome, Berlin, and Tokyo, if only given a free hand, would in fact do what they had long promised to do—attack Russia. Stalin and the Moscow Politburo played the same game in reverse against the Western powers during the period of the Nazi-Soviet pact, from August of 1939 to June of 1941.

Appeasement in this sense is an old and familiar device in the game of power politics. Its objective is to play the role of *Tertius Gaudens* or the "happy third." Its motto, in small boys' language is: Let's you and him fight! This is a possible and sometimes a highly practicable policy in a world of three or more powers. The test of its wisdom, like the test of any pattern of foreign policy, is the test of results. In the cases to which I refer, the results unfortunately did not correspond to anticipations and expectations. I did not believe at the time that they would, and yet there is a certain logic in this type of appeasement which we should not, I think, dismiss as either absurd or immoral, for it is neither.

This logic was bluntly expressed by an American Senator in late June of 1941 on the occasion of the Nazi invasion of Russia. Said the Senator: "If we see Germany is winning, we ought to help Russia, and if we see Russia is winning, we ought to help Germany, and in that way let them kill as many as possible." The Senator quoted was Harry S. Truman.

This logic also found expression, perhaps more vividly, in the old wartime story of 1943 according to which Churchill, Hitler, and Stalin all died and went to heaven and were greeted at the pearly gates by the

Archangel Michael who told them all that in view of their great services below they might each be granted the fulfillment of one worldly wish before entering into Paradise. Hitler, upon being asked his wish, said that he desired the extermination of all the Russians. Stalin, upon being asked his wish, said he desired the extermination of all the Germans. Churchill, upon being asked his wish, puffed his cigar and hesitated. He finally asked the Archangel if he intended to grant Hitler his wish and the answer was "yes." He then asked the Archangel if he intended to grant Stalin's wish. The answer was "yes." "Well then," said Churchill, "I'll be happy to settle for a Scotch and soda!"

How happy we should all be if Senator Truman's hope of 1941 and Mr. Churchill's apocryphal heavenly vision of 1943 had been fulfilled! The sad and sober fact, of course, is that the Fascist totalitarians whom the Western powers appeased in the hope that they would attack Russia, attacked the Western powers instead. And the same Fascist totalitarians whom Russia later appeased in the hope that they would continue to attack the Western powers, attacked Russia instead. So in this calculation also—the calculus of the happy third—appeasement as practiced by both the Western powers and Russia against one another a decade or more ago produced not peace and security but war and disaster. Small wonder, then, that both we and the Russians, remembering this experience, want no appeasement in the 1950's.

But appeasement in this second sense is not at all possible in a two-power world. A cannot appease B in the hopes that B will attack C, if there is no C but only A and B. The world of the 1950's is a bipolar or two-power world. We and the Russians, each for our own purposes, are striving mightily to make it a three-, four- or five-power world in which this type of appeasement may again become practical politics. But we have not thus far succeeded in our endeavor. Our world being still a two-power world, neither power can appease the other in the hope that it will attack a third, because there is no third.

Let me return to appeasement in its first aspect and invite you to reconsider the alleged analogy between the 1930's and the 1950's, with Communist totalitarianism substituted in our time for Fascist totalitarianism in the earlier times. The truth or falsehood of this analogy is, I believe, crucial and decisive in any effort at clear thinking about war and peace in the current reëxamination of American foreign policy, even though it is seldom mentioned and almost never discussed.

If we ask ourselves in this context the most general question possible, namely, "Do Fascist totalitarianism and Communist totalitarianism resemble one another?" the answer plainly is "yes." These two varieties of totalitarianism are quite alike in repudiating political democracy, personal freedom, and human dignity. They are alike in that both foster one-party rule, ideological intolerance, and dreams of global hegemony. If Fascist totalitarianism and Communist totalitarianism are alike in these respects, are they sufficiently alike in all respects to warrant our regarding them as identical? More important, can we reasonably conclude from these undeniable similarities that all negotiations with, and all bargains with, Communist totalitarianism in the 1950's are likely to have results comparable to negotiations and bargains with Fascist totalitarianism in the 1930's? In short, are we again in the position of trying to appease the unappeasable, to satisfy the insatiable, to reason with the irrational and to bargain with those whose object is not bargaining but annihilation?

The most popular answer to this question, or at any rate the most widely advertised answer, is an emphatic, emotional, and often hysterical affirmative. And this answer has much support in the words and deeds of the Communist totalitarians. From this answer, taken as a premise, the American War Party has drawn the only possible answer that can be drawn. That conclusion, quite starkly, is that we must destroy Soviet Communism or be destroyed by it. This answer, be it noted, long antedated Communist military aggression in Korea in June of 1950.

I mean by "the American War Party" all of those who accept this conclusion and demand that it be acted upon. I use the term in no invidious sense, but only in a descriptive sense. For the conclusion in question obviously means war—total war, war to the death, a war of annihilation in which the victors, if any, must, by the very definition of the issues at stake, destroy the vanquished utterly as the price of their own survival. I respect this conclusion even if I regret it, as all of us must. I respect it because it is well reasoned, highly logical, and quite correct if its premise is correct. It may be correct. If premise and conclusion are both correct, then our duty is clear, our future is manifest, and all further discussion is pointless.

But the question we want answered is the question of whether the conclusion of the War Party is right or wrong. Is it true or false that we must destroy Soviet Communism or be destroyed by it? This is not the kind of proposition which can be validated or invalidated conclusively by references to precise facts and exact knowledge. It is rather the kind of proposition which can be most certainly made true if enough people act as if it were true, and which quite possibly can be made false if enough people act as if it were false.

My own best judgment, as you may well guess from such past analyses of world affairs as I have been privileged to inflict upon you, is that the conclusion of the War Party is false, and that it would be altogether tragic if we were to act as if it were true. I do not believe that the rulers of Red Russia and Red China, in spite of their ineffable wickedness which seems to me to be as real as our own collective virtue and righteousness, are in quite the same position as the late rulers of Fascist Italy, Germany, and Japan. I do not refer, of course, to geographic or demographic or strategic position, though the difference here is also important. I refer to political, economic, social, and psychological position.

I do not believe that the structure of society and of the economy and of the organization of power in China and Russia, abominable and hateful as that structure seems to us, is sufficiently comparable to the structure of society and the economy and the organization of power in Fascist Italy, Germany, and Japan to justify the conclusion that the Communist oligarchs are inexorably and inevitably driven, regardless of risks and consequences, toward a course of militarism, aggression, war, and global conquest by arms.

The Communist economies, unlike the Fascist economies, are not dependent for their viability and stability on public spending for arms and war. The Communist ideology, unlike the Fascist ideology, does not glorify war as preferable to peace and, whatever its grim results in practice, does not repudiate in theory and aspiration all the moral values and social ideals of the Jewish-Greek-Christian tradition.

I cannot here support this judgment by any attempt to compare the economic systems and the social and political dynamics of Fascist and Communist totalitarianism. I would only recall the verdict of time. Fascist totalitarianism, once in power in major nations, meant war with the West within a very few years. Communist totalitarianism has been in power in Russia for 34 years. These have not been years of uninterrupted peace. During this third of a century the Western powers have twice sought by arms to destroy Soviet Communism, and the men of Moscow have repeatedly sought by propaganda, infiltration, and subversion but never by arms, to destroy the West. Both sides have failed. During the larger part, by far the larger part, of this third of a century, Soviet Communism and Western democracy have coexisted in peace, as George Kennan keeps reminding us now somewhat wistfully or even desperately.

These circumstances suggest to me the possibility, remote as it may currently seem to be, that peaceful coexistence rather than a total war of extermination might conceivably continue for a long time to come, or perhaps indefinitely, if our leaders and the Communist leaders could be brought to act on the assumption of this possibility. There would be risks in so acting. In times of crises there are risks in all action and all inaction. We have to try as best we can, if we still believe in the role of reason in human affairs, to weigh probable alternative risks.

The risks of acting as if peace were possible are many. Such action may encourage the enemy to new aggressions. It may play into the hands of domestic subversives. It may halt the inflationary war boom. It may infuriate the American War Party. There are doubtless other risks. There is only a single risk in acting as if war were inevitable—that is, to make it so. None of us who is a loyal citizen and patriot would shrink for a moment from inevitable war if it were clear that war was the necessary price of national survival and of the preservation of our freedoms, that the war, however appalling and destructive, could be won, and that our victory would represent a new and heartening triumph of liberty over tyranny. Our anguish of spirit is due to our knowledge that these things are by no means clear.

What gives us pause, what makes us doubtful and fearful, is the very high degree of probability that the war we are contemplating is not the price of freedom and survival, that once launched it may never be won nor even ended in a truce of mutual exhaustion short of the atomic annihilation of our civilization, and that it may, in its course and consequences, irreparably destroy the American way of life and deliver us to the evils of our own brand of the Garrison State, the Police State, and a neo-Fascist totalitarianism. So we have been warned by Joseph Kennedy, by Herbert Hoover, and by Robert Taft, among others, and their warnings can scarcely be brushed aside by calling them names. Walter Lippmann (Feb. 26, 1951) has recently written with regard to the danger of an excessive increase of our armaments:

> The temptation may become irresistible to embrace the hallucination that the third world war could be fought, won and finished and that after that the world would be happy again. The third world war can be fought. There is no prospect whatsoever that it could be finished. Nothing is so certain, no prophecy is so sure, as that once the third world war started it would spread like a prairie fire and would become an uncontrollable, inconclusive, interminable complex of civil and international wars. . . . To raise the level of armaments too high, to subject the country to an intolerable strain, is to make the great military mistake which has ruined so many other nations.

It is to arm past the point of no return. It is to create armaments that are so heavy to bear that they must be used in the hope of getting rid of the burden—wars that are inspired not by self-defense or by clear policy but by internal pressures and irrational hopes invariably end in ruin and disaster.

How can we strike a balance between risks? Each of us must do this for himself, bearing in mind his responsibility to his fellow-citizen and his duty to his country and mankind. For my own part I believe that the risks of acting as if peace were possible, many and grave as they may be, are less than the risks of acting as if global war were inevitable.

If we were as a nation to act as if peace were possible (and I am not very confident that we shall), then it seems to me we should have to revise somewhat drastically and painfully a number of our current attitudes and policies. To discuss such revisions in detail is quite impossible in what time remains, for very little time remains. The exercise may prove, at best, "academic"—which in our vocabulary still means impracticable, irresponsible, and crackpot. Therefore, I limit myself in conclusion to a few very broad and highly controversial suggestions regarding the prerequisites of effective action based on the assumption of the possibility of peace.

First, I believe we must come to recognize that if the great issues of power politics are not to be settled by war they can be settled only by diplomacy and in no other way at all, since there is no other way. Diplomacy requires bargaining and some measure of secrecy about the bargaining until it is concluded. It requires a trading of advantages *quid pro quo*. Let us be clear that if we choose to say that no bargaining is possible because all bargaining is appeasement, we are saying that no diplomacy is possible. And if no diplomacy is possible, then there is no alternative to war.

Second, we must come to recognize, as Hans J. Morgenthau has eloquently argued, that the only rational purpose of foreign policy is the protection and promotion of national interests, not the propagation and vindication of moral principles. To base foreign policy on ethical doctrines, however noble and exalted they may be, rather than on practical calculations of risks and advantages, is to please the heart, to betray the mind, and to expose the country and the world to all the horrors of religious crusades and Holy Wars in which the ethical doctrines themselves are the first casualties. If we deny, as we do and must, the Marx-given right of Moscow to impose its values and way of life on the world, let us not assert for ourselves some allegedly God-given right to impose our values and way of life on the world. This cannot be done. Let us also recognize that American world leadership cannot achieve any attainable goal if we define it in terms of a sacred mission to suppress sin all over the globe and to liberate all victims of injustice and tyranny all over the earth. Neither by propaganda nor by arms can we possibly achieve these desirable ends. Any effort to achieve them through war can only mean more sin, more injustice, and more tyranny all over the globe.

Third, we must come to recognize anew that collective security as a means of keeping the peace is an illusion, that the United Nations organization was never designed or intended to be an agency of collective security save on the basis of a concert of *all* the Great Powers, and that if we would preserve the United Nations as a possible basis for future world government, we must think of it and deal with it not as a police force to wage war, which it is not and can never be, but as a forum of discussion and an arena of diplomacy for the keeping of peace.

Fourth, we must come to recognize—as my late dear friend, Max Werner, the most brilliant military analyst of our time, continued to argue to the day of his death—that the security of Western Europe cannot be achieved by military means but only by diplomatic means. The policy of seeking to rearm Germany in the face of German and French opposition is to promote not security, but disaster. In my judgment, as in that of James Warburg, our rearmament of Western Europe can promote security and peace only on condition that Germany be demilitarized and neutralized by a diplomatic accord between East and West.

The issue here is starkly simple. I can state it in the form of an incident at the National War College in Washington where I have lectured from time to time. Several years ago, the chairman of the round-table discussion which followed a lecture was a distinguished American diplomat who was one of the first advocates of the policy of "getting tough with Russia." He opened the discussion by saying: "Our problem is an old one. Russian troops are in Central Europe. They have to be driven out. Russian troops have been in Central Europe before. They have always had to be driven out. This is our task." He was at once interrupted by a distinguished diplomatic historian, then on the staff of the War College, who said: "Why, Mr. Chairman, what are you saying? When have Russian troops ever been driven out of Central Europe?" The chairman could think of no case, since there is none. The diplomatic historian went on to point out that whenever in the past Russian troops have been in Central Europe they have finally been withdrawn.

by agreement among the Powers and have never been driven out. The chairman said that this didn't matter, the problem was still the same.

Unfortunately, it does matter. The problem of getting Russian troops out of Central Europe is hopelessly insoluble so long as it is thought of as a problem of driving them out. It is, in fact, a problem of getting them out by agreement, which requires diplomacy. The heart of the agreement, as I see it, will have to be an accord for the military evacuation and the demilitarization and neutralization of Germany within her present frontiers. I believe that no other course in the end will prove workable.

Fifth, we must come to recognize that in the long run no peace settlement in Korea, no peace treaty with Japan, no determination of the status of Formosa, no new dispensation in Indochina and Malaya is at all likely to endure except upon the basis of a negotiated accord throughout the Far East in which America, China, Russia, India, France, and the British Commonwealth are all equal partners and participants. Such a negotiated accord will require, it seems to me, that the United Nations and the United States deal with the actual government of China as the government of China. Such a negotiated accord may well provide by general agreement, since it would be to the advantage of all so to provide, for the demilitarization and neutralization of Korea, Formosa, and Japan, leaving America secure in its naval control of the Pacific and leaving Russia and China secure in their military control of those portions of the Asiatic mainland which are within their present frontiers.

The alternatives to this approach—namely, war with China or the unilateral use of Western military might to maintain the *status quo* in Korea, Formosa, Japan and Southeastern Asia—will, I believe, prove unworkable by the ultimate test of consequences.

Sixth, and finally, we must come to recognize that military power alone, essential as it is in a world threatened with anarchy, is wholly inadequate by itself to give us national or international security or to halt the continued expansion of Communism. Military aggression must be met with military resistance, as in Korea. But if such resistance is to accomplish its purposes, it must be the means toward attainable political objectives and not a mere rash and reckless use of violence without regard to political objectives.

Communist expansion by means other than military aggression cannot be hindered, and may indeed be furthered, by excessive reliance upon military might. It can be halted, to repeat a truism, only by a "bold new program" of developing resources, raising living standards, and promoting economic opportunity and social justice among the backward, impoverished and exploited masses of mankind, as the International Development Advisory Board so ably and eloquently urged in its report released last Sunday. Communism thrives on misery. War is always productive of misery. Communism therefore thrives on war, as we ought by now to know from the results of two world wars. A third world war will inevitably be productive of such appalling misery throughout most of the human community that the ultimate inheritors of the wreckage are far more likely to be the apostles of totalitarianism than the disciples of freedom.

Is it probable, is it even possible, that our policy-makers, our press, and our people as a whole will prove able and willing to face and to act upon these realities of the present and these prospects of the future in time to save the peace? The answer must be in the negative if we continue to reject all bargaining as appeasement and if we continue to act in terms of fear, hatred, catchwords, and multiple abstractions rather than in terms of a rational evaluation of our goals and purposes, our ends, and our means. The answer can be in the affirmative if we can somehow act in the name of sanity as Lewis Mumford has recently urged in the February issue of *Common Cause*. "We are witnessing," writes Mr. Mumford, "a collective outbreak of compulsive irrationality. . . . Men must recover the capacity for balanced judgment before they can halt the approaching catastrophe and bring about the conditions for peace. We must awaken ourselves from this nightmare. . . . In those countries like the United States and England, where men are not yet wholly imprisoned in an official ideology, the obligation to use that freedom is a command. Applied at the right moment, rationality may prove as infectious as madness."

This, our capacity for sanity, and nothing other than this, will, I am convinced, be the ultimate test of the fitness of the free world to survive and to save the future. If we lack it, we shall inevitably enter into the shadows of a long darkness, whatever the verdict of arms may be. If we possess it, we may yet live in hope of achieving One World at peace. This is our test. We are summoned, each of us individually and all of us together, to meet this test with all the talents for reason and justice at our disposal. Time grows short. But it is not yet too late to meet the test successfully.

The Defense of the Free World
Vannevar Bush

Dr. Vannevar Bush, the president of the Carnegie Institution of Washington since 1939, is an electrical engineer by training and an administrator by profession. He studied at Tufts College (B.S. and M.S., 1913) and at Harvard and the Massachusetts Institute of Technology (joint Eng.D., 1916). He taught engineering at M.I.T. from 1916 to 1917 and from 1919 to 1932 and then became Vice President and Dean of Engineering. He designed the first differential analyzer at the Institute and has made many notable contributions to scientific research.

During World War II Dr. Bush was Director of the Office of Scientific Research and Development. In 1947-48 he was Chairman of the Joint Research and Development Board of the National Military Establishment. His book, *Modern Arms and Free Men*, was published in 1949.

As a member of the Committee on the Present Danger, Dr. Bush delivered this address to a nation-wide radio audience on 4 March 1951.

MY FELLOW-CITIZENS:

The Committee on the Present Danger is beginning tonight a series of weekly broadcasts on the peril that faces the American people and on how it can be met. The committee is a nonpartisan group of citizens who have organized to work together as the nation prepares to safeguard freedom. I have never been a "joiner," as we call them on Cape Cod, but I believe so strongly in what this committee stands for that I am glad to be a member of it.

We believe the nation's preparation to meet the danger must be on the same scale as the danger itself. We believe balanced armed forces are the heart of such preparation. And we believe the utmost speed is essential. I have been asked to begin this series with a reckoning of the probabilities of the defense of the free world, and how the atomic bomb affects them.

There is no doubt of the desire of the American people—and of our friends. We wish to avoid war. We wish to preserve our freedom and the free way of life. In a world where aggressive dictators are still at large, there is but one way to achieve these ends. That way is—to be strong. I am confident that the American people realize this. But we need to study just how to build that needed strength.

The key to the matter, in my opinion, is the A-bomb. At the end of the war our allies were exhausted. We disarmed. We know what has happened. Russia moved in. Working by intrigue and by the subversive overthrow of governments, she took over enormous territory and millions of people. But Russia stopped. Russia stopped at the boundary where the Kremlin was sure there would be war with us if it proceeded further. We saw the matter tested out at the time of the airlift in Berlin, and we know when we confronted the Russians with true strength they did not force the issue.

The deterrent is nearly as powerful today as it was then. If Russia sent its armies rolling across the German plains tomorrow, we with our A-bombs and the planes to carry them would destroy Russia. We could do it without question, as matters stand today. We could destroy not only the key centers from which her armies would be supplied, but also political centers and the communications of the armies on the march. Initially equipped with weapons and supplies, those armies might keep rolling for a time, but there would be no Russia behind them as we know it today.

The answer to this is that the armies will not roll. No all-out war is in sight for the immediate future unless they or we make some very serious error indeed. If Russia knows that she cannot go beyond certain boundaries without provoking a war, she will not pass those bounds; no war will occur. This has been well shown in recent years. The only apparent exception is in Korea, and there we did not make our position clear.

The difficulty is that we cannot count indefinitely upon strategic bombing as the sole means of averting war. Today, it gives us a military stalemate. To maintain that stalemate is the real problem.

Defenses against strategic bombing have been mounting ever since the war. Jet pursuit ships controlled by ground radar can be enormously effective in bringing down high-flying bombers. Russia with its vast distances can have extensive early warning radar networks to alert its defenses. She can have great fleets of jet pursuit ships for defense, accurately controlled from the ground night and day. She can also have about her key positions modern anti-aircraft artillery and also perhaps ground-to-air guided missiles.

Russia in time can thus protect her key points. Note that I say "in time." She cannot do it now. She cannot at any time safeguard all the places in Russia we might wish to attack. But in time there is a strong probability that she can defend key points to the extent that we could not penetrate to them without prohibitive attrition. She is also building a stock of A-bombs of her own. The deterrent of our A-bombs is real. But we cannot count on its remaining fully effective forever. I trust we have time—time to prepare the defenses that will continue the balance and avert war. But we do not have time to waste.

These defenses center in an allied army in Europe capable of holding a defensive line, stopping the Russian hordes if they should ever start, and so dissuading them from starting. That army must be well trained and it must be supplied with the very best of weapons of every sort. It must be created before our present enormous atomic advantage is seriously lessened. Of course it needs to be combined with continued development of our striking air force and support of our Navy to keep the seas open, but there must be an army in being and on the spot capable of holding back the hordes of Russia. Such an army does not now exist.

This need by no means be a matter of opposing hordes by hordes. We have no idea whatever of invading Russia by land, nor should we develop any such idea. Ours should be a defensive line, a line to hold back the hordes while we strike by other means.

Many elements enter into this. In the first place, take the matter of tanks. Russia has 40,000 tanks of various sorts. All her military doctrine revolves about the use of tanks and artillery. But there have been developed in the last few years antitank weapons of great power. Relatively small recoilless antitank guns mounted on a jeep or handled by four men can put a heavy tank out of business, with a high probability of doing it before the enemy can get off his first shot, even at ranges of 1,500 to 2,000 yards. These guns can be built in quantity by the hundreds for the cost of a single heavy tank.

When the countryside is infested by stingers of this sort no tanks are going to roam that countryside long. There will still be a function for the light tank and for armored vehicles of various sorts. But the big tank has met its match, and unless techniques change in a way that I do not now see it will become a liability rather than an asset in due time. I do not say that the big tank is now obsolete; I do say we can make it obsolete if we put our minds to the job and build the things to counter it. With that problem settled, the defense of Europe is simpler.

There is another factor, moreover, which is of enormously great importance. Out in the Nevada desert there have recently been a number of explosions. Presumably they mean the testing of new types of A-bombs developed by the Atomic Energy Commission during the past five years. I will not speculate as to their nature, but we can certainly assume that we have not been idle and that we have more effective bombs today than we had five years ago. They may indeed be far more adaptable for a very important purpose.

We have thought of the A-bomb as a means for attacking great military production facilities or centers of political power. The A-bomb can also have important tactical uses. Suppose that a war were to break out three or five years from now and that the Russian hordes were held up by a much smaller number of well-disciplined and well-armed divisions. If the line were not too thinly held, if it were defended in depth with the land mines, antitank obstacles, artillery, and other weapons that we can have if we choose, how would the Russians break it?

They could do so only by a huge concentration of armies, artillery and tanks—the kind of thing the Nazis did in 1944 just before the Battle of the Bulge. But with A-bombs in existence this becomes a very different matter. An A-bomb delivered upon such a concentration by an airplane, or possibly by use of a gun or a guided missile, would be devastating. In its presence, concentration of this sort would not make sense. Tactical use of the A-bomb thus will help to make the defense of Europe with reasonable numbers of men a practical matter.

Further, Europe is regaining courage and spirit. The mission of General Eisenhower and the evident determination of the American people are aiding greatly in that regard. We can join our strong and well-trained troops with those of our allies in Europe—we must assemble them in such numbers that they can hold the line. When enough men are mustered, there are important technical innovations to enable them to hold such a line against vastly superior numbers. It is not a matter of meeting hordes with hordes. Yet with even the most subtle of modern weapons there must be men to maintain the line and men to wield the weapons if they are to be effective.

I trust, therefore, that in our provision of manpower we will look well to the future. There is no thought in my mind that the men we bring in for training now will have to fight soon. Rather, I think they will be the beginning of a well-trained, well-organized reserve. We need not only an army in being on the spot, but also behind it masses of trained men who can be called, if it becomes necessary, without a long period of indoctrination. If total war ever comes again, it will break suddenly. I believe that the way to accomplish this purpose is to induct 18-year-olds to have approximately two years' training and service and thereafter to go into the reserve to build up the essential body of trained men.

We cannot build the forces we need without sacrifice. This sacrifice must come in many ways—in forgoing some of the pleasures we like to enjoy, in increased taxes and heavier burdens, and above all in the selflessness of our youth as they devote a part of their lives to training for the defense of decency and freedom. In my opinion we shall produce less interruption in the life of the youngster if we train him in the years of 18 and 19, after he has finished high school and before he launches his permanent career. Moreover, the earlier the training starts, the longer will men be available for the reserve. It takes young men to fight a war.

As I said when I started this talk, the object of the free world is not to fight a war but to avoid the necessity of fighting. If we are wise, I feel sure that we can avoid that necessity. We have today an able group of military leaders. We have a strength which Russia fears. The Kremlin will not strike unless it makes a mistake or unless we by the utmost foolishness cause it to make a false move in the belief that it can do so without bringing our retaliation upon it.

We must keep such strength that we cannot be overwhelmed, such strength that to attack us would be suicidal. If we do, the attempt will no be made and we can live without a World War III. The sacrifices we shall make to that end, heavy though they may be, will be small indeed compared to the sacrifices we would make if through weakness or hesitancy we allowed a war to come upon us.

Nor does America stand up to Russia alone. Russia today faces the entire free world, of enormous production capacity and enormous numbers of men, a vigorous, free world. The free world has no idea of making war on Russia. But it is determined to live in peace, and to be strong in order to do so. We of the United States have great allies. They are temporarily in some distress, for they suffered grievously during the war.

But their might is rising. France is rising with all of its great traditions of strength and independence. Britain is rising with its pride at having maintained the peace of Europe by its strength for many years. So are other allies as well. Their growing strength combined with ours can be made ample to stand off the present danger. If it is held in check, that danger will in time fade. We will face the threat shoulder to shoulder, and facing it thus we will keep the peace.

Peace in the Atomic Era

Albert Einstein

Dr. Albert Einstein, foremost theoretical physicist, was born in Germany in 1879. He studied in Munich, Aarau and Zurich, Switzerland, and became a world-renowned figure by his discovery of the theory of rela-

Albert Einstein

tivity, for which he was awarded the Nobel Prize in 1922. He came to the United States in 1933, was naturalized as an American citizen in 1940. Since 1933 he has been a life member of the Institute for Advanced Study at Princeton, New Jersey.

Aside from his scientific writings Dr. Einstein is known for his books of general interest, such as *Living Philosophies* (1931); *The World as I See It* (1934); and *The Evolution of Physics* (with Leopold Infeld, 1938).

This address was given by Dr. Einstein on 19 February 1950 over a national radio network from his home in Princeton, New Jersey.

I AM grateful to you for the opportunity to express my conviction in this most important political question.

The idea of achieving security through national armament is, at the present state of military technique, a disastrous illusion. On the part of the United States this illusion has been particularly fostered by the fact that this country succeeded first in producing an atomic bomb. The belief seemed to prevail that in the end it were possible to achieve decisive military superiority.

In this way, any potential opponent would be intimidated, and security, so ardently desired by all of us, brought to us and all of humanity. The maxim which we have been following during these last five years has been, in short: security through superior military power, whatever the cost.

This mechanistic, technical-military psychological attitude had inevitable consequences. Every single act in foreign policy is governed exclusively by one viewpoint.

How do we have to act in order to achieve utmost superiority over the opponent in case of war? Establishing military bases at all possible strategically important points on the globe. Arming and economic strengthening of potential allies.

Within the country—concentration of tremendous financial power in the hands of the military, militarization of the youth, close supervision of the loyalty of the citizens, in particular, of the civil servants by a police force growing more conspicuous every day. Intimidation of people of independent political thinking. Indoctrination of the public by radio, press, school. Growing restriction of the range of public information under the pressure of military secrecy.

The armament race between the U.S.A. and the U.S.S.R., originally supposed to be a preventive measure, assumes hysterical character. On both sides, the means to mass destruction are perfected with feverish haste—behind the respective walls of secrecy. The H-bomb appears on the public horizon as a probably attainable goal. Its accelerated development has been solemnly proclaimed by the President.

If successful, radioactive poisoning of the atmosphere and hence annihilation of any life on earth has been brought within the range of technical possibilities. The ghostlike character of this development lies in its apparently compulsory trend. Every step appears as the unavoidable consequence of the preceding one. In the end, there beckons more and more clearly general annihilation.

Is there any way out of this impasse created by man himself? All of us, and particularly those who are responsible for the attitude of the U.S. and the U.S.S.R., should realize that we may have vanquished an external enemy, but have been incapable of getting rid of the mentality created by the war.

It is impossible to achieve peace as long as every single action is taken with a possible future conflict in view. The leading point of view of all political action should therefore be: What can we do to bring about a peaceful coexistence and even loyal coöperation of the nations?

The first problem is to do away with mutual fear and distrust. Solemn renunciation of violence (not only with respect to means of mass destruction) is undoubtedly necessary.

Such renunciation, however, can only be effective if at the same time a supranational judicial and executive body is set up empowered to decide questions of immediate concern to the security of the nations. Even a declaration of the nations to collaborate loyally in the realization of such a "restricted world government" would considerably reduce the imminent danger of war.

In the last analysis, every kind of peaceful coöperation among men is primarily based on mutual trust and only secondly on institutions such as courts of justice and police. This holds for nations as well as for individuals. And the basis of trust is loyal give and take.

What about international control? Well, it may be of secondary use as a police measure. But it may be wise not to overestimate its importance. The times of prohibition come to mind and give one pause.

The Road to Peace
Trygve Lie

Trygve Lie was born in Oslo, Norway on 16 July 1896 and was graduated from the Law School of the University of Oslo in 1919. He became active in the Norwegian labor movement and in 1926 was elected national executive secretary of the Labor party. He was elected a member of the Norwegian Parliament in 1935 and was reëlected in 1945. In June 1940 he escaped to England with the Norwegian government and in 1941 was appointed Foreign Minister.

In April 1945 Mr. Lie was elected chairman of the Norwegian delegation to the United Nations conference in San Francisco, where he served as chairman of Committee III, dealing with the powers of the Security Council. In February 1946 he was elected Secretary-General of the United Nations.

The text below is the complete version of the address of the Secretary-General to the General Assembly of the U.N. on 17 November 1950 introducing his Memorandum on a Twenty-Year Program for Achieving Peace through the United Nations.

What was the effect of the Secretary-General's Memorandum? On 20 November 1950, after five meetings of debate, the General Assembly decided that the proper bodies of the United Nations should consider the ten points. The vote on the nine-power resolution was 51 in favor, 5 against, and 1 abstention. The resolution called attention to the progress already made in the Fifth Session of the General Assembly on certain items of the memorandum. Mr. Lie was commended for his initiative in preparing the document and the Assembly reiterated its desire that all the potentialities of the charter should be explored to achieve peace. The Assembly voted down a plan offered by the Soviet delegation entitled a "Proposal for a Twenty-Year Program for Achieving Peace through the United Nations."

On 1 November 1950 the General Assembly extended Mr. Lie's term of office for a three-year period beginning 1 February 1951. The vote was 46 in favor, 5 against, and 8 abstentions. The Soviet proposal to defer consideration and to request the Council to continue its study of a recommendation was rejected by a vote of 9 in favor, 37 against, and 11 abstentions. The resolution finally adopted expressed the need for guaranteeing the continued operation of the office and pointed out that the Security Council had first recommended Mr. Lie in 1946.

IT MAY be useful at the beginning of the general debate on this item to recall the circumstances in which my "Memorandum of Points for Consideration in Development of a 20-Year Program for achieving Peace through the United Nations" originated.

Early last spring it seemed to me—as I am sure it did to most of you—that the United Nations was in grave danger. The deadlock over the representation of China came at the end of a chain of events that had progressively weakened faith throughout the world over a period of three years in the United Nations approach to the problems of war and peace.

There had been a steadily growing tendency to relegate the United Nations to a secondary position in international affairs and to give first priority instead to the old, familiar expedients of arms and alliances.

I believed that this fatal tendency toward loss of faith in the United Nations as the principal means of preventing war must be, and could be, arrested.

I never had any doubt that the peoples of the world would continue to support the United Nations with all their hearts, if given a chance to demonstrate their loyalty to its humane and universal aims. I also believed that the Member governments—all of them—wanted the United Nations to succeed. But the many and dangerous conflicts of interest and ideology were making all of us the prisoners of a vicious circle of charge and countercharge, of force and counterforce, in which distrust and hatreds mounted month by month.

Somehow a way had to be found by the Member governments to break out of this vicious circle. I felt it was clearly my duty as Secretary-General to do what I could to help. It was with these considerations in mind that I prepared my Memorandum on the Development of a 20-Year United Nations Peace Program.

"A New and Great Effort"

In this Memorandum I declared my belief that the atmosphere of deepening international mistrust could be dissipated and that the threat of universal disaster of another war could be averted by a new and great effort to employ to the full the resources for conciliation and constructive peace-building present in the United Nations Charter.

I personally handed the Memorandum to the President of the United States, Mr. Truman, on April 20 in Washington; to the Prime Minister of the United Kingdom, Mr. Attlee, on April 28 in London; to the Prime Minister of France, M. Bidault, on May 3 in Paris; and to the Prime Minister of the Union of Soviet Socialist Republics, Generalissimo Stalin, on May 15 in Moscow.

I discussed the Memorandum, and my reasons for preparing it, with them and with other leaders of their governments, including the Secretary of State of the United States, Mr. Acheson; the Foreign Secretary of the United Kingdom, Mr. Bevin; the Foreign Minister of France, Mr. Schuman; and the Vice Premier of the Union of Soviet Socialist Republics, Mr. Molotov, and the Foreign Minister of the Union of Soviet Socialist Republics, Mr. Vyshinsky.

My talks with these statesmen during my visits to the capitals of the four Great Powers were entirely preliminary and exploratory. All of the talks—without exception—were most friendly and cordial. I neither asked for nor received commitments on specific points in the Memorandum.

While it was indicated to me that each of the four governments might have reservations or amendments concerning some of the points of view expressed, it became equally clear that the approach I was making could provide an acceptable initial basis for discussion to all four governments.

As a next step, therefore, I communicated my Memorandum on June 6 formally to all the Members of the United Nations, together with a covering letter in which I amplified my Memorandum on points concerning atomic energy, trade restrictions and discriminations, and the desirability of universality of Membership and support for the specialized agencies as well as for the United Nations itself.

The North Korean Attack

Less than three weeks later came the attack from North Korea upon the Republic of Korea. I do not today need to recall here the momentous events in the life of the United Nations that have occurred since then.

The United Nations action in Korea and the further steps toward the creation of collective security that have been taken at this session of the General Assembly are, however, not in conflict with, nor do they diminish in the slightest degree, the importance of the many other approaches to peace prescribed by the Charter and suggested in the Memorandum. It is just as important now as it ever was that the United Nations serve as a center for harmonizing the actions of nations toward achieving the purposes of the Charter—perhaps even more so.

The United Nations works best when negotiation, mediation, and conciliation succeed in preventing breaches of the peace such as the one that occurred in Korea.

Once a breach of the peace has occurred, the United Nations can succeed on three conditions: first, that the breach of the peace be suppressed by effective collective action; second, that full collective assistance be given to rehabilitate and reconstruct the country that is the victim of aggression; third, that steps toward genuine and lasting reconciliation be undertaken as rapidly as possible after peace has been restored in that area.

With these considerations in mind, I went ahead with my plan to place my Memorandum on the agenda of this session of the General Assembly, and I so informed the Member governments in my Annual Report.

I am glad that the General Assembly decided to consider my suggestions in plenary meeting. My Memorandum is, of course, not in itself a program. It is, rather, a working paper that suggests an approach to what I hope may develop in time into a 20-Year United Nations Peace Program. It is a reaffirmation of the United Nations approach and an appeal to the Member governments to renew their efforts to make the United Nations work as the only tolerable and civilized alternative to that barbarous thesis of despair—the thesis of irreconcilable conflict.

I believe that detailed consideration of the points in my Memorandum can most fruitfully be undertaken by those organs of the United Nations particularly concerned under the Charter. This consideration —by the Security Council, the Economic and Social Council, the Trusteeship Council, and by appropriate Commissions of the General Assembly—will lead, I hope, during the coming year, to specific action by these organs in their respective fields of responsibility and to the formulation of definite and concrete proposals.

Historic Assembly Decisions

Already, this session of the General Assembly has made several historic decisions that reflect the will to employ to the full the resources for peace and for political, economic, and social progress available under the United Nations Charter, which I had in mind in suggesting the development of a 20-Year United Nations Peace Program.

Let me now proceed to discuss briefly each of the ten points in my Memorandum.

The first point is: *Inauguration of periodic meetings of the Security Council, attended by foreign ministers, or heads or other members of governments, as provided by the United Nations Charter and the rules of procedure; together with further development and use of other United Nations machinery for negotiation, mediation, and conciliation of international disputes.*

There have been no periodic meetings of the Security Council so far, either because, until 1948, the Council of Foreign Ministers met regularly, or because, until this year, there have been two General Assembly sessions each year, or for other reasons. The Charter says there "shall be" such periodic meetings, separate and distinct from the regular continuous session. The Charter also says that the Security Council may hold meetings "at such places other than the seat of the organization as in its judgment will best facilitate its work."

Such periodic meetings, in my opinion, should be inaugurated and used for a general semiannual review at a high level of outstanding issues, particularly those that divide the Great Powers. These meetings should not be expected to bring great decisions every time. They should not be held primarily for public debate. They should be used mainly for consultation—much of it informal—for efforts to gain ground toward agreement on questions at issue, to clear up misunderstandings, to prepare for new initiatives that may improve the chances for definitive agreement at later meetings.

In this connection, I hope that the Security Council and the General Assembly will be able to settle the question of the representation of China in the near future.

We need more direct and regular contact between the men who are responsible for policy-making. Periodic meetings of the Security Council will enable the foreign ministers of the five Great Powers to talk among themselves and to have the benefit of the views of the foreign ministers of the six nonpermanent members, who represent the interests of all the smaller Member states of the United Nations in the Security Council. They have often demonstrated their effectiveness in conciliating and moderating Great Power disputes.

Rotation of Meetings

I suggest that the special periodic meetings normally be held away from the Permanent Headquarters in New York, where the Security Council meets in regular session. The periodic meetings might appropriately be rotated among the other four permanent members of the Security Council, as well as held in other Member countries. Among other advantages, this practice would bring the physical presence of the United Nations closer to all the peoples of the world.

I believe that the inauguration of a series of periodic meetings of the Security Council may not only revive negotiation on Great Power policies and differences, but could also bring about the progressive development over the next few years of other United Nations resources for the prevention, as well as the mediation and conciliation, of disputes of all kinds between Member nations.

The Security Council has well established its role as a place where international controversies can be publicly debated. It has, however, only made a beginning at using its meetings for negotiation as effectively as for debate.

I hope that the practice of using Presidents of the Council as *rapporteurs* for purposes of mediation and conciliation will be encouraged, together with regularly established and functioning machinery for private consultations by the Big Five representatives among themselves as well as with other Members—as this session of the General Assembly has unanimously recommended.

At San Francisco the Big Five representatives met every day. That was one of the means through which unanimous agreement was ultimately secured on the United Nations Charter.

The General Assembly has demonstrated its unique role as the main instrument through which world public opinion on international issues can be determined and given effective political expression. The General Assembly has surpassed in this respect the expectations of the founders at San Francisco. Likewise it has proved to be an ideal forum in which the statesmen of the smaller countries can exert upon conflicts of power an important and even decisive mediating and moderating influence.

Building on Experience

We must build on this experience. The principle of equal rights of states, large and small, is fundamental in the United Nations approach to peace. The smaller states not only have the right to be consulted on all matters in which their interests are involved, but they can often contribute substantially toward results that will strengthen the United Nations influence for peace.

The second point *in a United Nations 20-Year Peace Program is a new attempt to make progress toward establishing an international control system for atomic energy that will be effective in preventing its use for war and promoting its use for peaceful purposes.*

There is no prospect of any quick or easy solution of this most difficult problem—a problem that goes to the very heart of the greatest conflict of power and ideology in the world at the present time. I do believe in the possibility of a definitive solution, but I believe that such a solution probably will be found only at the end—rather than at the beginning—of a long series of difficult negotiations toward settlement of wider issues.

In the meantime, I hope that negotiation on the problem of atomic energy itself can be resumed, in line with the directive of the last session of the General Assembly: "to explore all possible avenues and examine all concrete suggestions with a view to determining whether they might lead to an agreement."

It may be that satisfactory interim or step-by-step agreements on atomic energy control could be worked out that would at least be an improvement on the present state of affairs, when we have an unlimited atomic arms race, even though they did not afford full security. Even such initial steps could be of great importance.

Problem of Armaments

Perhaps the General Assembly and the Security Council, in periodic meeting or otherwise, should reëxamine the decisions to establish two separate Commissions—the Atomic Energy Commission and the Commission on Conventional Armaments—or at least consider the advisability of linking their work more closely together.

I recall the statement made by President Truman in this hall on United Nations Day, when he said in this connection: "One possibility to be considered is whether their work might be revitalized if carried forward in the future through a new and consolidated disarmament commission."

This brings me to the third point *in the Memorandum—a new approach to the whole problem of bringing the armaments race under control, not only in the field of atomic weapons, but in other weapons of mass destruction and in conventional armaments.*

We should not forget that a single raid in World War II using so-called conventional blockbuster and incendiary bombs killed more people than the atomic bomb. The destructive power of existing lethal chemical and bacteriological weapons has not been tested, but such weapons may well be even more deadly than any atomic bombs so far made.

It is understandable and in conformity with their responsibilities to their own peoples that Member governments, when faced with the failure to make peace and the consequent delay in establishing a United Nations collective security system, should look to their own defenses.

In an atmosphere such as exists today strong national defenses are a necessary evil. Disarmament can come only as part of a collective security system and in an atmosphere of mutual confidence such as prevailed among the Allies during the war.

Reducing Tensions

But it is also true that any progress at all toward agreements on the regulation of armaments of any kind would help to reduce tensions and would thus assist in the adjustment of political issues.

We do not need to delay, and should not delay, work on the vast amount of study, discussion, and planning that is required to complete preparation of an effective system of international control for all armaments.

Neither efforts at political settlement nor efforts at regulation of armaments will wait upon the other. Both must go hand in hand.

The fourth point *in my Memorandum is a renewal of serious efforts to reach agreement on the armed forces to be made available under the Charter to the Security Council for the enforcement of its decisions.*

Negotiations on this issue have been stalemated for almost three years in the Military Staff Committee. The problem is clearly one of a political nature. This is an issue that needs new consideration by the Security Council, first of all, probably, at one of the proposed periodic meetings.

The important action taken by this session of the General Assembly in recommending to Member states that they have forces available for United Nations service on the recommendation of either the Security Council or the General Assembly does not in any way diminish the need for and desirability of new efforts to establish the United Nations forces that the Charter says should be on call of the Security Council under Article 43. The Assembly has itself explicitly recognized this.

The fifth point *is acceptance and application of the principle that it is wise and right to proceed as rapidly as possible toward universality of membership.*

Fourteen nations are still awaiting admission to the United Nations. Some of them have been awaiting for three years. Some have been kept out by one negative vote, some by abstentions by the majority in the Security Council.

Arguments have been advanced against the conduct or nature of each of these governments by one side or the other. But it seems to me that the tests provided by the Charter for membership should be applied with wisdom and with generosity, bearing in mind first of all the interests of the peoples concerned rather than the nature of their governments.

Showing Responsibility

I believe it is better for every nation to be inside the United Nations than outside it. I believe it is better both for the United Nations and for the people of the country seeking admission. I do not think it is wise to discourage intercourse and coöperation with the rest of the world that United Nations membership helps to promote. Membership entails the sharing of responsibility for upholding the obligations of the Charter that rests upon each Member.

The United Nations is made weaker, not stronger, when countries of Asia that have newly won their independence are kept outside and when Europe also is grossly underrepresented because of the continued absence of nine European countries that have long ago applied for membership.

I look forward to the day when all the peoples of the world will be represented in the United Nations. I include not only those countries awaiting admission now, and others who may apply, but also Germany and Japan as soon as the peace treaties have been completed.

The sixth of the ten points *is a sound and active program of technical assistance for economic development and encouragement of broad-scale capital investment, using all appropriate private, governmental, and inter-governmental resources.*

The fundamental purpose of such a United Nations program is to help the people of every country to raise their standard of living by peaceful means. A good start has been made during the present year with the inauguration of the $20,000,000 United Nations expanded program of technical assistance for economic development and social welfare.

Encouraging Self-Help

A United Nations program of technical assistance that will produce a basis for sound economic development and social progress must be practical and realistic; it must aim at encouraging self-help. If carefully planned and sensibly administered it will help greatly toward the type of economic development which will increase production, increase purchasing power, and expand the markets of all producers of industrial and agricultural products. The mutual interests of well-developed and underdeveloped nations in such a program are apparent to everyone.

But such a program is only a beginning.

In addition to technical assistance, the underdeveloped countries require financial assistance. The Second Committee of this Assembly has unanimously adopted a resolution declaring that the volume of private capital now flowing into underdeveloped countries cannot meet their needs for economic development.

In this same resolution the Economic and Social Council is asked to consider practical methods for achieving the expansion and steadier flow of foreign capital, both private and public. I hope that the steps taken by this session of the General Assembly will lead next year to real progress in solving the problems of financing economic development on an adequate scale.

It may be that what is needed is a strengthening of the resources of the International Bank and other international organizations operating in this field. On the other hand, it is probable that additional methods of financing certain types of capital expenditures in underdeveloped countries will be needed. I confidently look forward to the establishment of what has been called during this Assembly a "United Nations Recovery Force" through which all the nations will join in a mutually beneficial effort to raise the unspeakably low living standards of more than half of the human race.

In this connection, I warmly welcome the initiative of the Second Committee in calling for an examination of those features of agrarian life, such as outmoded systems of land tenure, which are an obstacle to economic development. The campaign to raise the standard of living of the underdeveloped countries must be fought on many fronts. Next to the preservation of peace, it is the greatest undertaking to which we have put our hands. It must succeed.

The seventh point *of the Peace Program is the more vigorous use by all the Member governments of the specialized agencies of the United Nations, to promote—in the words of the Charter—"higher standards of living, full employment, and conditions of economic and social progress."*

The United Nations family of specialized agencies is by far the most effective machinery that the world has ever had for organized international action to eliminate human misery through persistent, day-to-day, practical programs. The specialized agencies have quietly gone ahead in the past four years, right in the middle of the grave world crisis and with very limited resources, with the development and putting into operation of hundreds of such programs. It is not too much to say that almost everybody in the world has been helped by one or more of the programs undertaken by these agencies. They have become vitally necessary tools in a long-range program aimed at eliminating the economic and social causes of war.

Need for Support

The specialized agencies, however, like the rest of the United Nations peace system, are not self-operating. They need wider and more constructive support from all Member governments of the United Nations. It is very much to be regretted that they have not had this support in all cases in the past. I hope that all the Member governments will be prepared, as time goes on, to participate fully in the work of the specialized agencies and to increase their resources.

Much has already been done to achieve better coördination so as to prevent overlapping and thus effect economies and improve programming. A more important place for the specialized agencies in the policies of governments would produce better leadership in achieving these objectives, while at the same time putting to greater use some of the best tools the world has yet devised for reducing the causes of war.

I wish once again to call the attention of representatives to the statement to which the Directors-General of the specialized agencies and I subscribed in Paris last May, reaffirming the principles of universality and urging that "the greatest efforts . . . be directed towards achieving in fact true universality in the membership and programs of the United Nations and of those of the specialized agencies which are founded on that principle."

The eighth point *is the continued and vigorous development of the work of the United Nations for wider observance and respect for human rights and fundamental freedoms throughout the world.*

The attention of the world has been so concentrated during the past four years upon contests of political interest and ideological dogmas that the significance of the growing demand throughout the world for better observance of human rights has not been fully understood.

Evidence is already accumulating that the Universal Declaration of Human Rights is destined to rank in history with such great documents as the Magna Carta, the Declaration of Independence of the United States, and the Declaration of the Rights of Man. It goes beyond these declarations in two important respects. First, it is international—the first worldwide declaration of human rights in history. Second, it proclaims economic and social rights along with the traditional political and religious liberties—such rights as the right to work, the right to a decent standard of living, and the right to social security, in conformity with what should now be the universal standard.

Most of the peoples of the world do not yet enjoy most of these rights.

Peaceful Revolution

The United Nations has the resources to achieve a peaceful revolution during the next twenty years by securing much wider observance of these rights in all parts of the world. This effort may take many forms: international covenants on individual rights or groups of rights designed to mobilize the power of national and international law behind the observance of such rights; development of other methods to promote implementation of these rights; assistance to governments to help them create conditions in which economic, social and cultural rights particularly can be enjoyed by greater numbers of people; separate action toward such ends as promoting freedom of information and rights of women; and fighting discrimination against minorities, slavery, and the use of forced labor.

These and many other programs of action through the United Nations and the specialized agencies deserve the fullest possible support from all the Member governments and peoples of the United Nations.

The ninth point *is the use of the United Nations to promote, by peaceful means instead of by force, the advancement of dependent, colonial or semicolonial peoples toward a place of equality in the world.*

I firmly believe that such great changes as have been taking place since the end of the war—fundamental changes in the relationships of whole peoples and even continents—can be prevented from tearing the world apart only by using the universal framework of the United Nations to contain them within peaceful bounds.

Since the United Nations was founded, nine countries of Asia with a population of 600,000,000 people have gained their independence.

In Africa, the United Nations is assisting the former Italian colonies of Libya, Eritrea, and Somaliland to achieve independent status.

The United Nations, through its Trusteeship System and the provisions of the Charter relating to other Non-Self-Governing Territories, offers the Administering Powers and the peoples under their jurisdiction the best opportunity to move forward by peaceful means toward an era of coöperation for their mutual welfare.

This opportunity needs to be more fully used and I am glad to note the progress that is being made in this direction.

The tenth and last point *in the Memorandum is the active and systematic use of all the powers of the Charter and all the machinery of the United Nations to speed up the development of international law for a universal world society.*

This work is in progress. It needs more vigorous support from the Member governments and from the peoples. The General Assembly adopted unanimously in Paris in 1948 the Convention outlawing genocide—the crime of destroying a national, ethnical, religious, or racial group of human beings as Hitler tried to destroy the Jews. This Convention has only just now secured the number of ratifications required to bring it into force.

The codification and embodiment in similar conventions of the laws of the Nürnberg Tribunal under which the Nazi war criminals were punished should also be pressed forward by the Member governments.

Other conventions widening the scope of world law—like the protocol extending the control of narcotic drugs to the new synthetic drugs and the proposed conventions on human rights—should be pressed. The constitutional scope and authority of the United Nations system will be enhanced by each such convention or treaty as it comes into force as law.

Toward a World Law

If during the next twenty years, the General Assembly, the International Court of Justice, the International Law Commission, and other appropriate organs of the United Nations can proceed systematically in the development of international law, by the end of that time we may have at least the essential beginnings of a system of enforceable world law directly applicable to individuals as well as governments on all matters essential to the peace and security of mankind.

In the meantime I hope that the Member governments will continue the trend of the past year towards greater use of the International Court of Justice both for the juridical settlement of disputes and for the handing down of advisory opinions and interpretations of the United Nations Charter.

I have placed my Memorandum before you as a preliminary working paper. The suggestions it contains are, of course, not in any way final or complete. I am grateful for the many expressions of sympathy, interest, and support that I have received since the circulation of my Memorandum last June from the foreign ministers and representatives of Member states.

I welcome the draft resolution by the sponsoring powers to refer the Memorandum for further study and action to the appropriate organs. I hope that other constructive ideas and suggestions will be brought forward during this debate and will be given full and equal consideration.

The suggestions I have made carry with them an appeal to the Member governments to make the United Nations the primary instrument of their foreign policies in all ways—in the creation of collective security against armed aggression, in the prevention and peaceful settlement of disputes, in all international efforts toward disarmament, expanding world trade, raising living standards, promoting human rights for individuals and equal rights for peoples.

One of the things the world needs more than anything else today is a continuing reaffirmation by the Member governments that the United Nations is the right road to peace, and the only road now open to mankind.

We cannot foresee today what the next twelve months will bring. But of one thing I am certain—it is still possible for the Member governments to win peace, and to win it for a long time to come if they will follow that road.

Part Two

The United States and

Foreign Affairs

GENERAL

The Fulcrum of Western Civilization
Arnold Toynbee

In the fall of 1950 Dr. Arnold Toynbee delivered three lectures at Stanford University and at the Commonwealth Club in San Francisco. The text below is based upon the stenographic transcription made at the first lecture and later published in the *Christian Science Monitor* for 22 December 1950. Dr. Toynbee has gone over the newspaper version and has made certain revisions. In a letter to the editor dated 5 March 1951 he explains: "I always speak only from notes; I have no scripts."

Author of the monumental six-volume work, *A Study of History* (1934-39), Dr. Toynbee has been director of studies at the Royal Institute of International Affairs, London since 1925. He was born in London in 1889 and educated at Winchester College, at Balliol College, Oxford, and at the British Archeological School. From 1919 to 1924 he was professor of Byzantine and Modern Greek language, literature, and history at the University of London and is now professor of international history there.

The title of this text was suggested by the *Monitor* article. Dr. Toynbee's other two lectures in California dealt with "True Religion in Contrast to Communism" and "The Need of Becoming Supranationally Minded."

IT SEEMS to me that the domestic politics of the United States have now become the government of the Western world as a whole. This has happened since World War II, though there were symptoms of it even in World War I. I do not know how far people in this country realize this. No doubt it is an extra complication for you and an extra annoyance to you.

It is very awkward for you; you did not wish that, you did not ask for that, when you created your Constitution and worked out your party system and your way of governing yourselves; you did all this for yourselves and for your own national purposes. You never asked or wished that your domestic politics should become of vital importance to the Western world as a whole.

And yet, owing to the central and preponderant position of the United States in our common Western community, we in my country, Great Britain, and the rest of us in all the other countries of the Western world or countries that are even remotely associated with the Western world, follow your politics, I think, with greater interest and with greater anxiety nowadays than we follow our own local politics.

Why this interest in American politics outside the United States? It is because we have all come to realize that American politics have become a matter of life and death for us. We have not votes, but, though we cannot vote for the President of the United States, he is the most important executive official that we possess. We have no voice in who is to be Secretary of State, but he is the most important diplomatic officer that we possess. You did not ask for it; we did not ask for it; but that is the situation, and I do not quite see how that can last as between peoples who are all accustomed to democratic processes of self-government, and who prize this heritage of self-government almost as highly as they prize life itself.

A union of the democratic Western nations around the United States is, I believe, now a paramount necessity for all of us. But this union cannot, I also believe, really be placed on a sound, healthy, satisfactory, and lasting basis unless we face a problem from which we all shrink. We shrink from it because it clashes so much with our traditional national feelings. It is the problem of creating some kind of common government for our Western community on a democratic basis—a democratic government for the Western community as a whole.

During the last four or five hundred years, we Westerners have been insisting on these national differences of ours. We have been digging the dividing lines between one Western nation and another deeper and deeper, and we have been trying to make each of these national fractions of our Western Christendom into a separate and self-contained universe. Our respective nations have in a sense become idols. They have become perhaps the real gods that we Westerners worship under the nominal surface forms of our traditional Christianity. It seems to me that we now have to undo and reverse the whole of what you might call this secessionist movement from our common Western Christendom. We have all been guilty of this during these last four or five centuries. We must all coöperate now to rebuild the common house that we have all had a hand in breaking up.

That is very difficult because it brings us into conflict with national group emotions that have become consecrated by time and that are particularly difficult to cope with because they are not based on reason.

It might well take four hundred years for so deep-rooted an institution as national sovereignty to be uprooted from peoples' hearts. If it takes three generations to change your nationality (in the sense that immigrant families are assimilated into the American scene), it might take ten generations or fifteen generations to give up some very cherished idea like national sovereignty or local independence and to accommodate ourselves to the idea of world government. Yet current history is forcing the pace and speeding up the rate of change in our feelings. If you or I today are thinking of what is happening in Korea, and if, in connection with that, we say the word "we," I think we would find ourselves meaning a much bigger "we" than we used to mean when we said "we" about war or politics. We used to mean just "we Americans," "we French," "we British"; now we mean "we Westerners."

Of course, we mean more than that. We mean not only us peoples of the Western world; we mean all freedom-loving people in the world, Western or non-Western, whatever the color of our skins, whether we are inhabitants of the New World or of the Old World, whether we are Christians or Jews, or Mohammedans or Hindus or Buddhists. We mean all of us who share the same ideas and ideals about freedom and justice and the supreme value of the individual soul.

But within that happily wide group of peoples there is a smaller group with a closer and longer past in common—the Western group—and I think we feel and know today that the Western community is a reality. Outsiders still recognize that we are in some sense a single society, a common family. But we ourselves, when we grew strong at the beginning of the modern age, found it easy to ignore the rest of the world and to indulge in the luxury of emphasizing our domestic national differences from each other. Now that we Westerners no longer have an unchallenged and unquestioned monopoly of power in the world, our consciousness of our unity is, I believe, happily, and just in time, beginning to come back to us, and we are groping about for common institutions to express this unity once more—to give it a practical expression to meet our common need for standing together in a world that has become once again a dangerous place for the West and for its ideals.

If I am right about this, then I think we cannot be content with having just our present local, national governments on a democratic footing, while we leave our all-important common Western government to be carried on without a common parliamentary control. Of course we might shirk that problem, but we shall shirk it at our peril in the world as it is today.

Perhaps it is legitimate—I am sure it is both legitimate and wise to look at what one's adversary is doing when he has perhaps done, rather well and successfully, something that is also important for us. Well, we might learn something from what the Soviet Union has done about this problem of nationalities.

Let us give to nationality in our Western world a wide scope in all linguistic, cultural, and educational lines and in the field of sports, but do not let us—because we cannot afford this in face of our present Russian adversary—do not let us leave any edged tools in the hands of these local fractions of our Western world; let us place the edged tools under the control of a central Western authority. If our Western community can crystallize around North America on a footing of democratic self-government for central as well as for local purposes, we shall be so irresistibly strong that neither Russia nor anybody else outside will be able to challenge us.

Let us begin by building up the necessary common institutions behind our new common Western army as far as efficiency demands, and that will carry us very far towards a common self-government. But when we have got that far, we cannot just rest there. On the one hand, I feel it would be a mistake to think that we can shirk the question of a common political constitution. On the other hand, it would be equally a mistake if we were to develop our common institutions on lines that would be unnecessarily provocative to the national sentiments that are so deeply planted in the hearts of all Western peoples.

Let us take the moderate, statesmanlike way but, in taking it, let us not shirk the problem of providing, not merely a common Western army, but a common democratic form of self-government for our threatened and precious common Western world.

The National Interest of the United States
George F. Kennan

Northwestern University celebrated its centennial in 1951. On 30 January the committee in charge sponsored the first of a series of academic conferences designed to highlight the anniversary. It was devoted to the subject, "International Understanding," and the principal speaker was George F. Kennan.

Born in Milwaukee in 1904 and a graduate of Princeton in the class of 1925, Mr. Kennan has served as a foreign service officer in Hamburg, Tallinn, Riga, Kovno, Berlin, Vienna,

Prague, Lisbon, London, and Moscow. He accompanied Ambassador Bullitt to Moscow in 1933 and became minister-counselor of the embassy there in 1945.

Mr. Kennan, the author (designated as "X") of the article, "The Sources of Soviet Conduct," in the July 1947 issue of *Foreign Affairs*, joined the policy planning staff of the Department of State in 1947. In June 1949 he became the chief long-range adviser to the Secretary of State. In the fall of 1950 he resigned and became a member of the Institute for Advanced Study at Princeton, New Jersey. His book, *American Diplomacy 1900-1950—and the Challenge of Soviet Power*, was published in the fall of 1951. Toward the close of 1951, President Truman named Kennan to be Ambassador to the Soviet Union and he departed for Moscow in spring 1952.

The text here reproduced represents the last third of a 6300-word lecture. For the full version the reader is referred to the January-February 1951 issue of the *Illinois Law Review*.

NONE OF US can really see very far ahead in this turbulent, changing, kaleidoscopic world of foreign affairs. A study of the great decisions of national policy in the past leaves the historian impressed with the difficulty of analyzing the future clearly enough to be able to make really reliable calculations of the consequences of national action. It also reveals that too often the motives of national action are ones dictated for government by developments outside of its control. Its freedom of action, in these cases, lies only in the choice of method—in the *how* rather than the *what*.

Let no one underestimate the importance in this life of the manner in which a thing is done. It is surprising how few acts there are, in individual life, which are not acceptable if they are carried out with sufficient grace and self-assurance and above all with dignity and good manners and with respect for the feelings and rights of others. I would say that these rules alone, if consistently applied, would save a man or a nation from at least two-thirds of the worst mistakes they might otherwise make. On the other hand, there are few acts, however commendable in purpose, which cannot be rendered unacceptable and unfortunate in their results if carried out in the wrong way, with the neglect of these principles.

And I would remind you that this question of method affects not only the outward consequences of our acts, but it has the deepest and most important effect on ourselves. Our life is so strangely composed that the best way to make ourselves better seems sometimes to be to act as though we were better; and the man who makes it a point to behave with consideration and dignity in his relations with others, regardless of his inner doubts and conflicts, will suddenly find that he has achieved a great deal in his relations with himself. The tenor and manner of our behavior toward others, as a nation, is therefore going to have an important effect on the character of our development here at home.

For these reasons we would do well to learn to think of the conduct of foreign affairs as a problem of style even more than of purpose. Where purpose is dim and questionable, form comes into its own. There are situations in this world in which good manners and proper modalities of action, while they may seem to be an inferior means of salvation, may be the only means of salvation we have at all. This is my reason for maintaining that if national interest relates to our purpose in world affairs, it relates more importantly to the dignity and propriety of our conduct—to the methods by which we pursue those aims which necessity, public feeling, and good judgment press upon us.

Today, of course, we face a world of which I think it fair to say that it is more troubled and more complicated, more potentially dangerous to us, than any we have ever known. And the dangers are not only outside ones but are in part within ourselves. What lessons would this view of national interest, which I have outlined here this evening, hold for us in the light of the problems which are crowding in upon us today?

I would say that the first lesson it holds for us is the necessity of a realistic appraisal at all times of the danger that confronts us. We are all steamed up about a possible Soviet attack. It is right that we should prepare for all eventualities and be able to deal with them if they come. Perhaps we will be faced with such an attack. But we do not know that for sure. So far, Russia has attacked no one with her own forces since the recent war; and those who know most about her intentions feel that it would be no less foolish to stake our future on a certainty that Russia means to go to war than to stake it on a certainty that she does *not* mean to. We simply do not know. The only thing we do know is that to act as though war were inevitable, and unavoidable, when we have no proof of that assumption, is the best way to substantiate the Soviet thesis that we are aggressors and are planning war ourselves, and the best way to bring war nearer to us. Let us reckon with the possibility that war may come and let us be prepared accordingly; but let us not sell our souls to that prospect. For if we do, it will almost certainly become reality; and we shall never be able to be sure that we did not have a part in bringing it to pass.

Secondly, some of us in government find ourselves being reproached for not "getting mad" and for not adding our voices to the thundering assertions of anger and indignation with which the air is already full. I hope we will never yield to those pressures. The public would be well advised not to listen to the people who strain in that direction. One of the prerequisites for dealing successfully with the sort of problem we have before us today in the form of Soviet Communism is an ability to keep cool and to rise above petty irritation. Dealing successfully with the pressures of Bolshevism is like tennis or any form of contest that requires cool nerves—rage doesn't help; the adversary has ways of taking advantage of it.

Let us repudiate, therefore, these easy reactions. Let us repudiate idle invective and empty gestures and pinpricks. These are only forms of petulance and self-indulgence. Let us reserve our power for the things that are really necessary and the things that can really advance our interests. We can have our emotions, and we can have our conviction that those who are now agitating the world with their irresponsible and provocative actions, and I am thinking here of the Chinese Communists, will live to regret this unnecessary resort to violence, these childish tantrums, and this reckless squandering of the good will of the American people. But it will be *actions*—wise, temperate, well-chosen actions, for which the end is in sight before the beginning is made—which will determine the outcome, not words or breast-beating or saber-rattling or storming around.

Next, in our dealings with friendly nations, and particularly with those who find themselves most closely associated with us in world affairs, let us be fair and tolerant in this difficult moment. It is the mark of real self-assurance, the sign of inner strength, to be conciliatory and respectful and understanding of the neighbor's point of view. There is no uglier tendency in American nature than the quickness to moral indignation and to wild suspicions of bad faith which many of us display when other people do not think as we do. These questions which are now agitating international life are ones about which there are deep and troubled differences of opinion among us here at home. Is it surprising, then, that other nations, which have different interests and outlooks, should not see them just as we do? When I see the shallow self-righteousness with which many of us condemn our closest friends for taking different views of world realities than we do in matters which are admittedly questions of judgment and opinion, I cannot help but hear again the well-known admonition of Cromwell to the General Assembly of the Kirk of Scotland: "Is it therefore infallibly agreeable to the word of God, that which you say? I beseech you, by the bowels of Christ, think it possible you may be mistaken."

And finally, my friends, if we succeed in laying upon ourselves this forbearance and restraint in our dealings with the nations we are trying to collaborate with, let us then see whether we cannot find a little of it left for our dealings with ourselves. You know and I know that this country rings from end to end today with angry voices charging all sorts of failings and iniquities, eager to smash not only the reputations but the public usefulness of people, over these questions of foreign policy and national interest. Is it impossible for us to get it into our heads that we are dealing with an extremely complicated environment; that the choices are *not* simple, are *not* obvious; that none of us is capable of seeing very clearly all that is involved; and that for that reason not a single one of us has the right to certainty or to self-righteousness and to uncharitableness toward others who do not think as he thinks? I have been in Washington, and I have been in and out of this business of the formulation of foreign policy for years on end; and I do not know one person in a responsible position in the government of the United States who is not animated in these dark days by the most earnest, and in many instances anguished, sense of devotion to the interests of this country of ours. Who has the right to treat these men as reprobates or criminals because he does not agree with them? The air has been full of charges of dereliction toward the interests of this country; but I tell you that I know of no greater dereliction from duty to the American people in this day and age than to be quick to undermine their faith in the decency and good will and patriotism of other Americans over matters of opinion so deeply problematical that only almighty God could be sure he had the right answers. You can listen day in and day out to these disputes about the merits of this policy or that, and you will never be able to be entirely sure as to who is right and who is wrong, for only time will tell; but there is one man you may depend upon it is wrong, and that is the man whose mind is preoccupied, and whose voice is hoarse, with destructive criticism and fulminations and accusations against others.

I would plead, then,—if you will—for concepts of national interest more modest than those with which we are accustomed to flatter our sensibilities, but for a greater dignity and quietness and self-discipline in the implementation of those concepts. I would plead, particularly at this genuinely crucial moment in American history, for cool nerves and a clear eye, for the husbanding of our strength, and for an iron self-discipline in refusing to be provoked into using that strength where we cannot see some plausible and reasonably promising end to what we are beginning. I would plead for the restoration of a sense of comradeship and tolerance in our public life and public debates, and for a recognition of the fact that Americans may be wrong without being evil, and that those wrong ones may even conceivably be ourselves.

If we can achieve these things we need not be too exacting in our demands for a definition of national interest. We will then have done the best we can do to bring the world closer to that state of understanding to which this Centennial celebration has been devoted: an understanding based necessarily more on respect than on intimacy, but fortified by mutual restraint and moderation, and all the more durable and serviceable for its modesty of concept. Therein—not in the world of hatred or of intolerance or of vainglorious pretense—lies the true glory and the true interest of this nation.

Tensions Between the United States and the Soviet Union

Dean Acheson

This address was delivered at the University of California at Berkeley on 16 March 1950 in connection with the Conference on International Coöperation for World Economic Development. Mr. Acheson spelled out for the first time and in specific detail the seven principal areas of disagreement between the United States and the U.S.S.R. The speech did much to allay the criticism that the State Department had failed to communicate its policies to the American people.

Dean Gooderham Acheson was born in Middletown, Connecticut in 1893, the son of an Episcopal bishop. He studied at Yale (A.B., 1915) and Harvard Law School (LL.B., 1918) and from 1919 to 1921 was private secretary to Supreme Court Justice Louis D. Brandeis. He served for six months as Under Secretary of the Treasury in 1933 and as Under Secretary of State from August 1945 to July 1947. He succeeded General Marshall as Secretary of State in January 1949.

I WISH TO make a report to you about the tensions between the United States and the Soviet Union.

Now, the right and obligation of the Secretary of State to speak to his fellow citizens, or to the representatives of other nations, about our foreign relations is not derived from any claim on his part to special knowledge or wisdom which makes him right and other people wrong. It is derived from the fact that our forefathers by free choice worked out and approved a Constitution. This Constitution, with the amendments and interpretations which have made it a living and growing thing, has survived to this day as an expression of the will of the entire people. A President is duly elected under this Constitution with a heavy and solemn responsibility to direct the foreign relations of the American people. The President has, in accordance with law and with the advice and consent of the Senate, appointed a man to serve as Secretary of State to assist him in the conduct of our foreign affairs. This right to speak on your behalf results directly from the constitutional processes by which the American people provide a government for themselves in an orderly, clear, and democratic manner.

A little over thirty years ago there came into power in one of the great countries of the world a group of people who also claim the right to speak on your behalf. That claim was based not on any constitutional procedure, or on any expression of the will of those whose representatives they professed to be. It was based on a claim which those men made to a monopoly of the knowledge of what was right and what was wrong for human beings. They further profess that their claim is based on a body of thought taken over in large part from the writings of a mid-nineteenth-century German economist and theorist, Karl Marx.

I have no desire to debate here the errors of one version or another of what is today called "Marxism." But I think it must be recognized in the light of the experience of the last hundred years that many of the premises on which Marx based his thought have been belied by the known facts of what has actually happened in the decades since Marx made his studies. Marx's law of capitalist accumulation, his law as to the rate of profit, his prediction of the numerical decline of the middle classes, and of the increase of the class struggle: none of these calculations has been borne out by the experience of the societies of the West. Marx did not foresee the possibility of democratic solutions.

Furthermore, the body of doctrine now professed by the Moscow-controlled Communists is only tenuously identified with Marx's writings and is largely overlaid with Russian imperialism. We certainly cannot accept the thesis that such a doctrine can serve as the justification for the right of a small group of individuals to speak for the great masses of human beings who have never selected them as their spokesmen and whose own opinions they have never consulted.

Now for three decades this group of people, or their successors, has carried on as the rulers of that same great country. They have always, at the same time, maintained the pretense that they are the interpreters of the aspirations of peoples far beyond their borders. In the light of that professed philosophy they have conducted, as masters of the Russian state, a foreign policy which now is the center of the most difficult and troublesome problems of international affairs, problems designed to keep the peoples of the world in a state of deepest apprehension and doubt. In addition to this, they have operated within the limits of the Soviet state on the basis of a domestic policy founded, they say, on the same philosophy.

There are many points in this philosophy, and particularly in the way in which it has already been applied in practice in the Soviet Union and elsewhere, which are not only deeply repugnant to us, but raise questions involving the most basic conceptions of good and evil —questions involving the ultimate moral nature of man. There is no use in attempting to ignore or gloss over the profundity of this conflict of view.

The free society values the individual as an end in himself. It requires of him only that self-discipline and self-restraint which make the rights of each individual compatible with the rights of every other individual. Individual freedom, therefore, implies individual responsibility not to exercise freedom in ways inconsistent with the freedom of other individuals, and responsibility positively to make constructive use of freedom in the building of a just society.

In relations between nations, the prime reliance of the free society is on the strength and appeal of its principles, and it feels no compulsion sooner or later to bring all societies into conformity with it.

It does not fear, rather it welcomes, diversity and derives its strength from freedom of inquiry and tolerance even of antipathetic ideas.

We can see no moral compromise with the contrary theses of international communism: that the end justifies the means, that any and all methods are therefore permissible, and that the dignity of the human individual is of no importance as against the interest of the state.

To our minds, these principles mean, in their practical application, the arrogation to individual human leaders, with all their inevitable frailties and limitations, of powers and pretenses which most of us would be willing to concede only to the infinite wisdom and compassion of a Divine Being. They mean the police state, with all that that implies; a regimentation of the worker which is hardly distinguishable from slave labor; a loss to society of those things which appear to us to make life worth living; a denial of the fundamental truths embodied in all the great religions of the world.

Here is a moral issue of the clearest nature. It cannot be evaded. Let us make no mistake about it.

Yet it does not follow from this that the two systems, theirs and ours, cannot exist concurrently in this world. Good and evil can and do exist concurrently in the whole great realm of human life. They exist within every individual, within every nation, and within every human group. The struggle between good and evil cannot be confined to governments. That struggle will go on, as it always has, in the wider theater of the human spirit itself.

But it also does not follow from this coexistence of good and evil that the two systems, theirs and ours, will necessarily be able to exist concurrently. That will depend largely on them, for we ourselves do not find impossibility in the prospect of coexistence with the Soviet system.

However much we may sympathize with the Soviet citizens who for reasons bedded deep in history are obliged to live under it, we are not attempting to change the governmental or social structure of the Soviet Union. The Soviet regime, however, has devoted a major portion of its energies and resources to the attempt to impose its system on other peoples. In this attempt it has shown itself prepared to resort to any method or stratagem including subversion, threats, and even military force.

Therefore, if the two systems are to coexist, some acceptable means must be found to free the world from the destructive tensions and anxieties of which it has been the victim in these past years and the continuance of which can hardly be in the interests of any people.

I wish, therefore, to speak to you about those points of greatest difference which must be identified and sooner or later reconciled if the two systems are to live together, if not with mutual respect, at least in reasonable security. What is it which the leaders of international communism could do to make such coexistence more tolerable to everyone?

There are a number of things they could do, which, while leaving much yet to do, would give the world new confidence in the possibility of peaceful change, in the principle and processes of peaceful settlement as an effective means of finding workable solutions in areas of disagreement.

Let us look first at the points where we and they are perhaps most closely in contact, and where the establishment of peace in its narrowest, most limited sense is dangerously impeded by the absence of common ground.

One: Definition of Terms of Peace

It is now nearly five years since the end of hostilities, and the victorious allies have been unable to define the terms of peace with the defeated countries. This is a grave, a deeply disturbing fact. For our part, we do not intend nor wish, in fact we do not know how, to create satellites. Nor can we accept a settlement which would make Germany, Japan, or liberated Austria satellites of the Soviet Union. The experience in Hungary, Rumania, and Bulgaria has been one of bitter disappointment and shocking betrayal of the solemn pledges by the wartime allies. The Soviet leaders joined in the pledge at Teheran that they looked forward "with confidence to the day when all peoples of the world may live free lives, untouched by tyranny, and according to their varying desires and their own consciences." We can accept treaties of peace which would give reality to this pledge and to the interests of all in security.

With regard to Germany, unification under a government chosen in free elections under international observation is a basic element in an acceptable settlement. With that need recognized and with a will to define the terms of peace, a German treaty could be formulated which, while not pretending to solve all of the complex and bitter problems of the German situation, would, nevertheless, go far toward a relaxation of a set of major tensions.

With regard to Austria, that unhappy country is still under occupation because the Soviet leaders do not want a treaty. The political and economic independence of Austria is being sabotaged by the determination of the Soviets, camouflaged in technicalities, to maintain their forces and special interests in Eastern Austria.

With regard to Japan, we feel that the Soviet leaders could recognize the interest which nations other than the members of the Council of Foreign Ministers have in a Japanese peace treaty and could refrain from taking positions and insisting on procedures which block progress toward a treaty.

In the Far East generally, there are many points where the Soviet leaders could, if they chose, relax tensions. They could, for example, permit the United Nations' Commission in Korea to carry out its duties by allowing the Commission's entry into North Korea and by accepting its report as the basis for a peaceful settlement of that liberated country's problems. They could repatriate Japanese prisoners of war from Siberian camps. They could refrain from subverting the efforts of the newly independent states of Asia and their native leaders to solve their problems in their own way.

Two: Use of Force

With regard to the whole group of countries which we are accustomed to think of as the satellite area, the Soviet leaders could withdraw their military and police force and refrain from using the shadow of that force to keep in power persons or regimes which do not command the confidence of the respective peoples, freely expressed through orderly representative processes. In other words, they could elect to observe, in practice, the declaration to which they set their signatures at Yalta concerning liberated Europe.

In this connection we do not insist that these governments have any particular political or social complexion. What concerns us is that they should be truly independent national regimes, with a will of their own and with a decent foundation in popular feeling. We would like to feel, when we deal with these governments, that we are dealing with something representative of the national identity of the peoples in question. We cannot believe that such a situation would be really incompatible with the security of the Soviet Union.

This is a question of elementary good faith, and it is vital to a spirit of confidence that other treaties and other agreements will be honored. Nothing would so alter the international climate as the holding of elections in the satellite states in which the true will of the people could be expressed.

Three: Obstruction in the United Nations

The Soviet leaders could drop their policy of obstruction in the United Nations and could instead act as if they believe the United Nations is, as Stalin himself has recently called it, a serious instrumentality for the maintenance of international peace and security. They are simply not acting that way now.

Their policy of walkout and boycott is a policy that undermines the concept of majority decision. Indeed, they seem deliberately to entrench themselves in a minority position in the United Nations. This was illustrated last fall when they voted against the Essentials of Peace Resolution which solemnly restated and reaffirmed the principles and purposes of the United Nations Charter and which pointed to practical steps which Members should take to support the peace.

A respect for the expressed will of the majority is as fundamental to international organization as it is to democracy. We know that a majority of the General Assembly has generally not agreed with the Soviet Union, whereas we ourselves have generally been on the majority side. There is nothing artificial about this situation. It has not been the result of any sleight of hand or pressures on our part. We do not have any satellites whose votes we control. The significant fact is that proposals which have commended themselves to a majority of the members of the United Nations have also commended themselves to us.

Let the Soviet Union put forward in the United Nations genuine proposals conducive to the work of peace, respectful of the real independence of other governments, and appreciative of the role which the United Nations could and should play in the preservation of world stability and the coöperation of nations. They will then doubtless have a majority with them. We will rejoice to see them in such a majority. We will be pleased to be a member of it ourselves.

Four: Effective Control of Atomic Energy

The Soviet leaders could join us in seeking realistic and effective arrangements for the control of atomic weapons and the limitation of armaments in general. We know that it is not easy for them under their system to contemplate the functioning on their territory of an authority in which people would participate who are not of their political persuasion.

If we have not hesitated to urge that they as well as we accept this requirement it is because we believe that a spirit of genuine responsibility to mankind is widely present in this world. Many able administrators and scientists could be found to operate such an authority who would be only too happy, regardless of political complexion, to take an elevated and enlightened view of the immense responsibility which would rest upon them. There are men who would scorn to use their powers for the negative purpose of intrigue and destruction. We believe that an authority could be established which would not be controlled or subject to control by either ourselves or the Soviet Union

Five: Attempts at Undermining Established Governments

The Kremlin could refrain from using the Communist apparatus controlled by it throughout the world to attempt to overthrow, by subversive means, established governments with which the Soviet government stands in an outward state of friendship and respect. In general, it could desist from, and could coöperate in efforts to prevent, indirect aggression across national frontiers—a mode of conduct which is inconsistent with the spirit and the letter of the United Nations Charter.

Six: Proper Treatment of Diplomatic Representatives

The Soviet leaders could coöperate with us to the end that the official representatives of all countries are treated everywhere with decency and respect and that an atmosphere is created in which these representatives could function in a normal and helpful manner, conforming to the accepted codes of diplomacy.

The standards of conduct of our own representatives are known from more than a century and a half of American diplomatic experience. These standards are such that all countries which have accepted our representatives in a spirit of respect and confidence over periods of many decades have certainly remained none the worse for it. The independence of those countries has not been undermined; their peoples have not been corrupted; their economies have not been scathed by sabotage.

When we now find our representatives treated as criminals, when we see great official propaganda machines reiterating that they are sinister people and that contact with them is pregnant with danger—we cannot believe that such insinuations are advanced in good faith, and we cannot be blind to the obvious implications of such an attitude.

Seven: Distortion of Motives of Others

In general, the Soviet leaders could refrain, I think, from systematically distorting to their own peoples the picture of the world outside their borders, and of our country in particular.

We are not suggesting that they become propagandists for any country or system other than their own. But the Soviet leaders know, and the world knows, with what genuine disappointment and concern the people of this country were brought to the realization that the wartime collaboration between the major allies was not to be the beginning of a happier and freer era in the association between the peoples of the Soviet Union and other peoples.

What are we now to conclude from the morbid fancies which their propaganda exudes of a capitalist encirclement, of a United States craftily and systematically plotting another world war? They know, and the world knows, how foreign is the concept of aggressive war to our philosophy and our political system. They know that we are not asking to be the objects of any insincere and effusive demonstrations of sentimental friendship. But we feel that the Soviet leaders could at least permit access to the Soviet Union of persons and ideas from other countries so that other views might be presented to the Russian people.

These are some of the things which we feel that the Soviet leaders could do, which would permit the rational and peaceful development of the coexistence of their system and ours. They are not things that go to the depths of the moral conflict. They are not things that promise the Kingdom of Heaven. They have been formulated by us, not as moralists but as servants of government, anxious to get on with the practical problems that lie before us, and to get on with them in a manner consistent with mankind's deep longing for a respite from fear and uncertainty.

Nor have they been formulated as a one-sided bargain. A will to achieve binding, peaceful settlements would be required of all participants. All would have to produce unmistakable evidence of their good faith. All would have to accept agreements in the observance of which all nations could have real confidence.

The United States is ready, as it has been and always will be, to coöperate in genuine efforts to find peaceful settlements. Our attitude is not inflexible, our opinions are not frozen, our positions are not and will not be obstacles to peace. But it takes more than one to coöperate. If the Soviet Union could join in doing these things I have outlined, we could all face the future with greater security. We could look forward to more than the eventual reduction of some of the present tensions. We could anticipate a return to a more normal and relaxed diplomatic atmosphere, and to progress in the transaction of some of the international business which needs so urgently to be done.

I fear, however, that I must warn you not to raise your hopes. No one who has lived through these postwar years can be sanguine about reaching agreements in which reliance can be placed and which will be observed by the Soviet leaders in good faith. We must not, in our yearning for peace, allow ourselves to be betrayed by vague generalities or beguiling proffers of peace which are unsubstantiated by good faith solidly demonstrated in daily behavior. We are always ready to discuss, to negotiate, to agree, but we are understandably loath to play the role of international sucker. We will take the initiative in the future as we have in the past in seeking agreement whenever there is any indication that this course would be a fruitful one. What is required is genuine evidence in conduct, not just in words, of an intention to solve the immediate problems and remove the tensions which divide us. I see no evidence that the Soviet leaders will change their conduct until the progress of the free world convinces them that they cannot profit from a continuation of these tensions.

So our course of action in the world of hard reality which faces us is not one that is easily charted. It is not one which this nation can adopt without consideration of the needs and views of other free nations. It is one which requires all the devotion and resolve and wisdom that can be summoned up. We have had and continue to have the assistance and advice of distinguished leaders in all walks of life. We have the benefit of the great public discussion which has been proceeding in the democratic way, by free inquiry and free expression.

It is my purpose in talking with you to point a direction and to define the choices which confront us. We need to stand before the world with our own purpose and position clear.

We want peace, but not at any price. We are ready to negotiate, but not at the expense of rousing false hopes which would be dashed by new failures. We are equally determined to support all real efforts for peaceful settlements and to resist aggression.

The times call for a total diplomacy equal to the task of defense against Soviet expansion and to the task of building the kind of world in which our way of life can flourish. We must continue to press ahead with the building of a free world which is strong in its faith and in its material progress. The alternative is to allow the free nations to succumb one by one to the erosive and encroaching processes of Soviet expansion.

We must not slacken, rather we must reinvigorate, the kind of democratic efforts which are represented by the European Recovery Program, the North Atlantic and Rio Pacts, the Mutual Defense Assistance Program, the Point Four Program for developing the world's new workshops, and assistance in creating the conditions necessary to a growing, many-sided exchange of the world's products.

We must champion an international order based on the United Nations and on the abiding principles of freedom and justice, or accept an international society increasingly torn by destructive rivalries.

We must recognize that our ability to achieve our purposes cannot rest alone on a desire for peace, but that it must be supported by the strength to meet whatever tasks Providence may have in store for us.

We must not make the mistake, in other words, of using Soviet conduct as a standard for our own. Our efforts cannot be merely reactions to the latest moves by the Kremlin. The bipartisan line of American foreign policy has been and must continue to be the constructive task of building, in coöperation with others, the kind of world in which freedom and justice can flourish. We must not be turned aside from this task by the diversionary thrusts of the Soviet Union. And if it is necessary, as it sometimes is, to deal with such a thrust or the threat of one, the effort should be understood as one which, though essential, is outside the main stream of our policy.

Progress is to be gained in the doing of the constructive tasks which give practical affirmation to the principles by which we live.

The success of our efforts rests finally on our faith in ourselves and in the values for which this Republic stands. We will need courage and steadfastness and the cool heads and steady nerves of a citizenry which has always faced the future "with malice toward none; with charity toward all; with firmness in the right, as God gives us to see the right."

The State of the Union (1952)
Harry S. Truman

Harry S. Truman was born in Lamar, Missouri on 8 May 1884. He attended the public schools of Independence, Missouri and studied at the Kansas City School of Law from 1923 to 1925. He was elected to the United States Senate from Missouri in 1934, reëlected in 1940, and was elected Vice-President of the United States on 7 November 1944. He succeeded to the Presidency upon the death of Franklin D. Roosevelt on 12 April 1945. In November 1948 Mr. Truman defeated the Republican presidential candidate, Governor Thomas E. Dewey (popular vote 24.1 millions to 21.9 millions; electoral college vote 303 to 189, 28 states to 16), upsetting practically all predictions.

In a surprise announcement on 29 March 1952 Mr. Truman declared he would not seek reëlection.

This annual State of the Union message was delivered by the President in person to the Senate and the House of the Eighty-second Congress on 9 January 1952. It was followed by a reading of his economic message on 16 January and the budget message on 21 January. The address is in two parts, the first being devoted to international affairs and the second to domestic matters. In this respect it differed from the 1951 message which centered on foreign affairs almost to the exclusion of home affairs. But, as Mr. Truman pointed out, most of his 1952 domestic proposals were directly linked with "our program for peace."

The speech required forty minutes, during which the President was interrupted eleven times for applause. His standing ovation upon entering the House chamber lasted one minute.

An unusual feature was the presence in the gallery of Prime Minister Churchill and Foreign Secretary Anthony Eden, sitting in the box reserved for members of the President's family. Another was the speaker's departure from his prepared text to stress the importance of the Point Four program for underdeveloped countries. He inserted his contention that a third of the expenditures for World War II could have "created the developments necessary to feed the whole world so we would not have to stomach Communism. That's what we've got to fight."

Reactions to the speech were mixed. Perhaps because it contained no new surprises and most thoughts were turned to the coming political conventions, the enthusiasm it generated was only mild. As *The New York Times* leading editorial for 10 January 1952 stated: "This is the time when it is most painful to call upon the electorate to make individual sacrifices for the national good." The same writer repeats a frequently expressed judgment: "Unfortunately, Mr. Truman lacks the inspired eloquence and the personal magnetism that could be usefully employed in such a time as this to pull all groups and all factions together in heroic fashion for a common effort. His premises are sound enough, but his message loses its way among side issues and inconsequences."

The President began preparation for this address as early as mid-November when he worked on a rough draft while vacationing at Key West, Florida. At that time his press secretary, Joseph Short, said that White House staff members had been assigned various parts of the speech in compliance with a general plan.

For a remarkable account of how the President and his aides work on an important address the reader is referred to John Hersey's article, "A Weighing of Words," in the *New Yorker* for 5 May 1951. It describes in detail how the final revision was made for Mr. Truman's address of 15 December 1950 announcing the national emergency.

MR. PRESIDENT, MR. SPEAKER, MEMBERS OF THE CONGRESS:

I have the honor to report to the Congress on the state of the union.

At the outset, I should like to speak of the necessity for putting first things first as we work together this year for the good of our country.

The United States and the whole free world are passing through a period of grave danger. Every action you take here in Congress, and every action that I take as President, must be measured against the test of whether it helps to meet that danger.

This will be a Presidential election year—the year in which politics plays a large part in our lives—a larger part than usual. That's perfectly proper. But we have a great responsibility to conduct our political fights in a manner that does not harm the national interest.

We can find plenty of things to differ about without destroying our free institutions and without abandoning our bipartisan foreign policy for peace.

When everything is said and done, all of us—Republicans and Democrats alike—all of us are Americans; and we are all going to sink or swim together.

We are moving through a perilous time. Faced with a terrible threat of aggression, our nation has embarked upon a great effort to help establish the kind of world in which peace shall be secure. Peace is our goal—not peace at any price, but a peace based on freedom and justice. We are now in the midst of our effort to reach that goal. On the whole, we've been doing very well.

Last year, 1951, was a year in which we met and threw back aggression, added greatly to our military strength, and improved the chances for peace and freedom in many parts of the world.

This year, 1952, is a critical year in the defense effort of the whole free world. If we falter, we can lose all the gains we have made. If we drive ahead, with courage and vigor and determination, we can by the end of 1952 be in a position of much greater security. The way will be dangerous for the years ahead, but if we put forth our best efforts this year—and next year—we can be "over the hump" in our effort to build strong defenses.

When we look at the record of the past year, 1951, we find important things on both the credit and the debit side of the ledger. We have made great advances. At the same time, we have run into new problems which must be overcome.

Now let us look at the credit side first.

Peace depends upon the free nations sticking together, and making a combined effort to check aggression and prevent war. In this respect, 1951 was a year of great achievement.

In Korea, the forces of the United Nations turned back the Chinese Communist invasion—and did it without widening the area of conflict. The action of the United Nations in Korea has been a powerful deterrent to a third world war. However, the situation in Korea remains very hazardous. The outcome of the armistice negotiations still remains uncertain.

In Indo-China and Malaya, our aid has helped our allies to hold back the Communist advance, although there are signs of further trouble in that area.

In 1951, we strengthened the chances of peace in the Pacific region by the treaties with Japan and the defense arrangements with Australia, New Zealand, and the Philippines.

In Europe, combined defense has become a reality. The free nations have created a real fighting force. This force is not yet as strong as it needs to be; but it is already a real obstacle to any attempt by hostile forces to sweep across Europe to the Atlantic.

In 1951, we also moved to strengthen the security of Europe by the agreement to bring Greece and Turkey into the North Atlantic Treaty.

The United Nations, the world's greatest hope for peace, has come through a year of trial stronger and more useful than ever. The free nations have stood together in blocking Communist attempts to tear up the Charter.

At the present session of the United Nations in Paris, we, together with the British and the French, offered a plan to reduce and control all armaments under a foolproof inspection system. This is a concrete, practical proposal for disarmament.

But what happened? Vishinsky laughed at it. Listen to what he said: "I could hardly sleep at all last night—I could not sleep because I kept laughing." The world will be a long time forgetting the spectacle of that fellow laughing at disarmament.

Disarmament is not a joke. Vishinsky's laughter met with shock and anger from the people all over the world. And, as a result, Mr. Stalin's representative received orders to stop laughing and start talking.

If the Soviet leaders were to accept this proposal, it would lighten the burden of armaments, and permit the resources of the earth to be devoted to the good of mankind. But until the Soviet Union accepts a sound disarmament proposal, and joins in peaceful settlements, we have no choice except to build up our defenses.

During this past year, we have added more than a million men and women to our armed forces. The total is now nearly three and one-half million. We have made rapid progress in the field of atomic weapons. We have turned out $16,000,000,000 worth of military supplies and equipment, three times as much as the year before.

Economic conditions in the country are good. There are 61,000,000 people on the job; wages, farm incomes, and business profits are at high levels. Total production of goods and services in our country has increased 8 per cent over last year—about twice the normal rate of growth.

Perhaps the most amazing thing about our economic progress is the way we are increasing our basic capacity to produce. For example, we are now in the second year of a three-year program which will double our output of aluminum, increase our electric power supply by 40 per cent, and increase our steel-making capacity by 15 per cent. We can then produce 120,000,000 tons of steel a year, as much as all the rest of the world put together.

This expansion will mean more jobs and higher standards of living for all of us in the years ahead. At the present time, it means greater strength for us and for the rest of the free world in the fight for peace.

Now, I must turn to the debit side of the ledger for the past year.

The outstanding fact to note on the debit side of the ledger is that the Soviet Union in 1951 continued to expand its military production and increase its already excessive military power.

It is true that the Soviets have run into increasing difficulties. Their hostile policies have awakened stern resistance among free men throughout the world. And behind the iron curtain the Soviet rule of force has created growing political and economic stresses in the satellite nations.

Nevertheless, the grim fact remains that the Soviet Union is increasing its armed might. It is still producing more war planes than the free nations. It has set off two more atomic explosions. The world still walks in the shadow of another world war.

And here at home, our defense preparations are far from complete.

During 1951, we did not make adequate progress in building up civil defense against atomic attack. This is a major weakness in our plans for peace, since inadequate civilian defense is an open invitation to a surprise attack. Failure to provide adequate civilian defense has the same effect as adding to the enemy's supply of atomic bombs.

In the field of defense production, we have run into difficulties and delays in designing and producing the latest types of airplanes and tanks. Some machine tools and metals are still in extremely short supply.

In other free countries, the defense build-up has created severe economic problems. It has increased inflation in Europe and has endangered the continued recovery of our allies.

In the Middle East, political tensions and the oil controversy in Iran are keeping the region in a turmoil. In the Far East, the dark threat of Communist imperialism still hangs over many nations.

This, very briefly, is the good side and the bad side of the picture.

Taking the good and bad together, we have made real progress this last year along the road to peace. We have increased the power and unity of the free world. And while we were doing this, we have avoided world war on the one hand, and appeasement on the other. This is a hard road to follow, but the events of the last year show that it is the right road to peace.

We cannot expect to complete the job overnight. The free nations may have to maintain for years the larger military forces needed to deter aggression. We must build steadily, over a period of years, toward political solidarity and economic progress among the free nations in all parts of the world.

Our task will not be easy; but if we go at it with a will, we can look forward to steady progress. On our side are all the great resources of freedom—the ideals of religion and democracy, the aspiration of people for a better life, and the industrial and technical power of a free civilization.

These advantages outweigh anything the slave world can produce. The only thing that can defeat us is our own state of mind. We can lose if we falter.

The middle period of a great national effort like this is a very difficult time. The way seems long and hard. The goal seems far distant. Some people get discouraged. That's only natural.

But if there are any among us who think we ought to ease up in the fight for peace, I want to remind them of three things—just three things.

First: the threat of world war is still very real. We had one Pearl Harbor—let's not get caught off guard again. If you don't think the threat of Communist armies is real, talk to some of our men back from Korea.

Second: if the United States had to try to stand alone against a Soviet-dominated world, it would destroy the life we know and the ideals we hold dear. Our allies are essential to us, just as we are essential to them. The more shoulders there are to bear the burden the lighter that burden will be.

Third: the things we believe in most deeply are under relentless attack. We have the great responsibility of saving the basic moral and spiritual values of our civilization. We have started out well—with a program for peace that is unparalleled in history. If we believe in ourselves and the faith we profess, we will stick to that job until it is victoriously finished.

This is a time for courage, not for grumbling and mumbling.

Now, let us take a look at the things we have to do.

The thing that is uppermost in the minds of all of us is the situation in Korea. We must—and we will—keep up the fight there until we get the kind of armistice that will put an end to the aggression and protect the safety of our forces and the security of the Republic of Korea.

Beyond that, we shall continue to work for a settlement in Korea that upholds the principles of the United Nations. We went into Korea because we knew that Communist aggression had to be met firmly if freedom was to be preserved in the world. We went into the fight to save the Republic of Korea, a free country, established under the United Nations. These are our aims. We will not give up until we attain them.

Meanwhile, we must continue to strengthen the forces of freedom throughout the world.

I hope the Senate will take early and favorable action on the Japanese peace treaty, on our security pacts with the Pacific countries, and on the agreement to bring Greece and Turkey into the North Atlantic Treaty.

We are also negotiating an agreement with the German Federal Republic under which it can play an honorable and equal part among nations and take its place in the defense of Western Europe.

But treaties and plans are only the skeleton of our defense structure. The sinew and muscle of defense forces and equipment must be provided.

In Europe, we must go on helping our friends and allies to build up their military forces. This means we must send weapons in large volume to our European allies. I have directed that weapons for Europe be given a very high priority. Economic aid is necessary, too, to supply the margin of difference between success and failure in making Europe a strong partner to our joint defense.

In the long run, we want to see Europe freed from any dependence on our aid. Our European allies want that just as bad as we do. The steps that are now being taken to build European unity should help bring that about. Six European countries are pooling their coal and steel production under the Schuman Plan. Work is going forward on the merger of European national forces on the Continent into a single army. These great projects should become realities in 1952.

We should do all we can to help and encourage the move toward a strong and united Europe.

In Asia, the new Communist empire is a daily threat to millions of people. The peoples of Asia want to be free to follow their own way of life. They want to preserve their culture and their traditions against Communism, just as much as we want to preserve ours. They are laboring under terrific handicaps—poverty, ill health, feudal systems of land ownership, and the threat of internal subversion or external attack. We can and we must increase our help to them.

This means military aid, especially to those places like Indo-China which might be hardest hit by some new Communist attack.

It also means economic aid, both technical know-how and capital investment.

This last year, we made available millions of bushels of wheat to relieve famine in India. But far more important, in the long run, is the work Americans are doing in India to help the Indian farmers themselves raise more grain. With the help of our technicians, Indian farmers, using simple, inexpensive means, have been able since 1948 to double the crops in one area in India. One farmer there raised sixty-three bushels of wheat to the acre, where thirteen bushels had been the average before.

This is Point Four—our Point Four program at work. It is working —not only in India—but in Iran, and Paraguay, and Liberia—in thirty-three countries around the globe. Our technical missionaries are out there. We need more of them. We need more funds to speed their efforts, because there is nothing of greater importance in our foreign policy. There is nothing that shows more clearly what we stand for, and what we want to achieve.

My friends in the Congress, less than one-third of the expenditure for the cost of World War II would have created the developments necessary to feed the whole world so we would not have to stomach Communism. That's what we've got to fight. And unless we fight that battle and win it we can't win the cold war nor a hot one either.

We have recently lost a great public servant who was leading this effort to bring opportunity and hope to the people of half the world. Dr. Henry Bennett and his associates died in the line of duty on a Point Four mission. It's up to us to carry on the great work for which they gave their lives.

During the coming year, we must not forget the suffering of the people who live behind the iron curtain. In those areas, minorities are being oppressed, human rights violated, religions persecuted. We should continue to expose those wrongs. We should continue and expand the activities of the Voice of America, which brings our message of hope and truth to those peoples and other peoples throughout the world.

I have just had an opportunity to discuss many of these world problems with Prime Minister Churchill. We have had a most satisfactory series of meetings. We thoroughly reviewed the situation in Europe, in the Middle East, and in the Far East. We both look forward to steady progress toward peace through the coöperative action and teamwork of the free nations.

Now, turning from our foreign policies, let us consider the jobs we have here at home as a part of our program for peace.

The first of these jobs is to move ahead full steam on the defense program.

Our objective is to have a well-equipped, active defense force large enough—in concert with the forces of our allies—to deter aggression and to inflict punishing losses on the enemy immediately if we should be attacked. This active force must be backed by adequate reserves, and by the plants and tools to turn out the tremendous quantities of new weapons that would be needed if war came. We are not building an active force adequate to carry on a full-scale war, but we are putting ourselves in a position to mobilize very rapidly if we have to.

This year I shall recommend some increases in the size of the active force we are building, with particular emphasis on air power. This means we shall have to continue large-scale production of planes and other equipment for a longer period of time than we had originally planned.

Planes and tanks and other weapons—what the military call "hard goods"—are now beginning to come off the production lines in volume. Deliveries of hard goods now amount to about $1,500,000,000 worth a month. A year from now, we expect that rate to be doubled.

We shall have to hold to a high rate of military output for about a year after that. In 1954, we hope to have enough equipment so that we can reduce the production of most military items substantially. The next two years should therefore be the peak period of defense production.

Defense needs will take a lot of steel, aluminum, copper, nickel, and other scarce materials. This means smaller production of some civilian goods. The cutbacks will be nothing like those during World War II, when most civilian production was completely stopped. But there will be considerably less of some goods than we have been used to these past two or three years.

A very critical part of our defense job this year is to keep down inflation.

We can control inflation if we make up our minds to do it.

On the Executive side of the government, we intend to hold the line on prices just as tightly as the law allows. We will permit only those wage increases which are clearly justified under sound stabilization policies; and we will see to it that industries absorb cost increases out of earnings wherever feasible, before they are authorized to raise prices. We will do that, at any rate, except where the recent amendments to the law specifically require us to give further price increases.

Congress has a tremendous responsibility in this matter. Our stabilization law was shot full of holes at the last session. This year, it will be one of the main tasks before the Congress to repair the damage and enact a strong anti-inflation law.

As a part of our program to keep our country strong, we are determined to preserve the financial strength of the government. This means high taxes over the next few years. We must see to it that these taxes are shared among the people as fairly as possible. I expect to discuss these matters in the Economic Report and the Budget Message which will soon be presented to the Congress.

Our tax laws must be fair. And we must make absolutely certain they are administered fairly, without fear or favor of any kind for anybody. To this end, steps have already been taken to remedy weaknesses which have been disclosed in the administration of the tax laws. In addition, I hope the Congress will approve my reorganization plan for the Bureau of Internal Revenue. We must do everything necessary in order to make just as certain as is humanly possible that every taxpayer receives equal treatment under the law.

To carry the burden of defense, we must have a strong, productive, and expanding economy here at home. We cannot neglect those things that have made us the great and powerful nation we are today.

Our strength depends upon the health, the morale, the freedom of our people. We can take on the burden of leadership in the fight for world peace because, for nearly twenty years, the government and the people have been working together for the general welfare. We have given more and more of our citizens a fair chance at decent, useful, productive lives. That's the reason we are as strong as we are today.

This government of ours—the Congress and the Executive both—must keep on working to bring about a fair deal for all the American people. Some people will say that we haven't the time or the money this year for measures for the welfare of the people. But if we want to win the fight for peace, this is a part of the job we cannot ignore.

We will have to give up some things; we will have to go forward on others at a slower pace. But, so far as I am concerned, I do not think we can give up the things that are vital to our national strength.

I believe most people in this country will agree with me on that.

I think most farmers understand that soil conservation and rural electrification and agricultural research are not frills or luxuries, but real necessities in order to boost our farm production.

I think most workers understand that decent housing and good working conditions are not luxuries, but necessities if the working men and women of this country are to continue to outproduce the rest of the world.

I think our business men know that scientific research and transportation services and more steel mills and power projects are not luxuries, but necessities to keep our business and our industry in the forefront of industrial progress.

I think that everybody knows that social insurance and better schools and health services are not frills, but necessities in helping all Americans to be useful and productive citizens, who can contribute their full share in the national effort to protect and advance our way of life.

We cannot do all we want to in times like these—we have to choose the things that will contribute most to defense—but we must continue to make progress if we are to be a strong nation in the years ahead.

Let me give you some examples.

We are going right ahead with the urgently needed work to develop our natural resources, to conserve our soil, and to prevent floods. We are going to produce essential power and build the lines we have to have to transmit it to our farms and factories. We are going to encourage exploration for new mineral deposits.

We are going to keep on building essential highways and taking any other steps that will assure the nation an adequate transportation system—on land, on the sea, and in the air.

We must move right ahead this year to see that defense workers and soldiers' families get decent housing at rents they can afford to pay.

We must begin our long-deferred program of Federal aid to education—to help the States meet the present crisis in the operation of our schools. And we must help with the construction of schools in areas where they are critically needed because of the defense effort.

We urgently need to train more doctors and other health personnel, through aid to medical education. We also urgently need to expand the basic public health services in our home communities—especially in defense areas. The Congress should go ahead with these two measures immediately.

I have set up an impartial commission to make a thorough study of the nation's health needs. One of the things this commission is looking into is how to bring the cost of modern medical care within the reach of all the people. I have repeatedly recommended national health insurance as the best way to do this. So far as I know, it is still the best way. If there are any better answers, I hope this commission will find them. But of one thing I am sure: something must be done and done soon.

This year we ought to make a number of urgently needed improvements in our Social Security Law. For one thing, benefits under Old

Age and Survivors Insurance should be raised $5 a month above the present average of $42. For another thing, the states should be given special aid to help them increase public assistance payments. By doing these things now, we can ease the pressure of living costs for people who depend on those fixed payments.

We should also make some cost-of-living adjustments for those receiving veterans' compensation for death and disability incurred in the service of our country. In addition, now is the time to start a sensible program of readjustment benefits for our veterans who have seen service since the fighting broke out in Korea.

Another thing the Congress should do at this session is to strengthen our system of farm price supports to meet the defense emergency. The "sliding scale" in the price support law should not be allowed to penalize farmers for increasing production to meet defense needs. We should also find a new and less costly method for supporting perishable commodities than the law now provides.

We need to act promptly to improve our labor law. The Taft-Hartley Act has many serious and far-reaching defects. Experience has demonstrated this so clearly that even the sponsors of the act now admit that it needs to be changed. A fair law—fair to both management and labor—is indispensable to sound labor relations and to full, uninterrupted production. I intend to keep on working for a fair law until we get one.

As we build our strength and defend the freedom in the world, we, ourselves, must extend the benefits of freedom more widely among all our own people. We need to take action toward the wider enjoyment of civil rights. Freedom is the birthright of every American.

The Executive Branch has been making real progress toward full equality of treatment and opportunity—in the armed forces, in the civil service, and in private firms working for the government. Further advances require action by Congress, and I hope that means will be provided to give the members of the Senate and the House a chance to vote on them.

I am glad to hear that home rule for the District of Columbia will be the first item of business before the Senate. I hope that it, as well as statehood for Hawaii and Alaska, will be adopted promptly.

All these measures I have been talking about—measures to advance the well-being of our people—demonstrate to the world the forward movement of our free society.

This demonstration of the way free men govern themselves has a more powerful influence on the people of the world—on both sides of the iron curtain—than all the trick slogans and pie-in-the-sky promises of the Communists.

But our shortcomings, as well as our progress, are watched from abroad. And there is one shortcoming I want to speak about plainly.

Our kind of government above all others cannot tolerate dishonesty among public servants.

Some dishonest people worm themselves into almost every human organization. It is all the more shocking, however, when they make their way into a government such as ours, which is based on the principle of justice for all. Such unworthy public servants must be weeded out. I intend to see to it that Federal employees who have been guilty of misconduct are punished for it. I also intend to see to it that the honest and hard-working great majority of our Federal employees are protected against partisan slander and malicious attack.

I have already made some recommendations to the Congress to help accomplish these purposes. I intend to submit further recommendations to this end. I will welcome the wholehearted coöperation of the Congress in this effort.

I also think that the Congress can do a great deal to strengthen confidence in our institutions by applying rigorous standards of moral integrity to its own operations and by finding an effective way to control campaign expenditures—and by protecting the rights of individuals in Congressional investigations.

To meet the crisis which now hangs over the world, we need many different kinds of strength—military, economic, political, and moral. And of all these, I am convinced that moral strength is the most vital.

When you come right down to it, it is the courage and the character of our nation—and of each one of us as individuals—that will really decide how well we meet this challenge.

We are engaged in a great undertaking at home and abroad—the greatest, in fact, that any nation has ever been privileged to embark upon. We are working night and day to bring peace to the world and to spread the democratic ideals of justice and self-government to all people. Our accomplishments are already remarkable. We ought to be full of pride in what we are doing—and full of confidence and hope in the outcome. No nation ever had greater resources, or greater energy, or nobler traditions to inspire it.

And yet, day in and day out, we see a long procession of timid and fearful men who wring their hands and cry out that we have lost the way—that we don't know what we are doing—that we are bound to fail. Some say that we should give up the struggle for peace, and others say we should have a war and get it over with. That's a terrible statement, though I have heard it made. They want us to forget the great objective of preventing another world war—the objective for which our soldiers have been fighting in the hills of Korea.

If we are to be worthy of all that has been done for us by our soldiers in the field, we must be true to the ideals for which they are fighting. We must reject the counsels of defeat and despair. We must have the determination to complete the great work for which our men have laid down their lives.

In all we do, we should remember who we are and what we stand for. We are Americans. Our forefathers had far greater obstacles than we have, and much poorer chances of success. They did not lose heart, or turn aside from their goals. In the darkest of all winters in American history, at Valley Forge, George Washington said: "We must not, in so great a contest, expect to meet with nothing but sunshine." With that spirit, they won their fight for freedom.

We must have that same faith and vision. In the great contest in which we are engaged today, we cannot expect to have fair weather all the way. But it is a contest just as important for this country and for all men, as the desperate struggle that George Washington fought through to victory.

Let us prove, again, that we are not merely sunshine patriots and summer soldiers. Let us go forward, trusting in the God of Peace, to win the goals we seek.

THE WAR IN KOREA

Background of Korea
John M. Chang, Edward A. Ackerman, Niles Bond, and Arthur C. Bunce, Jr.

This University of Chicago Round Table radio discussion took place on 3 September 1950. Messrs. Ackerman, Bunce, and Bond were in Washington and the Ambassador from Korea, Dr. John M. Chang, spoke from New York. Dr. Edward A. Ackerman is professor of geography at the University of Chicago. Niles Bond was in charge of North East Asian Affairs in the Department of State. Dr. Arthur C. Bunce, Jr. was chief of the Economic Coöperation Administration mission in Korea.

From Washington

MR. ACKERMAN: The latest news on Korea, which is still on the news wires, reads: "Northern Front, Korea. Communist forces are surging toward the supply base of Taegu and the east-coast port of Pohang in heavy new attacks along the entire northern front. One drive has carried the Reds to within less than ten miles of Taegu. Toward the east, they have punched a wide gap through our defenses, recapturing Kyongju and cutting the Taegu-Pohang highway seven miles to the south.

"For the first time in two months, Communist planes have taken to the air to blast American positions on the southern front."

You were in Korea a few days ago, Mr. Bunce, what do you think about the condition of things there now?

MR. BUNCE: I am not a military expert, but the recent news certainly emphasizes General MacArthur's appeal to the United Nations for more troops. It is my hope that that appeal will be met speedily.

Apart from the military situation, however, there are other problems which are very serious in the small area which we have under our control. For example, the population of that area has almost doubled with a tremendous influx of refugees. These people are without food or clothing. They have to be taken care of medically in order to avoid typhus and typhoid and smallpox spreading very rapidly. Winter is coming on; the housing is going to be a serious problem.[1]

I would like to say that arrangements have already been made among the United Nations, ECA, and the War Department to take care of many of these immediate problems. And the whole ECA program has been changed and redirected in order to meet this problem which the civilian population is facing.

MR. ACKERMAN: You are an expert in the recent history of Korea, Mr. Bond, and you are the State Department official in charge of Korean affairs. On today's Round Table, the listeners and I want to learn all that we can about Korea. Did the United States fail in occupation of South Korea? Why did we withdraw our troops? Why did the invasion by the North Korean forces occur? Was Syngman Rhee running a police state? What efforts did we make in the last four years to get the Russians to agree to a unified Korea? How much did we do to help the people of Korea toward democracy and land reform? These and other questions are what I would like to get answers to. So let us start at the beginning and get the full story. How did we get into Korea?

MR. BOND: Although official relations between the United States and Korea extend back to the 1880's, nearly thirty years before the Japanese annexation of Korea, the current phase of our interest in Korea may be said to date from the Cairo Declaration of December, 1943. In that declaration the United States, Great Britain, and China, in defining their war aims in the Pacific, expressed their collective determination that in due course Korea should become free and independent. That pledge was reaffirmed by the same three powers in the Potsdam Declaration of July, 1945, and (and this point should be noted) was subscribed to by the Soviet government in its declaration of war against Japan in the following month.

American military forces first landed in Korea on September 8, 1945, some four weeks after the capitulation of Japan, for the limited pur-

---

[1] "Estimates of the refugee population in Southern Korea are not as yet complete, but a figure of 1,500,000 persons is generally regarded as reasonably authentic. The condition of hundreds of thousands of these unfortunate people is pitiable. Sickness and disease are rife among many thousands of them. A very large proportion, indeed, are without shelter and lack covering or blankets of any description. They are reduced to the clothing in which they stand. At present, and for the next two months, there are sufficient food stocks available for the government of the Republic of Korea to provide them with a bare minimum subsistence. Later, however, there will be need for essential provisions from external sources" (*United Nations Bulletin,* September 1, 1950, p. 198).

pose of accepting the surrender of Japanese troops in that part of Korea lying south of the thirty-eighth parallel.

MR. ACKERMAN: On the University of Chicago Round Table discussion of Asia on July 30 Mr. Hoskins told how the decision was made to divide the country at the thirty-eighth parallel. North Korea was not given to the Russians at Yalta; but there is still the question in our minds of why we made it the thirty-eighth parallel.

MR. BOND: The circumstances surrounding the establishment of this notorious line have somehow become the subject of one of the most prevalent and tenacious of misconceptions. Stated briefly, this misconception consists of the idea that the United States and the Soviet Union agreed at Yalta to the partition of Korea along the thirty-eighth parallel. As you have just said, the fact is that no arrangements relating to the division or joint occupation of Korea were made at Yalta or at any other wartime international conference. The establishment of the thirty-eighth parallel line was part of an overall military plan drawn up in Washington during the closing days of the war—the sole purpose of which was to define the areas in which American, Russian, and other Allied forces would accept the surrender of Japanese troops throughout the Japanese-occupied areas of the Far East.

MR. ACKERMAN: Why did we not allow the Russians to accept the Japanese surrender in all Korea?

MR. BOND: Well, even though our disenchantment with our Russian allies was, at that time, still in its very early stages, I imagine that it was felt that the fulfillment of our pledges on behalf of Korean independence would be rendered immeasurably more difficult if Korea were to be occupied in its entirety by Soviet forces. One virtue of the particular line which was chosen was that it placed Seoul, the historical capital of Korea, and the port and communications center of Pusan in the United States zone.

I would add that, from the point of view of the United States, the establishment of such a line in Korea was rendered particularly important by the fact that the nearest available American troops were many hundreds of miles and several weeks away, in Okinawa and the Philippines, while Russian forces were poised on the very borders of Korea and did, in fact, enter North Korea while the thirty-eighth parallel line was still under discussion.

Far from permitting the Soviet Union to take over a part of Korea from which it could be excluded, the thirty-eighth parallel therefore provided a holding line, without which the entire Korean Peninsula could have been occupied by Soviet forces, long before American troops could have been put ashore.

MR. ACKERMAN: You were adviser to General Hodge, Mr. Bunce, and spent many months in Korea. What is your view on these circumstances at the beginning of the occupation of Korea?

MR. BUNCE: Following the establishment of the thirty-eighth parallel, we very rapidly found out that, although it was set up only as a line to demark areas in which surrender would be accepted, the Russians closed the border completely. Persons, goods, and even money was stopped from flowing over that border. As a result, we went to Moscow; and there the Moscow decision was made, in which an agreement was set up to establish a Joint Commission on Korea. When was the Moscow decision on Korea?

MR. BOND: The Moscow Agreement was announced in December of 1945, if you recall.

MR. BUNCE: Following that announcement we had a conference in Seoul. The Russians came down. The Americans took the position that we wanted to establish free movement of people and goods over the border and establish a uniform currency. None of these programs were accepted by the Russians. As a result, the only thing which we got out of that conference was the exchange of mail between North and South Korea.

Following this conference, of course, the Joint Commission met in 1946, and I was a member of both sessions of the Joint Commission. At the first Joint Commission meeting, the Russians took the position that any party which had opposed the Moscow decision, which included the concept of trusteeship, could not be admitted for consultation in a consultative assembly, which was to be established under this decision.

MR. ACKERMAN: How did the Communist party stand on the matter of trusteeship?

MR. BUNCE: At the very beginning the Communist parties were just as opposed to it as were the non-Communist parties, and there was a very interesting incident. They were having a parade; and the Communists got orders at the last minute that they were to support trusteeship, so half of them had banners opposing trusteeship, and half of them had banners supporting it. But all the non-Communist parties were overwhelming in opposing trusteeship.

The Americans took the position that if these people were to have something to say about their government and if they wanted to oppose trusteeship, they should be given the opportunity to do so.

The first Joint Commission was completely futile. Russia said anybody that opposed this trusteeship concept could not be invited for consultation, which eliminated everything except the Communist parties.

Following this breakdown in the Joint Commission, the Secretary of State and the Minister of Foreign Affairs of the Soviet government exchanged letters, and a new basis admitting freedom of speech was established. But in the second session of the Joint Commission, when the Soviet command found that the non-Communist parties would sign a pledge stating that they would coöperate with the Joint Commission, the Soviet delegates immediately took the position that they would not admit them, because they had to be jointly approved by the American and Russian members.

In other words, they established a unilateral veto of any of the powers, parties, or social organizations which wanted to join in this consultative assembly. We had taken the position that the parties and social organizations from North Korea would be accepted, and those Communist parties in South Korea. This would have given them, as a matter of fact, about 40 per cent of the seats in that consultative assembly. The Russians would not accept it. The only thing which they would accept was over 51 per cent. The whole thing broke up again.

MR. ACKERMAN: So, the only thing which came from all the conferences with the Russians was an exchange of mail, which was an agreement made at the very beginning?

MR. BUNCE: That is right.

MR. ACKERMAN: This brings us to the time of the North Korean invasion of last June 25. For an analysis of the issues of this conflict, the Round Table is fortunate in being able to present, at this time, a distinguished official of the South Korean government, Dr. John M. Chang, Ambassador from Korea to the United States.

From New York

AMBASSADOR CHANG: It is a great honor for me to take part in the University of Chicago Round Table discussion on Korea.

I shall not attempt to give any background facts on Korea, because I am sure all of you are already quite familiar with them. In discussing the conflict currently waging in Korea, I might explain what happened in my country and why it happened.

As for what happened, the answer is not far to see. The men in the Kremlin decided to test the strength of the free world. What is happening in Korea is not a civil war; it is Communist aggression. I shall tell you why.

Background of Korea

North Korea is, and since August, 1945, has been, a captive area. From 1945 to the present time, it has not been so much a satellite as a puppet state. What it does is what Moscow tells it to do. To misunderstand that fact, or to fail to grasp its meaning, is to misunderstand the situation which we confront. When the Soviet Union moved into Korea in 1945, she did so with her plans carefully laid. Communist expatriate Koreans were brought back; and, with them as a nucleus, a Communist police state was set up in Korea. Over two million loyal and patriotic Koreans in North Korea refused to knuckle down to this totalitarian regime, and they fled secretly across the border. Upon those who remained, the police state was ruthlessly imposed. They were forced into the lockstep of totalitarianism. It goes without saying that the army of North Korea was equipped with tanks, planes, and artillery supplied by Russia. This is the regime and this is the army which at dawn on a peaceful Sunday struck, without warning, upon the Republic of Korea.

That day will be well marked by historians. It was that day which resolved the doubts which beset the free world and resolved the issues of our time. It clarified the minds of men as nothing has done since the defeat of the Axis powers. The brutal attack of that day brought sharply into focus the danger which the free world faces and which it must overcome.

I wish now to turn to the question of why this mad attack was launched. The briefest answer, and perhaps the best, is contained in a phrase used by Mr. Paul Hoffman, director of ECA, when he called the Republic of Korea a "bastion of democracy in Asia." The continued existence of the Republic of Korea could not be tolerated by the Communists. It was too much of a success. The Republic of Korea was the only part of northern Asia which was not in Communist hands. So long as the Republic of Korea continued to exist, the people of Asia would know that the United States, and the rest of the free world, renounced aggression.

To our witness stand to testify to the degree of success which the Republic of Korea has been making since 1948, we could bring the United Nations Commission on Korea, which has certified our two general elections—one held in 1948 and one held in May of this year—as both fair and free.

I wish also to cite the words of a great American, Mr. John Foster Dulles, who visited Korea just one week before the blow was struck. In explaining to the American people why he thought the attack was made, he said that the Communists struck in force because the society was so wholesome that it could not be overthrown from within. He further said, "I was in Korea and saw with my own eyes that the Republic of Korea was a land of freedom."

We Koreans realize, with full solemnity, the great global will to peace which has drawn so many people to our side. In all our four thousand years of history, the Korean people have never fought an aggressive war. We have no designs upon the territory, the rights, or the security of any nation. All that we want is the restoration of our own homeland under a government of our own free choice. We have had a government of our own free choice since 1948, and this the Russian-inspired, Russian-supported, and Russian-directed invasion sought to crush.

If aggression is encouraged by one triumph, it will seek still more. Surely this is one lesson which the twentieth century has had much cause to learn. A true and a lasting peace can be effected only when the aggressors are completely subdued and disarmed. Only then would our compatriots in North Korea be able to enjoy freedom and democracy.

To say that the people and the government of the Republic of Korea are grateful for the generous and sacrificial support of the overwhelming majority of the members of the United Nations, who have placed themselves at our side, is but a weak way of saying what is in our hearts. Our feelings are especially deep and warm for the great contribution of the people of the United States, whose armies fought in our behalf during the last war and whose sons are now giving their lives in our homeland to safeguard the cause of freedom.

We cannot believe that such a devotion, such sacrifices, will be in vain. We can only believe that they mark the eventual dawn of a new day when peace and security will be restored to all the yearning people of the world.

From Washington

MR. ACKERMAN: Thank you, Ambassador Chang.

The Ambassador from Korea has said that the continued existence of the Republic of Korea could not be tolerated by the Communists, because it was too much of a success. Do you agree?

MR. BOND: I certainly do. I believe that the existence of a working example of the advantages of democracy over totalitarianism, on the very periphery, posed a threat which the Communists felt they could no longer tolerate.

MR. ACKERMAN: On the other hand, it has been reported that the United States record in Korea is not a successful or a happy one. It is said that we failed to understand the tremendous popular Korean demand for independence and reform, while the Russians in the north set up an all-Korean Communist government, avoiding direct intervention in Korean affairs. When General Hodge landed in Seoul, we proclaimed that in South Korea a military government is the only government. We then continued to employ Japanese police and officials and failed to push for land reforms quickly enough. Did the American government fail in aiding the Korean government toward a development of democracy? What do you think about this?

MR. BUNCE: It is rather strange to have this statement that the Russians avoided direct intervention in Korean affairs, while in South Korea, we did the opposite. I have known many of the two million refugees who came down from North Korea, fleeing from the Soviet regime, and the one thing which they always told me when they came to South Korea was, "Here you can speak freely; here there is freedom. In North Korea we are under a police reign of terror." And that is true.

MR. ACKERMAN: On the other hand, did they not get land reform in North Korea?

MR. BUNCE: They had land reform in North Korea, which was quite different from the one which we had in South Korea. In South Korea we took a little longer to do some of these things, but the basic direction in which we were going was sound and toward democracy and freedom for the people.

MR. ACKERMAN: How did it compare with the North Korean land reform?

MR. BUNCE: In South Korea we took the Japanese land, and we distributed it to a half-million farm peasants. They paid 20 per cent for fifteen years. In North Korea they never got any deeds to the land, and they paid 35 per cent per year in taxes. In other words, they were much worse off in North Korea under the North Korean system than they were under the South Korean land reform.

MR. ACKERMAN: Almost twice as badly off in other words?

MR. BUNCE: Yes.

MR. ACKERMAN: But you have mentioned that Japanese-owned lands were distributed. Was that the only reform which was carried out?

MR. BUNCE: No. Following that reform, the Korean government put in its own land-reform law, which was passed in 1949 and which was being implemented very rapidly. By November of this year, if we had not had the invasion, tenancy would have been wiped out in Korea, as it has been known in the past. There would have been only 5 to 10 per cent of the farmers left as tenants, and they would have been tenants of state-owned land.

MR. ACKERMAN: And that is a normal rate of tenancy in any event, is it not?

MR. BUNCE: You have to have a small amount of tenancy in changing over landownership from one person to another.

The other things which we did in military government, for example, were to set up a Korean interim government. The Americans became advisers; they were not directors any longer. And we also developed the basis upon which there was a free election held under the United Nations auspices. Criticisms of the police have been made, but again we were trying to build up a police system, and it was not perfect.

MR. ACKERMAN: One thing which is often said about Rhee's government is that Rhee was running a police state. You do not agree with this, Mr. Bunce?

MR. BUNCE: I think that you have to look at it two ways. The idea of the police state is something which would make it completely impossible to have a free election. Do you not agree, Mr. Bond, that the last election was relatively free?

MR. BOND: I do. It seems to me that the "police state" charge can be pretty effectively answered by recalling the circumstances surrounding the Korean elections of 1948 and 1950, both of which were observed by United Nations commissions and both of which were found, by those commissions, to have been fair and free elections.

MR. ACKERMAN: You have said that the elections in 1948 and 1950 were fair and free. But it is reported that the 1948 elections in Korea were preceded by 589 political deaths, and an estimated 10,000 arrests; that the elections were boycotted by all parties of the left and center. Because these parties abstained voluntarily, the United Nations Commission recognized the election. But how representative or how popular is the Rhee government on the basis of such an election?

MR. BOND: I am not familiar with the figures which you cite, but I would refer again to the judgment of the UN Commission on Korea, an international and presumably an impartial body. I would point out, also, that the 1948 balloting was held in the face of Communist threats to break up the elections—by force, if necessary—and that reasonable precautions were not only wise but essential.

MR. BUNCE: I want to make one comment on this police system and the police threat. One thing which we have to recognize is that during this period the Communists were moving down from North

Korea. They would attack police boxes; they would shoot the policemen. They would then take the families of the policemen and shoot them and burn their homes. And the police retaliated. Force begets force. It is not something which we desire, but it is something, it seems to me, which we have to face up to realistically.

MR. BOND: With respect to the boycotting of the elections by the left and center parties, which you mentioned, while it is true that certain middle-of-the-road groups boycotted the 1948 elections for fear of perpetuating the division of their country, it is worth noting that these same groups not only participated in the 1950 elections but, according to the report of the UN Commission, made the most significant gains in the balloting.

MR. ACKERMAN: Other than promoting free elections and the beginning of democracy in Korea, what else have we done to help the Korean people? That is, we need to have support for democracy economically, for instance.

MR. BUNCE: In economics I think that we have developed, under ECA, a program of rehabilitation. We have been developing their coal resources, power resources, building new railroads, developing their fishing fleet. We have increased industrial production at least 50 per cent. We have irrigation projects, forestry projects. When one looks over the whole picture of South Korea as it was, the land reform and the increased agricultural production which has increased 20 per cent meant that the farmers were better off than they have ever been in their lives before. We did not achieve as much for the workers as we would have liked.

The Frank and Candid Light
Ben C. Limb

This speech was delivered before the Political Committee of the General Assembly of the United Nations at Lake Success on 9 December 1950. It is published here as an official Korean view of the hostilities in Korea. The speaker is the Permanent Representative of Korea to the United Nations and the former Foreign Minister of the Republic of Korea.

Colonel Ben C. Limb was born in Seoul, Korea on 26 October 1893, the son of a Korean educator, Yunsung Limb. He attended the Seoul School of Chinese Classics, the Posung Junior College, and the Royal Foreign Language School. He came to the United States as a youth, attended the Mount Hermon School, and graduated in 1918. He studied agriculture at Ohio State University in 1918-19. In this latter year he was elected general secretary of the All-Korean Congress in the United States and became private secretary to Dr. Syngman Rhee, president of the provisional government of the Republic. Upon the return of Dr. Rhee to Korea in 1946, Colonel Limb was appointed his successor as Chairman of the Korean Commission in Washington. He attended the 1947 session of the U.N. General Assembly in New York, was appointed Minister for Foreign Affairs in February 1949, and late in that year was named a delegate to the Council on National Affairs in Seoul.

On 3 June 1951 Colonel Limb was awarded an honorary LL.D. degree by Gustavus Adolphus College. His scholarly and critical article, "The Pacific Pact: Looking Forward or Backward," appeared in the July 1951 issue of *Foreign Affairs*.

An excellent biographical sketch of Colonel Limb appears in the *United Nations World* for April 1951. It is written by S. M. Vinocour and is entitled "Big Little Diplomat."

MR. CHAIRMAN:

In the tense and difficult situation which now confronts us, we cannot afford the luxury of self-deceit. Neither can we longer endure the unpalatable diet of untruth which has been fed to us with reckless abandon in regard to the recent events in my country. Unless we open our eyes and our minds to the real facts, we shall not be able to confront and deal with them. While we live in a fog of deception, it is only natural that we cannot see our course plainly. We have walked half-blinded in this misty and murky atmosphere of lies long enough, and for more than long enough. It is high time that we emerge into the frank and candid light of truth.

In my country, the Soviet Union refused to permit the reunification of the north and the south, as by its solemn declaration at Potsdam and in its declaration of war against Japan, it was bound to do. When the General Assembly of the United Nations voted to reunify Korea and to observe elections in all parts of the nation, the Soviet Union flatly refused to permit this program of peace and of justice to be carried out in the area under the control of its armed forces. Instead, the Soviet Union conducted farcical elections and set up a farcical puppet regime in northern Korea. It called this puppet regime a "government," and asserted that it was the chosen instrument of the people themselves. In the writings of certain "liberals," who seem to pride themselves in their "scholarly fairness," this manipulated puppet regime was in fact accepted as a real government.

Thus the minds of many innocent and honest people were clouded. They read of "two governments" in Korea. One was legally and properly established by the vote of the United Nations and was elected in free and fair balloting under full United Nations observation. The other was covertly and secretly erected by the Soviet Union, behind the hard barrier of an iron curtain, with the United Nations and all other foreign observers shut out, and with the people marched to the polls under police scrutiny to present their forced concurrence with a single slate of hand-picked candidates.

Despite all the facts—despite what honest men knew beyond any question to be the facts—the pretense was accepted, and repeated in seemingly reputable publications, that there were indeed "two governments"—one north, and one south, in Korea. Following this same blind path of self-deception, some people have persisted in speaking of the government of South Korea (when they meant the officially approved, recognized, U.N.-sponsored Republic of Korea), and they balanced this misbegotten phrase with its evil twin—the government of North Korea.

This was a type of self-deception which had a very confusing effect upon the thinking of many, in the world's community of free nations. It led to speculations as to why one part of the Korean people should choose to attack another part.

Fortunately, this self-deception did not poison the thinking of the majority of delegates here in the General Assembly, where you have been kept fully informed by your own Commission in Korea. You have known full well that the so-called "government" in northern Korea was merely a puppet regime established in complete violation of the will of the Korean people by the Soviet Union, to serve its own purposes, in violation of the judgment of the United Nations, as well as in violation of the direct pledges of the U.S.S.R. Most of you have not been in any degree deceived by this pretense of "two governments." But some segments of public opinion have been deceived. And because of that fact, the task of the United Nations and the efforts of the Republic of Korea have been rendered far more difficult.

It is high time that that kind of deception should be denounced and exposed. It is past time for us to unveil the kind of shoddy thinking—if it is no worse—of those spurious "scholars" who have blandly and blindly written of "two Korean governments." The truth, of course, is that there has been only one Korean government, plus an armed puppet regime in the north, which was wholly under the control of the Soviet Union, and which existed from the beginning for the single purpose of serving the selfish interests of the Soviet Union.

When the attack of June 25 (1950) was launched against the free government and the free people of Korea, more lies were spoken and written, and more self-deception was indulged in by some honest and innocent people.

The attack was interpreted as having been launched by the north Korean regime, although all fact and reason indicated, beyond any doubt, that it was launched and directed by the Soviet Union. The lie was broadcast in the Security Council itself—that the Soviet Union had nothing to do with the attack, and that it had not even provided the weapons with which the attack was launched. This lie was spiked by the capture or destruction of huge quantities of Russian-made weapons on the field of battle.

Yet, in the interests of peace, the Republic of Korea and the United Nations were willing for a time longer to pretend to accept the fiction that the Soviet Union was not the direct force which was waging a war of naked and fierce aggression. We pretended to accept that lie in the hope that the masters of the Kremlin would make the lie come at least partly true by withdrawing their aggressive program when they saw that they had aroused the entire free world to resist their designs.

The next lie that was blandly spoken, and that, in form, at least, was for a time accepted, was that the Chinese Communists, who were hurled into the struggle to turn the tide of battle, were not really organized troops, but were merely miscellaneous "volunteers." This lie, too, was accepted on the surface at least, in the bare hope that the Chinese Communist puppets of Moscow might come in time to see the madness of the course they were pursuing, so that they might withdraw their armies before war should become general and inevitable.

On the one hand, the free nations of the world accepted the Communist lie; and in doing so, refrained from attacking the area of Red China, just as though Red China were not actually engaged in the fight. On the other hand, the free nations did frankly recognize that the Red Chinese regime was directing the new attacks, and did appeal to the Peiping regime to desist. Promises were made to the Red Chinese of full safety, if they would withdraw the forces, which they still declared they had not sent into the battle. A large part of Korean sovereignty was offered up in sacrifice, in the vain hope of persuading the Russian and Chinese Communist forces to withdraw from the struggle. The Republic of Korea was restrained from operating north of the thirty-eighth parallel. Power from the Yalu River dams was offered to the Red Chinese, in return for their withdrawal from the war they had already launched. A buffer strip of Korean territory was suggested in some circles as a further guarantee to the Chinese Communist regime.

Every effort was made by the peace-loving nations of the world to make the lie of Chinese nonintervention come to be the truth! But these efforts to avoid the facing of honest facts were of no avail.

Gentlemen, all the efforts that have been made to avert the crisis by a certain amount of self-deception, and by at least a seeming acceptance of the Communist lies, have proved of no avail.

What has chiefly resulted has been an unfortunate confusion in the minds of the Allies themselves! Our people have suffered the double anguish of having to endure the terrible devastation and tragic casualties of battle without even knowing for certain that the fighting was aimed to accomplish the goal of reunification and freedom for which it was being fought. The free nations of the world, represented in this great body of the United Nations, were asked to provide troops and to make sacrifices for a cause which was not clearly defined. One terrible result was that the men who were forced to endure the horrors of war on the battlefields could not have a clear understanding of what their sacrifices were intended to achieve.

This confusion was supposed to serve a good purpose. The motives of the democracies have been of the purest. The desire to avoid a direct struggle by pretending that it does not exist is a worthy desire. But it has not accomplished its aim. The enemy still pours destruction upon us. The foe continues to build up its strength and to drive ahead. Our efforts to pretend that this is a limited war have not prevented the enemy from continuing to fight it as a war of extermination.

The time has come to face the simple fact that surrender and appeasement and self-deception are not leading, and will not lead, to peace. The Communist empire cannot be bought off from its design of conquest by a weak surrender in Korea of the position that the United Nations has taken there. Instead, the facts must be dealt with for what they are.

My country has become a battleground for the contending forces of freedom and justice on the one side, and for brutal aggression on the other. This issue should not and cannot be blinked.

To surrender now would be to make an ironic mockery of the sacrifices which have been endured by my people and by the soldiers of the United Nations. To surrender now would be to offer up the free government and the freedom-loving people of Korea as a living sacrifice to the savage hordes of the Communist empire, in the vain hope of buying at this awful price a reasonable willingness to negotiate. We know the emptiness of this hope, for we know that negotiation is fruitless unless it is conducted honestly and openly by the free will of both sides. Finally, to surrender now to the demands of the Communists in Korea would constitute a disastrous repudiation of the position already firmly and clearly taken by the United Nations.

Mr. Chairman, the Republic of Korea wants nothing less than to be a cause of war. The aim of my government and my people has been only to live in peace, as a free and democratic member of the world community of free and peaceful nations. We have refused to surrender ourselves to conquest by the Communists. We have done our best to hold intact our own particular segment of the world-wide front of free democratic peoples. We have done our duty as best we can in helping to defend the freedom of liberty-loving peoples all over the world. It is our misfortune that the struggle has been joined on our soil, in our cities, and among our civilian population.

It has been our great good fortune that the free nations of the world have viewed our defense as a part of the defense of freedom everywhere. As Stephen Decatur, an American patriot said, "He who fights for freedom anywhere fights for freedom everywhere." I am confident that this solidarity between our people and the rest of the free world will endure. I am confident that the Communist empire no longer can successfully pursue its plan of separating the nations of the free world from one another, so that it can safely destroy and conquer them one by one.

Weakness has not served as an effective defense against Communist conquest. The only adequate defense must lie in strength—in strength of purpose and in fighting force.

We Koreans do not feel ourselves to be helpless. We want to fight in defense of our own homes and of our own lives. We have the young men who are eager to bear arms. But we do not have arms to put in their hands. Our plea, therefore, is twofold. We plead with the free nations of the world to stand firm in the defense of freedom, on the battleground of Korea, where the issue has been joined. And we plead for the supply of arms and other equipment to be placed in the hands of our own people, so that we may more effectively fight by the side of the United Nations troops, to win the victory which is indispensable for us all.

The watchword for this hour is not vaccilation or despair, but determination and action. When we take our stand for freedom and justice, with courage and with a clear vision of our duty, we know that our cause shall win.

Mr. Chairman, there is no retreat from, and no compromise with, the espousal of a moral principle. This great body adjudged the northern

Korean Communists guilty of illegal aggression. How can the present Chinese Communist aggressors be other than equally culpable?

Guilt is not subject to percentage rule. Neither a nation nor an individual can be "a little bit guilty."

The United Nations acted bravely, boldly, and righteously, when it detected and proved the guilt of the first aggressors in Korea. The guilt of the second aggressor is brazen and contemptible. His emissaries sit in your midst, while his soldiers, in overwhelming force, shoot, kill, capture, and enslave the brave men on the wintry battlefields of Korea— the very men who are fighting to restore peace and security under the banner of the United Nations.

There is no possibility of appeasing the aggressor in Korea. One cannot negotiate with rattlesnakes. The aggressor believes that might is right, and that brute force will triumph. He is on the march for world conquest. Should he subjugate Korea, he will pause only long enough to regroup, to rearm, to attack.

Sir, the acceleration of Communist aggression will be in direct proportion to the acceleration of defeatism or appeasement in Korea. The consequences of appeasement will be appalling not only to peace and democracy in the Orient, but to peace and democracy in the remainder of the world as well.

When right and justice are disregarded, and expediency is embraced in their stead, disaster is all the more invited and made inevitable, even though it may seem to have been postponed!

Have we forgotten what happened when, in 1931, Japan seized upon Manchuria because the world was then unwilling to act in concert against the aggressor?

Cannot we recall how Hitler and Mussolini and other dictators of the past score of years, felt free to commit one excess after another? They went on, and on, and on—until the entire world was plunged into war. Cannot we remember Munich? Yet, that war could have been averted, had the concept of collective security been invoked, and had the other nations acted with speed and decision in behalf of justice.

When, last June, the Security Council of this great body did invoke the concept of collective security, and did activate it with armed resistance, the peoples of the free nations of the world rejoiced. It was the first time in history that the great powers had kept their promise to a small nation. The prestige of the United Nations enhanced a hundred times. Its authority became a reality! The world looked to it and cheered. All the world began to repose faith and trust in the United

Nations. The United Nations dare not go back on that precious faith of the world. It must not become another League of Nations!

The forces of the United Nations fought first a magnificent defensive action against tremendous odds. They then turned their retreat into a sweeping offensive, which brought victory within their grasp. Peace and security were actually reëstablished throughout most of Korea. The initial aggressor had been beaten and disarmed.

Then followed one of the grossest acts of international immorality, the wanton invasion of the land of a peaceful neighbor by hundreds of thousands of trained and armed Chinese Communists.

The spokesman for the masters of the Kremlin terms this a great "volunteer" movement to rid Korea of the "American aggressor." Once again the free world recognizes this new aggression of the Chinese Communists for just what it is—Russian in origin, Russian in direction, Russian in execution! Once again Korea is being subjected to all the hideous devastation of modern war, plus the inevitable starvation for a great portion of its population.

But the people of Korea have not lost hope. They will be heartened by the "no appeasement" pronouncement of President Truman and Prime Minister Attlee. They will be further heartened when, as I firmly believe, this great organization, the United Nations, again will act boldly and decisively on behalf of right and justice. The people of Korea will fight on to the end, for they know that, if a death warrant is served upon them as a nation, it will be the prelude to other death warrants served singly upon other free and democratic nations throughout the world. Should we forget the fate of a democratic Czechoslovakia? Of Poland? Of the souls of all the other now-satellites?

History can be a harsh and brutal teacher. It is so in Korea today. The lesson of collective security—of all for one, and one for all, against the aggressor—is being written in Korea in letters of blood, the blood of heroic men of many a United Nations country, the blood of our own brave Korean soldiers. These men died for freedom and decency. They must never be regarded as "expendables"! Were this ever to come to pass, and I pray that it never shall, the world of free men would have to bow its head in shame.

The Korean army has been more than willing to make the heaviest of sacrifices in combating Communist aggression. Our civilian population also has had to pay an awful toll. But our resolution to resist this mad force unleashed against a peaceful world has been in no way diminished. Though denied membership in this great organization by a Soviet veto—we have felt a sense of real kinship, for we shall always remember the interest of the United Nations in the re-creation of our Republic. We shall always treasure your kindly counsel and genuine assistance in helping to restore to us our rightful place among the family of civilized and democratic nations. We shall never forget your prompt and vigorous action when the brute force of Communist aggression was first launched against us and imperiled our very existence.

Now, a second time, our life as a free nation is in grave danger. Now, a second time, brute force of magnitude bears down upon us. Once more we call upon you to help us resist the aggressor.

Our fight is your fight—more so now than ever. It is the fight of free men anywhere and everywhere in the world, to preserve liberty and to destroy tyranny! It is a struggle which can never be encompassed by any single geographical area, no matter how seemingly remote. We share a common cause, a holy cause.

You did not fail us in the past. I know you will not fail us now.

An Address to the Security Council of the United Nations

Wu Hsiu-Chuan

The text below is taken from the United Nations Security Council Official Records, Fifth Year, 527th Meeting, 28 November 1950, No. 69. It is the second half of a long speech given on that date by General Wu Hsiu-Chuan of the Central People's Government of the People's Republic of China and is published here as representing the official view of the government of Communist China.

An account of the proceedings of the day is to be found in the *United Nations Bulletin* for 15 December 1950. General Wu declared in the early part of his reading that on the instructions of his government he was there in the name of the 475,000,000 people of China to accuse the United States government of the unlawful and criminal act of armed aggression against the territory of China—Taiwan (Formosa) and the Penghu Islands. He said he would not, of course, participate in the discussion of that part of the Council's agenda concerning the complaint of aggression against the Republic of Korea.

The writer of the leading editorial in *The New York Times* for 30 November 1951 commented on the speech as follows: "Mr. Wu read his piece like the automaton he probably is, without a flicker of expression or a change of intonation. His charges of American invasion of Formosa, where we maintain a force of forty-two men, came strangely from a government that has poured 250,000 into Korea, but the Russians have accustomed us to this kind of fantasy. What is intolerable is the vicious attempt to besmirch the whole American record in China."

THE ARMED aggression of the United States government on our territory, Taiwan, is not accidental. It is the inevitable consequence of the United States government's policy of aggression against China to interfere in China's internal affairs and to seek exclusive domination over China—a United States imperialist policy of long standing.

In the entire history of China's foreign relations, though the peoples of the United States and China have always maintained friendly relations, in their relations with China the American imperialists have always been the cunning aggressor.

The American imperialists have never been the friends of the Chinese people. They have always aligned themselves with the enemies of the Chinese people. They have always been the enemies of the Chinese people. However shamelessly the American imperialists claim to be friends of the Chinese people, the historical record which distinguishes friend from foe cannot be altered.

Before the Second World War, because of the advantage gained by other imperialists in China, the American imperialists adopted what was known as the "open door" and "equal opportunity" policy, which though ostensibly different from the policies of the other imperialist powers, was in fact an aggressive policy aimed at sharing the spoils with other imperialists.

After the Second World War, mainly because of the efforts and sacrifices of the Chinese people and of the Soviet Union in the Second World War, the power of Japanese imperialism in China was smashed, and that of the other imperialists in China weakened. Taking advantage of this opportunity, the United States government stepped up the execution of its policy of sole dominance over China. But the difficulties in realizing this policy were formidable, for those who favored this policy were only the Kuomintang reactionary clique, while the entire Chinese people were opposed to it. Therefore, in order to carry out their policy, it was necessary for the American imperialists to support the Kuomintang reactionary clique and to oppose the Chinese people with all their power.

After the surrender of imperialist Japan in 1945, the United States government immediately adopted a policy of open intervention in China's internal affairs, using every means to smooth the way for the Kuomintang reactionary clique to launch a bloody civil war to slaughter the

An Address to the Security Council of the United Nations

Chinese people. The United States government mobilized 113,000 men of its naval, ground, and air forces to make landings in the major ports of China, to grab important strategic points from which the Kuomintang reactionary clique could launch the civil war, and to assist the Kuomintang reactionary clique by transporting one million troops to the fronts on which the civil war was to be launched. Moreover, the United States government equipped, at one time or another, 166 divisions of Chiang Kai-shek's reactionary army, as the main force for the invasion of the Chinese people's liberated areas; it helped Chiang to equip nine squadrons consisting of 1,720 aircraft; it supplied the Chiang navy with 757 vessels, it gave material and financial aid to Chiang in the amount of over six thousand million U.S. dollars, although the United States government admits only one-third of this figure.

It is only because of the large-scale aid it received from the United States government that the Chiang Kai-shek Kuomintang reactionary clique dared and was able to carry out a civil war against the people unprecedented in China's history for its scale and cruelty, and to slaughter with United States arms several millions of the Chinese people. During Chiang Kai-shek's bloody civil war against the Chinese people, apart from the fact that the United States government had sent over 1000 military advisers to Chiang Kai-shek to plan the civil war, United States troops stationed in China in fact participated directly in the civil war, and invaded the Chinese people's liberated areas more than forty times. During this period, the United States government and the Chiang Kai-shek Kuomintang reactionary clique signed all kinds of unequal treaties and agreements which reduced China to the status of a colony and military base of the United States. These included such military agreements as the "Aviation Agreement" and "Naval Agreement," and such economic treaties and agreements as the "Sino-American Treaty of Friendship, Commerce and Navigation," the "Bilateral Agreement between China and the United States," and the "Sino-American Agreement on Rural Reconstruction."

Furthermore, on the basis of these treaties and agreements, the United States government secured many naval and air bases in Kuomintang China and gained control of the military, political, financial, and economic branches of the Kuomintang government. American goods flooded China's markets, causing China's national industries to fall into bankruptcy. The monopoly capitalists of the United States, through the four big families of Chiang, Soong, Kung, and Chen, controlled the lifestream of China's economy. In fact the Chiang Kai-shek

Kuomintang reactionary regime was nothing more than a puppet whereby American imperialism controlled China. The Chinese people are completely justified in entering all the tyrannical crimes of Chiang Kai-shek on the account of the American imperialists. The Chinese people will never forget their blood debt against the American imperialists. American imperialists decidedly cannot escape the grave responsibility which they must bear for all the crimes committed by the Chiang Kai-shek brigands against the Chinese people. The hands of the American imperialists are stained with the blood of the Chinese people. The Chinese people have every right to indict the United States government for the bloody crimes of slaughtering the Chinese people and enslaving the Chinese nation through its puppet, Chiang Kai-shek.

However, all the efforts of the United States government have failed. A relatively complete record of this failure can be found in the White Paper entitled *United States Relations with China,* compiled by the State Department of the United States. But the United States government, still reluctant to admit that this is its final defeat, has converged for the time being all its activities of aggression against China on Taiwan Island, the lair of the Chiang Kai-shek remnant clique in its last desperate struggle.

Shortly after the Japanese surrender, the United States armed forces had already started making various preparations for aggression against Taiwan under the pretext of assisting the Kuomintang regime in "accepting surrender" and "repatriating war prisoners." What the United States did in Taiwan through the Kuomintang regime, just as what it did in Japan, was first of all to keep intact all Japanese fascist forces and military installations. During the second half of 1947, under the direction of the United States government, Hasegawa Kiyoshi, former Japanese Governor of Taiwan, and Yoshisuke Aikawa, former president of the Japanese Manchuria Industrial Development Corporation, who was released by order of MacArthur from Lugamo Prison, as well as other notorious war criminals of the aggressive war against China, were sent to Taiwan under United States protection. They were sent there to participate in planning the construction of military bases in Taiwan and, under United States instructions, to help train Chiang Kai-shek's troops to slaughter Chinese people.

During this period the United States successively established air bases, liaison radio stations, and other installations at Taipei, Sungsan, Taichung, Tainan, and Hsinchu airfields. Military aircraft of the United States Thirteenth Air Force in the Pacific were sent out to photograph the topography of the whole of Taiwan Island and to make meteorological surveys. Furthermore, United States military aircraft were constantly stationed in the various airfields in Taiwan. Hsinchu airfield, originally the largest air base in Taiwan during the Japanese occupation, became, after the Japanese surrender, the base of the United States aggression forces—the Thirteenth Air Force.

Meanwhile, the United States gradually converted the ports of Keelung and Kaoshiung in Taiwan into its own naval bases. In the spring of 1948, Admiral Charles M. Cooke, Jr., arrived in Taiwan with the United States West Pacific Fleet under his command and compelled the Kuomintang regime—which had intended to cover up the fact that it had sold China's seaports—to declare officially that Keelung as well as Tsingtao were ports open to the United States Navy.

From that time onward, vessels of the United States Navy have continually violated the territorial waters of our country around Taiwan and have been stationed in the various ports of Taiwan. In the port of Kaohsiung alone, at one time there were stationed as many as twenty-seven United States naval vessels. In regard to land forces, the United States "Joint Military Advisory Group" long ago sent a large staff of officers in active service to be stationed permanently on Taiwan. In accordance with the joint war plans of the United States and Chiang Kai-shek, this military staff is responsible for organizing, equipping and training the so-called "new army" of the Kuomintang to be used to attack the Chinese people. Thus, the United States has, in reality, taken over the military role of Japan, put Taiwan under its control and converted it into a military base of the United States.

Economically, the United States government and American monopolies such as the Westinghouse Electric Company, the Reynolds Metal Company, the American Express Company, and others, have, through various devices, jointly dominated Taiwan's main industries—electric power, aluminium, cement, fertilizer, and others—controlled the economic life of Taiwan, and actually reduced it to a colony of the United States. Under such conditions, it is natural that the United States will not lightly give up Taiwan. Consequently, in order to realize its aim to dominate Taiwan, the United States government has long been engaged in a variety of vicious political conspiracies. The instigation by the United States of the "Taiwan Separation Movement" reached such a height of brazenness that an American government official in Taiwan openly declared that, if the people in Taiwan wanted to relieve themselves of China's rule, the United States was ready to help them. The Chinese people of Taiwan have witnessed with their own eyes all these conspiracies of the United States government in league with the Kuomintang reactionary remnants. Hence, in the last five years, they have repeatedly launched great national liberation movements directed against the United States government and its puppets. The glorious uprising of the Chinese people of Taiwan on 27 February 1947 declared to the whole world that just as they had not accepted the rule of Japanese imperialism, so they would never accept the rule of United States imperialism. The people of Taiwan fervently demand their return to the fold of their already liberated motherland and are at this very moment engaged in hard and heroic struggles for the liberation of Taiwan.

In 1949, the Chinese People's Liberation Army completed the liberation of the mainland of China. The vestiges of Chiang Kai-shek's clique fled to Taiwan to use it as a lair for their last desperate struggle. In spite of President Truman's hypocritical statement on 5 January, this year, of "nonintervention in the Taiwan situation," the United States government has, in fact, intensified and stepped up its support for the Chiang Kai-shek remnant clique herded together in Taiwan. The United States government continues, through the Kuomintang remnant clique, to try to prevent the People's Republic of China from liberating Taiwan, so that Taiwan may remain under the actual domination of the United States.

But why does not the United States government continue this course of action—this relatively covert form of aggression through the Chiang Kai-shek puppet regime—instead of adopting the form of open and direct armed aggression to attain its objective of controlling Taiwan? There is only one reason—the growing might of the Chinese people and the imminent collapse of the Chiang Kai-shek reactionary remnant regime have made it impossible for any indirect form of aggression to ensure the attainment of the United States objective. Thus we can see that the United States act of open armed aggression against China's territory, Taiwan, is the inevitable outcome of the development of the United States imperialist policy of aggression against China, a policy of long standing.

The act of armed aggression against China's territory, Taiwan, by the United States government serves only to prove once again to the Chinese people that United States imperialism regards with hostility all victories of the Chinese people and that it is the most deadly enemy of the Chinese people.

I must further point out that the armed aggression of the United States government against the Chinese territory, Taiwan, is not an isolated affair. It is an integral part of the overall plan of the United States

An Address to the Security Council of the United Nations

government to intensify its aggression, control, and enslavement of Asian countries and the peoples of Korea, Viet-Nam, the Philippines, Japan, etc. It is a further step in the development of interference by American imperialism in the affairs of Asia.

During the five years following the Second World War, General MacArthur, Commander in Chief of United States forces in the Far East, has adopted a series of unlawful measures, abusing the power granted to him as Supreme Commander of the Allied forces in Japan, and completely violating the Potsdam Declaration jointly signed by China, the United States, the United Kingdom, and the Union of Soviet Socialist Republics, and the "Basic Post-Surrender Policy toward Japan" of the Far Eastern Commission. MacArthur arbitrarily sets free the Japanese war criminals whom the people all over Asia hate bitterly. He revives the power of Japanese fascism, suppresses the movement of the Japanese people for independence and liberation, and refuses to bring about an early overall peace treaty with Japan. He attempts to gain sole domination over Japan, to enslave the Japanese nation, and to reduce Japan to a United States colony as well as a United States base for a new aggressive war. This policy of the United States government towards Japan damages not only the interests of the Japanese people but also the common interests of the Chinese people, the Korean people, and the other peoples of Asia. The Chinese people cannot but strongly protest and resolutely oppose this reactionary policy of the United States government. Since the Chinese people won their victory on the Chinese mainland, the United States government has still more frantically carried out a policy of rearming Japan to oppose the Chinese people and the other Asian peoples. At present, the United States government has not only turned Japan into its main base in the Far East in preparation for aggressive war, but it has already begun to use this base as a means to launch aggressive wars against a series of Asian countries. The headquarters of the United States government for its aggression against Korea and Taiwan is in Japan.

Under the pretext of the Korean civil war, which was of its own making, the United States government launched armed aggression simultaneously against Korea and Taiwan. From the very outset, the United States armed aggression against Korea gravely threatened China's security. Korea is about 5000 miles away from the boundaries of the United States. To say that the civil war in Korea would affect the security of the United States is a flagrant, deceitful absurdity. But there is only a narrow river between Korea and China. The United States armed aggression in Korea inevitably threatens China's security.

That the United States aggression forces in Korea have directly threatened China's security is fully borne out by the facts.

From 27 August to 10 November 1950, the military aircraft of the United States aggression forces in Korea have violated the territorial air of Northeast China ninety times; they have conducted reconnaissance activities, strafed and bombed Chinese cities, towns and villages, killed and wounded Chinese peaceful inhabitants, and damaged Chinese properties. The details are set out in a separate list. This list has been translated into English and I hope that the Secretary-General will distribute it to the members of the Security Council.

Here I should point out in addition that from 10.30 hours on 10 November to 13.10 hours on 14 November, thus within 100 hours, United States airplanes violated China's territorial air for as many as twenty-eight times. On nine of these occasions they bombed and strafed. The total number of invading planes was 339. In ten of these raids more than ten planes took part. On one occasion the number of invading planes was sixty-eight. Six Chinese were injured and 168 houses destroyed by bombing and strafing. During the five days from 15 November to 19 November, United States airplanes again violated Chinese territorial air thirty-three times. The total number of invading planes was 218. On 20 September naval craft of the United States aggression forces against Korea opened fire on and forcibly inspected Chinese merchant shipping on the high seas.

All these acts of direct aggression against China by the United States aggression forces in Korea are an insolent provocation which the Chinese people absolutely cannot tolerate. The Central People's government of the People's Republic of China has repeatedly lodged accusations with the United Nations demanding that it immediately take measures to stop such outrageous acts of the United States government and to bring about the withdrawal of the United States aggression forces from Korea so that the issue may not assume more serious proportions. Although, because of the resolute support of the representative of the USSR, our charge was placed on the agenda of the Security Council on 31 August, yet, owing to the manipulation and obstruction of the United States government, the Security Council has up until now refused to admit the representative of China to state the case and participate in a discussion of this item.

Now the United States forces of aggression in Korea are approaching our northeastern frontiers. The flames of the war of aggression waged by the United States against Korea are swiftly sweeping towards China. Under such circumstances the United States armed aggression against

An Address to the Security Council of the United Nations

Korea cannot be regarded as a matter which concerns the Korean people alone. No, decidedly not. The United States aggression against Korea gravely endangers the security of the People's Republic of China. The Korean People's Democratic Republic is a country bound by close ties of friendship to the People's Republic of China. Only a river separates the two countries geographically. The Chinese people cannot afford to stand idly by in the face of this serious situation brought about by the United States government's aggression against Korea and the dangerous tendency towards the extension of the war. The Chinese people have witnessed with their own eyes Taiwan fall prey to aggression and the flames of the United States war of aggression against Korea leap towards them. Thus stirred into righteous anger, they are volunteering in great numbers to go to the aid of the Korean people. Resistance to United States aggression is based on the self-evident principles of justice and reason. The Chinese People's government sees no reason whatever to prevent voluntary departure for Korea to participate, under the command of the government of the Korean People's Democratic Republic, in the great liberation struggle of the Korean people against United States aggression.

The United States armed aggression against Taiwan is inseparable from its interference in the internal affairs of the Viet-Nam Republic, its support of the French aggressors and their Bao Dai puppet regime, and its armed attack on the Viet-Nam people. The people of the entire world know that France is the aggressor against Viet-Nam and that the Bao Dai regime is a typical puppet regime which cannot possibly win any confidence and support from the Viet-Nam people. In supporting this aggressor and this puppet regime against the people of Viet-Nam, the United States government aims not only at aggression against Viet-Nam but also at threatening the borders of the People's Republic of China. The Chinese people cannot but be deeply concerned with the unfolding of the aggressive plot of the United States government against Viet-Nam.

In making Japan its main war base in the East, launching armed aggression against Korea and Taiwan, carrying out active intervention against Viet-Nam, and tightening its control over other countries in Asia, the United States government is systematically building up a military encirclement of the People's Republic of China, in preparation for further attack on the People's Republic of China, and to stir up a Third World War.

The truth of the matter is not difficult to understand: after the Second World War, the United States imperialist policy on the Chinese mainland met with miserable failure. The great victory of the Chinese people's revolution points to the oppressed peoples and nations throughout Asia the way of driving imperialism out of Asia and achieving national independence. It shows them with living facts that it is possible to defeat American imperialism, and that without imperialist oppression, the Asian peoples not only can survive but will live a much better life. The great victory of the Chinese people's revolution has inspired and encouraged the oppressed peoples throughout Asia in their struggle of liberation for national independence. But American imperialism cannot resign itself to the shattering of its dream of exclusive domination over Asia, nor can it acquiesce in its withdrawal from Asia. Hence, American imperialism regards the victorious People's Republic of China as the most serious obstacle to its sole domination over Asia.

American imperialism is hostile to all liberation struggles of Asian peoples, and is particularly hostile to the great victory of the Chinese people. It has, therefore, resorted to the form of open and direct armed aggression to realize its fanatic design of attacking new China and dominating the whole of Asia. The American imperialists claim that the United States "defense line" must be pushed to the Yalu River, to the Straits of Taiwan, and to the mountainous border regions between China and Viet-Nam, or the United States will have no security. This is the reason why, they claim, the United States has conducted armed aggression against Korea and Taiwan and intensified its intervention in Viet-Nam. But in no sense whatever can it be said that the Korean people's struggle for liberation, or the exercise of sovereignty by the People's Republic of China over its own territory, Taiwan, or the volunteering of the Chinese people to resist the United States and aid Korea, or the struggle for national independence of the Viet-Nam Democratic Republic against French imperialism and its puppets affect the security of the United States in North America 5000 miles away. The Chinese people, steeled by hardship and sufferings, know full well that the United States government has taken this series of aggressive acts with the purpose of realizing its fanatic design of dominating Asia and the world. One of the master-planners of Japanese aggression, Tanaka, once said: to conquer the world, one must first conquer Asia; to conquer Asia, one must first conquer China; to conquer China, one must first conquer Manchuria and Mongolia; to conquer Manchuria and Mongolia, one must first conquer Korea and Taiwan.

Ever since 1895, the course of aggression taken by imperialist Japan has exactly corresponded to the Tanaka plan. In 1895, imperialist Japan invaded Korea and Taiwan. In 1931, imperialist Japan occupied the whole of Northeast China. In 1937, imperialist Japan launched the war of aggression against the whole of China. In 1941, it started the war aimed at the conquest of the whole of Asia. Naturally, as everyone knows, before it had realized this design Japanese imperialism collapsed. American imperialism, by its aggression against Taiwan and Korea, in practice plagiarizes Tanaka's memorandum and follows the beaten path of the Japanese imperialist aggressors. The Chinese people are maintaining a sharp vigilance over the progress of American imperialist aggression. They have already acquired the experience and learned the lesson from history as to how to defend themselves from aggression.

American imperialism has taken the place of Japanese imperialism. It is now following the old track of aggression against China and Asia on which Japanese imperialism set forth in 1894-1895, only hoping to proceed with greater speed. But after all, 1950 is not 1895; the times have changed, and so have the circumstances. The Chinese people have arisen. The Chinese people who have victoriously overthrown the rule of Japanese imperialism and of American imperialism and its lackey, Chiang Kai-shek, on China's mainland, will certainly succeed in driving out the United States aggressors and recover Taiwan and all other territories that belong to China. In the course of fifty-five years, as a result of the victories of the great socialist October Revolution of the Soviet Union, of the anti-fascist Second World War, and of the great revolution of the Chinese people, all the oppressed nations and peoples of the East have awakened and organized themselves. Regardless of the savagery and cruelty of the American imperialist aggressors, the hard struggling people of Japan, the victoriously advancing people of Viet-Nam, the heroically resisting people of Korea, the people of the Philippines who have never laid down their arms, and all the oppressed nations and peoples of the East will certainly unite in close solidarity. Yielding neither to the enticements nor to the threats of American imperialism, they will fight dauntlessly on to win the final victory in their struggle for national independence.

The armed aggression against the territory of China, Taiwan, and the extension of the aggressive war in Korea by the United States government have multiplied a thousandfold the Chinese people's hatred and indignation against American imperialism. Since 27 June, the thousands upon thousands of protests against this base act of aggression committed by the United States government—raised by the various democratic political parties, people's organizations, national minorities, overseas Chinese, workers, peasants, intellectuals, industrialists, and business men throughout China—have demonstrated the irrepressible wrath of the Chinese people. The Chinese people love peace. But if the United States aggressors should take this as an indication of the weakness of the Chinese people, they would be making a grave mistake. The Chinese people never have been, and never will be, afraid of a war of resistance against aggression. Regardless of any military measures of obstruction by the United States government, and no matter how it may arrogate for its purpose the name of the United Nations, the Chinese people are firmly determined to recover Taiwan and all other territories belonging to China from the grip of the United States aggressors. This is the irrevocable and immovable will of the 475 million people of China. The United States must bear the full responsibility for all consequences that may arise from its invasion and occupation of Taiwan.

In order to safeguard international peace and security and to uphold the sanctity of the United Nations Charter, the United Nations Security Council has the inalienable duty to apply sanctions against the United States government for its criminal acts of armed aggression upon the territory of China, Taiwan, and its armed intervention in Korea. In the name of the Central People's government of the People's Republic of China, I therefore propose to the United Nations Security Council:

First, that the United Nations Security Council should openly condemn, and take concrete steps to apply severe sanctions against, the United States government for its criminal acts of armed aggression against the territory of China, Taiwan, and armed intervention in Korea.

Second, that the United Nations Security Council should immediately adopt effective measures to bring about the complete withdrawal by the United States government of its forces of armed aggression from Taiwan, in order that peace and security in the Pacific and in Asia may be ensured.

Third, that the United Nations Security Council should immediately adopt effective measures to bring about the withdrawal from Korea of the armed forces of the United States and all other countries and to leave it to the people of North and South Korea to settle the domestic affairs of Korea themselves, so that a peaceful solution of the Korean question may be achieved.

These proposals have been translated into English. We request the Secretary-General of the United Nations to distribute them to members of the Security Council, keeping one copy for himself. We ask that a copy should not be given to the reactionary Kuomintang representative, disowned by the people of China.

Finally, I wish to declare that the President of the Security Council has taken advantage of the fact that the representative of the Central People's government has only just arrived at Lake Success and is not familiar with the procedure here and of the fact that my government is still not a member of the Security Council. He has conspired with the United States representative in arranging an unreasonable procedure with regard to our speaking before the Council. The President has thus deprived the representative of the Central People's government of the right which is due to him to speak first before the Council. I wish to lodge a strong protest against this action.

On Assuming Command of the Eighth Army
General Matthew B. Ridgway

Shortly after General (then Lieutenant General) Matthew B. Ridgway succeeded the late General Walton H. Walker on 26 December 1950 as Commander of the Eighth Army in Korea, he issued the statement published below to his command. It is reproduced here as the field commander's answer to the questions uppermost in the minds of the combat troops.

On 11 April 1951 President Truman relieved General MacArthur as Supreme Commander, Allied Powers; Commander in Chief, United Nations Command; Commander in Chief, Far East; and Commanding General, United States Army, Far East. Secretary of Defense Marshall said in his message to General Ridgway appointing him to these commands: "It is realized that your presence in Korea in the immediate future is highly important, but we are sure you can make the proper distribution of your time until you can turn over the active command of the Eighth Army to its new commander [Lieut. Gen. James A. Van Fleet]."

General Ridgway was born at Fort Monroe, Virginia on 3 March 1895 and was graduated from the United States Military Academy in 1917. During World War II he commanded the 82nd Infantry Division (1942), the 82nd Airborne Division in Sicily, Italy, and Normandy (1942-44), and the 18th Airborne Corps in Belgium, France, and Germany (1944-45). From 1946 to 1948 he was the senior U.S. Army member of the Military Staff Committee of the U.N. In 1949 he was appointed Deputy Chief of Staff for Administration of the United States Army.

In his General Order issued from Headquarters Eighth United States Army Korea, dated 26 December 1950, General Ridgway stated in part: "I have, with little advance

General Matthew B. Ridgway

notice, assumed heavy responsibilities before in battle, but never with greater opportunities for service to our loved ones and our nation in beating back a world menace which free peoples cannot tolerate. It is an honored privilege to share this service with you and with other comrades of the navy and air force. You will have my utmost. I shall expect yours."

IN MY brief period of command duty here, I have heard from several sources, chiefly from members of combat units, the questions: "Why are we here?"—"What are we fighting for?"

What follows represents my answers to those questions:

The answer to the first question, "Why are we here?" is simple and conclusive. We are here because of the decisions of the properly constituted authorities of our respective governments. As the Commander in Chief, United Nations Command, General of the Army Douglas MacArthur said publicly yesterday: "This Command intends to maintain a military position in Korea just as long as the statesmen of the United Nations decide we should do so." The answer is simple because further comment is unnecessary. It is conclusive because the loyalty we give and expect precludes any slightest questioning of those orders.

The second question is of much greater significance, and every member of this command is entitled to a full and reasoned answer. Mine follows:

To me the issues are clear. It is not a question of this or that Korean town or village. Real estate is, here, incidental. It is not restricted to the issue of freedom for our South Korean allies, whose fidelity and valor under the severest stresses of battle we recognize, though that freedom is a symbol of the wider issues, and included among them.

The real issues are whether or not the power of Western civilization, as God has permitted it to flower in our own beloved lands, shall defy and defeat communism; whether rule of men who shoot their prisoners, enslave their citizens, and deride the dignity of man, shall displace the rule of those to whom the individual and his individual rights are sacred; whether we are to survive with God's hand to guide and lead us, or perish in the dead existence of a Godless world.

If these be true, and to me they are, beyond any possibility of challenge, then this has long since ceased to be a fight for freedom for our Korean allies alone, and for their national survival. It has become, and it continues to be, a fight for our own freedom, for our own survival, in an honorable, independent national existence.

The sacrifices we have made, and those we shall yet support, are not offered vicariously for others, but in our own direct defense, wherein certain principles mean more than life.

In the final analysis, the issue now joined right here in Korea is whether communism or individual freedom shall prevail, and make no mistake, whether the next flight of fear-driven people we have just witnessed across the Han River, and continue to witness in other areas, shall be checked and defeated overseas, or permitted, step by step, to close in on our own homelands, and at some future time, however distant, to engulf our own loved ones in all its misery and despair.

These are the things for which we fight. Never have members of any military command had a greater challenge than we, or a finer opportunity to show ourselves and our people at their best—and thus be an honor to the profession of arms, and a credit to those who bred us.

I would like each commander to whom this is addressed, in his own chosen ways of leadership, to convey the substance of this message to every single member of his command, and at the earliest practicable moment.

Preventing a New World War
Harry S. Truman

On 11 April 1951 the President of the United States relieved General of the Army Douglas MacArthur of his Far East commands in the following order:

I deeply regret that it becomes my duty as President and Commander in Chief of the United States military forces to replace you as Supreme Commander, Allied Powers; Commander in Chief, United Nations Command; Commander in Chief, Far East; and Commanding General, United States Army, Far East.

You will turn over your commands, effective at once to Lieut. Gen. Matthew B. Ridgway. You are authorized to have issued such orders as are necessary to complete desired travel to such place as you select.

My reasons for your replacement will be made public concurrently with the delivery to you of the foregoing order, and are contained in the next following message.

The address printed below was delivered to a nation-wide radio and television audience on 11 April and is in the nature of an explanation of the reasons prompting the decision of the Commander in Chief.

I WANT TO talk plainly to you tonight about what we are doing in Korea and about our policy in the Far East.

In the simplest terms, what we are doing in Korea is this: We are trying to prevent a third world war.

I think most people in this country recognized that fact last June.

And they warmly supported the decision of the government to help the Republic of Korea against the Communist aggressors. Now, many persons, even some who applauded our decision to defend Korea, have forgotten the basic reason for our action.

It is right for us to be in Korea. It was right last June. It is right today.

I want to remind you why this is true.

The Communists in the Kremlin are engaged in a monstrous conspiracy to stamp out freedom all over the world. If they were to succeed, the United States would be numbered among their principal victims. It must be clear to everyone that the United States cannot—and will not—sit idly by and await foreign conquest. The only question is: When is the best time to meet the threat and how?

The best time to meet the threat is in the beginning. It is easier to put out a fire in the beginning when it is small than after it has become a roaring blaze.

And the best way to meet the threat of aggression is for the peace-loving nations to act together. If they don't act together, they are likely to be picked off, one by one.

If they had followed the right policies in the 1930's—if the free countries had acted together, to crush the aggression of the dictators, and if they had acted in the beginning, when the aggression was small—there probably would have been no World War II.

If history has taught us anything, it is that aggression anywhere in the world is a threat to peace everywhere in the world. When that aggression is supported by the cruel and selfish rulers of a powerful nation who are bent on conquest, it becomes a clear and present danger to the security and independence of every free nation.

This is a lesson that most people in this country have learned thoroughly. This is the basic reason why we joined in creating the United Nations. And since the end of World War II we have been putting that lesson into practice—we have been working with other free nations to check the aggressive designs of the Soviet Union before they can result in a third world war.

That is what we did in Greece, when that nation was threatened by the aggression of international Communism.

The attack against Greece could have led to general war. But this country came to the aid of Greece. The United Nations supported Greek resistance. With our help, the determination and efforts of the Greek people defeated the attack on the spot.

Another big Communist threat to peace was the Berlin blockade.

That too could have led to war. But again it was settled because free men would not back down in an emergency.

The aggression against Korea is the boldest and most dangerous move the Communists have yet made.

The attack on Korea was part of a greater plan for conquering all of Asia.

I would like to read to you from a secret intelligence report which came to us after the attack. It is a report of a speech a Communist army officer in North Korea gave to a group of spies and saboteurs last May, one month before South Korea was invaded. The report shows in great detail how this invasion was part of a carefully prepared plot. Here is part of what the Communist officer, who had been trained in Moscow, told his men: "Our forces," he said, "are scheduled to attack South Korean forces about the middle of June. . . . The coming attack on South Korea marks the first step toward the liberation of Asia."

Notice that he used the word "liberation." That is Communist double talk meaning "conquest."

I have another secret intelligence report here. This one tells what another Communist officer in the Far East told his men several months before the invasion of Korea. Here is what he said: "In order to successfully undertake the long awaited world revolution, we must first unify Asia. . . . Java, Indo-China, Malaya, India, Tibet, Thailand, Philippines, and Japan are our ultimate targets. . . . The United States is the only obstacle on our road for the liberation of all countries in southeast Asia. In other words, we must unify the people of Asia and crush the United States."

That is what the Communist leaders are telling their people, and that is what they have been trying to do.

They want to control all Asia from the Kremlin.

This plan of conquest is in flat contradiction to what we believe. We believe that Korea belongs to the Koreans, that India belongs to the Indians—that all the nations of Asia should be free to work out their affairs in their own way. This is the basis of peace in the Far East and everywhere else.

The whole Communist imperialism is back of the attack on peace in the Far East. It was the Soviet Union that trained and equipped the North Koreans for aggression. The Chinese Communists massed 44 well-trained and well-equipped divisions on the Korean frontier. These were the troops they threw into battle when the North Korean Communists were beaten.

The question we have had to face is whether the Communist plan of conquest can be stopped without general war. Our government and other countries associated with us in the United Nations believe that the best chance of stopping it without general war is to meet the attack in Korea and defeat it there.

That is what we have been doing. It is a difficult and bitter task.

But so far it has been successful.

So far, we have prevented World War III.

So far, by fighting a limited war in Korea, we have prevented aggression from succeeding and bringing on a general war. And the ability of the whole free world to resist Communist aggression has been greatly improved.

We have taught the enemy a lesson. He has found out that aggression is not cheap or easy. Moreover, men all over the world who want to remain free have been given new courage and new hope. They know now that the champions of freedom can stand up and fight and that they will stand up and fight.

Our resolute stand in Korea is helping the forces of freedom now fighting in Indo-China and other countries in that part of the world. It has already slowed down the timetable of conquest.

In Korea itself, there are signs that the enemy is building up his ground forces for a new mass offensive. We also know that there have been large increases in the enemy's available air forces.

If a new attack comes, I feel confident it will be turned back. The United Nations fighting forces are tough and able and well equipped. They are fighting for a just cause. They are proving to all the world that the principle of collective security will work. We are proud of all these forces for the magnificent job they have done against heavy odds. We pray that their efforts may succeed, for upon their success may hinge the peace of the world.

The Communist side must now choose its course of action. The Communist rulers may press the attack against us. They may take further action which will spread the conflict. They have that choice, and with it the awful responsibility for what may follow. The Communists also have the choice of a peaceful settlement which could lead to a general relaxation of tensions in the Far East. The decision is theirs, because the forces of the United Nations will strive to limit the conflict if possible.

We do not want to see the conflict in Korea extended. We are trying to prevent a world war—not to start one. The best way to do that is to make it plain that we and the other free countries will continue to resist the attack.

But you may ask: Why can't we take other steps to punish the aggressor? Why don't we bomb Manchuria and China itself? Why don't we assist Chinese Nationalist troops to land on the mainland of China?

If we were to do these things we would be running a very grave risk of starting a general war. If that were to happen, we would have brought about the exact situation we are trying to prevent.

If we were to do these things, we would become entangled in a vast conflict on the continent of Asia and our task would become immeasurably more difficult all over the world.

What would suit the ambitions of the Kremlin better than for our military forces to be committed to a full-scale war with Red China?

It may well be that, in spite of our best efforts, the Communists may spread the war. But it would be wrong—tragically wrong—for us to take the initiative in extending the war.

The dangers are great. Make no mistake about it. Behind the North Koreans and Chinese Communists in the front lines stand additional millions of Chinese soldiers. And behind the Chinese stand the tanks, the planes, the submarines, the soldiers, and the scheming rulers of the Soviet Union.

Our aim is to avoid the spread of the conflict.

The course we have been following is the one best calculated to avoid an all-out war. It is the course consistent with our obligation to do all we can to maintain international peace and security. Our experience in Greece and Berlin shows that it is the most effective course of action we can follow.

First of all, it is clear that our efforts in Korea can blunt the will of the Chinese Communists to continue the struggle. The United Nations forces have put up a tremendous fight in Korea and have inflicted very heavy casualties on the enemy. Our forces are stronger now than they have been before. These are plain facts which may discourage the Chinese Communists from continuing their attack.

Second, the free world as a whole is growing in military strength every day. In the United States, in Western Europe, and throughout the world, free men are alert to the Soviet threat and are building their defenses. This may discourage the Communist rulers from continuing the war in Korea—and from undertaking new acts of aggression elsewhere.

If the Communist authorities realize that they cannot defeat us in Korea, if they realize it would be foolhardy to widen the hostilities beyond Korea, then they may recognize the folly of continuing their aggression. A peaceful settlement may then be possible. The door is always open.

Then we may achieve a settlement in Korea which will not compromise the principles and purposes of the United Nations.

I have thought long and hard about this question of extending the war in Asia. I have discussed it many times with the ablest military advisers in the country. I believe with all my heart that the course we are following is the best course.

I believe that we must try to limit the war to Korea for these vital reasons: to make sure that the precious lives of our fighting men are not wasted; to see that the security of our country and the free world is not needlessly jeopardized; and to prevent a third world war.

A number of events have made it evident that General MacArthur did not agree with that policy. I have therefore considered it essential to relieve General MacArthur so that there would be no doubt or confusion as to the real purpose and aim of our policy.

It was with the deepest personal regret that I found myself compelled to take this action. General MacArthur is one of our greatest military commanders. But the cause of world peace is more important than any individual.

The change in commands in the Far East means no change whatever in the policy of the United States. We will carry on the fight in Korea with vigor and determination in an effort to bring the war to a speedy and successful conclusion.

The new commander, Lieutenant General Matthew Ridgway, has already demonstrated that he has the great qualities of military leadership needed for this task.

We are ready, at any time, to negotiate for a restoration of peace in the area. But we will not engage in appeasement. We are only interested in real peace.

Real peace can be achieved through a settlement based on the following factors:

One: the fighting must stop.
Two: concrete steps must be taken to insure that the fighting will not break out again.
Three: there must be an end to the aggression.

A settlement founded upon these elements would open the way for the unification of Korea and the withdrawal of all foreign forces.

In the meantime, I want to be clear about our military objective. We are fighting to resist an outrageous aggression in Korea. We are trying to keep the Korean conflict from spreading to other areas. But at the same time we must conduct our military activities so as to insure the security of our forces. This is essential if they are to continue the fight until the enemy abandons its ruthless attempt to destroy the Republic of Korea.

That is our military objective—to repel attack and to restore peace.

In the hard fighting in Korea, we are proving that collective action among nations is not only a high principle but a workable means of resisting aggression. Defeat of aggression in Korea may be the turning point in the world's search for a practical way of achieving peace and security.

The struggle of the United Nations in Korea is a struggle for peace.

The free nations have united their strength in an effort to prevent a third world war.

That war can come if the Communist rulers want it to come. But this nation and its allies will not be responsible for its coming.

We do not want to widen the conflict. We will use every effort to prevent that disaster. And in so doing we know that we are following the great principles of peace, freedom, and justice.

Address to the Congress
General of the Army Douglas MacArthur

Douglas MacArthur was born in Little Rock Barracks, Arkansas in 1880, the son of Lieutenant General Arthur MacArthur, and was graduated as first in his class at West Point in 1903. During World War I he commanded the 42nd (Rainbow) Division and was twice wounded in action. He was Chief of Staff of the United States Army from 1930 to 1935. He commanded the U.S. armed forces in the Far East from 1941 until 11 April 1951.

General MacArthur arrived back in the United States in the week following his dismissal amid tumult and glory. Celebrations of unprecedented fervor marked the trip from Tokyo to Honolulu to San Francisco to Washington. Here on 19 April he addressed a joint session of the Congress and a national radio and television audience of unprecedented size and interest. The text below is based on a stenographic transcript furnished by the Associated Press.

President Truman took occasion to refute some of General MacArthur's views in an address before a dinner of the Civil Defense Conference in Washington on 7 May 1951. It was entitled "Why We Need Allies."

Mr. President, Mr. Speaker and distinguished members of the Congress:

I stand on this rostrum with a sense of deep humility and pride—humility in the weight of those great architects of our history who have stood here before me, pride in the reflection that this home of legislative debate represents human liberty in the purest form yet devised.

Here are centered the hopes and aspirations and faith of the entire human race.

I do not stand here as advocate for any partisan cause, for the issues are fundamental and reach quite beyond the realm of partisan considerations. They must be resolved on the highest plane of national interest if our course is to prove sound and our future protected.

I trust, therefore, that you will do me the justice of receiving that which I have to say as solely expressing the considered viewpoint of a fellow American.

I address you with neither rancor nor bitterness in the fading twilight of life, with but one purpose in mind: to serve my country.

The issues are global, and so interlocked that to consider the problems of one sector oblivious to those of another is to court disaster for the whole. While Asia is commonly referred to as the gateway to Europe, it is no less true that Europe is the gateway to Asia, and the broad influence of the one can not fail to have its impact upon the other. There are those who claim our strength is inadequate to protect on both fronts, that we cannot divide our effort. I can think of no greater expression of defeatism.

If a potential enemy can divide his strength on two fronts, it is for us to counter his effort. The Communist threat is a global one. Its successful advance in one sector threatens the destruction of every other sector. You can not appease or otherwise surrender to Communism in Asia without simultaneously undermining our efforts to halt its advance in Europe.

Beyond pointing out these general truisms, I shall confine my discussion to the general areas of Asia.

Before one may objectively assess the situation now existing there, he must comprehend something of Asia's past and the revolutionary changes which have marked her course up to the present. Long exploited by the so-called colonial powers, with little opportunity to achieve any degree of social justice, individual dignity, or a higher standard of life such as guided our own noble administration in the Philippines, the people of Asia found their opportunity in the war just past to throw off the shackles of colonialism and now see the dawn of new opportunity, and heretofore unfelt dignity, and the self-respect of political freedom.

Mustering half of the earth's population, and 60 per cent of its natural resources, these peoples are rapidly consolidating a new force, both moral and material, with which to raise the living standard and erect adaptations of the design of modern progress to their own distinct cultural environments.

Whether one adheres to the concept of colonialization or not, this is the direction of Asian progress and it may not be stopped. It is a corollary to the shift of the world economic frontiers as the whole epicenter of world affairs rotates back toward the area whence it started.

In this situation, it becomes vital that our own country orient its policies in consonance with this basic evolutionary condition rather than pursue a course blind to reality that the colonial era is now past and the Asian peoples covet the right to shape their own free destiny. What they seek now is friendly guidance, understanding, and support, not imperious direction, the dignity of equality and not the shame of subjugation.

Their prewar standard of life, pitifully low, is infinitely lower now in the devastation left in war's wake. World ideologies play little part in Asian thinking and are little understood.

What the people strive for is the opportunity for a little more food in their stomachs, a little better clothing on their backs, and a little firmer roof over their heads, and the realization of the normal nationalist urge for political freedom.

These political-social conditions have but an indirect bearing upon our own national security, but do form a backdrop to contemporary planning which must be thoughtfully considered if we are to avoid the pitfalls of unrealism.

Of more direct and immediate bearing upon our national security are the changes wrought in the strategic potential of the Pacific Ocean in the course of the past war.

Prior thereto the Western strategic frontier of the United States lay on the littoral line of the Americas, with an exposed island salient extending out through Hawaii, Midway, and Guam to the Philippines. That salient proved not an outpost of strength but an avenue of weakness along which the enemy could and did attack. The Pacific was a potential area of advance for any predatory force intent upon striking at the bordering land areas.

All this was changed by our Pacific victory. Our strategic frontier then shifted to embrace the entire Pacific Ocean, which became a vast moat to protect us as long as we hold it. Indeed, it acts as a protective shield for all of the Americas and all free lands of the Pacific Ocean area. We control it to the shores of Asia by a chain of islands extending in an arc from the Aleutians to the Mariannas, held by us and our free allies.

From this island chain we can dominate with sea and air power every Asiatic port from Vladivostok to Singapore—with sea and air power, every port, as I said, from Vladivostok to Singapore—and prevent any hostile movement into the Pacific.

Any predatory attack from Asia must be an amphibious effort. No amphibious force can be successful without control of the sea lanes and the air over those lanes in its avenue of advance. With naval and air supremacy and modest ground elements to defend bases, any major attack from continental Asia toward us or our friends in the Pacific would be doomed to failure.

Under such conditions, the Pacific no longer represents menacing avenues of approach for a prospective invader. It assumes, instead, the friendly aspect of a peaceful lake.

Our line of defense is a natural one and can be maintained with a minimum of military effort and expense. It envisions no attack against anyone, nor does it provide the bastions essential for offensive operations, but properly maintained, would be an invincible defense against aggression.

The holding of this littoral defense line in the western Pacific is entirely dependent upon holding all segments thereof, for any major breach of that line by an unfriendly power would render vulnerable to determined attack every other major segment. This is a military estimate as to which I have yet to find a military leader who will take exception.

For that reason, I have strongly recommended in the past, as a matter of military urgency, that under no circumstances must Formosa fall under Communist control. Such an eventuality would at once threaten the freedom of the Philippines and the loss of Japan, and might well force our Western frontier back to the coast of California, Oregon, and Washington.

To understand the changes which now appear upon the Chinese mainland, one must understand the changes in Chinese character and culture over the past fifty years. China up to fifty years ago was completely nonhomogeneous, being compartmented into groups divided against each other. The war-making tendency was almost nonexistent as they still followed the tenets of the Confucian ideal of pacifist culture.

At the turn of the century under the regime of Chang Tso-lin efforts toward greater homogeneity produced the start of a nationalist urge. This was further and more successfully developed under the leadership of Chiang Kai-shek, but has been brought to its greatest fruition under the present regime to the point that it has now taken on the character of a united nationalism of increasingly dominant aggressive tendencies.

Through the past fifty years the Chinese people have thus become militarized in their concepts and in their ideals. They now constitute excellent soldiers, with competent staffs and commanders. This has produced a new and dominant power in Asia, which, for its own purposes, is allied with Soviet Russia but which in its own concepts and methods has become aggressively imperialistic, with a lust for expansion and increased power normal to this type of imperialism.

There is little of the ideological concept either one way or another in the Chinese make-up. The standard of living is so low and the capital accumulation has been so thoroughly dissipated by war that the masses are desperate and eager to follow any leadership which seems to promise the alleviation of woeful stringencies.

I have from the beginning believed that the Chinese Communists' support of the North Koreans was the dominant one. Their interests are at present parallel with those of the Soviet, but I believe that the aggressiveness recently displayed not only in Korea but also in Indo-China and Tibet and pointing potentially toward the south reflects predominantly the same lust for the expansion of power which has animated every would-be conqueror since the beginning of time.

The Japanese people since the war have undergone the greatest reformation recorded in modern history. With a commendable will, eagerness to learn, and marked capacity to understand, they have from the ashes left in war's wake erected in Japan an edifice dedicated to the supremacy of individual liberty and personal dignity, and in the ensuing process there has been created a truly representative government committed to the advance of political morality, freedom of economic enterprise, and social justice.

Politically, economically, and socially Japan is now abreast of many free nations of the earth and will not again fail the universal trust. That it may be counted upon to wield a profoundly beneficial influence over the course of events in Asia is attested by the magnificent manner in which the Japanese people have met the recent challenge of war, unrest, and confusion surrounding them from the outside and checked Communism within their own frontiers without the slightest slackening in their forward progress.

I sent all four of our occupation divisions to the Korean battlefront without the slightest qualms as to the effect of the resulting power vacuum upon Japan. The results fully justified my faith.

I know of no nation more serene, orderly, and industrious, nor in which higher hopes can be entertained for future constructive service in the advance of the human race.

Of our former ward, the Philippines, we can look forward in confidence that the existing unrest will be corrected and a strong and healthy nation will grow in the longer aftermath of the war's terrible destructiveness. We must be patient and understanding and never fail them, as in our hour of need they did not fail us.

A Christian nation, the Philippines stands as a mighty bulwark of Christianity in the Far East, and its capacity for high moral leadership in Asia is unlimited.

On Formosa, the government of the Republic of China has had the opportunity to refute by action much of the malicious gossip which so undermined the strength of its leadership on the Chinese mainland. The Formosan people are receiving a just and enlightened administration with majority representation in the organs of government, and politically, economically, and socially they appear to be advancing along sound and constructive lines.

With this brief insight into the surrounding areas, I now turn to the Korean conflict.

While I was not consulted prior to the President's decision to intervene in support of the Republic of Korea, that decision, from a military standpoint, proved a sound one. As I say, it proved to be a sound one, as we hurled back the invader and decimated his forces. Our victory was complete, and our objectives within reach, when Red China intervened with numerically superior ground forces.

This created a new war and an entirely new situation, a situation not contemplated when our forces were committed against the North Korean invaders; a situation which called for new decisions in the diplomatic sphere to permit the realistic adjustment of military strategy. Such decisions have not been forthcoming.

While no man in his right mind would advocate sending our ground forces into continental China, and such was never given thought, the new situation did urgently demand a drastic revision of strategic planning if our political aim was to defeat this new enemy as we had defeated the old one.

Apart from the military need, as I saw it, to neutralize sanctuary protection given the enemy north of the Yalu, I felt that military necessity in the conduct of the war made necessary (1) The intensification of our economic blockade against China, (2) The imposition of a Naval blockade against the China coast, (3) Removal of restrictions on air reconnaissance of China's coastal area and of Manchuria, (4) Removal of restrictions on the forces of the Republic of China on Formosa, with logistical support to contribute to their effective operations against the Chinese mainland.

For entertaining these views, all professionally designed to support our forces in Korea and to bring hostilities to an end with the least possible delay and at a saving of countless American and Allied lives, I have been severely criticized in lay circles, principally abroad, despite my understanding that from a military standpoint the above views have been fully shared in the past by practically every military leader concerned with the Korean campaign, including our own Joint Chiefs of Staff.

I called for reinforcements, but was informed that reinforcements were not available. I made clear that if not permitted to destroy the enemy built-up bases north of the Yalu, if not permitted to utilize the friendly Chinese force of some 600,000 men on Formosa, if not permitted to blockade the China coast to prevent the Chinese Reds from getting succor from without, and if there was to be no hope of major reinforcements, the position of the command from the military standpoint forbade victory.

We could hold in Korea by constant maneuver and in an area where our supply line advantages were in balance with the supply line disadvantages of the enemy, but we could hope at best for only an indecisive campaign with its terrible and constant attrition upon our forces if the enemy utilized its full military potential.

I have constantly called for the new political decisions essential to a solution.

Efforts have been made to distort my position. It has been said in effect that I was a warmonger. Nothing could be further from the truth.

I know war as few other men now living know it, and nothing to me is more revolting. I have long advocated its complete abolition, as its very destructiveness on both friend and foe has rendered it useless as a means of settling international disputes.

Indeed, the second day of September, 1945, just following the surrender of the Japanese nation on the Battleship Missouri, I formally cautioned as follows:

> Men since the beginning of time have sought peace. Various methods through the ages have been attempted to devise an international process to prevent or settle disputes between nations. From the very start workable methods were found in so far as individual citizens were concerned, but the mechanics of an instrumentality of larger international scope have never been successful. Military alliances, balances of power, leagues of nations, all in turn failed, leaving the only path to be by way of the crucible of war. The utter destructiveness of war now blocks out this alternative. We have had our last chance. If we will not devise some greater and more equitable system, our Armageddon will be at our door. The problem basically is theological and involves a spiritual recrudescence and improvement of human character that will synchronize with our almost matchless advances in science, art, literature, and all the material and cultural developments of the past 2000 years. It must be of the spirit if we are to save the flesh.

But once war is forced upon us, there is no other alternative than to apply every means to bring it to a swift end. War's very object is victory, not prolonged indecision.

In war indeed there can be no substitute for victory.

There are some who for varying reasons would appease Red China. They are blind to history's clear lesson, for history teaches with unmistakable emphasis that appeasement but begets new and bloodier wars. It points to no single instance where this end has justified that means, where appeasement has led to more than a sham peace. Like blackmail, it lays the basis for new and successively greater demands until, as in blackmail, violence becomes the only other alternative. Why, my soldiers asked me, surrender military advantages to an enemy in the field? I could not answer.

Some may say to avoid spread of the conflict into an all-out war with China. Others, to avoid Soviet intervention. Neither explanation seems valid, for China is already engaging with the maximum power it can commit, and the Soviet will not necessarily mesh its actions with our moves. Like a cobra, any new enemy will more likely strike whenever it feels that the relativity of military and other potentialities is in its favor on a world-wide basis.

The tragedy of Korea is further heightened by the fact that its military action was confined to its territorial limits. It condemns that nation, which it is our purpose to save, to suffer the devastating impact of full naval and air bombardment while the enemy's sanctuaries are fully protected from such attack and devastation.

Of the nations of the world, Korea alone, up to now, is the sole one which has risked its all against Communism. The magnificence of the courage and fortitude of the Korean people defies description. They have chosen to risk death rather than slavery. Their last words to me were: "Don't scuttle the Pacific."

I have just left your fighting sons in Korea. They have done their best there, and I can report to you without reservation that they are splendid in every way.

It was my constant effort to preserve them and end this savage conflict honorably and with the least loss of time and a minimum sacrifice of life. Its growing bloodshed has caused me the deepest anguish and anxiety. Those gallant men will remain often in my thoughts and in my prayers always.

I am closing my fifty-two years of military service. When I joined the army, even before the turn of the century, it was the fulfillment of all of my boyish hopes and dreams. The world has turned over many times since I took the oath at West Point, and the hopes and dreams have all since vanished, but I still remember the refrain of one of the most popular barracks ballads of that day which proclaimed most proudly that old soldiers never die; they just fade away. And like the old soldier of that ballad, I now close my military career and just fade away, an old soldier who tried to do his duty as God gave him the light to see that duty. Good-by.

THE FAR EAST

United States Policy Toward Asia
Dean Acheson

This address was made by Secretary Acheson at a luncheon in his honor at the Commonwealth Club in San Francisco on 15 March 1950. It brings together some of the fundamental assumptions and explanations of American policy towards China and the countries of Southeast Asia. A new departure in Far East policy was announced by Assistant Secre-

Dean Acheson

tary Dean Rusk in a speech on 18 May 1951 in New York (his speech, "Chinese-American Friendship," begins on page 165 of this book).

For an unofficial appraisal of our policy in the first half of 1951 the reader is referred to the University of Chicago Round Table broadcast of 29 April 1951 entitled "What is the Basis of American Far Eastern Policy?" The discussants were Professors John K. Fairbank and Arthur N. Holcombe of Harvard University, Phillips Talbot of the Institute of Current World Affairs, Professor Donald F. Lach of the University of Chicago, and Professor Ralph E. Turner of Yale University.

In the *Foreign Policy Bulletin* for 26 January 1951 Professor Henry Steele Commager explained "What the United States Must Do to Implement Current Policy." In the same publication for 23 February 1951 Professor Arthur Schlesinger, Jr. discussed "The Path between Moralism and Retreatism."

Mr. Acheson spent several days in June 1951 testifying before the Senate committees investigating the recall of General MacArthur. In the Sunday *New York Times* for 17 June 1951 William S. White reported from Washington that the testimony and the oral presentation of the Secretary of State "was, by almost common consent, the most finished and technically impressive since that of the general himself." He goes on: "The paradox of his [Mr. Acheson's] service has been deepened; he is, in a fairly general view, the most persuasive unpersuasive man in the Truman administration. This is so in spite of the fact that Mr. Acheson's testimony, though shaken a bit here and there by that of his old Cabinet antagonist, the former Secretary of Defense, Louis Johnson, has been in no way really broken."

FIRST OF ALL, let me remind you that the foreign policy of a free nation in relation to other free nations should be rooted in the fundamental attitudes of the peoples on both sides and in the facts as they exist.

So far as we are concerned, we know that we are interested in the peoples of Asia as people. We want to help them as people. We do not want to take anything from them for ourselves. We do not want to deny them any opportunity, any freedom, any right. We do not want to use them for any purpose of our own.

On the contrary, we want to help them, in any sensible way we can, to achieve their own goals and ambitions in their own way. We want to do this, because we believe that what the peoples of Asia earnestly desire will make for the kind of a free and productive world in which we and they can live out our lives in peace.

We know that this is our attitude, and we say this without qualification of any sort. But we must understand that others will judge us and our intentions not by what we say but by what we do. Actions have always spoken louder than words. Today, amid the welter of distortion which hostile propaganda pours out about us, actions best proclaim our purpose and our intentions.

So it is vitally important that our actions are clear reflections of our purposes. It is vitally important that muddied or emotional thinking should not result in equivocal and mistaken courses. We may know that such actions spring from good hearts, but confused thinking. To others, they will be unmistakable proof of ulterior purposes. And have no doubt that there will be no lack of willing tongues to further that message. The end result will be the loss of the priceless asset we have—the confidence of hundreds of millions in our integrity.

Now what are the fundamental attitudes of the Asian peoples? And what are the basic facts in Asia?

We must understand that a new era is in full course in Asia. That whole great region, containing more than half the population of the world, is changing profoundly. The significance of that change, the reason the change is irrevocable, is that it is brought about by a deep and revolutionary movement of the peoples of Asia.

Now that movement, that powerful conviction, is made up of two dominant ideas. The first of these is revulsion against misery and poverty as the normal condition of life. The second is revulsion against foreign domination. These ideas meet and fuse in the positive conception of national independence. This is both the symbol of aspirations and the means by which they may be achieved.

The desire for national independence is the most powerful spontaneous force in Asia today. It is the common tie among the diverse peoples of Asia, the tie between them and the free peoples of other countries, including the United States. Since the end of the war, more than 500 million people have achieved national independence and self-government—in the Philippines, India, Pakistan, Ceylon, Burma, Southern Korea, and Indonesia. The people of Indo-China are also moving along this same road, developing with the French a new relationship expressive of their own national aspirations and resting securely on a basis of mutual consent. We welcome this development and shall continue in the future as in the past to encourage it.

In China, the same strong longings of the people have reached a different end. Since before the overthrow of the Manchu dynasty in 1912, the Chinese people also have striven for freedom from infringement on their sovereignty and for improvement of their lives. For years, they struggled with unbelievable courage, endurance, and patience against the adversities of nature; against internal division and strife; and against foreign enemies until the end of the war seemed to bring almost within their grasp the achievement of the hopes for which they had been striving.

Then the failure of their government to respond to their needs, its ineptitude and blindness destroyed all their confidence and support. The Nationalist government was overthrown in China not by force of arms. It collapsed from its own inherent weakness and the withdrawal of the people's support.

The Communists won by default, not by what they offered. They employed the well-known Communist technique of probing for weakness and, on finding it, exploiting it to the full. The result is that today the Nationalist government exercises authority only on the islands of Formosa and Hainan.

The revolutionary movement in China, which began a half century ago as an expression of the aspirations of the Chinese people, has been captured, for the present, by the Communists. Their seizure of power has reversed the true purposes of the revolution. For while neighboring peoples, some of them for the first time in centuries, are at last achieving true national independence, China, with its long proud history, is being forced into the Soviet orbit as a dependency of the Soviet political system and the Soviet economy.

Since I spoke in January on the Far East there has been one new and clear indication of Soviet Russia's intentions in China. We see it in the published terms of the Sino-Soviet Treaty of Friendship, Alliance and Mutual Assistance of February 14, 1950, and the other agreements concluded and announced at the same time.

The Soviet Union and its most ardent supporters in China may have temporary success in persuading the people of China that these agreements refute the contention of the non-Communist world that alliance with Soviet Russia holds an evil omen of imperialistic domination. These agreements promise help in the rehabilitation of China's war-torn and impoverished economy. They promise, in particular, assistance in the repair and development of China's railroads and industry. The Chinese people may welcome these promises and assurances. But they will not fail, in time, to see where they fall short of China's real needs and desires. And they will wonder about the points upon which the agreements remain silent.

Now, let us examine these assurances and promises of economic aid. First, Soviet Russia has promised to return certain Manchurian property but not the industrial equipment robbed by the Red Army in 1945.

Is this aid? Is it even a belated admission of a theft which deprived not only China but all of Asia of some 2 billion dollars worth of productive capacity?

Second, Soviet Russia extends to China a 300-million-dollars 5-year credit at an interest rate of 1 per cent yearly. This works out at 60 million dollars each year. This announcement was made only to be followed by the news that the ruble was to be revalued, thus cutting down the effective aid by one-fourth if the new dollar-ruble rate should be applied to this credit. Thus, the Chinese people may find Soviet Russia's credit to be no more than 45 million dollars per year. They can compare this with a grant—not a loan—of 400 million dollars voted by the American Congress to China in the single year 1948.

China's needs are great and pressing. China today faces a prospect of 40 million people suffering from hunger between now and the next crops. Millions may die. And yet, food moves from China to the Soviet Union.

China's need for development capital runs into billions of dollars. In its issue of February 25, the *London Economist* makes the following penetrating analysis of Chinese needs and hopes and the extent to which they have been dashed by the agreements with Moscow:

. . . it has not been the purpose of modern-minded Chinese to stagnate in the backwardness of a pre-industrial era; for many years they have been possessed by the dream of a rapid industrialisation whereby China would break out from its old weakness and poverty and take a place among the nations more in keeping with its vast population and considerable natural resources. There is, indeed, no sign at all of a great programme of industrialisation to be carried through with Russian aid; the idea seems rather to make China's economy more "colonial" than before, so that it can provide foodstuffs and raw materials for the new industrial areas of Siberia.

The more fanatical of the Communist leaders may be content with this, but it must bring a bitter disillusionment to many progressive Chinese who have supported the Communists against the Kuomintang in the belief that the new revolution would clear away obstacles to China's economic development. The new rulers of China have deliberately cut off their country from the possibility of American economic assistance which would have been forthcoming for a United China on a far larger scale and with fewer strings attached than the loan now received with so much official gratitude from Moscow. If any Chinese really thought that Peking could obtain an unconditional and unstinted bounty by turning from Washington to Moscow, the experience of Yugoslavia might have warned him that there are more kicks than halfpence in dependent association with the Soviet empire.

And now, as to the political and territorial assurances contained in the agreements. Can the Chinese people fail to observe that, whatever may be the promises for the future, under the terms of the treaty and agreements recently concluded at Moscow, the U.S.S.R. has special rights in China which represent an infringement of China's sovereignty and which are held by no other foreign power? It is Soviet Russia which, despite all the tawdry pretense of the treaty terms, occupies the role of empire builder at China's expense.

These are the realities that must be faced by the Chinese people. In facing them, they can well consider what it means to brush aside an established friendship for new-found and voracious friends. Our friendship has been founded on the belief that anyone who violates the integrity of China is the enemy of China and is hostile to the interests of the United States. We have fifty years of history and a world war to prove that this belief is not a mere matter of words. This belief has been proved by deeds. We can and shall stand on the record.

We now face the prospect that the Communists may attempt to apply another familiar tactic and use China as a base for probing for other weak spots which they can move into and exploit.

As old friends, we say to the Chinese people that we fully understand that their present unhappy status within the orbit of the Soviet Union is not the result of any choice on their own part, but has been forced upon them. We understand that the Communist basis for their government is similarly not the result of any free choice of their own. We do not intend to tell them what ideologies or form of government they should have. We do not intend to engage in any aggressive adventures against them. The American people will remain in the future, as we have been in the past, the friends of the Chinese people.

But they should understand that, whatever happens within their own country, they can only bring grave trouble on themselves and their friends, both in Asia and beyond, if they are led by their new rulers into aggressive or subversive adventures beyond their borders. Such adventures would violate not only every tradition and interest of the Chinese people, they would violate the traditions and interests of their Asian neighbors, of the American people, and—indeed—of all free peoples. They would violate the United Nations Charter. They would violate the peace which the Charter was designed to preserve.

I say this so that there may be no mistake about the attitude of the United States; no opportunity to distort or twist it; and so that all in China may know who would be responsible for all that such adventures might bring to pass.

Again, as old friends of the Chinese people, we say to them that the representatives of our country are leaving them not by any wish of ours. They are leaving because the normal and accepted standards of international conduct have not been observed by the Chinese Communist authorities in their treatment of our representatives and because they have, in effect, even been summarily ejected from their own offices in Peiping. Under such conditions, our representatives could not fulfill their normal functions. We regret this leaving by our people, but our Chinese friends will understand again where the responsibility lies.

One more word about China—on the subject of trade—in which you here in San Francisco have played such an important part in the past. Our policy is the traditional American one. We have traded with China since before there was a United States of America. In fact, our country was discovered by people seeking a shorter trade route to the Far East. We have traded with China under many regimes and are willing to continue to do so. But here again the decisions do not lie entirely with us.

Trade requires certain standards of conduct. Ships, planes, and traders must be received under conditions of security and decency. Contracts must be honored. There must be some medium of exchange reasonably regulated.

Under these conditions, your government is entirely willing that Americans, in the future as in the past, should buy Chinese goods and sell American goods. It does not propose that Americans should sell goods which may be used to harm us. Nor does this government propose to give credits or gifts to those who declare their hostility to us and all we stand for. We Americans should be willing to trade with China, as our forefathers did, whenever and in so far as it is made possible in China.

I want to make it entirely clear that we have no desire to thrust this trade upon China, nor is China in a position to extort it from us. In the period 1946-1948 the United States supplied over 50 per cent of China's imports and bought approximately a quarter of China's exports. Yet, those same exports from America were less than 5 per cent of our total exports and our purchases from China were a mere 2 per cent of all we bought abroad. If the present rulers of China wish to believe that we depend on trade with China, we are entirely willing to leave it to the test of experience to prove whether they are right or wrong.

Passing from the difficult problems of China, we come to the problems of Southeast Asia, which certainly seem no less complex. The circumstances which, added together, create these difficulties are largely common to the area.

They flow, first, from the fact that, except in Thailand, the governments are governments which are new. They are experiencing the difficulties of organizing and administering the new-found independence of these countries. Problems come, second, from serious economic dislocations. Some of these flow directly from the ravages of war; others from the disruption of trade routes and trade connections. Thirdly, another group of difficulties throughout this whole area stems directly from years of Japanese occupation which broke down many longstanding habits of life, of industry, of government, with resulting internal strife.

It would be difficult enough, even under the best of circumstances and with the undivided help of their friends in other continents, for these new countries of Southeast Asia to find their feet and make progress along the difficult road before them. It is, therefore, tragic that, on the contrary, they find themselves in the path of a main thrust of Soviet subversion and expansion. They are subject to influences designed to produce division within each of the countries and subject to propaganda designed to turn them against those who might be able to help.

An important objective of Soviet propaganda has been to deceive and confuse the world concerning the policy of our government toward the newly established nations of Southeast Asia. The United States consistently has supported and will continue to support the movement of these peoples toward self-government and national independence. Since the late nineteenth century, when we ourselves first became responsible for territories in the Pacific, we have fostered national independence and the growth of free democratic institutions. In our dealings with nations who had similar responsibilities in the Far East, we have urged them to do likewise and have given substantial and tangible assistance in order that such objectives might be realized. We cite our record in regard to Philippine independence. Our recent participation through the United Nations in the Dutch-Indonesian settlement is a more recent example of this policy.

The people of Asia must face the fact that today the major threat to their freedom and to their social and economic progress is the attempted penetration of Asia by Soviet-Communist imperialism and by the colonialism which it contains. The reactionary character of this effort is illustrated by comparing the miserable fate of the European satellites with the emergence of the free nations of Pakistan, India, Burma, Ceylon, Indonesia, and the Philippines, with the full consent and coöperation of those who had earlier exercised control over them.

In speaking to the Press Club in Washington, I pointed out that American assistance can be effective in Southeast Asia, as elsewhere, when it is the missing component in a problem which might otherwise be solved. Where the will and the determination exist, where the people are behind their government, American help may be the indispensable element required to produce constructive results. There is no guarantee that it can produce those results, but it has a good chance of succeeding if these other components are present.

President Truman has declared his belief that it must be the policy of the United States to support free peoples who are resisting attempted subjugation by armed minorities or by outside pressures and that we must assist free peoples to work out their own destinies in their own way.

The aid we extend must be of a kind appropriate to the particular situation; it must be fitted into the responsibilities of others, and it must be within the prudent capabilities of our resources.

In some situations, it will be military assistance. In others, it may be grants or loans, such as the recent 100-million-dollar credit to the Republic of the United States of Indonesia. In still other cases, the need may be for technical assistance.

These are not new principles nor is the application of them to the Far East a new departure. In Japan, Korea, the Philippines, Indonesia, and Thailand, for example, we have been demonstrating our desire to help where such help can strengthen the cause of freedom.

It has been a great disappointment that help which we rendered on a massive scale to China did not result in bringing peace and economic recovery to the Chinese people as we had hoped. That does not mean that the attempt to help was wrong, nor does it mean that we should not help others who seek to maintain their freedom and independence. It merely underlines that our help can only reinforce the efforts which others are prepared to make on their own behalf.

A recent expression of our desire to assist in specific and concrete ways in Southeast Asia has been the dispatch of a mission composed of technicians under the direction of R. Allen Griffin of California, formerly Deputy Head of the China ECA mission. This mission will determine, by spot surveys, what type of projects is most immediately needed and which ones might be got under way almost immediately. The mission has been instructed not only to determine suitable projects for quick action but also to attempt to lay some of the groundwork for the anticipated Point Four program.

We recognize our special ties with the Philippines. There is much still to be repaired in the economy of the Islands torn by war. At the request of President Quirino, we are going to send out an economic mission to work with the Philippine government to determine how best to consolidate the gains already made and to lay out what still needs to be done to develop their resources. There will doubtless be situations where our aid added to energetic measures by the Philippine government will accomplish what otherwise could not be done.

In acting to strengthen the forces of freedom in Asia, we shall work in the spirit and within the framework of the United Nations and in coöperation with other free nations which are in a position to assist.

The free nations of Asia are proceeding with their programs for political stability and economic development aided by the United States and other free nations. There is need for effort, but there is no need to be discouraged. There are sound elements in the situation on which these peoples may build. Their newly won responsibilities are calling up enthusiasm, pride, and patriotic support for their own institutions. If they lack, at the moment, the technical and administrative experience and training they need, these can be overcome by the application of their own energy and demonstrated intelligence. Their countries have rich natural resources which can provide a basis for a flourishing trade with the rest of the world. As stability is achieved, as experience is accumulated, and technical and financial assistance becomes effective, I have no doubt that the peoples of Asia will be able to participate fully and equally in the international community both politically and economically.

It is encouraging to see growing agreement about the nature of the problem in Asia. For example, we were much interested in a statement on Australian foreign policy made to the Australian House of Representatives by Mr. Spender, the Minister for External Affairs, on March 9.

Mr. Spender concluded with an enumeration of six principles through which the real democracies of the world could avoid war and preserve their way of life. They must (1) understand the true causes of present international tension, (2) realize that the preservation of their own way of life calls for a sustained and determined effort in all fields, (3) accept the fact that appeasement is completely ineffective and even dangerous, (4) put their own domestic houses in order, (5) coöperate in the many international agencies which already exist to preserve the values in which they believe, and (6) give thought to the creation of more effective methods of coöperative action in those areas where their vital interests are affected.

From what I have said today about our own attitude toward the problems in Asia, it is evident that we believe these points are soundly taken. We welcome the statement of them.

I would like to stress here a point I have made before but which cannot be stressed too often. We frequently hear that the United States is striving to halt the spread of communism. That is far too negative a way of putting it. Of course we want to halt the spread of communism, not because we want to dictate to the Asian people or to any other people what their political and economic institutions should be. We are opposed to the spread of Soviet communism because it is the means, the tool, by which Soviet Russia is attempting to extend its absolute domination over the widest possible areas of the world.

The Asian peoples, for the past several decades, have been engaged in a revolution in which they have been trying to throw off the poverty and oppression of past centuries. They have been striving for independence, better education, more widespread ownership of the land, and control over their own destiny.

It is no accident that their goals and our goals are the same. The American people have been the leaders in a revolution that has been going on for a century and a half, a revolution by the common people. And the basic objective of American foreign policy is to make possible a world in which all peoples, including the peoples of Asia, can work, in their own way, toward a better life. That is why we are opposed to the spread of communism not only in Asia but elsewhere. It is because this tool of Soviet imperialism perverts the real democratic revolution that has been going on all over the world since long before communism as a world conspiracy had been thought of.

The American people, and we believe the Asian peoples, when they have an opportunity fairly to appraise their interests, oppose Soviet communism for the same reason that they opposed Nazism, Japanese imperialism, or any other form of aggression—that is, because it denies to the people whom it engulfs the right to work toward a better life in their own way. This is why we must unceasingly in all we do and say affirm the positive goals of free peoples. We are for something positive, for the most fundamental urges of the human spirit. We are not and must not allow ourselves to appear merely negative, even though that negation is directed against the most corrupting force now operating in the world.

Chinese-American Friendship
Dean Rusk

Dean Rusk was born in Cherokee County, Georgia in 1909. He studied at Davidson College (A.B., 1931) and as a Rhodes Scholar at St. John's College, Oxford (B.S., 1933; M.A., 1934). He taught at Mills College and was dean of the faculty from 1934 to 1940. During World War II he served as a colonel in the China-Burma-India theater. In 1946 he became special assistant to the Secretary of State and from 1947 to 1949 was director of the Office of United Nations Affairs. He became Deputy Under Secretary of State in May 1949 and subsequently Assistant Secretary of State for Far Eastern Affairs. In December 1951 Mr. Rusk resigned from the Department of State to become President of the Rockefeller Foundation.

This speech proclaims a new concept in State Department policy on Asia. The occasion was a dinner sponsored by the China Institute of America at the Waldorf-Astoria Hotel in New York on 18 May 1951. Senator Paul Douglas of Illinois and Ambassador John Foster Dulles also made important pronouncements at the same meeting.

Mr. Rusk gave great encouragement to the anti-Communist Chinese when he stated that they would have "tremendous support from free peoples in other parts of the world" as soon as they "move to assert their freedom and to work out their destiny in accordance with their own historical purposes."

In his speech, also entitled "Chinese-American Friendship," Mr. Dulles stated: "My own official concern today is the Japanese Peace Treaty. I can assure you that, in negotiating that treaty, we shall not consider that the voice of Mao Tsetung is the voice of China. . . . I am not advocating 'slow motion' in the case of China. On the contrary, it is imperative that we move quickly, while we still have many friends, not only on Formosa but on the mainland, and possibilities of access to them. But we must not only start fast, we must start with long vision and endurance because we cannot overnight undo what has been accomplished by the best brains and skills of the Soviet Communist Party working with substantial resources over a span of thirty years."

I SHOULD LIKE, first of all, to congratulate the China Institute on its quarter century of splendid public service and to compliment you who are responsible for this timely chance to recall the warm friendship which has marked the relations between the Chinese and American people throughout the last two centuries.

Something of what we have in mind this evening is contained in a

Concurrent Resolution which passed the Senate on May 4 and which is now before the House of Representatives, which reads in part:

> Resolved by the Senate (the House of Representatives concurring), That the Congress of the United States reaffirm the historic and abiding friendship of the American people for all other peoples, including the peoples of the Soviet Union, and declare—
>
> That the American people deeply regret the artificial barriers which separate them from the peoples of the Union of Soviet Socialist Republics, and which keep the Soviet peoples from learning of the desire of the American people to live in friendship with all other peoples and to work with them in advancing the ideal of human brotherhood; and
>
> That the American people and their Government desire neither war with the Soviet Union nor the terrible consequences of such a war.

Despite the artificial barriers which now separate us from most of the peoples of China, we meet to reaffirm the historic and abiding friendship of the American people for the people of China.

Most of you here this evening are better qualified than I to explore the origins and elements of Chinese-American friendship. Over the centuries this friendship has come to be taken for granted; cordial sentiments between a free China and a free America became strong and durable because they were constantly nourished by common purposes and common practical interests.

We and the Chinese, for example, have had a vital interest in the peace of the Pacific. Each of us wants security on our Pacific flank and wants to be able to look across those vast waters to find strength, independence, and good will in its great neighbor on the other side. It was inevitable that the driving force of Japanese militarism would sooner or later bring China and America together to oppose it, just as we had moved forty years earlier to support China's independence and integrity against threats from Europe. The same issues are now posed again —and are made more difficult to deal with because foreign encroachment is now being arranged by Chinese who seem to love China less than they do their foreign masters.

We meet here this evening to reaffirm our friendship with the Chinese people—but not merely as a routine and elegant expression of good will. For the friendship we have taken for granted for so long is now being attacked with every available weapon by those who have come to power on the mainland of China. Their sustained and violent effort to erase all evidence of this friendship bears powerful witness to the validity and strength of the bonds between our two peoples. American influence among the Chinese people is intolerable to those in power in Peiping and Moscow because they know, and quite rightly, that the idea of national and individual freedom which is at the heart of American political thought is the greatest threat to their own evil purposes.

Is the message of this meeting this evening to our friends in China prompted solely by narrowly conceived American interests? That important American interests are involved, there can be no doubt. But our historical relations with China have always reflected a high regard on our part for Chinese interests and it is these we ask our friends in China now to consider.

The independence of China is gravely threatened. In the Communist world there is room for only one master—a jealous and implacable master, whose price of friendship is complete submission. How many Chinese, in one community after another, are now being destroyed because they love China more than the Soviet Union? How many Chinese will remember in time the fates of Rajk, Kostov, Petkov, Clementis, and all those in other satellites who discovered that being Communist is not enough for the conspirators of the Kremlin?

The freedoms of the Chinese people are disappearing. Trial by mob, mass slaughter, banishment as forced labor to Manchuria, Siberia, or Sinkiang, the arbitrary seizure of property, the destruction of loyalties within the family, the suppression of free speech—these are the facts behind the parades and celebrations and the empty promises.

The territorial integrity of China is now an ironic phrase. The movement of Soviet forces into Sinkiang, the realities of "joint exploitation" of that great province by Moscow and Peiping, the separation of Inner Mongolia from the body politic of China, and the continued inroads of Soviet power into Manchuria under the cloak of the Korean aggression mean in fact that China is losing its great northern areas to the European empire which has stretched out its greedy hands for them for at least a century.

Are our Chinese friends reflecting upon the maps of China now being published on the mainland which show Sinkiang, Inner Mongolia, Manchuria, and areas in the west and southwest as something distinct from China? Are our friends in China impressed by trade union buttons appearing on the streets of Peiping which no longer show Sinkiang and Inner Mongolia on the map of China? Have the authorities in Peiping themselves fully considered what it means for them to have Soviet troops on Chinese soil, in the light of the experience of the miserable satellites of eastern Europe?

The peace and security of China are being sacrificed to the ambitions of the Communist conspiracy. China has been driven by foreign masters into an adventure of foreign aggression which cuts across the most fundamental national interests of the Chinese people. This action stands condemned by the great world community in which the Chinese people have always aspired to play a worthy role.

Hundreds of thousands of Chinese youth are being sacrificed in a fiery furnace, pitting their waves of human flesh against the fire power of modern weapons—and without heavy equipment, adequate supply, or the most elementary medical attention. Apart from Korea, the Chinese are being pressed to aggressive action in other areas—all calculated to divert the attention and energies of China away from the encroachments of Soviet imperialism upon China itself.

I find it hard to believe that the Chinese people will acquiesce in the kind of future which their masters are now preparing for them. I find it impossible to believe that our friends in China have given up their desire to live at peace with their neighbors, to play a major role as a peaceful member of the international community of nations, to trade freely with all the world, to improve their own conditions in accordance with their own needs, aspirations and traditions, to maintain their independence as a nation, to preserve their territorial integrity and to live out their lives in dignity and with the respect of their fellow men.

Events in China must surely challenge the concern of Chinese everywhere—in Formosa, on the mainland, and in overseas communities. There is a job to be done for China which only the Chinese can do—a job which will require sustained energy, continued sacrifice, and an abundance of the high courage with which so many Chinese have fought for so long during the struggles of the past decades. The rest of us cannot tell them exactly what is to be done or how. We cannot provide a formula to engage the unity of effort among all Chinese who love their country. But one thing we can say—as the Chinese people move to assert their freedom and to work out their destiny in accordance with their own historical purposes, they can count upon tremendous support from free peoples in other parts of the world.

It is not my purpose, in these few moments this evening, to go into specific elements of our own national policy in the present situation. But we can tell our friends in China that the United States will not acquiesce in the degradation which is being forced upon them. We do not recognize the authorities in Peiping for what they pretend to be. The

Peiping regime may be a colonial Russian government—a Slavic Manchukuo on a larger scale. It is not the Government of China. It does not pass the first test. It is not Chinese.

It is not entitled to speak for China in the community of nations. It is entitled only to the fruits of its own conduct—the fruits of aggression upon which it is now willfully, openly, and senselessly embarked.

We recognize the National government of the Republic of China, even though the territory under its control is severely restricted. We believe it more authentically represents the views of the great body of the people of China, particularly their historic demand for independence from foreign control. That government will continue to receive important aid and assistance from the United States. Under the circumstances, however, such aid in itself cannot be decisive to the future of China. The decision and the effort are for the Chinese people, pooling their efforts, wherever they are, in behalf of China.

If the Chinese people decide for freedom, they shall find friends among all the peoples of the earth who have known and love freedom. They shall find added strength from those who refuse to believe that China is fated to become a land of tyranny and aggression and who expect China to fulfill the promise of its great past.

A World in Revolution
William O. Douglas

William O. Douglas was born in Maine, Minnesota in 1898. He was educated at Whitman College (A.B., 1920) and at Columbia University Law School (LL.B., 1925). He has been an Associate Justice of the Supreme Court since 1939. Mr. Douglas taught law at Columbia (1925-28) and at Yale (1928-34), and then served on the Securities and Exchange Commission from 1934 to 1939, first as director of the protective committee study and later as a commissioner and as chairman.

Justice Douglas made extensive tours of the Mediterranean, the Middle East, and the Far East in the summers of 1949, 1950, and 1951, often traveling by horseback, and talked with the governed and their governors in many lands. The address published below was made on his return from the second of his trips, before a joint meeting of the Rotary Club and the Bar Association of Tucson, Arizona on 14 February 1951.

For further accounts of his observations the reader is referred to the article, "Mr. Justice Douglas on Iran," in *Life* for 18 June 1951 and to his book, *Strange Lands and Friendly People*, published in the fall of 1951.

A World in Revolution

I BELIEVE it was Chesterton who said that travel narrows one. It does that to Americans in the sense that one who returns from travel abroad loves his country even more than before and cherishes to a greater degree its institutions of liberty. Travel these days, however, has other effects also. At least it does if one goes to the back countries of the world and loses himself in the villages of Asia for weeks on end. When I did that, I was profoundly disturbed. The America I love was not the America the people of Asia see. The attitudes we express, the words we use, the policies we pursue too often injure rather than help the cause of freedom-loving people. The reason is that we live in one world, the people of Asia in a different world. We must know their world, if we are to fulfill our destiny.

The world is different than we in America have thought. Wendell Willkie and many other reporters who traveled the back countries told us what was happening; but we did not listen. The plain fact is that the world is in a revolution which cannot be bought off with dollars. There are rumblings in every village from the Mediterranean to the Pacific. A force is gathering for a mighty effort. We think of that force as Communistic. Communists exploit the situation, stirring every discontent and making the pot boil. The revolutions which are brewing are not, however, Communist in origin nor will they end even if Soviet Russia is crushed through war. The revolutionaries are hungry men who have been exploited from time out of mind. This is the century of their awakening and mobilization.

What I saw and heard as I traveled this vast territory that lies under the southern rim of Russia reminded me very much of what I had read about other revolutions. The spirit which motivates these people is pretty much the same as the one which inspired the French and the American Revolutions. The abuses against which our American forebears protested in 1776 were piled high. They are listed in our Declaration of Independence: dissolution by the King of legislative bodies; corruption of judges; maintenance of a standing army and quartering of troops among the people; imposition of taxes without the consent of the colonies; transporting citizens beyond the seas for trial of offenses committed here. These and other practices of the King brought our people to a boiling point; and we declared ourselves free.

The complaints of the peasants of Asia are just as specific as those in our own Declaration of Independence; and to the people involved they are just as important. I have talked with them in many places across this wide belt and found them alive not only to their problems but to the solutions as well. These people, though illiterate, are intelligent.

The people of Asia have a catalogue of specific complaints. The absence of medical care always comes first. The absence of schools is always second. Then comes land reform. These people have a passion for land-ownership that Americans can understand. We expressed it in our homestead laws and in the great westward movement that built a nation out of the wilderness. Next comes the desire to learn how to farm the modern way. The right to vote, the right to elect a representative government, the power to expel and punish corrupt officials—these too are important claims to reform. Finally, they have a new sense of nationalism. It reflects itself in many ways—the growing sentiment in some countries of the Middle East to nationalize their oil and keep the profits for themselves; the desire to have local capital a partner with foreign capital in developing the nation; an exultant feeling of independence and resentment against intermeddling by outside powers.

There are professional agitators who stir this brew of discontent; but the force comes from the masses. I have not seen a village between the Mediterranean and the Pacific that was not stirring uneasily.

American foreign policy has never been addressed to the conditions under which these revolutions flourish. Democracy, peace, aggression are important words to us; but to those in the hinterland they are apt to be hollow and meaningless. America's voice when heard in this poverty and disease-ridden belt often sounds coarse and cheap—not because we intend it but because we do not know the world in which we live.

We tell about our high standard of living, how well our workers eat, the fine houses they live in. And it sounds like boasting and bragging.

We send technical experts abroad to help in seed selection, soil conservation, malaria control, and the like. But we never raise our voice for reforms of the vicious tenancy system of Asia under which increased production inures to the benefit of a few. We seem to forget that health programs unrelated to land distribution projects, minimum wages, maximum hours of work, and the like merely increase the number of people among whom the existing poverty must be rationed.

We talk about democracy and justice; and at the same time we support regimes whose object is to keep democracy and justice out of the reach of the peasants for all time.

We put billions of dollars behind corrupt and reactionary governments which exempt the rich from income taxes and fasten the hold of an oligarchy tighter and tighter on the nation.

The fact is that America has been so engrossed in providing a defense against Communism that we have lost the initiative. Our great weakness has been our negative attitude. We have been anti-Communist. We have been pledged to root it out and expose it for all its ugliness. We have taken up the hunt inside the country for every human being who was, is, or may be a Communist. Yet no matter how feverish our efforts, the red tide of Communism seems to spread abroad. We are seized with panic as the waters lap at feeble dikes. So we rush to the support of every group which opposes Soviet Communism. That puts us in partnership with the corrupt and reactionary groups whose policies breed the discontent on which Soviet Communism feeds and prospers.

This negative attitude, the policy of merely defending against Communism, is one reason for our default. The other basic reason is that we have relied more and more on our military to do our thinking and planning for us. Beginning in 1945 with the fall of Japan, we entrusted most of our attitude towards Asia to the Army. The military made policy for us. It is no reflection on the military to deplore that fact. The situation in Asia is delicate and complex. It requires astute handling at the political level—the best that we can muster in skill and understanding.

As a consequence of our negative attitude and military approach to problems, the tide of Soviet Communism has picked up momentum. The trend will continue; and the part of the world on which Communism has not fastened itself will become smaller and smaller as long as our policy is merely negative or dominated by military thinking. The Communists are not merely anti-status quo. They have concrete programs of political action in every country. If we are to regain the initiative, we must be prepared with equally idealistic and equally specific programs of reform. We, too, must use our ingenuity to invent ways to aid the peasants in their revolutionary aims. We must take over the guidance and direction of these revolutions if we want a free world.

We have thought we could save the world from Communism by dollars. It is, however, ideas not dollars that count the more in this campaign. Dollars are secondary. They must be conserved until an honest, progressive government comes into power. Then they can be used in select ways to help the natives build a new economy.

America is fitted by tradition for directing and guiding the revolutions that sweep the earth. We won our freedom by revolution and set the example which today inspires the peasants of Asia. We cannot remake the world in our image; but we can help those who are seeking an escape from squalor to find alternatives to Communism. We cannot do it by talking democracy to these people. We can do it only by making our foreign policy understandable in terms of their aspirations: medical care, education, distribution of land to the peasants, modern agriculture, free elections, independence from foreign domination. If we took that stand not only in rhetoric but in action, the political implementation of the program would be relatively easy. The Philippines, already the show case of Asia, could be transformed into a healthy, prosperous, democratic community.

India and Israel are examples of the strength and stability that democratic forces can mobilize. These nations have domestic programs that make Communism internally an empty threat. What Israel and India have done can be done elsewhere.

There are liberal forces in practically all of the Asiatic countries which can do the same. At times they are either in a minority position in the cabinet or outside the government completely. But each country has men who have the dream of a new freedom for their people, who have the character and ability to rid the nation of the feudal system that has existed from time out of mind. In other words, there is both the leadership and the energy within these countries to accomplish the necessary programs of social reconstruction.

A striking example is Persia. The present Shah has extremely liberal ideas for the reconstruction of his country and has recently announced the sale of the royal lands to the peasants. The Persian government, headed by Ali Razmara, has the highest degree of competence and the most liberal viewpoint in recent Persian history. His cabinet is composed of strong men with Western leanings.

Yet if some day soon the papers carry the news that Persia has swung into the Soviet orbit or has taken a position of pro-Soviet neutrality, it will not be because the Persians have embraced Communism. Communists in Persia are few and far between. The reason for such a tragedy will be that the Soviets have a program of political action which we do not match.

If we undertook to match the Soviets in a program of political action, the chances of success would be considerable. One reason is that the revolutions which sweep Asia are basically incompatible with Communism.

1. The people of this area are mostly God-fearing folks, while Communism is atheistic.
2. The people of this area want free elections and a free press; they

want to be rid of gendarmes and soldiers who break up their political meetings and tell them how to vote or who close their newspapers. Communism merely substitutes one group of armed, political censors for another.

3. The peasants of this area (and they comprise the vast majority of the population) want to be rid of their landlords; they want to own their own land—to fence it and call it theirs, to cultivate it and keep the produce for themselves and their families. The Communists merely substitute one landlord (the state) for another.

4. The people of this area are increasingly nationalistic. Most of them have only recently gained their independence from foreign domination. They are now offered the first chance in centuries to develop their own culture, to fashion their own laws, to shape their own destiny. Communism is Soviet inspired and controlled. Communist satellites lack the independence the people of the Middle East crave. They do not want to be the tool of any foreign power. They know that Communism would seek to make them the tool of the Kremlin.

This is why Soviet Communism works under great handicaps in this region. It is a creed that is hard to sell; its converts are few and far between; the number of rock-bottom Communists between the Mediterranean and the Pacific is extremely low—certainly less than 1/10th of 1 per cent. The fact that precious few people have rallied to the hammer and sickle must be discouraging to the Politburo, for it has changed its tactics. Today the Communists in the Middle East pose as an outright reform party—liberal, progressive, democratic. They espouse the causes which the elder La Follette, Woodrow Wilson, Franklin D. Roosevelt espoused here. They make revolution under slogans as staid and respected as minimum wages, price control, food rationing, reduced rents, and the like. They won several countries in Eastern Europe that way. It is that way, rather than by invasion, that they hope to win the Middle East.

Communism can win by this political technique only if it has no political competition. It has been gaining in great strides because it has been operating mostly in a political vacuum. It has had little competition in the political field. We in America talk democracy, peace, and justice at home. In Asia we either support the reactionaries and the corrupt forces who make democracy, peace, and justice impossible; or we fail to support to the hilt our real friends such as Nehru in India and Razmara in Persia.

If we persist in our present attitude, Communism will slowly spread and the free world will continually contract. Soviet Russia will continue to pick up country after country.

We cannot possibly defend with our armies the wide perimeter stretching from Japan to Cairo. We have not the men to do it. Anyone who has seen the jungles of Malaya and the swamps of Indo-China knows we could easily lose our armies in them. Soviet Russia's military strategy takes this into account. She does not plan to dissipate her own strength in that way. Behind her military strategy is a program of political action. Her aim is to get native Communists in control of every country. Then these countries will become neutral in a pro-Soviet sense or raise local armies (Korean style) to fight her battles for her. We cannot defeat those tactics by military action, for we are too small and the military theaters are too scattered. We can counter that military strategy only by a program of political action of our own.

We must be and remain strong as a military power in case Russia shifts from political to military action. But meanwhile our only real defense against Communism is a political offensive, a political offensive with action rather than with rhetoric.

The hour is late; but so long as World War III has not struck, it is not too late.

Let Us Make Peace

John Foster Dulles

John Foster Dulles was born in Washington, D. C. in 1888. He was graduated from Princeton in 1908, spent the following year in study at the Sorbonne in Paris, and then finished his legal studies at George Washington University in 1911. He has practiced in New York since that year. In 1945 he was appointed a member of the U.S. delegation to the San Francisco conference on World Organization and has taken part in various United Nations meetings, including the Moscow meeting of the Council of Foreign Ministers in 1947 and the United Nations General Assembly in Paris in 1948. He was appointed an interim United States Senator from New York by Governor Thomas E. Dewey in 1949, but was defeated for a six-year term in the 1950 election.

Mr. Dulles made this address at the Japanese Peace Conference at San Francisco on 5 September 1951. It represents the views of the American delegation on the proposed treaty of peace for Japan.

In his address at the China Institute dinner in New York on 18 May

1951, Mr. Dulles reminded his listeners: "Generally, and particularly in the Orient, great results are not achieved quickly and those who would succeed must dedicate themselves to a sustained effort."

WE HAVE met here for a consecrated purpose. We shall here make peace. "Blessed are the peacemakers." But the most blessed of this peace are not those of us who assemble here. The foundation for this peace was laid by the many who gave up their lives in faith that the very magnitude of their sacrifice would compel those who survived to find and take the way to peace.

We are here to redeem, in some small measure, the vast debt we owe.

That task is not a simple one. Victory usually gives power greater than should be possessed by those who are moved by the passions that war engenders. That is a principal reason why war has become a self-perpetuating institution.

The treaty before us is a step toward breaking the vicious cycle of war—victory—peace—war. The nations will here make a peace of justice, not a peace of vengeance.

True peace is possible because of what has been accomplished by six years of Allied occupation. That Occupation was calm and purposeful. Japan's war-making power was destroyed. The authority and influence of those who committed Japan to armed conquest was eliminated. Stern justice was meted out to the war criminals, while mercy was shown the innocent. There has come freedom of speech, of religion, of thought; and respect for fundamental human rights. There has been established, by the will of the people, a peacefully inclined and responsible government, which we are happy to welcome here.

The Allied occupation goals set forth in the Potsdam Surrender Terms have been met, with the loyal coöperation of the Japanese people. It is now time to end that Occupation, and make a peace which will restore Japan as a sovereign equal.

It is possible now to make that kind of a peace, to make this a peace of reconciliation, because the Japan of today is transformed from the Japan of yesterday.

The past is not forgotten or excused. Bitterness and distrust remain the sentiment of many. That is human. Those who have suffered less have no warrant to set themselves up as moral judges of those who have suffered more. But time, and the good use to which it has been put in Japan, have somewhat healed the scars of war. New hopes have gradually displaced old fears. Now, by an effort of self-control which is perhaps unprecedented in history, the Allies present to Japan a treaty which shows no trace of angry passion.

That is not merely an act of generosity toward a vanquished foe, it is an act of enlightened self-interest. For a treaty warped by passion often becomes a boomerang which, thrown against an enemy, returns to strike its authors.

For this treaty we are deeply indebted to the man who led the Allied Powers to victory in the Pacific. After that victory he devoted five and one-half years to service in Japan as Supreme Commander for the Allied Powers. As such he showed not only magnanimity, but strength without which magnanimity is counted weakness. He provided the Occupation with moral leadership which has been the impulsion for the kind of peace we make. The present generation and generations to come owe much to General MacArthur.

In framing the peace, the United States has taken an initiative. That was plainly our duty.

Some now find it expedient to disparage the role played by the United States in the Pacific War. None did so in the hour of victory. Then, by a unanimous Allied act, the United States was given the exclusive power to name the Supreme Commander for all the Allied Powers and to direct the Occupation which would prepare Japan for the peace to come. That Allied act put us in a position uniquely to judge *when* the Japanese were prepared for peace. It surely entitled us, indeed it obligated us, to take timely steps to bring our Occupation responsibilities to their normal predestined end.

We first moved in this matter four years ago. In 1947 the United States proposed a preliminary conference of the governments represented on the Far Eastern Commission to consider plans for a Japanese Peace Treaty. That proposal was blocked by the insistence of the Soviet Union that the treaty could only be considered by the Council of Foreign Ministers where the Soviet Union would have veto power. The Soviet Union continued stubbornly to adhere to that position.

Last year the United States decided to abandon the conference method, which afforded excessive possibilities of obstruction, and to seek peace through diplomatic processes which no single nation could thwart. That has been done with the hearty coöperation of most of the Allies and has resulted in a finished text.

The negotiations began about a year ago when the Allies principally concerned were gathering to attend the United Nations General Assembly in New York. The various delegations principally concerned had frequent consultations at that time. Then came conferences at many capitals and many written exchanges of views. A United States Presidential Mission toured the globe, visiting ten capitals of countries especially concerned. Meanwhile, the United Kingdom was exploring the problem within the Commonwealth, and its representative will tell you more of that.

The first round of discussions dealt with the question of whether it was *time* for peace and, if so, what basic *principles* should be applied. In this connection the United States outlined seven principles which it felt ought to govern the framing of the treaty.

We found complete agreement to the urgency of prompt peace and general agreement as to the basic principles. So, in January of this year, the United States undertook to make the first draft of a text which would translate the agreed principles into treaty words. That draft was circulated last March, and was subjected to intensive study by over twenty countries. These included not only the Far Eastern Commission countries, but others which had expressed interest. The American states were kept informed, as was their due. Mexico had actively participated in the Pacific War, as had Brazil in the European War. All had made important political, economic, and moral contributions.

Meanwhile, the United Kingdom produced a text of its own, drafted in the light of the Commonwealth Conferences. Then in June, the United States and the United Kingdom combined their parallel efforts and jointly drafted a text to reconcile and reflect still more fully the different views that had been developed. This text was circulated to Allied Powers during the first half of July and was kept open for further changes until mid-August.

Throughout this period, the Soviet Union took an active, though reluctant, part. We had several conferences with Yakov Malik and our governments have exchanged ten memoranda and drafts.

Every nation which has constructively interested itself in the treaty can claim authorship of important parts of the present text. Also each of these nations can claim the equally honorable distinction of voluntarily subordinating some special interest so that a broad base of unity might be found. The Allied Powers have been conducting what, in effect, is an eleven months' peace conference participated in by so many nations as to make this treaty the most broadly based peace treaty in all history.

Any who are interested in studying the evolutionary processes which have been at work can compare our March draft with the present text. To make that comparison easy, a parallel-column document has been prepared for distribution here. It shows how our conference methods have worked.

The treaty remains, as first agreed, a non-punitive, non-discriminatory treaty, which will restore Japan to dignity, equality, and opportunity in the family of nations. But it has been found increasingly possible to do justice to particular situations without violating these basic concepts.

I now turn to a consideration of the principal provisions of the text.

The Preamble is an important part of the treaty. It affords the Japanese nation the opportunity to record intentions and aspirations which the whole world welcomes.

Japan declares its intention to apply for membership in the United Nations; to conform to the principles of the Charter; to adhere to the new ideals of human rights and freedoms which have become implanted in the Constitution and legislation of Japan; and, in public and private trade and commerce, to conform to internationally accepted fair practices.

If Japan's intentions in these respects are sincere, which we believe, and if they are pursued with resolution, they will go far to restore good will between the Japanese and Allied people.

It may be asked why, if that is so, the treaty does not attempt to put the Japanese under legal compulsion in these respects. There are good reasons for not doing so. Japan, when it applies for membership in the United Nations, should do so because it *wants* to be a member, not because the Allies compelled it. Eighty million people cannot be compelled from without, to respect the human rights and fundamental freedoms of their fellows. Fair trade practices cannot be made a formal obligation when they have not yet been spelled out in international conventions. In general, treaty obligations should only be such as can be precisely formulated, so that the parties will clearly know just what are their rights and what are their duties. Where applicable conventions exist, Japan will voluntarily adhere to them, as set out in the Declaration appended to the treaty.

Chapter I ends the state of war, with consequent recognition of the full sovereignty of the Japanese people. Let us note that the sovereignty recognized is the "sovereignty of the Japanese people."

What is the territory of Japanese sovereignty? Chapter II deals with that. Japan formally ratifies the territorial provisions of the Potsdam Surrender Terms, provisions which, so far as Japan is concerned, were actually carried into effect six years ago.

The Potsdam Surrender Terms constitute the only definition of peace terms to which, and by which, Japan and the Allied Powers as a whole are bound. There have been some private understandings between some Allied Governments; but by these Japan was not bound, nor were other Allies bound. Therefore, the treaty embodies Article 8 of the Surrender Terms which provided that Japanese sovereignty should be limited to Honshu, Hokkaido, Kyushu, Shikoku, and some minor islands. The renunciations contained in Article 2 of Chapter II strictly and scrupulously conform to that Surrender Term.

Some question has been raised as to whether the geographical name "Kurile Islands" mentioned in Article 2 (c) includes the Habomai Islands. It is the view of the United States that it does not. If, however, there were a dispute about this, it could be referred to the International Court of Justice under Article 22.

Some Allied Powers suggested that Article 2 should not merely delimit Japanese sovereignty according to Potsdam, but specify precisely the ultimate disposition of each of the ex-Japanese territories. This, admittedly, would have been neater. But it would have raised questions as to which there are now no agreed answers. We had either to give Japan peace on the Potsdam Surrender Terms or deny peace to Japan while the Allies quarrel about what shall be done with what Japan is prepared, and required, to give up. Clearly, the wise course was to proceed now, so far as Japan is concerned, leaving the future to resolve doubts by invoking international solvents other than this treaty.

Article 3 deals with the Ryukus and other islands to the South and Southeast of Japan. These, since the surrender, have been under the sole administration of the United States.

Several of the Allied Powers urged that the treaty should require Japan to renounce its sovereignty over these islands in favor of United States sovereignty. Others suggested that these islands should be restored completely to Japan.

In the face of this division of Allied opinion, the United States felt that the best formula would be to permit Japan to retain residual sovereignty, while making it possible for these islands to be brought into the United Nations Trusteeship system, with the United States as administering authority.

You will recall that the Charter of the United Nations contemplates extension of the trusteeship system to "territories which may be detached from enemy states as a result of the Second World War" (Article 77). The future Trusteeship agreement will, no doubt, determine the future civil status of the inhabitants in relation to Japan while affording the administering authority the possibility of carrying out

Article 84 of the Charter, which provides that "It shall be the duty of the administering authority to ensure that the trust territory shall play its part in the maintenance of international peace and security."

A peace which limits Japanese territory according to the Potsdam Surrender Terms, naturally leads one to ask, can a growing population, now numbering over 80 million, survive on the Japanese home islands? A clue to the correct answer is the fact that when Japan had a vast colonial empire into which the Japanese people could freely emigrate, few did so. Formosa, a rich, uncrowded land with temperate climate, attracted, in 55 years, a total Japanese population of about 350,000. Korea, under Japanese control since 1905, attracted a total Japanese population of about 650,000. In South Sakhalin there were 350,000 Japanese and in the Kurile Islands about 11,000. Japan's colonies helped assure Japan access to food and raw materials, but they were no population outlet. Japanese, like other people, preferred to live at home. So far as emigration is concerned, the territorial clauses of the treaty do not establish restraints greater than those which 98% of the Japanese people voluntarily put upon themselves.

Of course growing populations create problems in Japan and elsewhere. The Japanese will need to develop the capacity to perform services which others want, so that in exchange they can buy the food and raw materials they need. This calls for willingness on the part of the Japanese people to work hard, to work efficiently and to work with creative imagination so that they can anticipate the economic wants of others. Each of the Allied Powers also has a responsibility. The Surrender Terms promised the Japanese "access to raw materials" and "participation in world trade relations." Peoples who are ready and willing to work and to create what others want, should have the means to do so. Under such conditions the present territorial status of Japan is no cause for alarm.

Chapter III deals with security, a problem which has not been, and never is, automatically solved by victory. By Article 5, Japan undertakes to live peacefully, in accordance with the Principles set forth in the Charter of the United Nations. We hope that Japan will promptly become a member of the United Nations. If this were certain, Article 5 would be unnecessary. But, in the past, veto power has been used to block the admission of nations qualified for membership. So it is prudent to write into the treaty that, as provided by Article 2(6) of the Charter, Japan will settle its international disputes by peaceful means; will refrain in its international relations from the threat or use of force; and will give the United Nations every assistance in any action it takes in accordance with the Charter.

These provisions completely meet the desire which some nations have expressed that the treaty should bind Japan to peaceful processes and explicitly prohibit Japan from acting forcibly, alone or in coalition, against any other nation. There can be nothing more sweeping than the renunciation of offensive force expressed in Article 5(a) (ii) of the treaty.

In order, however, that this treaty, like the United Nations Charter, should make it perfectly clear that the prohibition against the use of force does not deprive Japan of the right of self-defense, subdivision (c) of Article 5 contains a recognition that Japan as a sovereign nation possesses what Article 51 of the Charter of the United Nations refers to as "the inherent right of individual or collective self-defense."

Article 6 of the treaty calls for ending the Occupation not later than ninety days after the treaty comes into force. However, Japan, as contemplated by Article 51 of the United Nations Charter, may enter into collective security arrangements, and these might, in part, be implemented by Allied elements which were in Japan when the treaty came into force. Accordingly, it seemed useful to make it clear that, under such circumstances, these elements would not have to be physically removed from Japan before they could serve as collective security forces. This would be a burdensome requirement, and a risky one, for it would for a time leave Japan wholly defenseless, in close proximity to proved aggressors possessed of great military strength. To avoid that danger, Article 6 provides that Occupation elements now in Japanese territory may stay on for Japan's defense, if this is wanted by Japan.

These remaining military elements would, of course, have characteristics and powers very different from what they had as occupation forces. They would have only such status in Japan as Japan would voluntarily have given them.

The security provisions which we have reviewed are necessary if the Treaty of Peace is honestly to restore sovereignty to Japan. It has been suggested that the treaty ought to deny to Japan "the inherent right of collective self-defense" and permit only a token right of "individual self-defense."

That kind of a peace, in this present kind of a world, would be a fraud. To give a sovereignty which cannot be defended, is to give an empty husk. Indefensible sovereignty is not sovereignty at all. An undefended and indefensible Japan would be so subject to the menace of surrounding power that Japan would not in fact be able to lead an independent existence.

It has been suggested that a collective security arrangement with the United States, such as Japan is considering, would not be a free act or what the Japanese people really want.

That is not a suggestion which will command credence here. Nearly two-thirds of the delegations here are from countries which either have, or are about to have, voluntary association in collective security arrangements which include the United States. These delegations will assume, and rightly assume, that the Japanese people are like their own people, and like most free peoples, in wanting the collective security which may deter aggression.

When I was in Japan last February this topic was discussed with the Japanese for the first time. I then said publicly that Japan, if it wished, could share collective protection against direct aggression. In order, however, to make perfectly clear our government's position in the matter I had this to say: "That, however, is not a choice which the United States is going to impose upon Japan. It is an invitation. The United States is not interested in slavish conduct. . . . We are concerned only with the brave and the free. The choice must be Japan's own choice."

No person in this room, and I mean that literally, honestly believes that Japan seeks collective security with the United States because it is coerced. That is palpably absurd.

As the President of the United States pointed out in his opening address to us, security in the Pacific area is being developed on a *collective* basis which, through combination, enables each nation to get security without making itself into what could be an offensive threat. That is one way to approach the problem. The other way is to prohibit collective security and to follow the policy of "let each country defend itself from aggressors as it likes or as best it can." That latter way, Generalissimo Stalin said, addressing his Party on March 10, 1939, means "conniving at aggression."

Any nation which seeks to deny to Japan the right to collective security and which insists that Japan must stand alone is, at heart, a conniver at aggression. Those who sign this treaty will not lend themselves to that design.

I have expounded the philosophy of the treaty with reference to security because it is a philosophy which has been challenged. I hope, however, that the time I have given to this subject will not lead any Delegations to feel that military matters are our principal preoccupation.

Security from armed aggression is a *negative* asset. Our dedication is to the *positive* side of national life and of individual life. Throughout the Occupation the effort has been to create a climate conducive to human development. To that end, the United States has made a tremendous moral investment. President Truman, in his opening address to us, emphasized the social revolution which has been taking place in Japan, the sweeping away of militarism, the establishment of universal suffrage, the extensive land reforms, and the rapid growth of labor unions. Also, we are not ashamed of the fact that it was under the Occupation that the Japanese people adopted a Constitution forever barring war as an instrument of their national policy. If today we are compelled to think in terms of a treaty which will enable Japan to protect its sovereignty and independence it is not because we seek a remilitarized Japan—that we have done everything in our power to prevent—but because social and economic progress cannot be achieved in the cold climate of fear.

An outstanding humanitarian feature of the Japanese surrender was the Allied promise to return Japanese prisoners to their homes. However, evidence produced before the United Nations General Assembly last September indicated that large numbers of Japanese soldiers, who had surrendered to the Soviet Union five years before, had not yet been repatriated. The United Nations expressed its concern and set up a Commission to study this matter. In order to make clear that the Allied undertaking to Japan survives until it has been performed, Article 9 of the Potsdam Surrender Terms has been incorporated into the Treaty of Peace. (Article 6(b)). We earnestly hope that it will be fulfilled, and tragic anguish be allayed.

Chapter IV deals with trade and commerce. The text is somewhat technical but the words add up to this: Japan is not subjected to any permanent discriminations and disabilities, her economy is unrestricted and no limitations whatever are placed upon her right to trade with each and every country.

The permanent relations between Japan and the Allied Powers, as regards trading, maritime, and other commercial relations (Article 12); as regards high seas fishing (Article 9); as regards international air transport (Article 13), are to be negotiated between Japan and Allied Powers so desiring. Pending the conclusion of such treaties, and for a four-year interim period, each Allied Power will be entitled to most-favored-nation treatment as regards customs duties, but only on a basis of reciprocity.

These are liberal treaty clauses. The fulfillment of the hopes placed in them will, however, depend on whether Japan lives up to its intention, proclaimed in the Preamble, "to conform to internationally accepted fair practices," and on whether the Allied Powers, by their domestic legislation, extend to Japan trading possibilities which are reasonable, having regard to their own domestic requirements. On these matters, a peace treaty can do no more than point the way to a healthy trade relationship and create the opportunity to go in that way. That this treaty does.

Reparations is usually the most controversial aspect of peace-making. The present peace is no exception.

On the one hand, there are claims both vast and just. Japan's aggression caused tremendous cost, losses, and suffering. Governments represented here have claims which total many billions of dollars and China could plausibly claim as much again. One hundred thousand million dollars would be a modest estimate of the whole.

On the other hand, to meet these claims, there stands a Japan presently reduced to four home islands which are unable to produce the food its people need to live, or the raw materials they need to work. Since the surrender, Japan has been two billion dollars short of the money required to pay for the food and raw materials she had to import for survival on a minimum basis. The United States had made good that two-billion-dollar deficit. We accepted that as one of our occupation responsibilities. But the United States is entitled to look forward to Japan's becoming economically self-sustaining, so as to end dependence on us; and it is not disposed, directly or indirectly, to pay Japan's future reparations.

Under these circumstances, if the treaty validated, or kept contingently alive, monetary reparation claims against Japan, her ordinary commercial credit would vanish, the incentive of her people would be destroyed and they would sink into a misery of body and spirit which would make them an easy prey to exploitation. Totalitarian demagogues would surely rise up to promise relief through renewed aggression with the help of those nearby who, as we have seen in Korea, are already disposed to be aggressors. The old menace would appear in aggravated form.

Such a treaty, while promoting unity among aggressors would promote disunity among many Allied Powers. There would be bitter competition for the largest possible percentage of an illusory pot of gold. Already, several countries have approached the United States with suggestions that their particular claims for reparation should be favored at the expense of others.

A treaty which on the one hand encouraged division among the non-aggressive states and on the other hand, brought recruits to the side of the aggressive states, would be a treaty which would recklessly squander the opportunity of victory. The parties to such a treaty would expose themselves to new perils greater than those which they have barely survived.

These conflicting considerations were fully discussed, until there emerged a solution which gives moral satisfaction to the claims of justice and which gives material satisfaction to the maximum extent compatible with political and economic health in the Pacific area.

The treaty recognizes, clearly and unambiguously, that Japan *should* pay reparation to the Allied Powers for the damage and suffering caused by it during the war.

It then goes on to dedicate to the implementation of that principle, certain assets which Japan does have in surplus and which could be put to work to help to compensate those nations which suffered the most from Japan's wartime acts.

Japan has a population not now fully employed, and it has industrial capacity not now fully employed. Both of these aspects of unemployment are caused by lack of raw materials. These, however, are possessed in goodly measure by the countries which were overrun by Japan's armed aggression. If these war-devastated countries send to Japan the raw materials which many of them have in abundance, the Japanese could process them for the creditor countries and by these services, freely given, provide appreciable reparations. The arrangements could cover not merely consumer goods but machinery and capital goods which would enable underdeveloped countries to speed up developing their own industry, so as hereafter to lessen their dependence on outside industrial power.

This is, in essence, the formula expressed in Article 14(a)1. It results from prolonged exchanges of views, particularly with such countries as the Philippines and Indonesia, which were occupied by Japanese forces and injured in a way which places on the Allied Powers as a whole, and on Japan, a very clear duty to seek all means of reparation which are realistic.

I am frank to say that the treaty is a better, fairer treaty than first drafted. That results from the proper insistence of some governments that all possibilities of reparation should be exhaustively explored. That has been done, and the result is a fresh demonstration of the worth of the free processes of free and equal people. Those processes have here produced a treaty formula which serves the ideal of justice within an economic framework which can benefit all concerned.

In addition to this source of future reparation, the treaty validates the taking, by Allied Powers, of Japanese property within their jurisdictions.

By Article 16, Japanese property in neutral and ex-enemy countries is to be transferred to the International Red Cross for the benefit of former prisoners of war and their families, on the basis of equity, to make some compensation for undue hardships suffered, often in violation of the Geneva Conventions. The United States, in response to some Allied inquiries, has indicated that, since its own prisoners of war have received some indemnification out of proceeds of Japanese property we seized, we would assume that equity would require first distribution to those who have had no comparable indemnification.

Allied property within Japan is to be returned. Where this cannot be done, because of war damage, there will be compensation in blocked yen in accordance with pending Japanese domestic legislation.

Article 21 makes special provision for Korea. The Republic of Korea will not sign the treaty of peace only because Korea was never at war with Japan. It tragically lost its independence long before this war began, and did not regain independence of Japan until after Japan surrendered. Many individual Koreans steadfastly fought Japan. But they were individuals, not recognized governments.

Nevertheless, Korea has a special claim on Allied consideration, the more so as it has not yet proved possible for the Allies to achieve their goal of a Korea which is free and independent. Korea is, unhappily, only half free and only half independent; and even that fractional freedom and independence has been cruelly mangled and menaced by armed aggression from the North.

Most of the Allied Powers have been seeking to make good their promise of freedom and independence and, as members of the United Nations, to suppress the aggression of which Korea is the victim. By this treaty, the Allies will obtain for Korea Japan's formal recognition of Korea's independence, and Japan's consent to the vesting in the Republic of Korea, of the very considerable Japanese property in Korea. Korea will also be placed on a parity with the Allied Powers as regards postwar trading, maritime, fishing, and other commercial arrangements. Thus the treaty, in many ways, treats Korea like an Allied Power.

The absence of China from this Conference is a matter of deep regret. Hostilities between Japan and China first began in 1931 and open warfare began in 1937. China suffered the longest and the deepest from Japanese aggression. It is greatly to be deplored that the Sino-Japanese war cannot be formally terminated at this occasion. Unhap-

Let Us Make Peace

pily, civil war within China and the attitudes of the Allied governments have created a situation such that there is not general international agreement upon a single Chinese voice with both the right and the power to bind the Chinese nation to terms of peace. Some think that one government meets these tests. Some think another meets them. Some doubt that either meets them. No majority can be found for any present action regarding China. Thus, the Allies were faced with hard choices.

They could defer any peace with Japan until they could agree that there was in China a government possessed of both legitimacy and authority. It would, however, be wrong, cruel and stupid to penalize Japan because there is civil war in China and international disagreement regarding China.

As another approach, each Allied Power could refuse to sign a treaty of peace with Japan unless a Chinese government of its choice was co-signer with it. That, we ascertained, would leave Japan at war with so many Allied Powers that Japan would get only a small measure of the peace she has earned. Indeed, there is no reason to believe that Japan, an essential party, would willingly coöperate in a program leading to that end. To exert compulsion, in this matter, would create resentment in Japan, and it would activate and aggravate Allied division in the face of a grave world-wide menace which requires maximum unity.

The remaining choice was for the Allied Powers generally to proceed to conclude peace without any present Chinese co-signature, leaving China and Japan to make their own peace, on terms, however, which would guarantee full protection of the rights and interests of China.

That is the choice reflected by the present treaty. By Article 26, China is given the right to a treaty of peace with Japan, on the same terms as the present treaty. The victorious Allies, which sign the treaty, take nothing for themselves that they do not assure equally to China. Also, by Article 21, China, without need of signature, gets the sweeping renunciation by Japan (Article 10) of all Japan's special rights and interests in China, in accordance with a formula suggested by the Republic of China. Also, China receives automatically, and without need of signature, the benefit of Article 14(a)2 which validates the seizure of Japanese property subject to its jurisdiction. The treaty preserves, in full, the rights of China as one of the Allied victors in this war.

Chapter VII contains clauses which are largely matters of protocol. Of these Article 23, dealing with ratification, gives those signatories to the treaty which have been actively concerned with the Occupation, a special position, for nine months, regarding the bringing of the treaty into force. But after nine months all of the Allied Powers stand on an equal footing as regards bringing the treaty into force as between themselves and Japan.

Such, in broad outline, are the main aspects of the treaty that awaits our signature.

It contains, no doubt, imperfections. No one is completely satisfied. But it is a good treaty. It does not contain the seeds of another war. It is truly a treaty of peace.

We may hear a suggestion that we should not now complete, by signature, this product of a year's negotiation, but resort to new procedures, with new parties. It may be pretended that thereby we can gain greater unity and more perfection. At first that may sound plausible and tempting. It may seem to offer the partially dissatisfied a chance for great satisfaction.

In some Allied countries there are organized groups which urge that the treaty could be changed merely to benefit them, leaving everything else intact. If all of these proposals were to be brought together, it would be apparent that the cumulative effect would be destructive of any agreed peace.

Fortunately, there are also in most of the Allied countries those who see with truer vision. They know that this treaty is good to the point where it cannot be made better without its becoming worse. Better words might theoretically be found; but to seek these is to let escape what is now within our grasp. There come times when to seek the perfect is to lose the good. This is such a time.

There is greater unity now than we are apt to find if there is renegotiation. The treaty has been painstakingly built by the delicate processes of diplomacy, helped by an unusual display of self-restraint and good will. But it is not wise to assume that those qualities will be ever present and that differences can always be composed.

There is a larger measure of satisfaction now than we can ever get again. Delay will inevitably set in motion corroding forces and contradictory efforts which will block each other and frustrate the possibilities inherent in a common effort of good will.

In terms of Japan's future, delay would cost a price which makes petty all the sacrifices incident to present action. The great goals of victory will have been made unattainable.

It was our common hope that, out of the fiery purge of war, there would rise a new Japan. That was no foolish hope. Japan has a great culture and tradition which are capable of producing distinctively, but no less authentically, those virtues which all nations and peoples must possess if there is to be a world-wide commonwealth of peace.

In order, however, that that potentiality shall become actuality, Japan needs free political institutions in a climate conducive to their vigorous growth; social progress; an equal administration of justice; an awareness of human dignity; a sense of self-respect, of respect for others.

Above all, Japan needs the will to live at peace with others as good neighbors.

All of this is possible, if we make peace now. It becomes impossible, or at best improbable, if Japan's long deferred hopes are now blasted.

There are, in Japan, new born institutions of freedom. But they will not flourish if military rule continues indefinitely to be supreme.

Dignity cannot be developed by those who are subject to alien control, however benign.

Self-respect is not felt by those who have no rights of their own in the world, who live on charity and who trade on sufferance.

Regard for justice rarely animates those who are subjected to such grave injustice as would be the denial of present peace.

Fellowship is not the mood of peoples who are denied fellowship.

The United States, which since the surrender has directed the Occupation on behalf of all the Allies, says solemnly to each of the Allies: unless you now give Japan peace and freedom on such honorable terms as have been negotiated, the situation will rapidly deteriorate.

The Surrender Terms have served their every legitimate purpose. Under them "the authority of the Emperor and the Japanese government to rule the state shall be subject to the Supreme Commander of the Allied Powers." To perpetuate that subjection which has existed for six years, into more years, would be to pervert the Occupation into an instrument of imperialism and colonialism. The United States wants none of that, and we know that most of you want none of that.

It is time to end the subjection of the Japanese government to Allied command. It is time to end the Occupation and to recognize that, henceforth, it is the Japanese people who exercise complete sovereignty in Japan. It is time to welcome Japan as an equal and honorable member of the family of nations.

That is what the pending treaty will do.

No nation is bound to sign the treaty. This is no Conference that wields legal compulsion. The only compulsion is the moral compulsion of grave circumstances. They unite to cry aloud: Let us make peace.

RUSSIA AND COMMUNISM

An Interview with a Pravda Correspondent
Joseph Stalin

This discourse represents an interview by a *Pravda* correspondent with Premier Stalin. It was broadcast on 16 February 1951 by the Moscow Radio and heard in London. The English text, supplied by the Associated Press, is that which appeared in *The New York Times* for 17 February 1951.

In a sense this rare pronouncement by the Russian leader continues at some points the discussion begun on 30 January 1949 when a United States news agency put to Stalin four important questions on world policy. He said at that time that his government was ready to consider the publication of a joint Soviet-American declaration that the two countries had no intention of waging war against each other. He reiterated his view that the Soviet government was willing to institute a gradual disarmament. He stated that his country would not object to removing transport restrictions between Berlin and the Western zones of Germany providing the United States, Great Britain, and France would lift both trade and transport restrictions between the Western and Soviet zones and pending a conference of the Council of Foreign Ministers to discuss the problems. Finally, he asserted that he was available to meet President Truman for discussion of these problems.

This present interview is astutely analyzed by Louis Fischer in the *United Nations World* for April 1951 in the article, "Stalin Needs a New Line." Mr. Fischer believes that the interview "reflects tension between Russia and China" and tells us that in the light of subsequent developments the most significant sentence in the interview reads: "If Britain and the United States reject finally the proposals made by the People's Government of China, the war in Korea can only end in a defeat of the interventionists." This means, according to Mr. Fischer, "that the door to negotiations with China remains open." He continues: "Stalin's interview indicates that he is troubled. He is troubled not only by Chinese pressure but also by world-wide anti-Soviet trends which militate against Russia's chances of winning further triumphs. Stalin interviewed himself for *Pravda* in the hope of reversing these trends."

Joseph Vissarionovich Djugashvili (his real name) was born on 21 December 1879 at Gori, Georgia, in Transcaucasia. The name Stalin, meaning "Steel Man," was given to him by Nicolai Lenin. As Chairman of the Council of Ministers of the U.S.S.R., Stalin wields supreme power. He is also general secretary of the Communist Party of the Soviet Union, Minister for the Armed Forces, and a member of the Supreme Soviet of the U.S.S.R. He was named Generalissimo in June 1945.

Among Stalin's published works are the following: *Foundations of Leninism* (1924), a chapter (IV) on dialectical and historical materialism in the *History of the Communist Party of the Soviet Union* (1938), and *War Speeches, Orders of the Day and Interviews to Foreign Correspondents during the Great Patriotic War* (1945). For an analysis of the strategy of Communism, based on the writings of Lenin and Stalin, the reader is referred to *The Operational Code of the Politburo*, edited by Dr. Nathan Leites (1951).

According to Maurice Hindus: "When he [Stalin] speaks he seldom lifts his voice above a conversational tone. He never attempts to arouse an audience with gestures or rhetoric. He is no orator at all. He hesitates, makes lengthy pauses like a school teacher. His language is so simple that everybody can understand him, and while speaking he drinks endless glasses of water."

QUESTION: How do you estimate the latest statement made by British Prime Minister Attlee in the House of Commons to the effect that after the termination of the war the Soviet Union did not disarm, i.e., did not demobilize its troops and that since then the Soviet Union is constantly increasing its armed forces?

ANSWER: I estimate this statement made by Prime Minister Attlee as a slander against the Soviet Union. It is known to the whole world that the Soviet Union demobilized its troops after the war. As is known, demobilization was carried out in three stages: the first and second stages, in the course of the year 1945; the third stage, from May to September, 1946. In addition, the demobilization of older age groups of the personnel of the Soviet army was carried out in 1946 and 1947.

Such are the facts known to everyone.

If Prime Minister Attlee were competent in financial or economic science, he would have realized without difficulty that not a single state, the Soviet Union included, could develop civilian industry to the full, launch great construction projects like the hydroelectric power stations on the Volga and Dnieper and the Amu Darya, which demand scores of hundreds of thousands of millions in budget expenditure, continue the policy of systematic price reduction for consumer goods which also demands scores of thousands of millions in budget expenditure, invest hundreds of thousands of millions in the restoration of the national economy destroyed by the German invaders, and together simultaneously with this multiply its armed forces and develop war industry.

It is not difficult to understand that so reckless a policy would have led any state to bankruptcy.

Prime Minister Attlee should have known by his own experience as well as by the experience of the United States that the multiplication of a country's armed forces and an arms race lead to developing war industry, to curtailing civilian industry, to stopping civilian construction work, to increased taxation, to a rise in prices for consumer goods.

It stands to reason that if the Soviet Union is not reducing but on the contrary is expanding its civilian industry, is not winding up but on the contrary expanding the construction of new civilian hydroelectric power stations and irrigation systems, is not stopping but on the contrary continuing the policy of price reduction, it cannot simultaneously with this inflate war industry and multiply its armed forces without risking finding itself in a state of bankruptcy.

If despite all these facts and scientific considerations, Prime Minister Attlee considers it nevertheless possible openly to slander the Soviet Union and its peaceful policy, this can only be explained by the fact that by slandering the Soviet Union he thinks it is possible to justify the armaments race in Britain now being carried out by the Labor government.

Prime Minister Attlee needs a lie against the Soviet Union, and it is essential to him to depict the peaceful policy of the Soviet Union as an aggressive one and the aggressive policy of the British Government as a peaceful one in order to mislead the British people, to impose upon them that lie about the U.S.S.R. and thus to draw them by means of deceit into the new world war being organized by the ruling circles of the United States.

Prime Minister Attlee represents himself to be a supporter of peace. However, if he is really in favor of peace, why did he reject the proposal of the Soviet Union in the United Nations Organization for the immediate conclusion of a peace pact between the Soviet Union, Britain, the United States of America, China, and France?

If he truly stands for peace, why did he reject the proposals of the Soviet Union for an immediate start on the reduction of armaments, for the immediate prohibition of atomic weapons?

If he is really in favor of peace, why does he persecute the fighters of peace, why did he prohibit the peace congress in Britain? Can a campaign in defense of peace threaten Britain's security?

It is obvious that Prime Minister Attlee is not in favor of preserving peace, but of unleashing a new aggressive world war.

QUESTION: What do you think of the intervention in Korea? How could it end?

ANSWER: If Britain and the United States reject finally the proposals made by the People's Government of China, the war in Korea can only end in a defeat of the interventionists.

QUESTION: Why, is it possible that the American and British generals and officers are worse than the Chinese and the Korean ones?

ANSWER: No, they are not worse. American and British generals and officers are in no way worse than the generals and officers of any other country.

As to the soldiers of the United States and Britain, as is known, they showed themselves in the best light in the war against Hitlerite Germany and militarist Japan. Wherein lies the crux of the matter then? It lies in the fact that the soldiers regard the war against Korea and China as unjust, whereas they regarded the war against Hitlerite Germany and militarist Japan as completely just.

The matter at issue is that this war is extremely unpopular among the American and British soldiers. Indeed, it is difficult to convince the soldiers that China, which is not threatening either Britain or the United States, and from which the Americans appropriated the island of Taiwan (Formosa), is the aggressor, whereas the United States, which appropriated the island of Taiwan and brought its troops to the very boundaries of China, is the party defending itself.

It is difficult to convince the soldiers that the United States of America is entitled to defend its security on the territory of Korea and at the frontiers of China, whereas China and Korea have no right to defend their security on their own territory or at the frontiers of their states. This is the reason why the war is unpopular among the Anglo-American soldiers.

It stands to reason that the most experienced generals and officers can suffer defeat if the soldiers regard the war imposed upon them as profoundly unjust and if, as a result of this, they perform their duties on the front in a formal way without faith in the righteousness of their mission and without enthusiasm.

QUESTION: How do you estimate the decision of the United Nations Organization which proclaimed the Chinese People's Republic an aggressor?

ANSWER: I estimate it as a shameful decision. Indeed, one must lose the last vestiges of conscience to contend that the United States, which appropriated Chinese territory—the island of Taiwan—and which invaded Korea close to the frontiers of China, is the party defending itself, whereas the Chinese People's Republic, which is defending its frontiers and is striving to secure the return of the island of Taiwan appropriated by the Americans, is the aggressor.

The United Nations Organization, created as the bulwark for preserving peace, is being turned into an instrument of war, into a means of unleashing a new world war.

The aggressive core of the United Nations is represented by the ten member countries of the aggressive North Atlantic Pact and twenty Latin-American countries.

The representatives of these countries now decide the fate of war and peace in the United Nations. It was they who carried in the United Nations the shameful decision on the aggressiveness of the Chinese People's Republic. It is characteristic of the present-day regime in the United Nations that, for instance, the small Dominican Republic in America, whose population hardly amounts to two millions, has the same weight in the United Nations as India and much more weight than the Chinese People's Republic, which is deprived of the right to vote in the United Nations.

Thus, being turned into the tool of aggressive war, the United Nations Organization is at the same time ceasing to be a world organization of nations enjoying equal rights.

As a matter of fact, the United Nations Organization is now not so much a world organization as an organization for the Americans, an organization acting on behalf of the requirements of the American aggressors.

Not only the United States and Canada are striving to unleash a new war. The same stand has also been taken by twenty Latin-American countries, the landowners and businessmen of which are craving for a new war somewhere in Europe or Asia in order to sell goods to the belligerent countries for excessively high prices and to earn millions from that sanguinary business.

It is not a secret for anyone that twenty representatives of twenty Latin-American countries now represent the most solid and obedient army of the United States of America in the United Nations Organization.

The United Nations Organization is therefore taking the inglorious road of the League of Nations. In this way it is burying its moral prestige and dooming itself to disintegration.

QUESTION: Do you consider a new world war inevitable?

ANSWER: No. At least at the present time it cannot be considered inevitable.

Of course, in the United States of America, in Britain, as also in France, there are aggressive forces thirsting for a new war. They need war to obtain super-profits, to plunder other countries. These are the billionaires and millionaires who regard war as an item of income which gives colossal profits. They, these aggressive forces, control the reactionary governments and direct them.

But at the same time they are afraid of their peoples who do not want a new war and stand for the maintenance of peace. Therefore they are trying to use the reactionary governments in order to enmesh their peoples with lies, to deceive them and to depict the new war as defensive and the peaceful policy of the peace-loving countries as aggressive. They are trying to deceive their peoples in order to impose on them their aggressive plans to draw them into a new war.

Precisely for this reason they are afraid of the campaign in defense of peace, fearing that it can expose the aggressive intentions of the reactionary governments. Precisely for this reason they turned down the proposal of the Soviet government for the conclusion of a peace pact, for the reduction of armaments, for banning the atomic weapon, fearing that the adoption of these proposals would undermine the aggressive measure of the reactionary governments and make the armaments race unnecessary.

What will be the end of this struggle of the aggressive and peace-loving forces?

Peace will be preserved and consolidated if the peoples will take the cause of preserving peace into their own hands and will defend it to the end. War may become inevitable if the warmongers succeed in entangling the masses of the people in lies, in deceiving them and drawing them into a new World War.

That is why the wide campaign for the maintenance of peace as a means of exposing the criminal machinations of the warmongers is now of first-rate importance.

As for the Soviet Union, it will continue in the future as well firmly to pursue a policy of averting war and maintaining peace.

What Are the Real Issues in Our Fight Against Communism?

Louis Fischer and Harold H. Velde; George V. Denny, Jr., Moderator

This discussion was broadcast over America's Town Meeting of the Air from Scott Field, Belleville, Illinois on 10 October 1950.

Louis Fischer is a writer and lecturer. He was born in Philadelphia in 1896. Following his graduation from the Philadelphia School of Pedagogy in 1916, he taught in the Philadelphia public schools. Since 1921 he has been a foreign correspondent. His first assignment was with the *New York Evening Post* at Berlin. Among his books are *Gandhi and Stalin* (1947) and *The Life of Stalin* (1950).

Harold H. Velde was born at Parkland, Illinois in 1910. He graduated from Northwestern University in 1931 and then taught for a few years in the Hillsdale Community High School. He gained his LL.B. degree from the University of Illinois in 1937. In World War II Mr. Velde served as a private in the Signal Corps. He also became a special agent for the Federal Bureau of Investigation in the sabotage and counterespionage division. Prior to his election as a Republican to Congress from the 18th Illinois district in 1948, Representative Velde served as a judge in Tazewell County, Illinois.

MODERATOR DENNY: Good evening, neighbors. Colonel Ogden, we of Town Hall extend our heartiest congratulations to you and General Harper for the magnificent training program you are giving the men in our Air Force, and we are happy indeed to be here at Scott Field, headquarters for this tremendously important activity. We know that the men under your command are deeply interested in tonight's subject—the real issues in our fight against Communism—as are the American people out of uniform. This very basic question has many of us baffled.

Perhaps one reason why we are so confused is our willingness to let the enemy name the terms. They call it Communism. In reality, it's simply another form of despotism, which we first fought in 1776, again in 1812, and again in 1917 and '18. We just finished fighting it in three of its most hideous forms: Nazism, Fascism, and Japanese imperialism.

Perhaps a better way to ask tonight's question is, "What are the real issues in our fight against aggressive despotism?" We freedom-loving Americans like to say, "Let every country have the kind of government it wants, provided they let us alone." But the trouble with despotism in any of its forms is that it will not let others alone. Like a cancer, it feeds on normal tissue.

We've learned to outlaw smallpox, leprosy, and other contagious diseases. Has the time come for us to outlaw dangerous despotisms that threaten world peace? We want nothing Russia has, and the men of Moscow say they despise our way of life. What, then, are the real issues? They are far deeper than those that appear on the surface.

To help us explore this subject we've invited two experts, a United States Congressman who is a member of the Un-American Activities

What Are the Real Issues in Our Fight Against Communism?

Committee, and a distinguished scholar, author, and foreign correspondent who has spent many years in Russia. It's understood, of course, that the opinions expressed here are those of the individual speakers and have no relation to Air Force policy.

We hear first from Congressman Harold H. Velde, Republican of the 18th Congressional District of the State of Illinois and a member of the Un-American Activities Committee of the House of Representatives. Congressman Velde.

CONGRESSMAN VELDE: My friends, the meaning of Communism is as varied throughout the world as Joseph's coat of many colors. The leaders of the Communist party are actually practicing deception and fraud on their citizenries by calling their government a Communist government. As you say, Mr. Denny, they call it Communism, when in reality it is a simple form of despotism.

The followers of the original theory of Communism as set down by Karl Marx and others believe it is an economic, political, and social plan for sharing the wealth, thus making each person—man, woman, child, merchant, beggar, or thief—equal in wealth and position.

The real leaders of the Communist party, here and abroad, know differently, however, and they are happy with their success in confusing the minds of some 800 million people who are now under the iron hand of Communism.

Mr. Fischer, we who know Communism for what it actually is know that its policies are directed by a few members of the Politburo in the Kremlin. We are certain that it is a carefully laid-out and treacherous scheme for the establishment of a totalitarian dictatorship of world-wide scope.

The real issue of Communism is, then, that it is a most vicious fraud; not only a fraud on the peoples ruled by the Kremlin, but an attempted fraud on all freedom-loving peoples of the world. Most treacherous of its concepts is the belief that despotic dictators are all-powerful; yes, even more powerful than God.

Our problem, then, is twofold: First, to expose the true nature of the Communistic fraud and then spread this knowledge to all peoples of the world, that republican constitutional government and the free enterprise system of economy are the only political and economic systems that can possibly bring them to the same high standards of living that we here in the United States enjoy.

In other words, we must teach the basic concept of the dignity of the individual man as opposed to the belief that man is a slave and tool of the state. We must teach that man—every man—is capable of controlling his own destiny and must be given that opportunity.

The second problem is this: How can we in America defend ourselves, as well as the other free nations of the world, against aggression and ultimate domination until our first objective is accomplished?

We have seen in the last five years the expenditure of some 13 billion dollars of American taxpayers' money to contain Communism in Europe, but we let it knock at, and almost let it enter, the back door in China and the Far East. At the same time, we have witnessed in our country the foothold gained by Communism in such socialistic schemes as deficit spending, increasing our taxes beyond all reason, and increasing controls with them—the very things that the Politburo is hoping for.

Surely, then, our relief program and our foreign policy have been wrong. It is my firm belief that we cannot teach the world the benefits to be derived from our form of government by allowing its destruction from within by the very persons we are fighting in foreign fields. To help others we must remain strong ourselves.

And so it becomes increasingly important that we place in political leadership in America men who are not chained in any manner to the schemes of a Communist dictator. We must be certain, especially, that those in charge of our foreign policy in the State Department and other executive branches are loyal Americans, capable of establishing and carrying out a straightforward foreign policy.

Furthermore, we must make certain that, as the famous Justice, Learned Hand, recently said, "we are not divided in counsel, that we are not overextended in foreign affairs, and finally, that we are not on the brink of financial disaster here at home."

MODERATOR DENNY: Thank you, Congressman Velde. Our next speaker, whose voice is familiar to Town Meeting listeners, spent fourteen years in Russia as a foreign correspondent and has covered most of the hot spots in the world during the past thirty years. His most recent book, *The Life of Mahatma Gandhi,* has just hit the best-seller list. Another of his fourteen other books is *Soviets in World Affairs,* a two-volume history of Soviet foreign policy. So, we're happy to welcome back to our platform Mr. Louis Fischer. Mr. Fischer.

MR. FISCHER: Mr. Denny and friends. The key issue in our struggle against Communism is Soviet imperialism. It is Russia's expansion since 1939 and her seizure of a vast empire that present a danger to the security and peace of mind of America and other democracies.

What Are the Real Issues in Our Fight Against Communism?

Our first task, therefore, is to check all forms of Soviet aggression as we have done in Greece and Berlin and Iran and as we are now doing in Korea, because if the Communists succeeded in these places they would be encouraged to go further and imperil our safety. Accordingly, we and the other free nations, working whenever possible through the United Nations, must be strong militarily.

But the democratic world might possess thousands of atomic bombs, thousands of warships, tens of thousands of planes, and millions of fighting men and yet be defeated by Communism. The strength of Communism lies not only in Russia. Communism is also an idea. It stands for a certain kind of economic system and for a government which is a dictatorship.

We dislike the idea, and the tyrannical shape it takes in practice is repugnant to us. Yet Communism does have an appeal to millions of people in France, Italy, and other countries, and especially to the people of Asia—one billion strong, all of them colored.

The Congressman would probably like to suppress the Communist parties of France and Italy, but they are too strong. They cannot be made illegal, nor will arrests and shootings kill Communism in Asia. The British arrested Mahatma Gandhi and his followers many times, but in the end the British had to get out, and India won her independence.

Force and persecution are blunt weapons against the hungry, the unhappy, the unpriviledged, and words about the blessings of American free enterprise will mean nothing to them. In fact, Congressman, if you mislead the people of Asia, Europe, Africa, and Latin America into thinking that the welfare state is Communism, they may go for Communism, for the very thing they want is a state that is going to look after their welfare. And because they know about the blessings that the American people enjoy, they feel that it conflicts with the dignity of the individual and with public decency, when we live so richly while hundreds of millions of them starve.

We must prove ourselves by good deeds. I believe in the Voice of America, and in words; but we must show by our good deeds that we believe in the dignity of man, whether he is white, yellow, or brown. The American cause suffers, for instance, when our boys disparagingly call the Koreans "gooks," and when we behave superior to colored people at home or abroad.

The real issue in our struggle against Communism is to win the majority of mankind to our side. And to do that, we have to give them friendship and understanding, as well as material help. We must convey to them the message that Communism is a fraud, which it is, but we must also show them that we have a spiritual message which guides our inner lives.

Unlike Congressman Velde, I'm not afraid of Communism in the United States. If any Communist, American or other, tries to spy on us, or steal secrets, or filter into the government, we must have agencies like the FBI and loyalty commissions to deal with him adequately and legally by applying law, not mud and smear. But we are a strong, prosperous, and happy nation, and I do not think that the handful of misguided, pathological Americans who believe in Communism endangers our democracy by its writings or speeches or parades. Let them talk.

What we mean is that the real issue is how to make democracy more pure, more spiritual, and more effective in allowing every individual to achieve the full flower of his personality without fear. Individualism should depend not on how much you have, but on what you are; not on property, but on personality. It is this kind of democratic individualism that will kill Communist dictatorship.

MODERATOR DENNY: Thank you, Mr. Fischer. Congressman Velde was an FBI agent before he got into Congress, so he is in a very appropriate position to comment on what Mr. Fischer has just said.

CONGRESSMAN VELDE: Well, Mr. Fischer, I think I can generally agree with your position as far as Communism in foreign fields is concerned, but I certainly cannot agree with your ideas about fighting Communism here at home. If we remember some of the cases that have been tried recently—if we remember, for instance, what was contained in the confessions of Julian Wadleigh, Elizabeth Bentley, and Whittaker Chambers and what the evidence produced in the trials of Alger Hiss, Judy Coplon, Valentin Gubitchev, and the eleven Communists; and if we remember the facts of the espionage cases of Klaus Fuchs and Harry Gold—we'll certainly realize that it's more of a problem here in this country than can be handled properly with milk and honey.

Certainly not all these people that I mentioned can be called misguided pathological Americans. We're going to have to do something more. We're going to have to have laws to handle this problem here in America. And more than that, my friend, we're going to have to have enforcement of those laws, and strict enforcement.

MR. DENNY: Thank you, Congressman Velde. Mr. Fischer.

MR. FISCHER: Congressman, don't you contradict yourself? You said that Hiss and Wadleigh and the others had been prosecuted, and the eleven Communists have been put on trial and sentenced. In other words, we had laws to deal with these things, and we are making other laws. And I believe in those laws, and I believe in having the FBI; but I also believe that democracy, in combating Communism, in combating dictatorial means, must remain democratic. We must not lose our democracy in fighting for democracy.

And now, Congressman, I'd like to put a question to you. You may have noticed that I like to hit straight from the shoulder, and I don't like to beat around the bush. Now, you made a reference to our need of political leaders that are not chained to Communist dictators, and by implication you suggested that there were such people in our present government. Now, is that so, and would you name them?

CONGRESSMAN VELDE: No, I certainly do not care to name any of the Communists in our present government at the present time. I will say, however, for your benefit, Mr. Fischer, that the Un-American Activities Committee is making an investigation at the present time, and I'm sure that there will be a finding of Communism in the State Department, but until we find those facts definitely, we certainly will not reveal the names of any Communists.

And furthermore, I would like to comment just a minute on your statement in reference to me. Mr. J. Edgar Hoover, I think it was, once said that every Communist in this country is a potential saboteur and a potential espionage agent. Now, once upon a time, Alger Hiss and some of the others that I mentioned a while ago were just mere, ordinary, everyday Communists, but look what's become of them.

MR. DENNY: All right, Mr. Fischer.

MR. FISCHER: I want to come back to this question. You said that we must get rid of Communists in our political leadership. Now do you mean that there are Communists who are heads of departments in our government, who are perhaps secretaries?

CONGRESSMAN VELDE: As I said before, I don't care to comment on that until we've made a complete investigation and ascertained all the facts relative to it. I claim that anybody who is employed by the federal government and who is a Communist is dangerous, whether he is in a position of high political power or low political power.

How Communists Make Converts
Benjamin Gitlow

Benjamin Gitlow was born in Elizabethport, New Jersey in 1891. He is the former secretary of the American Communist Party and was twice the

Benjamin Gitlow

party candidate for Vice-President of the United States and once the candidate for Mayor of New York City. He was expelled from the Communist Party of the U.S. and the Communist International "for defiance of Stalin."

On 24 April 1951 Mr. Gitlow testified in Washington before the Subversive Activities Control Board in effect that as early as 1921 and to the present there has been an unbroken continuity of Soviet domination of the Communist Party in the United States. The hearings were designed to discover whether the Communist Party members in the United States should be forced to register under the terms of the 1950 Internal Security Act.

Mr. Gitlow spent three years (1919-21) in Sing Sing and Dannemora Prisons in New York on a five-year conviction of criminal anarchy. Before he was pardoned, while still in prison, he was elected an honorary member of the Moscow Soviet.

The address was delivered before the Economic Club of Detroit at the Book-Cadillac Hotel on 11 December 1950. Only the second half of the text is published here.

COMMUNIST AGGRESSION didn't begin with rifles and tanks and bombs. Communist aggression began with ideas, the ideas directed to the mind. It started as an attack upon the mind by Communist ideas. When those ideas penetrated and Communism gained influence, when Communism overcame resistance to its ideas, then came the tanks, the guns, the brutality, the violence, the bloodshed and war which are attributes of Communism.

We therefore notice, as a result of the persistent efforts of the Communists in the field of ideas, a degeneracy in American intellectual life, with the result that in intellectual fields and on the cultural front, the Communists have made tremendous progress. I am often asked the question: "How does it come that people who have a college education—professors and intellectuals, who know how to read and think—are attracted in such large numbers to the Communist Party?" I think responsible for that are a number of factors. One is that we in the United States were so busy carrying on business and making money that we never gave serious consideration to the question of ideas and their importance in our make-up. Second, we were caught in the depression of 1929 and the early thirties—a depression which played havoc with the middle classes in the United States, particularly with the intellectuals, who suddenly discovered that the very basis of existence was taken from under them. During the great depression the Communists were able to attract large numbers of individuals on the claim that they were the only organization that had a way out of the depression, that wanted and intended to do something for the underdog. The intellectuals who were imbued with the Communist philosophy, whose whole outlook on life was changed, the overwhelming majority of them continue to be valiant supporters and strong props to the Communist movement. The Communists always made and continue to make a special effort to attract intellectuals into their camp. Though they proclaim themselves as a working-class movement, and make their major appeal to the workers in the country, the leadership of the Communist movement comes not from the ranks of the working class but from the ranks of the intellectuals. The intellectuals are attracted first on the idealistic appeal. Then they are transformed into Communists and pivoted into positions of leadership. They are early given positions of importance and recognition in the movement and soon become the outstanding champions and effective leaders of Communism in America.

Then again, Communism in recent years has been helped by the unprincipled and shameless opportunism of a large section of American political life. Many of our politicians curried the favor of Communists because it meant getting additional votes. We had a national administration that did not reject Communist support, but instead welcomed Communists into the administration and into the government. The results are only now beginning to be felt. Politicians, who should know the traitorous roles of Communism, up to this very date are ready to do business on the political field with the Communists, thus greatly contributing to the influence and strength of the Communists. We had a demonstration recently in Detroit, at a Democratic district convention which is part of the same picture of political unprincipledness that plays right into the hands of the Communists. Walter Reuther, head of the auto workers' union, took it upon himself with the aid of his "goon squad" to nullify the will of the democratic process regarding enrolled Democrats and their delegates in this section of the State of Michigan. He took over by force and in violation of the election law, a Democratic Party convention so he could nominate his own personal nominees. That was a defiance of our democracy by using Communist tactics that destroy the very foundations of our political structure. Using force and gangster methods to eject duly elected delegates to a district convention was a tremendous disservice to America and a great aid to Communism. In no other way can we characterize this high-handed action of Reuther and his trade-union machine.

Apropos the question of the politicians who have trucked favor with the Communists, with the result that many Americans were attracted to the Communist movement, I can only mention briefly the role of Henry Wallace in the organization of the Progressive Party, and his support of Soviet international policies; the role of Harold Ickes, who wrote an article in the *New Republic* suggesting that we erect a monument to Agnes Smedley, a Soviet spy and traitor to the United States; and the associations and relations of the Roosevelt family with known Communists and Communist fellow travelers in the United States. It was all part of a pattern which confused the American people. It enabled the Communists to use support of most distinguished Americans to approach good Americans from one end of the country to the other, and to attract them and to enroll them in the Communist Party.

Let us now turn to our schools and colleges. I'm not going to deal with the theater, with the motion picture, with the radio field—all the elements used in the cultural approach to the American people. How does it come that in the schools and colleges there is such a misunderstanding of the Communist issue? How does it come about that in the schools and universities of our country the Communists have made such headway? How can we account for the fact that so many professors and distinguished professors in our leading universities have been drawn into Communist-front movements, and have aided Communist causes year in and year out? I have here the record. I want to read it to you. It makes an amazing story. Yale University—35 professors: 157 affiliations with 82 Communist fronts. University of California, Stanford University, and California Institute of Technology. What is the result? University of California—33 professors: 126 affiliations with Communist-front organizations. Stanford University—22 professors: 104 affiliations with Communist-front organizations. California Institute of Technology—5 professors: 32 Communist-front affiliations—and from that university a couple of atomic spies have been arrested and indicted. We go to the University of Chicago—60 professors: 133 Communist-front affiliations. Harvard University—76 professors: 124 Communist-front affiliations. Columbia University—87 professors: 589 affiliations with 229 various Communist fronts. That tells a story. Then you wonder why, when your son and daughter return from a university, you find no common ground with your son and daughter? The answer is obvious. Because of the Communist infiltration of our schools of higher learning Communism has exerted a marked influence on the intellectual life of America.

Let us now proceed to the question of religion. The Communists are atheistic. They claim that religion is the opium of the people. Nevertheless, they infiltrate religious institutions, regardless of their denominations. On the religious field the Communists conduct an anti-Catholic campaign—trying to arouse the Protestants against the Catholics. They conduct a campaign against racial and religious discrimination in the United States. They want to get the Jews into a position where they believe that every anti-Communist is an anti-Semite. Nevertheless, in the Soviet Union, the government as such—the Communist government—has destroyed all vestiges of Jewish cultural life, and in recent months has engaged in the deportation of Jewish families from their homes on the Western borders of Russia to the wastelands of the North and to Siberia.

The whole attitude of Communism in Russia is directed against the Jewish masses. Nevertheless, in the United States they carry on, for the express purpose of creating divisions in our population, a campaign, the purpose of which is to instill a belief that we are a disunited people, motivated by prejudices, a people so intolerant that we are ready to fly at one another's throats.

The Communists seek converts on the basis of civil rights. But if the Communists get power, there will be no civil rights. Are there civil rights in Russia? None whatever. Can you publish a newspaper in Russia? Not at all. Only the government—the Communists—have that right. Can you hold a meeting in Poland of a group in opposition to the government? You can't. Only the Communists can hold meetings in Poland. The Communists, if they get control in the United States, will throw the Bill of Rights into the ashcan, will impose a Communist dictatorship, will take over all the newspapers, all the radio stations, all avenues of public information, and convert them into a monopoly in the hands of the Communists.

Finally, the Communists seek their most important recruits in the basic mass-production industries of our country. In the Manual on Organization the Communists say, "We must concentrate in the basic industries." These are the industries that produce steel, have control of the means of transportation, power, oil, the natural resources and chemicals of our country. Why do the Communists seek to enroll the masses of workers in the basic industries into their organization? Because that gives them economic power—the power economically to cripple our country in an emergency. They, at the present time, in the United States are not interested in providing for the welfare of our community. What they want to grasp in their hands is that domination of the trade unions in the basic industries that will give them the power to stop the wheels of industry from moving, and to cripple our economic life.

They have shown that in control of C.I.O. unions in the past. Particularly in the city of Detroit were they able to do that. If they succeed in their major plan for domination of the trade unions, they will have a weapon of great power against the United States.

Communism must not be underestimated in this country. I know a lot of you will say: "What is this man talking about? We never meet up with a Communist. The Communists are few in numbers in the United States. Why should we worry about the Communists? We have a job to do. We have our businesses to take care of." I want to ask you a simple question. Czechoslovakia was a democracy. They had private enterprise in Czechoslovakia. I met many Czechs. They looked just like you do. They operated big businesses. Where are these Czech businessmen today? What firms do they represent? Can you conceive of a meeting of this kind, attended by Czech businessmen in Prague? Impossible. What happened to the businessmen and the business executives in Poland? Where are they at the present time? What happened to the industrial giants of Czarist Russia? Where are they today? What happened in Communist China? Where are the Chinese businessmen? Where are the Chinese industrialists? How many representatives of American business have we in China today, where we did good business with China years ago? Why? Because—wherever Communism gains the upper hand, there everyone and everything connected with free enterprise and a free system disappears from the scene. Even were I to grant that the Communist Party in the United States today is not numerically strong, nevertheless, that Communist Party is part of a world-wide organization—an organization backed up by the power of a great nation, with a population of millions, with a mighty army. The American Communists can afford to wait, particularly until situations are developed that will make it possible for the Communist Party in the United States to grow by leaps and bounds and to challenge Americans for the rule of their own country.

If you examine the sweep of Communism historically you have to admit that never in history has a force gained in so short a time such extensive dominion over large sections of the globe. Thirty-three years' time: Stalin the Communist chieftain dominates a large portion of Europe and Asia. You know the old saying: "Nothing succeeds like success." The success of Communism has an attractive power right here in the United States. There are many in America who are anxious for power, for an opportunity to rule, who see in the colossus that is sweeping over the world an opportunity to satisfy their ambition for rule and power. Many who today profess their loyalty to America and its ideals may in the future be the instruments for sweeping Communism into power in America.

You will say: What can we do to combat this Communist menace? Well, I would say that if I was delivering this talk twenty years ago I could map out an educational program and an organizational program that would suffice to counter the inroads of Communism in America. But the time is too late. We're not in that kind of a situation today. Civilization hangs in the balance. We are at the turning point of history. We have to meet a menace that marches with the boots of militarism—immediately. We can't adopt a long-time program of careful prodding and work to meet the Communist issue.

Something happened in Asia. We lost a continent to Communism. We woke up one day and found that 450 million Chinamen were under a Communist dictatorship. By looking into the question a little further we find that our Communist enemy, who is determined to destroy us in order to gain dominion over the world, now covers a land area—a continuous land area—of 12½ million square miles. The United States controls a land area of 3,700,000 square miles. Communism has under subjection in Europe and Asia a population of 800 million people, unlimited manpower to pit against the United States. We thought we had the North Koreans licked, and we discovered on the Manchurian border the legions of Communism, one million strong, arrayed against us—and in back of that million there are millions more. This land mass covers the world's richest territory—a territory rich in all kinds of resources—giving the Communist overlords access to raw materials and labor power by which they can build up the mightiest military machine in the world.

They have more. The Communists have a fifth column: members of the Communist Party outside the Soviet Union. How many members have we in the Communist fifth column—in America? In Latin America? In Africa? In Asia? In Europe? There are 18 million members of the Communist Party. The Communist Party in Italy has close to 5 million members and controls the trade unions, and no man can work in Italy unless the Communist Party gives him the O.K. that he can go to work. They have the economic power in their hands in Italy. The same is true of France. Here is a tremendous fifth column at the disposal of the Communist Party.

What is its military strength? Let me give you a few figures on the military strength of the Communist Party. In China, 4,500,000 troops; North Korea, 150,000 troops; Indo-China—guerrillas—75,000; Japan, unknown numbers of Communists—the figure is unknown; the Philippines, 10,000 Communist guerrillas; on the Russian border of China, 27 Russian divisions, fully armed, 5,250 first-rate planes; in Europe, close to 6 million Chinese under arms—and the British report that by 1954 the Soviet Army will have a man pool of from 12 million to 13 million soldiers. That is a force that must be reckoned with.

Can we defeat this force with the atom bomb? We cannot. In order to defeat Communism we have to meet the Communist ideas and Communist psychological warfare with our ideas and our psychological warfare techniques. General Eisenhower was absolutely correct when he stated that in a war against Communism we cannot win by military action alone; that our armies in Russia would be bogged down in the mud and climate of Russia; that we didn't have the manpower through military action alone to invade, to occupy, and to conquer Russia. Nevertheless, the Russians are determined to destroy us. They hold that war between us and the Communist regime is inevitable; that between the two conflicting systems of society there is no compromise possible. And they are working day and night, organizing every way possible, for the eventual struggle of the two systems—the world of Communist slavery, and the democratic world of freedom, represented by the United States. They are feverishly preparing for the gigantic global war—a war that will determine what system of society, what set of ideas, and what philosophy, what spirit, is going to dominate the world.

We've made a lot of errors in dealing with world Communism. We made errors because our politicians didn't have the time, or were opposed, to finding out the true nature of Communism. Our policies on the international field were motivated not by an objective understanding of the situation but by the well-wishes of those responsible for our policy, and by a conscious support of the interests of Communism in Europe, in the Near East, and particularly in Asia. At the end of World War II—in a war in which we adopted a set of principles, moral principles—in the Atlantic Charter we violated those principles. We got rid of one tyrant, Hitler; then we threw into the arms of a worse tyrant, a more diabolical force, millions of people who looked up to us for freedom; and for these violations of principle, for this abandonment of moral issues, we in the United States will have to pay dearly with our own blood, and we're beginning to pay dearly at the present time.

What must we do to overcome the Communist menace? The first thing we must do is to overcome our ignorance of Communism. Communism is a complex problem. It is a new factor in world politics, and we have to deal with it in an entirely new fashion. Since we are facing a formidable enemy, who is set upon our destruction, we have no room in the United States for Communists; we must permit no toleration of Communist fellow travelers; and we must root out all Communist infiltration in our government. Finally, we must rekindle a faith in American ideals. We must renew our understanding of the foundation upon which American freedom and the American system rests. And in a situation where gangster methods prevail in international affairs, the United States, which is the only country that has the resources, the wealth, and the technical ability to save mankind—the United States, which has spent billions in defense of civilization—must act resolutely and courageously. It is about time that Uncle Sam stands on his two feet, acts like a lion and not like a mouse.

In Korea we cannot tolerate appeasement. Acceptance of the terms of Attlee for the appeasement of China and the giving up of Formosa would play right in the hands of Stalin. We must prevent Stalin and his Communist hordes from ensnaring us into situations, particularly in Asia, that become bleeding operations to weaken the American people. We need a change in our foreign policies. We must eliminate from our government the advocates of appeasement, those who support Soviet policy. We must pursue a firm, courageous policy on behalf of America.

In conclusion, I think we have to start with America in meeting the Communist issue. It is impossible for us to put our destiny completely in the hands of a world organization made up of bankrupt nations that live on our support. These nations, cowardly and hesitant in the face of the Communist danger, attempt to hamstring us with policies which weaken us, undermine our national will and security and prevent us from pursuing a course that will save America, and through the saving of America, save the entire world.

I think we have something to offer the world. I have been to Europe in 1949, and also in the Near East. There is no country on the face of the earth that has so much at stake as the United States. We have in our short history, through our system, demonstrated that we could overcome crises and provide the best well-being for the largest numbers of our population. We have always been a progressive and a dynamic nation. That doesn't mean that everything in the United States is perfect, that there is no room for improvement. There is, however, no room for complacency at the present time. Only by defeating Communism can we open up new horizons for America, achieve peace, and make progress in the betterment of mankind.

The United States, Russia, and the Atomic Bomb

Frederick Osborn

Frederick Osborn is a native New Yorker, born in 1889. Following his graduation from Princeton in 1910, he began a career in business management. During World War I, he was vice-president in charge of traffic and treasurer of the Detroit, Toledo, and Ironton Railroad. From 1921 to 1938 he was a partner in a New York banking firm. In the Second World War he headed the Morale Branch of the Army and later became director of the Information and Education division, serving until 1945 with the rank of Major General. He was appointed deputy representative of the United States to the U.N. Atomic Energy Commission in 1947.

When Mr. Osborn spoke in Detroit on 8 January 1951 before the Economic Club, he was introduced by James W. Parker, president of the Detroit Edison Company and former chairman of the Industrial Advisory Group of the United States Atomic Energy Commission. Mr. Parker said: "I think you will agree with me that here is a man who brought to the tasks he will now tell us of an unusual education and preparation. He is a man of uncommon intellectual stature—and if I may be pardoned this personality—a man of uncommon physique. This is important, gentlemen, considering the fact that facing up to the potentialities of atomic energy release makes almost unprecedented demands upon a man's physical as well as his moral and mental stamina."

The text that is reprinted below is the main part of the speech given by Mr. Osborn in Detroit. He also answered a number of questions from the audience and expressed his belief that, "for the first time in five years," in the event of a Russian attack "we have at least a good fighting chance. A year or two from now it may be better still. But for the first time I feel somewhat comfortable and relieved."

WHEN MR. BARUCH went in as United States representative on the Atomic Energy Commission of the United Nations, at their very first session he proposed that the discussions of the committee should be based on the points of the plan which he laid out, under which all atomic energy installations which were dangerous, and all dangerous materials, would be taken over by an international agency, as our chairman has said, and would be operated by that agency for the benefit of all the nations participating. And, of course, all nations would be prohibited from making atomic weapons; but, they also would be prohibited from making atomic materials, so that they would be entirely out of that field.

When the Russians spoke they proposed what must have been a very carefully considered plan on their part, namely, that all nations should immediately sign a covenant agreeing that they would cease making atomic weapons and never use atomic weapons. That didn't seem to the majority of the Commission very much of a proposal. Here was a weapon which in the hands of any group of men, if nobody else had it, could control the world and the Russians were proposing blandly to go ahead and make atomic materials and simply prohibit their use as weapons.

The Commission adopted the Baruch proposals as the basis for its work. They put them together in the form of a report, and on the end of December of that year, 1946, approved them by a large majority. During this period there were a number of committees working, and one of them was a scientific committee, composed of scientists from all the major countries. They were an eminent group of men and a very fine group of men. The Russian representative was Dr. Alexandroff. Dr. Alexandroff was a well-known physicist of world-wide reputation, quite a friend of a great many of the other physicists on the committee. This subcommittee of scientists was asked, among other things, to report on whether there was any way of controlling atomic energy, unless the dangerous large plants were actually owned and managed by an international agency. In other words, would inspection be enough to assure that explosive materials weren't being stolen?

The committee studied this question while the General Assembly was in session and Mr. Gromyko and Mr. Vishinsky were very much engaged in the General Assembly and apparently didn't watch their delegation because, in the haste to get the report of the Atomic Energy Commission out, the committee reported, and reported unanimously, with the signatures of all these scientists, including that of Dr. Alexandroff, that the only way that atomic energy could be controlled would be to put the dangerous facilities in the actual operating hands of an international agency, and that inspection would not be enough. This report was signed and turned in to the Commission and there was to be a meeting of the Commission the next day. Dr. Alexandroff became sick during the night and was unable to attend the meeting of the Commission. And Dr. Alexandroff remained so sick that he never was able to attend another meeting of the Commission and had to go back to Russia, where he has been so sick ever since that he has never been heard from, by any of his international physicist friends.

That was my introduction to the Atomic Energy Commission. I took Mr. Baruch's place shortly afterwards and we were charged then with taking the general principles of the first report, which the Russians had not vetoed—they had simply abstained from voting—and whipping those general principles into a real, detailed formula for setting up such an international agency, and assigning quotas to the various nations, arranging for judicial reviews, and that sort of thing. We started to work very seriously on this program. We had been at it a couple of weeks when the Russians came in with a series of amendments to the first report. Now, the first report had been adopted by a vote of all of the nations concerned, except the Russians, who had abstained, and their satellite, who had abstained. It didn't seem appropriate to go back and rework the first report. The amendments looked pretty good at first. They didn't look as if they meant very much. Maybe there were language difficulties. But they were beautifully drawn amendments, and as we studied them—and I have been restudying them recently for an article I've been working on—these amendments took all of the life out of the plan which had been adopted in the first report of the Commission, and put it back exactly on the basis the Russians had first proposed, namely, that there should be a prohibition of atomic weapons and no control over them. And each of these amendments was designed to do that, without giving itself away.

I was hopeful that with good will and patience we would be able to come to some understanding. Certainly it looked as if that would be sensible and reasonable on the part of the Russians. But as the debate went on I was struck with a number of things. In the first place, while the Russians debated and supported these amendments, they didn't tell the truth about them. In fact, it didn't seem that telling the truth was a part of their way of doing business. After a while I realized that these fellows were professionally trained not to tell the truth. They were trained solely to try and confuse the issue.

It seemed to me—and I have since by the work of a group of sociologists, who have divided up the actual time spent in the Commission meetings, ascertained that my first views were correct—that the Russian delegates spent one-half of all of the time spent talking, and the other ten delegates spent the other half. That is the way the time was divided. If you divide the speeches by subject matter, 20 per cent of the time of the Russian delegates was spent in questioning the motives of the other delegates. None of the other delegates are on record as having questioned the motives of the Soviet delegate at any time. That wasn't their idea of how to handle things.

The United States, Russia, and the Atomic Bomb

These Soviet speeches were extraordinary. These speeches were about the control of the United States by a small group of conspirators in Wall Street. As I have a lot of friends in Wall Street, and know the extent to which they wished they had a little more influence to affect things that go on in Washington, I was always amused by these statements of the control of the United States by a small group of conspirators in Wall Street. And then onto that, the control of this same group over all the other countries which voted with the United States, with never the glimpse of an admission that it was the behavior of the Soviet which was making the other countries vote with the United States. These speeches were in a form. They had a regular set way of making them. I have no doubt that those forms were learned by heart in Communist schools for diplomats, because they never varied.

I was amused last month, during the session of the General Assembly, to read in the newspaper a speech by Vishinsky which I knew almost by heart because I had listened to it so often in the mouths of Gromyko and Vishinsky three years ago. The same speech. The same proposals. They did this endlessly.

In this same study which we made, of what the discussions on atomic energy were like, the other delegates spent some 40 per cent of their speaking time in discussing the proposals and saying why a proposal should be made in this way, and why such and such a control should be set up. The Russians spent about 2 per cent of their time discussing the proposals.

There were some very amusing aspects to these debates. The new Russian scientist was a man named Dr. Skobeltzyn. Dr. Skobeltzyn was an elderly man who had lived in France and taught there for some years, a physicist of the old regime. He was not in good health. His heart was bad and often he had to lie down after meetings of the Commission. The poor fellow was sick, and his wife was sick. The first year we worked very long hours, through a very hot summer—late in the evening, often. We were all very tired. Skobeltzyn came to me in the middle of August and said, "Mr. Osborn, don't you think we could get a little vacation? The Security Council is taking two weeks off; why couldn't we finish our work and get a little vacation?" I said, "Fine, it would certainly suit me. We have really finished our work." Skobeltzyn came after me two or three times on this and finally I said, "Well now, Dr. Skobeltzyn, if you would like me to, I would be very glad to propose to the Commission that we close the debate and finish our work because it's all finished. Everybody knows that, and we might as well vote it. We have two weeks vacation." He said, "That would mean so much to me. My wife is sick and we have been asked to go to the mountains. It would be wonderful if we could go. That would be very nice, Mr. Osborn." So at the next meeting of the Commission the next day I got up and I said that I thought at last I had a proposal which we could get unanimous agreement on: that if we could finish the debate in the next three days, the Commission could adjourn for two weeks while the Security Council was adjourned, and we could have a vacation. Gromyko leaped to his feet and he said, "Here is a typical proposal of the warmongers of Wall Street, who control the destinies of the people of the United States. They propose to stop this work for the people. They propose to allow atomic energy to remain in the hands of Wall Street to hold as a threat. They propose to stop." And so on, and so on. "The Russians will never give up. We will sit here and work on this problem until we have reached a solution." Poor old Skobeltzyn was sunk down in his chair looking awful beaten. I guess he had told Gromyko about this and Gromyko was all ready for me, so I withdrew my proposal. Afterwards, it was several days before Skobeltzyn had gotten his nerve up to come and speak to me about his mistake. I think he was quite sincere. He really thought that maybe he could get a vacation.

One of the very extraordinary things the Soviet delegates did in the Commission, and did consistently, and still do, in every meeting of the General Assembly, is to antagonize, apparently intentionally, anybody who opposes them in any way—especially the smaller nations, and this has always been a great puzzle to me. There are many examples. When we went to the General Assembly in Paris to get a vote on the second report of the Atomic Energy Commission, Mr. Ramadier took over from the very able French representative, and Mr. Rolin, who was a Senator in Belgium, and an important political figure, took over from the able Belgian representative. Both Mr. Rolin and Mr. Ramadier wanted to make a move towards a compromise. They hadn't been through this thing. They didn't know it very well. It all happened rather suddenly. Both the French and the Belgian delegates were much disturbed. They said these were great men but they don't know the subject, and they are going to make compromising speeches which may be very embarrassing. These fine elderly men got up and made beautiful pleas for a compromise and said they would be willing for their countries to compromise. That the position of the Russians was stiff, and the position of the United States stiff, and that we must find some middle ground. My heart sank. I thought, "Now, we're going to be in trouble, because if the Russians are smart they will accept this proposal.

They will say, 'See, we told you the United States was taking too stiff a position.' And then they will handle it in such a way as to put us in the wrong and yet offer us an impossible proposition." Vishinsky asked for the floor immediately and he said, "I am accustomed to the enmity of men like Cadogan and Austin, who represent the enemies of the peoples of the world, and I can stand it because that is an honest fight, but what I despise are these sycophantic followers of the warmongers of Wall Street, who come from little countries and have no position in the world, and make suggestions at the request of the powers who control them." Rolin and Ramadier came to me after this, both red with anger. They said, "Mr. Osborn, we didn't know what you have been up against in the last year and we certainly are voting with the United States." Why was that? What sense did it make? In the following session, a year later, of the Assembly, there was a very fine representative from Lebanon and he made a mistaken proposal for compromise. In fact, it was a very dangerous proposal. But it was done with the best intentions and with great sincerity—a very fine man. Vishinsky again got up and attacked this poor little fellow from Lebanon for being a follower of the warmongers and proposing a compromise. I never have understood. Even without that, these delegates in the small countries, who are a fine group of people, finer representatives perhaps than any of you would expect unless you worked with them, have inevitably been drawn closer together by the intransigence of the Soviet delegates. Working with these men for three years one has a sense of unity and solidarity and friendship and mutual respect which is hopeful and very inspiring. Some of the best friends I have are men from countries that you wouldn't expect to send representatives with whom you could have that kind of a friendship. I won't go through the list. I'm thinking particularly perhaps of Fawzi Bey of Egypt, a very sincere and a very fine man that you could always count on to do the honest, square, decent, and intelligent thing—and many others from the Arab states. For all their anger at our behavior about Palestine, and they were very angry, and you can quite understand that, you still felt—and they told you constantly—the basic solidarity they had with the West, because they said, "Somehow we can get along with the United States and England. We can't get along with Russia. If Russia should ever come in, there would be no Arab states."

We were able to reach no solution with the Soviet Union. If this arrangement, this agreement for an international agency, had been entered into with a country whose rulers were still determined to subvert all other governments and take control of all other governments, it would have been, I suppose, impossible to make the agreement work. And this thing that we're working with represents too great a danger to mankind to make a false step with. The atomic bomb and the strategic bomber which carried it represent the culmination of the development of weapons. And it is a very strange and frightening culmination. The knight in armor on horseback for some time was the equal of many foot soldiers and struck terror into the men on foot. The English developed the bow and arrow and its wide use, and every ordinary man on foot could learn to shoot a bow and arrow, and they defeated the armed knights of Europe. And the musket and rifle are the weapons of the common man. The American farmer with a musket in his hands was a better soldier than the trained British Redcoat. But then the machine gun came and one man with a machine gun could hold off a hundred men with rifles. That was the beginning of this series of weapons which are terribly expensive and terribly powerful, and of which the strategic bomber and the atomic bomb, and perhaps later the hydrogen bomb, are the culmination. And if those weapons ever should get into the hands of an aggressive group of dictators, when nobody else had them, those men could rule the world for as long as they stuck together, without any possibility of revolt anywhere, so long as they were tough enough. And I tell you that we have seen Hitler, and we have seen Stalin, and there are men tough enough to control the world by that means. And they wouldn't have to send a policeman to Detroit. They would say to Detroit: "You will do so and so." They would say it to them from Moscow. They could say to Detroit: "If you don't do it there won't be any Detroit"—if they had a monopoly of these weapons.

Now, as long as the world is constituted as it is—I say the "world" meaning all the world's peoples—that makes for a dreadfully dangerous situation, because the world is in an extraordinary shape. A little group of people—originally only 60 million Europeans—started about 400 years ago and made this extraordinary advance, which we call civilization. I suppose it is. It has extended the life of man to an average expectancy of 70 years. It has given us a security such as mankind has never known before; physical well being and health; material things in great quantity; medicine; education for the masses; and all these other things which we enjoy. That advance is still solely limited to this little group of originally 60 million Europeans, and now some 400 million people of European descent. And the advance hasn't touched the rest of the world's people. They are still on the margin of starvation. They are still wholly without possessions. Now, I'm talking about the great mass of the other billion six or eight hundred thousand people: the Indians of South America, the Africans of Africa, the mass of the people of India, the mass of the people of China, and so on. They are wholly without education. Most of them are on the verge of being without food. They have only the clothes they wear on their backs. And in this world are this group of people of European descent who are wealthy beyond the imagining of the rest of the world; and the American and Canadian groups, who are twice as wealthy as those still living in Western Europe. Naturally, the peoples of the world are jealous of us, and naturally that jealousy can easily be turned into hatred by an aggressive group of dictators. That is just the situation we have today. The men in the Kremlin are spending all their energies, with a cunning and a thoroughness beyond our conception, to teach these people to hate us— and they already control not very far from half the people of the world, who are not allowed to hear anything else. So, it is a plenty dangerous world for us, and it will be for a long time to come because while the Kremlin dictatorship is probably the most dangerous that we'll ever know, the best trained and the most subtle, there will be other dictatorships in other countries, and the dictators will always hate the United States. They will hate it, not for its wealth but for its revolutionary doctrines because, after all, this is the country of the revolution. The Soviet leaders long ago betrayed the revolution which was meant to be for the benefit of mankind—and betrayed it immediately they came in power because their purpose was always to retain themselves in power, rather than to advance the revolution. And they know that as long as the United States holds out the picture of what can be done for the common man by a government controlled by the people, the dictator is insecure. So the dictator has plenty of reason for hating us, and plenty of reason for his teaching his people that they must hate us.

The only people in the world who share our interests, our understanding, have the same Judeo-Christian ideals of life, have any experience of self-government, have any form of effective mass education, are our fellow Europeans. Now, these Europeans are stuck on the edge of the Eurasian land mass—the biggest piece of land in the world, which is occupied by about one billion eight hundred million people. They are quite easy to count up—the people who live on the Eurasian land mass: 400 million Chinese; 400 million Indians; 200 million Russians; 200 and something million Central Europeans; 250 million Western Europeans; you add up to a great deal more than half of the population of the world. The only people close to us are the Western Europeans on the edge of it. We have got to work with them. We have got to keep them in a separate, independent existence. I don't care whether we like them or not. I think the question of our liking or not is a question that is very similar to a family row—you row with your family but when somebody else comes along you side with your family. We've got to get along with them because if they should be taken over by the Soviet, the whole Eurasian land mass would go with them. In Western Europe there is one-quarter of the production of goods in the world. In the United States there is half of the world's production of goods. And in the Soviet Union—these are very general figures—there is one-quarter of the world's production of goods. Let the Soviet Union take over Western Europe and the Soviet Union will then control half of the world's production of goods. And in time of war that means war goods. And instead of having odds of three to one in our favor on production, we will be about even at the start on production, and probably falling behind quite rapidly.

And on manpower, where we are today the odds are somewhat in our favor: a little more than 50 per cent of the world's manpower is still among the free nations. If Europe is taken over, the Middle East will go with Europe inevitably, and the oil of the Middle East. And one by one the rest of the smaller nations on the Eurasian land mass, and then the preponderance of power will be against us.

I have always had great confidence in the United States, and I think we would go down fighting, but I don't believe that we would emerge victorious from a world war in which we controlled at the start just about half of the world's production and had a great deal less than half of the world's people on our side.

So, we have no alternative. We have no alternative today, in these dangerous days, but to go back to what has always been the instinctive self interest of the American people, and that is to adopt as our foreign policy, in its simplest terms, to coöperate with other freedom-loving, independent nations to maintain national independence against aggression. And in all our consideration of matters of foreign affairs, let's keep in mind that we're no longer big enough or strong enough to go it alone. And we must somehow manage to coöperate with those who, however weak, however punished in past wars, however in our minds mistaken in their utterances or behavior, nevertheless are the only people in the world who share our aspirations and our hopes for a decent world for humanity.

THE DEFENSE OF EUROPE

A Report to the Nation
General of the Army Dwight D. Eisenhower

This address was made by General Eisenhower to the American people by radio and television on 2 February 1951 after a month of intensive preparation in establishing the Supreme Headquarters Allied Powers Europe (SHAPE). During January 1951 he toured the countries which signed the North Atlantic Pact and, as Premier René Pleven of France said at the time, "he brought out the best in all of us, and thus gave substance to the idea of unification of effort."

The speech below is unique in that it was delivered apparently without notes or prepared manuscript. At least no text was visible to the television audience. Actually General Eisenhower read the speech from huge cards with sentences printed in large-size letters, and placed just behind the television cameras. The pace was rapid and the conversational quality and directness were remarkably good. The explanation of the method of delivery was made public after the address.

General Eisenhower was born in Denison, Texas in 1890, although he is now claimed as a Kansan because he spent his boyhood in Abilene, Kansas. He was graduated from West Point in the famous class of 1915 and during World War I served as a Lieutenant Colonel in the Tank Corps. Early in 1942 he was appointed Assistant Chief of Staff in the Operations Division of the War Department General Staff. On 8 November 1942 he was designated Allied Commander in Chief, North Africa. He became Commanding General, Allied Forces, European Theater of Operations on 31 December 1943. At the close of the war he served as Chief of Staff, United States Army and in February 1948 became President of Columbia University. He was recalled to active duty at the end of 1950. A temporary headquarters was quickly established at the Hotel Astoria in Paris and General Eisenhower began with great zeal the task of welding together a command structure for the armed forces of the United States and the countries of Western Europe. In 1952 he became a strong candidate for the Presidency.

In this speech, as Anne O'Hare McCormick writing in *The New York Times* for 3 February 1951 points out, "the voice of the soldier warned us that it is as much our business to stimulate faith and courage in countries where they are in short supply as it is to build up military force."

Fellow Americans:

As a soldier, I have been given an Allied assignment that directly concerns the security of the free world, with special reference to the countries bordering upon the North Atlantic Ocean. I have approached the task, aiming at the good of the United States of America, conscious that a strong, solvent America is the indispensable foundation for a free world. While I have reached certain conclusions, the subject of the free world's security is so vast and complex that no man could hope to master its elements to the last critical item or, in a quarter hour, to answer all questions in his fellow-citizens' minds. Consequently, though I speak to you out of deep conviction, I do so in all humility, trusting to your sympathetic consideration.

Our hope remains the achievement of peace based on understanding and forbearance, the only sure foundation for peace.

We must never lose faith that such a peace can be ultimately established. We seek such a peace and no one can honestly interpret our current modest preparations otherwise.

But we should examine the current situation fearlessly and clearly, neither shutting our eyes to obvious dangers nor permitting fear to warp our judgment. America's record and America's strength certainly should prevent hysterical apprehension of the future.

Today we are faced by an aggressive imperialism that has more than once announced its implacable hostility to free government. Therefore, we strive to erect a wall of security for the free world behind which free institutions can live. That wall must be maintained until Communistic imperialism dies of its own inherent evils.

One of the great questions before us is the will and capacity of Europe to coöperate effectively in this aim. Unless there exists in Europe a will to defend itself, no amount of outside help can possibly make it secure. A nation's defense must spring from its own soul; and the soul cannot be imported.

For years we have heard that Western Europe is plagued, confused, and divided far more seriously than we are; we have heard that in their homes, in factories, on the street, millions of honest workmen are daily subjected to Communist bullying; that their days and nights are haunted by the specter of invading hordes whom they cannot hope to equal in numbers or physical strength.

Furthermore, the discouragement, destruction, and confusion visited upon the peoples of Europe by two World Wars sapped their productive capacity and, in some instances, reduced them to levels of near-starvation. More than this—their spirit was smothered in war-weariness.

That is a story often told. If it were the whole story, then all I could honestly do would be to recommend that we abandon the NATO Treaty and—by ourselves—attempt, however futilely, to build a separate fortress against threatening aggression. Two striking facts make such a recommendation, for me, impossible.

The first fact is that the utter hopelessness of the alternative requires our participation in European defense. We can all understand that America must be strong in air and sea power. These elements are vitally essential to the defense of the free world and it is through them that we protect the approaches to our homeland and the routes of commerce necessary to our existence.

But this alone is not enough. Our ships will not long sail the seas, nor our planes fly the world airways, if we stand aside in fancied security while an aggressive imperialism sweeps over areas of the earth with which our own future is inseparably linked.

Western Europe is the cradle of our civilization; from her originally we drew our strength, genius, and culture. But our concern in Europe is far more than sentimental. Our own security is directly involved. Europe is a highly developed industrial complex with the largest and most varied pool of skilled labor on earth. This huge potential would be a rich prize for a totalitarian invasion. Its direct importance to us is the stark fact that its possession by Communistic forces would give them opportunity to develop a preponderance of power. Even this disaster would not tell the whole story.

If Western Europe should be overrun by Communism, many economically dependent areas in Africa and the Middle East would be affected by the debacle. Southeastern Asia would probably soon be lost. Thus, we would be cut off from the raw materials of all these regions—materials that we need for existence. World destiny would then be dictated by imperialistic powers whose avowed purpose is the destruction of freedom.

The second fact bearing upon our participation in European defense is that the people of Europe are not spiritually bankrupt, despite the validity of many pessimistic reports. Great sections of its population have for years labored on and fought the creeping paralysis of Communism. Now, the North Atlantic Treaty has brought new fuel to the flames of hope in Europe. It has noticeably lifted morale, the fundamental element in this whole situation—the force which powers all human progress.

In every capital, there is growing a desire to coöperate in this mutual security effort. All the governments that I have recently visited agreed that their defense programs must be stepped up despite economic and other difficulties—in spite of preoccupations that constitute abnormal drains upon particular nations. For example, France now wages a relentless and costly war against Communism in Indo-China. Britain, still existing on an austerity level, shoulders heavy burdens in Malaya. However much those nations may differ from us in their diplomatic thinking with respect to Asiatic states, there is no question concerning their solidarity in opposing Communistic aggression.

They and others on the continent are taking measures to effect substantial increases in their defense establishments. Within the past few days, Britain has stepped up drastically its rate of preparation. The new military service program in France bars all exemptions, of every kind whatsoever. The Norwegians impressed me with their unshakable determination that never again will they be victims of occupation. To them, a fighting resistance, even to their own destruction, is preferable. And in Italy, there are unmistakable signs of a stiffening courage and determination. The same is true of Belgium, Holland, Denmark, Portugal, Luxembourg, and Iceland.

In every country, I saw heartening evidence of a regeneration in Europe's spirit. Its morale, its will to fight, will grow with every accretion to physical strength. The arrival in Europe of new American land and air units, though modest in protective influence by themselves, will certainly produce added confidence and accelerate the production of military force throughout the member nations.

The European nations must, of course, produce and maintain the great bulk of the land forces necessary to their defense.

For this purpose the most immediate need of Europe is munitions and equipment. Every one of the continental nations I visited can rapidly and markedly increase its resistance power if it can be promptly furnished additional supplies of this kind. To fill this need, our loyal neighbor, Canada, with Britain and others, is shouldering part of the load.

In military potential, the free nations have everything they need—natural resources, industrial genius, productive capacity, and great reservoirs of leadership ability. Given the ingredient of morale—the determination to combine for mutual protection—the military strength necessary will be produced at a speedy pace. With every increase in strength, there will be an upward thrust in morale, resulting in an ever-mounting spiral of confidence and security.

With respect to time, no man can know at what hour, if ever, our defensive organization may be put to the ultimate test. Because our purpose is entirely defensive, we must be ready at the earliest possible moment. Only an aggressor could name the day and hour of attack. Our current mobilization, properly adjusted to our peaceful security needs, should be as rapid as any required by the emergency of war.

To you, the people of America, I repeat—as I have to the Congress and to the President—that I believe:

First, the preservation of free America requires our participation in the defense of Western Europe.

Second, success is attainable. Given unity in spirit and action, the job can be done.

Third, while the transfer to Europe of American military units is essential, our major and special contribution should be in the field of munitions and equipment.

By no means do I believe that we Americans can support the world militarily or economically. In our own interest, we must insist upon a working partnership with every nation making the common security its task of first priority. Every one of the member nations must realize that the success of this combined effort to preserve the peace rests as directly upon America's productive, economic, and political strength as it does on any amount of military force we can develop. Only coöperative effort by all of us can preserve for the free world a position of security, relative peace, and economic stability.

Attainment of this result is largely a matter of morale and the human spirit. The free world now must prove itself worthy of its own past.

If Frenchmen can rise to the heights their fathers achieved at Verdun in 1916; if Italians can recapture the fervor of Vittorio Veneto; if the British can relive the days of 1940 when they stood alone against Hitler; if our other Allies can react to today's threat in the mode of their own revered patriots; if we here in America can match the courage and self-sacrifice of the ragged, freezing members of Washington's Army at Valley Forge; indeed, if each of us now proves himself worthy of his countrymen fighting and dying in Korea, then success is sure—a glorious success that will bring us security, confidence, tranquillity.

Each of us must do his part. We cannot delay, nationally or individually, while we suspiciously scrutinize the sacrifices made by our neighbor, and through a weasling logic seek some way to avoid our own duties.

If we Americans seize the lead, we will preserve and be worthy of our own past. Our children will dwell in peace. They will dwell in freedom. They will read the history of this decade with tingling pride and, from their kinship with this generation, they will inherit more than can be expressed in millions, in acres, or in world acclaim.

It is not my place as a soldier to dwell upon the politics, the diplomacy, the particular treaty arrangements that must accompany and go forward with such an effort. But I do conceive it my duty to report from time to time, both to this government and to all others in the coalition, as to progress achieved. Thus our own and all other peoples may constantly review their decisions and plans—and, if necessary, revise them.

This evening, I come back to you only as one with some experience in war and peace, of some acquaintanceship with our friends of Western Europe, to bring you what is in my heart and mind. I shall go about my own task in this undertaking with the unshakable confidence that America will respond fully when the basic issues are understood. We know that 150 million united Americans constitute the greatest temporal force that has ever existed on God's earth. If we join in a common understanding of our country's role today and wholeheartedly devote ourselves to its discharge, the year 1951 may be recorded in our history in letters as bright as is written the year 1776.

A Statement
before the Senate Armed Forces Committee and the Senate Foreign Relations Committee
General of the Army George C. Marshall

A fortnight after General Eisenhower's address to the nation, on 15 February 1951, the Secretary of Defense, General George C. Marshall, testified as below to the two Senate committees considering the problem of military assistance to Western Europe.

General Marshall's reputation as a lucid and succinct pleader was established during World War II when he frequently presented the strategy of the war to congressional committees.

At the age of seventy and when he had for the second time returned to private life General Marshall was recalled to duty. In September 1950 he replaced Louis Johnson as Secretary of Defense. He had previously (1947-49) served as Secretary of State.

When General Marshall finally retired on 12 September 1951, President Truman called attention to "the tremendous strides that have been made, under your direct leadership, in establishing a sound basis for our military manpower and production program which has already increased our defensive strength." The President recalled that in all his varied assignments General Marshall "gave great talent and wisdom. In fact, no man ever has given his country more distinguished and patriotic service than have you."

IN REGARD TO the question under consideration this morning, it seems to me that fundamentally the real issue is what should we do, the United States, in our own self-interest as a nation.

Whatever we do in the way of giving military assistance to Western Europe naturally requires the wholehearted support of the nation. The trouble seems to be somewhat a state of confusion in the public mind, and for evident reasons, as to just what the situation is and, more specifically, what are the military necessities.

In one sense, this is not a new issue for you gentlemen to be discussing in this room because many of you considered much the same issue when the Senate Foreign Relations Committee was considering the Vandenberg Resolution, S.R. 239 of the 80th Congress.

Much the same issue also was before you a few months earlier when I was called to testify here in support of the European Recovery Program.

The action of the Senate in 1949 when it voted 82 to 13 in favor of the North Atlantic Treaty, and then 55 to 24 in favor of the Military Aid Program was, I took it to be, a confirmation of the view that the independence of the North Atlantic community of nations was of vital importance not only to the further development of free and democratic governments but also to the security of this country. To be more specific, in enacting the Military Aid Program, your committee added to the basic legislation a requirement that the bulk of the funds to carry out the program would not be available until there had been prepared and then approved by the President integrated plans for the defense of the North Atlantic area.

Since then there have been five meetings of the Defense Ministers of the North Atlantic Treaty Nations, at the fourth of which I presided. In addition, there have been numerous meetings of the military committee in which General Bradley represented the United States and a number of meetings of the North Atlantic Council at which the Secretary of State represented the United States. Further, the standing group consisting of one representative from the United Kingdom, one from France, and one from the United States—General Bradley representing this country—has been in almost daily session.

Out of all of these meetings has emerged, as Congress expressly stipulated, a plan for the integrated defense of the North Atlantic area—a plan which will succeed or will fail, depending upon two fundamental factors: first, the support which it receives from this country and the other nations associated with us; and second, the ability with which it is carried out by General Eisenhower and the staff he is now assembling. Regarding the second point, I am sure I am right in the belief that none of you have any misgivings. It is the first point to which your deliberations here appear to be addressed.

Please permit me to state the issue as I see it, in a rather different form. I assume that no one will differ from my belief that the United States will be safer—that is, more secure—if governments friendly to the United States are in power throughout the North Atlantic community. If this is correct, the question then resolves itself into the problem of how the nations of the North Atlantic community can best protect their independence. This is the problem to which the North Atlantic Treaty was addressed and it is the problem to which all of our discussions under that treaty have been addressed.

In my opinion, the course outlined by our planning is the logical one. We are building up in the United States and in each of the nations of the North Atlantic community stronger armed forces. We are not building up these stronger forces for any aggressive purpose, but in order to enable us to defend ourselves if we should be attacked. Also our aim is primarily to deter aggression if that be possible and to defeat aggression if, in spite of all our efforts, the actions of the Soviet Union or its satellites should precipitate another world war.

Fundamental to all of our efforts in this regard is the immediate start toward the creation in Western Europe of strong and integrated forces—land, sea, and air—in such proportions to one another as appear reasonable and practicable.

As General Eisenhower pointed out in his recent testimony here, the United States forces will constitute only a minor portion of these proposed integrated forces—the major portion being furnished by the Western European nations. This is particularly true in the matter of ground forces. Because of the great amount of discussion which has been centered on the subject of ground forces, I have obtained the express permission of the President to discuss with you the specific strength of the ground forces which the United States has planned to maintain in Europe in the present emergency.

I take this step reluctantly because of the security considerations involved—but I have reached the conclusion that there is a greater peril to our security through weakening the morale of our Allies by a debate based upon uncertainties, than there can possibly be through the public disclosure of our planned strength figures.

To be specific, the Joint Chiefs of Staff have recommended to me, and I have so recommended to the President—and the President has approved—a policy with respect to our forces in Europe which looks to the maintenance by us, in Europe, of approximately six divisions of ground forces.

We already have there, on occupation duty, about two divisions of ground forces. Our plans, based on the recommendation of the Joint Chiefs of Staff, therefore contemplate sending four additional divisions to Europe.

While this number does not appear to represent in pure fighting power a large contribution to the immediate defensive strength of Western Europe, it does represent a small Army unit of high efficiency and we believe a tremendous morale contribution to the effectiveness and build-up of the projected ground forces the North Atlantic Treaty nations are undertaking to develop under General Eisenhower's direction and command.

As President Truman pointed out in his announcement on September 9, 1950, "The basic element in the implementation of this decision is the degree to which our friends match our actions in this regard. Firm programs for the development of their forces will be expected to keep full step with dispatch of additional United States forces to Europe."

General Eisenhower outlined to you the responsibility which he possesses, and which he intends to exercise, to assure that all members of the North Atlantic Treaty contribute the maximum amount of strength which their geographic, economic, and manpower situations permit. In the key position to which he has been named at the request of the nations which make up the North Atlantic Treaty Organization, General Eisenhower will be in a position to insist that all members of the North Atlantic Treaty play their full parts in this vital undertaking.

Proportionately, the American contribution will be greater in air and in naval forces than in ground forces, for the greater strength of the United States is in the air and on the sea. Proportionately also, our contribution will be greater in the production of munitions than in the provision of manpower—for the industrial capacity of the United States is the greatest of any of the member nations of the North Atlantic Treaty.

In all that we are doing, as just outlined, we are specifically carrying out the instructions of the Congress with respect to the preparation, and the approval by the President, of integrated plans for the defense of the North Atlantic area. As a result of the various steps outlined earlier, these plans are now well advanced, and General Eisenhower as you know has assumed Supreme Command.

In order for him to succeed in this most difficult and critical of assignments, it is essential that he not be deprived of that freedom of action which is so necessary to a military commander. I realize, of course, that whenever this issue of flexibility is raised, some people will say, "If the fighting starts in Europe, the military commanders will be given complete freedom of action."

But what we want above everything else is something infinitely more important, namely, a certain freedom of action to establish a deterrent against the development of a general war.

Moving in an international setting in a military way is at best fraught with many and often great difficulties. We had them throughout the last World War but we successfully overcame the problems and proceeded to a victorious conclusion of the war. In this situation though, we have a far more delicate and more dangerous situation to deal with. The most important, the greatest factor in the creation of military strength for Western Europe in my opinion is the build-up of morale, of the will to defend—the determination to fight if that be necessary. And because of the events of the past few years and the increasing threat presented by the Soviet Union, we have an exceedingly difficult situation with which to deal, in the way of preparations which we hope will enable us to avoid war and will help us to take the necessary action, if war is thrust upon us. Under these conditions, having in mind the various measures which have been taken by the Senate in regard to the North Atlantic community, the fewer limitations you impose upon the military establishment the better off we will be. And incidentally I would say, gentlemen, that it is not a question today of having large bodies of troops ready to march down to the docks and embark for Europe. Our problem is the creation of troops. The limiting factor today, by far the most critical factor, is the long time yet required to do this.

Those of you who are members of the Armed Services Committee have been addressing yourselves to this problem for many weeks and I will therefore not repeat here what we are doing to achieve this build-up as rapidly as possible.

A Report from the President of France
Vincent Auriol

The text below is the translation of the address made by the President of France, Vincent Auriol, to Congress on 2 April 1951.

René Pleven, the then Premier of France, had preceded M. Auriol with a visit to the United States some weeks earlier. Speaking before the National Press Club in Washington on 30 January, M. Pleven asserted: "Really, if something is specially noteworthy in France today, it is the cold determination of a people who, having suffered two wars and an invasion, calmly face the present situation with all its responsibilities and dangers."

In this speech M. Auriol dealt directly with the two issues often debated in Congress on the question of more American aid to Europe. He met the charge that France and other European countries were not doing their share towards their own defense and the corollary argument that we should not give more aid until the countries themselves made greater contributions. He also argued that the United States should not hold back ground troops from Europe and permit the Russians to occupy the Continent while we in this country prepared gigantic air attacks designed to cripple Russian industrial centers.

M. Auriol, who was born at Revel, Haute Garonne, France in 1884, became the first President under the constitution of the Fourth Republic on 16 January 1947. He was elected to the Chamber of Deputies as a Socialist member for Muret in 1904 at the age of twenty and was regularly reëlected up to the fall of France in 1940. He protested against Marshal Petain's efforts to establish a dictatorship and for several months was imprisoned by the Vichy government. In October 1943 he escaped to England where he joined the Free French government. In November 1945 General de Gaulle appointed him a minister of state without portfolio.

The United Nations correspondent of *France Presse*, Louis Foy, has written an illuminating sketch, "Vincent Auriol: Fighting President" in the April 1951 issue of *United Nations World*.

Mr. President, Mr. Speaker, Senators and Members of Congress:

I am deeply moved by the exceptional honor you are rendering me in allowing me to appear before this assembly and to address you from this glorious rostrum. It will touch the heart of the people of France to whom, through me, this homage and this warm welcome are directed.

I am the more deeply moved that my visit is the first one made by a President of the French Republic, in the name of France to the Republic of the United States, and that it recalls to me two historic visits to our country made by two of your illustrious statesmen: Benjamin Franklin in 1776, and, a century and a half later, after the first World War, President Wilson.

It gives me an opportunity to pay tribute to your heroic young men who under the command of their glorious leaders twice rushed to our ravaged country to share with our own sons in the fight.

These memories illustrate our common history, and this history already long and always friendly is a history of freedom.

In recalling these memories in the presence of the Congress of the great American democracy, I want to express our constant and heartfelt sympathy to all the families whose sons have died for our common ideal and are resting forever in French soil, side by side with the sons of France and of the other Allied nations. Through you representing the forty-eight States of the union, I wish to tell the American people of our grateful and loyal friendship and of our unshakable attachment to the great human principles France has always proclaimed—principles embodied both in your Declaration of Independence and in our Declaration of the Rights of Man and of the Citizen, principles which, three years ago, after so many trials and contests, have received the unanimous consecration of the United Nations.

These sacred achievements of man which are not only the most precious values in our civilization but also the conditions for all future improvement, for all individual and social progress, are today threatened—we are sorrowfully obliged to admit this—only six years after our two peoples made sacrifices never before equaled in history, for the attainment and organization of a just and tranquil peace.

Confronted with this situation, far different from what we had wanted and expected, with our security threatened, any nation worthy of her freedom must face reality and take stock of her own responsibilities. Today I have come to tell you what France thinks and what France seeks.

Gentlemen, you are the representatives of a people who insist upon truth. Your opinions are based on facts and your judgments on acts and not on words.

This is why I will ask you this question: When in the defense of her independence and the sacred cause of liberty a nation has lost 1,357,-000 men from 1914 to 1918, 575,000 dead from 1939 to 1945—(240,-000 perished in uniform in the first and the last battles for freedom—112,000 were shot or were killed by bombing—182,000 died deported to Germany for belonging to the underground and 40,000 died in enemy labor camps); when, for the same cause, the same nation, fighting at the door to Southeastern Asia, in Indo-China, a war which has lasted more than four years, does not hesitate to reaffirm her faith in international law by sending to Korea officers and men whose heroism makes them the worthy comrades of your officers and men; then I ask you, who could seriously question her determination? In fact, what nation has ever proven better her love for independence and for peace and her will to defend both?

The attitude which has been given the barbarous name of "neutralism" has always been foreign to the French soul, not only because it is a moral absurdity—can anyone be neutral between servitude and liberty, between good and evil?—but because it is geographical and historical nonsense. Our people have experienced the frailty of their exposed land and sea frontiers. Almost alone in 1914 and again in 1939 they have met the first shock of armies so powerful that each time it has taken four years of ceaseless effort and a coalition of the world's forces to defeat them.

Therefore they know that right without might is powerless. They know that isolation is death. They know that neutrality, whether declared, armed, or disarmed, has protected neither Belgium, the Netherlands, Norway, nor Denmark and that an aggressor would never stop at a frontier post, even should it be surmounted with a dove holding the branch of an olive tree.

Finally, they know that France is not simply the western extremity of Europe in the Mediterranean and the Atlantic, but that the French Union extends its influence and civilization to all parts of the world and that in the common strategy for freedom and peace, France has courageously accepted the tasks and responsibilities of a great world power. They know also that once France has fallen, the whole of Europe will be in chains with all her potential strength in the service of the invader and that the whole world, indeed civilization itself, will be in mortal danger.

I shall always remember the clear warning when, in 1919, as a young Deputy, I heard it stated from the rostrum of our own Parliament by the President of the United States that France still stands at the frontier:

". . . here is where the blow fell because the rulers of the world did not sooner see how to prevent it . . . they know that the only way to do this is to make certain that the same thing will not always happen that has happened this time, that there never shall be any doubt or waiting or surmise, but that whenever France or any free people is threatened, the whole world will be ready to vindicate its liberty . . ."

Because they did not establish this union in time; because they did not organize soon enough and at the most vulnerable points a collective defense prepared for instant action, the democratic nations with their decisions delayed by the interplay of their institutions or by the scruples and indiscipline of freedom were once more thrown into the most destructive of wars. One after the other, nations fell which would have been saved had they joined their forces. And France herself, who entered the fight faithful to her word, was wounded on the ramparts, imprisoned for four years, and almost destroyed.

If our people had given up, if for a single moment they had hesitated between resistance and collaboration with the enemy, if they had not been willing to subject themselves to an implacable oppression, had not chosen to destroy, often with their own hands, their properties and their tools, rather than work for the enemy; if they had permitted him at times when the fortunes of war were in the balance to have a free disposition of their remaining resources and forces in metropolitan France and in her overseas territories, what would Europe and the world be today?

After such common fights and sacrifices, the achievement of the final victory must not make us forget the perils to which we were led by an uncoördinated diplomacy and strategy. It is the very old story of the Horatii and the Curiatii. For the goal to be reached is not to liberate a Europe which may once more be occupied, enslaved, exploited, and ravaged and whose name, you may be sure, would only recall the final ruin of a civilization, but rather, by shielding her against aggression, to protect the whole community of the free nations and in this way to save peace.

In putting into practice an effective union, in which risks as well as efforts must be shared, France has a clear understanding of her duties and of her rights.

Her contribution to the defense of freedom and of peace is first of all her own recovery.

Undoubtedly, gentlemen, our people are sometimes disparaged, and they are sometimes guilty of self-disparagement. But those of you whom we have had the joy of welcoming in our country have been able to see the road covered since the liberation.

In 1944, the country was bled white, the state disrupted, 90 per cent of our departments were in ruins, our lands were laid fallow, our industrial equipment was pillaged or obsolete, our ports, our means of communication were in shambles, more than two million houses were destroyed or damaged, our economy and our finances were ruined.

In 1951, there is an increased population, republican institutions are reëstablished, our production has been raised to the level of 133 as compared with a 100 in 1938, our commercial balance is in equilibrium and our currency stabilized before the rise in prices of raw materials could compromise the equilibrium thus gradually attained, our homes have been built again, and the specter of social troubles and of despair has been pushed aside.

Gentlemen, it is with pride that I speak of the accomplishments of our workers, of our engineers, of our leaders of enterprise, of our farmers, of our administrators, of all Frenchmen, and of their representatives. The generous aid that you have given us through the Marshall Plan, for which I am happy to thank you today publicly, has not been extended to us in vain. In giving a decisive impulse to our paralyzed economy, it has again opened for us the way to work and to hope, and by driving away the threat of unemployment and misery, it has preserved us from those social upheavals which are the breeding ground for adventure and tyranny.

Though a great deal remains to be done, this first balance sheet of our recovery testifies to the courage of our people, supported by your brotherly assistance.

Our next contribution to the cause of freedom and peace is our rearmament effort which our Parliament has voted by a huge majority without hesitation or reservations. This has been done in spite of the already enormous burden of our reconstruction and reëquipment and of our military expenditures. It is certainly not the fault of our two nations if world collective security has not been organized, though we consider this failure as merely temporary.

The spirit of aggression is foreign to both Americans and Frenchmen. But in the face of threats of totalitarian expansion and the formation of certain mighty groups of powers whose policies and armaments are not subject to the free control of the people, we have turned thoughtfully and inflexibly to regional pacts and especially to the regional pact of the North Atlantic which, conforming to the statutes of the United Nations, has but one aim—to deter aggression and to strengthen the peace. Thus, by our reciprocal undertakings that we shall from now on pool together our resources of arms and troops at all threatened and strategic points, we have made the Atlantic community a solid foundation of our common security and of peace.

For us, indeed, the effort for peace and the effort for defense are not contradictory; they complement each other. With the prudence and firmness dictated by our said experience, we shall never cease to answer negation, procedural obstructionism, and propaganda, in the language of right, of truth, and of sincerity.

Let us not fail to speak clearly, frankly, and firmly. Let us put at the service of peace and freedom, side by side with our material forces as long as those are needed, the invincible moral forces which always animate free people aware of the righteousness of their cause.

We shall not tire, on our part, of repeating the conditions that are necessary for the reëstablishment of trust and coöperation among all peoples. Does everyone sincerely want peace? In that case, everyone must respect the commitments subscribed to in the Charter of the United Nations by all the allies of yesterday; in that case, certain countries must stop interfering in the internal affairs of others in an effort to weaken their freely chosen regimes, to provoke troubles, to paralyze production, and to pour daily insults upon their governments.

In that case, international and permanent control by the United Nations Organization of armaments, of all armaments, in all countries, must be accepted, in order to limit fairly and later to destroy all classic or atomic weapons.

In that case, the national armies must be progressively replaced by a United Nations army as provided by the common Charter.

In that case, every country must agree to the free movement of wealth, ideas, and persons as well as the free and sincere expression of view, under international control, of peoples on whom regimes have been imposed by force.

Here are, among so many others, the questions to which answers must be found. And so that they may be answered clearly, I am asking them here, clearly and publicly, before the legislature of a great nation which is ridiculously accused every day, as is ours, of warmongering, and I am certain that I speak in the name of all the men who want peace with liberty, the only peace worth living for.

Finally, our effort to unite and organize Europe must be considered a contribution to the defense of peace and liberty by all who believe that it is not sufficient to guarantee the security of nations and of individuals but that we must also, by assuring welfare and justice, enrich their existence and increase their attachment to society.

France is working towards this goal by the creation of communities of production of which the coal and steel pool, that bears the name of its moving spirit, President Schuman, is but a beginning and a preface for others that we are preparing. France is working towards this goal through the Council of Europe and the Strasbourg Assembly which she initiated. She is working towards it in seeking the formation of a European army—the nucleus of a future international army—to take its place, first of all, in the great Atlantic army whose illustrious leader General Eisenhower I wish to salute here today.

Passionately devoted to the realization of a European federation which will put an end to secular antagonisms, France has put aside her legitimate resentment against the enemy of yesterday, demanding of it only that it bring to the cause of coöperation the admission of its responsibilities as well as the proof of its redemption through the repudiation of its old regime and the sincere attachment to the cause of democracy. Convinced of the need for supranational institutions, France has declared herself prepared to grant to those bodies, in conformity with her Constitution and under condition of reciprocity, part of her sovereignty.

And she hopes to convince the still hesitant nations that they will not curtail their sovereignty but on the contrary strengthen it by associating it with others, by uniting their resources and labor to increase their forces, by developing and coördinating their industrial and agricultural economies, by widening their markets, by raising the standard of living of their workers, in a word, by making the old divided Europe, slow of decision, torn with antagonisms, mistrustful of herself, a new and harmonious organism animated by one soul and adapted to the needs and exigencies of the modern world.

Patiently and untiringly, we shall pursue the realization of these United States of a free Europe which, with full respect for the independence and dignity of all nations, will join the United States of America to work still more effectively for the welfare and peace of the world. In this way, we shall translate into actuality the prophecy of Victor Hugo who said, seventy-five years ago, on the eve of the Philadelphia Exhibition: "The future is already foreseeable. It belongs to a united and peaceful democracy. And you, our delegates to the Philadelphia Exhibition, you are beginning under our eyes the superb realization which the twentieth century will witness: the union of the United States of America and of the United States of Europe . . . Go, workers of France, go, workers of Paris who know how to think, go, girl artisans of Paris who know how to fight, useful men, brave women, go and carry the good news, go and tell the new world that the old world is young. You are the ambassadors of fraternity. The two continents will exchange not only their products, their trade, their industries, but also their ideas and the progress they make in justice as well as in prosperity."

Gentlemen, I would be happy if, today, I could have been one of those useful ambassadors of friendship and of peace.

The Integration of Europe
Konrad Adenauer

Dr. Konrad Adenauer, the Chancellor of the Federal Republic of Germany, was born in Cologne on 5 January 1876. Following his university education at Bonn, Munich, and Freiburg, he served as a town Councillor of Cologne and in 1917 was elected Lord Mayor. He founded the University of Cologne in 1925. During the Hitler regime he was arrested and detained for a period in the Brauweiler concentration camp. Dr. Adenauer became President of the Bonn Assembly in 1948 and on 15 September 1949 was appointed Chancellor. On 20 October 1950, when he addressed the first annual congress of the Christian Democratic Union at Goslar, Dr. Adenauer reaffirmed his view that Germany belonged to the West and would never acquiesce to Russian rule.

The address below was delivered over the German radio from Bonn on 18 September 1951. It suggests the difficulties of the problem of West German remilitarization. By 22 December 1951 when the Chancellor published the annual report of his government he was able to say: "It cannot be the sense of an all-German policy to step down to the level of the Soviet-occupied zone. Our policy must rather lift our brothers and sisters out of Soviet slavery to the level of the democratic freedoms."

THE FOREIGN Ministers of the United States, of France, and of Great Britain, have issued communiqués concerning the discussions held by them in Washington on 14 September 1951. These communiqués are of outstanding importance for us Germans, though not for us alone, but also for all of Europe and for the entire world. These communiqués stress, first and foremost, the participation of Germany in the defense of the West and the integration of Europe. The hope is expressed that negotiations with the Federal Government may result in agreements between the four governments which would lead to the participation of Germany in the European defense community which is being prepared at present. These communiqués furthermore state that the entry of the Federal Republic into a European community on the basis of equality, and the participation of the Federal Republic in the measures that are being envisaged, would not be feasible without a complete change in the nature of the relations now existing between the three powers and the Federal Republic. The High Commissioners have been instructed by their governments to inaugurate negotiations with the Federal Government as soon as possible concerning all the facts I have sketched above. These negotiations will start after the return of the High Commissioners, in all probability on the 24th September. In their communiqués, the three Foreign Ministers say that they agreed on the general principles on which the negotiations of the High Commission with the Federal Government are to be based.

We are not yet informed respecting the details of the instructions given to the High Commissioners. It would, therefore, be premature to discuss details at this moment, much less to pass judgment on them. It is, however, appropriate to comment on the intentions of the Western Allies as expressed in their communiqués, and, above all, on the point of view from which the new epoch that is now at hand must be judged. The communiqués strongly express the firm determination of the Western Allies to offer to us a full partnership with equal rights. This information can only cause real pleasure to us Germans. Let us refrain from venturing upon all kinds of considerations concerning the detailed instructions which, as said above, are yet unknown to us. Concerning these, there will be genuine negotiations. Let us await these negotiations. When entering into them we shall take account of the paramount viewpoints which must guide our decisions. We are privileged to enter into these negotiations with optimism and with confidence. It would not be right to judge this great initiative exclusively by the fact that the Occupation Statute and the intervention rights will be abolished. Rather should we, in order to arrive at a fair judgment, take into account the political developments during the past years, the growing tensions throughout the world, and the tendencies which have become apparent in recent months.

Since the breakdown of Germany, i.e., since 1945, Soviet Russia has been the only state which has continued to arm. Contrary to what happened in Russia, the Western Allies reduced their armaments after the breakdown of Germany. It was only last year, when the case of Korea revealed Soviet Russia's intentions to the world, that the Western Allies and the nations of the North Atlantic Treaty Organization started rearming. It is only since the outbreak of this war in Korea that the world has clearly realized Soviet Russia's true aims.

There is something else I must point out here: Since 1945, Soviet Russia, by the methods of the cold war has linked the following countries to herself: Albania, Bulgaria, Roumania, Poland, Hungary, Czechoslovakia, and the eastern half of Germany. In this eastern part of Germany, Soviet Russia has been maintaining over twenty-five highly armed divisions only for the purpose of striking fear into our hearts, and of making us subservient. She maintains fifth columns in the Federal Republic and in other European countries. As I have just pointed out, the eastern half of Germany has already fallen a victim to Soviet Russian policies. The Soviet Zone is a satellite state of Russia, its government is one of Russia's publicity agents. At the same time, the Federal Republic of Germany is a no man's land from both a political and military point of view. It is completely disarmed. It is not a sovereign power. It is suspended between the Eastern bloc and the Western Allies without in any way being able to protect and defend itself. In the long run, this is an impossible situation. A conclusion of treaties with the Western Allies as envisaged in the above-mentioned communiqués of 14 September, would put an end to this situation which, I insist again, is impossible and unbearable in the long run. Once these treaties are concluded, the Federal Republic would be a treaty partner of the Western Allies for mutual defense against any attack upon Germany or Europe. At the same time, the Federal Republic would recover its full sovereignty. In this case, Soviet Russia would suffer as decisive a defeat regarding her Western policy as she did in San Francisco regarding her Eastern policy through the Japanese peace treaty. The aim of Soviet Russian world policies is perfectly clear. She wants to perpetuate the present uncertain situation of German political and military affairs because this will prevent an integration of Western Europe. The Soviet Union calculates that the United States would no longer be interested in a Western Europe that is falling to pieces, and, without unification and integration, Western Europe is crumbling away and the Western European states are more or less powerless. The Soviet Union assumes that the United States would no longer be interested in a weak Europe and would withdraw from Europe. The Soviet Union would then, without a war, draw not only the Federal Republic, but also the other Western European countries, into the sphere of its influence, and would finally dominate the whole of Europe. We know very well what would be in store for us in that case. We only need remember Czechoslovakia, Hungary, Poland, and the other satellite states. Germany would then certainly be doomed. All Europe would then be politically an appendix to that part of Asia which is ruled by the Soviet Union. Communism in its Asiatic form would descend upon us with all its horrors. All those things that are sacred and dear to us would be destroyed. There would be no freedom for anyone. Christian civilization of the occident, and Christianity itself, would be destroyed. If Germany remains a no man's land, and if at last, after all, hostilities commenced in Europe, Germany would become the battlefield for the clashing powers. The fate of unhappy Korea would then be our fate. Up to now battle has swept backwards and forwards over Korea seven times.

The declaration of the Foreign Ministers, and the result of the negotiations based on it, will truly bring decisions of the greatest historic consequences. Either we remain a no man's land politically and militarily, or, as a free state with equal rights, we become partners in the European, and thus in the North Atlantic defense system against any aggression from the Soviet Union. This is the viewpoint under which we conduct and must regard negotiations. All those who, whether here in Germany or in France or elsewhere in the world, take exception to this or that, express this or that worry or fear, who would allow their decisions to be governed by this or that retrospect into the past, are applying an absolutely wrong set of values at this historic hour. It is necessary again and again to try to see events and situations clearly and simply. Things that are not really of a decisive character should not be allowed to cause confusion. Most important, however, is that the situation of Germany should be contemplated by weighing up and assessing the entire world situation with an absolutely cool and intelligent mind, disregarding all considerations and objectives of party politics. Party-political concessions and party-political considerations would amount to a crime against the German people and against Europe at this moment.

Now you will ask me: Is it not the very policy of the integration of Europe, the policy of the Federal Republic's joining the European defense community which, in its turn, is to be linked to the North Atlantic Treaty Organization—as I said just before—is it not this policy that will lead to war with the Soviet Union? I think I can answer this question, and I am convinced that I can answer it by saying emphatically NO. The character of the European defense community is absolutely defensive, as is evidenced by its internal structure. It is absolutely impossible that it could in any way have offensive intentions. It is absolutely impossible that it could appear as an aggressive power to the Soviet bloc, so that a hot war would be unleashed by its coming into being. All I have said of the European defense community also applies to the North Atlantic Treaty Organization. Organizations consisting of over a dozen member states can never pursue aggressive but only defensive policies. In addition, the three Foreign Ministers expressly declared the following in their publications of 14 September: "The three Ministers reaffirm that this policy, which will be pursued jointly with the other free nations, aims at creating and maintaining a lasting peace founded upon law and justice. Its aim is to promote the prosperity and the security of Europe without in any way changing the purely defensive character of the North Atlantic Treaty Organization. They reaffirm their determination not under any circumstances to permit the use of such an agreement for the pursuing of an aggressive policy."

May I point out to my listeners that the Soviet Union, though constantly talking about peace and freedom since 1945, is the only great power that, since 1945, has deprived so many peoples of peace and freedom, and constantly menaces us. I have just mentioned that the Soviet Union cannot regard a European defense community as in any way aggressive. Nor could she regard the Atlantic Treaty Organization in any different way, although she again and again says that she feels threatened. Though Soviet Russia is consistent and methodic in her foreign policy, she is also cautious, and does not want to run any serious risks. If Europe and the United States unite for common defense, however, it would be more than dangerous for Soviet Russia to start a war with this combined force. I am convinced that negotiations with Soviet Russia will also be possible then, in order to give the world lasting peace. One may view the present situation, and view it repeatedly, and reflect on it again and again; one always comes to the same conclusion: What the free peoples of the world have now initiated is the surest way of preserving world peace.

Now, after the declarations of the three Foreign Ministers in Washington, Herr Grotewohl suddenly comes along, and directs his appeal to the German Bundestag. He says he wants to carry through All-German elections for a National Assembly for the establishment of a uniform, democratic, and peaceful Germany. In a long speech he delivered before the Volkskammer in the Eastern Zone he demands, just as he did formerly, that all occupation troops be withdrawn, and praises Soviet Russia's power and love of peace in loudest tones. Herr Grotewohl already used the same little phrase on a former occasion and has even done so repeatedly. The Federal Government and the Bundestag have over and over again expressed their opinion on the same problem and have done so very precisely, very exactly, and very decidedly, and this on 22 March 1950, 14 September 1950, 15 January 1951, and on 9 March 1951. On 26 May 1950, and on 9 October 1950, the three High

The Integration of Europe

Commissioners of the Western powers, on the proposal of the Federal Government, addressed letters to the Chairman of the Soviet Control Commission, in which they supported the demands of the Federal Republic of Germany. The Soviet Zone government never followed up these declarations of the Federal Republic nor did the Soviet Control Commission make any answer. We stand by the declarations the Federal Government and the Bundestag have made so far and mean to stick to them. Herr Grotewohl's present appeal is a counterpart to the note addressed by the Soviet Russian government to the French government before the Conference of San Francisco. In this note the Soviet Russian government made every effort possible to keep France from signing the peace treaty with Japan. In its present appeal the SED, or rather their leader, Herr Grotewohl, by order of Soviet Russia, try to prevent the integration of Europe. This attempt will not be successful. The entire situation is so clear, it is too clear for anyone to be taken in by this note.

We want peace! We do not want Germany to become a battlefield. We wish to reënter the community of nations on an equal footing with the others. That is why we desire the integration of Europe. It is only through this integration that peace can be saved. In this way, in this peaceful way, we shall reëstablish the unity of Germany.

Now that the peace treaty with Japan has been concluded, the consolidation of the Western world must also make progress. The cold war must also cease. The world should settle down quietly once more. Peace can be saved and secured. It will not be saved by being blind and undecided, but only by a clear and unwavering policy. If things are allowed to drift on, then war will one day break out. Neither the plan of a European defense community—let me repeat this once more—nor the North Atlantic Treaty Organization, aim at aggression against any power. What they are striving for is peace, and this is also what we desire, such is our aim.

Part Three
The United States and
Home Affairs

PROBLEMS OF MOBILIZATION AND MANPOWER

Mobilizing America's Strength for World Security

W. Averell Harriman

W. Averell Harriman was chairman of the United States mission to Moscow in 1941 with the rank of Ambassador and again from 1943 to 1946 was the American Ambassador to Moscow. From April to October 1946 he was Ambassador to Great Britain. He has since served as Secretary of Commerce and as the U.S. representative in Europe under the Economic Coöperation Act of 1948. He was President Truman's Special Assistant on International Affairs at the time of this address. A year later, on 31 October 1951, he was sworn in as Mutual Security Administrator, a position which gives him full control over the flow of American arms and economic assistance to European countries.

Mr. Harriman is a Yale graduate of the class of 1913. Prior to entering the public service he served as vice-president of a railroad, partner of a banking and investment business, and as chairman of the board of the Merchant Shipbuilding Corporation.

Early in 1951 Mr. Harriman made available his country estate at Harriman, New York to Columbia University for the establishment of the American Assembly, an organization designed to provide for serious study of world problems. The first conference was held in late May 1951 and was devoted to the subject "The Relationship of the United States to Western Europe." The effects of inflation were discussed in 1952.

In introducing Mr. Harriman as the keynote speaker at the nineteenth *New York Herald Tribune* Forum on 23 October 1950 at the Waldorf-Astoria Hotel in New York, Mr. Whitelaw Reid, the editor of the *Herald Tribune*, said in part: "Since last spring the country has been dealt a sledge-hammer blow. Our collective eyes have been jolted open and focused on the machinations of world Communism backed by force. Our immediate military potential has been shown perilously slim. And we are today faced not with the pleasant task of perfecting the economy as a model for community living, but with the nightmare of calling on it for another miracle, for setting right the balance of democratic strength in the world."

It is a high honor for me to have the privilege of opening this nineteenth *Herald Tribune* Forum. For this Forum, under the guiding genius of Mrs. Helen Reid, has not only become one of the great institutions of this country but one which attracts the attention of the world.

The theme this year is "Mobilization of American Strength for World Security."

To mobilize our strength for security in this age of crisis, we must establish so impregnable a moral position that everywhere men of good will may find in our objectives the fulfillment of their yearnings for peace, freedom, and abundance.

It would be fatal for us to believe that security can be attained merely from a preponderance of military weapons. For security is rooted in the minds and hearts of free peoples. It dwells in the zeal with which they cherish their freedom and in the will with which they defend it.

While military strength fortifies a nation's will to resist aggression, it does not inspire that will. The will to resist is grounded in the conviction that freedom offers to man his most promising opportunities for a fuller life. It stems from the conviction that man's yearnings can be realized only in a community of free nations whose objectives embody the aspirations of their peoples.

If we would nourish these convictions, then we must dedicate ourselves to the proposition that mankind possesses the wisdom, the moral strength, and the resolve to bring out of this divided world a community in which men can live in peace, in dignity, and in freedom.

We can never accept the proposition that war is inevitable. But if war is not inevitable, neither is agreement easy. In our pursuit of peace we must prepare for a long, arduous, and costly struggle.

But we need never lose faith. The free nations of the world possess a preponderance of economic and moral strength. And we have now joined in a common effort to mobilize our military force for defense. If we approach the difficult years ahead with resolution, we can look forward with confidence to the outcome.

We Americans have been actively engaged in the task of constructing world security and the conditions of world security ever since the early days of the war.

We began our effort in 1941 when President Roosevelt met at sea with Prime Minister Churchill to draft in the Atlantic Charter a statement of the fundamental principles by which nations must live if they are to live together in peace and freedom. In this charter, the American people allied their objectives with the aspirations of mankind. We constructed a moral foundation on which men might, in the words of the charter, "base their hopes for a better future for the world." In January, 1942, twenty-six countries, including the Soviet Union, subscribed to this Atlantic Charter when they signed the declaration by united nations. These were the first in the series of steps by which we took leadership in the creation of the United Nations, whose fifth anniversary we celebrate tomorrow.

During the war it was the hope of our government that the nations united in war to destroy the Axis would remain united in the common purpose of maintaining peace.

We recognized that we would encounter great difficulties with the Soviet Union once the war ended.

Now while our prime objective in our wartime relations with the Russians was to maintain them as effective allies—and of course they were effective allies—we currently entered and conducted negotiations and discussions with them on those specific political matters where difficulties were most likely to occur. These discussions were culminated at the Yalta conference. There certain definite agreements were reached by the United States and the United Kingdom with the Soviet Union.

We foresaw that once the Red Army occupied the countries of Eastern Europe and the Balkans, the Soviet Union might exercise its power to dominate them. We therefore negotiated agreements with the Soviet government to respect the sovereignty of these countries and to permit free and unfettered elections to establish independent democratic governments. It was at Yalta that the Soviet Union finally undertook those commitments.

Would that these commitments had been carried out. The world would be quite different today if they had been. Now, in addition, the Soviet Union pledged itself at Yalta to enter the war against Japan at an early date. This undertaking it honored, at the eleventh hour. We always were convinced that the Russians would enter the war against Japan before it was over. Stalin, in fact, told me so when I saw him in 1942. The question was whether the Russians would come into the war in time to do us good, or whether it would just hold off until it was easy going and they could take what they wanted. It was obvious that they could occupy Manchuria and could, of course, dominate it.

Now, it was at Yalta that the Soviet Union agreed not only to enter the war against Japan at an early date, but to enter into an agreement of friendship with the Chinese National government and to recognize the sovereignty of that government over Manchuria.

I would like to quote some sentences from the treaty of friendship which the Soviet Union and the Chinese National government subsequently signed, implementing the Yalta agreement: "To work together in close and friendly collaboration after the coming of peace and to act according to the principles of mutual respect for their sovereignty and territorial integrity and of non-interference in the internal affairs of the other contracting party." And again in another provision: ". . . The U.S.S.R. agrees to render to China moral support and aid in military supplies and other material resources, such support and aid to be entirely given to the National government as the central government of China."

Unfortunately, the Soviet Union broke these agreements as they related both to Europe and to China. This marked the beginning of our postwar difficulties.

The strength of our moral position today rests upon the fact that we made every effort to reach an understanding with the Soviet Union.

The failure to honor these agreements revealed the duplicity and designs of the Soviet Union.

Although we continued our efforts to resolve our differences by negotiation in good faith, we began to take firm measures to resist aggression and to strengthen the free world.

In 1946, we joined in supporting Iran when its borders were threatened. We followed with military aid to Turkey when she was under pressure. We helped Greece to preserve its independence. We thwarted the Soviet attempt to seize Berlin.

Nor were we concerned solely with military matters. We handled our domestic affairs in such a way as to produce a stable and expanding economy which was fundamental to world economic recovery. Through loans, grants, and other forms of economic aid, we helped nations in many parts of the world to rebuild their peacetime economies. Through the Marshall Plan, we have assisted war-torn Western Europe to recover its economic strength and vitality. The concept of Point Four has given hope to the peoples of the underdeveloped areas. During the last five years we have seen six free nations emerge from dependence status.

Confronted by the increasing threat of Soviet military strength, we joined in 1949 with eleven other nations in the North Atlantic Treaty to form a common defense against aggression. At the same time we undertook to help rearm these countries and other free nations for our common defense.

During all those years we worked unceasingly to strengthen the United Nations and to support the principles of its charter.

In June we faced our greatest crisis when the Republic of Korea was invaded. The American people met this crisis with boldness and determination. Fifty-three nations joined us in the United Nations decision to meet force with force. Such unity on the part of nations was unprecedented in history.

We can see now that we have built well. By our acts during the last nine years we have inspired the trust, the confidence, and the unity of the free world.

By our efforts to resolve differences between nations by peaceful means, by the help we have given others to regain their strength, by the determination with which we have fulfilled our obligations under the United Nations Charter, we have established our position on a firm moral foundation.

The years ahead will be difficult. Our task is to persevere on the course we have set.

Our faith that we can succeed is justified. For the first time in history, the most powerful nation in the world is dedicated to peace and in partnership with other nations is mobilizing its moral force and its resources for world security.

The Moral Core of Military Strength
Brigadier General Charles T. Lanham

At the time this address was delivered, on 16 February 1949, General Lanham was Director of the Staff, Personnel Policy Board, Office of the Secretary of Defense, in Washington. He was appointed Chief of Public Information by General Eisenhower in Supreme Headquarters Allied Powers Europe early in 1951.

This speech attracted wide attention and within a year more than 100,000 copies were distributed to American businessmen. The text was reprinted by the Command and General Staff College, Fort Leavenworth, Kansas, and was used by the faculty in connection with a study of the problems of manpower.

Charles T. Lanham was born in Washington, D. C. and was graduated from the Military Academy in the class of 1924. During World War II General Lanham served with distinction as a regimental commander and as an assistant division commander. He was awarded the Distinguished

Service Cross and the Silver Star with Oak Leaf cluster for bravery, the Legion of Merit, and several other decorations. From November 1945 to July 1948 he was chief of the Information and Education division of the War Department Special Staff. He is the coauthor with Major Richard Tindall of *Infantry in Battle*, published in 1934.

THE EVILS that attend us today are abundantly evident wherever we look. In this, the fourth year since the destruction of the Axis powers, we have found neither peace nor tranquillity. On the rubble of broken cities and in the desolation of ravaged countrysides, weary and bewildered men scrabble for food and for hope, while the first fruits of their labor are still claimed by the mechanisms of death that dominate our shrunken planet. This is the true face of the obscene impostor that for four long years has worn the bright name of peace.

In our broad land the picture is different, but only in degree. For even here 1,600,000 men are diverted from the fruitful tasks of America and apprenticed to the barren profession of arms. Nor does the bitter paradox that we maintain this military might in the name of peace lessen our yearning for a sane and stable world free from the tramp of marching men, free from the shadow of the bomber's wing, free from the unseen death that moves beneath the oceans.

Nonetheless, we are confronted with this fact and we must learn to live with it. As a free people, our most compelling concern is to cauterize the vast potential for evil that is inherent in this as in any other great concentration of power. We have learned that lesson thoroughly, and there is little likelihood that we will forget it now. At the same time we must avoid the equally grave danger of building a barrier of distrust and suspicion between the civil community and the amazingly young men who now make up our armed forces. To allow such a situation to develop will more than counterbalance all the billions we are currently devoting to the dreadful paraphernalia of war. For an army derives its moral strength from the people it defends—from their confidence, their affection, their institutions, their beliefs.

There is no substitute for this. The nation's will is our will; the nation's faith is our faith; the nation's virtues are our virtues. Even those countries that are the most barren politically and the most retarded morally recognize that fact and strive endlessly to create the illusion of civic virtue and moral rectitude. For they understand that neither a nation nor its army is any stronger than its beliefs. The centuries have underscored this truth with blood and ruin for those leaders, both civilian and military, who have ignored it. Over and over again, gigantic concentrations of physical power have gone down in defeat before a lesser strength propelled by conviction; over and over again, the Goliaths have perished at the hands of the Davids.

Therefore, without deprecating our armed might and the evil circumstances that make it necessary, I contend that we must be increasingly vigilant lest we come to evaluate our strength and our security exclusively in terms of material power. Our true strength resides in the philosophy upon which our country stands and the degree of understanding and acceptance of that philosophy by our people. Here lies our fundamental security whether the threat be external or internal, by ideology or by force. And about this hard and enduring moral core must we build our military strength. To do otherwise is to build a colossus of straw.

Until the eve of World War II this basic consideration played no significant part in our military thinking. Until that time we had taken for granted the ancient virtues of our people—a deep knowledge of our freedoms, an almost instinctive awareness of dangers that threatened those freedoms, a broad fund of factual information from our amazing press and radio, and a public school system that had always been the source of our civil strength and unity. In mid-1941, these complacent assumptions came down like a house of cards. For in that year we found that the young men in our expanding army were divided and confused. We found that great numbers of them were literally ignorant of the catastrophic events in Europe and the dark portents in Asia. And since they saw no danger, they saw no compelling reason why the Congress had decided to retain them in the service. In common with many of their fellow citizens, they appeared to be unaware of the human values at stake in a collapsing civilization—values which they would soon be called upon to preserve at the ultimate price of their lives.

Somewhere, somehow, a perverted philosophy had found its way into our national blood stream; a philosophy that placed peace before freedom, comfort before sacrifice, self before the common good, and rights without obligations. It is not likely that any nation which embraces such principles will long endure; and it is certain that any military force so motivated will collapse at the first shock of battle, no matter how magnificently it may be equipped.

Pearl Harbor automatically restored all of us to our good senses and united us as we have never been united before. Nevertheless, the great gaps in the moral armor of our young fighting men had been made clear. Anger and indignation at Japanese treachery had served to unite us, but anger and indignation were not substitutes for an understanding of the freedoms we were committed to preserve or the moral issues involved or the nature of the dark forces that were loose in the world. Therefore, the army undertook to remedy these grave defects as best it could.

This was a strange and unfamiliar mission; and since it was strange and unfamiliar, mistakes were made and acceptance was slow and difficult. But the important thing lies in the fact that the army had at long last come to recognize that its fighting strength depended completely and utterly upon the understanding and acceptance of an idea. That idea was the preservation of freedom and the fearful consequences of failure. We recalled belatedly that even in our own war for independence General Washington had engaged Tom Paine to do an identical job—to keep the idea of freedom burning like a beacon before his little army. We recalled that the philosopher Spinoza had observed that "men fight better with ideas on the ends of their bayonets." We remembered that nearly every great captain in history had testified that the decisive factor in war lies in the moral field, in the will to win. Not all our billions can arm one man with this determination; nor can all our fabulous machines of war make good its absence. That ineluctable power is derived from the spiritual and moral roots of our country. It carries no price tag.

Thus were our traditional military patterns shaken. Today our concepts are beginning to crystallize. We realize now that we can no longer live in our former military isolation, walled up in forgotten garrisons and divided spiritually and intellectually from the civil community. We realize, too, that we are citizens first and soldiers second; that we cannot exist as a separate organism divorced from the context of citizenship and the social fabric of our country.

Similarly, we have taken a long, hard look at our human relations within the military establishment. Here, too, a new philosophy is beginning to take on form and substance. At the moment, we see it shaping up toward four broad objectives; these I should like to discuss briefly.

At the head of the list we set as our number-one goal the preservation of the dignity and the identity of the individual soldier. This is the very foundation of our system of government; it must also become the solid foundation upon which our military structure rests. For man can suffer no greater indignity than the loss of his identity. He can sustain no heavier spiritual blow than the thought that his life or death is of no consequence. Too often has the conviction that the individual is of no importance led the soldier to the collateral belief that his individual effort is of no importance either. If this thought be generated in enough men in an army, the end result in battle is obvious. Therefore, we are striving to build an officer corps that will recognize, honor, and preserve the dignity and the identity of the humblest soldier. At the same time, we use every device available to us to convince the soldier himself that his well-being, his aspirations, his service are all matters of prime importance to his country and his army. Thus do we seek to fulfill the desire in every human heart to count for something, to be needed.

Our second aim is to provide an answer to the soldier's inevitable and eternal question "Why?" We base this on the fact that the American soldier can be led but not driven; and to lead him he must have an adequate and an intelligent explanation of the things he is called upon to do. You will recognize, of course, that this does considerable damage to that ancient school of thought which contended "Theirs not to question why; theirs but to do or die." Enlightened leaders have always done their best to answer this ever-present question, whether it was spoken or unspoken. Now, as it should be in the army of any free people, it is a fundamental requirement of command.

Strangely enough, this policy has been questioned not only by some of our military men but by some of our civilian critics, too. This, in common with the rest of the philosophy I have been describing to you, has been indicted as "mollycoddling." It has been categorically charged by some that such procedures will destroy the discipline without which an army cannot exist. It appears to us that these critics are mistaking the shadow for the substance. Quite apparently, they are advocates of that brittle counterfeit of discipline which is based upon fear. We seek as a matter of fundamental policy the tougher, more enduring discipline rooted in understanding. This, the true discipline, by its very definition renders an army propaganda-proof and subversion-proof. Nothing short of it has ever produced a first-class American fighting unit and nothing short of it ever will.

The third goal is to bring to our young men an understanding and appreciation of the American ideal, to nourish that ideal and to build an abiding belief in the future of our country and the democratic process. Here lies the very bedrock of motivation, the hard, enduring core of our military strength. Sometimes it is contended that this is not our business, that our business is to develop a body of trained fighting men for the Republic and nothing else. But for our part, we contend that love of country must live in the heart of every fighting man and that anything we can do to strengthen it we should do. No one group should have a monopoly on civic education; it is a job for all of the people all of the time.

The army's fourth objective is to keep our men aware of the great national and international issues that confront us from day to day in order that each man may understand the vital interest those matters hold for him as a soldier and a citizen. The military man, just as much as the civilian, is entitled to a free flow of information. But for reasons I have cited earlier, we believe those matters to be of such vital import to the soldier that we cannot leave the question of his current knowledge entirely to chance or inclination. Therefore, in addition to providing him with broad access to the American press and radio, we make positive provisions to bring him objective presentations of the more important matters occurring in his country and in his world and, then, encourage organized discussion of those matters on duty time. There is no attempt to influence his thinking. On the contrary, every effort is made to encourage him to think for himself and to discuss his views with his fellow soldiers.

The many activities and many programs that bear directly on the attainment of these good ends justify the statement today that our army is the best informed and the most objectively informed in the world.

You will not find perfection in the army of today. You will not find that every officer is an Eisenhower or a Bradley or even a competent practitioner in the difficult art of leading his fellow soldiers. But you will find that the doors and windows of the army are open and that a clean, invigorating wind is blowing away the cobwebs of a narrow and fruitless traditionalism. A good start has been made. But it cannot continue without the interest, the understanding, and the help of our fellow citizens. It cannot succeed if young America comes to the army imbued with a hatred for it and a contempt for the corps of officers. Nor can it succeed without first-class leaders who enjoy the confidence of their country and of their men.

It might be well to pursue this thought a bit further. It seems significant to me, for example, that three key groups in our country are under ceaseless attack—our representatives in Congress, our business, our military leaders. These three groups are made the butt of endless ridicule; vicious stereotypes unendingly depict them as fools or scoundrels or advocates of the blackest reaction. The fact that completely honest and worthy citizens are occasionally involved in this practice does not disguise the treacherous inspiration nor hide the treacherous intent to undermine confidence in our political, industrial, and military leadership.

We of the military establishment are particularly handicapped by this attack since we cannot strike back. Our defense, therefore, must be left in the hands of others. For our part, we have nothing to apologize for. The professional officers of our army are justly proud of their service to the American people. Our senior officers find it difficult to believe that their fellow citizens regard them as incompetents, as unscrupulous seekers after a tarnished glory, or as heartless and inhuman martinets. We are unwilling to believe that after a hundred and seventy years, the American people have suddenly come to regard success as shameful and mediocrity as an ideal. For four years, the attempt has been made to drive these vicious wedges between the corps of officers and their fellow soldiers and between the corps of officers and the civil community. That way lies disaster for any army any time anywhere.

It would also be well to remember that a man of ability in a free society will not elect a profession that promises no reward for achievement. Our whole society is based on incentives. Competition and personal initiative have carried us to the pinnacle of the world. Dare we set these aside for the military profession and still expect to attract men of ability or hold those we have? I submit that this is a matter of profound concern now and in the future.

For a considerable period of time we have concentrated almost exclusively on the enlisted soldier. Perhaps it is time we gave a little sober thought to the men who may some day have to lead him in battle and upon whose ability and wisdom and judgment his life will depend. Therefore, while we strive to build a more perfect army about the central core of our way of life, let us remember that such armies are not built by second-rate leaders with second-rate minds. Nor have our wars ever been won by such men. It is the devout hope of all of us that we may never again be engulfed in war. But if we should be, let us hope that the policies we adopt today will attract to our ranks the Eisenhowers and Bradleys of tomorrow.

The Present Danger
James B. Conant

James B. Conant was born in Dorchester, Massachusetts in 1893. He took his Ph.D. at Harvard in 1916 and after a distinguished career in organic chemistry was elected twenty-third president of Harvard in June 1933. His recent books, *On Understanding Science* (1947), *Education in a Divided World* (1948), and *Science and Common Sense* (1951) have attracted wide and favorable comment.

Dr. Conant gave this brief radio address for the Committee on the Present Danger on 7 February 1951 just as the Congress was beginning its debate on the problems of the draft and military manpower.

The Committee on the Present Danger, of which Dr. Conant is the chairman, is composed of some sixty leading citizens who possess "the deep conviction that the United States and its present way of life are greatly threatened by Soviet aggression." The Committee's program to avert the present danger includes the following measures: defense against aggressors everywhere, Europe and Asia alike; supporting General Eisenhower in Europe; keeping political tensions at home from weakening us in the face of the Soviet enemy; fighting apathy and complacency in ourselves; advocating universal military training and service; legislating strength to ourselves and to our allies; and confronting the aggressors with a power they will not dare attack.

On 3 June 1951, in his final talk of a thirteen-week series of broadcasts, Dr. Conant concluded: "We have emphasized the need for partial mobilization of America, the rearmament of Europe, the defense of the free world against military aggression. We do not believe World War III to be inevitable. Quite the contrary. The measures we advocate are designed to build a road out of the atomic age—a road to peace."

FELLOW CITIZENS, the United States is in danger. Few would be inclined to question this simple statement. The danger is clearly of a military nature. On this much we can all agree. The Congress of the United States has, with almost no dissenting voices, authorized a vast program of rearmament and mobilization.

But as to the exact nature of the danger which confronts us there is far from being complete agreement among the citizens of this Republic. Nor are we by any means of one mind as to how we should mobilize the young men of the nation. Indeed some few question even the need for an army of the size announced.

Now, if we are going to ask the youth of the country to serve two years in the armed forces—as I believe we must—if the government is going to ask this sacrifice of them, each one of us who supports this program must be prepared to answer one simple question—"why?"

Why must we look forward to a period of austerity, of partial mobilization, of more weapons for war, fewer tools for peace?

The answer to these questions seems to me to be summed up in General Eisenhower's recent statement that we must build a secure wall for peace.

The free world has entered a new period—a highly disturbing and dangerous period. Let me recall to you the signals which announced the arrival of this new stage in our history in which prompt and bold measures are required for our survival.

The first clear sign was a year ago last September, when President Truman announced that the Soviet Union had exploded an atomic bomb. This marked the end of our monopoly of a weapon on which the security of the free world in no small measure depended.

The grim atomic age had dawned far sooner than all of us had hoped. It was evident that before long two major powers would have atomic bombs in sufficient quantity to constitute a military threat to one another. Whether such time was three or five years off might be a matter of opinion, but it was hardly to be questioned that the balance of power between the free world and the Soviet Union was about to be upset. This first clear danger signal could be read by all of us some fifteen months ago.

The second signal flashed last June. Up till then the spread of Soviet Communism had been by subversion and internal revolution as in the case of Czechoslovakia, not by military aggression. The aggression of the North Koreans established a new pattern. It could hardly be argued any longer that the dwellers in the Kremlin never intended to use military means to gain their objective, that their sole concern was with a battle of propaganda, of intrigue, and sabotage.

The third signal was the action of Communist China and the justification of this action in the United Nations by the official representatives of the Soviet Union.

In short, within less than eighteen months the free world has been confronted with two highly unpleasant facts. First, the Soviet military power is beginning to mount in terms of the most modern type of warfare—the United States monopoly of the atomic bomb has ended; second, the Soviet allies, at least, have shown a readiness and willingness to gain their ends by force of arms.

Place these facts against the background of the postwar military situation on the European Continent and you can see the outlines of the present danger—a danger to the entire free world, a clear danger to the United States. The background is quite as important as the signals. Indeed the latter are so obvious as to warrant little comment, but the situation on the Continent is far harder to understand.

Let me give you my analysis if I may. For on the appraisal of this situation by each and every one of us as Americans, the course of history in the twentieth century may well depend.

Let me start with a question. Why has the Soviet Union not extended its power to the English Channel since the close of World War II? A few may argue that the failure is evidence of a lack of interest on the part of the Soviet Union—that the rulers in the Kremlin have no desire to spread their doctrine. In the light of recent history any such assumption appears not only improbable but highly dangerous. Others may think the failure reflects the inability of the Communist Party in France, Italy, and the Low Countries to pull off another revolution of the Czechoslovakian type. Certainly no such revolutions have occurred, and we Americans can take satisfaction in the fact that aid through the Marshall Plan has been of prime importance. But surely the one deterrent to direct military aggression has been and is today, the overwhelming destructive power of the United States strategic air force armed with the atomic bomb.

Let me spell out this last point. If Russia tomorrow should move its troops toward the Atlantic Ocean, European territory would be conquered, but the Russian industrial centers would be destroyed from the air. This would be a bad swap from any point of view. It seems clear that we could strike a devastating series of blows against the Soviet's vital centers. Or so I read the newspapers, and so I believe the Russian rulers read their own sources of intelligence. As long as the United States strategic air force is in this commanding position, the danger of Russian troops marching to the channel is relatively slight.

But as the years go by, the deterrent power of strategic bombing will meet an ever-mounting counterthreat—a threat to the industrial centers of Great Britain and the United States, to the continental cities themselves. Any doubt about our being engaged in an arms race has certainly disappeared. The Russians are building up their offensive strength and doubtless likewise their own defenses against strategic bombing. The time may well come when these defensive measures are far more effective than at present. Under their totalitarian system they have been able to direct as much of their industrial strength as they desired into the manufacture of military equipment; they have been able to concentrate on building radar networks, jet planes, and antiaircraft weapons.

Now an arms race today is a highly technical affair. Both sides have equipment on the production line, new developments being tested, blueprints of designs not yet off the drawing boards. No one can say with certainty when one side or the other has the predominance; for few military men will challenge the statement that the battle alone is the pay-off. But what determines the course of history is the estimate of men in control of national destinies as to the chances of success in a future war. Therefore the danger of a third global war, I am convinced, turns on the fact that a few years hence the handful of men who rule Russia may decide that the power of our strategic air force has been largely canceled out. If at that time Europe is defenseless on the ground, the Russian hordes will begin to move. Strengthening the defense of Europe in terms not of a deterrent threat against Russian cities but in terms of armies to stop an advance—this seems to me the top item on the agenda of the free nations of the world. Only then can we achieve a true global stalemate.

We need not only trained manpower but, as Dr. Vannevar Bush says, the most modern weapons for our men to use. We shall have them, perhaps including tactical atomic weapons. There will be a tactical air force. We shall not meet hordes with hordes. We can and must maintain superiority in the quality of weapons for perhaps a generation. Our defense establishment must be geared up to do the best possible job in research and the development of new instruments of war.

But at this point some listener may object. He or she may say it is impossible to defend Europe against the vast manpower of Russia and its satellites. This clearly is a question which only military men are capable of answering with authority. General Eisenhower, whose professional competence no one can challenge, has just returned from an inspection of the situation. If he believed Europe to be indefensible he would, as he said, "recommend that we abandon the North Atlantic Treaty alliance and—by ourselves—attempt however futilely, to build a separate fortress against aggression." He made no such recommendation. Quite the contrary. Such a recommendation, he said, was for him impossible. He reports, "In every capital, there is growing a desire to coöperate in this mutual security effort." The governments are taking measures to build up their defense establishments.

"On every side," General Eisenhower said, "I saw heartening evidence of a regeneration in Europe's spirit. Its morale, its will to fight, will grow with every accretion to physical strength."

"The preservation of free America," General Eisenhower said, "requires our participation in the defense of Western Europe."

"While the transfer to Europe of American military units is essential," General Eisenhower continued, "our major and special contribution should be in the field of munitions and equipment."

"The arrival in Europe of new American land and air units, though modest in protective influence by themselves, will certainly produce added confidence and accelerate the production of military force throughout the member nations."

"Success," he held, "is attainable. Given unity in spirit and action, the job can be done."

That is General Eisenhower's conviction after a first-hand appraisal of the situation.

What must we do here at home?

What is required of the United States, if we are to play our part in the defense of the free world—in building this wall of security of which General Eisenhower has spoken? Clearly, the rapid production of arms and military equipment—and on this we are well embarked. But we must also be in a position to furnish men as well as arms.

To quote General Eisenhower once again: "We have to devise a scheme that we can support if necessary over the next twenty years, thirty years, whatever may be the time necessary, as long as the threat, the announced threat of aggression remains in the world."

In other words, General Eisenhower says that we in the United States must be prepared to stand by in a partially mobilized state for a long period of years. To this end we must have a system of universal military service.

Let me talk for a moment about universal military service and training. As you know, Congress now has before it a universal military service bill. The Committee on the Present Danger is supporting this bill. This measure needs to be understood by the American public, for there is much confusion as to what is in fact involved.

In any discussion of universal military service, it is important to separate certain issues which can all too easily become entangled. In the first place, we are not talking about the type of legislation which would be needed to mobilize the manpower of the country on a total basis if we became engaged in a global war. That is another subject. What would be required in such an eventuality would be a national service act such as was proposed in the closing days of World War II but never became law. I am not discussing this evening mobilization for an all-out war. I am discussing rather, partial mobilization for a long, drawn-out period of international stress and strain. I am discussing the method of maintaining over many years three and a half to four million men in our armed forces.

What the situation requires is a universal military service act which will call into the armed forces all able-bodied young men when they graduate from high school or reach eighteen years of age, whichever is later. This is a vital point in the argument; this is the essence of the bill which must not be destroyed by amendment. Those of us who support the bill believe that the interruption of a young man's education should be before college, not during college, and for those who go direct from high school to a job, before starting in an occupation.

After they have completed the twenty-seven months of military service, these young men will be ready to enter college or go to work. The problems which bedeviled us in World War II in regard to deferring special types of students or essential men in industry will be eliminated if military service is performed between the ages of eighteen and twenty. To my mind, it is quite clear that a man's military service had best be done before he enters the productive life of the country or before he begins his collegiate or professional education.

On this point we have the testimony of Dr. William C. Menninger, who was chief psychiatrist of the Army in World War II.

"From the point of view of the mental health of our young men," Dr. Menninger said, "a program of universal military service and training is far more practical than our present system of selective service. The present system engenders hostility in the man who is selected because he must carry an unfair share of the burden. Because it is selective, it tends to stimulate men to seek deferment on whatever grounds they may be able to plead."

"With our present system," he continues, "a man of draft eligible age lives in uncertainty from mail to mail. The result is great unrest in our youth of this age, not only in colleges but in industry and business."

Dr. Menninger concludes that: "A system which begins at a definite age, which distributes equally the responsibility and privileges among all youth, and which runs for a definite length of service, is far superior, from the mental health point of view, to our present indefinite and discriminatory system under the selective service law."

That is the testimony of the psychiatrist, Dr. William Menninger.

Now, there is one obvious difficulty in a scheme of universal service between eighteen and twenty. How is one to provide from each age group the required number of officers and specialists? I have become persuaded, contrary to my first opinion, that in order to accomplish the training of officers and specialists a small fraction of each age group should be selected after basic training by a civilian board and sent to the colleges for specialized education. This feedback proposal, which first came before public attention as a result of recommendations of the Association of American Universities, is incorporated in the bill now before the Congress. The inclusion of this feedback meets the objections that many educators first raised to a universal military service program.

Some scientists have been disturbed lest the passage of this bill strike a serious blow at the national defense by interfering with the continuous flow of trained men. I venture to think they are mistaken and I call as an expert witness Dr. Vannevar Bush, who headed all our scientific work during the last war.

Dr. Bush appeared before the Senate Armed Services Committee to urge the passage of this universal military service and training bill, and this is what he said:

"We should call all young men at eighteen without exception, adjusting standards to defer only those who cannot be used somewhere in the widely varied efforts of the military establishment. Once the system is in full operation, the process of choice of men to receive advanced training to become officers or to develop new weapons, to maintain our public health, or to perform other professional duties should be on a secure basis of fair competition. There will be adjustments needed in a transition period, for it would be absurd to denude our laboratories just when we need them most, and it would be short-sighted to deny to industry the engineers it must have to build new weapons in adequate quantities in the next year or two.

"But when the system is in full operation," Dr. Bush went on, "every youth on reaching eighteen should expect to go into the service of his country, with his subsequent advancement and the nature of his assignments during the entire age period until he emerges from the reserves and goes his own way determined by competitive tests and the judgment of fair men."

I heartily agree with Dr. Bush. And it is hardly likely we shall be foolish enough to draft out of the colleges today students who are well on their way toward the completion of their specialized training.

Let me emphasize the distinction between universal service and selective service, for this point is often misunderstood. The bill before Congress is a real universal military service bill and not merely an extension of the Selective Service Act to include eighteen-year-olds. The power given the President to call up men by age groups and the establishment of a large reserve are the distinguishing features. When the call goes out for an age group the draft boards will make no deferments in this group on grounds of occupation or dependencies. When the program becomes fully operative the services could count on at least 700,000 to 750,000 men from each age group, and another 100,000 for limited service by lowering the present physical and mental standards for induction.

In addition to providing a force in being the continual flow into the armed forces of those who reach eighteen and their release after about two years will provide over the years a pool of trained manpower—a large body of men in reserve status. I believe this to be imperative. The danger of all-out war is so serious that all our young men must have military training for their own protection as well as for the protection of their country.

The present selective service law expires in June. Clearly before that date Congress must act on the bill that is now before it. But one may hope that the matter may be settled in the coming weeks. Delay will not reassure the free peoples of the Continent; it will not contribute to the morale of our young men. Quite the contrary. Until it is settled how we are to recruit our armies there will be a feeling of uncertainty and confusion in many families throughout the land. I suppose all of us who are urging the rapid rearmament of the United States would agree that there is nothing we like about the whole business. Universal military service is a bitter pill to swallow, and I for one have come most reluctantly to support such a program. But the desperate need to build up our military strength cannot be denied. One of the chief reasons for the existence of the committee under whose auspices I speak tonight is the belief that we must take immediate steps to meet the national danger. We urge all our citizens to impress upon the Congress and the administration the imperative need for prompt and adequate action. We have no time to lose.

Many of us remember with what shock we read of the fall of France in 1940 and with what fear we awaited the outcome of the battle of Britain. Our military men, we know now, were full of apprehension as to what would be the consequences to the United States of the loss of the British Isles. The margin of victory then was narrow enough, we all recall. But with the weapons of the 1950's an enemy in control of the channel ports would be far more dangerous, perhaps impossible to stop.

In short, while the defense of Europe is essential for the survival of Europe, it is just as essential for the survival of a free United States. Again on this point General Eisenhower speaks with authority:

"Western Europe," he reminds us, "has the greatest pool of skilled labor in the world and a vast industrial capacity second only to that of the United States. Now if we take that whole complex with its potential for military exploitation and transfer it from our side to another side, the military balance of power has shifted so drastically that our safety would be gravely imperiled."

Note carefully General Eisenhower's use of the words "gravely imperiled," which he repeated to emphasize the seriousness, to his mind, of the possibility of the loss of Europe. Europe lost—just sketch the outline of such a world and fill in the details yourself, all the terrible details. Imagine as in a nightmare the Soviet Union in control directly or through puppets of all of Europe, the Middle East, and the North of Africa—Great Britain neutralized, this hemisphere alone. Think in terms of military strategy, think in terms of raw materials, think in terms of Western civilization. However you look at it the picture is too terrifying for contemplation.

What is the alternative? A third global war? Not to my mind. It may be forced upon us any day—that one must admit. Conceivably the masters of the Soviet Union have already decided to start World War III and given the necessary orders. If so, a global war is indeed inevitable. But otherwise peace or war hang precariously in the balance of the future. I believe there is still a chance, a good chance, of avoiding World War III—a war which can lead only to wholesale destruction with no clear victory possible for either side. I believe there is a good chance of avoiding this catastrophe, but only if Europe is made defensible and without delay. For today we are dealing with an inherently unstable situation. To be sure the free world has the ability to punish an aggressor who moves his troops by destroying his cities from the air. But matching possible retaliation against possible invasion provides no true opposition of military strengths; it provides no basis for successful negotiation. Not that we should cease discussing with the Soviet Union the settlement of disputed points in Europe. We must continue to explore every road to peace. But we cannot approach the heart of the present tensions, the technological arms race, we cannot even consider steps toward disarmament until the free peoples of Europe can be defended and feel secure.

I venture to conclude on a note that I trust will not seem unduly optimistic. If the United States will show leadership, be both calm and strong, prove that freedom can endure even long years of partial mobilization, then there is hope for the second half of the twentieth century. I see a radically altered international situation a decade or more hence, a free world secure on its own frontiers, a Soviet Union with vastly diminished ambitions and pretensions, yet itself secure against invasion. Under such conditions, the United Nations might well function as those who founded it first dreamed. Under such conditions, steps toward disarmament would no longer be regarded as utopian; the terror of modern weapons might slowly vanish from the skies.

But while the present danger lasts the peoples of the free world must be armed and ready. As General Eisenhower has so well said, we must meet the fearful unity of totalitarian force with a higher unity—the unity of freemen that will not be defeated.

Mobilizing and Training a Citizen Army
General Mark W. Clark

This address was presented on 25 October 1950 at the nineteenth annual *New York Herald Tribune* Forum. In introducing General Clark Mr. Whitelaw Reid said: "One of the Forum's long-time objectives has been a talk by our next speaker. We originally hoped he could tell us of his experience in trying to work with the Russians while serving as United States High Commissioner for Austria. Their doctrines of obstruction and aggression became plain to him in short order and he met them with statesmanship and firmness. Because of this experience, in addition to his brilliant record in Africa and Italy, he has seemed the ideal man to head the training of our troops. It's a special pleasure to welcome to this platform General Mark W. Clark, Chief of Army Field Forces, whose recent book, *Calculated Risk*, you will probably all want to read."

After graduation from West Point in 1917 General Clark served in World War I as a battalion commander and was wounded while fighting in the St. Mihiel and Meuse-Argonne offensives. In World War II he commanded the U.S. Fifth Army and later the Fifteenth Army Group (U.S. Fifth Army and British Eighth Army). At the close of the war he was made Commander in Chief of the U.S. Occupation Forces in Austria. General Clark holds numerous American and foreign decorations including the DSC, DSM, Legion of Merit, and Grand Officer of the Legion of Honor.

On 26 June 1951 General Clark revealed changes in the army troop training program in an address before the convention of Lions International at Atlantic City, New Jersey. He explained: "We are placing greater emphasis on night fighting, and one third of our training is now conducted during hours of darkness. We are also emphasizing anti-guerrilla and anti-infiltration tactics."

MY JOB as Chief of the Army Field Forces includes responsibility for the training of our army in the United States and determining the combat readiness of our troops both at home and abroad. In carrying out these responsibilities, I am vitally concerned with the impact of the Korean war upon our military establishment, the special considerations which must guide us at this time in the conduct of our training, and the organization and equipment with which we have to fight. In the time allotted me, I shall touch briefly on each of these matters.

First, I should like to say a few words about the regular army. Our troops in Germany, Austria, and Trieste, which I recently inspected, are highly trained and well led, but their numbers are wholly inadequate for the job which may confront them. I am glad that the President has indicated his determination to augment these forces in Western Europe. Back here in the United States, our regular army has been seriously affected by the extensive levies made upon it to build up the strength and effectiveness of our forces in the Far East.

At the outset of the Korean war, our ten active regular army divisions were understrength and underequipped, primarily because of budgetary limitations. General MacArthur was, therefore, initially under a severe handicap. His troops had been organized and trained to perform occupational duties. It is no wonder that it was necessary to supplement piecemeal his depleted units which were fighting on wide fronts when he was catapulted into combat in Korea. To do this, we had to scrape together and send over nearly everything we could lay our hands on in this country, including men, units, and material. The record of achievement that was written in the face of such odds is one of the finest in our military history and is a tribute to General MacArthur's magnificent leadership.

Despite our success in Korea, however, the larger picture is not good. I tell you frankly that the depletion of our regular army strength has progressed to an extent which leaves it barely capable of serving as a mobilization base upon which to build new units and reconstitute a general reserve sufficient to implement our war plans should combat be forced upon us by new acts of aggression.

In an individual contest—perhaps staged in Madison Square Garden—between an American division and one of the probable enemy, we would win hands down; but we can't measure our combat readiness in this way since the forces of Communism have at their disposal many times the divisions that we have or could reasonably hope to raise. Fortunately, we are by no means dependent entirely on our regular army. It always has been our national military policy to place our main reliance on our citizenry in times of emergency. That's what we are doing today, and I can assure you that once more, but in a shorter time than ever before, we will have an army that will have the know-how and the will to fight, and of which you will be proud. I have great confidence in our citizen soldiers. It was my privilege in Italy to command not only regular army but also National Guard and Organized Reserve divisions and other units. All conducted themselves with great credit on the field of battle.

To reconstitute the reserve in the shortest space of time, we have brought into the Federal service certain units of our civilian components. Four of our twenty-seven National Guard divisions are now in camps with about 60 per cent of their war-time strength. We also have brought many smaller units of both the guard and the Organized Reserve Corps. Bringing these inducted units up to a state of combat readiness is somewhat simplified by the fact that many of their officers and a substantial number of their noncommissioned officers had battle experience in World War II.

These units are being expanded to full strength by the induction of new men from civil life by way of the selective service. They will then embark on an extensive training program. It will take about seven months to bring these National Guard units to operational readiness and from seven to nine months to fully train the Organized Reserve Corps units.

Our training job at this time is complicated by factors which did not exist when emergencies confronted us in 1917 and 1941.

First, there is the ruthlessness of the enemy who now opposes us and who is of the type that would be most likely to oppose us in any general war. He cheats, murders, abrogates his solemn pledges, kills our wounded and prisoners on the field of battle, and flaunts the accepted rules of land warfare.

Secondly, the evil forces of Communism will give no warning of attack. Their well trained, well equipped and well led divisions are available for immediate combat.

Thirdly, this aggressor directs his entire peacetime economy to preparation for war with little consideration for the welfare of its citizens.

These considerations lead us to the conclusion that we must eliminate all the frills in our training and concentrate on the minimum essentials to insure the combat readiness of our army at the earliest possible date.

There has been much controversy and some criticism concerning the amount of training new men receive before they are sent into combat. I want to make it clear that our soldiers are being given thorough training. All men who come into the army without previous training now go to one of our replacement training centers or to unit training centers. They receive fourteen weeks of intensive training, during the first six weeks of which they are taught basically to be soldiers and to fight with infantry weapons. For the following eight weeks they are trained as specialists in the infantry, artillery, and armor—or as specialists in the supporting technical and administrative services.

The training of individuals and units of all three components is rugged and realistic. Live ammunition is used in rifles, machine guns, and artillery firing over the heads of our trainees to condition them mentally and physically for the noise and confusion of battle. We are teaching the individual soldier to react normally when confronted by the enemy, to protect himself in the heat of battle, and to function as a member of a highly coördinated team. Elimination of nonessentials has been effected by cutting out all instruction that does not have a direct and positive bearing on preparing the soldier to give a good account of himself in combat or in support of combat.

We are placing great emphasis on the training of our troops for air-ground operations. I know from my own combat experience in the Mediterranean that unless an army fighting on the ground is adequately supported by combat aviation its chances for success are greatly reduced. This fact also has been strikingly emphasized in Korea. It is absolutely essential that proper planes be developed and produced to provide this ground support and that air-ground teams be trained so that smooth and efficient liaison and communications will be assured in combat.

To further improve training, I have sent teams of officer observers from my staff to Korea to make certain that we are constantly up to date on the lessons learned from actual combat. The information gathered by these teams has been studied, evaluated, and disseminated so that troops will be thoroughly oriented in the kind of warfare they are likely to encounter wherever they meet this same type of aggressor.

With respect to equipment, it is unfortunate that prior to the outbreak of the Korean war there were many unwarranted optimistic pronouncements with regard to new and unconventional weapons that would be available in the event an emergency occurred. Many people were prone to believe that push-button, secret weapons would be brought into play and that they would be so decisive as to relegate the unglamorous role of the infantryman to the background. Nothing could be further from the truth. It is usually true that we enter a new war with most of the equipment with which we ended the last one. Some of the old equipment has been modified and it is good. We won the last war with it and we are winning the war in Korea with it.

Scientists have been working with the military on planning and developing new equipment. But the cold fact is that we never have enough money in peacetime to produce newly developed weapons in quantities required to equip the entire army.

The new weapons you have heard so much about are in the various stages of development—from an idea in a scientist's mind, to a blueprint, to a prototype, and, in some instances, to limited production. Since the war was thrust on us in Korea, additional sums of money have been made available. Emergency programs have been initiated, designed to accelerate the production of new and better equipment. But this takes time, and much of this equipment will not begin to roll from the assembly lines for several months, and some of it not for several years.

In conclusion I would like to point out three major problems which confront us in the mobilization and training of a new and bigger American army:

First: It is the army's task to train our sons for battle and to develop them into determined fighting men. The army can give them confidence in themselves and in their weapons, knowledge of their job, and endurance and stamina. But the army has no time available in which to mold in a man all the traits of character he will need on the battlefield. This we ourselves must do as private citizens, in our homes, and in our schools. We must instill in our sons the courage to tackle any job and the determination to stick to it once it is undertaken. We must teach them appreciation and respect for discipline and, at the same time, develop their initiative and aggressiveness. Proper rearing and training of our American youth, who are accustomed to the free and easy way of American life, will make the transition to the arduous life of a soldier far less abrupt. It will also give us men who are ready in any emergency to take part in the defense of their country with eagerness and pride.

Second: I firmly believe that the one indispensable element in the winning of wars is the doughboy with plenty of guts, a stout and courageous heart, and his rifle and bayonet. By saying this, I mean no reflection on our sister services, for I am a firm believer in unification. The air force and the navy are essential elements in our three-part military team, and the whole team is required to win a war. But I still say that it is the infantryman on the ground who is the dominant factor in battle, and it is around him that we must build the national military team.

Third: We must be on guard against phony peace proposals. We must not permit ourselves to be lulled again into a false feeling of security. We must go full-steam ahead along the course on which we have embarked.

By the commitment of ground troops in Korea, our President and the United Nations have shown determination and courage which caused the Communist leaders to make a reappraisal of the world situation. These fellows only respect and understand force, for they came into power through forceful action and revolution, and they maintain themselves through force. They despise weakness. So we must show them strength and force in the form of blue chips at this poker game in which we have been cheated during the last five years. Possession of those blue chips—if they represent divisions, battlewagons, and airplanes—will enable us to give notice to the world that anyone who brings war upon us will do so at risk of his own destruction.

Let us make it clear to would-be aggressors, as well as those detestable people in our own country who seek to change our form of government through treacherous and underhanded methods, that by the grace of God we intend to keep the blessings and privileges and the freedom for which you and I fought and which even now are being preserved through the shedding of American blood on the fields of battle in Korea.

CONTROL OF PRODUCTION

The Present Crisis and the American Economy
Roy Blough, Robert A. Taft, and Richard Weil, Jr.

This radio discussion was a broadcast of the University of Chicago Round Table.

Dr. Roy Blough is a member of the President's Council of Economic Advisers and is on leave from the University of Chicago where he has been professor of economics since 1946.

Robert A. Taft, the son of President William H. Taft, is the senior United States Senator from Ohio and an avowed candidate for the Presidential nomination in 1952. Prior to his election to the Senate he served in the Ohio House of Representatives (speaker, 1926) and the Ohio Senate (1931-32). His book, *A Foreign Policy for Americans*, was published in the fall of 1951.

Richard Weil, Jr. is vice-president of R. H. Macy and Company of New York. During World War II he served as a lieutenant colonel in the Army of the United States.

MR. BLOUGH: I believe that there is general agreement in this country that the nation must rearm. But I believe, also, that there are misgivings about the effects which this rearming may have upon the American economy, both immediately and for the longer run.

SENATOR TAFT: I fully agree that we are going at least to double our military preparation. The question which I raise is whether we have a sufficiently definite plan. Up in Congress we cannot decide what to do about drafting men, about levying taxes, until we know approximately what the plan is and what it is going to cost. There is the budget figure, but that seems to be a mere estimate. I have been figuring that we might have to have a total budget of 75 billion dollars. Now Mr. Wilson comes along, the night before last, and says that he is going to spend 50 billion dollars for equipment alone every year. That would mean a total budget running up to 70 billion dollars for the army and 100 billion dollars for everything else.

It seems to me that the time has come for all these people to get together; it is time for our economic mobilizers and our military people to sit down together and give us an intelligent guess. Of course it is a guess; but we ought to know it. Otherwise, we cannot make this plan which ought to be made to cover the tremendous emergency program which we face.

MR. BLOUGH: Weil, you are a businessman. How does business look at the problem of rearming?

MR. WEIL: Business, of course, supports the program and will do its part in producing and in meeting these problems. Business, I would say, has certain understandable fears in connection with this program, on which I hope we will spend some time in discussion. Business, being business, has fears having to do with money; fears about taxes; fears about margin squeezes; fears about squeezes if prices are set and wages go up. Then business has fears about good will, having to do with manpower shortages and its difficulties in rendering proper services. And, lastly, businessmen have fears about their economic independence. They have reached their present high level of activity in this country and the resulting standard of living through enjoying certain rights as business. They would like to feel sure that the rearmament program will not unduly endanger those rights.

MR. BLOUGH: Granted that the rearmament program is not so well defined as it will undoubtedly be in the course of the next few weeks and months, we must recognize that a great deal has already been done to define it. Certainly, whatever the size, within the anticipated magnitudes we are going to have a problem of adjusting our economic system to it.

Our problem is to deal with this emergency without permanent impairment of the system. How can we do this without hurting ourselves needlessly? Now you have mentioned some fears, Weil. What specifically do you see as the dangers which the rearmament program can bring to the economic system?

MR. WEIL: The biggest fear, I believe, on the part of all of us is inflation. I think that inflation is more than a bugaboo. The American people understand what happens if the purchasing power of the dollar is eroded and diminished. Whatever controls and whatever regimentation are going to be necessary to avoid inflation, or to minimize inflation, if we can satisfy ourselves that they are effective in combating inflation, are something which are eminently necessary.

SENATOR TAFT: There is one other danger of which I think. That is that we do not get in the state of being a perpetual military mind—that we do not make ourselves into a great imperialist nation, as many nations have in the past. We must realize that this is a temporary matter.

MR. BLOUGH: You think that controls and regimentation are also feared by business. I gathered from your earlier remarks, Weil, that you consider that fairly serious also.

MR. WEIL: Yes, I think that there is no question about that. The difficulties which were experienced with price controls alone during World War II and the technical difficulties of drafting the present control order indicate that it is always possible, with the best intentions in controlling prices, to drive people out of business, to create black markets, and to run into very serious evils of that sort.

SENATOR TAFT: Even more than that, today thousands of people with new ideas start new businesses every day, and this business of control practically chokes that initiative. There is not that great opportunity. Many of those things fail, but many of them build themselves up into new ideas and new businesses.

MR. WEIL: Do you not think, Senator, that the price-control problem hurts new business less than the tax problem? New business always wants a special tax base in wartime, and understandably, I think.

SENATOR TAFT: Yes. But by the time they get through they have to have allocations and things, and it is awfully hard to start on a new business if these controls are in full effect.

MR. BLOUGH: We have learned a good deal in the last ten years about how to handle an emergency situation. But in some respects our problem is more difficult even than it was at the beginning of World War II. For one thing we have had a high level of employment and production, which gives us somewhat less room in which to expand our production as needed. And, in the second place, rather than looking forward to a short, sharp crisis, after which we would presumably have peace, full peace, we are looking forward to a long period of tension. Both of those things, it occurs to me, make it more difficult at this time even than it was when we had a not much bigger effort at the beginning of World War II.

Now, our purpose here today is to talk about the policies by which these rearmament needs might be met and yet the economy might be protected. I am sure that you have given a lot of thought to that problem, Senator Taft. What do you see as these dangers?

SENATOR TAFT: In the first place, I think that it is important that we do not assume to do more than we can do and still keep some basic principles in our economy. So I think that we have to examine the magnitude of the program with great care. I have, for instance, just a suggestion. It seems to me that our military establishment is unduly wasteful. In time of war we cannot do much about it. If this crisis is going to last for ten years and eat up 70 per cent of our budget, somebody ought to make a thorough examination to study this problem to see if we cannot get the same results with less money.

Then, of course, I think that we have to do all that we can to increase production, so that we can take care of the civilian economy on the basis we want to do it and also take care of this war program, at least after we have built up the preliminary equipment which is necessary. In the third place, of course, we want to prevent inflation by limiting credit, by balancing the budget, by levying necessary taxes.

I myself think that we cannot levy too high taxes, though, without creating the very inflation we are fighting. There is a limit even to taxation, even though we can balance the budget. And, finally, we ought to do all these things in such a way as always to look forward to a return to a normal economy.

MR. BLOUGH: Let us take up these particular points which you have mentioned in the order you have mentioned them.

First, you mentioned the need for greater economy and efficiency in the military effort. Of course, in addition to that, there is the whole question of how large the military effort should be. There is obviously some weighing that has to be done. Do we dare sacrifice military security to reduce the risks which the expanded program would have on the economy? Must not the economy really support whatever is necessary for military security?

SENATOR TAFT: Well, in principle yes, but what *is* necessary for military security? That is about as elastic a figure as anybody can dream of. Complete military security would probably require us to spend 150 billion dollars a year, beyond an all-out war status, and put us into a garrisoned state. I do not think that we can do that now because we are facing the possibility of actually having peace for the next ten years with war preparations. We have to get a program, as opposed to a war program, for which people will stand for ten years. People will pay high taxes in the middle of the war when the boys are fighting and when they think it is going to be over in a year or two, but, when it comes to paying them for ten or fifteen years, there is going to be a tremendous protest.

MR. WEIL: I am wondering, Senator, how you would treat, in that connection, a problem such as radar protection for both our coasts, which costs several billion dollars and which is not complete security even after we have it. It is a good illustration of the kind of thing on which you were just commenting.

SENATOR TAFT: The relative importance of these things, of course, is, I admit, a military question, so far as what kind of things will defend us and what will not. But the only point which I am trying to make is that military security is a judgment of people. We take the same thing with people in wartime. We postpone, for example, the construction of all school buildings. Well, I do not think that people are going to be willing to postpone that type of activity for a period of ten or twenty years.

We are willing to choke new businesses off by controls for a short time; but we have to alleviate them somehow to let new businesses come in and share in raw materials and so forth. Black markets are much more likely to arise in peacetime. People will stand for price and wage controls in war, but it is going to be a tough job to impose those controls in time of peace.

Thus not only is military security elastic. What do we need for military security? Let us take right now. Is it necessary for our military security that we are spending billions in Korea and that we have over a hundred thousand soldiers in Korea fighting? Is that necessary or not? That is a question of security which has to be decided. Everybody agrees, for instance, that we are not apparently going to send soldiers to Indo-China or Tibet. That is something which probably would help our military security, but we cannot afford it. In other words, this military security decision is a relative thing. I do not want to raise the general question at this time, but that is why I have taken the position that we ought to emphasize the sea and the air in our defense and that we ought to go very slowly on high land commitments in Europe and Asia.

MR. BLOUGH: I do not feel that I am qualified, as a military strategist, as to what will give us security. But I do not think that it is purely a question of any man's judgment, one against another, as to what will give us security.

It seems to me that the problem here in connection with the economy is that we want the maximum security for the long pull. It is a question, to a considerable extent, of how soon our maximum effort might be required and for how long a period of time we must be prepared to give that maximum effort. Within the economy itself we obviously should not concentrate our effort too greatly on actual military expenditures if it will actually reduce our total security. But I cannot agree that security is simply a matter of judgment.

SENATOR TAFT: But the things we do for security *are* a matter of judgment. Certainly as to how far the protection of Western Europe is necessary for the security of the United States is a matter on which we have all sorts of opinions. Somebody has to make up his mind. It is not a military question ultimately. It is really a civilian question, and somebody has to decide that.

My only point is that we cannot go too far and wreck the economy. In the last war we spent about 50 per cent of our total national product on war, and I think that we can do it again in another actual war. The scope of the present program seems to be about 25 per cent of the national economy—about half what we did in actual war. Yet I think that it is sufficient to insure as much military security as we can hope to have in time of peace.

MR. BLOUGH: Whether or not we can get agreement on the point, it is clear that part of our economic problem is to increase the total production of the country. How can we increase the total production?

MR. WEIL: I felt that during World War II there was one question which was often discussed but never squarely enough put up to the people so that they could voice their opinion on it. That is the question of which they prefer—a longer work week, whatever the week may be, forty-four hours, forty-six hours, and at whatever pay, or the other sacrifices which they have to make in shortages of goods which are not produced if they do not work longer. I would like to see, as part of our present rearmament program, a more elaborate and more comprehensive effort made to find out what people really think—not just managements of business, not just heads of labor unions, but people. I am quite uncertain in my mind as to which they would prefer. I have no proposal to make as to which would be better for the country—a longer work week or more shortages of goods. I think the people should be given a chance to become articulate.

SENATOR TAFT: In the last two years I have walked through, oh, several hundred plants in Ohio, and I have come to have much more admiration for the forty-hour week than I had before. I think that it is awfully hard, in an industrial plant, to raise this week over forty hours. I do not say that it cannot be done. It can be done in wartime. But I do think that it ought not to be approached with any light idea that we just increase the hours of labor without some substantial damage to the morale of the people and the health of the people.

MR. WEIL: I thoroughly agree that it cannot lightly be done, and I agree thoroughly that it might not be desirable. But it is something on which attention should again be carefully focused and the reactions analyzed. I have one other point which I had in mind in connection with production. Part of increasing our production is creating new plants. Some of the new plants have to be created in critical industries, and some of those industries are reluctant to put up this added plant capacity. I believe that we can view some of these added plants as industrial cadres—a term which became very familiar to most people during World War II as nuclei in the armed forces from which they could rapidly expand into larger numbers of armed men. If we have the nuclei, or cadres, in the industrial system for defense, and then if we give some of these critical additional plants which we call "cadres" special advantages in taxation and government financial support so that we have a "mothball fleet," if you like, of plants, as well as of ships, that might help to solve our problem.

MR. BLOUGH: The increase in production, in any event, is a pretty important part of meeting the needs of the emergency without too much control and too much restriction of the economic system. The failure to get larger and larger production will, of course, be reflected in a number of different ways. Certainly one of the ways in which it is going to be reflected is in inflation and in lack of stability in the economy. The increase in production obviously is not the only way to try to fight the problem of inflation. In fact, it is not fully successful, because people's incomes increase along with the production. But everybody recognizes it to be important.

But now there are other ways that we can attack this problem of inflation which, in many people's minds, has come to be one of the most serious problems of the present time. Suppose we examine, for a little while, what can be done about inflation. Is enough being done? Is the situation being taken care of?

SENATOR TAFT: In general, it seems to me that we ought not to permit people to spend money which they do not have. That is to say, we ought to limit credit. And we ought to prevent the government from spending money that it does not have. In other words, we ought to balance the government budget. The first thing to look at is to cut the government expenditures as much as they can be cut. I certainly do not think that we ought to undertake any new programs—many of which are included in the present budget. There are various respects in which we can cut down on personnel. I said that I do not want more than forty hours a week in industrial work; but it seems to me that in office work the extra four hours on Saturday is exceedingly useful. I think that it ought to be undertaken in the government to save personnel. Then, finally, as I suggested, I think that a very fundamental study, under a civilian with military and naval advice, ought to be made to cut this tremendous expense of military preparation. We ought to be able to get the same results with less money, I believe.

MR. BLOUGH: I have seen very few people and talked to very few people who would not be very happy to see government nondefense expenditures further reduced. It is a lot easier, however, to talk about reducing them than it is actually to get them reduced, because, as I understand it, the budget is based pretty much on what appear to be the minimum public demands for the services of the government.

SENATOR TAFT: But if we are going to ask every citizen to cut his expenditures—and that is what we are doing by increasing the taxes on him—at least during this temporary period of very heavy, heavy production, it seems to me fair to ask the government also to cut back on some of the things which it has been doing.

MR. BLOUGH: Well, yes, if the citizens are willing to have those cuts made. That is the real problem.

SENATOR TAFT: We are going to cut their own expenditures, whether they are willing or not. I think that they would rather have the government expenses cut than they would their own, as a matter of fact.

MR. WEIL: I certainly agree with you on that. It is rather difficult for the citizen as an individual to express himself on what parts of government expenditures should or should not be cut; but I think that they would all be delighted if nondefense expenditures were cut and the burden, therefore, was reduced on taxes.

MR. BLOUGH: My observation is that they would all be delighted to have the expenditures cut which go to benefit somebody else but not the expenditures which benefit them. And let us not forget that the expenditures of government do not go for the pleasure and edification of the government. They are for the service of the public; and it is public programs which will be cut if these expenditures are cut. I do not mean to suggest that I am against cutting expenditures. I am in favor of cutting them, except that I am not too optimistic about its being done.

That, then, is the expenditure side of the picture. The other side is taxes. As already has been mentioned here, we ought to have a balanced budget—a balanced budget through tax collections too. And the Administration program is to do that. We had two tax increases last year. The Secretary of the Treasury and the President have asked for new taxes this year—ten billion dollars to be passed as soon as possible and the balance necessary after it is clear just what that balance will be. Is that in harmony with what the business community is thinking about this, Weil?

MR. WEIL: I find myself somewhat puzzled as to how to speak for the entire business community because I have never known them to be unanimous about anything. I think that this added tax burden, whatever it may be, which should be paid, raises, at least in my mind, one question which I want to discuss here. It would be possible, I believe, with this heavy added tax burden on personal incomes to consider a program of a certain portion of that tax being refundable to the individuals who paid the tax at some considerably later date when the inflationary dangers were substantially less. I am thinking of that not just as an emergency measure but as a permanent measure in our tax program. It is one on which I am not prepared to express a final opinion, except to say that I know that the individuals who pay the taxes would pay them with greater alacrity if they knew they were going to get some of them back at some later time.

SENATOR TAFT: It sounds to me like compulsory saving. Is that what you mean?

MR. WEIL: That is not exactly what I mean, in terms of what was proposed in the Treasury in 1943, although I agree with you that there is some relationship between the two proposals.

MR. BLOUGH: The Treasury did not propose compulsory saving; it suggested the possibility of a refundable tax, which I think is about what you are suggesting. The tax field is an extremely large one. We could also talk about excise taxes on durable goods as a method of cutting down consumption and production of such goods; and we could talk about the excess profits tax, and so on.

But let us move from taxes to the credit area. Senator Taft, you have already indicated the importance of not having credit expansion.

SENATOR TAFT: I was just looking over the figures. Consumer credit in the last twelve months, in spite of some controls toward the end of reduction, increased over three billion dollars. That means those consumers spent three billion dollars which they did not have to spend. Then, the banks have increased their loans and private securities about twelve billion dollars—a billion a month. That is four times anything which they have done in past years. And that money has been spent when people did not have it to spend, so that a big purchasing power was put in against the same old production. The production only built itself up very slowly, and obviously that has been a material factor in the increase in prices which has occurred. It seems to me that there should be selective controls on consumer credit. Housing credit has probably increased five or six billion. The government has taken steps toward control in that direction, and correctly so, I think. I do think that the Federal Reserve Board ought to be given the right to refuse to buy government bonds from the banks at par. I think that they ought to let those bonds go to their natural level, which actually may not be much different from par, so far as I can see, in any event. It seems to me that if the banks cannot cash in practically every government bond, it will help check the situation. The present policy permits them to monetize the government debt, and that means that they can increase their reserves without restraint. And I think that it would be a substantial check on government lending if these bonds were permitted to drop, well, say, to 95, or so.

MR. BLOUGH: That is an extremely technical and difficult subject to handle in a few seconds. But I simply raise the question as to whether we really will get less monetization of debt under that program than under the program which has been followed in the past. I am sure, however, that we would all agree that a reduction in bank credit, or at least the holding-down of increases in bank credit, would be very helpful in this anti-inflation program.

SENATOR TAFT: In a general way, it does seem to me that, if we can balance the government budget and prevent any unreasonable increase in credit, we ought to be able to hold prices without controls, once this distortion of the new military production program is over.

MR. BLOUGH: We really have not mentioned price and wage control. They certainly have an important part in any stabilization program. But I gather from the emphasis which we have been putting on it that we look upon price and wage controls as being relatively minor in the long-run part of this problem.

MR. WEIL: I do not think that they are minor. I think that the one thing which should be said about price control is that, at least in my opinion, it must be on all segments of the economy in order to work at all. And I believe that we must have it.

MR. BLOUGH: And you think that we must have it as part of an anti-inflation program.

Let us come back, in conclusion, to our general question: What can we do now to come back to normal when this emergency is over?

SENATOR TAFT: Of course, we ought to do the things which we have pointed out already. Above that, I think that we ought to create the psychology that this, after all, is a temporary thing which we are doing and that we are not going to change our economy permanently. We are going to stick to the free system. I feel, for instance, that, when we pass these various laws, they ought to be laws with definite termination dates, so that they expire three, four, or five years from now. We can take up then the question whether it is necessary to resume them. We must maintain the fact that we are going to stick to the American system and get back to it as soon as we can.

MR. WEIL: I agree with Senator Taft on that, and I think that nothing which we have discussed cannot be discarded when the emergency is over.

MR. BLOUGH: It seems to me that we have had a good deal of agreement here that we can do a great many things during this emergency period so that we keep the economy from getting permanently out of line from the system which has been accepted by all of us as most desirable for the long run.

Mobilizing for Defense
Charles E. Wilson

Charles E. Wilson, who was born in New York City in 1886, has been president of the General Electric Company since 1940. During World War II he served as Executive Vice-Chairman of the War Production Board. He was appointed to the post of Defense Mobilization Director by President Truman in December 1950. In late March 1952, after weeks of fruitless negotiation over steel prices, he resigned and charged in a letter to the President: "You changed the plan we agreed upon."

Mr. Wilson was a leading participant at the opening exercises of the twentieth annual *New York Herald Tribune* Forum held at the Waldorf-Astoria on 22 October 1951. In introducing the speaker Whitelaw Reid, the editor of the *Herald Tribune*, stated: "Some months ago when he left his post as head of General Electric to take the helm of defense production, the acclaim his appointment received was universal. Since then he has weathered stormy times and kept the country's mobilization on course. We are very glad he can be with us tonight to plot our present position and perhaps even, as they say in navy lingo, to give us an exact 'fix.'"

THE *Herald Tribune* Forum, with its wide renown, offers me an opportunity to emphasize the wherefores of defense mobilization—how we conceived the program, how far we have gotten, and where we are going.

The war in Korea unfortunately has become something of a habit after sixteen months. The heroism of our soldiers draws very few banner headlines.

It is therefore well to make it clear that it was not the Communist invasion by itself that caused us to mobilize for defense. That invasion was merely the latest of a long list of aggressions by Communist imperialism in furtherance of its deep-laid plans to gain supremacy over the earth.

We have seen the imperialists of the Kremlin reduce nation after nation to slavery, as in Poland and Czechoslovakia. We have seen them instigating civil war, as in Greece and Indo-China; testing and challenging us, as in Berlin; making impossible demands, as in Turkey; promoting the spread of militant Communism, as in China; undermining our economic assistance, as in France and Italy; sabotaging the United Nations, as in repeated meetings of the Council and Assembly; spreading the big lie and the little lie about us, as in their daily propaganda broadcasts, and everywhere stimulating the subversion of free governments through their henchmen, as in this hemisphere. Throughout we have seen them strengthening their armed forces, and those of their satellites, even in the face of our own demobilization. We have seen them spending upon their armaments a percentage of their national income that to us would be intolerable.

We have begun to appreciate the nature of the terrible danger that confronts us. We have become aware that if we shrank from meeting the challenge, the ambitious men of the Kremlin would push into every existing area of weakness until finally we would have to accept their gage in conditions of frightful inferiority.

We have therefore acted. We joined with other United Nations countries to throw back the invaders in Korea, we completed a security system with our friends in the North Atlantic, and we began our rearmament program.

Therefore, what happens in Korea must not influence the bases of our defense mobilization. If while I am talking here tonight a firm truce were to be signed, I say to you that we must not deflect by one whit from our inflexible determination to become strong, and remain strong.

We are still in grave danger. We will be in danger throughout the winter. We may be in graver danger next spring, still graver danger next summer. Not until the men of the Kremlin say to themselves, "If we attack it means the end of us," can we stop to breathe.

We have recognized the possibility that our present twilight relationship with Russia may last over a period of years—who knows, ten, perhaps fifteen, perhaps twenty. We have planned accordingly. And we must act accordingly.

When we laid the premises for the program there were those who said, "Let us build to a peak in one year or a year and a half." But fortunately there were more who said that such an effort—spending $150,000,000,000 for armaments in such a period—might wreck us internally.

Accordingly we agreed on a three-year program of $150,000,000,000 spent for military goods, the delivery of which would spread out over a period somewhat longer than three years. At the end of three years we and our allies would be so strong that only the most reckless of reckless men in the Kremlin would think of attacking us—and if they did we could shatter their assaults.

After the first year we would be greatly strengthened and capable of a very rapid expansion of our might if the showdown came. That year is now past and we are now in that position.

After the summit of strength had been reached we would maintain the peak at much less effort; military production could taper off in quantity while continuing to stress quality and invention; and civilian production could resume its normal upward climb.

Thirteen months after the passage of the Defense Production Act of September, 1950, that is still our plan. I have seen nothing develop to warrant its alteration. But more than ever it requires understanding and patience.

Some people have said the three-year plan was an open invitation to the Kremlin to attack us in the meantime. But our strength is already at the point where the Soviet leaders ought to hesitate long before challenging it. The powerful wheels of American production are turning ever faster, and he who would thrust his sword into them may find it broken.

Further in line with our graduated approach we are carrying out two principles:

One is that, while turning out planes, tanks, and guns, we are developing further production lines, so that, in the event all-out war comes, we can swing to all-out production in relatively short time. In essence, we would fight the war right from the production lines.

For instance, our program may call for the production of 15,000 or 18,000 planes a year, but we are also installing production lines with a capacity for 50,000 planes a year, if needed.

The second principle is that we are expanding the production of our basic metals, particularly steel and aluminum, so that, in due course, we can provide for military goods largely from the new production. For example, we shall nearly double our production of primary aluminum.

This three-pronged effort—military goods production, establishment of extra military goods production lines, and expansion of our basic metals production—is the greatest demand upon our abilities and resources the United States has ever seen except in all-out war.

Often those who protest that we are not producing this airplane or that tank fast enough forget to mention the two other programs we are carrying forward simultaneously.

It is not our intention to cover the State of Texas with myriads of tanks and planes and guns, there to become obsolete.

Moreover, I am in accord with the willingness of the armed services to halt production of a given item when a new design is conceived that will materially improve that item.

Our production plans, in fact, are satisfactory to the Department of Defense. The production picture on the whole is encouraging. Month by month America's military might grows. Looking ahead through next year the outpouring of military material will steadily increase and in 1953 it will pour from the production lines of America in a mighty torrent—enough to submerge an enemy if need be.

Our rearmament program is facing us now with mountainous problems in finding and wisely distributing the requisite materials. The present quarter and the first two quarters of 1952 will find us straining our whole economy to the utmost.

The crucial period ahead will call for sacrifices and understanding from all of us. Sharp bites are being made into the materials allocated for civilian durable-goods production. Within ten days new taxes go into effect.

This is the winter that will test our character. To my mind one of the highest aspects of character is restraint. The savage knows no restraint—he goes out with a club to get all he can. But the more civilized a man is, the more he knows how to exercise restraint.

This, I hope, will be a winter of restraint. There will be powerful temptations for one group and another—especially the organized groups, agriculture, business, and labor—to come forward and claim special considerations in prices, wages or allocations of materials.

But I want to remind them that this nation is finer and mightier than all of its components. The whole is greater than the sum of all its parts.

The next eight months will test our national character in the crucible of an historic emergency. This period will test whether we are ready for the role of world leadership that has been thrust upon us. Have we the character and unity necessary, are we ready to accept the sacrifices and pay the economic price required? The price of security is admittedly high even for the richest nation on earth.

Aside from the material sacrifices, are we bulwarked with the spiritual and moral forces so vital to a political democracy engaged in so gigantic a task? I believe the answer is affirmative if the American people understand the terrible threat of imperialist Communism to dominate the world. The dangers that beset us must—I believe will—strengthen our unity, bolster our national character, and heighten our moral and spiritual powers.

As a thoroughly united nation we will go forward to build our strength, determined to fulfill our destiny—to preserve our priceless heritage of liberty and freedom, bought with the blood of our sons from 1776 to Korea, 1951—and to help other freedom-loving people whose strength and dependence is also in Almighty God, and who, like ourselves, are willing if need be to fight and die that liberty and freedom shall not vanish from the earth according to the blueprint of the godless crew of the Kremlin.

Acting from a foundation of spiritual, moral, and military strength, and with the help of God, we may well be able to prevent World War III and to lead the people of the world to a realm of fruitful, lasting peace.

How Can We Stop Rising Prices?
Michael V. DiSalle, Walter P. Reuther, and Herschel D. Newsom; George V. Denny, Jr., Moderator

This discussion took place in Fredericksburg, Virginia on 20 February 1951. Mr. DiSalle was unable to be present and he therefore spoke from Washington. The program, presented by America's Town Meeting of the Air, was sponsored by the Fredericksburg Chamber of Commerce and Mary Washington College of the University of Virginia.

Michael V. DiSalle was appointed Director of Price Stabilization of the Economic Stabilization Agency by President Truman on 1 December 1950 and resigned that post on 23 January 1952. He is a lawyer by profession and prior to assuming his duties in Washington had served as a member of the Ohio legislature, the City Council of Toledo, and as Mayor of Toledo. He served as first president of the Ohio Association of Municipalities in 1949. Later he became chairman of the United States Conference of Mayors. As a delegate of this group he was one of a party of four United States mayors designated to attend the 1949 International Union of Cities meeting in Geneva.

Walter P. Reuther is president of the International Union of United Automobile, Aircraft and Agricultural Implement Workers of America, CIO. He began his career as an apprentice tool and die maker at the Wheeling Steel Corporation in 1924. From 1927 to 1932 he worked in Detroit at plants of the Briggs Manufacturing Company, the General Motors Corporation, and the Ford Motor Company. Following a three-year tour of Europe and the Orient by bicycle, he returned to the United States in 1935 to organize automobile workers. He was elected vice-president of his union in August 1942 and president in March 1946 and again in 1947.

Herschel D. Newsom was elected master of the National Grange in November 1950. He is a member of the policy committee of the United States Chamber of Commerce and also served on the Public Advisory Board for the Economic Coöperation Administration. Born on a farm in Indiana in 1905, Mr. Newsom has long been identified with the campaign for better farming methods and better living conditions. He was graduated with a degree in chemistry at Indiana University in 1926. He now owns and operates a large farm near Columbus, Indiana.

MODERATOR DENNY: Good evening, neighbors. How can we stop rising prices? Well, this certainly is the jackpot question. I'm sure Michael DiSalle, Walter Reuther, Herschel Newsom and every American citizen would like to know the answer. And don't let us forget, friends, that we wouldn't be facing this emergency if we had found the right answers to the problem of peace-making in 1945.

The Defense Mobilization Act, prompted by Korea, was passed by Congress late last summer. The basic price-control order was issued on January 26 last, which set ceilings at the highest prices charged between December 19 and January 25. But it was something like clamping controls on with a sieve as there were so many exceptions. In the area of food, for instance, the law forbids real ceilings on farm products selling below parity. Union labor complains that there is no stabilization program except wage stabilization.

Hence, we have invited Herschel Newsom, head of the Grange, Walter Reuther, President of the United Automobile Workers, C.I.O., to discuss this question with Mr. DiSalle, Director of Price Stabilization of the Economic Stabilization Agency.

Mr. DiSalle, former Mayor of Toledo, who has also seen service in the Ohio State Legislature and the Toledo City Council, must be a man of high good humor and a great patriot, indeed, to undertake his present job. We're delighted to welcome him to Town Meeting, although he speaks to us tonight from Washington. Mr. DiSalle.

MR. DISALLE: Thank you, George Denny. I regret that I have to make this broadcast from Washington because it deprives me of certain pleasures that I had anticipated. One would be to come down and visit with the good folks in Fredericksburg, the other would be to renew the acquaintanceship of my good neighbor from Detroit, Walter Reuther, and then the opportunity of meeting Herschel Newsom. However, many times we're deprived of those things that we want most.

The Director of Price Stabilization has much in common with the modern American college football coach; he has more downtown coaches judging his every action than possibly even the coach at Ohio State University.

I have been asked the question many times, why didn't we control prices earlier than January the 26th. The answer is that the American people hate controls. When I took the job as Price Stabilizer on December the 12th we knew it was a momentous thing to impose peace-time controls on the American economy. We approached the job with great caution.

Inflationary pressures, the prices of food, wool, cotton, tin, steel, and rubber were building up toward the danger point. But as we dug into the job of price stabilization we could not help but be impressed with the case for voluntary controls. We tried the voluntary program first but it didn't work. Prices continued to go up; therefore on January 26 we put the general freeze on prices. This action definitely slowed the upward rise.

I know that Mr. Reuther, Mr. Newsom, and all you good people listening tonight want to know why prices have continued to go up after the freeze. You and I realize that we cannot simply apply the brakes suddenly to a truck going seventy miles an hour without a smash-up. You have to apply the brakes gradually. We must be fair to three million business concerns selling more than eight million items. And we must protect 152 million American consumers.

We remember that prices continued to rise for over a year after OPA's general maximum price regulation. This was even after a year of what was called "jawbone control," and the issuance of over one hundred price schedules. Our price freeze is less than a month old with our very first action, the issuance of voluntary standards, dating back to December the 19th.

Our general price regulation puts ceilings on practically all commodities and goods at all levels of processing, distributing, and retailing. We are working out special regulations for retailers, wholesalers, and manufacturers. We are working out specific meat regulations. But the Defense Production Act requires that ceilings cannot be applied to agricultural commodities until prices reflect parity or the minimum price required by law. Rents are covered by a separate act.

I am deeply concerned with the need to give the farmer a fair share of the national income, Mr. Newsom. Consequently, I have publicly

How Can We Stop Rising Prices?

taken the position that we should have more experience with price controls, before we make recommendations with reference to the present parity provisions of the Defense Production Act. But should the next two or three months indicate that the parity concept interferes with our efforts to hold the price line, we shall have to recommend to Congress that the parity provisions be modified.

All Americans have a responsibility to help stabilize prices. The business man cannot expect business as usual. He must do his best to hold prices down. Workers should not press for wage increases that would cause additional rises in prices.

We are all consumers, we are all in this fight together, and let me make a personal appeal to each of you. Buy only what you need. There are no shortages of necessities. Buy only at legal ceiling prices. Do not hoard or buy through fear. Buy carefully and wisely, using and saving wherever you can.

MODERATOR DENNY: Thank you, Mr. DiSalle. Walter Reuther is both president of the United Automobile Workers, the largest union in the country, and a vice-president of the C.I.O., as well as one of the outstanding spokesmen for organized labor. Mr. Reuther is deeply concerned about tonight's question and we are happy to welcome him back to America's Town Meeting. Mr. Walter Reuther.

MR. REUTHER: Good evening. Mr. DiSalle, you suggested that we had to proceed on the price control front with great caution. I believe that if our fighting men had proceeded with equal caution on the battle fronts that we would have lost Korea. To defend freedom we must fight both Communism on the battle front and profiteering and runaway prices on the home front with equal courage.

The recent so-called price control order is a fraud upon the American people. Prices were frozen at the stratospheric levels to which they had soared. The government has rolled back the prices of Cadillacs and scrap iron but the price of food keeps going up. In Detroit, hamburger and stew beef are 79 cents a pound. There is no substitute for effective price and rent control. The halfway, halfhearted steps taken to date will not do the job and the cost of living will continue to rise. Yes, Mr. DiSalle, Americans hate controls but they hate inflation much more.

Congress must take immediate action to amend and strengthen price control by putting teeth into the law and rolling back prices.

We must attack inflation on every front. Congress must enact the pay-as-you-go tax program, based upon ability to pay. The present tax law forces low income families to pay more than their fair share. The proposed tax bill is even worse. Families of less than $5,000 income are now paying as much in taxes as they paid during the last war, while a family with a $500,000 income is paying $40,000 less. A fair tax program must first reduce the standard of luxury of wealthy families, before it cuts into the standard of living of low income families. Corporations must pay a larger share of the tax burden out of their scandalous profits.

Effective control of the cost of living and a fair tax program are the key to wage stabilization. American labor recognizes the need and is prepared to accept wage stabilization as a part of an overall economic stabilization program. Realistic wage stabilization must provide for wage adjustments to compensate for increases in the cost of living, the correction of substandard wages, the right of workers to share in the benefits of technical progress; and, finally, the government should not upset or tamper with existing collective bargaining contracts. Industrial stability and high levels of production are not possible unless they rest upon equity and justice for workers and their families.

Working farmers like city workers are entitled to economic justice. Fair prices for the farmers should be guaranteed through parity with subsidy payments, where necessary, to prevent price increase to consumers. We must reduce the tremendous gap between what the farmer gets and what the city consumer must pay.

Maximum production is a powerful anti-inflation weapon. To get full production we must break the bottlenecks of monopoly. Eight months of delay and inflation have already cost us 20 billion dollars. Mr. DiSalle tells us prices are going up at least five per cent more. This will cost us another 12 billion dollars.

America must and can stop rising prices. The government must demonstrate the same courage fighting inflation at home as our men in Korea are demonstrating in the fight against Communist tyranny and aggression. Thank you.

MODERATOR DENNY: Thank you, Walter Reuther. The new Master of the National Grange is the owner and operator of a 472-acre farm near Columbus, Indiana. He attributes his recent election as head of the Grange to his opposition to "excessive governmental control of farm products and our daily lives." It's important, therefore, that we hear his voice on tonight's subject and we're happy to welcome to America's Town Meeting of the Air, Mr. Herschel D. Newsom.

MR. NEWSOM: Thank you, Mr. Denny. Mr. DiSalle indicates that if food prices rise more he may ask for a change in the Stabilization Act. Presumably this would mean that farm prices now below parity may be frozen at lower than equitable prices. I want to point out that

How Can We Stop Rising Prices?

ceilings that yield the producer a less price than cost of production may help the consumers to buy more temporarily, but surely they'll not be helpful when production is lower, and, we should hasten to add, we are informed that this is likely to be a long-time effort.

Mr. Reuther has well said that we must attack inflation vigorously through a tax program. I would point out that a sound tax program, in this respect, means assessing income tax liability at the individual level and not in the form of hidden taxes through the businesses of the country, which are passed on to the consumers without any regard to their ability to pay.

The National Grange is made up of 850,000 rural people who for the most part operate family farms. They represent a cross section of American agriculture. They are as much concerned about inflation as you are.

Farm families buy more things on the average than the family living in town. And the farmers' costs have gone to record highs. At the same time, prices received by farmers have advanced, since Korea, only 21 per cent. Prices of other commodities have increased much more during this period—tin, for example, 138 per cent; chemicals, 27 per cent; textiles, 32 per cent; aluminum, 78 per cent, and so on.

As we in the National Grange see it, the surest protection consumers have against exorbitant food prices is the will that farmers have to produce abundantly, which is as dependable and as determined as the burst of spring itself. Farmers have already embarked upon a production program aimed at producing the greatest volume of food, without exposing our precious land to destruction through misuse.

I must point out, however, that in my opinion we are in real danger of falling short. Only last week I was back on my farm in Indiana and while there was asked to fill out six applications for recommendation to industries and the local community that are planning to employ people that have worked and operated farms in my neighborhood.

Most of us agree, I believe, that meats are the most discussed recent food price increases. None of the increases resulted from the imposition of a parity formula or support prices. In fact, prices of red meats, as well as other agricultural commodities, have increased principally because of rising consumer demands. Even so, the USDA predicts as individuals we will eat this year, including meat, more than at any time since 1947. Specifically, we are expected to have three pounds more meat per person this year. Official reasons are given for this: higher employment, longer working hours, and more spendable income for food because of cutbacks in civilian goods.

Much has been made of the fact that farm commodities selling below parity are free to rise and thus increase the cost of living before becoming subject to control. But if all commodities now below parity should reach the parity level, consumer food costs would rise less than 5 per cent, and this would mean a 2 per cent rise in the overall cost of living.

In direct answer to some suggestions which have been made that farm prices be frozen at levels below parity, I submit that unprofitable production cannot be maintained in a free-enterprise system. We must, if necessary to control inflation, control wages, prices, and profits. But we must recognize that price and wage controls are sound only when used to adjust purchasing power to supplies. They are unsound when used to limit or reduce the price of goods and services to a point where demand and purchasing power exceeds supply.

Freezing farm prices at levels below parity would penalize each farmer and, in my opinion, seriously jeopardize the only effective control of high prices, which is abundant production.

MODERATOR DENNY: Thank you, Mr. Newsom. Well, gentlemen, now that we have this general idea of your views perhaps you would like to have a little discussion up here around the microphone among yourselves, before we take the questions from this fine Virginia audience. We know that Mr. DiSalle is standing by in Washington ready to join us and if Mr. Reuther and Mr. Newsom will join me here, we'll have a little three-way conversation. How about it Mr. DiSalle in Washington?

MR. DISALLE: Ready.

MR. DENNY: Yes sir. Your comment or question.

MR. DISALLE: A question. I'm sorry that I can't be there because I'd like to see the expression on Walter Reuther's face.

MR. DENNY: It's very pleasant, I assure you.

MR. DISALLE: Well, he's a pleasant-looking fellow. But I think in discussing this matter we ought to remember, that in making American policy, all segments of American society express opinions and then, from joint discussions, we arrive at what ultimately is policy. I know of no fighting man, no matter how brave he might be, who deliberately walks into a machine-gun nest. He doesn't accomplish too much by it. And I'd like to ask Walter this question. Since he says that labor will accept wage stabilization providing that they get the improvement factor, and cost-of-living increases, and nobody cuts across the collective bargaining contracts, just what sacrifice is being made there?

MR. REUTHER: A great deal of sacrifice. The workers of America have been fighting. I, personally, appeared before a Congressional com-

How Can We Stop Rising Prices?

mittee, eight months ago, fighting for effective price control. Now the escalator clause that we have doesn't increase the purchasing power of the worker—it merely protects him, ninety days late, against increases in prices. The working people of America are prepared to carry their part of the load. But they're not going to have an arrangement in Washington, such as we have now, where you freeze the worker with a rabbit and you freeze the management, the industry people, who have too much, with a horse. We believe you can mobilize a free people on the basis of a program of equality of sacrifice, in which all tighten their economic belts together and we all sacrifice in the common struggle to defend freedom in the world.

MR. DENNY: Thank you. Mr. Newsom, do you want to get in on this?

MR. NEWSOM: Well, I don't know that I, especially, want in on that one, but there was a question raised a moment ago, that I didn't get a chance to answer, as to the cause of inflation, whether farmers have caused it or perhaps somebody else. I want to point out that it is a matter of supply and demand. This three pounds of extra meat, that the farmers of this nation have provided this year, for each consumer in the land, over and above that supply which was available last year, just isn't adequate to match the increased demand—the increased purchasing power that they have in the form of dollars to purchase that meat and we must recognize those two causes of inflation.

MR. REUTHER: I'd like to say that I think every American appreciates that the job taken on by Mr. DiSalle is a very difficult one. And most of the trouble is not in his hands. It's in the hands of Congress because they have not given him adequate tools to work with. I would like to pose a question, which came up during the last war, when we were working under OPA. You see, when you control the price of goods, that's only half the problem. You've got to control the quality, because we learned, under OPA, if they control the price of a pair of shoes for the children, at $5.00, and the price was fixed, but the quality of shoes wasn't fixed, and that pair of shoes would normally last six months, but then the manufacturer chiseled on the quality, and he put paper soles on instead of leather soles, and they lasted only three months. So really while you were paying $5.00 for a pair of shoes, it wasn't the same pair of shoes. Now we plugged those holes in OPA; we worked hard at it. The present law specifically does not permit controlling quality standards. I want to know how you can make a law work that does not protect the consumer and guarantee that for the same price, he's getting the same quality of goods.

MR. DISALLE: I'll answer that question for Walter. I've never claimed that price controls had all the answers to all the problems that we face. I want to say this to Walter—I appreciate what he said about Americans realizing what a difficult task this is, I just want to say, Walter, as one American, I realize it more than any other American that I know, that's Mr. DiSalle—on the problem that you raised, we must work with other defense agencies in hitting those fundamental problems. On the day that we issued our general freeze order, Charles Wilson issued from the Office of Defense Mobilization, an order directed to NPA to coöperate with us on the channelization of materials, the freezing of models, and an order designed to preserve low end items, and we hope through those devices to help preserve quality of merchandise.

MR. REUTHER: I was just going to say, Mike, it's going to take much more than hope. It's going to take some effective price policing machinery because we found that out under OPA.

MR. DISALLE: Well, we're going to give it to you.

MR. DENNY: All right, thank you. Mr. Newsom, do you have a comment? Mr. DiSalle, anything for the speakers here?

MR. DISALLE: Not right now. I'd like to answer some questions.

MR. DENNY: All right. We're going out in the audience now for questions.

SCIENCE AND RESEARCH

The State of Science
Karl T. Compton

This address was delivered at the Massachusetts Institute of Technology Mid-Century Convocation in Boston on 31 March 1949.

Karl T. Compton, ninth president of M.I.T. from 1930 to 1948, is a distinguished physicist, educational administrator, and government research director. During World War II he served as a member of the National Defense Research Committee, as chairman of the U.S. Radar Mission to Great Britain, and as chief of the Office of Field Service of the Office of Scientific Research and Development. He resigned the presidency of M.I.T. in late 1948 to become Chairman of the Research and Development Board of the National Military Establishment.

The volume, *Mid-Century,* giving the verbatim account of the discussions held at M.I.T. on the occasion of the Mid-Century Convocation, 31 March and 1, 2 April 1949, is dedicated to Dr. Compton. The editor, John E. Burchard, describes him as "a distinguished scientist, a man of great heart, an understanding boss, and a tolerant friend."

One of three brothers who became university presidents, Dr. Karl Compton was born in Wooster, Ohio in 1887. He was graduated from the College of Wooster in 1908 and received his Master of Science degree there in 1909. Princeton awarded him the Ph.D. degree in 1912. He taught at Reed College and at Princeton (1915-30) where he became a full professor in 1919 and chairman of the department of physics in 1929.

In this address, one of the most significant at the Mid-Century Convocation, Dr. Compton analyzes and evaluates the accomplishments of science during the first half of the twentieth century. This assessment admirably complements the appraisal of world political events made by Winston Churchill and published as the leading address of this volume.

As I contemplated the task of preparing for this occasion an evaluation of science at the mid-century, I quickly came to a conclusion which became more firmly established as I proceeded, and which I shall now demonstrate to you. It is that I am inadequate for the task. I am reminded, by analogy, of the Negro sprinter who, when complimented on his running 100 yards in $9\frac{1}{2}$ seconds, replied: "I could run that race in 9 seconds if it wasn't for the longness of the distance and the shortness of the time." I am handicapped by the bigness of the subject and the smallness of my capacity to do it justice.

Were I a man from Mars, visiting our planet à la Orson Welles, I should have certain advantages. In the first place I should undoubtedly be very intelligent, else I could not have contrived to make the journey and land safely. In the second place I could view this scene objectively. For the attempt to stand off, in time or space, and survey objectively our accomplishments and our shortcomings is a difficult one. Our sincerest efforts toward objectivity are unconsciously colored, not only by our own convictions and philosophy, but by those fields to which we have allied ourselves, so that the statesman tends to view everything as a political problem, the priest, as a spiritual one, the economist, as a social one, and the scientist, as a problem for his laboratory. Nor am I, as we shall see later, any exception to this rule.

But for the moment, let us look at the world through the eyes of the man from Mars. This, his latest invasion, is timed for the rounding of the mid-century, an accounting time when one tends to review the past for the progress made to date and to contemplate the future speculatively as to what may lie ahead.

Let us suppose our Martian had prepared himself for his trip by a study of history. He would first of all be struck by the long existence of the earth itself as a physical entity in contrast to the brief span of time in which man has played a significant role, an estimated two or three billions of years for the earth and a brief million and a half for man. He would be further astonished by the tiny fragment of time we call "history" in contrast to the endless millennia of prehistory. He would note that all that modern man knows of prehistoric man has been cleverly deduced from the mute evidence left by his ancestors, often hidden in caves and dry river valleys. And finally, he could not fail to be astonished by the unequal march of history itself—the long eras during which man fought and struggled and moved along, to the slow pedestrian pace of two to four miles per hour—in contrast to this century in which he has accelerated his pace until it has exceeded the speed of sound.

Our Martian's perusal of history would have acquainted him with the various stages of civilization and culture through which man has passed—the nomadic civilization of the early Semitic tribes, the intellectual ages of Greece and Rome, the primitive agrarian culture of the middle ages, the emergence of the crafts and guilds, the cultural renaissance of the Western world, and the rise of exploration and sea travel. And finally, he would view with some astonishment, no doubt, the industrial revolution of the last hundred years and its kaleidoscopic impact on the succeeding decades.

But he would be unprepared, I think, in his global survey, for the strange inconsistencies and incongruities of the modern world. Having observed in his study of history a slow progression through nomadic, agrarian, handicraft, and industrial stages of economy, he would likely be surprised to find examples of all these stages still extant in various parts of the world. Or, if he had been particularly interested in the social and political emergence of man, how would he account for the vestigial remains of ancient tyranny, the oppressive burden of autocratic rule, still existing side by side with the democracies of the modern world? In short, to borrow a figure from the biologists, he would find our present-day civilization the phylogenesis of human history.

We might assume that this mid-century convocation on the social implications of scientific progress, which opens today, has convened for the purpose of explaining to the man from Mars the achievements, the trends, the problems, and the anomalies of our times. And in so doing perhaps we shall be able to gain for ourselves a better understanding of the multiplicity of forces which have a bearing on our lives, and so achieve a better orientation for the resolution of those discords which threaten further progress.

For my part, I am happy to be today the special pleader for the role of science in modern society. For I hold that science and technology are largely responsible for much that we find good in the world, and are capable of being the common denominator of many things we seek to accomplish in the decades ahead.

To our visitor from Mars I would point out that the scientist and engineer are busy not only in the laboratory and library, but in many strange places on, above, and below the surface of the earth. On one of the highest mountain peaks in America one group of scientists measures the effects of cosmic radiation, while many feet below the surface of the earth, in a dark tunnel or at the bottom of a lake, other scientists check on the cosmic bullets that pierce the surface of the earth. In bathyspheres, as strange in appearance as though they themselves had come from Mars, men try new fathoms of the ocean depths. And missiles of extraordinary shape and size hurtle hundreds of miles above the earth to seek new data on the upper atmosphere and the spheres that lie above it. So that if to our neighbor, Mars, we appear as a race of ants, busy with a complex and remarkable division of labor, we must also appear as the possessors of an extraordinary intellectual curiosity —examining every aspect of our tiny globe and then projecting ourselves beyond it into the infinities of space.

The marvels thus uncovered have been so numerous and so dazzling in recent years that we have come to accept each new announcement with a certain complacency—almost indifference—as though nothing were to be wondered at. Yet these things to which we adjust ourselves so quickly as to be almost unconscious of change, and which we quickly come to count as necessities and "rights" of life, are often things which were entirely unknown to our grandparents or our parents.

It is not inappropriate, then, that we should take stock, at the midcentury, of exactly where we do stand in scientific achievement, and what is yet to be accomplished. For the scientist is not apt to find himself in the predicament of Alexander the Great, who wept because there were no more worlds to conquer. We shall see, I think, that much needs to be done on an ever-widening scale toward meeting the physical needs and opportunities facing mankind, and that science is responsive, also, to those who see in it a method of approach to the deeper social problems of our times.

In assessing the status of science and society today, it is a temptation to use as a point of comparison the middle of the last century. Politically, the world then turned in an aura of unrest, not unlike that in which we today find ourselves. The revolutions which had swept across central Europe in 1848, with an upsurge of liberalism and self-determination, had been succeeded by counterrevolutions and strong reaction in 1849 and 1850. To those seekers of freedom who had sought to introduce new concepts of human rights into the ancient monarchies of Europe, it must have seemed that their work and sacrifices had been in vain. The efforts for a democratic federation of states in Germany had failed; Austria had regained autocratic domination of central Europe; and the progress that had been made in Italy had been lost in the tide of reaction.

Men like Garibaldi, Lamartine, and Louis Kossuth became the displaced persons of their day, and many of them sought refuge in the United States. Yet though all may have seemed lost to these valiant liberals, the receding tide of revolution had left its mark, and the smell of change was in the air.

In Great Britain Queen Victoria had only just completed the first decade of her long reign. Things were relatively stable politically, and the industrial revolution had passed its first stage. The long train of miserable social conditions which the first impact of the machine age had brought to the working classes had only begun to be ameliorated. But thanks to the zeal of social reformers and enlightened industrialists, such as Robert Owen, Britain was learning how better to utilize this vast new giant in its midst and, above all, was coming to realize that economic stability was intimately associated with well-being, and that increased ability to produce on the part of working people was basic to any improvement in their standards of living.

It is hard for us now to realize from what depths these living standards have risen thanks to the applications of science which produced the machine age. Just prior to the introduction of steam power, men, women, and children labored between fourteen and sixteen hours a day in poorly equipped factories, enjoyed no transportation of any kind, lived in windowless and unheated houses, and could not afford the luxury of candlelight because candles were taxed. Even the least fastidious today would be horrified at the unhygienic conditions which everywhere prevailed in the absence of even the most primitive types of sanitary facilities. In the long, six-day weeks there was neither money nor leisure for any kind of recreation. The average number of a man's acquaintances during his entire lifetime was of the order of only a hundred. Intellectual and cultural activities among the poor were unheard of. The rate of infant mortality was enormous and estimated life expectancy was about thirty years. Moves to better these conditions can be traced in part to the strong emotional appeal of such tales as *Oliver Twist, Bleak House,* and *Martin Chuzzlewit.*

In 1850 the first industrial exposition in the world was held in the Crystal Palace in London under the patronage of Queen Victoria and the Prince Consort.

For the United States, which abounded in its great expanses of unexploited land and endless national resources, there were no very difficult adjustments to make to get into the swing of the industrial revolution. It was just coming into full stride as a nation. Politically the sectional strife between the abolitionist North and the slave-holding South had come to an uneasy lull, based upon the compromise of 1850. For the time being, violently partisan points of view were submerged in the common desire to take advantage of a rapidly expanding economy.

Arthur M. Schlesinger, in his chapter on mid-century America, writes as follows concerning that mid-century economy:[1]

> The amount of capital invested in manufacturing (including fisheries and mines) doubled, totaling more than a billion dollars on the eve of the Civil War. First in order of importance was the making of flour and meal, then boots and shoes, cotton textiles, and lumber

[1] Arthur Meier Schlesinger, *Political and Social Growth of the United States, 1852-1933* (New York, The Macmillan Company, 1933), p. 4.

products, with clothing, machinery, leather and woolen goods forging rapidly to the fore. In 1849, for the first time, the patents granted for new inventions passed the thousand mark, to reach nearly six times that number in 1860.

He also points out that "Of the new mechanisms employed in industry the census officials in 1860 characterized the sewing machine as 'altogether a revolutionary instrument.'" From where we stand today, it is difficult to realize that a century ago perhaps the most significant tool in American industry was the sewing machine.

With respect to science and invention, the world at the last mid-century stood at the threshold of far-reaching and significant discoveries which were to render the ensuing century unparalleled in human progress.

Whitehead has observed that the greatest invention of the nineteenth century was the invention of the method of invention. He goes on to say,[2] "In order to understand our epoch, we can neglect all the details of change, such as railways, telegraphs, radios, spinning machines, synthetic dyes. We must concentrate on the method in itself; that is the real novelty, which has broken up the foundations of the old civilization. The prophecy of Francis Bacon has now been fulfilled; and man, who at times dreamt of himself as a little lower than the angels, has submitted to become the servant and the minister of nature."

In physics, at the last mid-century, the scientific world stood firmly on the solid foundation of Newtonian mechanics, unaware that just ahead a series of events was taking shape which would effect a revolution in traditional thinking. In electricity, the basis had been laid by Franklin and Volta, while Oersted, Faraday, and Henry had shown the relation between electricity and magnetism. Fresnel had established the wave theory of light, and Joule had just proved the equivalence of heat and work.

But in 1850 the great evolution of the science of physics was about to begin. Dr. Robert A. Millikan summarized these events last year on the occasion of the Centennial of the American Association for the Advancement of Science by mentioning three great advances: (1) the establishment by Joule, Kelvin, Mayer, and Helmholtz of the first and second laws of thermodynamics; (2) the quantitative proof of the kinetic theory of gases by Clausius, Boltzmann, and Maxwell; and (3)

[2] Alfred North Whitehead, *Science and the Modern World* (New York, The Macmillan Company, 1926), p. 141.

the publication by Maxwell in 1867 of his classic paper on electromagnetism. Millikan calls Maxwell the greatest ornament of his age and points out that "Maxwell's book has created the present age of electricity in much the same way in which Newton's *Principia* created, a hundred years earlier, the mechanical age in which we are still living."[3]

The century drew to a close with four very great discoveries which have profoundly affected our own times. They are: (1) Roentgen's discovery of x-rays in 1895; (2) Becquerel's discovery of radioactivity in 1896; (3) J. J. Thomson's demonstration in 1897 of the electron as a fundamental constituent of all the atoms of the universe; and (4) the quantum theory of radiation enunciated by Planck in Berlin in 1900.

During the period in which such strides were being made in physics, the other sciences, notably chemistry, biology, and medicine, were not standing still. But, whereas research in physics had enjoyed a steady growth for the two centuries preceding the opening of the nineteenth, the other sciences lagged somewhat in their development. This was partly because in both chemistry and biology there had been a strong tendency to cling to the classical teachings of the past. But, more significantly, progress in these fields and in medicine also was dependent to a large extent on the tools and processes being evolved by modern physics.

If one were to review even a partial list of the great names in the growth of chemistry prior to this century, it would be necessary to mention the Norwegians, Guldberg and Waage, who stated the law of mass action; the great Swedish chemist, Arrhenius, who advanced the theory of electrolytic disassociation; and the American, Willard Gibbs, whose phase rule contributed so much to the development of industrial chemistry. There would be the Russian, Mendelyeev, who first classified the elements in the periodic table, and the Polish Marie Sklodowska who, with her French husband, Pierre Curie, made the important discovery of radium. Von Liebig and Wöhler would stand for organic chemistry, and mention should be made of Hofmann, who may be regarded as the father of the German dye industry. To aspiring young scientists of today it should be of interest to note that one of Hofmann's students, W. H. Perkin, a boy of seventeen, is credited with discovering the first synthetic dye. The chemical industry in the United States to-

[3] Robert A. Millikan, "The Progress of Physics from 1848 to 1948," *Science,* Vol. 108, No. 2081 (September 3, 1948), p. 231.

day owes much of its start to basic work in dyes and synthetics which was done in Germany prior to World War I.

The emphasis which modern industry and modern warfare also have laid upon physical sciences has tended to obscure somewhat in the public eye the less spectacular advances of biology and medicine. The use of atomic power for both constructive and destructive purposes has greater interest for the public imagination than that mysterious process by which green plants convert the energy of the sun into the substance of life. But who can say whether the answer to the secret of photosynthesis may not have more far-reaching effects on our lives and on those of generations to come?

C. E. Kenneth Mees, whose book, *The Path of Science*,[4] presents a succinct review of the growth of scientific ideas, places the beginning of modern biology in 1838 with the publication by two Germans, Schleiden and Schwann, of the cell theory.

Biological sciences developed enormous impetus from the publication in 1859 of Darwin's *Origin of Species,* but Darwin died without ever learning of the important work of Gregor Mendel, whose great study of heredity shed such interesting light on Darwin's theories. The science of genetics, which rests upon the foundation so brilliantly laid by Mendel, owes much to the Belgian zoölogist Beneden, who discovered the double sets of chromosomes in each nucleus except the reproductive cells.

It was also in this latter half of the nineteenth century that the great German pioneer bacteriologist, Robert Koch, discovered the bacilli of anthrax and tuberculosis, that the great French chemist, Louis Pasteur, did his pioneering work on germs and ferments, and the British Lord Lister developed antiseptic surgery.

Astronomy at the end of the nineteenth century was largely observational, with the discovery and cataloguing of stars and nebulae, examination of the appearance of sun and planets, and precise calculations of orbits. Stellar spectra and brightness were measured with routine persistence but without interpretive theories to guide and give significance to the observations.

In the foregoing sketch of science up to the beginning of our twentieth century I have made no attempt at complete coverage; I have even omitted entire fields of science, like geology and psychology. I have not discussed practical applications, like engineering and medi-

[4] C. E. Kenneth Mees, *The Path of Science* (New York, John Wiley & Sons, Inc., 1947).

cine. I have only used these few examples to serve as "springboards" for the jump into the twentieth century, in which scientific progress has forged ahead with ever-increasing acceleration, and in which the fields of science, hitherto almost separate in their development, have merged more and more toward a single all-inclusive and all-interrelated science of the forces and materials of nature.

The physicists and the chemists both started their twentieth-century research with the atom. The physicists have looked into the atom to discover how it was constructed and how its parts behaved. The chemists piled atoms together to form molecules of all degrees of complexity. The work of each reacted on the other, and physicists had to learn more chemistry and chemists more physics. And the discoveries of each provided new tools for both.

The major interest of physical science in the first dozen years of the century was in the attempt to explain natural phenomena by the behavior of electrons under the influence of electric forces. Such theories were very successful for some phenomena, and had some very important practical applications, namely our entire modern electronics industry. But the electron alone was far from adequate to account for the universe.

Then Lord Rutherford proved that each atom has a heavy nucleus of positive electricity surrounded by electrons. Moseley in England proved by x-rays that these atomic nuclei are characterized by simple numbers: 1 for hydrogen, 2 for helium, 3 for lithium, and so on up to 92 for uranium, and these numbers were soon identified with the electric charges on the nuclei or the number of electrons outside the nuclei in the respective atoms. Thus quantitative meaning was given to the periodic table of the chemists. Next, Bohr in Denmark and Sommerfeld in Germany applied the quantum theory to the Rutherford-Moseley atom and found the basis for the explanation of the spectra of light and x-rays. Henceforth spectroscopy became the most powerful tool for further atomic structure research, and such research became a major preoccupation of physicists in the 1920's.

But all during this time other scientists were experimenting with radioactivity, an interesting and puzzling subject whose only practical uses had been for making watch dials luminous in the dark and treating with moderate success certain types of cancer. But when Rutherford in 1920 succeeded in transmuting one chemical element into another by bombarding it with fast particles from a radium source, and thus made real the ancient dream of the alchemists, a new era in science opened up. It opened slowly at first, and it was not until 1931 that such a transmutation was effected by the use of a high-voltage machine. This was done by two pupils of Rutherford's in Cambridge University. In that same year Ernest Lawrence at the University of California invented the cyclotron, which has proved the most productive of all the atom-smashing machines to date. Also in the same year Chadwick in England discovered another very important subatomic particle, the neutron. And still in that same year Fermi in Italy showed that neutrons are extremely potent in producing atomic transformations in the atoms which they strike.

The quick result of the atomic nuclear research stimulated by these discoveries was the new discovery, or production in the laboratory, of more than twice as many species of atoms as had been previously known to exist. Furthermore, although it was formerly thought that only a very few of the heaviest types of atoms were radioactive, it is now possible in these "atom-smashing" machines to produce at least one radioactive modification, or isotope, of every kind of chemical atom, and several radioactive modifications in many cases.

Now we jump to the fateful time, just ten years ago, when the discovery of nuclear fission opened the way to the atomic bomb and atomic energy. In early January, 1939, two Germans, Hahn and Strassmann, found that an isotope of barium is produced when uranium is bombarded by neutrons. This news promptly reached Copenhagen, where it was given the true explanation as being a hitherto unsuspected phenomenon, nuclear fission, by two refugee scientists, Robert Otto Frisch and Lise Meitner, who had fled Germany to work with the great Danish scientist, Niels Bohr.

On January 19, Bohr arrived in the United States to deliver some lectures, and brought with him the news of this discovery of nuclear fission. By January 26 this discovery had been confirmed and extended in four laboratories in the United States, in Copenhagen, and in France, and there had been a scientific conference on the subject in Washington. All of this had happened within the short space of less than one month. By the end of a year more than one hundred scientific articles on nuclear fission had been published.

Then, in 1940, the clouds of war shrouded the further developments in a degree of secrecy never before imposed in the field of science. This secrecy was at first entirely self-imposed by the scientists themselves, who conceived of the military applications of nuclear energy before either officialdom or industry even knew of the existence of this new phenomenon. The project barely survived the skepticism with which it was initially received by many of the non-nuclear scientists and engineers who became concerned with it, but by the end of 1942 its potentialities had become well established and the great Manhattan Project was undertaken, with close collaboration between the carefully selected scientific groups in the United States, the United Kingdom, and Canada.

The rest of the story is now written into the history of the dramatic ending of the war with Hiroshima and Nagasaki; of the efforts to turn atomic energy into an instrument, through international control, for the maintenance of permanent peace; and of the current work under our Atomic Energy Commission to develop peacetime uses of atomic energy and radioactivity which are already beginning to influence the processes of industrial production and medical practice, and to open entirely new fields of exploration in chemistry, geology, metallurgy, physiology, botany, and agriculture. On the horizon, still uncertainly, loom the possibilities of useful production of power for ship or aircraft propulsion or other special applications of heat and power.

In this story we see the sudden merging of the results of many lines of investigation which had previously proceeded almost independently: fifty years of research on radioactivity; twenty years' development of high-voltage machines; the equivalence of mass and energy announced by Einstein as early as 1905 as part of his theory of relativity; several decades of study of cosmic rays; fifty years' development of electronics; the whole modern art of chemical separation; the science of radiology, whose impetus had come from medical applications of x-rays and the rays from radium; the most modern refinements of metallurgy, of chemistry, of electrical engineering. And the practical consummation of the atomic energy objectives has called upon the highest skills in engineering design and instrumentation. It is truly an exciting picture!

I might have described many other scientific achievements of our century, such as the synthesis of complicated organic chemicals; the developments in aerodynamics or those like radio, radar, and television in the field of communications; the exciting new discoveries of hormones and their influence on physiological and emotional processes in animals and man; or the growth of the automobile industry which has so profoundly influenced our personal lives and our business operations. But I elected to dwell at length on this story of atomic energy for several reasons. It is the most striking scientific and technological development of our century; it best illustrates the methods of scientific discovery and its practical application; from it can be drawn many lessons, some of which I would mention.

The *first lesson* is the *coöperative character of scientific progress,* depending on the stimulating interplay of ideas and the accumulation of facts and skills contributed by many scientists. In my survey of nuclear science progress I mentioned only some of the most significant steps in this progress, but back of it all and filling in the gaps was the work of some thousands of other research workers.

A *second lesson* is the *unpredictable and uncontrollable origin of the new ideas and discoveries which produce scientific progress.* It was to emphasize this point that I mentioned the origins of the major discoveries which led up to the atomic energy program. Many scientists from many parts of the world contributed the building blocks which, piled each on the ones below, completed the structure. The fact that it was done so quickly is explained by the *quick and free channels of communication,* often supplemented by personal acquaintance, which have traditionally characterized the scientific fraternity the world over. *It is more than tragic that any nation should seek to restrain the great flow of knowledge across the world or, within national boundaries, should seek to direct its course or make it subservient to the current politics of the state.* That such a policy will ultimately stifle the birth and development of scientific ideas is scarcely open to dispute. For nowhere more than in science is Donne's statement true: ". . . every man is . . . a part of the maine," and the killing off of scientific ideas in one area impoverishes the world.

Engineering developments can usually be carried through in accordance with a plan carefully prepared in advance, and often this can be done most effectively by a competent self-contained group like a company or a bureau. *But scientific discovery, in its very nature and as proved by experience, does not progress according to preconceived plan and is stifled if attempts are made to control the free initiative of the research workers or to limit the freedom of their communication.* This is one reason why most of the fundamental new scientific discoveries have originated in the free environment of the universities, rather than in the quite properly more controlled atmosphere of industrial or governmental laboratories. When, however, it comes to practical applications and engineering developments, then thorough planning and control are essential to efficiency. Thus the *third* lesson which I would draw is this: *to the extent that we wish fundamental science to advance, we must maintain the maximum of opportunity for competent scientists to follow their own bent and to communicate freely with each other.*

The *fourth lesson* is, at first sight, in apparent contradiction with the last, but actually it is not. It is that *teamwork has proved extraordinar-*

ily effective in producing results. To a certain extent, of course, teamwork implies control, which I have just decried. But what I mean by a team is a group of competent and imaginative project leaders whose skills and knowledge supplement each other and are supported by the technical assistance required to carry out their ideas. Such groups actually provide the maximum opportunity for quick initiative and for stimulating exchange of ideas. As science becomes more complex, or as its practical applications come more and more to the fore, the advantages of such team organization become more pronounced.

The *fifth lesson,* which needs no amplification, is the *increasing extent to which a basic advance in theory or technique in one branch of science is likely to provide new concepts, or new tools, which can open up new frontiers for exploration and exploitation in other fields of science or art.* This is not a new idea. It was for this reason, for example, that the Rockefeller Foundation established, under the National Research Council, the great program of National Research Fellowships which were largely effective, within a decade or two, in raising the United States from a third-rate, perhaps a fourth-rate, to a first-rate position in science. The Rockefeller Foundation hoped, by this stimulating advance in the fundamental sciences, to uncover new avenues of approach to the medical sciences—a hope that has been brilliantly justified. And another lesson which can be drawn comes from the realization that an astonishing proportion of today's leaders in American science, and of the project leaders who were the key men in our great scientific program during World War II, were men who had received their inspiration and training in independent research under this National Research Fellowship program.

Let me now conclude this address by a look to the future. I might discuss this in terms of current scientific programs. I could describe the race between the cosmic ray scientists who, from mountain top, airplane, and balloon, seek to utilize the still unknown energies of the cosmos to search out even more of nature's fundamental secrets of matter and energy, and the high-energy-machine scientists who, with Van de Graaff generator, cyclotron, betatron, and synchrotron, are reproducing cosmic ray phenomena in the laboratory. It remains to be seen which group can discover the most for the fewest millions of dollars. This much can be said: both groups are meeting with exciting successes, and each stimulates and supplements the other.

Or I could try to describe some of the opportunities for the use of radioactive chemical isotopes, produced by cyclotrons and atomic piles, as tools in other lines of research. Of this Dr. Shields Warren, Director of the Division of Biology and Medicine of the Atomic Energy Commission, said at the Eighth Annual Science Talent Dinner in Washington this month:

> ... an event, the scope of which can be but dimly appreciated, has recently occurred: the development of atomic energy. First, a revolutionary concept in physics has been developed, proved; active experimentation as to its potentialities is well under way. Second, a method of tagging atoms by radioactivity so that chemical and biologic processes can be followed through in great detail is now at hand. Through this radioactivity accurate measurement of minute quantities is now feasible, for as little as one million billionth of an ounce of radio phosphorus may be detected. Third, advances in knowledge of biologic effects of radiation permits changing some hereditary characteristics in plants or animals.

Or I could venture on some speculations on the possible future role of synthetically manufactured hormones which, administered like insulin to a diabetic, could control the tendency to cancer, or produce a race of giants, or turn a general into a pacifist, or cure a schizophrenic.

Or I might review the interesting theories of the universe. Is it finite; is it expanding; is it still being created; what maintains the heat of the stars and how old are they; what is their internal constitution and what forces and energies account for their condition?

But such considerations are ruled out by the limitations of both my time and my knowledge. I shall therefore approach the future more as I introduced the past, in terms of some of the problems which face our society and in whose solution science may be able to assist.

In view of the prodigious strides which science and technology have made in our century, what remains to be accomplished? From our own point of view the United States might appear to be at the summit of its industrial greatness. The young country which, in 1849, was sending its first railroads across an undeveloped territory and pouring eager thousands of its citizens into the frantic California gold rush, in 1949 has spread across a continent and developed the land from coast to coast. Its teeming agriculture has reached new heights of productivity, so that we have been able to feed not only ourselves but much of the war-torn world as well. Our industries thrive, the majority of our people are employed at good wages, and the chief danger seems to be that we may overextend ourselves and push prosperity beyond the point of stability. At a glance, this picture would not seem to leave much for our creative energies.

A closer examination of the facts leaves less room for complacency.

Not only do we have left to solve many problems of our own areas, but we have facing us also the inescapable fact of one world. Even if we were disposed to pursue our own destiny, unmindful of the rest of mankind, we have recognized that it is impossible to do so, and that our national good is strongly linked to the good of the rest of the world. This has been the philosophy underlying the Marshall Plan and much of our postwar thinking.

One of our principal causes of concern, as scientists, is the grave interruption that foreign science suffered by the war, and we are anxious for its rehabilitation. The destruction of institutions and implements of learning has been a source of distress to scholars throughout all the ages, and American scientists have viewed with a sense of personal loss the destruction of libraries, laboratories, and other important tools of learning, as one of the sad by-products of the war.

We should like to see foreign science restored to its prewar vigor, not only in the interest of fundamental knowledge everywhere, upon which we and everyone else may draw, but also because of the way in which a healthy body of science can contribute to the economic and social recovery of all nations.

To my way of thinking, it would be a helpful and legitimate thing if those countries whose progress in scientific research was most seriously disrupted by the war would see fit to include funds for the rehabilitation of those programs in their requests for United States aid under the provisions of the Foreign Assistance Act of 1948. I believe that such requests should be sympathetically received, since sound plans for economic development must rest upon technology supported by fundamental research. It is not difficult to envisage the ultimate practical good to be derived from renewed investigation in such fields as: utilization of human resources, food and nutrition, medical sciences, chemistry, physics, metallurgy, geology, meteorology, hydrology, engineering, soil mechanics, etc. If only a small proportion of Marshall Plan funds were invested in this manner, I believe there can be no doubt that rich returns of a long-range nature in material matters and in good will could be anticipated, beneficial alike to the countries concerned and to the United States.

The purposeful employment of science and technology to aid in economic reconstruction following a period of disaster is not a new thing.

Louis XV established the first significant school for civilian education in engineering as part of a program prudently directed to restoring the French economy from the depression brought on by the extravagances of Louis XIV. In similar fashion, the great École Polytechnique was established in Paris in 1795 as part of the government's program of scientific and technical education to repair the economic ravages of the French Revolution. For a century, at least, L'École Polytechnique was the world's outstanding center of pure and applied science, and profoundly influenced French social and economic progress.

In Germany, where the statesmen had a peculiar appreciation for the practical values of technological education, this type of school was established in part as a recovery program from the economic chaos brought on by the Napoleonic Wars, and in part as an aid in competing with Great Britain in industry and trade. The famous technical schools in Germany became the very foundation stone of its industrial progress, and of them Whitehead has said:

> . . . the Germans explicitly realized the methods by which the deeper veins in the mine of science could be reached. They abolished haphazard methods of scholarship. In their technological schools and universities progress did not have to wait for the occasional genius, or the occasional lucky thought. Their feats of scholarship during the nineteenth century were the admiration of the world. This discipline of knowledge applies beyond technology to pure science, and beyond science to general scholarship. It represents the change from amateurs to professionals.[5]

Closer to our own day, we have the admirable example of the British, who, following World War I, established the million-pound research fund for stimulating renewed industrial activity. This marked the beginning of a great program of scientific research, under private management but with government support, which, in the results of fundamental research and creative invention, has been claimed to exceed that of the United States, at least on a per capita basis.

It follows, then, that one important task confronting science and technology today is to assist in rescuing world-wide economy from the setback suffered by the war. This applies not only to the other war-devastated countries, but also to our own country, where also the war seriously diminished the normal supply rate of new scientists and engineers and of new scientific discovery for those stockpiles of trained

[5] A. N. Whitehead, *Science and the Modern World*, p. 142.

technologists and new ideas which should be our most important future asset.

It is to be hoped that our leaders of public affairs, in government and business and the professions, will be no less far-sighted than were those statesmen of earlier days. The postwar interest in research shown by our military departments, the favorable prospects for a National Science Foundation, and above all the recently increased liberality of American industrial corporations in support of fundamental research within and without their organizations, are all encouraging signs.

An aspect of such problems which is in the traditional spirit of American altruism, but which is also of long-range bearing on our own welfare, was ably stated by the President in Point Four of his Inaugural Address when he said:[6]

> ... we must embark on a bold new program for making the benefits of our scientific advances and industrial progress available for the improvement and growth of underdeveloped areas.
>
> More than half the people of the world are living in conditions approaching misery. Their food is inadequate. They are victims of disease. Their economic life is primitive and stagnant. Their poverty is a handicap and a threat both to them and to more prosperous areas.
>
> For the first time in history, humanity possesses the knowledge and the skill to relieve the suffering of these people.

Already notable steps along such lines have been undertaken by a number of industrial companies which have been convinced that their long-term profitable business in relatively undeveloped areas is closely linked to the improvement in the living standards of the populations of those countries, for reasons both economic and political. Hence we see skillful programs in progress, not only to raise wages but, more importantly, to apply the most modern arts of medicine and public health, soil utilization, seed selection and agricultural technique, education, and recreation for improving the health, prosperity, and morale of the peoples with whom they deal. The more of this that is done, the better and safer the world will be.

One of the lessons of history is that the improvement of man's physical and environmental well-being does much to contribute to the elimination of political and social unrest, and that the reverse promotes revolution. We know also that the constructive applications of science do improve man's environmental well-being if the gains from science

[6] Harry S. Truman; January 20, 1949.

are fairly distributed among the people. Hence we see, in the program advocated by the President, not only a program of altruism but also of utilizing technology in the interests of political stability and peace.

This subject will be given expert treatment in one of the panel discussions tomorrow. So, in fact, will many other goals of our current technological programs, about which I had originally thought of speaking. And I can obviously do little justice to much in my few remaining minutes. I would therefore simply state my credo and my conclusions by quoting two paragraphs from my recent Wallberg Lecture at the University of Toronto:[7]

> The people of our countries crave peace and security. They want protection against the perils of nature, like floods, hurricanes, earthquakes, and droughts; and against man-made perils of transportation, fire, and group violence. Labor strives for steady employment at higher wages, shorter hours, and more comfortable working conditions. They want the quality of goods to go up and prices to go down. People want better and more adequate housing. Those in business want larger profits. Governments, in our expanding civilization, need more tax money. Everybody wants better health. Those who think much beyond the present envisage ahead what I believe to be the greatest ultimate challenge to mankind, and that not many generations in the future. It is the problem of maintaining our growing populations in the face of rapidly depleted natural resources without descent into a final world epoch of struggle for bare survival.
>
> If we were to take the time to examine into all these needs and desires of men we would discover two facts. One is that science and engineering have positive contributions to make to every one of these requirements. The other is even more striking. I believe that technological progress is the only common denominator to them all—the only solution which can simultaneously satisfy these statements of human needs. Laws, ideologies, economic theories, ethics, and brotherly love can provide orderly distribution, reduce waste, and promote good will among men, but they can not create the wherewithal to satisfy all the apparently conflicting demands listed above.

We must be prepared to take each step as it comes in these vast new fields that are opening before us. The fact that all the answers are not immediately at hand is no reason for pessimism. It is in the American

[7] Karl Taylor Compton, *The Scientist and the Engineer,* The Second Wallberg Lecture (Canada, The University of Toronto Press, January 11, 1949), p. 21.

spirit of things to want to accomplish everything overnight, and in view of past triumphs of technology perhaps we may be forgiven for being sanguine of success in this venture. In the long run, I think it is not likely that this confidence will be disappointed.

In any event, today, as in every other time, the scientist still stands on the threshold of the unknown. Perhaps that is his greatest joy—what Huxley more than half a century ago called "the supreme delight of extending the realm of law and order ever farther towards the unattainable goals of the infinitely great and the infinitely small, between which our little race of life is run." [8]

Science, Technology, and National Security
Louis N. Ridenour

Dr. Louis N. Ridenour, physicist, is a graduate of the University of Chicago (B.S., 1932) and the California Institute of Technology (Ph.D., 1936). He has been professor of physics and dean of the Graduate College of the University of Illinois since 1947 and has also served as a leading consultant to the United States Air Force.

This address was given at Cabell Hall, University of Virginia, Charlottesville, on 12 July 1950 at the annual Institute of Public Affairs. Because of space limitations only the first half of the address is given here.

MR. CHAIRMAN, DISTINGUISHED GUESTS, LADIES AND GENTLEMEN:

As affairs in Korea show us very well, atomic energy—although vital to our military position in the grim world of today—is by no means the key to all our problems. Even if we had no troubles in connection with our development of atomic energy for military purposes (which is far from the present case), we should still be faced with the gravest difficulties in ensuring and advancing our national interests in these uncertain times.

Therefore, however inadequate to the task my information and my talents may be, I wish to discuss with you tonight the larger question of the interaction between science and technology, on the one hand, and national security, on the other. By "national security" I shall mean the ability of this country to maintain its political integrity without

[8] T. H. Huxley, *The Advance of Science in the Last Half-Century* (New York, D. Appleton and Company, 1887), p. 20.

domination by either the application or the threat of application of outside force. Of course, we all recognize that genuine long-term national security demands that we honestly take part, as one nation among many, in the erection of a sound and workable world order. It seems clear that we are sincerely doing everything we can to move toward that goal. It seems equally clear that the time has not yet come when all the peoples of the world are ready to join unreservedly in such a sound and workable order. That being so, it is our duty to keep in mind the goal of world organization on a fair and peaceful plane, and, while working toward it, to protect the human values and the political forms that we have come to cherish.

As you know, the civilization of this country—and, to a lesser degree, the civilization of the present world—is increasingly shaped by advancing technology. The frightening thing about this increasing domination of society by men's increasing engineering competence is not that it is occurring (though that is frightening enough), nor yet the present pace of that development (though that is dizzying). The most frightening aspect of the social change being caused by technological advance is that it is going on at an ever-increasing rate. As our scientists and engineers have won victories over nature, each new discovery or advance has increased the power and scope of the methods used to make discoveries. The result has been that we have been adding to our store of knowledge and technical competence not in arithmetical progression, but in geometrical progression, since each advance contributes to quickening the pace of later progress.

Everyone knows the fable of the modest man who did a favor for a prince, and asked as his reward no greater fee than the amount of wheat which could be put on a chessboard by putting one grain on the first square, two on the second, four on the third, and so on—doubling each time. The ruler eagerly accepted this innocent-sounding proposition, the story runs, not having performed this simple calculation: There are 64 squares on a chessboard, so that the number of grains that would have to be put on the last square is the number 2 multiplied by itself 63 times, or about 10 million billions of grains.

So much for the intractability of geometrical progressions, which rapidly get out of hand. The most wildly various human activities are found to be changing according to an exponential law. To be sure, new things grow more rapidly than old ones, in general; and whole technologies can be replaced, and therefore die. But things are changing, and they are changing fast. The total aspect of society alters substantially in a time which is short compared with the life of any one of us.

Science, Technology, and National Security

The aspect of warfare similarly alters; for total war is nothing but the concentration of all society on a single central objective.

Though I expect that you are fully aware of the ever-increasing rate of social change, let me give a few specific examples of the way in which the pace of development is speeding up. These are chosen on no uniform scheme, but only because statistics on them are accessible to me.

The total assets of all life-insurance companies of the United States have increased in a geometrical progression which has caused their doubling every decade. In 1900, they were 1.8 billions of dollars; today they are some 70 billions.

For the last half-century, the number of long-distance telephone messages has doubled every 7.5 years, rising from 7 millions per year in 1900 to over 300 millions today.

Since the Wright brothers first flew at Kitty Hawk in 1903, the gross weight of aircraft in common use has doubled every seven years, having risen to over 300,000 pounds today. Speed and range of military aircraft have similarly increased according to a geometrical progression.

These examples could be multiplied almost indefinitely. I ask that you accept my assurance that not only is society being changed by science and technology, but also this change is occurring at a rate which continually increases.

Of course, all this has had a profound effect on the tools and methods of warfare. Former Secretary Patterson pointed out that we finished World War II with weapons which were more than 90 per cent new. That is, more than nine out of ten of the weapons in the hands of our troops at the end of the last war were new either in the sense that they had been designed *de novo*, or very completely redesigned, since the beginning of that conflict. The weapons suggested by World War I, of which the Maginot line was perhaps the epitome, were of little use in the second World War. By the same token, we must expect that our ideas of weapons and strategies based on World War II are likely to be incomplete or misleading as guides to the future of armed maneuver and of warfare.

These lessons, of course, were not lost on our military leaders and our lawmakers. The pitch of federal support for science and engineering, including support from the military services, is greater today than it has ever been in nominal peacetime. Scientists are taking their places in the federal service—in the Department of Defense and its armed services, in the State Department, and in the new National Science Foundation—to a far greater extent than ever before. Preoccupation with the scientific and technical "secrets" of atomic weapons is so extensive as to be frightening to any reasonable man. There can be little doubt that the technological theme of our present civilization is appreciated in the sense that we are frightened of science, if in no other way.

Nevertheless, there are serious deficiencies in our present national cultivation of science for the common good. These deficiencies arise, for the most part, from an imperfect understanding of the nature of science and the way in which it is best cultivated for the purposes of national security. Let us examine what we are doing now, and what we had better do, to make sure that science and technology are fully exploited for the nation's good, and fully enlisted in the cause of advancing the national security.

To do this, we must make some assumptions about the unknown future. This is a chancy business, and I shall not pretend that the assumptions I make here are more reliable, or better informed, than the assumptions which might be made by any reader of the daily papers. With this preamble, and in all humility, I suggest the following assumptions regarding our national situation.

First, that our long-term aim is to work toward a supranational world political organization which can abolish war. There are many critics of our participation in the United Nations, but I am persuaded that we have been pursuing this purpose with determination and good will. I believe that most people are persuaded that in this direction, and only in this direction, lies international stability.

Second, that events clearly show that the time for full idealism is not yet here. The behavior of Russia, in and out of the United Nations, makes it clear that that great power is not yet ready to join the other nations of the world in implementing the goals of a global political organism, unless, indeed, that organism is erected on Russia's terms. We are similarly intransigent about the principles that we hold dear.

Third, that in the present uneasy period we must constantly be prepared to fight an all-out war, but that for the near future we can expect instead to be involved in far more limited actions, such as the one in Korea has been to date. A declared and total war seems some time off; the only thing we can be sure of is that peace is even farther.

Fourth, that American supremacy over possible enemies must be qualitative, not quantitative, in nature. Our limited resources in manpower and our respect for human life will not permit us to suppose that we can match the numberless divisions of a powerful enemy. Instead, we must base our plans upon a clear-cut technical superiority which makes of every man the greatest use.

From these assumptions, and some knowledge of the nature of technical development, we can assess the present performance of our nation, and specify the future lines of effort that will be of greatest use. This is attempted in what follows.

Among other things, we see that it is most important for us to avoid being stampeded by the press of events into a short-term plan for the exploitation of technology for national defense. When the immediate need is obvious and great, there is a great temptation to make a "practical" assessment of the utility of the scientific and engineering developments being pursued in universities, industry, and government; and to weed out ruthlessly any work that is not obviously contributing to the needs of the moment. This is often suggested, sometimes done, and always misguided. It neglects two important factors: first, that all appearances suggest we are in for a trying time for several years; and second, that the time lag between an unexpected scientific discovery and its practical application is now very short. A few decades ago, twenty-five years elapsed between the fundamental discovery of radio waves by Heinrich Hertz and the transmission of the letter "S" across the Atlantic by Marconi; from the fundamental discovery basic to atomic energy to the practical application of that discovery was a little over five years. As the pace of technological advance increases, the time lag between scientific discovery and practical application is shortened also. Since, by definition, we cannot know in which direction there lies a scientific discovery of the greatest practical importance, it follows that we reduce fundamental scientific work at our peril, even in a time of what seems immediate stress.

This principle has several immediate corollaries. One of the most important of those corollaries has to do with the activities of university scientists, who still make up a majority of the top-ranking scientists of the country, despite the cultivation of science and advanced technology by industry and government.

At the time of the excitement about the hydrogen bomb, in the beginning of 1950, several of the most able academic physicists gave serious thought to moving to Los Alamos to work on it. Some of them actually did go. It is my opinion that this action on their part may have been unwise. For, if we are indeed to expect a long period of strained international relations, then there may be and probably are many weapons and devices better suited to our needs than is the hydrogen bomb, even assuming that its development will succeed. Further, if the present crisis lasts as long as it well may, then it will be most important for us not to abandon the competent advanced training of our youth which is the proper business of the universities.

To mobilize all our resources for a short-term war when a long one is in prospect is unwise; to mobilize too soon is to put our emphasis on work which may, as our experience increases, prove ill-calculated to serve the national security. There is no doubt that the academic scientists and engineers of the nation can make a contribution of the first importance to the problems faced by the military, but we must remember that they can make, and are routinely making, a contribution of the first importance to society as a whole, including the military, by their efforts in support of advanced education and research in their home institutions.

Scientific Manpower
Henry D. Smyth

Dr. Henry D. Smyth was born in Clinton, New York in 1898. He studied at Princeton (A.B., 1918; Ph.D., 1921) and at Cambridge University in England (Ph.D., 1923). From 1940 to 1945 he was a consultant on war research projects to the National Research Council and to the Office of Scientific Research and Development. He also served as a consultant on the Manhattan District project (the atomic bomb) from 1943 to 1945.

This speech was delivered at the 117th meeting of the American Association for the Advancement of Science in Cleveland on 28 December 1950. The text below represents only the last third of the address.

Dr. Smyth is the author of *Atomic Energy for Military Purposes* (1945), more commonly referred to as the Smyth Report, and was appointed a member of the Atomic Energy Commission in 1949. He is at present on leave of absence from Princeton University where he has been chairman of the department of physics since 1935.

I PROPOSE the establishment of a Scientific Service Corps directed by a Scientific Manpower Board and based on a national roster of scientists. These organizations would be concerned only with scientists who have completed their education, not with students. Nevertheless, two categories are concerned: men of military age, normally subject to call for military service, and older scientists. Both categories would be under the general supervision of the Scientific Manpower Board and both would be listed in the roster. At present, only the scientists of military age would be required to join the Scientific Service Corps, and only the members of this corps would be subject to orders from the Scientific Manpower Board. For older scientists the board would act in an advisory capacity only.

This Scientific Service Corps would be a civilian organization without ranks or uniforms. I believe it would be most effective if it were guided by that curious mixture of coöperation and discipline that characterizes most civilian organizations in this country. The principal function of the Board in charge would be to get the right man in the right job and often this man's own judgment should carry great weight. The Scientific Manpower Board, although a civilian organization, would need to have real authority over the members of the Service Corps. It would need power to keep them out of the army, navy or air force, or to put them in. It should have power to return men from military to civilian service or vice versa, or to shift them from one project to another, or to return them to universities. But I hope that most of the orders issued by this board would be merely formal endorsements of voluntary agreements. Coöperation will serve us better than force.

For scientists not in the Service Corps, the Scientific Manpower Board would act only in an advisory capacity. With information on the full scope of national defense research projects, it could be an invaluable guide for men who wanted to be sure they were making the best use of their abilities.

The Scientific Manpower Board should be responsible to the President, not to the Department of Defense. The quality, wisdom, and powers of this board would be the key to the success or failure of the whole scheme. Their ideal should be guided coöperation with the scientists, not rigidly organized direction of them. The board members and staff would require access to complete information on all technical and scientific phases of our military activities and of the supporting civilian economy. They would also have to know the scientific community—not just the names and numbers in a card file, but the men themselves. This suggests the need for regional branches of the Board.

Turning to the question of stock-piling, that is, the training of new scientists, we have quite a different problem. Various schemes have been proposed for the deferment of students. Most such schemes do not make it clear that we are aiming at a positive goal, not a negative one. We are not interested in helping individuals escape the duty of military service just because they are bright boys or happen to have played with chemistry sets as children. We are interested in developing a group of men with trained minds and disciplined imaginations who can strengthen the country over the next twenty years. That some of them will be doing very nearly what they would choose to do in peacetime is irrelevant except insofar as it may make them more effective.

Can we not have something more positive than draft deferment for brilliant students of science, medicine, and engineering? The continuance of their education in such times as these, implies obligation, not privilege. I propose a student scientific corps with enrollment beginning in the freshman year and continuing through graduate training. The requirements of native intelligence and industry in such a student corps would be high and the requirements of sustained performance higher still. Students who did not keep up would be continually weeded out. Men of excellent technical competence but lacking in imagination and originality would be carried only through their undergraduate training and then released to the armed services or to industry. Others would be continued through graduate training. Some recruits should occasionally be added to the student corps from the services or industry or project research to receive more education.

Administration of this student scientific corps should be, it seems to me, decentralized as much as possible. Professors in the universities would be best fitted to take the responsibility of making judgments within the established criteria. No amount of statistical data, intelligence tests, or examinations can replace the intimate knowledge a university professor should have of his good students. The student scientific corps or training program or whatever it is called should perhaps be under the general jurisdiction of the National Science Foundation. Coöperation with the Scientific Manpower Board and with Selective Service would be essential but the problems are sufficiently great and sufficiently different to suggest separate authorities.

Although the programs I have discussed are intended to meet both short-range and long-range requirements for scientific manpower and are not meant to be dependent on the present system of recruiting under the Selective Service Act, they may appear in conflict with other proposed systems of recruiting for the armed services. One such system is the plan to put all eighteen-year-old men into military service. It is estimated that if these men were kept in service for two years, the country would have a total of three million men constantly under arms and would shortly build up a large trained reserve. Once their period of service was over, these men could feel confident that they could pursue their education and begin their professional careers without interruption unless large-scale war broke out.

The first effect of this proposal on the training of young scientists appears to be bad. All men now eighteen would defer their education two years with a corresponding interruption in the supply of engineers and scientists four to eight years later. To some degree these effects could be counteracted by acceleration or by special training of men still in service or by reduction of the length of service for obviously talented men. On the good side would be the smaller probability of interruption for men already started on their professional careers. In the long run, that is, the ten- or twenty-year period I have been talking about, these effects would largely disappear, with one exception: the dozen or so students of really outstanding brilliance who appear each year—and there are seldom more—might be lost to science or have their early and most productive years spoiled.

There is another danger. The young men who had been in service might be kept in some sort of reserve; in fact, they should be, or much of the point of their military service would be lost. However, they constitute a whole generation of manpower, the manpower that is needed for the innumerable civilian activities as essential to success in total war as the army or navy or air force. It would be wise to put the control of this reserve manpower in civilian hands at the highest level.

As to the use of mature scientific manpower, this 18-20 service proposal seems to have only secondary effects. It might relieve the pressure for direct military service on some of the younger scientists. In the long run, it might help stabilize the universities. It does not remove the need of a Scientific Manpower Board, a Scientific Service Corps, or a student corps. While I believe the Scientific Manpower Board should be vested with great authority from the first, the proposed military service for eighteen-year-olds might lessen the danger of too hasty and too arbitrary exercise of that authority.

I have tried to put before you the problems of stock-piling scientific manpower and rationing it, in the best interest of the country, just as we would any other essential resource. I have proposed for this purpose a student scientific corps to insure a continuing supply of scientists. For men of military age, I have proposed a Scientific Service Corps to be directed by a Scientific Manpower Board. For men above the age of military service, I have suggested widespread voluntary coöperation with the Scientific Manpower Board.

These may not be the best solutions to this problem, but they are possible ones. Any system to be established must obviously be flexible and subject to change with experience and with changing international conditions. Either the organization I have suggested, or a better one, should be set up now before we repeat the errors of the last war.

I believe there is real danger that nothing will be done or that a system will be set up and will fail. Scientists can best understand the nature of this danger. They know very well that a thoughtless bureaucracy with centralized control can threaten the independence, imagination, and clarity of mind needed for creative work. Scientists know also that a haphazard system of recruitment can lessen their value to the country. I suggest that the members of this audience and their associates throughout the country have a peculiar duty to work for the adoption of a sensible system for the wise use of scientific manpower, to talk to their friends of the need for such a system, and to make such a system work. You know what needs to be done. Give the foresight and leadership to achieve it.

Such questions as these cannot be left entirely to the government. They are everybody's business. What John Curran said in 1790 is still true: "It is the common fate of the indolent to see their rights become a prey to the active. The condition upon which God hath given liberty to man is eternal vigilance; which condition if he break, servitude is at once the consequence of his crime and the punishment of his guilt."

Nuclear Energy Development and Military Technology

Alvin M. Weinberg

Dr. Alvin M. Weinberg is a mathematical biophysicist. He was born in Chicago in 1915 and was educated at the University of Chicago (A.B., 1935; M.S., 1936; Ph.D., 1939). He taught and conducted research at the university from 1939 to 1945. For the next three years he worked at the Clinton Laboratories, Oak Ridge, Tennessee. During 1948-49 he was director of the physics division and in 1949 he was appointed Research Director of the Oak Ridge National Laboratory.

This address in longer form was delivered in the McIntyre Open-Air Theatre at the annual Institute of Public Affairs held at the University of Virginia, Charlottesville, on 17 July 1950.

MY PURPOSE this evening will be to retell a story which I suppose has been much dulled by repetition—the story of where our country stands in trying to extract something useful from nuclear fission. Of the various conceivable products and by-products of nuclear fission—such as atomic and hydrogen bombs, radioisotopes, controlled power, not to speak of scientific culture, loyalty probes, and billion-dollar budgets, I shall concern myself mostly with nuclear power—where it will come, when, and without being facetious, why. For even now, more than ten years since the discovery of nuclear fission, not one single kilowatt of useful mechanical energy has been extracted from uranium—at least not in this country, and so far as I know, in no other country.

The main reason we have no atomic engines or nuclear-power reactors today is because it is hard to make atomic engines—much harder, it seems, than to make atomic bombs. But the technical difficulties are tremendously increased by the circumstance that, until rather recently, it was not completely clear to people connected with the effort why we —or anyone else—might really want nuclear reactors. What was lacking was motivation for the development of nuclear engines.

Briefly, it is taking a cold war to give motivation to the development of nuclear reactors for power in much the same way that it took a hot war to give motivation and point to the development of the original nuclear bomb.

But before I dwell on nontechnical aspects of nuclear-energy development, I should like to summarize those scientific facts about nuclear fission which explain on the one hand why nuclear reactors are hard to build, and on the other hand why it is taking the pressure of cold war to force on us so-called peacetime benefits of atomic energy.

It is simplest, in reëxplaining nuclear energy, to compare a nuclear fire with an ordinary chemical fire—or if you will, a nuclear reactor with a coal furnace. Prior to December 2, 1942, all man-released energy resulted ultimately from the rearrangement of extranuclear electrons. When a piece of coal burns in air, electrons of carbon and electrons from oxygen undergo rearrangements which cause the release of heat, light, and products of combustion. Almost all of our energy economy has until now been based on ordinary combustion—on electronic or chemical rearrangement.

When the first man-made nuclear chain reaction was established in Fermi's knob-shaped atomic pile, mankind succeeded in causing rearrangement of the nuclear constituents of matter on a scale comparable to that involved in ordinary chemical combustion. Since the forces which hold constituents of the nucleus together—the neutrons and the protons —are enormously stronger than those which hold the extranuclear electrons in their orbits, it is to be expected that the energy liberated when a uranium nucleus is split is tremendously greater than when a carbon atom combines with an oxygen atom. And in fact the characteristics which distinguish nuclear fire from chemical or electronic fire all stem directly from the enormous disparity in internal energy—or tightness of binding—between the atom and its nucleus.

I have already mentioned that when an ordinary chemical fire burns it gives off heat, light, and products of combustion; in addition it requires oxygen and an original charge of fuel. In analogous fashion, when a nuclear fire burns (or when a nuclear reactor "reacts"), *it* gives off heat, a sort of light, and products of nuclear combustion; in addition it requires original fuel (U^{235} or Pu) and, in a sense, *it* requires an atmosphere of neutrons rather than of oxygen. It is instructive to compare the chemical fire and the nuclear fire with respect to each of these characteristics; and to indicate which kind of energy is more convenient in each of these respects.

1. *Heat:* With respect to heat, nuclear fire at first sight wins hands down. Everybody is familiar by now with the fact that one pound of U^{235} has as much heat energy as 1260 tons of coal. As columnist Sam Grafton once said, there is enough atomic energy in a battleship to drive a toothpick twice around the world, or something. But while nuclear fuel wins by a walk as far as its *compactness* as a heat source is concerned, it does not do so well as far as the temperature at which its heat is easily and practically available. The situation is complicated but boils down to this: materials limitations. As you know, to extract mechanical power heat must be delivered at high temperature. Practically, the temperature at which heat can be extracted from an energy-producing system—either nuclear or chemical—depends on the temperatures which the coolant and the firebox can withstand. In a furnace a firebrick is chosen only on the basis of the temperature it can withstand. In a nuclear furnace, the firebrick is chosen not only for adequate thermal properties but also for adequate nuclear properties. Thus, the materials available for constructing a nuclear power system are in principle somewhat limited, and therefore just for this reason it is more difficult though probably not impossible to extract heat at as high a temperature from a nuclear reactor as from a chemical reactor.

2. *Light:* Chemical burning is accompanied by light. If the fire is hot enough, it may give off ultraviolet light which might hurt one's eyes. Nuclear burning also gives off light but nuclear light has far shorter wave lengths than chemical light; it manifests itself as x-rays or even gamma rays which, in the large doses given off by a nuclear reactor, are deadly. For this reason a high-powered nuclear reactor must be shielded by heavy concrete walls which add to the bulkiness and to the expense of a nuclear reactor.

3. *Combustion products:* A coal furnace produces ashes and smoke, both of which are nuisances which however can be dealt with rather easily. A nuclear reactor produces ashes too—the so-called fission products—but these are enormously radioactive, and disposal of this waste is a problem of major magnitude.

On the other hand, certain types of nuclear reactors—such as the atomic piles at Hanford—produce plutonium, a new fissionable material, as the old kind, U^{235}, is used up. Thus, in the ashes of nuclear combustion are the terribly deadly radioactive fission products and also the very useful new fissionable material.

The fission products tend to use up the neutron atmosphere which is required to maintain a nuclear chain reaction. It is therefore necessary to remove the fission products at regular intervals. This cleaning process is far more drastic than the cleaning of an ordinary furnace. It involves dissolving the reactor parts in acid, extracting the uranium, converting the resultant oxide to metal, and refabricating the metal into the required shapes.

4. *Atmosphere:* A chemical fire requires oxygen to burn. A nuclear fire requires neutrons to burn. Moreover the nuclear fire supplies its own neutrons. It is in this sense that a nuclear reactor is self-sustaining or chain-reacting. The fact that a chain reactor needs no oxygen means that in principle it is possible to use nuclear power for submarines or for high-altitude aircraft.

Let us summarize then the relative advantages and disadvantages of nuclear fires and chemical fires. The major advantages of nuclear energy are its fantastic concentration, its independence of atmospheric oxygen, and its capacity for regenerating new fuel as it burns its old. The major disadvantages are great expense, temperature limitations, tremendous shielding requirements (which tend to counterbalance to some extent the advantage of compactness), the nuisance and hazard of dealing with the radioactive by-products, and the need to recover and reprocess unused fuel at frequent intervals.

The apparent postwar lull in nuclear-power development has its origin in a variety of causes. In the first place, the atomic energy effort in this country suffered immediately after the war because so many of the technical staffs wanted to demobilize—to go back to their universities or industrial laboratories. The resulting uncertainty was to some extent increased by the reorganization necessitated by the transfer of the whole works from the Manhattan District to the Atomic Energy Commission. It is only within the last year or so, I believe, that the situation has settled; that the large atomic-energy laboratories have been staffed by personnel who have made long-term intellectual commitments to careers in nuclear-energy development; and that the permanent organizational pattern under the AEC has emerged.

But there was a much deeper reason for the postwar lull in reactor development, namely, that when the time came to ask for the many millions needed to build reactors, there were few who rose vigorously to say the country needs nuclear-power reactors—reactors which are expensive, perhaps dangerous, certainly far more complicated than coal —and needs them badly enough to pay the millions required to finance them. In explanation, it must be remembered that the unfortunate pattern of international relations in which the world now muddles did not become clear immediately after the war. The pressure for development of military gadgetry such as nuclear reactors was not as great in 1946 as it is now.

And, in fact, it was precisely the demands of the military which have put vigor and push into the terribly difficult and expensive job of extracting useful power from uranium fission. The disadvantages of nuclear power—the radioactivity, the expense, the fuel reprocessing which make private power companies remarkably disinterested for the time being are for certain military purposes outweighed by the advantages —compactness and independence of oxygen supply.

Two major military locomotion problems are the development of faster and longer-range aircraft and faster and longer-range submarines. In principle, nuclear energy should be applicable for both these purposes. Since a nuclear reactor requires no oxygen, it should be possible to adapt a nuclear-energy engine to propulsion of a submarine which can travel under water for essentially indefinite periods of time. There are now two reactor projects: one sponsored by Westinghouse in collaboration with the Argonne National Laboratory and the other by General Electric for the accomplishment of nuclear submarine propulsion. The nuclear submarine project does not appear to be a particularly difficult one, at least by nuclear-energy standards, and it is expected that a nuclear submarine might be in operation within a few years.

In somewhat different category stands the airplane propulsion project. If the shield weight around a reactor can be reduced sufficiently, it should be possible to construct a nuclear engine which will fit on an airplane—although a large one. Such an airplane would combine unlimited range, tremendous speed, and probably very high altitude. It would be a strategic weapon of very great potentiality. While it seems possible, in principle, to build such an airplane, the technical difficulties—such as reducing the shield weight to manageable proportions and coping with the extraordinarily high radiation and heat intensities inside the reactor—make it hardly certain that a nuclear airplane can fly. But the military advantage which accrues to the possession of a nuclear aircraft is so great that we can ill afford not to try to overcome the technical problems. A large project involving ORNL and the NEPA project at Oak Ridge, and the NACA at Cleveland, has been working for some time trying to solve the many problems connected with nuclear flight. One of the most important of the problems—the change in properties of materials inside a reactor because of the intense radiation bombardment—will be studied in the so-called Materials Testing Reactor which is being built now at Arco, Idaho—an atomic oven in which materials can be exposed to the high radiation intensity present in an aircraft reactor.

Our present unhappy existence is a strange mixture of military and nonmilitary. Every phase of our life seems more and more to be affected by the state of half-war in which we are. It is not too surprising nor too much to wonder at that our nuclear-energy effort is a military one nor that a large fraction of our total technological research and development bill is being paid out for military research and development. With whole industries such as the aircraft industry supported by the military there is little point to question the purity of motivation for atomic-energy development.

Nor is this in principle a new situation. The large-scale technologies such as radio or gas turbines which have developed either directly or indirectly from war or from fear of war are too many to enumerate. The only difference now is that our military technologies are becoming so demanding that an increasing proportion of our *total* technological culture—increased in men and in money—is devoted to military development.

With our technology so highly developed, with it so perfected, with it so enormous in scope, it is apparent that large segments of it can be adequately challenged only by the enormously difficult and expensive demands of the military art—that without such demands, with an end to military motivation, we might expect a shrinkage of our technology for sheer lack of problems of adequate difficulty and magnitude. After all, the difficulties of making a nuclear bomber, or of detecting a high-speed submarine, or of building an H-bomb, are orders of magnitude greater and involve much greater size of effort than the difficulties, say, of perfecting color television.

But, perhaps in microcosmic reflection of our current semimilitary civilization in which the threads of peace and war are unavoidably and intimately intermingled with each other, so our nuclear military technologies are even now closely mingled with our nonmilitary science. The national atomic-energy laboratories—Argonne, Brookhaven, Oak Ridge, and even Los Alamos—which in a fundamental sense are military laboratories, are also great centers of scientific learning. Their influence on scientific culture in the regions they serve is already significant and will grow. Already the direct by-products of nuclear energy, the radioisotopes, have given much of nonmilitary value. Already the scientific results from the nuclear military laboratories, e.g., the discovery of connection between arteriosclerosis and cholesterol have been significant in the nonmilitary segment of our life.

We who are alive today are unhappy victims of circumstance. We see our technology—yes our civilization—being transformed inexorably into a military civilization, into a caricature pictured by George Orwell in his book *1984*. This we of the West choose as an evil which we hope is temporary but which in any case is lesser than the evil which faces us if we do not accede to this trend. The path of development in nuclear power is after all only a reflection of this larger trend. But it is by no means certain that this trend will continue always. It is presumptuous for me or for any man to claim real validity for predictions about a matter as complicated as war and peace or as nuclear energy.

Today we nuclear technologists complain of the difficulty and the expense of extracting nuclear power—difficulties and expense so great that we can find adequate support for our efforts only by appeal to the military. But it is much too early to say that nuclear-energy extraction will always be expensive, will never find a place in our power economy comparable to the present position of chemical energy. Even now there are lines of research and development carried out in the atomic-energy laboratories which may culminate in nuclear power which is economically competitive with coal even if it does not produce nuclear explosives as a by-product.

Today our nuclear-energy effort is a military effort—as our civilization is a semimilitary civilization. It is possible that tomorrow our planet will regain its senses and return to the ways of peace—that tomorrow we will look upon our trend toward Spartanism as an unpleasant fiction described only in books such as George Orwell's *1984*.

For the atom to fulfill its latent promise to man, we scientists must of course show technically that there is in the atom such promise; but we men must also bring the world out of its present chaos so that the way of the atom can indeed be the way of peace. Should we succeed in both of these—and it is wrong for me to say that we cannot—then, to paraphrase H. G. Wells, the world will be set free by the atom—but only *after* the world sets both itself—and the atom—free.

HEALTH AND MEDICINE

Stress and Disease
Jerome Conn, M.D., Albert Dorfman, M.D., and Hans Selye, M.D.

The discussion below was presented over a National Broadcasting Company network on 10 December 1950 as a program of the University of Chicago Round Table.

Dr. Conn is professor of medicine at the University of Michigan. Dr. Dorfman is assistant professor of pediatrics at the University of Chicago. Dr. Selye, who was born in Vienna, is professor and director of the Institute of Experimental Medicine and Surgery at the University of Montreal.

DR. DORFMAN: Almost two years have now elapsed since the announcement of the discovery of the effects of ACTH and cortisone on rheumatoid arthritis. During this time many patients have been treated with these drugs, and experiments have been conducted in attempting to understand their action better. It has been clear to everybody that they represent a very major change in our entire thinking about disease.

You have had a great deal of experience, Dr. Conn, both experimentally and in treating patients with these drugs. How do you feel about the impact of this discovery?

DR. CONN: There are, in my opinion, two major potentials regarding the use of these compounds. First, there is the employment of these substances as experimental tools, so to speak, with which it may be possible to learn many of the fundamental mechanisms about disease —what a disease is all about. And the second potential is the use of these substances as medicines in the actual treatment of disease. I think that the use of these substances as research tools probably represents their greatest potential. That is to say, we now have at our disposal materials which allow us to turn a disease on and off again. And so it ought to be possible for researchers to find out what is going on in the body with respect to a particular disease.

DR. DORFMAN: Dr. Selye, you have long been interested in the effect of hormones on the disease process. How do you feel about this?

DR. SELYE: To me the most important part in these discoveries is that I hope these substances will give us efficient tools with which to study adaptation—the adjustment of our bodies to any change such as disease, or cold, or heat, changes which we might encounter in everyday life, including even nervous and psychic distress.

DR. DORFMAN: Our listeners have heard a great deal about the miraculous cures of certain things, or at least changes in certain diseases by the use of these hormones. They have been well publicized in the public press. But today we want to discuss a little more about the impact of their discovery upon our thinking in medicine in general. Dr. Selye, you speak of the adaptation to the effects of stress. How did you relate these hormones to the effects of stress?

DR. SELYE: Well, Dr. Dorfman, you have mentioned that ACTH and cortisone are hormones. That is to say, they are chemical messengers, one might say, which the glands produce and by which various organs in the body are regulated. Now, in 1936, I was trying in my laboratory to isolate chemically some new hormones from endocrine glands—from these hormone-producing glands. My associates and I prepared an extract which was very impure. It was a toxic, impure extract which we injected into animals, and we found that that extract stimulated the adrenal very much. Not only the microscopic structure but their appearance in general changed. These glands seemed to be not only large but also extremely active. And this adrenal enlargement was associated with various other changes in the body.

DR. DORFMAN: How were the changes in the adrenal different from any others?

DR. SELYE: During stress and strain and damage, the body suffers. One loses weight, for instance. The individual cells of the body—the cells in each organ lose weight—and show what we call signs of damage. Only the adrenal glands seemed to be different in this respect. They seemed to flourish on stress. They became larger, and they were stimulated by stress.

So, as we studied these changes, we thought that perhaps this adrenal change, together with changes in other organs, represented what they call, in medicine, a syndrome—that is to say, a set of symptoms or manifestations which belong together somehow. We felt that this may be a syndrome of adaptation. We called it the "adaptation syndrome." We felt that that syndrome represents the expression of an effort to adjust ourselves to change. We were able to produce that same syndrome, including that adrenal enlargement, with such different agents and different types of stress as drugs, infections, nervous strain. We were able to produce it with cold. One could not say, though, that it was really due to cold as such, because the same syndrome was produced by heat. So, we came to the conclusion that here we were dealing with the syndrome of stress, a syndrome caused by a stress in which the adrenal enlargement was particularly obvious.

DR. CONN: You had some notion, did you not, of what would make the adrenals enlarged, by what mechanism the adrenals might enlarge?

DR. SELYE: In the beginning we did not have very much of an idea about that. We thought that perhaps the nerves, which go to the adrenal, might be responsible; but if you cut the nerves, that did not change anything. Stress would still stimulate the adrenals. So, a little later, stimulated mainly by the work of Dr. Evans in California and of Dr. Philip Smith in New York, who had been working on the pituitary and had found it to have something to do with the regulation of adrenal function, we removed the pituitary from animals. Then we found that after the pituitary was removed, the adrenal did not respond to stress any more. So, we felt that perhaps during stress the pituitary is stimulated to produce something, to discharge something into the blood, adrenocorticotrophic hormone, as one calls it now, or ACTH, which would be the agent, the chemical messenger, which tells the adrenal that there is an increased need for its work and for its activity. Under the influence of that ACTH, the adrenals would produce what we call corticoid compounds, and the cortisone which you mentioned, Dr. Dorfman, is one of these corticoid substances which the adrenal produces.

Now then, at that time, of course, we did not have any cortisone or any other pure adrenal cortical hormones; but we had adrenal extracts. And when we injected those into animals, we imitated some of the changes which occur during stress. But if you removed the adrenals, then these same changes were not produced by stress. So, gradually, as you can see, this concept developed that, perhaps during stress, the pituitary is stimulated to produce ACTH. That in turn acts on the adrenal and causes it to produce corticoids. All that, we felt, must be somehow useful for defense and resistance and adaptation or adjustment to stress, because if you interfere with the mechanism at any point, by removing either the pituitary or the adrenal, then the resistance to stress is at a low ebb.

So we arrived at the conclusion that the pituitary and the adrenal play an important role in the adaptation syndrome; that the adaptation syndrome is perhaps a useful response necessary for adjustment—adjustment during disease, for instance; and that perhaps by helping that reaction by injecting some of the hormones produced by the pituitary and the adrenal, one could fight the stress factor in disease and help adaptation to what causes disease.

DR. DORFMAN: We have spoken a good deal about the things which happen in the experimental animal as a result of stress and the role of an adrenal hormone, such as cortisone, in protecting the animal against the effects of stress.

The problem of ACTH and cortisone and the thing which is so striking to everybody were its effects on certain human diseases of which we knew very little. These diseases, of course, are now well known to everybody, particularly rheumatoid arthritis, rheumatic fever, a number of related diseases, a number of allergies.

Some of the people who have been interested in these diseases from an entirely different point of view, in a way not unlike your diseases of adaptation, Dr. Selye, have considered these diseases as diseases which result from the reaction of the body to some type of unknown stimulus, whether we call it stress or some bacterial infection. They are different from the diseases such as pneumonia, which results specifically from the action of a particular microbe or bacterium. ACTH and cortisone are hormones which affect these particular diseases very strikingly.

Dr. Conn, you have had a great deal of experience with their use. Have we gone far enough to say anything about what they really do? Are they really the miracle drugs which most people have been led to believe they are?

DR. CONN: I would say that, from the point of view of the clinician, he sees some very miraculous results when he gives ACTH or cortisone in a wide variety of diseases—things which the physician has never seen before. On the other hand, certain definite generalizations can now be made, after a period of experience of almost two years with these drugs. First, we actually do not cure the disease when we give ACTH or cortisone, because when these drugs are stopped, the disease comes back to its former state, even though the patient has received these materials for many months. It appears that we balk the clinical manifestations and symptoms of a disease which is actually still present.

DR. DORFMAN: What do you mean by these changes which you see? What sort of changes does one actually see when these drugs are administered?

DR. CONN: If a patient has severe arthritis and is bedridden, one frequently finds that the swelling of his joints disappears in several days and that a man who otherwise would not be expected to be able to walk is up walking, with normal temperature and a good appetite—and, as we say clinically, he feels very well. Then when the drug is stopped, within a few days, sometimes several weeks, he is essentially back to the same place that he was before. So that we have not actually hit the underlying disease.

DR. SELYE: From the experimental point of view we have made the same type of observation. For instance, in experimental animals you can easily imitate arthritis by injecting a little bit of some irritating substance into the joint region which will cause swelling of the joint and will be an experimental simulae of human arthritis. If you give ACTH or cortisone, the same irritating injection will not cause an arthritis. So, just as you say, one can, I believe, conclude that the manifestations of the abnormal reaction are inhibited by these drugs. In the sense in which I tried to introduce our own interest in this subject I would interpret it as indicating that the actual causative agent is not eliminated. The cause of the disease is not eliminated, but its manifestations are eliminated in the sense that we adjust to it.

DR. CONN: But you would agree that no one yet has discovered the actual fundamental mechanisms by which these manifestations of disease are made to disappear under the influence of these hormones?

DR. SELYE: No. I think that the actual mechanism is entirely unknown.

DR. DORFMAN: What we can say and what seems to fit and to give us a certain unity of this is that here we have a wide variety of diseases (in some cases we know something of the causes or the remote causes of these diseases), and, although they have many different causes, we have, in some way, stopped the diseases from becoming apparent. All we can say at this stage of the game is that we have, in some way, changed the body so that it no longer shows the usual reactions and symptoms. But what we have actually done, I do not think, Dr. Selye, I can say any more about that than you can, and I doubt whether many people are willing to say that at this time.

DR. CONN: One of the difficulties with which all of us have to contend is that there does not appear to be any evidence at the present time that any of these diseases, which respond so dramatically to these hormones, have as a basis a deficiency of these hormones. That is to say, the amounts of materials which are required in order to make a disease go into so-called remission are far in excess of what we usually expect to find clinically. And so, it is difficult to think of ACTH and cortisone as substituting for something which the body does not make.

DR. DORFMAN: So that this is not comparable to using insulin in diabetes, where we supply artificially the amount of insulin which is required. There is some other kind of effect with which we are dealing, you think.

DR. CONN: I think so, because compared with the amounts of ACTH or cortisone which are needed for replacement in conditions where there actually is a deficiency of these hormones, the amounts required for these other diseases, like arthritis, are far in excess of that.

DR. SELYE: I wonder what you would think about the possibility that here we might be dealing with a relative deficiency of these hormones. That is to say, under normal conditions we need a certain amount of ACTH and a certain amount of cortisone to get along and to meet the daily stresses of ordinary life. But if we acquire some disease which would seriously affect one part of the body, for instance, a joint, we would need very much more to meet it, without showing manifestations of a local reaction. So that actually, in the final analysis, perhaps it would still be a sort of deficiency—a deficiency in comparison with the increased amount needed.

DR. CONN: That is very possible; in fact, I think that it is very likely, but there is very little evidence at the moment with which we could support that.

DR. DORFMAN: You spoke of the fact that these drugs act to mask certain symptoms. Is this always a desirable thing? Do we have any adverse effects?

DR. CONN: Yes, I think so. I think that we are coming now to see an increasing lack of resistance to infection by patients under long, continued treatment with either ACTH or cortisone. In this respect there is experimental evidence in animals to back that up as well. It probably is wise, in view of what we are learning now, therefore, to use some of the antibiotic agents, such as penicillin, in association with long, continued use of ACTH or cortisone which seem to lower resistance to invading organisms.

In addition to that, there appear to be definite changes in the pituitary glands of people who have received cortisone at least, for a week or two. Whether these changes are important still remains to be seen.

There are also other things which bother me a little bit. It certainly still remains to be found out whether the masking of some of the clinical manifestations of a disease is a desirable thing.

DR. DORFMAN: What you are saying, then, is that these agents apparently prevent certain types of reaction in the body. Sometimes these reactions are undesirable and produce disease; and sometimes these reactions help us get rid of disease. And when they prevent the reactions which help us get rid of disease, they are undesirable and lead to undesirable conclusions, such as spread of infections and dangers of various kinds which we encounter. So that these are agents which have to be used with a great deal of caution.

Do you think at the present time that they can be used freely, safely?

Are there some special things which have to be observed in their use?

DR. CONN: By what I have said I do not mean to discourage the use of these compounds to alleviate suffering in many patients, but I mean simply to point out that we are dealing with extremely potent materials, the precise activities of which are not yet fully understood. If these materials are used carefully, with a full knowledge of our present background, and with rigid control of the patient, one can feel a reasonable degree of safety, but not completely, because no one yet knows which way these things are going.

DR. DORFMAN: And one of the critical questions, of course, if they are going to contribute to our knowledge of disease, is how they do act in the body. And this, of course, is a question which has occupied all three of us and many other people.

Dr. Selye, do you have any way by which you think these pieces fit into a general concept by which we can better explain what they all mean?

DR. SELYE: Meanwhile we can only express thoughts and formulate theories. I do not think that anybody would want to make any very definite and final statements, but from what has been said around this table here, it seems pretty obvious that, wherever we give cortisone or ACTH, there is always some question of helping adaptation or adjustment under abnormal conditions—helping adaptation or adjustment to something which would be able to cause disease. And it is in this sense that one might interpret that action.

You will recall, perhaps, that when we first worked with a cortical hormone, the first one which was available to us in large enough quantities, it happened to be one of those cortical hormones which have, in a sense, antagonistic, opposite, effects to ACTH. About five years ago, we injected large amounts of these hormones into animals, and we produced the same kind of disease which can now be beneficially influenced with cortisone or ACTH in man. So there seems to be a sort of balance between the various types of cortical hormones; and I think that this balance may help us to adjust and to adapt to our surroundings.

The diseases which we have produced experimentally by the hormones which seem to be opposite to cortisone are of the rheumatic and hypersensitivity type. And it is again in this same type of disease that cortisone and ACTH can be effective.

So that I think that, although this is not a final explanation and is somewhat vague, the easiest way to unite our knowledge and express some sort of a uniform opinion about it would be to say that these hormones of the adrenal help to adjust the response of various tissues to change, to injuring, to the stress of disease, to the stress of daily life.

DR. DORFMAN: Then you would emphasize that what we are really doing with these things is that we are essentially increasing the amount of substance available to the body to combat disease—in the same way that the body does physiologically under conditions of stress. But, for some reason, which at the moment is unknown to anybody, certain individuals do not have enough or the right balance of substances; and for that reason they develop disease. If we give to these individuals, artificially, as medicine, some of these compounds, we accomplish the same purpose.

Dr. Conn, do you feel that this would fit in with your concept of how these drugs act?

DR. CONN: Well, in general; but I am not at all certain that it fits with all the things which we see clinically. That is, if one gives ACTH or cortisone to a patient with ordinary pneumonia, the manifestations of that disease seem to disappear, although the pneumonia keeps on going. And then, when one stops this ACTH or cortisone, the patient again manifests the clinical evidence of pneumonia.

I have difficulty in applying all the basic concepts that Dr. Selye has mentioned, to some of the things that we see clinically, although they are obviously applicable in others. I think, as I said earlier, that the greatest contribution that these drugs can give to the clinical investigator is the ability to turn off and on a disease and to get into the middle of it and to find out what is going on.

DR. DORFMAN: From our own experience here in our laboratories in experimental work, the thing which impresses me is that in some way we create by giving these compounds an almost abnormal animal which is no longer capable of getting a normal reaction. Now, that normal reaction in some individuals, or in presence of certain disease stimuli, is undesirable; and if we prevent the animal from getting that reaction, we have prevented, or at least suppressed, as you say, the disease. On the other hand, that normal reaction, under other conditions, is highly desirable; and, when we suppress it, we do a highly undesirable thing. So, it would seem to me from our own experience that we can sum up our own feeling of the mechanism of action that we are creating a hyperadrenal animal.

Why some individuals should get these diseases, even though at least by present techniques we cannot find any evidence of deficiency of the reaction of the adrenal, is something which none of us know.

We ought to make it clear that we are, in this last part of our discussion particularly, all speculating and that there is a great deal more evidence and that we all may change our minds a great deal with future knowledge.

Dr. Selye, would you like to summarize your views and what you feel our present state is now, almost two years after this great discovery? What does it all mean to us now?

DR. SELYE: For one thing, I think, thanks to the observations made at the Mayo Clinic which showed us the clinical applicability of ACTH and cortisone in the treatment of rheumatoid diseases, we can now say, with some measure of assurance, that adrenal and pituitary hormones act essentially in the same way in the human being as they do in animals. If I had to summarize somehow our own participation in this research, I would say that the most important outcome of it is that we are imitating a natural, a normal defense reaction which helps adjustment and adaptation to the stress of various diseases.

DR. DORFMAN: There is little question that our experience during the last two years indicates that we now have new powerful drugs to use in the treatment of a wide variety of diseases, including rheumatoid arthritis, rheumatic fever, and many allergies. Although ACTH and cortisone probably do not act to cure these diseases, they do change their course in a dramatic way. They relieve much human suffering, and sometimes they save life. These drugs, of course, have many undesirable side effects, which mean that they must be used with caution and under conditions of careful control. But, when so used, their benefits may be great.

The wide range of diseases on which ACTH and cortisone act has brought about a new synthesis in our thinking in medicine. We begin to see, for the first time, the close connection between diseases with widely different symptoms. Thus, the work of specialists, previously working in widely separated fields of medicine, is now coming closer and closer together. In fact, we are now beginning to see the manner in which a variety of stresses—such as heat, cold, physical exhaustion, emotional disturbances—affect the tissues of the body. We see that all these stimuli influence the body through common pathways.

We are only at the early stages of thinking about this new concept, but the future should provide a much better understanding of man's reaction to his environment and how these reactions may be controlled to his benefit.

An American Medical Association Presidential Inaugural Address
Elmer L. Henderson, M.D.

Dr. Elmer L. Henderson was born in Garnettsville, Kentucky in 1885. He received his M.D. at the University of Louisville in 1909. Since 1911 he has practiced general surgery in Louisville and since 1942 he has been a special surgical consultant to the office of the Air Surgeon of the U.S. Air Force. In 1941-42 Dr. Henderson was president of the Kentucky State Medical Association. For the past twelve years he has served as a member of the Board of Trustees of the American Medical Association.

This address, delivered on the occasion of the inauguration of Dr. Henderson as the president of the American Medical Association, was broadcast on 27 June 1950 from the Palace Hotel in San Francisco over the ABC and the Mutual radio networks.

DR. IRONS, DR. BAUER, MR. SPEAKER, MEMBERS OF THE AMERICAN MEDICAL ASSOCIATION, AND FELLOW AMERICANS:

In the annals of American medicine, this is an historic occasion.

Tonight, the American Medical Association, in its inaugural ceremony, is speaking not just to doctors, but to the American people—on two nationwide radio networks, reaching into every State and into every corner of the country.

There is a vital reason for this new policy. Our affairs are no longer just medical affairs. They have become of compelling concern to all the people.

American medicine has become the blazing focal point in a fundamental struggle which may determine whether America remains free, or whether we are to become a socialist state, under the yoke of a government bureaucracy, dominated by selfish, cynical men who believe the American people are no longer competent to care for themselves.

In light of the challenge which confronts us, it is with a deep sense of responsibility that I begin my year of stewardship as president of the American Medical Association.

American medicine, which has led the world in medical advances, and which has helped to make this the healthiest, strongest nation on the face of the globe, has been made the first major objective of those ambitious men in Washington who would make the American people walk in lockstep under a rigidly controlled, government-dominated economy.

The American medical system has been made a target for the barbs and criticisms of a comparatively small group of little men—little men whose lust for power is far out of proportion to their intellectual capacity, their spiritual understanding, their economic realism, or their political honesty.

These men of little faith in the American people propose to place all our people—doctors and patients alike—under a shabby, government-dictated medical system which they call "Compulsory Health Insurance." And this, factually, is socialized medicine, regardless of how hard they try to disclaim it.

But it is not just "socialized medicine" which they seek; that is only their first goal.

Their real objective is to gain control over all fields of human endeavor. Their real objective is to strip the American people of self-determination and self-government and make this a socialist state in the pathetic pattern of the socially and economically bankrupt nations of Europe which we, the American people, are seeking to rescue from poverty and oppression.

This we must all recognize: There is only one essential difference between Socialism and Communism. Under State Socialism human liberty and human dignity die a little more slowly, but they die just as surely!

Never will our people accept the socialist program that grasping men in our government have planned for them, if they once understand that fundamental fact.

And tonight I call upon every doctor in the United States, no matter how heavy the burdens of his practice may be, to dedicate himself, not only to the protection of the people's physical health, but also to the protection of our American way of life, which is the foundation of our economic health and our political freedom.

The moral and spiritual health of a people certainly is of equal importance with their physical well-being.

It is not American medicine which has failed to measure up to its obligations. It is not American business nor American agriculture which has failed, nor the fine, loyal working people of America who have failed.

It is the administrative arm of our government in Washington which has failed us in this generation—a government which is sick with intellectual dishonesty, with avarice, with moral laxity, and with reckless excesses!

That condition we simply must change, if we are to survive as a strong, free people, and all of us—every one listening to me tonight, regardless of what his way of life may be—shares the responsibility.

There are many who recognize this need.

Only two days ago, newspaper publishers of the National Editorial Association, which represents 5,200 country newspapers in every section of America, made a pilgrimage to Plymouth Rock to rededicate themselves to the principles and the ideals on which this country was founded —and to consecrate themselves anew to the fundamental freedoms of our America.

Tonight, in behalf of American medicine, I want to pay tribute to the American press for its staunch devotion to the welfare of our people.

If it were not for leadership of the American press, in defending our fundamental liberties, American medicine, even now, might be socialized —and under the heel of political dictation.

The newspapers of America, with comparatively few exceptions, have taken a strong stand, not only against socialized medicine, but against all forms of state socialism in this country—and the doctors of America are proud to take their stand beside the fighting editors of America in the battle to save our freedom and the system of individual initiative which maintains it.

I am taking office as president of the American Medical Association at the half-way mark of the fabulous twentieth century—and I want to review briefly some of the advances we have made before turning to the goals which lie ahead.

The history of American medicine is a vibrant, continuing story of human progress. Because of that progress, millions of Americans are alive today who otherwise would have died at birth, during infancy, in childhood, in youth, or in middle age.

The story of never-ending medical progress in this country is not just a story of so-called "miracle drugs" and "miracle discoveries."

The real miracle of American medical progress is the miracle of America itself—the motivating power of the American spirit, of free men, unshackled and unfettered, with freedom to think, to create, to cross new frontiers.

Part of the great miracle that is America is our freedom to share, to coöperate, to work together for the common good.

That is the spirit which not only has provided the motive power for American medicine, but which has permeated the entire fabric of our American life—inspiring labor and business and industry, science and education, and all our fields of endeavor.

It is only the course of wisdom and common sense, therefore, to examine the past, present, and future of our medical system—to appraise what has been done, what is being done, and what can be done.

For if government—under the guise of misleading promises of health "security"—finally regiments physicians, dentists, nurses, druggists, scientists, hospitals, medical schools, and patients under a totalitarian plan which Washington directs and the people pay for—the spirit of individual initiative not only will be killed in the realm of health. Gradually, it will die in all phases of American life, just as it is dying today in other nations which first embarked on socialized medicine and then took the final, irrevocable steps down the path of state socialism.

Let's look at the facts: In America, since the turn of this century, the death rate has been cut almost in half. In 1900, the average life expectancy at birth was only 49 years. Today, newborn babies have a life expectancy of more than 68 years—a gift of 19 years of life!

For American mothers and babies, the risks of childbirth have been greatly reduced. Both the maternal and infant mortality rates are the lowest in our history.

The death rate for mothers in this country is the lowest reported by any nation in the world!

I wonder whether the politicians who want control over medicine can point to any comparable achievement.

At the turn of the century, pneumonia and influenza, taken together, and tuberculosis were far out ahead as the leading causes of death. Today they have been pushed down to sixth and seventh places, respectively, with death rates less than one-fifth and one-sixth of what they were in 1900.

If our would-be overseers in Washington had made similar progress in the art of government, we might look upon their pretensions in the field of health with less fear of the consequences!

Dread diseases like typhoid fever, diphtheria, and smallpox—which fifty years ago took a heavy toll in sickness and death—virtually have been eliminated as national health problems. And all of the infectious diseases have been brought under effective methods of prevention, control, and treatment.

The fight against disease and premature death is of significance and dramatic interest to every man, woman, and child in our country.

It is being waged today with weapons which were largely unknown or undeveloped in 1900—new and revolutionary methods of examination, diagnosis, and treatment; new drugs, new anesthetics, new surgical techniques, new vaccines and serums, new facts about nutrition, new kinds of equipment and facilities, new methods of sanitation, public hygiene, and medical education.

A vital part of the great advance has been the continual expansion and improvement of our hospital system, and the constant raising of standards in our medical schools.

Yet only recently, the advocates of a government-controlled medical system had the amazing effrontery to castigate American medicine because, they asserted, there were more schools of medicine in 1900 than there are today!

The truth is that in 1900, the American landscape was dotted with scores of unaccredited, second and third-rate medical schools, many of which were actually diploma mills for the production of quack doctors!

Is that the condition to which these political medicine men would have us return?

Today, as a result of the American Medical Association's fight for higher standards, that dangerously deplorable situation has been eradicated—and we now have 79 Class A medical schools with approximately 25,000 students. And the number of doctors in America is increasing at a more rapid rate than the general population!

The misleading propaganda which has emanated from Washington on this issue is an affront to the American people's intelligence. Typical of this flagrant misrepresentation is the attempt to create a crisis over an alleged "doctor shortage" in this country.

The simple truth is that the ratio of doctors to population is higher in the United States than in any nation on earth except Israel, where the unfortunate refugee doctors of all Europe are gathered. It is equally true, as we are confident most of the people are aware, that the individual physician today can provide far more medical service than even a decade ago, because of technological improvements.

Now let's look at a half-century of progress in the hospital field.

In 1900, there were less than 1,000 approved hospitals, with approximately 400,000 beds.

Today there are more than 6,300 registered hospitals, with almost 1,500,000 beds, serving more than 16,000,000 patients a year. And the number of hospitals also is increasing steadily.

Finally, in the field of medical economics, the past twenty years have given our nation the new instrument of voluntary health insurance to provide people with prepaid medical care and thereby take the economic shock out of illness. Today, hundreds of excellent voluntary health insurance plans are available. There are nonprofit plans sponsored by doctors and hospitals. There are commercial plans offered by insurance companies. There are fraternal group plans, labor-sponsored plans and industry-sponsored plans.

This has been one of the great advances in medicine in our times, because it is increasing the availability of medical care to people in all income groups.

Compulsory health insurance is not the answer to this problem. The voluntary way is the American way to cope with the problem—and the people, by their support of the voluntary systems, are demonstrating that fact.

In 1946, there were 40 million Americans enrolled in the voluntary health insurance plans. In 1949, the number had increased to 61 million —and now it is approximately 70 million.

Within the next three years, in the opinion of leading medical economists, 90 million persons will be enrolled in the voluntary prepaid medical plans—and when that number has been reached, the problem will have been largely resolved.

This, then, is a brief, overall picture of just one chapter of American accomplishment—the stimulating, hopeful march of medical progress in the past half-century.

Mindful of that astounding progress, we can look forward to even more amazing medical progress in the next half-century, if the American spirit of freedom, initiative, and adventure is kept alive.

The doctors believe that solutions to current problems of medical care and service can be reached without recourse to legislation, without compulsory payroll taxes, and without political pressure!

In the half-century ahead, I think we can expect that doctors and their scientific allies will achieve victory over cancer.

I think we will conquer infantile paralysis, arthritis, rheumatic fever, premature heart disease, and high blood pressure.

It is reasonable to expect that pneumonia, influenza, tuberculosis, the common cold, and other infectious conditions will be reduced to an absolute minimum by new methods of prevention, control, and treatment.

And certainly the years ahead will bring a wealth of new knowledge concerning the human mind as well as the human body.

We are on the threshold of great progress which will do much to alleviate human suffering and to prolong human life. But if we are to achieve this maximum progress in the future, we must keep alive the American spirit and the American methods which have made possible the progress of the past and present!

This is the spirit, and these are the very methods, which government domination of medical practice would destroy!

In behalf of American medicine, I want to express my deep appreciation of the wonderful support the medical profession has received from civic groups all over America in its fight for liberty.

Today nearly 10,000 national, State, and local organizations, with many millions of members, have taken positive action against socialized medicine—and there is a rapidly broadening front against all forms of state socialism as a result of the fight that American medicine has been making.

We are proud to have such outstanding organizations as the American Farm Bureau Federation, the American Legion, the National Grange, the Veterans of Foreign Wars, the General Federation of Women's Clubs, the American Bar Association, the American Council of Christian Churches, and thousands of other groups, standing beside us in this battle for good medicine and sound Americanism!

With the help of God and the American people, the medical profession will continue to minister to the sick, to relieve human suffering—and to uphold the ideals which have made America the hope of freedom-loving people everywhere.

Weighed in the Balance
Hamilton W. McKay, M.D.

This presidential address was delivered at the forty-fourth annual meeting of the Southern Medical Association, at St. Louis on 13 November 1950.

Dr. Hamilton W. McKay was born in 1885 in Sumter, South Carolina. He studied at Davidson College (B.S., 1906) and at Jefferson Medical College in Philadelphia (M.D., 1910). After interning in New York and Philadelphia he taught at the North Carolina Medical College from 1913 to 1917. Following service as a Major in the Medical Corps in World War I, he studied at the Sorbonne (1919) and then returned to Charlotte, N.C., where he has continued to practice as a urologist. Dr. McKay served as a committee member and as an officer in various medical societies and associations prior to his election to the presidency of the Southern Medical Association in 1950.

IT IS difficult for us to realize and visualize the revolutionary changes which have taken place in business and professional circles in the past few years. I refer to changes in the thinking of the average American, the changes which apply to the creation of an attractive environment for the public to do business in and the entirely new approach to customers from the standpoint of public relations.

The following statistics, which were released by Ralph Brubaker of the Los Angeles Sales Executive Club, indicate the reasons for the rapid changes in the thinking of the average citizen during the past ten years and show the necessity of setting our sights on a much higher level:

Since 1940

1. 13½ million old customers have died;
2. Over 17 million marriages have taken place;
3. Over 30 million babies have been born;
4. Over one-third of all present families in the United States have been formed;
5. Out of the 140 odd million people in the United States today, 63 per cent do not remember World War I;
6. Fifty-two per cent do not remember a Republican administration in the White House;
7. Forty-eight per cent do not remember what conditions were like before World War II;
8. Forty-four per cent are consciously experiencing for the first time a free market in which they can buy what they want from normal assortments.

To enlarge upon these statistics and to further indicate why this "new" thinking public has come into being, stroll through the business district of your city or town. First, enter your bank. You may or may not realize it, but the bars and grillwork are demolished. Open counters and attractive surroundings replace them. Perhaps some junior officer approaches you with a smile and asks if he can serve you. These radical changes did not just happen but were brought about by the leaders in the banking business who, twenty years ago, felt a need for good public relations and did something about them. To me, modern merchandising is fascinating beyond description. The proper psychological display of merchandise will even make you buy items that you do not need. Air conditioning, special shopping guides to aid customers, free parking for his or her convenience: you just cannot get away from it. In a modern place of business, the customer is always right or is made to think he or she is. In dealing with the great air lines of this country, you will encounter courtesy and accommodation that are revolutionary in the field of transportation. As doctors, I think it is a good idea to leave our offices and hospitals once in a while and think, as we have been thinking, about the world along Main Street, the world of bankers, merchants, hotel managers, and air-line representatives. I believe there is much for doctors to learn along Main Street. The great and important truth we learn is that these persons are schooled and trained in business administration, and that they believe and practice good public relations because it is essential to building for the future and success.

Today, everything is being "weighed in the balance" by the people of America. Our town is no longer an isolated little island in an agricultural sea. We hear the news of the world simultaneously with our fellow Americans everywhere. We even see the World Series games in our homes as they are played. We move across the face of the earth or fly to far away places at speeds undreamed of a very few years ago. We are linked commercially and professionally in an amazing network that crosses the boundaries of the past as if they were no longer there at all.

As a consequence, the people of America have come to expect miracles of progress as a matter of course. And woe be unto any sector of American life which fails to keep pace, for it will be weighed in the balance of public opinion and will be found wanting.

What about the world of medicine? Is it really a world apart? Or must it also take its place in this new world that we have seen on our walk along Main Street? Has it any grillwork and bars which must be torn down? Does it, too, stand in need of some air conditioning and renovating? Let us consider these questions.

Certainly we should begin by crediting our profession with the advancements it has admirably achieved. We know that it is true that more people get better medical care today in America than in any other country in the world. We know that we have a program of medical education second to none. We know that we have a system of hospitals, clinics, and medical centers, small and large, that is the envy of the whole world. All of these and many more are measurable facts that stand above dispute.

But the trouble with most of us is that we stop our thinking at this point. We do not realize that it is not enough to be better than somebody else. Most of the American people do not know much about the levels of medical care and attention in other parts of the world, and most of them care less. We may think our fellow citizens are ungrateful in this; but no matter how much we think it, we still cannot change the fact that they are weighing us in an altogether different set of balances.

We are being weighed against the balance of strictly American standards. Our public relations are being weighed against the public relations standards which Americans have come to respect in other pursuits. Our competence is being weighed against the American standard of competence in other professions. Our charges are being weighed against the budgetary demands of other services which are essential to life and happiness in America. What we need is a revolutionary change of direction in our own thinking. We must break from our traditional defensiveness, our backward glances at the distance we have come, our comparisons with Europe and Asia. We must accept the challenge of the American mind. We must weigh ourselves against the standards of American demands!

What, exactly, does the American public think of American medicine? I wish I knew. Actually that is a question it is impossible to answer. It would depend, for one thing, on the segment of the public you were talking about. Level of family income, geographic location, cultural background, all these and many other factors would condition the answer.

But, if you will forgive me for generalization, I will tell you that it is my opinion that something is radically wrong between the medical profession and the people of America.

True enough, the people have not yet permitted the obstructing hand of the politician to lay itself upon the free practice of medicine by the individual doctor. But the only thing that has saved us so far from political control of medicine has been the statesmanlike efforts of hundreds of unselfish medical leaders like Dr. Elmer L. Henderson, president of the American Medical Association, and his co-workers, plus the spending of huge sums of money in our defense. We are deeply grateful for the services which our leaders, teachers, and practitioners are rendering wherever they may dwell. The battle is not yet won. It is only well begun.

I assume that it is as clear to you as it is to me that the loss of freedom in medical care would be an American tragedy. Why, then, is it not equally clear to the people, who, in the end, would bear individually the awful burden of the loss?

Well, it is tempting to conclude that they are simply ignorant of the consequences of socialization. It might even be comforting to us to shift the whole burden upon the people by taking the cynical position that the American spirit of self-reliance is vanishing and they are seeking collective security rather than individual responsibility in all areas of life.

To some degree, these criticisms may be justified. But I, for one, believe that they have been vastly overestimated by many medical men.

I believe, if I am correct in my premise, that there is something radically wrong between the people and the doctors; then it follows that we must be prepared to accept our rightful share of the blame for this situation.

Edward Bulwer-Lytton spoke a great truth when he wrote a long time ago, "The easiest person to deceive is one's own self." Have we been guilty of self-deception? Have we been blinded to our own faults and deficiencies? Is our traditional attitude of defensiveness mute evidence of our own reaction? If so, it is high time we changed our attitudes in favor of self-analysis, correction, and a positive program of constructive public relations. Or, to express it somewhat more simply, we must bring the doctor back to the people and the people back to the doctor. This is the grass-roots problem. This is the fundamental task; and unless we get on with it, medicine is sooner or later doomed to political control.

So much for generalizations. Now let us get down to some practical suggestions in the direction of these objectives.

Let us begin with medical education itself; and what better place is there to make our beginning?

Many institutions, organizations, and individuals play an important role in the training of a doctor. And each one is busily and constructively engaged in current debate concerning the length of time a man should be occupied in the various stages of his medical training. Personally, I do not believe that the time can be shortened and I have no criticism to offer of the scientific training program. What I am concerned about is the lack of evidence that our educators are aware of the tremendous need for training in human and public relations.

A streamlined 1950 model of the well-trained doctor can make a difficult diagnosis and direct the therapy. If he is trained to do a lung or brain operation, he can do it well. In short, he is a first-class scientific product, "ready and willing to go." But, he has not been taught, either in medical school or in the hospital, to become a part of the community, one of the people. There is a gulf, deep and wide, between him and his potential patients. In his office, he is like a babe in the woods. He knows little or nothing of office organization, of handling patients, or of how to charge and collect. He simply does not know that it is not enough to do a good scientific job; he is a bungling novice in the art of human relations with his patients, who are, after all, his greatest assets and medicine's stock in trade.

In the community at large, he is no better. He tells his fellow citizens that he does not have time to help with the character-building agencies and civic enterprises that make the town or city a better place for his wife and children to live in. He believes that the Chamber of Commerce, which brings many potential patients to him and his fellow doctors, should be run and supported by laymen or somebody else. When the self-sacrificing solicitor for the Community Chest finally runs him down, he makes a token gift much as if he were tossing small change in a collection plate. Such criticism is meant to be constructive and is to emphasize the lack of training in this area rather than to belittle the young doctor.

Such conduct, in and out of the office and hospital, is well known, too, and frequently discussed by the lay people of his community. If he were the only one who suffered as a result, it might be simple justice. But, the fact is that it is just such failures in the realm of personal and public relations that have nearly cost us our medical freedom.

Somewhere along the road between admittance to a medical school and completion of hospital internship and residency, a period of twelve to fifteen years and a cost estimated between $20,000 and $35,000, provision must be made to teach the young scientist the practice of good personal and community relations. It is vital not only to his own welfare but to the future of free medicine itself.

Another area in which we have done a sorry job is in professional self-discipline. The doctor who has a license to practice medicine and joins a county medical society is usually fixed for life. Unless he is convicted by a court for some criminal offense, he can continue to enjoy the rights and privileges of responsible doctors even though he, himself, practices overcharging, neglect of patients, and nonsupport of organized medicine.

Such practices should not only be considered intolerable by the good doctors, but should be condemned and properly dealt with by an honest, competent and nonpartisan court of medicine. Grievance committees are now operating in more than twenty States and the American Medical Association is taking steps in the right direction. All of this constitutes one of the most interesting experiments of modern times.

A third area in which we need to clean our own house is in the medical practice acts which in many States permit doctors to carry out procedures, operative or otherwise, for which they are neither trained nor competent. I am not speaking about criminal abortion, violation of the Harrison Narcotics Act, or other like offenses. Neither am I thinking about the honest mistakes that each of us makes every day. I am referring to the medical man or surgeon, usually in the small hospital, who cannot or will not make proper studies to arrive at a diagnosis or have a diagnosis made. Often these men are responsible for the health of hundreds of people.

These antiquated medical practice acts which license a man to practice medicine and surgery and give him the permission of the State to do anything on anybody, constitute another grievance against medicine; for the results of incompetence in high places of medicine and surgery are beginning to become known to the people. To illustrate, *Reader's Digest* carried an article in December 1947 on this subject which must have been read by countless millions. In substance, it reported to the people "the shocking fact that many of the nine million surgical operations performed annually in America are unnecessary."

It should be perfectly clear to anyone that if the people cannot convince themselves that organized medicine is taking vigorous steps to correct its own shortcomings, they will insist that the initiative for action be transferred to other hands.

Now, in summary, here is what we have done: we have observed wonderful progress which has been made by other groups along the Main Streets of America in overcoming serious public relations problems; we have reminded ourselves that it is not enough for us to compare the American medical system with similar systems in other parts of the world; we have seen that we are being weighed in the balance of public opinion against strictly American standards; we have recognized that something is radically wrong between the people and the doctors; we have accepted our share of the blame for this situation; and we have suggested three areas in which we should make immediate beginnings toward improvement: education in the art of human relations, professional self-discipline, and modernization of the medical practice acts.

These suggestions by no means exhaust the possibilities for progressive action. But, they do serve most capably the primary purpose of this discussion, which is to make it as clear as I possibly can that ultimate responsibility for the freedom and welfare of American medicine rests squarely upon the individual doctor and his friends in related organizations in the field of general medicine. The term "organized medicine" has no meaning except as it be defined in terms of individual responsibility. Unless and until the doctor on Main Street faces up to the deficiencies of his profession and wants these weaknesses corrected, there will be no progress.

We can win the fight for medical freedom if and when we decide to look after our own business. This means sacrifice, hard work, and devotion to organized medicine. Above all else, it means that liberty is possessed only by those who earn the right to be free and employ that freedom in such a fashion as to maintain and enhance the respect and confidence in which the physician is held by his community.

What Health Insurance Would Mean to You
Oscar R. Ewing

The text below is a slightly revised version of a radio address delivered by Oscar R. Ewing, the Federal Security Administrator, on an American Broadcasting Company network on 14 November 1949. It is printed here as an official statement of the Truman administration on national health insurance, or "socialized medicine," as the plan is called by its opponents. President Truman took occasion to challenge these opponents when he dedicated the Clinical Center of the National Institute of Health at Bethesda, Maryland on 22 June 1951. He asserted: "Since 1945, I have been proposing to meet this problem [of rising medical costs] by national health insurance. This proposal has generated a great deal of controversy. I still believe it is sound and that the nation would be greatly strengthened by its adoption."

Oscar R. Ewing was born in Greensburg, Indiana on 8 March 1889. He studied at Indiana University (A.B., 1910) and Harvard Law School (LL.B., 1913). Following a period of legal practice in Indianapolis (1915-16), he joined the law firm of the late Chief Justice Hughes in New York, became a partner in 1920, and is now a member on leave of Hughes, Hubbard, and Ewing. In August 1942 he was appointed Vice Chairman of the Democratic National Committee. He was in charge of the prosecutions of the Silver Shirts leader, William Dudley Pelley, for sedition (1942) and of Douglas Chandler for treason (1947). Appointed by President Truman as Federal Security Administrator in 1947, Mr. Ewing soon became the target of vigorous attacks by the American Medical Association and other organizations.

GOOD EVENING. I want to talk to you tonight, not about the nation's health, but about your own health. Suppose that tomorrow morning, you should become suddenly ill—seriously ill. Suppose you found that you needed an operation, with special medical care, and all kinds of x-rays and drugs. Suppose you had to stop working for some months while you went through your operation and your convalescence. Suppose the doctor's bill, the hospital bill, the bills for special laboratory services and medicines, added up to hundreds of dollars—maybe even thousands. Would you be able to afford it?

If you are like most other people in this country, I can tell you the answer just as quickly as you would tell it to me if I were sitting there in the room beside you. The answer, for most of us, is one word: No.

Most of us are neither very rich nor very poor. People who are very rich don't need to worry about their medical bills, any more than they need to worry about whatever other bills they run up. On the other hand, people who are very poor do generally get medical treatment in the United States, because we have charity care which does make doctors and hospitals available to the real needy. But, if you are like the majority of Americans, you are somewhere between those two extremes. You've got a job. You've got your self-respect. And you like to stand on your own two feet. But you're not made of money; and when sickness strikes, when you wake up one morning with acute appendicitis, or when your old folks get sick, or when your child comes home from school restless and feverish, you have two worries—your first worry is that they should get the best treatment in town; and your second worry is how you're going to pay for it.

If you have ever been lying in a hospital bed after an operation, worrying about where the money to pay the bills would come from, you know what I mean. If you have had to go to a loan company and borrow money to pay a hospital bill, you know what I mean. If you have ever received a note from your child's school, telling you that your little boy or your little girl needs adenoids or tonsils out, and wondered how you'd pay for it, you know what I mean. If your wife has noticed a lump in her breast, but puts off going to the doctor because of the cost, you'll know—and she'll know—what I mean.

We have a problem in this country, and we're grown-up enough to face it squarely. Here we have some of the finest doctors and hospitals in the world, and we have the benefit of the magnificent research laboratories of America. True, we should be spending more money on medical research, but just with what we've done, we have already made such huge progress in medical research that we could call our times the Age of Giant Advances in Medicine. Yet, right now, thousands of sick people are not receiving the benefit of these giant advances because they cannot afford it. Every physician knows the torment he must go through when a patient comes in with a disease that could be cured if only that patient had the money to pay for x-ray treatments, or expensive specialists, or costly new drugs or equipment, that would make him healthy again.

In America today, there is a barrier between the doctor and the patient. That barrier is the dollar bill.

This is our problem—to remove the barrier of dollars, to bring the patient and the doctor together, and in this way, to make medical care

What Health Insurance Would Mean to You

available to all our people, not just the very rich and the very poor, but *all* our people.

Now, we could simply say, "Oh, we've gotten along okay so far, why change things? If people worry, why, they've always worried, haven't they? If people have died for lack of medical care, why, they've always died, haven't they? So what?" Or we might take another line and say, "Anyway, there are systems of voluntary health insurance to take care of those who want to provide for themselves." Yes, we *could* say these things—if we had the heart to do so. But we aren't the kind of people who can say, "So what?" when we hear that one out of every two mothers who died in childbirth in this country this very day, November 14, died unnecessarily, and that her life could have been saved if known medical measures had been fully applied. It might have been your wife. We can't say "So what?" when we know that one out of every three babies who died in this country today, November 14, could have been saved if known medical measures had been fully applied. It might have been your baby.

The voluntary plans for health insurance are fine as far as they go. But how far do they go? In the first place, most of them stop short of giving the amount of medical care you need. For example, most of them won't pay the bill if you have to call the doctor to your home or even if you go to his office. And if you have a serious chronic ailment at the time you enroll, then they will make a particular point of *not* giving you protection for that ailment. There are various other limitations in voluntary insurance policies which I won't take time to recite because these two examples illustrate what I mean.

Another reason why the voluntary health insurance may be impracticable for you is that the premiums for this type of insurance are not adjusted to your income. Whether you earn $50 a week or $200 a week, you pay the same amount.

But most important, in voluntary health insurance you generally get a poor return for your money because overhead and profits of the insurance company eat up huge chunks of the premiums you pay. Many commercial companies in the hospital, surgical, and medical insurance business sell only *group* policies. Generally speaking, this means that there must be a group of 25 or more employees of a concern who want the insurance. By dealing with a group, the cost of selling the insurance is reduced and bookkeeping costs are largely eliminated, since the employer keeps all the wage records. However, companies selling group insurance pay out on the average 30% of their group-insurance premium receipts for overhead and profits, leaving only 70% for payment of benefits. But you can't get *group* insurance if you are a clerk in a small store or if you are a farmer or if you are a small businessman. Unless you work for some large business, you must probably buy insurance from a company which sells individual policies. Now, here's the catch. On individual policies these companies spend for overhead and profits an average of about 60% of what you pay them and only about 40 cents of your premium dollar goes for benefits to policyholders. Obviously, such insurance is a mighty poor buy.

Under voluntary nonprofit insurance plans, Blue Cross hospitalization plans paid back 85 cents of the premium dollar in hospital benefits last year, and Blue Shield surgical-medical plans paid back in benefits 77 cents on the premium dollar paid.

We ought to be able to do better than that. We *can* do better than that. That is why we are proposing a plan for national health insurance. There has been a lot of loose talk about this proposal. I think you will want to have the straight facts on how this plan would work for you personally.

Under national health insurance, if you get sick, or anyone in your family gets sick, you would call your family doctor, just as you do now. He would examine you in order to decide the treatment he should prescribe. Your doctor would know that he can freely use x-ray and any kind of laboratory tests he thinks desirable. He may decide you should see a specialist or go to the hospital. Possibly you need eyeglasses or a hearing aid or maybe you need an expensive medicine like streptomycin. Under national health insurance, your doctor is free to give you the best that medical science has to offer without giving a thought to what it will cost because this cost is met, not by you personally, but by the insurance fund.

But, you naturally wonder, where does this insurance fund come from. Well, if you are employed, your employer will pay into the fund an amount equal to 1½% of your salary, and another 1½% will be deducted from your pay check. This deduction is only taken from what you earn up to $4800 a year. If you earn $50 a week, you would pay a premium of 75 cents. The maximum premium for any employee, no matter how high his salary, would be $1.40 a week. If you are self-employed, your premium would similarly be worked out on the basis of how much your income was. These payments cover home and office calls by the doctor, treatment by specialists, hospital and nursing care for at least sixty days, eyeglasses, hearing aids, cost of expensive medicines, x-rays, laboratory tests, and dental services to the extent available—for yourself and your family.

What Health Insurance Would Mean to You

You can see from this that national health insurance would affect you and your family in three ways: First, all the bills for medical services will be paid by the insurance fund and not by you; second, you will get more and better medical care; and, third, your contributions to the insurance fund would be in the form of small regular deductions from income when you are well and working, and best able to pay. No longer would you have to pay large doctor and hospital bills when you are sick or convalescing and least able to pay. And you would be getting the most for your money. Remember the figures I gave you before—group policies that pay out in benefits about 70 cents on the dollar, individual policies that pay out only about 40 cents on the dollar, nonprofit hospital plans that pay out about 85 cents on the dollar, nonprofit surgical and medical care plans that pay out about 77 cents on the dollar. Overhead under national health insurance would cost no more than 5 to $7\frac{1}{2}\%$—which means that from $92\frac{1}{2}$ to 95 cents of every dollar in premiums would go to pay for the medical care you need.

The reason estimated overhead costs for national health insurance are so much lower than those of the voluntary companies is that under national health insurance (a) there would be no selling costs; (b) the Federal Security Agency is already keeping the wage records of some 90 million workers and health insurance records would add comparatively little to this cost; and (c) the Treasury Department already is collecting social-security payroll deductions, and deductions for health insurance could be collected with comparatively little added cost.

Now, what about the doctor under national health insurance? You hear a lot of talk about regimenting doctors, about doctors spending long hours making out reports, socialization of medicine, etc., etc. You can put all that talk down as just plain "baloney." The proof of this is very simple. Today, the doctors are almost all plugging for voluntary health insurance. But under voluntary health insurance, doctors have the same problems regarding the making of reports, arrangements for payment of their services, handling of hypochondriacs, etc., as they would have under national health insurance. The only difference between national health insurance and voluntary health insurance, so far as the doctor is concerned, is that his bill would be paid by a check from a national insurance fund instead of from a private insurance fund.

Maybe you're worrying about red tape. Maybe you are asking yourself, "Who's going to run this thing?" Well, here's the answer: It would be run right in your own home town, right in your own State, by your local doctors, and by local people representing you as partners in national health insurance. There would be no more red tape than you find today in the voluntary plans for health insurance, and probably less. The day-to-day administration of the program would be in the hands of local doctors and laymen—not here in Washington.

You may have heard some criticism of health insurance. Most of it comes from people who may mean well but who just haven't taken the trouble to find out what the plan involves. Many doctors, I'm sorry to say, have been misled by people who tell them all kinds of horrible stories about what it would do to their profession. When someone tells you one of these wild stories, ask him just to find out what we are really proposing. The plain fact is that this program, when it comes into force, will be the greatest boon to the medical profession since the discovery of anesthesia; for it will help the doctors to practice better medicine for more people. It is just an honest-to-goodness attempt to remove the dollar barrier that separates you from your doctor and prevents you and your family from having the best medical care that money can buy. It is pretty much like Social Security and not much different, in theory, from life insurance, or fire insurance, or accident insurance.

What would national health insurance mean to you? It would mean that, when someone asks you, as I ask you, "Can you get all the medical care you and your family really need?" you could answer with confidence and relief, "Yes, under national health insurance I can."

Prepayment Plans
Paul R. Hawley, M.D.

Dr. Paul R. Hawley, the director of the American College of Surgeons, delivered the talk below to the Clinical Congress of the American College of Surgeons meeting at the Civic Auditorium in San Francisco on 5 November 1951. The speaker points out that "as yet little has been done toward the solution of the real problem, which is that of prolonged and really expensive illness."

Dr. Hawley was born in West College Corner, Indiana on 31 January 1891. After graduating at Indiana University (A.B., 1912) he studied medicine at the University of Cincinnati (M.D., 1914) and at the Johns Hopkins University (Dr. P.H., 1923). He was commissioned a First Lieutenant in the Army Medical Corps and advanced through grades to Major General in 1944. From 1943 to 1947 Dr. Hawley was Chief Medical Director of the Veterans Administration. Prior to assuming his present position he served as chief executive officer of the Blue Cross and Blue Shield Commissions.

Prepayment Plans

To USE a favorite expression of my father's, when he ventured into the field of prediction, I want to open my remarks with the statement that "I am neither a prophet nor the son of a prophet." It would be the height of temerity for me to make any categorical statement upon either the future of prepayment plans or their influence upon the hospitals of the future.

I do think that one firm prediction can be made, and this is that prepayment plans are here to stay, and the only question about their general pattern is whether they will be voluntary or compulsory in type. If the voluntary type is to prevail, it must meet the reasonable needs of the people; and no type of prepayment plan can survive unless it have a strong social conscience. The lack of a social conscience is the greatest weakness of commercial health insurance today. While it is absurd to expect any kind of prepayment plan to operate at a financial loss, the profit motive alone will never produce a satisfactory prepayment plan against the costs of medical and hospital care.

While I decline to offer any prediction upon the future of prepayment plans, I do hold certain personal convictions upon the problems to be solved by prepayment plans, and I have no hesitation in offering them to you for what they may be worth.

The Ewing Plan of national, compulsory health insurance is dormant for the moment. I would like to think that it is dead, but this is entirely too optimistic. It is, however, sufficiently comatose that we may do a biopsy upon it without awakening it—although I would much prefer a complete autopsy.

In the first place, the Ewing Plan was both praised and damned entirely upon emotional grounds. No one really knew what they were talking about. The very problem had not, and has not yet, been defined. The proponents of the Ewing Plan confined their arguments almost exclusively to the field of catastrophic illness. Their examples of the burdens imposed by illness were limited almost entirely to the costs of chronic illness or acute illness of long duration. Yet the Ewing Plan itself did not meet this problem. It provided only for a limited period of hospital care.

On the other hand, too much of the opposition to the Ewing Plan ignored the existence of some rather obvious problems in the field of medical care, and offered no constructive suggestions as to their solution.

My association with these problems, which has placed me in contact with a great many people in this country, has convinced me that both the proponents and the opponents of the Ewing Plan, taken together, constitute less than one-half of our people. I am convinced that the majority of our people today are in the very intelligent position of not knowing the solution of the problem for the very sound reason that the problem has never yet been clearly defined. These are the people who will make the ultimate decision; and it is my hope that their patience will endure until the problem can be thoroughly explored and clearly set forth in its essentials.

There is a rapidly growing conviction that the crucial aspect of the problem is limited to the need of truly expensive medical and hospital care. For generations the average family has devoted a certain percentage of its income to medical care. This figure has been placed at around 6 per cent. The vast majority of people have been, and still are, able to meet such costs out of current income, or without serious hardship. However, when the cost of medical care amounts to 15 or 20 per cent of income, it does present a formidable problem to the low income group.

This raises the question as to whether we have attacked the problem of cost of medical care at the right place. Until this time, with the exception of a very restricted catastrophic coverage recently offered against the cost of poliomyelitis, all prepayment plans, both nonprofit and commercial, have been restricted to the field of illnesses of short duration. I am beginning to feel that we have—as an old friend of mine likes to say—that we have backed into this problem.

There are very good reasons for this mistake, if indeed it has been a mistake. One reason is that illnesses of long duration affect only a very small proportion of people—probably not over 5 per cent—whereas almost all of us are subject to illnesses of short duration. The early voluntary plans were started by groups of employed people, largely free from prolonged illness at the moment. They were young people, to whom chronic illness seemed a remote possibility. So, their attention was quite naturally focused upon illness of short duration.

Another reason is that no one had the faintest idea of the proper price to be charged for protection against the costs of medical and hospital care—whether for illness of long or short duration. However, it was obvious to these pioneers that there was less chance of financial disaster if benefits were limited to short periods than there would be if unlimited protection were attempted.

So, we now have reasonably satisfactory plans for protection against the costs of illnesses of short duration. They are not perfect, but they are improving all the time. However, we are beginning to realize that this is not the critical aspect of the problem, and that as yet little has been done toward the solution of the real problem, which is that of prolonged and really expensive illness.

Steps are now being taken to attack this problem. Several commercial carriers are offering insurance against specified lists of chronic diseases. Blue Cross is studying the problem. However, the single obstacle to the development of this much-needed protection is that no one knows exactly what catastrophic illness is, nor how often it occurs. Consequently, no one knows what to charge for such protection. A study of this problem is just now being launched by an unprejudiced research agency, and I am hopeful that it will produce the necessary information for the rapid development of this type of insurance.

All voluntary insurance against the costs of medical and hospital care is seriously threatened today by flagrant abuses. Not only has the cost of hospital operation more than doubled in the past 15 years, but the utilization of Blue Cross benefits has increased about 50 per cent in the same period. This has forced the cost of Blue Cross to levels which threaten its expansion—and it must be greatly expanded if voluntary insurance is to succeed.

I have almost reached the conclusion that it is a serious mistake to offer complete coverage against the costs of medical and hospital care. I think that, to minimize abuses, there must be a considerable degree of coinsurance in such protection. The patient must have a stake in his use of benefits. The insurance must always take the curse from these costs, but the only way we can prevent serious abuses is for the patient to pay a part of the bill. Whether Blue Cross and Blue Shield will come to this conclusion, I do not know. If they do, I am sure it will be with considerable reluctance; but it seems to me to be inevitable if we are to keep the cost of voluntary protection at a reasonable level.

To summarize, I think the future will bring us much more knowledge about the essential factors of health insurance. It may well be that the emphasis will be shifted from protection against the costs of illness of short duration to those of illness of long duration. There is no reason why we should not develop both. However, all development in this field will be seriously restricted until we have solved the problem of protecting prepayment plans from abuses.

EDUCATION

Where Do We Go from Here in Education?
Robert M. Hutchins

Dr. Hutchins spoke to the Economic Club of Detroit on 12 May 1947. He had just returned from a trip to Europe and in the address below he further expounded his educational theories. In addition to numerous articles and speeches Dr. Hutchins has written the following important books: *No Friendly Voice* (1936), *The Higher Learning in America* (1936), and *Education for Freedom* (1944).

For a more recent address by Dr. Hutchins the reader is referred to "The Freedom of the University," originally given as the Hillman Lecture at Columbia University on 21 November 1950. It was published in *Ethics* for January 1951 and in the *American Association of University Professors Bulletin* for Summer 1951.

MR. CHAIRMAN, MR. LOVETT, GENTLEMEN:

I appreciate Mr. Lovett's remarks very much indeed. From one point of view I do deplore them. I deplore them because of the emphasis on the word "new." I must say that I feel very far from "new." Now that Nicholas Murray Butler is out of the way, I am the senior executive in the American Association of Universities, closely pushed by that young man at Ann Arbor, Mr. Ruthven, who had the misfortune to be elected president of the University of Michigan four months after the University of Chicago had the misfortune to elect me.

From the gray eminence which I occupy, I survey American education with a detachment, a disinterestedness, and, I may add, a pessimism which nobody, except possibly Mr. Ruthven, in the State of Michigan can approach.

I have worked long, and occasionally hard, and have seen very little done. My one solid accomplishment I owe to Michigan—it procured a team which defeated mine 85 to 0. Because of this, I was able to abolish football in Chicago.

For this and many other favors, I shall never cease to be grateful to you.

Now, in the twenty-five years, and more, that I have been in American education, I have noticed that it has certain permanent and abiding problems. They are caused by various paradoxes or contradictions in our educational system, and in our attitude toward it. It is about these problems, paradoxes, and contradictions, that I wish briefly to speak.

The first paradox appears in our national behavior in the support of education. It is often said that American education is the American substitute for a national religion, but many countries have been able to reconcile support of an official religious establishment with disregard of its principles, and American support of education often appears to be of this kind. The devotion seems to be to the symbol, rather than to the activity, and is rather rhetorical than real.

Popular education is a splendid subject for a Fourth of July address; yet, 350,000 teachers have been driven from the profession by the pitiful salaries now offered.

In some parts of this country, a teacher may count herself fortunate if she receives $500 a year, and we can be certain, I think, that if there is another depression the experience of the last one will be repeated. The expenditures on the schools will be the first cut and the last restored.

I have come to Detroit directly from the plane that brought me home from a month in England. There is a country in which there is a shortage of all goods; a country whose empire, if not dissolving, is at least changing its shape; a country which has neither manpower, building materials, books, nor paper.

What is it doing?

It is putting into effect the provisions of the Education Act of 1944, the main result of which is an extension of the period of compulsory education from fourteen to fifteen years of age. I do not say that this is a wise decision, or that a mere increase in the school-leaving age produces necessarily sound educational results. I do say that this action which, under the circumstances, is so courageous as to be almost reckless, shows that the British really mean what we say about education.

They mean that education is important; it is more important than food, tobacco, or even beer; more important than capital equipment, military equipment, or houses. They mean that man does not live by bread alone, and that an intelligent nation is more likely to succeed economically and militarily than one which has great material resources but does not know what to do with them.

It is true that our own country is now committed, in the GI Bill of Rights, to the greatest educational expenditure in the history of the race. The appropriations for educational purposes under the GI Bill of Rights will run between ten and fourteen billion dollars. This legislation originated, not in the desire to educate veterans, but in the forebodings of the economist that there would be six to eight million unemployed within six months after the war.

The genesis of the National Youth Administration during the depression was the same. It did not result from the conviction that young people must be educated even if the stock market falls, but from a desire to keep young people off the labor market.

I applaud the expenditure and the consequences of the National Youth Administration, and the GI Bill of Rights, although I must say it will be a little unfortunate if the young men now studying under the GI Bill of Rights come to the end of their grants and the end of their studies in a period of unemployment.

I am concerned here, not with what such measures accomplish, but with what they reveal of the American attitude toward education. They do not require any revision of my thesis that the American people, whatever their professions, do not take education very seriously. And, in the past there has been no particular reason why they should.

This country was impregnable to enemies from without, and apparently indestructible. It could not be destroyed even by the hysterical waste and mass stupidity of the people and its government. Foreign policy, for example, could be the blundering ground of nice old southern lawyers, and education could be regarded as a means of keeping children off the street; the schools kept young people out of worse places until we were willing to have them go to work.

Now, when the Russians have the atomic bomb—which I am happy to say was not solely the product of the University of Chicago—and the Russians certainly will have it within five years; Langmuir's prediction is about a year and a half—when the Russians have the atomic bomb, the position of the United States automatically undergoes a dramatic change. The position of the United States, then, is very little beyond that of Czechoslovakia before the war—one false step in foreign policy can mean the end, not only of our institutions, but also of civilization. In a war in which both sides have atomic bombs, the cities of both sides will be destroyed.

And, we cannot place our hope on those agreements for the control of atomic energy, which are just around the corner in the sense in which Mr. Hoover remarked, in 1932, that prosperity was just around the corner. These agreements are absolutely imperative; but they will simply guarantee, if they are effective, that the next war will end with atomic bombs instead of beginning with them. And, if these agreements are ineffective, they will simply increase the element of surprise which the atomic bomb has added to the arsenal of the aggressor. And, if it becomes possible, as it theoretically is, to manufacture atomic bombs out of helium and hydrogen, all plans for control based on the control of uranium must fail.

We have now reached the point where we cannot have war and civilization, too!

Last week in Paris, I met with a staff of the United Nations Scientific and Cultural Organization. There is a group operating, by the way, on an annual budget which is about 25 per cent of the amount which the United States government spent every year during the war at the University of Chicago alone for the production of new weapons. And, this group is dedicated to the proposition that, since war begins in the minds of men, and since education is supposed to have some effect on the human mind, the way to prevent war is to do something about education.

I put it to you that this proposition is sound; that education, as the British have decided, is the most urgent business before us; and that we must show, by our actions rather than by our speeches, that we regard it in this light.

Now, while we are about it, we might attack another paradox in Amercan education, which is that a system, nominally democratic, operates in an oligarchical way. An oligarchy, I need not remind you, was a form of government based on wealth.

American education is founded on the belief that democracy is served if its schools, colleges, and universities charge low fees, or none; and if, at the same time, there is no discrimination among students in terms of their intellectual ability.

We have democratic education, then, if we do not charge for it, and if we make clear that every citizen is entitled, as a matter of right, to as much free education as every other citizen.

This assumption is false in all its parts.

Actually, the important cost of education is not fees. It is the cost of the pupil's subsistence if he lives away from home, and the loss of his earning power. In this country, however, scholarships given by private foundations rarely cover more than fees.

The educational institutions, managed by local and State governments, feel they have performed their full duty if they charge low fees, or none. The books of the University of Chicago will show an expenditure on student aid of more than $600,000 a year, but the figure is meaningless, for almost every cent of this money is paid back to the University in the form of fees by the students who receive it.

Universal education in America has, therefore, meant that all those who could afford to continue in school have been able to, and those who have not had the money, have not.

Hence the paradox, that in a country which provides free education for all, the length of a young person's education varies directly with his capacity to pay; and since, at these age levels, at least, and probably at all age levels, there is no relation between intellectual ability and capacity to pay, the educational system has been overwhelmed with students who are not qualified for the work they are supposed to be doing, and whose presence inevitably dilutes and trivializes the whole program.

Every study that has been made in this country shows that there are more good high school graduates out of college than in. The reason is that the ones who go to college are the ones who have the money to go, and it would be undemocratic to say they were not bright enough to go. And, those who are bright enough to go, cannot go unless they have the money to go, because we have no adequate system of financial aid to those who are bright, but impoverished.

Here I think it is safe to say that we fall behind every country in the Western world.

Until the National Youth Administration and the GI Bill of Rights, nothing was ever done by anybody to recognize the cost of living as an element in the cost of education.

Before the war, we used to boast that a student could go to the University of Illinois for $75 a year. He could. That is, he could, if in addition, he could command not less than $750 a year to live on, and if his family could do without his earnings.

By contrast, every European country has long since made provision that those who show themselves qualified through a rigorous system of competition to receive aid in their education shall receive aid which enables them to live as well as to study.

As a self-supporting student, who tried to live first and study afterwards, I can testify that the combination is possible only because the American university demands so little study.

If we had in this country real intellectual competition in our universities, it would at once become apparent that it is not possible for a boy to work eight hours a day in a factory, as I did, and get an education at the same time. Under those circumstances it must be clear that I did not get an education; I simply graduated from college, which is quite a different thing.

What we need is an adequate system of financial aid for those who deserve it, a national system of competitive scholarships—scholarships which are large enough to enable the student to study as well as live.

We also need a system by which those students who are not qualified for university work may be effectually excluded from the university. The basic task of education for citizenship should be performed outside the universities. The universities should be devoted to advanced study, professional training, research, and the education of leaders. Therefore, the university must be limited, if it proposes to succeed in any of these tasks, to those who have demonstrated their qualifications for advanced study, professional training, research, or leadership.

The notion that any American, merely because he is one, has the privilege of proceeding to the highest university degree must be abandoned. A six-year elementary school, a three- or four-year high school, a three- or four-year college, locally organized, would give us a system which would take care of the fundamentals of education, and would relieve the university of the necessity of doing so. Students graduating from this system would come to the end of it between the ages of eighteen and twenty, and only those who had demonstrated their qualifications to go on should be permitted to do so—at least at the cost of the taxpayer.

In order to induce the others not to go on, I should be perfectly prepared to have them receive the Bachelor's degree at the age of eighteen or twenty.

I have, in fact, a good deal of sympathy for the proposal of Barrett Wendell of Harvard, that every American citizen should receive the Bachelor's degree at birth.

With a six-year elementary school, a three- or four-year high school, and a three- or four-year college, from which only carefully selected graduates should be permitted to proceed to the university, we might have a truly democratic system of education, democratic in the purest Jeffersonian sense.

Jefferson's proposals for the University of Virginia contemplated a rigorous selection of students, the like of which has never been seen in this hemisphere.

There is nothing undemocratic about saying that those who are to receive education at public expense should show they are qualified for it. On the contrary, it is most undemocratic to say that anybody can go as far as he likes in education, when what it actually means is he can actually have all the education he can pay for.

The creation of local colleges as the culmination of the six-four-four, or six-three-three system of education would give us a chance to develop institutions devoted to liberal education, free from the domination of the university, and would give us a chance to develop universities free from the domination of collegiate interests.

We should then have an intelligently organized educational system, democratically operated, and equipped to play its part in the new world that is struggling to be born; but, when all this is done, we shall be left confronting a third paradox, namely, the paradox presented by what the people expect of education.

Our country, in which the rapidity of technical change is more dramatically presented than anywhere else in the world, has an educational program which largely ignores the rapidity and inevitability of such change.

Now, vocational training assumes that the machinery on which the boy is trained will be in use when he goes to work. Actually, the machines and the methods are likely to be so different that his training will be a positive handicap to him.

As our experience in wartime shows, the place to train hands for industry is in industry. The aircraft companies produced better mechanics in a few weeks than the schools could produce in years. And, it must be obvious that education on a democratic basis cannot supply social standing, as Gilbert and Sullivan pointed out, when "Everybody is somebody and nobody is anybody."

Moreover, these who seek education for financial success are doomed to disappointment. Direct training for the purpose of producing financial success, like a course in how to make money, is obviously a fraud, and the number of occupations, I regret to tell you, in which what are known as college conditions are more of a help than a hindrance is certainly limited. Yet, the belief that education can in some way contribute to vocational and social success has done more than most things to disrupt American education.

What education can do, and about all it can do, is to produce a trained mind.

Now, getting a trained mind is hard work. As Aristotle remarked, "Learning is accompanied by pain." Those who are seeking something which education cannot supply are not likely to be enthusiastic about the pain which what it can supply must cause; and, since our false sense of democracy requires us to admit them to education anyway, then something must be done with them when they get into it, and it must, of course, be something which is not painful. Therefore, it must be something which interests them.

The vocationalism of our schools results, in part, from the difficulty of interesting many boys and girls in what are known as academic subjects, and the whole apparatus of football, fraternities, and fun is a means by which education is made palatable to those who have no business to be in it.

The fact is that the best practical education is the most theoretical one. This is, probably, the first time in human history in which change on every front is so rapid that what one generation has learned of practical affairs, in politics, business, and technology, is of little use to the next, just as what the father has learned of the facts of life is almost useless to his son. It is principles—everlastingly principles—which are of practical value today; not data, not methods, not facts, not helpful hints, but principles are what the rising generation requires if it is to find its way through the mazes of tomorrow. No man among us can tell what tomorrow will be like; all we know with certainty is that it will be different from today.

We can also see that it is principles which the adults of May 12, 1947, must understand if they are to be ready for May 13. The notion that education is something concerned with preparation for a vocational and social success, that it is composed of helpful hints to housewives and bond salesmen, has permeated the education of adults in the United States.

Adult education, in general, is aimed at making third-rate bookkeepers into second-rate bookkeepers by giving them classes at night; and in the general population, this process has not aroused much enthusiasm because we have thought of education as something for children, anyway; we have thought of it as something like the measles—having had education once, one need not—in fact, one cannot—have it again.

Apart from mathematics, metaphysics, logic, astronomy, and similar theoretical studies, it is clear that comprehension comes only with experience. A learned Greek remarked that young men should not listen to lectures on moral philosophy, and he was right. Moral philosophy, history, political economics, and literature, can convey their full meaning only in maturity.

Take Macbeth, for example. When I taught Macbeth to boys in preparatory school, it was a blood and thunder story—a very good blood and thunder story, one well worth reading, but a blood and thunder story still. Macbeth can mean what it meant to Shakespeare only when the reader has had sufficient experience, vicarious or otherwise, of marriage and ambition to understand the issues and their implications.

It happens that the kind of things we need most to understand today are those which only adults can fully grasp. A boy may be a brilliant mathematician, or a musician—and I have known several astronomers who contributed to the international journals at the age of thirteen—but, I never knew a child of that age who had much that was useful to say about the ends of human life, the purpose of organized society, and the means of reconciling freedom and order. But it is subjects like these about which we are most confused, and about which we must obtain some clarification if our civilization is to survive.

The survival of civilization, if the Russians are to have the atomic bomb in five years, depends on those who are adults today. We cannot wait for the rising generation to rise. Even if we succeeded in giving them a perfect education, it would be too late.

Therefore, it is imperative that we enter upon a program of mass adult education such as we have never contemplated before. The beginnings of this program are already under way. They can be seen here in Detroit, in the efforts which your library and universities are making to force the consideration of fundamental issues through the study of the Great Books of the Western World. At the rate at which this program is now expanding, I expect to see fifteen million people in it within five years.

I do not suffer from the illusion that, if fifteen million Americans are studying the Great Books of the Western World within five years, we shall avert the next war. Education alone cannot avert war; it may increase the chances of averting it. Nor do I deny that, if by reading the Great Books, or otherwise, the hearts of the Americans are changed, and the hearts of the Russians remain unchanged, we shall merely have the satisfaction of being blown up with changed hearts rather than unchanged ones. I do not expect the American audience to have enough faith in the immortality of the soul to regard this as more dubious consolation. But, if we do not avert war by this kind of education, we can at least provide ourselves, in the time that is left to us, with some suitable alternative to liquor, the movies and—if I may say so in Detroit—running around the country in second-hand cars, and catching glimpses of the countryside between the billboards.

At the age of 48 I can testify that all forms of recreation eventually lose their charm. I mean all! Partly as a result of the universal recognition of the great truth that eventually all forms of recreation lose their charm—partly in recognition of this great truth, the Great Books discussion classes have now begun to sweep the country from New York to Seattle.

Another explanation of their success is that the people are beginning to realize the shortcomings of their own education. They see now that the books they never read in school or college, the issues they never discussed, the ideas they never heard of, are the books, discussions, and issues that are directly relevant here and now. It may be that this generation of parents will see to it that the shortcomings of their children are overcome so that the American of the future may not have to get all his education after he becomes an adult.

The final paradox of American education which I wish to mention will become apparent when you look at what the world requires, and what American education has to offer.

American education excels in every technological activity, every applied sphere, and it excels as well, in pure science. The British, French, or German physician or engineer who had a chance to study in the United States would be a fool to decline the opportunity; but, he should be educated first and not count on the possibility of getting an education afterward. In every technological, applied, scientific field, the United States is, without question, preëminent today.

We know, therefore, one thing with certainty about the American university—it can produce weapons of war. Any time that you would like to have weapons of war produced, the American universities will undertake to supply them, and they will be bigger, better, and more deadly than ever.

On the other hand, another great segment of the American university, the modern medical school, has done almost as much to lengthen life as the schools of engineering and physics have done to shorten it.

In short, wherever the material conditions of existence are in question, the American university can deliver the goods. If you want better bombs, better poison gases, better medicine, better crops, better automobiles, you will find the American university able—and usually willing —to help you.

Where the American university cannot help you is where you need help most. Because of the paradoxes I have listed, because of our indifference to the real purposes of education, and because of our preoccupation with the trivial, frivolous, and immediately impractical, the American university is gradually losing its power to save the world. It has developed the power to destroy it; it is ill-equipped to save it.

What is honored in a country will be cultivated there. A means of cultivating it is the educational system. The American educational system mirrors the chaos of the modern world. While science and technology, which deal only with goods in the material order, are flourishing as never before, liberal education, philosophy, and theology, through which we might learn to guide our lives, are undergoing a slow but inevitable decay.

It is not enough to say, then, "Let us have lots of education," or even, "Let us have lots of expensive education." We must have universal education—let it cost what it may—of the right kind, and that is the kind through which we may hope to raise ourselves by our own bootstraps into a different spiritual world; that is the kind which places a sound character and a trained intelligence above all other aims, and which gives the citizen a scale of values by which he can learn to live. Only by such a scale of values, rationally established and firmly held, can a democratic individual hope to be more than a transitory phenomenon lost in the confusion of a darkening world.

In a democratic country there is a sense in which there is never anything wrong with education. A democratic country gets the kind of education it wants. I have no doubt that, if the people of the United States understand the urgency of education today, and understand the kind of education they must have, they can get it. I hope they will make the effort to get it before it is too late.

The Citizen's Stake in Academic Freedom
Quincy Wright

Quincy Wright is professor of international law and a member of the Committee on International Relations at the University of Chicago. He spoke at the spring meeting of the Ohio State University chapter of the American Association of University Professors held at the Faculty Club in Columbus on 30 April 1949.

Born in Medford, Massachusetts in 1890, Dr. Wright is a graduate of Lombard College (A.B., 1912) and the University of Illinois (A.M., 1913; Ph.D., 1915). After serving as an instructor at Harvard he taught at the University of Minnesota (1919-23) and has been at the University of Chicago since 1923. Among his books are *The Causes of War and the Conditions of Peace* (1935), *Legal Problems of the Far Eastern Conflict* (1941), and *A Study of War* (1942).

This address was published as the leading article of the October 1949 issue of *The Journal of Higher Education* and is reproduced here in shorter form.

IN DISCUSSING the citizen's stake in academic freedom, we have first to ask, What is a citizen? I suppose we might answer, a person who feels responsible for his community. We then have to ask, What is a community? and that may not be easy to answer. The citizen today lives in his town, he lives in his state, he lives in his nation, and he lives in the world. Certainly, from the material point of view every citizen is today vulnerable to various inconveniences which may proceed from the most distant parts of the world. He may be assaulted by ideas, by propaganda attacks. Even the Russian citizen cannot entirely evade the "Voice of America," despite the fact that there has been an unusual effort to jam these radio beams.

He is also subject to economic attack. Every citizen uses materials which come from distant places. Even Russia cannot get along entirely in economic isolation. I believe that the manufacture of a Ford automobile requires materials from forty different countries. The channels of trade which are sources of our daily necessities may be shut off by people in distant parts of the world to our great discomfort. Also, we now have the far-flying airplane that may carry atomic bombs from this country to others and can today carry lesser weapons from other countries to us, making possible rapid elimination of large populations. That vulnerability of every one to influences from everywhere means that the citizen must recognize the world as a community, at least in the material sense.

Morally, we think of ourselves primarily as citizens of a nation—of only a small part of the world. But the condition of universal vulnerability has meant that each nation has had to become a more integrated unit. Each has had to organize or regiment itself in order to defend its citizens from these distant sources of attack. Every state, every government, is assuming larger functions than it did during most of the nineteenth century in organizing the economic life of its citizens, in organizing their education and their ideas, as well as their defenses. Some states have gone further in that direction than others, but all states have intensified their administration, making their citizens more aware of their national loyalty.

We have here a very peculiar situation. The world is becoming more of a community, in the sense that there is a relationship of every part to every other part. Yet the nation is becoming in a more real sense the community that attracts the loyalty of its citizens. The world, it would seem, is moving in opposite directions at the same time. The very intensification of national loyalties is creating higher tensions and is giving many people a sense of the necessity of creating a world society, or even a world government. But the very effort toward such creation has meant that many nationalists have felt that their peculiar loyalties were subject to attack. Consequently they have sought to strengthen the organization of, and the sentiment for, the nation. There is a reciprocal action and reaction which means that, on the one hand, we are moving toward one world, and, on the other hand, we are moving toward a multiple world, perhaps a bipolar world of high tensions. We are all faced by the question of whether we must think of ourselves primarily as national citizens or as world citizens.

There is a change not only in regard to the area, but also in regard to the character, of the community of which we are members. The world citizen must think of himself, if he thinks of himself in that light at all, as a citizen of a community which is a complex of many values. This is a markedly different conception of the community from that of primitive man. He thinks of the community as a projection of his own personality, which has been so shaped by the culture of the tribe that there is an identity between the individual and the community. This community is what Ferdinand Tonnies called a *Gemeinschaft,* a natural society in which there is this identity of the group and its members. It is that identity which the totalitarian states of our day have tried to reproduce in some respects. It is an identity which exists in the beehive or the anthill. It is an identity which cannot exist to the same extent in our interdependent world, especially in a liberal nation. As the size of the community increases, it is inevitable that more and more cultural differences become incorporated within it.

Consequently, it is more and more necessary for the individual, if he thinks of himself as a citizen of this large community, to appreciate a multiplicity of values and not to identify himself absolutely with a single culture. Such appreciation is difficult. Perhaps the difficulty of identifying oneself with such a diverse, multifarious, and varied community as the world is one of the roots of modern totalitarianism. People long to be members of a community which is a projection of their own personalities. Consequently, they seek to "escape from freedom," as Eric Fromm said. They are willing to allow themselves to be guided and coördinated and submerged in the life of the totalitarian community by their leaders. I think, however, we can appreciate that that is impossible in our world community. The great problem of citizenship is therefore, it seems to me, to see the world as a community, and to see that that community must include many cultures and many values.

To do this, modern man must learn about varied cultures. He must know something about the way people think in China, in India, in Russia, in Western Europe, in Latin America, and in the Arab countries. They are all parts of this enlarged community of which we must all be members, from which we cannot escape. It is extremely difficult to acquire that breadth of knowledge, but there is something more difficult. The world citizen not only must know something about these varied cultures but he must recognize that they are all developments of a common human nature. It is the natural impulse, when one sees persons from a very different culture, to consider that they are unnatural. They are freaks. They in some way distort human nature. The "natural" way to behave is the way the people that I was brought up with in my childhood behaved. The citizen of the world must make an effort to transcend this impulse. He must see that these great varieties of cultures, beliefs, opinions, and values are possibilities of a human nature which is also his human nature. And finally, he must realize not only that these many cultures and values are possible developments of a common human nature but that they all contribute to progress. They are, it is true, different from his own culture and his own values, but it is in the complex of different values and through an appreciation by each of the values of the others that a world community which will protect every one from the vulnerabilities of which I have spoken will be possible.

Why is it necessary for us to get this broader conception of citizenship? First, because there are no alternatives. No nation can escape into isolationism; there is no probability of either a universal empire or universal faith. We can, however, look at the matter in a more practical way. This broader conception is necessary if the world is to solve the two great problems which face it—war and poverty—problems which, if not solved, threaten civilization, if not mankind itself.

These two problems are related. Total war impoverishes large areas, and poverty encourages revolutionary opinions likely to lead to war, particularly if the impoverished people doubt the inevitability of their condition. People can live and starve for generations if they do not know that anybody is in a better condition, or if they have never been in a better condition themselves. But our modern world of communication makes it extremely difficult to keep that secret. The impoverished masses of Asia are aware that the West lives better and, in spite of all that Stalin can do to keep the news from penetrating the iron curtain, there are vast numbers of Russians who know that the West lives better than they do. Revolutionary conditions inspire revolutionary opinions, and those inspire war.

War probably springs primarily from differences in group value systems. I do not agree with the theory which Karl Marx stated, which has been accepted by a great many non-Marxists, that war flows primarily from economic conditions. It flows primarily from differences of opinions about values. Economic conditions may influence important differences of opinions, but they are only one of many influences. Leadership, effective propaganda, historic traditions, can affect the opinions of groups. Wars arise primarily because a large group cleaves to a certain opinion which is incompatible with the opinion entertained by another large group. Each has a vision of the world, and both visions cannot be realized. Wars are, in a certain sense, always religious wars or ideological wars. If groups that have different opinions are in contact and each considers its values absolute, a cold or a hot war is almost inevitably the relationship. And the war becomes hotter as the contacts and material dependencies become greater. Consequently, the coexistence of sovereign nations, the people of each tending to think of its national ideals as absolute, and their closer contact with one another in a shrinking world have created a condition of cold war which is likely to become a hot war unless a greater sense of world citizenship is developed among all the peoples.

Poverty springs from the inadequacy of production to feed the population in a given area. Of course, there are many other factors in poverty —mistakes of government, inequity of distribution, war and catastrophe —but, in the broad sense, the problem of poverty is the problem of maladjustment of population and production. The population is ahead of the food supply in many areas, in fact in more than half of the world. Many of us have been alarmed by some of the books which have come out recently, pointing to the gradual, or in many places rapid, removal of the fertile topsoil into the ocean, while the world's population increases by twenty-one million people a year. We read that two-thirds of the world's population today is suffering malnutrition. Presently available sources of food and energy are getting less and less. Population is growing. Two-thirds of us are already starving; what are we coming to? Sometimes, when one goes into these pessimistic prognostications, it seems as though the problems of Russia and the cold war are insignificant compared with the problem of poverty.

It is clear that neither of these problems of war and poverty can be solved nationally. It is also clear that there can be no solution by restoration of the past. We cannot un-invent the airplane, or the atom bomb, or the radio, or the economic interdependencies which have sprung up in the wake of the numerous factors which have shrunk the world. Nor can we solve the problem in a radical method by fixing our gaze upon some utopia, some constitution of world government, some world structure which is oversimple and which will not win the general consent of all peoples of the world.

Now, what has academic freedom got to do with all this? It seems to me that academic freedom, and the kind of universities which spring from academic freedom, are necessary conditions for developing the kind of world community within which the great problems which confront mankind may be solved. Academic freedom makes possible a university which is a microcosm of the world, a university within which coming citizens and leaders can become acquainted with the varied and complex conditions of the world. Within such a university the potential citizen can become aware of all the cultures, all the parties, all the aspects of human nature. He cannot get that awareness if the university is regimented in accord with a particular culture or a limited set of ideas.

Academic freedom means the security of the university and of the teacher. It means that the teacher can teach what he has learned by his study, and that the university can stand on its own feet as a community of teachers and scholars. This implies that a university enjoying academic freedom will have within it a variety of opinions, all of which may be presented to the student. Such a university will shelter a variety of ends, of values, and of interests, and in that respect it may be like the world of which the student is going to be a citizen. But it will be united in its search for understanding, for awareness, for insight, and for accommodation, and so will resemble the world which good citizens want.

There are some who think that a university should cultivate only certain values, that it should provide only studies of the tradition and culture which immediately surround it, and that it should search for the basic values of that culture in order to instruct the student in them and their implications. Others suggest that the university should devote itself exclusively to scientific method, that it should assume that truth can be found only by the application of techniques of experiment and observation and by analysis of propositions which can be verified by such techniques. Some think that the university should accept values which are fixed by the policies of the state in which it exists. We have been made aware of universities that have become handmaids of the state. In the Middle Ages the university was the handmaid of the church, and it has been feared that at times in this country universities might become handmaids of large business corporations. A university that has a single set of values or is the instrument of any particular institution is not free. Such a university does not respect academic freedom in the widest sense of the term. It cannot be, in any sense, a microcosm of the world. The various reforms of the nineteenth century, it seems to me, attempted to narrow the university to a particular philosophy. I doubt whether a university that is going to fit students for life in our varied world can ever be of that kind.

The kind of university I have in mind will think of truth as a process which develops by contact of different ideas and by free discussion. I do not know whether that corresponds to the conception of truth as experiences of the human soul which are irreducible. Are either the things experienced or the human soul that experiences them ever the same in different times and places? It seems to me that truth is always dated. It is always growing. The university where academic freedom prevails cannot have a static conception of truth. Truth is continually being created by the coming together of different approaches.

The university which is to be a microcosm of the world must create new truths as the world, in the contacts, and discussions, and conflicts of its parts, is continually creating history. This implies that in a university there must be a spirit of toleration. A variety of opinions can only exist if people have the virtues of world citizenship—if they recognize that many values exist, and are all products of human nature, and that, while some may be preferable to others in particular situations, all have some possibility of contributing to progress. This kind of university, and only this kind of university, can be in a position to criticize the other great institutions of society. Mutual criticism is essential if absolutist conceptions and lethal conflict among them are to be avoided. The university must be in a position to criticize the state, the church, the business organizations.

I do not know of any other institution which can be a microcosm of this varied world and a critic of its elements. If the university does not do it, no institution can. The state has practical tasks. It must use coercive methods to carry them out. Business is dominated by the necessities of production. And the church seeks to orient its members to a particular view of the world. The university must be broad enough to criticize these other institutions and to realize the possibilities which exist in all of them and the limitations in each of them.

In this country we have individuals who do not appreciate this conception of a university. In my State of Illinois some bills have been introduced in the Legislature to prevent teaching by people who belong to organizations vaguely described as subversive or as Communist-front organizations. The author of these bills has been described as a very honest man, with very sincere convictions, whose views are, however, somewhat narrow. We have all met honest citizens of this country who have rather narrow conceptions of Americanism. I had a discussion with such a gentleman recently. There were a lot of people in America who were not Americans in his view, perhaps somewhere between a half and two-thirds of the population. It is a dangerous thing to have such a narrow conception of Americanism. It gets increasingly dangerous as the world contracts, as one finds oneself living in a world community where there are many people even more remote from that narrow conception of Americanism. That narrowness of vision is the thing which the university must combat. It must do it without sacrificing loyalties to ideas and to institutions which in our experience we have found adapted to our lives and our society. Can one be a loyal, patriotic American citizen and still recognize and appreciate the great varieties in our civilization and the greater varieties in the wider world of which we are a part? If the answer is no, there is little hope for a world society within which the problems of war and poverty might be solved. I believe that it is the task of the university to find an affirmative answer to that question. I do not see how an answer can be found except in a university which respects academic freedom.

Man Thinking
A. Whitney Griswold

This is the inaugural address of Dr. Griswold as the sixteenth president of Yale University as given in New Haven on 6 October 1950.

Born in Morristown, New Jersey in 1906, the descendant of a long line of Yale graduates, Alfred Whitney Griswold studied at Hotchkiss School, was graduated from Yale (A.B., 1929; Ph.D., 1933) and has taught there continuously since 1935. He became professor of history in 1947.

Yale under its new president was the subject of articles in both *Time* and *Newsweek* for the week of 11 June 1951. The writer of the *Time* article thus describes Mr. Griswold as a teacher: "He was a vivacious lecturer with a flair for mimicry. Pacing back and forth with theatrical grimaces, he could be Jefferson or Silas Deane or Talleyrand, and students flocked to hear him. He was both irrepressibly merry and irrepressibly concerned."

WE ARE met here today to renew the life of an old and honourable institution. In a few months we shall celebrate our two hundred and fiftieth anniversary. The "Collegiate School" founded at Parson Russel's house in Branford in 1701 has become a great university, the second oldest in the United States, the ninth oldest in the English-speaking world. Its fame has no national boundaries. The work of its scholars and teachers is known and respected in every quarter of the globe. In American higher education its prestige and influence are second to none. This is the trust we receive here today and that our presence here pledges us to maintain. It is a great responsibility, one that calls upon each of us for the best effort of which he is capable, and upon all of us for a common sense of the direction those efforts must take.

The times are not auspicious for learning. They are times of war, and war imposes a terrible burden of proof on everything that does not directly serve its ends. Just and noble as we believe those ends to be in our own case, war and the preparation for war are not conducive to the reflective life that produces great teaching and great scholarship. The teacher senses his remoteness from his fellow men. The scholar's thoughts stray to the battlefield. The Promethean secret of the atom breeds fear and suspicion in all our hearts, inclining us to dismiss the past, to dread the future, and to live in the present. There is indeed "no hiding place," no fortress, and no academic cloister from which we can escape the consequences of this latest knowledge we have wrested from the gods. It seeks us all out as indiscriminately as the Roman soldier who slew Archimedes in the siege of Syracuse, not knowing who his victim was or that the scientific knowledge that died with him would not be regained for nearly eighteen hundred years.

What price the scholar's life in times like these, or the university's, whose purpose is to foster that life? There have been moments in which we have all asked ourselves these questions, and at certain of those moments I, for one, have found no answers. Yet I wonder if we know our own strength. The briefest glance into history shows us that we are supported by powerful traditions—not symbols or legends, but vital forces with remarkable capacity for survival. I would cite three of these traditions this afternoon: the tradition of higher learning, the university tradition, and the tradition of American democracy. Any one of these should give us courage. The three together form a tower of strength.

I do not know who first questioned the value of the scholar's life: it may have been one of Socrates' disciples who watched his master drink the hemlock. Surely no calling has been so much questioned—and despaired of—since that memorable event; and just as surely none has contributed so much to Western civilization. What is the nature of this calling? Archimedes might have come down to us as a military strategist on the strength of the wonderful engines he contrived for the defense of Syracuse. But, says Plutarch, "he possessed so high a spirit, so profound a soul, and such treasures of scientific knowledge, that though these inventions had now obtained for him the renown of more than human sagacity, he yet would not deign to leave behind him any writing on such subjects; but . . . placed his whole affection and ambition in those purer speculations where there can be no reference to the vulgar needs of life-studies whose superiority to all others is unquestioned, and in which the only doubt can be whether the beauty and grandeur of the subjects examined, or the precision and cogency of the methods and means of proof, most deserve our admiration." The scholar, says Emerson, is the "delegated intellect" of mankind. In the degenerate state he becomes a "mere thinker, or still worse, the parrot of other men's thinking. . . . In the right state he is Man Thinking." To whom else do we owe our progress from savagery? To whom else do we pin our hopes of ending our periodic reversions to savagery and putting our engines of destruction to creative use? If the scholars of the past had waited for auspicious times to do their work, I doubt that we should be assembled here today. If they should now wait for total war to produce total peace, I doubt that our successors will be assembled here to mark Yale's three hundredth anniversary.

The scholar has always had to contend with his times. As we follow him through history, how thin his life line appears! The dreamer, the questioner, the restless migrant between past and future, he is seldom at home in the present or with the practical men of his generation. The practical men of Athens put Socrates to death; of Rome forced Galileo to deny what he had seen through his telescope; of Berlin drove a whole generation of scholars into exile; of Moscow frightened another generation into false witnesses and quacks. Anglo-American history embraces no such violent extremes. Yet even British and American scholars have suffered from test oaths—as they once did in the early days of both Oxford and Yale and do now in California; from economic adversity, with them an occupational disease; and from corrosively utilitarian national philosophies of life.

Higher learning is innate in Western civilization. Unorganized in the ancient world, it was carried on by individual Greek, Hebrew, and Roman scholars with such zeal and competence that it took European scholars a thousand years to catch up with their attainments. The phrase implies a parallel achievement. It was not. Medieval scholars rediscovered the works of the ancients and built on their foundations. Aristotle emerges as the intellectual colossus whose writings bridge the gap and restore continuity between the two civilizations. Far be it from me to pass critical judgment on these works. But I observe that they all possess this common significance: they represent a continuous effort to free the human mind from ignorance and superstition, a continuous voyage of discovery of the human imagination. The voyage is lonely, for great scholarship is an individual experience. Often it carries the voyager onto stormy seas. Yet no explorer ever felt its urge more powerfully than the true scholar feels it every morning of his life.

Since the revival of learning that ended the Dark Ages, the university tradition has strongly reinforced the tradition of higher learning. The university has been the scholar's home. In ways that point a fearful object lesson to us today, European civilization had been reduced nearly to their own level by the barbarians who destroyed the Roman empire. Learning, even in its most elementary forms of reading and writing, had been almost totally destroyed, and very likely would have been but for a few monasteries and cathedral schools. These kept the spark alive so that when Mohammedan scholars from Spain restored to Europe the works of Greek philosophers, mathematicians, and physicians, and the Justinian code of law, there were at least a handful of Europeans capable of understanding them. Toward the end of the twelfth century, groups of masters and students banded themselves together to exploit this newly rediscovered wealth of learning, first at Bologna, then at Paris, then at Oxford and Cambridge, calling their organizations *studia generalia, universitates,* and finally universities. We are the lineal heirs of Paris and the two English universities.

Historians consider the universities the outstanding intellectual achievement of the Middle Ages and credit them with determining the whole course of contemporary culture and thought. With manuscripts scarce and printing still two hundred years away, the part the earliest ones played in the general diffusion of knowledge is impossible to exaggerate. But it is for their institutional character that we take notice of them here. They brought together the study of the liberal arts (grammar, logic, arithmetic, geometry, astronomy, and music) with the pursuit of higher education in special fields (medicine, theology, law, philosophy). Thus they both deepened and broadened the higher learning. They deepened it by bringing this combination within the experience of a single individual, and they broadened it by making the experience available to much greater numbers of individuals. They did not attempt to cover every field of learning. That is neither the proper meaning of the word "university" nor, I submit, the proper policy for it to suggest to us. A group of men devoted to learning on the highest plane of intellectual and moral integrity would be an even more accurate historical definition of a university than an institution combining higher education with the liberal arts. But it is in their institutional design that we most clearly perceive the interlocking of the higher learning and university traditions and with it Yale's identity with the medieval universities.

I have said that we were the heirs of Paris, Oxford, and Cambridge. This is true in a very literal sense, as Oxford was founded by a migration of scholars from Paris about 1170, Cambridge by a migration from Oxford in 1209, Harvard by a group of Cambridge graduates in 1636, and Yale by a group of Harvard graduates in 1701. But there is more than antiquity in this lineage. In our graduate and professional schools we continue to extend our knowledge and project our imagination to the farthest frontiers of learning and beyond. And in our college of liberal arts we continue to prepare students for service on those frontiers. The importance of our graduate and professional schools, in our own day and age, is obvious. We can imagine the chaos and retrogression that would ensue in the arts and sciences and the professions if these schools, and others like them, should close their doors. The importance of the liberal arts is, if anything, even greater. Not only are they stepping stones to the professions. Generations of students have found them the best preparation for the ordinary work of the world.

This is particularly true in a democracy. The liberal arts inform and enlighten the independent citizen of a democracy in the use of his own resources. Broadened in our modern curriculum to include a wide range of humanistic, scientific, and social studies, they appeal to the most varied and subtle combinations of taste. Yet their fundamental purpose lies, not in their specific content, but in their stimulus to the individual student's powers of reason, judgment, and imagination. In a democracy, which rests upon the freedom and responsibility of the individual, they give that individual vision. They enlarge his capacity for self-knowledge and expand his opportunities for self-improvement. In a technological society whose working week is steadily shrinking, they render more profitable and more enjoyable the purposes to which he may put his steadily increasing leisure time. Even by the supreme practical test of modern warfare they have been judged the apprenticeship of the most alert and resourceful soldiers. They are the wellsprings of a free society.

It is in this way that the American democratic tradition forms the *tripos* with the traditions of higher learning and the university. Europeans and Englishmen have used their universities to train their intellectual and political leaders. We have conceived a broader purpose for higher education. This purpose regards all education as a preparation for life, and higher education but the culminating phase of a process that should be available to all who have the capacity to partake of it. By capacity we do not mean merely intellectual competence. We mean intellectual competence tempered by character, judgment, and moral responsibility. Our purpose does not assume equal capacity or equal attainment among men. It holds, rather, that if men are to be thrown upon their own individual resources in society, society should prepare them for that responsibility, and it should not allow that preparation to be limited by anything other than the individual's innate ability to benefit by it. This was Jefferson's corollary to popular sovereignty, his key to equal opportunity and a truly mobile, democratic society. This was the means whereby the people could not only instruct themselves in the use of the franchise but also produce their leaders and teachers in every sphere of life. It was education in this sense that Jefferson called "the most legitimate engine of government" and of which he said, in words that stand out vividly against the iron curtain, "If a nation expects to be ignorant and free, in a state of civilization, it expects what never was and never will be."

From this third great tradition Yale derives great strength. For if democracy depends upon education as its "engine of government," the proper functioning of that engine depends upon the maintenance of standards; and in this work Yale stands, with a few—a very few—of her sister universities, *prima inter pares*. Twenty-nine million children go to school in the United States and two and one-half million men and women to college. By 1960 our school population is expected to increase to 37,000,000 and our college to 4,600,000. Is this too much education? We might as well say there is too much health. Let us admit that under the weight of such numbers quality is bound to suffer; that the statistics cover a multitude of sins—underpaid and incompetent teachers, promising students neglected or allowed to fall by the wayside, others misdirected, others carried as supercargo beyond their proper destination, and an infinite variety of nature faking in the name of higher education. Let us say that relative to our resources—to what we could do if we wanted to—our American system of education varies as a company of infantry would vary if it went into action armed with everything from rockets to flintlocks. Still we can say that we have made the greatest effort to educate ourselves ever made by a free people, and that the hearts of our own people, and of every people in the world to whom it is given to know about it, are behind that effort.

How can we say that there is too much higher education when we think of it in these terms? Can we not afford it? We spend on higher education barely one-quarter of what we spend on tobacco, less than we spend on barber and beauty shops. Yale's entire plant and endowment together would not pay for two battleships like the *Missouri*. If our total college population should double by 1960 it would not increase the amount we spend on higher education, even assuming full employment and the consequent loss of students to the labor market, to much more than 3 per cent of the total gross product of our economy.

To argue saturation in higher education is to claim perfection for hundreds of educational institutions (not excepting Yale) that are far from it. Or it is to assume a narrowly vocational purpose for higher education and discredit it by pointing to momentary gluts in this or that profession. Or to believe that every American with the requisite ability gets to college. Or that those who lack that ability are routed into other channels. If we believe that higher learning, as we have deepened and broadened it, is not only a necessary preparation for the professions but the best preparation for a full, useful, and enjoyable life in a free society, how can we deny it to any citizen who is both able and eager to assimilate it? Are the liberal arts irrelevant to a mechanic? In our modern society, his material rewards and his store of leisure time make him their natural beneficiary. No one is born to drudgery in a democracy, and if drudgery is thrust upon any of us (as it is in some form or other upon all of us) the liberal arts are its antidote. We are all voters and as such all equally in need of as much enlightenment as education can give us. As men and women living in a state of civilization, the lives and welfare of all of us are identified with Man Thinking.

These traditions give us courage for the future, no matter how black it may look from day to day. These are the things Yale lives and works for, in war and peace. They are things to cherish and defend in times of war; to fight for, when there is fighting; and to return to when the fighting is over.

The Goals of Education Are Not Sufficient Today

Millicent C. McIntosh

Millicent Carey McIntosh, Dean of Barnard College, Columbia University, delivered this address at the *New York Herald Tribune* Forum on 19 October 1948. Before assuming the deanship at Barnard in 1947 Mrs. McIntosh taught English at Bryn Mawr and at the Brearley School in New York. She was awarded the Ph.D. degree at Johns Hopkins University in 1926. Mrs. McIntosh was married to Dr. Rustin McIntosh, a pediatrician, in 1932, and is the mother of five children.

NOTHING CAN be more important in a free society than the clear statement of goals for education. These goals, moreover, must constantly be reëxamined in the light of current conditions, so that education remains a dynamic force, effective in the lives human beings are called upon to live.

Our country is in great peril at this moment because of confusion as to what our educational institutions must achieve if our way of life is to survive. Our belief in sound intellectual training and scholarship may be undimmed, but we know that these are not enough. We have witnessed the destruction of a German culture which was fathered by the greatest university system and the most elaborate scholarship the world has ever known. We have lived through the dawn of a new age with the harnessing of atomic energy, and we know that research even into the ultimate secrets of science is not enough. We must somehow go further in educating the whole man, so that scholarship is made effective through harmonious personality and so that research is animated by an idealism which can use it for the good of mankind.

Strong voices of leadership have charted for us certain important areas. The progressive education movement, born under the aegis of Horace Mann and John Dewey, has aroused American teachers to realize the connection between the academic process and the development of personality, influencing even those who most disagree with them. Columbia College, after the first world war, set its standard firmly at the head of those who believed in education for citizenship in a democracy, a standard more recently taken up by the Harvard faculty, and in the last few days raised wholeheartedly by President Eisenhower.

I wonder whether even these important goals are enough. Those who have concentrated on the personality as such have succeeded often in developing superficial, egocentric young people, lacking in discipline and woefully ignorant of the great cultural and religious traditions through which man has emerged from group savagery into individual freedom and opportunity. The call to responsibility for citizenship in a democratic society, noble as it is, cannot create good citizens; nor can courses in contemporary civilization, social studies, current events—call them what you may—*in themselves* create the good life.

What goals then are needed which will make education truly effective for our time—the most difficult period, probably, in history? I believe that as teachers, at every level of the educational process, we must first come out of our ivory tower and face with candidness and humility the world for which we are educating our students. Suppose we can for a while forget the international picture and regard honestly our own culture. What are the characteristics of the present-day American scene?

We live in a world which, beyond a shadow of doubt, makes good living intensely difficult, especially for the young. Our mechanical genius has created a series of human problems which have not yet been adequately analyzed. Our overcrowded cities make life hectic and abnormal for a large proportion of our population. Our highly developed movie and radio industries provide entertainment which is too stimulating and often thoroughly artificial. The lack of quiet family routines and the difficulty of giving children responsibility in our complicated society all contribute barriers to the normal development of intellect and personality.

Thus we find that our highly esteemed civilization has resulted in an environment which destroys the very qualities which have produced it: initiative, independence, intellectual resourcefulness. Because young people are dependent on outside agents for their recreation and for the actual mechanics of living, many of them never learn to read nor to create for themselves a leisure which inspires creative activity or independent thought. A generation which has been born in confusion, suckled in tumult, reared with cars, radios, movies, comics, and picture magazines can hardly be expected to mature as reflective, sober, well-rounded young people.

Our first goal must, therefore, be to impart to young people the freshness of intellectual excitement, the opportunity for independent and creative activity, the delight in discussion and discovery that form an essential part of true education. A teaching staff in school or college who believe in their responsibility to impart these to their students will find ways of giving them, through constant reëvaluation of their subject matter and methods in the light of the needs of their time. I submit that the actual *content* of course is not so important as the *method* by which it is presented; that the material of the curriculum is insignificant in comparison with the quality of those who teach. Thus, Thomas Arnold of Rugby could influence hundreds of English boys to accept the call of duty and of citizenship not through expensive "integrated" courses but through the sheer force of his own conviction and the clarity of his own goals. So have devoted teachers through the ages met the challenge of their own time.

Even more difficult for young people than external complexities are the moral confusions of our time. A fundamental hazard lies in the frequent shift in parental standards from those in which a duty is performed to God and one's fellow men to those which estimate material success and pleasure-seeking as the ultimate goals in life. Adults have a right to live their lives in their own way so long as they do not hurt others; but the effect on children of such attitudes has not been honestly faced.

Important also is the change in attitude toward marriage and sex. No longer can children count on a home which will be kept intact. It is difficult now for parents to hand on to children clear-cut standards of what is right and what is wrong in the relations of the sexes and in the setup of a marriage. The air is blue with insistent voices, presenting "new" attitudes—stemming actually from the monkey and the cave man —analyzing behavior as "normal" which in the past we were accustomed to associate with the gutter. Our society may ultimately gain from these attempts to face honestly our own weaknesses; but at the moment the confusion is great, and society seems to deny all the premises which have given dignity to living.

What goal can possibly be established that will meet the situation presented here? Is it our business as educators to grapple with the problems of our generation and to provide a moral synthesis which can guide our students wisely through a mass of contradictory concepts? I believe that this moral synthesis should be a major objective of education, but that it can be provided only through freedom of inquiry and discussion, and by the personal idealism of the administrators and teachers who themselves cannot escape the necessity of coming to terms with the major problems of living. In this we are surrounded by a cloud of witnesses: great teachers, from Socrates to Whitehead and Toynbee, who were aware of the moral and spiritual implications of knowledge, and accepted fully the responsibility for passing these on to their students and to the world.

The greatest educational challenge of our time is thus formulated in the necessity of making teaching, on the school or college level, the great function which it has been historically, and which the urgency of our time demands. Graduate schools and colleges which glorify research and publication at the expense of the art of teaching are guilty of a grave and perhaps irreparable sin against civilization. Communities which spend millions for alcohol, cosmetics, tobacco, and amusements —and what is left over, for schools—are committing spiritual suicide. We, the educators of America, who meet endlessly to make and listen to speeches keyed to the superficial aspects of our problem, are convicted of letting our world slide into an abyss of technological and moral confusion while we have been concerned with what Professor Howard Mumford Jones calls the "polite fictions of genteel tradition."

Our high privilege, as well as our own duty, requires us to face the problems of our time with honesty and courage. Man can apparently rise to supreme heights only when faced with supreme crisis. To meet such a crisis we as teachers are called today. We shall not fail.

A High School Commencement Address
E. J. Thomas

This speech, delivered to the graduating class at East High School in Akron, Ohio on 7 June 1950, won first place in the Freedoms Foundations Awards for High School Commencement Addresses at the ceremonies held at Valley Forge, Pennsylvania on 22 February 1951.

Edwin Joel Thomas is the president of the Goodyear Tire and Rubber Company, Akron, Ohio. He was born in Akron in 1899 and was a student there at the Central High School (1912-16) and at the University of Akron (1918). Beginning as a stenographer at Goodyear in 1916, he successively held positions as assistant to the factory manager, personnel manager, superintendent of production, general superintendent, and finally in 1940 as president of the company.

YOUNG MEN and young women of the East High class of 1950, I greet you on this memorable evening with pride and neighborly affection.

I congratulate you, most warmly, on the record of achievement symbolized by the diplomas you are receiving here tonight.

From the bottom of my heart, I wish you well as you leave this gathering to face the trials and the triumphs, the obligations and the opportunities which lie ahead.

For you, these graduation ceremonies are an exciting, happy event, never to be forgotten, always to be cherished.

For me, the occasion is at once a privilege and a very pleasant trip down memory lane to one evening a third of a century ago when I reached my own commencement milestone at old Central High and started out, diploma in hand, to make my own way.

Let me assure you that the ensuing thirty-three years have been most engrossing. The horse and buggy was seen in greater numbers on Akron's streets than the automobile on that commencement night of 1917. Radio was practically unheard of, television was undreamed of, the flying machine was a mere experiment. You were lucky to get three thousand miles out of a set of very expensive tires and $1.75 was a pretty good day's pay.

The basic tasks of providing food, clothing, and housing called for the almost full-time efforts of the breadwinner in the average Akron family. Bathtubs were something of a luxury, influenza was a menace to the masses, and the washboard was a piece of basic equipment in every home.

Material progress during those years has been fabulous beyond human comprehension.

On that commencement night of thirty-three years ago, America was just emerging from a long era of self-containment and isolation from most of the rest of the world.

Akron, Ohio was still the center of the universe for my graduating class. Other parts of the world were generally conceived by members of the class as being remote, rather queer, and of no particular concern to us.

But army and navy recruiting stations were being opened in Akron on that graduation night. A draft law was being enacted which would impose unfamiliar limitations upon the youth of that day and it was beginning to dawn upon us that the freedom we had taken as a matter of course was not without its price tag.

The patterns which were taking form on that graduation night have developed in the ensuing years into a whole new fabric of prime concerns, restraints, responsibilities, and objectives for the American society of which we are part.

So what about it?

Has the rate of material accomplishment of the immediate past reduced the field of opportunity for the Class of 1950?

Has this new fabric of international relationships saddled you with unfair burdens and responsibilities?

Should you envy the comparative lot of the older generations?

These are academic questions but I can imagine they are bothering you to a certain degree.

I cannot give you the conclusive and categorical answers but I may, perhaps, be able to offer you some helpful counsel.

First of all, let me remind you that the significance of what your history books have undertaken to impart to you is of equal or greater importance than the factual incidents themselves.

It is more important to understand why Washington crossed the Delaware than it is to remember the exact dates and other factual details.

His crossing was not merely a piece of historic military tactics—it was a bid for the freedom and dignity of the individual American of that generation and of the generations to come, including yours and mine.

It is important, too, that you should understand the relationship of

America's march of progress and her future aspirations to those fundamental bases of individual freedom and dignity. Without them, there can be no true America.

The protection and preservation of these principles is not a new burden peculiar to tonight's graduating class. It is the *quid pro quo* of the heritage of every American generation since Washington. It is the obligation placed upon you by the older generations who, themselves assuming obligations to the future, thus discharged their obligations to the past.

Now please do not misunderstand my meaning. I am talking about the real substance of our way of life, the changeless principles of individual freedom and dignity. The forms which give expression to these principles are not fixed, cannot be fixed, and should not be fixed. The forms are always subject to enlightened change and improvement—that is progress. Because we have held fast to the basic principles of personal freedom and dignity, while improving the forms of their application, the material and cultural advantages accruing to your generation are, on the whole, superior to those of past generations.

I want most earnestly to make myself clear on that point.

If it is agreed that the burdens which must be assumed by your generation are much weightier than those of your forerunners, then it can be claimed that the processes of freedom work progressively to enhance the carrying capacities of succeeding generations. No generation has had greater potential capacity than your own.

Spectacular as has been our American progress, in contrast with that of other peoples of the earth, we have merely scratched the surface of the possibilities offered by those great human principles of liberty and dignity. You face a future of expanding, not shrinking opportunity if you will but keep the faith.

Let us take your own beloved East High as an illustration in point.

The structure itself represents a written-down value of around six hundred thousand dollars. That great sum did not come from government. Government merely transmitted it. It came from the productive efforts of your parents, your neighbors, your elder fellow citizens. It came out of their earnings and their accumulations.

It is a far cry from the little one-room schoolhouse of days gone by because your predecessors, working as coöperative individuals in an enlightened community, wanted something better for you than they had for themselves.

Within another year or two, I understand that improvements to East

High buildings will represent another million dollars or more in physical value—an additional value created by these same individuals. Don't think of those who pay the bill as vague and formless abstractions generally classified as taxpayers—think of them as persons, working and creating and striving for broad human betterment. Then you will recognize such obligations in their true perspective, and, probably, be more than willing to fit yourselves into this generous, enlightened continuing pattern of common effort.

Individual freedom and individual dignity just naturally breed that kind of spirit.

Let me remind you that your elders have worked and saved out from their earnings a total of between twenty and thirty millions of dollars to provide the land, buildings, and equipment for the Akron public school system from which you are now graduating.

There is an investment of almost three thousand dollars in tuition for each and every member of this graduating class.

When we think of these things, when we realize that they have been made possible by free men and free women working together for a better life for all of us, it becomes obvious that American idealism towers far above any other "ism" on the market today.

Yes, the significance of your courses in American history does take equal rank with the facts you have learned of who, when, and where.

But let us move on to the subject of mathematics. It, too, has great significance and the logic of your courses, if you will but grasp it, probably will mean more to you in later years than the tables and formulae you have learned.

I need not tell you that multiplication brings larger mathematical totals than division. But perhaps I should remind you that this truism of your textbooks applies with equal force in human progress.

Had we, as a people, followed the processes of division, there would have been no such thing as the magnificent structure known as East High. The best we could have hoped for through the philosophy of division would be an old-fashioned little red schoolhouse.

To spread human benefits, including facilities for mass education, we undertake to multiply what we have rather than to divide what we have.

We have multiplied the productivity of man to its present world-beating levels by spending less than we take in and investing the difference in improving our facilities and our methods. That has been our deliberate, our free choice. And it has worked! The proof is here for all to see.

The America of your heritage is not founded upon standards of mediocrity—the establishment of common levels through the processes of dividing things up.

Not at all! It is founded upon the urge to attain ever higher standards.

Superiority rather than mediocrity have been our goals and the results speak for themselves.

A large majority of the total population of the earth is on a mere subsistence basis, struggling for the bare essentials of food, clothing, and shelter. Here in America there is abundance. Here in America, we surround our daily lives with comforts and conveniences which are beyond the wildest dreams of most of the rest of the world. And we accept these benefits with casual off-handedness because we have long since become so accustomed to them.

Well . . . our forebears established the foundations for all of this when they fought for the principles of individual freedom and individual dignity.

On those foundations we have reared our structure of magnificent high-school buildings, material well-being, comforts, conveniences, and amazing productivity.

This heritage now goes to you.

Are you going to divide it up and quit?

Or are you going to continue in the philosophy of multiplication?

The choice is up to you.

And you will be making your choice as free individuals, as individuals who have been securely established in their personal dignity and rights.

The mass choice will be but the sum total of your decisions as individuals. Remember that, please—and always try to understand what it means in personal privilege and in personal responsibility.

Should you permit the compromise of your own freedom or your own dignity as an individual, you will contribute to the undermining of the foundations of the whole structure.

You young men and women will leave this gathering tonight and be on your way to a date with destiny.

Does the prospect occasion personal misgivings?

If it does, brush them aside. They just don't belong in your picture.

You have inherited the strength of free men—always remember that!

You have been trained, mentally and physically, to a high degree of fitness for the tasks which lie ahead.

You have, in fact, a head start on all of your contemporaries of other lands.

And you have, to a greater degree than these contemporaries, the opportunity to mold your own lives, to select your own goals, and to chart your own courses toward those goals.

But don't allow these reassuring facts to go to your head—take them to your heart and be humbly grateful.

What should you seek? ... Wealth? ... Power? ... Acclaim? That is up to you.

But above all, I earnestly counsel you, seek and strive to keep faith with your own selves.

Wealth, power, acclaim are but trappings and by-products. They are the marks of true success only if they have been attained without sacrifice of worthy standards of citizenship. True success is attainable without such trappings.

The real riches you will find in life are knowledge and understanding and friends. Seek them as you go on your way to that date with destiny.

And now in closing I should like to offer you a little philosophic guidepost to genuinely successful living. It was written by Robert Louis Stevenson many years ago and it will live on so long as America remains truly America:

> To be honest, to be kind—to earn a little and to spend a little less, to make upon the whole a family happier for his presence, to renounce when that shall be necessary and not be embittered, to keep a few friends but these without capitulation—above all, on the same grim condition to keep friends with himself—here is a task for all that a man has of fortitude and delicacy. He has an ambitious soul who would ask more; he has a hopeful spirit who should look on such an enterprise to be successful.

Good luck and God bless you.

PHILOSOPHY, LITERATURE, AND THE ARTS

New Problems, New Philosophers

Harry A. Overstreet

Harry A. Overstreet was professor of philosophy and head of the department of philosophy at the College of the City of New York from 1911 to

New Problems, New Philosophers

1939. He was born in San Francisco in 1875 and was educated at the University of California (A.B., 1899) and at Balliol College, Oxford University (B.Sc., 1901). He taught philosophy at the University of California (1901-11) and then for twenty-eight years at CCNY. His better known works include *Influencing Human Behavior* (1925), *About Ourselves—Psychology for Normal People* (1927), *Let Me Think* (1939), and *The Mature Mind* (1949).

The speech reprinted below was presented to the Tenth Conference on Science, Philosophy, and Religion, held at the Men's Faculty Club of Columbia University in September 1949.

IN MY paper presented at the Eighth Conference[1] I suggested that philosophy has, in the long past, had a powerful influence "in changing the outlooks of men and in building among them a new common consciousness." I still believe this to be true; and because I do believe it, I feel that philosophy can be a powerful means of building attitudes and points of view deeply needed in our present time of social crisis.

In the previous paper, I wrote that "our problem is that of saving man from his own suicidal inability to live with his fellows. It is a problem of helping him to get a new slant and a new grip on himself as a member of a world society." I would now amend that sentence by omitting the next to the last word. The problem, as I now see it, is that of helping man to a new slant and a new grip on himself as a *member of society*.

In this same article I recalled that for a generation and more philosophers had spent most of their energies examining the basic assumptions of the physical and mathematical sciences, but that today the time clock of science had struck the hour of the psychological and social sciences. The maturing of these sciences, I pointed out, coincided with a time of the world's greatest unhappiness and near-despair.

Philosophy, therefore, not only has this urgent task of helping man to become a productive rather than a destructive member of his kind, but it now has at its command scientific data that bear directly upon the problem of man's social ineptitude.

The urgency of the problem shows itself today on the world scene in a grave breakdown of the communicative processes. The so-called iron curtain symbolizes the fact that two peoples, in their governmental

---

[1] "Next: To Build a New Outlook," *Learning and World Peace,* Lyman Bryson, Louis Finkelstein, R. M. MacIver, editors, Conference on Science, Philosophy, and Religion in Their Relation to the Democratic Way of Life, Inc., New York, 1948, pp. 278-287.

forms, find it impossible to come to a common understanding. The processes of reason seem to have broken down and those of irrational fear, suspicion, and hatred seem to have taken over. Here is a problem for the "lovers of wisdom." Why the breakdown? How, if at all, might the lines of rational communication be restored?

Again, the urgency of the problem shows itself at the community level in the statistics of delinquency, crime, divorce, citizen apathy, civic and business corruption, political selfishness and stupidity. Plato invited philosophers to be kings—at least kings in their understanding of how men can best live together. The modern age invites the philosopher to examine the ways of man's life, to penetrate to his basic assumptions about himself and his fellows, and to find some answer to the puzzling question why, equipped with the high power of reason, man makes so sorry a mess of his conjoint life.

The philosopher, I take it, will approach these problems in full realization of the fact that there is a whole body of science now at his command to help him formulate his conclusions. He need not be a lone thinker meditating upon man's unhappy self-defeats. The psychological and social sciences give him at least a few pieces of information about this, that, and the other phase of man's living together. His philosophic task, I take it, is to get an over-view of these special knowledges and to formulate what seems to him to be a reasonable way of life.

I have the feeling that as philosophers seek for clues among the social and psychological sciences they will learn a new wisdom about the human problem of living together. These sciences are now at a stage where they can tell us much that we never knew before, at least in exact and demonstrated detail. Take, for example, the careful work that has been done in investigating the first years of the child's life. Here, it has been shown, is where we find the first causes of frustration, the first occasions for resistances, the first fear- and hate-breeding experiences of isolation, as well as, in happier cases, the first experiences of being welcomed into a human fellowship, the first triumphs of love. Take also the careful work done by a new breed of anthropologists in examining the psychological factors in the formation of various cultures—cultures that shape themselves into patterns of adult generosity and mutual hospitality, and, in contrast, cultures that shape themselves into patterns of adult hostility.

There is enough scientific material now at hand for the philosopher to make his search for a *determinative concept*. This, I take it, is the essential philosophic task: to find the concept that basically clarifies all our major problems of living together; that explains our defeats and directs us to a way of triumph. I myself seem to have found such a determinative concept in the idea of *psychological maturing*.

In every area of our life this concept seems to be the most fundamental of all. For example, the home is a place where psychological immaturity in the parents can (and does) do immeasurable damage to the character structure and later behavior system of the children. Instead of helping children to make their first contacts with life in such a way that they develop generous, outreaching attitudes and motivations, psychologically immature parents build fears, resistances, aggressivenesses, and hostilities. We now know that these first years of the child's life are of powerful influence in shaping his total outlook and behavior. Hence the question whether parents are psychologically mature or immature is of determinative significance for the shaping of what the human character is to be. Immature parents literally tend to create antisocial adults, and antisocial adults create a world at odds. If, in short, there is enough immaturity in parents, the reason why, in our social life, "we do it all so badly" is plain to see.

But the home is not an isolated institution. The four walls do not shut out the world. Forces from the outside world play in upon it. If these are predominantly forces of immaturity, there is all the more reason why the home should remain psychologically immature.

In the areas of economics and politics, of journalism, radio, the movies, the school, and the church, there is much to give us anxious pause. To what extent is the life of business, industry, and finance motivated by a fine maturity of outlook? It seems true to say—too tragically true—that the economic processes are basically egocentered. They are processes on a level comparable to the child's self-wantings. They are not yet on the level of the mature individual's concern about others and responsibility for others.

To what extent is politics motivated by a fine maturity of outlook? Here the psychological immaturity is notorious. The characteristic motivation in politics is the "I-win-you-lose" motivation. It is not the "You-and-I-can-work-together" motivation. In short, it, too, with few exceptions, is egocentric. Party politics is mainly partisan politics. National politics is, for the most part, nation-centered, not all-nation-centered. If there ever was a clear case of unfortunate causal sequence, it is found here in the political immaturities of men. Partisans who seek their own victory over their opponents, nationalists who seek their own country's advantage, are forces in the world that inevitably breed fear and hostility.

Here, then, is a determinative concept for the philosopher to clarify and apply. What would psychological maturity in politics mean? How would it begin to operate? In a world of disastrous political immaturity, the philosopher's wisdom must show itself in revealing the childishness of our typical political behaviors and in pointing the way to political maturity.

There are, too, all the forces of newspapers, radio, movies, magazines, books, comics, advertising, and the rest. They play in upon us daily and hourly. They are mind shapers, shapers of attitudes and motives. Are they mature enough to build mature people?

The answer is not a happy one, but it is the philosopher's task to seek out and make the answer. All these forces of communication are deeply determinative of our total life. To pass them by is to miss the chief character-forming elements of our life. Not only does "the eye see what it brings to the seeing," but what the eye sees and what the ear hears are what the character eventually brings to the building of its world. Here, then, are character-forming forces. The deepest question we can ask about them is: are they forces that encourage or discourage man's psychological maturing?

Then there are the school, the college, and the university. If we take "psychological maturing" as our determinative concept, our effort to appraise these is, I think, greatly aided. Appraisals of education come a dime a dozen. Every educator has his appraisal, and most educators have different ones—or at least appraisals differently expressed. The array of philosophies of education is now so bewildering that the average person pays no attention to them. I do not mean to speak with undue assurance, but I do believe that in the midst of this bewildering array of educational appraisals the concepts we have been considering might be of signal value. It seems wholly reasonable to say that the basic job of education should, first and foremost, be to help young people to grow up into a genuine intellectual, emotional, and social maturity (and to help adults to keep growing up). The curious thing is that this seems not to have been widely noticed in the schools, colleges, and universities, so that a recent writer (Bernard Iddings Bell) can speak of our educational system as largely responsible for "our dangerous juvenility."

Obviously, an educational system that has little or no success in turning immature into mature personalities—that does not even conceive this as its primary objective—does not yet possess the wisdom requisite for creating a socially effective citizenry.

Finally there is the church. Having just made a journey through the "Bible belt," I am aware of the terrifying amount of sheer infantilism that goes by the name of religion. It is terrifying because such religious infantilism is the source of fears, prejudices, intolerances, fanaticisms, group hostilities, and narrow-minded resistances to rational progress. What should religion be except the invitation for man to grow up into the full maturity of his emotional and spiritual powers? I can conceive of no greater service to the health of our culture than to bring into the church the concept of spiritually "growing up." Far too often the concept has been that of remaining the dependent child—taking orders from above, trusting that all good will come from above, awaiting the day when the Heavenly Parent will gather us to His fatherly bosom. The church, in many of its forms, has been one chief breeding place of intellectual, emotional, social, and spiritual immaturity. With our present insight into what it disastrously means to remain fixated on an infantile level, the goal of all religion must assuredly be to foster in man the purpose and the power to outgrow the dependence of the child and achieve the mature concern and responsibility of the grown man. "When I was a child, I spoke as a child" . . . those maturity-invoking words of Paul might well be applied to all religion.

When philosophers were chiefly concerned with the mathematical and physical sciences, their efforts were in the main directed toward clarifying certain key concepts: matter, mind, space, time, causality, infinity, and the rest. Today, when philosophers need to concern themselves with the psychological and social sciences, they will again direct their efforts toward clarifying key concepts. In this paper I have mentioned only one of them, the concept of psychological maturing. It seems to me that the clarification of this concept and its application in clarified form in the various areas of our life, constitutes a major task for today's philosophers. Even the definition of psychological maturing goes a-begging. When this concept is made clear, and when its application in the several areas of our life is made apparent, we may, I think, expect among ourselves not only a clearer understanding of the problems of living together, but more effective ways of bringing those problems to solution. To know that we do not yet know how to live together maturely, is the Socratic beginning of our wisdom. To discover how to live together maturely, is to be actively wise.

On Accepting the Nobel Award
William Faulkner

William Faulkner, born in New Albany, Mississippi in 1897, pilot in the British Royal Air Force (1918), student at the University of Mississippi (1922-24), postmaster at University, Mississippi (1922-24)—these details sketch the first half of his life. Beginning with *The Marble Faun* (1924) he has produced a steady stream of short stories and novels that have brought wide acclaim. The better-known titles include *As I Lay Dying, Sanctuary, Sartoris, Go Down Moses, Light in August, Absalom, Absalom!, Intruder in the Dust, Wild Palms,* and *The Hamlet.*

In November 1950 Mr. Faulkner was announced the winner of the Nobel Prize for literature held over from 1949. In that year the Swedish Academy failed to agree on a recipient and no prize was awarded in the field of literature. The brilliant response below was made on the occasion of the presentation of the award at Stockholm on 10 December 1950.

According to a story published by Leonard Lyon in his syndicated column on 3 April 1951, Mr. Faulkner did not know until the day of the ceremonies at Stockholm that he was expected to make an acceptance address. When congratulated after the delivery he explained: "If it was good, it was because I had such little time to prepare it. If I had been given longer notice, it would have been a longer speech—and worse."

I FEEL THAT this award was not made to me as a man but to my work —a life's work in the agony and sweat of the human spirit, not for glory and least of all for profit, but to create out of the materials of the human spirit something which did not exist before. So this award is only mine in trust. It will not be difficult to find a dedication for the money part of it commensurate with the purpose and significance of its origin. But I would like to do the same with the acclaim too, by using this moment as a pinnacle from which I might be listened to by the young men and women already dedicated to the same anguish and travail, among whom is already that one who will some day stand here where I am standing.

Our tragedy today is a general and universal physical fear so long sustained by now that we can even bear it. There are no longer problems of the spirit. There is only the question: when will I be blown up? Because of this, the young man or woman writing today has forgotten the problems of the human heart in conflict with itself which alone can make good writing because only that is worth writing about, worth the agony and the sweat.

He must learn them again. He must teach himself that the basest of all things is to be afraid; and, teaching himself that, forget it forever, leaving no room in his workshop for anything but the old verities and truths of the heart, the old universal truths lacking which any story is ephemeral and doomed—love and honor and pity and pride and compassion and sacrifice. Until he does so he labors under a curse. He writes not of love but of lust, of defeats in which nobody loses anything of value, of victories without hope and worst of all without pity or compassion. His griefs grieve on no universal bones, leaving no scars. He writes not of the heart but of the glands.

Until he relearns these things he will write as though he stood among and watched the end of man. I decline to accept the end of man. It is easy enough to say that man is immortal simply because he will endure; that when the last ding-dong of doom has clanged and faded from the last worthless rock hanging tideless in the last red and dying evening, that even then there will still be one more sound: that of his puny inexhaustible voice, still talking. I refuse to accept this. I believe that man will not merely endure: he will prevail. He is immortal, not because he alone among creatures has an inexhaustible voice, but because he has a soul, a spirit capable of compassion and sacrifice and endurance. The poet's, the writer's, duty is to write about these things. It is his privilege to help man endure by lifting his heart, by reminding him of the courage and honor and hope and pride and compassion and pity and sacrifice which have been the glory of his past. The poet's voice need not merely be the record of man; it can be one of the props, the pillars to help him endure and prevail.

The Stake of the Arts in the Democratic Way of Life

Walter Pach

Walter Pach, artist and author, was born in New York City in 1883. He was graduated from the College of the City of New York in 1903 and later studied at the New York School of Art and at the Académie Ranson in Paris. He has exhibited his paintings and etchings in many shows and they are in permanent collections at the Metropolitan Museum in New York, the Phillips Memorial Gallery in Washington, the New York Public Library, and in various private collections.

Walter Pach

The paper published below, a revision of a talk in 1941, was read at the Tenth Conference on Science, Philosophy, and Religion in their Relation to the Democratic Way of Life held at the Men's Faculty Club of Columbia University, New York on 6 September 1949.

EIGHT YEARS AGO, we were fighting Hitler's ideas, above all. But his disappearance has not meant the obliteration of totalitarian methods. On the contrary, Russia—to which country I already referred in 1941—is now offering an even clearer example of attempted control of thought and art by a government. Since education and the opportunities to understand art are far more advanced in Germany than in Russia, resistance by Germans to the autocratic domination of their thinking was stronger than what we have heard about in Russia, though the regimentation of the Germans was lamentable enough. Even so, if Hofer and Marcks were put under surveillance by the Nazis, as I described, no case has come to my notice of German artists condemning their own work as Prokoviev and Shostakovitch were forced to do after admonition from the commissar in charge of music. We know how the threat of punishing the family and associates of accused persons has extracted the most extraordinary confessions in Russia, and I cannot believe that when the two eminent composers promised to conform in the future and to give a more national and popular quality to their music, they were free of intimidation. Even if no physical suffering or imprisonment were threatened, the loss of government support might mean destitution in a country where art is so completely under official control.

An explanation somewhat along these lines is needed when we find Shostakovitch, as one of his country's representatives at the recent conference of scientific and intellectual workers, repeating his *mea culpa*, and thanking the authorities for putting him on the right track. Imagine Mozart uttering such ideas! Or, still more unthinkable would be self-condemnation by a man of Beethoven's independence.

A statement by Jan Christiaan Smuts, quoted by Dr. Irving J. Lee, comes to mind: "Amid the evils of the world today where the tendency is to follow slogans, to run after catchwords, to worship ideologies or exalt party politics, the sovereign remedy is . . . the spirit of science which exalts fact above sectional loyalties and ideologies."

If totalitarian governments have followed the reverse program, and flouted the spirit of science to the point of bending facts to suit their purposes, how much more is such a process to be feared when we come to the arts. There we are but rarely dealing with things as stubborn as facts. We deal with sensations and ideas so difficult to define that the obscuring of judgment, indeed the loss of judgment, is the price that will be paid for any deviation from impartiality.

Instead of allowing individuals to decide for themselves by what they can profit in the production of our time, a party line for art is established by official aestheticians such as V. Kemenov, whose article, "Painting and Sculpture in the Bourgeois West," was recently used by Togliatti in the magazine which is one of the organs of the Italian Communists. Condemning such men as Cézanne, Matisse, Picasso, Braque, Lipchitz, and Henry Moore, the article leads up to its climax in the words, "Today, Soviet culture is creating works of world importance following the road laid down by the genius of Stalin."

The "world importance" of the works referred to would be a more convincing matter if reported to us by someone less governed than Kemenov by the "tendency to worship ideologies or exalt party politics," so accurately described by General Smuts. The tying together of aesthetics and politics is subversive of the freedom necessary for artistic creation; and so clearly was this recognized in Italy that numbers of artists who had previously been Communists resigned from the party rather than accept Togliatti's dictation. I have confidence that Americans will be no less conscious of the truth than were the men whom we have noticed in Germany, France, and Italy. If, in those sorely tried lands, oppression was powerless to make artists give up their birthright, it would be strange indeed if our people, with their tradition of liberty, did not offer another affirmation of the artist's true position in society, his role in revealing the ideas in us which only his instinct, unhampered by political pressure, can bring to the light.

I want to stress that the foregoing remarks are not a criticism of Soviet policies on any point save the one discussed. No one, indeed, can quarrel with a genuine desire that art be accessible to the largest public willing to make the effort needed to understand and enjoy it. Such a result is not, however, to be accomplished by governmental dictation to artists, any more than people can be legislated into virtue or happiness. The urge toward such desiderata must come from within, not from without.

It seems to me that no understanding of the artist's relationship to society is possible unless we proceed from an acceptance of the fundamental fact that his mind is a free mind as far as the demands of temporal or spiritual employers are concerned. His freedom is limited only by the character of the race, the country, or the period to which he belongs, and never by the will of individuals or groups who tell him what to say. Even when he does say what is commanded of him, he does so because he believed it already: it is his own truth that he tells; but expressing what is deepest in his own sense of life, of proportion, of contrast, and balance, is also the best means of expressing such ideas as they exist, latent, in the mind of the generality of men. And it is for this that he has been esteemed.

It is through the properties of his art, which he can share with others only when he does his rightful work, that he conveys the great emotions we get on entering Chartres Cathedral, for instance. When we see that grand interior, with its perspective of shafts and arches, and its magic of light and shadow, we know that it is not to ecclesiastical or feudal lords that we owe the mighty stir of our blood that occurs every time we see that solemn beauty. It comes to us from architects, builders, and sculptors—those who carved each capital on the columns which the workmen placed where they needed to be placed, subtly varying the design which the *maître de l'oeuvre* had traced on paper, but in which no one could foresee the thousand accidents of space, material, and light. These could be orchestrated only by the quick sense for rightness of living men—who thus left a living work.

Compare Chartres with the churches along Fifth Avenue, for example. There, indeed, we get the result of acceptance by artists, or near-artists, of an authority outside their own minds.

Those minds are separated by many centuries from the current of thought and the special sensitiveness to materials (stone construction as compared to steel construction) which mark the difference between the period of real Gothic and our own period. And so today, when an order comes to an architect's office for a church in the style of Amiens, Bamberg, or Exeter, we know in advance that the thing will be stillborn; and its deadness will be only the more evident if we look just across the street to Radio City, and see with what alert and loving attention Raymond Hood and his associates watched the growth of the great shaft—the NBC building—in the center, and magnificently adjusted to its proportions the two small buildings which mark the approach to the tower. I need not tell you how the response of sightseers, as they look on this living work, differs from that which they make when dutifully observing the nearby churches produced by the school we might call that of Real Estate Gothic.

Someone may object that I am advocating a modernism so rabid as to exclude the acceptance of the great lessons of the past.

That is not so; and I will prove my affirmation by reference to an artist who carries on the essentials of that Gothic School which produced the masterpieces. He is a man now seventy years old [1] who, in his youth, so far obeyed the law of his profession—the law of the free mind—that he was classed with the group called *les fauves* (the wild beasts), for in the first years of the present century, so violently was it necessary to react against the pretended authority of the official bodies that that was the name invented by the academic crowd for men like Matisse, Derain, and Rouault. Rouault has never made the slightest change of direction from the course he was engaged on at the *fauve* period; but first one person and then another has become aware that his early training as a maker of stained-glass windows for churches, has remained with him, and that here was really new wine in old bottles. The wine has grown richer, headier, and stronger as the years have passed. The painting has gained in scope of color and in luminosity—both physical and spiritual; but while we recognize it always more readily as being uniquely the work of Rouault, our conviction grows apace that the artist is carrying on the spirit which animated the Gothic men, and thus giving one more confirmation to Van Gogh in his words, "Never say that the dead are dead; as long as men shall live, the dead shall live."

Returning to the question of the artist's relationship to society, and taking the instances where there is agreement between him and his employers, it is easy to see that his conception of his work should be the essential one, for it is a natural expression of the ideal inherent in the whole human group of which he is a part. But how does the matter stand when the artist is merely an instrument in the hands of a ruling class or an individual tyrant? History shows us many examples of such a condition, the chief one, for extent in time and for importance of result, being that of Egypt, with its thousands of years, during which the artist, but little above the rank of the slave—or perhaps differing from the other slaves only by the high degree of intelligence and training required for his work—produced that fabulously great sculpture which one may at times consider the supreme expression of art.

Taking other periods of history, almost at random, we can be sure that the Roman allowed very little freedom of choice to artists, either the ones who built his glorious aqueducts and amphitheaters, or the ones who recorded in portraiture the face and gesture of the conquering people. During the period which produced the greatest works of Christian art, the artist's role was stated by St. Bernardine when he decreed that the Church alone is to decide upon the content of works of art, and that the

[1] Rouault is now (in 1949) seventy-eight years of age; what I wrote of him, above, is even more the case than it was at the time of our meeting in 1941.

painter or sculptor shall simply execute the orders given him by ecclesiastical authority. Again, when we read about the haughty tyrants of the Renaissance, we may be sure that only a titan like Michelangelo could stand up to them. Raphael, though he has been called divine, times without number, appears to have been submissive on all occasions; and Leonardo, in his famous letter to the Duke of Milan, setting forth his qualifications in a way that would seem boastful if we did not remember his unparalleled intellect, is still the commoner humbly approaching a lord.

If I may take from a field adjacent to my own—the field of literature—a very specific example of the relationship between artist and patron, I would recall the dedication to a young prince which La Fontaine wrote for one book of his *Fables*. The great master speaks with such humility that he begs the acceptance of his work on the ground of its being unworthy of the time in which the prince himself could execute it—and far better than the poet—if his august lord were willing to absent himself from more important occupations. We get the significance of this when we recall that the prince was then six years old.

Let me also offer examples of the artist's attitude in more recent times. Jacques Louis David is, through his paintings, one of the instigators of the French Revolution, and, by his acts, one of the men who carried it to some of its most drastic manifestations. Yet he accepts Napoleon, not only as the brilliant general of the Revolutionary army, but as Consul and as Emperor, recording his coronation in a picture which is a prodigious masterpiece. Ingres continues the placid course of his art from the time of the old royal regime, through the periods of the Revolution, the Empire, the restoration of the Bourbons, the Second Republic, and the reign of the new Napoleon; at no time do the changes of society show in his work.

Under Napoleon III, Delacroix makes a sardonic entry in his *Journal*. He has just come home from a reception held by the sovereign; he snickers over the men who had been opposed to Bonaparte, and who now crowd his drawing room in order to stand well with him. "Whom did I see?" writes the painter, "Barye—the republican, Rousseau—the republican, Français—the republican." Then Delacroix mentions other artists for whom the change from the democratic to the autocratic form of government meant just as little.

It may seem that I am taking a very strange course, for one who speaks for the preservation of the democratic way of life; one might say that I am proving the artist to be quite aloof from society.

"Have patience," says Daumier's old lawyer to the client who is writhing under the denunciations of the opposing attorney, "have a little patience: presently I shall insult the whole family of your adversary."

That is what I am going to do; but first I must recall that statement which I called basic: that the mind of the artist is a free mind as far as the demands of temporal or spiritual rulers are concerned. If compelled to waive his republican principles when Napoleon III came to power, Barye's mind remained one of the freest that the human race has ever brought forth. Essentially a man of his time, typical of the nineteenth century in its magnificent power, he could at one moment so profoundly reorient us in the genius of Hellas that Théophile Silvestre called him "an Athenian," while at other moments Barye's rendering of the animals, his demonstration of the continuity between man and the animals, caused him to be denounced for making what we should today call propaganda in favor of the theories of Charles Darwin.

Ingres, by his evident lack of any political principles, provoked the sneers of that same Théophile Silvestre, a most admirable writer. But the mind of Ingres retained its limitless purity, its limitless freedom, whatever were the demands of temporal or spiritual rulers, throughout the eighty-seven years of his life.

David, in going from the Republic which he prophesied in his work and which he helped create, to the glorification of the Emperor, was the expression of the will and character of his people, and his work has, throughout its great expanse, that monumental quality given only to those whose utterance is that of a whole period. The authority of an artist's race is one that he must obey. Perhaps, in a superficial viewing, he seems to run counter to that authority, as Rembrandt did, in his maturity and old age—when he produced his supreme work—and paid the penalty of rejection by society. But that simply means that there are sometimes counter currents in a given time. The greater the artist, the more he will plunge to what is eternal in his race—as Rembrandt and Ruisdael did, while Frans Hals and Vermeer—though they are admirable masters—still remain nearer to the surface of things.

And now, getting back to La Fontaine: what did it cost him to write all his transparent flattery? Was anybody fooled, when he made his living as he did? Could you imagine any way in which he could have been more authentically the voice of France in her wisdom and poetry, and therefore one of the most beautiful voices of mankind?

So also those artists of the Gothic time: they took orders from their employers, but it is the genius of the workers themselves which gives to the cathedral its character, and makes it a universal thing. Renoir said that the craftsmen are the men to whom we must look in order to understand what is peculiar to a locality or a period, for the great artists go beyond the boundaries of space and time. And in saying that, Renoir, who himself had begun as a craftsman, unwittingly placed himself beside Aristotle, who said that art is not the imitation of the particular but of the universal.

The case for the artists of Rome and Egypt stands in just the same way. No matter how absolute were the Caesars, or the priest-kings from the time of Memphis to that of Sais, the laws which the artist followed in making an arch or making a man for his Roman master, in determining for his Egyptian master the scope of a pyramid, or in carving a hawk, or shaping a vase, were laws inherent in the nature of mankind. Essentially, therefore, these arts, like all arts, were democratic, even when the government was theocratic.

And that is what a vulgar parvenu of culture, such as Adolf Hitler, cannot understand. Amid the mass of his brutality and his ignorance, nothing stands out as more false and futile than his pretension to control the current of art. In a collection of popular German songs published under the Nazi regime, it was impossible to omit *Die Lorelei,* but in the space where the author's name should appear are the words, "Poet unknown." Of course every German knows that the poem was written by Heinrich Heine, and perhaps every German knows that for all the days to come, the printing of those words, *"Dichter unbekannt,"* will be futile in blotting out the name of a Jew, one who remains one of the glories of Germany.

But after all, the lie about Heine is only a little lie, a detail to which history will attend, for as Leibnitz says, God Himself cannot change the past. The big lie comes with the attempt Hitler so shamelessly and constantly made to falsify the processes of thinking, first among his own people, and then among the French and the Italians who were under his heel. The stupidity of Neville Chamberlain, for example, was above all in his blindness to the way in which Hitler had succeeded in corrupting Germany. Not a fanatical rouser of the rabble was to be dealt with, but a people fallen under the domination of its scum, and to a great extent already perverted in its mental processes by a philosophy of lies. The stupidity of our isolationists, who imagine they could keep out the ideas of the totalitarians by means of the oceans which surround us, may be compared only with the mental processes of that "pleasant gentleman," as John Milton calls him, "who thought to keep the crows out of his park by shutting the gates." The glorious defense of intellectual freedom which Milton gives in the *Areopagitica* is an example of the length of time during which the English-speaking peoples have cherished the democratic way of life. For in making his fight against censorship, the great poet was in effect asserting that authority in matters of literature and art resides not with individuals, who may have special interests or a system to uphold, but with the mass of mankind, that will decide through its own conscience what is good and what is bad.

But, someone may object, even if totalitarian ideas do seek to invade our country—by radio, to begin with, and then by means of the printed word, by the cinema, and the work of painters and sculptors—are you not joining the ranks of the defeatists, the men who have so little faith in America that they turn panicky over what they suppose to be its inability to defend itself? My answer to that question is no: President Roosevelt was not a defeatist when he decided that our defense begins with Iceland and doubtless other distant places yet to be designated; and we are no defeatists in calling attention to a menace to our way of life, a menace which is an integral part of the program of the dictators.

I will first glance at the case of Russia. Never having been in that country, I cannot testify at first hand as to the use of Russian museums by the present regime. But friends who have visited the country have brought me accounts of the placards on the walls of the galleries, and the so-called explanation by the guides, under whose supervision one is —or was—compelled to place oneself in order to see the pictures. The burden of both the printed and the spoken word in the museums was purely and simply Communist propaganda, a reiteration of Marxian principles as applied to the history and interpretation of art. Thus a Raphael Madonna was stated to belong to the period when the Church was manufacturing a specially insidious form of its "opium for the poor," the latter-day words for religion; other pictures were described as means for oppressing the masses by glorifying capitalist society—and so on.

But nauseating as such words were to every Russian of culture or of independent mind, the harm was small and temporary as compared with what occurred when the Soviets began to break up the collections which were the priceless heritage of the people, selling large numbers of masterpieces, like the *Alba Madonna* and the *St. George* of Raphael, now in the Mellon Collection at Washington, the great Van Eycks and the Watteau now in the Metropolitan Museum, and the Van Gogh of the *Café at Night* now in a New York collection.

The excuse for these sales was that the Soviets needed the money— to which we may reply that there are certain things one may not do for money. That is what all countries and all periods reply to the prostitute and the thief when they try to justify their way of life through the argument of necessity. Harsh as the reply may appear in individual cases, it is—along its general lines—the verdict of mankind.

The Nazis, in following the Bolsheviks, as they so often did, were a bit subtler in the statement of their case. From a museum in Berlin they sold the greatest piece of Gothic sculpture in all Germany, the glorious *Madonna and Child* now in the Cloisters, at Fort Tryon Park. But, they explained, this work is French, and they wanted to put works of German art in the place it had occupied. Perhaps that was also the excuse as to the Raphael portrait of a man from Munich, now in the Kress Collection at our National Gallery. We are pretty safe in saying, however, that all these examples of action by the dictators were motivated by the psychology of the kidnaper—to whom nothing is sacred if he can turn it into money. And if we think of the honor which the older Germany gave to learning, culture, and art, and then think that such outrages on the character and tradition of the people were tolerated in our day, we may well say that we are not dealing with an imaginary menace for America when we call upon its intelligent men and women to make themselves a barrier against the spread of this gangster psychology to a people like our own, whose necessary concern, till recently, with the clearing of a continent has not left time for such experience of art, such consideration of the value of art, as have been possible in the Old World.

But a more flagrant and dangerous poisoning of the wells of thought still remains to be noticed. I mean the branding of certain modern tendencies as degenerate, and the prevention by the government of work by the artists so stigmatized. Van Gogh has been dead for fifty years, and so the sale out of the country of great pictures by him has no more effect than to impoverish Germany by the loss of the actual works, the artist himself being beyond the range of persecution. One hopes the same is true of Derain, whose magnificent landscape of Vers has come to the Museum of Modern Art in New York, thanks to Hitler's incursion on one of the German museums. But this artist was in Paris, under Nazi rule—since one must recall that horrid fact. While no report has come as yet (1941)[2] of interference by the German authorities with the activities of French painters, it would be a simple step if there were what they call a coördination, a *Gleichschaltung,* of artists in the conquered territory with those in Germany itself. The best painter and the best sculptor,

---

[2] This date was taken from the original paper, written in 1941, "The Artist and the Democratic Way of Life," *Conference on Science, Philosophy and Religion,* Lyman Bryson and Louis Finkelstein, editors, Conference on Science, Philosophy, and Religion in Their Relation to the Democratic Way of Life, Inc., New York, 1942, pp. 493-505.

in that country today, Carl Hofer and Gerhard Marcks—to name them—are both so cut off from the public and so constantly visited by the police that their work has had to stop entirely.

Is it any wonder that the members of their profession in this country are—probably to a man—filled with loathing and contempt for a regime which supports itself by the sacrifice of what is best within its borders? Do not let it be suggested that these are temporary measures, like the sale of art works in Russia, which has now indeed prohibited such sales, and has even given orders for the repurchase of any of its works which might be obtainable.

The most vicious of the German activity was against ideas, especially those of freedom, because it has been, since the French Revolution, the chief aspiration of mankind. Crushed in the brave gesture it made in Spain, no one doubted—and Hitler least of all—that only force, in that country, will prevent its rise again. That rise has always been prophesied and led by the arts. Hence the Nazis' attempt to corrupt, prevent, or suppress them. Hence the identification I have been making between them and the democratic way of life. We have seen that the autocracies, the very theocracies of the past, representing the general understanding of the world of their times, operated in general harmony with the arts—which today are forced to seek refuge in the lands which have still kept their freedom, the condition understood by our time as the right one for humanity.

Let me make a final point in our question of the stake of the arts in the democratic way of life (and I would ask you to observe—in passing—that I have refrained from discussing, unless it be by implication, a subject even more vital, perhaps: I mean the stake which the democratic way of life has in the arts). My last point is that the present time is most particularly one when contamination of the arts at the hands of a political ideology, or by mere banditry, would be disastrous to a more than usual extent.

It is well known that the past hundred and fifty years have paralleled by the development of art the immense changes in the field of science. As to the latter, one would not expect even a Franklin, a Volta, or an Ampère to recognize himself or the results of his discoveries in the telephone, the airplane, or the radio, with their utter transformation of our concepts of space and time. Similarly, the painters of their period might well stand amazed at the externals of the art of today, even if we know to an absolute certainty that what made a picture good in the year 1800, or for that matter in 1500, is what makes it good today. But we can be sure that those great scientists of the earlier time would readily understand the latter-day marvels in their field if they had sufficient opportunity to trace the evolution since their own day, and grasp the thought of our day. In the same way, one can perfectly imagine Ingres, with his creativeness so closely conditioned by his study of the museums, coming to a full comprehension of Derain. The same words about creativeness within a tradition, which I have just used about Ingres (born exactly a hundred years before Derain), may be applied to our contemporary. Delacroix, recalling his journey to Morocco in 1832, and knowing his debt to the Orient for much of the color in his work, might well see the beauty of Matisse's color—with its own influence from Morocco and from other exotic lands.

The Goya who produced those frightful plates of the *Disasters of War* would, I am positive, hear his own voice in that terrible cry which Picasso utters in *Guérnica:* the great Spaniard of the earlier invasion and the great Spaniard of the recent invasion both preserve their respect for the laws of their art, and both extend the scope of those laws, even while hurling their imprecation against the enemies of that democratic way of life to which the people of Spain are so passionately devoted.

Schumann said that only genius perfectly comprehends genius. But if such comprehension of the modern masters as I have predicated for those older masters belongs to men of their stature alone, there is still a vast treasure of ideas and power to be derived by even average men from the great achievement of recent times. In a general way, we are coming to grasp this fact; and I am constantly finding myself astonished over the way the youngsters of today are seizing at once the ideas that the men of my generation came to only through the famous blood, sweat, and tears.

I have been speaking of the artists; but often I am more interested in laymen and, considering the creation of the Museum of Modern Art here, and the immense developments of the unspecialized museums of Boston, Chicago, and San Francisco (to take only the most widely separated cities), I do not think it in any way a self-deception to see a progressive closing of that unfortunate gap between the artist and the public which characterized the nineteenth century as no other before it.

For this beneficent process to continue, it is evident that a free movement of the spirit, undisturbed by totalitarian meddling, is essential. And so, though I cannot imagine how even the most blighting tyranny would cause the disappearance of the artist, although—as compared with him—it is the world in general that has most to gain by the preservation of the democratic way of life, I affirm that the artist needs it also, in order that he may, in the new era before us, no longer have to depend solely on his own strength, as he was forced to do for about a hundred years past, but may have the benefit of the understanding and support of his fellow men. In losing contact with him, they have—during the period which saw the creation of the museums—given their admiration to the things of the past. No loss of our love for the classics is required for us to enjoy the art of our own day, and when such enjoyment becomes general, when the artist is released from the isolation of the ivory tower and is again permitted a free exchange with his fellow men, he will make the great new advances for which his work in recent times has prepared him. Basing my convictions, therefore, on his own interest as well as what I know of his general outlook on life, I am proud to offer this testimony that the men of my profession stand solidly in support of the ideals of the present Conference.

LABOR AND INDUSTRY

Organized Labor and Current International Developments

Matthew Woll

Matthew Woll was born in Luxembourg in 1880 and arrived in New York as an immigrant at the age of eleven. As a young man he learned the photoengraving trade and from 1906 to 1929 was the president of the International Photoengravers Union of North America. He was a member of the National War Labor Board in 1942 and of President Truman's Labor Management Conference in 1945. At present he is the second vice-president of the American Federation of Labor and is chairman of four of the most important committees of the AFL: international labor relations, education, social security, and taxation and national defense.

This address was presented before the Economic Club of Detroit on 26 February 1951. Because of space limitations only the second half is published. In introducing Mr. Woll on this occasion Mr. Thomas C. Carroll said: "His ability as a debater is recognized by all who know him. He can hold his own with the best."

IN RECENT TIMES, the present world crisis has been described in some circles as a conflict between capitalism and socialism. That is nonsense. Indeed, there is a total lack of agreement as to defining of "capitalism" or as to what is implied by that term—and the same holds true of "socialism." These words have lost whatever meaning they may have had. Their content is no longer what it was at one time. The Bolsheviks and Nazis have destroyed the meaning of the words "socialism" and "capitalism." Modern socialists assert that there is no socialism in Russia in the old Marxian sense of the word. We know of no more severe critic of "socialism" in Russia than the militant socialist fighter of Germany—Dr. Kurt Schumacher—and the moderate socialist Prime Minister of England—Clement Attlee.

Our own country is said to be the model capitalist nation, the country of capitalism in its classical sense. But today we do not have capitalism in the United States either in the present European sense or what it was fifty years or more past in America. When we speak of free enterprise and personal adventure in the United States, we mean one thing; when Europeans or Asians speak of free enterprise, it means something quite different. In reality, our country, with its economy based on private enterprise and personal adventure, represents today an economy with a growing sense of social responsibility and with a growing recognition of labor's rights and responsibilities in the life of the nation. This is the economic and philosophic basis of our free society.

That is why labor of and in America prizes collective bargaining so highly. It provides the vital spirit and the most powerful vehicle for the extension of democracy in our economy. We hold to this principle and hold to it dearly, to this idea of contract—a meeting of minds of men and women individually and collectively coming together voluntarily into agreement. That is the basic philosophy underlying the structure, not only of our nation, but of the American economy—and which has made for the greatness of our people and the richness of our nation.

Here, in our country, alleged to symbolize capitalism in extreme form and control, organized labor enjoys far more and greater rights and prerogatives in the production policies than anywhere throughout the world. Despite all references to "Wall Street" and alleged great capitalists past and present, the workers of our country have a far greater and more effective voice in industry, in mining, and transportation than those of any other land. Let me cite a case in point, that of the International Ladies' Garment Workers' Union. This thriving labor organization has its own engineering department. In the collective bargaining agreement entered into by this organization, provision is made to the effect that when an employer does not produce well enough, the Union's Engineering Department has a right to examine his methods of production and to recommend and demand assurance of improvement in the manufacturing of garments. Then, too, if the employer pleads poverty and inability to pay adequate wages, then the accounting department of the Union has a right to examine the books of the employer and to check and establish the real facts. Examples of other trade unions might be cited in evidence of the coöperative relations existing here and as to the rights of labor in industry, and its participation with management.

When we compare the "rights" of labor in Russia with the rights of labor in America, we find, first and foremost, no real trade or labor unions exist in Russia or its satellite countries. The Russian worker has nothing whatever to say about choice, or change of jobs. The Russian worker is subject constantly to the most intensive exploitation and speed-up system. He is severely punished for the slightest infraction of factory rule or discipline. Lateness to work may even be punished by a prison term. Here is a good example of the dangers inherent in any society where both the economic and the political power are vested in a political government, and this danger is greatly enhanced where that political power is made the monopolistic political power in the nation; and then, furthermore, restricted to a comparatively few. God save us from that sort of system.

Clearly, the roots of the present crisis are deeply imbedded in the challenge of Soviet slavery to human freedom. This is the real menace of the Leviathan in the middle of the twentieth century. In this light, the struggle for human freedom has taken on a new meaning. Today, it is not merely a struggle to extend and expand freedom—it is a desperate struggle to preserve and protect freedom.

Let us face stern reality. In this crisis, Communist totalitarianism now has the initiative. It is the aggressor just as Nazi totalitarianism had been before. That is why the world is darkened by the clouds of war. That is why there is not an individual family in our nation or in any other free nation which does not have the growing danger of war first on its agenda of life and labor.

I am at a loss for words or energy with which to assure you that in this struggle to preserve, protect, and promote human freedom, American labor has done its part and will continue to do much more than its part. We of labor are cognizant of the fact that we have more to lose than any other group in society, if democracy is retarded or destroyed. Experience has clearly demonstrated that there can be no free labor without democracy. We sincerely hope and trust all other social, as well as industrial and economic, groups may come to understand that there can be no democracy without a healthy and powerful free labor movement.

If Communist totalitarianism should ever triumph, labor can win only one thing: the most brutal and brutalizing form of slavery.

It is this realization which has impelled us in the labor movement to be in the forefront of the fight for freedom. I do not say this as a boast. As a matter of fact, labor is best equipped to be the spearhead in the fight against every brand of totalitarian tyranny.

It is under the guise of proletarianism, in terms of labor parlance, as saviors of the workers that these crusaders of exploitation, of spoliation, of terroristic enslavement of body and mind are attempting to fasten the shackles of Communism upon the workers of the world, through their trade unions. It is labor which for centuries has been fighting against social injustice and economic exploitation which can, therefore, best meet these deadly marauders in the house and home of labor.

What has American labor done?

In America, labor, particularly the American Federation of Labor—and I speak solely in its behalf—has had a special role to perform in this contest for the survival of the rights of man. It is the A. F. of L. which opposed Bolshevism from its very inception. Our hostility to Communism has not been of recent origin or conversion. It has been unalterably opposed to Communism and any and all of its subverted movements and agencies at all times. We have never for a single moment yielded to, compromised, or associated with or made any concessions whatsoever to Bolshevism, Nazism, Fascism, Falangism, Peronism or any other form or character of dictatorship.

We turned a deaf ear to the Nazis when they posed as crusaders against Bolshevism. We considered them twin brothers of reaction—as the Stalin-Hitler Pact later disclosed. Even during the honeymoon days of our own country's partnership with Russia in the last war, the A. F. of L. was uncompromising in its vigorous hostility and intense opposition to Communism.

May I say that, from the moment on, that the Kerenski revolution was overthrown, and the Communists gained control of Russia, we petitioned not only President Wilson, but following him, President Harding; and then, Coolidge; and then, Hoover; yes, Franklin D. Roosevelt—not to recognize Soviet Russia. Fortunately, our appeals in the former instances were heeded; unfortunately, in the last case it was not heeded, much to the gripe of civilization of today. Had our government followed our advice, the whole of the world situation might have been different. By this recognition, we not only opened our doors wide to subversive propaganda and fifth-column activities and spies, but gave a world standing to this regime which would otherwise have been impossible.

As is well known, the A. F. of L. was the only labor organization in the world which never affiliated with and refused to have any association or dealings whatever with the so-called World Federation of Trade Unions. The A. F. of L. always considered the World Federation of Trade Unions as only a military espionage agency of Russia. We were delighted when recently the French government closed down this dangerous subversive agency. We hope other governments may follow that example.

For years, the A. F. of L. has carried on the fight against Communism and has brought this fight right into the camp of the enemy. We have fought and defeated the Communists on the field of labor, not only in our own country, but also abroad.

The American Federation of Labor immediately following the cessation of hostilities in the last world war set up special representatives to conduct its world-wide fight for democracy and against totalitarian despotism. We have and have had representatives in various countries, promoting the ideals of freedom, democracy, and of free trade unionism. We have and we are distributing abroad, publications of various kinds. We have provided American trade-union missions to go abroad and have made possible labor delegations from other countries coming to us to see our way of life, to get first-hand knowledge of our democratic procedures and institutions. Understand I am not speaking of these missions the government is bringing over; I am referring to missions that were financed by the American trade unions. And it was trade-union representatives from abroad that we invited over here, selected by the workers themselves.

In Germany we opposed our government's policy of several years past—a policy which gave the Communists the same rights as a democratic organization. Had we not fought this policy, the Communists would by now have had control of the trade-union movement today in Western Germany and all would have been lost in Europe. Today we have a labor movement in Germany of over five million trade unionists, dedicated to the principle of freedom and democracy, and engaged in the contest against Communism. We have exercised considerable influence in Germany and have fostered situations in which the democratic trade unions of that country are now independent of all political parties, with the trade unions increasingly breaking with the fetish of government ownership.

I must pause here to say that had it not been for the activities of the

American trade-union movement quite a different situation might prevail in Germany today. All familiar with the trade-union movement that existed prior to the regime of the Nazis, know that that movement then was adhering rigidly to the Marxian theory of economics. Today, German labor is shrinking from that theory. Today, German labor is urging co-determination. In that advocacy, one finds an acquiescence in and promotion of the idea of private property. Unfortunately, we have some of our trade associations here in America urging the government of Germany to disapprove of co-determination, and, in so doing, influence the German labor movement to return to the camp of Marxism.

In Italy we have been the primary force responsible for the breaking of the Communist strangle hold on labor and for getting together into an independent bona fide free trade-union federation one million workers of all democratic political denominations. Here, too, the trade unions are assuming more and more an independent course from political parties and bodies. We are actively concerned with the latest revolt inside the Communist Party against Russian domination.

In France we of the A. F. of L. have been the driving force leading to the establishment of the *Force Ouvrière*—a breaking away from the *Confédération Générale du Travail* (Confederation of Labor), of an independent free trade-union federation of over six hundred thousand members. Today, the Communist-controlled General Confederation in France is only half its former size and is no longer in the position to paralyze the economy of that unfortunate country.

In India we have been maintaining a bureau to promote better understanding of American labor and the American people—and we have our representative right on the ground, promoting the ideals of America.

In Formosa, and on the Chinese mainland, we are supporting the democratic forces. We are spreading the message of democracy.

In Japan we have been coöperating closely with the democratic trade unionists to help them clean house. Good results have been obtained here and an effective free trade-union movement is being formed in Japan, dedicated to the principles to which we have ascribed here in America.

We are now taking steps to organize a free trade-union training school in Indonesia.

In the Continental ports—mind you, and this is of importance—we have had a bitter battle with the Communists. They were determined to sabotage and prevent the shipment of Atlantic arms aid abroad. What is the use of our manufacturing arms and armament here in

America, if they cannot be landed in foreign ports? One of the first strategic moves of the Communists was to gain control of all the ports of the world, and thus control international commerce. In France they were determined to sabotage and prevent the shipment of Atlantic arms aid. We have beaten them decisively in this contest. In the port of Marseilles, once a great red stronghold, the Workers' Committee now consists of 35 democratic trade unionists and only 15 Communists or fellow travelers.

Whenever and wherever opportunity permits, we are on the offensive against the World Federation of Trade Unions and its affiliates. We have published a great volume of literature portraying in simple language the difference between democracy and Communism, between America and totalitarian Russia. On the basis of facts and not on the basis of rhetoric, we have exposed and fought the Communist monster.

Through our Free Trade Union Committee, we are publishing monthly a publication in English, French, German, and Italian. Scores of thousands of this monthly are sent to the homes of trade-union organizers and leaders throughout the world. Our "International Free Trade Union News" exposes the Communist despotism and explains American democracy.

In the United Nations we have exposed the Russian slave-labor system.

We have pioneered the creation of the International Confederation of Free Trade Unions—with more than fifty million workers in its ranks, pledged to the defeat and destruction of the Communist and every other brand of totalitarianism. This organization came into being last December, at the Conference in London. As I have previously pointed out, it embraces over fifty million wage earners throughout the world, dedicated to the idea of democracy and of freedom—a great world power now to carry on our fight against all forms of totalitarianism not only in Continental Europe, not only in the Middle East, not only in the Near East, but likewise in South and Central America and in Africa, as well.

We have not limited ourselves to the field of labor, broad as this field has been and is. The A. F. of L. has been very active in seeking to help our government develop a foreign policy which is vigorous and democratic. We have taken the initiative on a number of occasions and have blazoned the path for our government. We have not always agreed with our government. We have had to differ at times with our government in regard to Germany, China, and other areas. But we have also had occasions on which we were in full accord with our government's policies and have rendered invaluable services to their advancement.

Speaking of the Marshall Plan, certainly we have not only endorsed the Marshall Plan, but have done everything to help make it workable, possible, and feasible, not only within our own land, but also in the lands intended to benefit by it. We are even the pre-designer of the Marshall Plan, for in 1946, at our Chicago Convention, we laid the foundation for the ultimate development of the Marshall Plan. And, insofar as the Atlantic Pact is concerned, at our following Convention in San Francisco we urged the adoption of a plan somewhat similar to the Atlantic Pact. We have furthered that plan, not only here in America, but in all of the countries party to it.

More recently, at the Executive Council meeting of the A. F. of L., held but a month ago, we not only reversed our time-long-honored position against Universal Military Training, to the contrary we approved Universal Military Training—limited, however, as to time and extent—and not to be made part of our educational system, nor be brought into or made part of our industrial and civic life. More than that, we have urged that there be formed an Asiatic Protective Pact, and we hope our government will favorably consider and further that idea. We likewise have urged an Asiatic Conference for the prosperity of the peoples there. We are in hearty accord with Point Four in bringing relief and in building up the backward nations of the world.

It is our firm conviction that with world labor rallied vigorously on the side of democracy, neither the Communist nor any other brand of totalitarianism or slave statism can ever win or even dare to plunge the world into war. Towards this end, American labor, particularly the A. F. of L., has been and is completely dedicated.

It is because we have the most sound and best form of economy in the world—and I challenge anyone to disprove that—that we are potentially the strongest force against aggression and totalitarian enslavement. Our country was born out of a struggle for national independence. We have traditionally and unconditionally championed all democratic national independence movements. We are opposed to any and all forms of colonialism. We believe thoroughly in a government of the people, by the people and for the people, in reality and not merely by rhetoric.

We have no higher or more lofty ambition than our love for peace. If one wants proof of this, he need but look at the record of America and Russia. When at the height of our strength, when our military superiority over Russia was unquestioned, our government pursued a policy of pleasing and appeasing Russia. When we could have hit the Bolshevik dictators hardest and hurt them most, we helped and coddled the men in the Kremlin solely because we offered to and wished them every possible opportunity to live at peace with us and the rest of the world.

Our nation could not have proceeded in that fashion had we not been thoroughly humans, internationally-minded and imbued with the spirit of friendliness and peace. In addition, need I compare the way Moscow has treated defeated countries with our treatment of Japan and Germany.

Finally, let me state briefly what American labor intends doing in the present crisis.

While American labor will continue to foster and maintain a frankly critical spirit and constructive attitude towards our own political, social, and economic weaknesses and shortcomings, and we have them, and we intend to fight against them, we will at the same time intensify our activities to help strengthen the ranks of free labor and of other democratic forces abroad. We not only welcome the recent setbacks to Communism in Italy, India, Germany, and in other countries, but will continue every possible effort to still further advance this process of disintegration now taking place there and elsewhere.

It is our firm conviction that only America is strong enough to discourage, to defeat, and to destroy the aggressors and enemies of world peace. It is our definite belief that this is the historical mission of America to the human race. It is our determination to hold ourselves in readiness at all times to make available American know-how in health, industry, and self-government on a world scale to the economically underdeveloped countries and regions of the world, and to render every service possible to humankind.

In the field of ideology, the A. F. of L. and the American labor movement will redouble its efforts to advance the ideals of democracy and peace as against dictatorship and war, of freedom of enterprise as against state control, of freedom of expression and worship as against fear of persecution and intolerance.

Our enemy is strong, shrewd, and ruthless. Our enemy has a global approach. We will meet and defeat this enemy, not only by military force, but by all other economic, social, cultural, and political measures and weapons at our command and thus hold secure and advance human freedom and human well-being.

American labor has full confidence in the ability of our country and its people to provide dynamic and inspiring leadership in this world struggle for human freedom. In that struggle, the trade and labor organizations of our land will contribute more than their share to help our nation to perform its historical mission, and rally world labor for the triumph of freedom, of democracy, and of peace over tyranny, despotism, and war.

One final observation, and that is this: No matter what avocation we may follow, no matter what trade or occupation we may be engaged in, as Americans let us be happy that we are here, whether as native or foreign-born, for no other nation the world has ever known has offered the great heritage that is yours and mine—the heritage of freedom, the heritage to express ourselves as we please, the heritage of working out our problems as God intended they should be worked out, by the exchange of opinions, by understanding, by mutual coöperation. May that ever be so! God bless America, and may its blessings extend all over the world in the not far distant future!

Thank you, indeed, for this opportunity of presenting these few observations to you.

Labor's Role in Higher Education
Philip Murray

Philip Murray was born in Blantyre, Scotland in 1886. He came to the United States in 1902 and became a naturalized citizen in 1911. He has been president of the CIO since 1940 and president of the United Steelworkers of America since 1942. Since 1918 he has been a member of the Board of Education of Pittsburgh, Pennsylvania. He is a member of the executive committee of the National Association for the Advancement of Colored People, a trustee of the National Planning Association, and a director of the National Cancer Foundation and the American Red Cross.

This address was delivered by Mr. Murray at the Samuel Gompers Memorial Fund Dinner for Roosevelt College held at the Palmer House in Chicago on 8 December 1950.

Secretary Tobin, President Sparling, President Green, President Hayes, distinguished guests, ladies and gentlemen:

It is a great pleasure for me to participate in this Samuel Gompers Memorial Fund Dinner for Roosevelt College. I am glad to be with you because I hold the name, Samuel Gompers, in high regard and because I believe Roosevelt College to be one of our greatest institutions of higher learning.

Samuel Gompers was the father of organized labor in America. He was a friend of mine of long standing. I held him in the most affectionate esteem. I deem it only appropriate that the CIO officially, and I personally, coöperate in establishing a permanent memorial in his memory.

I believe in Roosevelt College, and the CIO does, because of Roosevelt College's policy of equal educational opportunities for all regardless of color, religion, or background. I believe in Roosevelt College because of its excellent Board of Trustees representing, as it does, both management and labor, and because of its outstanding Labor Education Division for the training of leaders in our movement.

I have long believed that labor must support and must participate in higher education if we are to safeguard and maintain our democratic rights.

It is important to remember that it was the working people of America who built the innumerable educational institutions which are now the glory of our country. They had instinctive faith in the future of America, and they had faith also in the value of formal education. They were dissatisfied, of course, with the way in which our economic system had treated them personally, but they were not resentful, and they didn't become embittered. They never lost confidence in the essential soundness of our American institutions. They were never class-conscious. They looked upon themselves first, last, and always as full-fledged citizens of the United States of America—citizens of equal dignity and equal worth in the eyes of God and in the opinion of their fellow men. If they themselves had been denied the advantages of a formal education, they didn't sour on the educational system itself. On the contrary, they made tremendous personal sacrifices to see to it that their children and their children's children should all have the fullest possible opportunity to be educated according to their native talents and abilities. More than any other group of our citizens they were responsible for building up the excellent educational facilities which are now America's.

You will forgive me, I am sure, if I suggest in passing that up until very recently our institutions of higher learning for the most part were either unfriendly to the cause of organized labor or, if not unfriendly, somewhat apathetic and aloof. I would be less than honest if I did not tell you very frankly that for many years the American labor movement was suspicious of many of our colleges and universities for this very reason. We believed wholeheartedly in higher education, as I have already indicated, and we were willing to make personal sacrifices to promote it to its present enviable position. But we frequently had the feeling that many of our colleges and universities were not very grateful for our interest and our assistance. We had the feeling that many of them were too snobbish to become associated in any way with the labor movement and too cautious and too conservative to present our side of the picture to their students and to the public at large.

I am extremely happy to say, however, that the situation is radically different today. Many of our institutions of higher learning are doing everything possible at the present time to bridge the gap between the classroom and the union hall and are offering a variety of services to our members. In this connection, I would be remiss in my duty as the president of the CIO if I did not pay grateful tribute to Roosevelt College and to its complete recognition from the very beginning of the College of the vital interest that labor has in higher education. The contribution which my good friend, President Sparling, and his many capable associates at Roosevelt College have made and are presently making to the cause of labor is deeply appreciated by the CIO. Thank you, President Sparling and the faculty of Roosevelt College, and be assured of our willingness to coöperate with your labor education programs and with your remarkable institution ever more closely as the years go by.

There is still another type of work that calls for the friendly and intimate coöperation of our colleges and universities with the labor movement and with the other social and economic organizations that go to make up our democratic society. I refer to the field of scientific research on the whole range of economic and industrial problems facing the United States. This *is* a relatively prosperous period, but there are still millions of people living at substandard levels, and we in the labor movement can see some very clear indications that the basic problem of maximum production and employment has not yet been solved in America. It has been temporarily postponed or alleviated, if you will, because of the recent war and the enormous public expenditures necessarily involved in the cold war which because of the aggressive attitude of the Soviet Union and its satellites, now has the United States and the rest of the world in such a critical state of nervous anxiety. But there are still many basic readjustments to be made in our economic system to guarantee full production and full employment on a permanent full-time basis.

The CIO is determined that these readjustments shall be made rationally and democratically. We do not believe—the American labor movement has never believed—that this problem of balancing the economy in the interests of the common good can be solved by government alone. Neither do we believe that it can be solved by management alone; or by labor alone. We do not believe in a government dictatorship or a management dictatorship. Nor, I hasten to add, do we believe in a labor dictatorship. We believe in good faith and coöperation among all the parties concerned. That's why we are requesting and shall continue to request—in spite of reactionaries, be they Communists or so-called free enterprisers—that organized labor be accepted by American industry as a full-fledged partner with an equal voice in deciding upon policies which will most effectively promote the general economic welfare. We shall continue to promote the CIO Industry Council Plan which was first suggested at our 1940 convention but which has received all too little public attention in the interim. Certain employers say that the Industry Council Plan is socialistic. The Communists say that it's a fascist program. We say that it's democracy at its best and the only alternative to either socialism or fascism.

In the light of all this you will understand why we are so determined to organize the unorganized workers of America and why we are so hopeful, too, that our colleges and universities will help to create a climate of informed opinion favorable to the basic purposes of trade unionism and favorable to the philosophy of the Industry Council Plan. We are convinced that workers need to be organized and want to be organized to protect their own economic interests. But we are also convinced—and this is all-important—that unless workers are organized into bona fide trade unions of their own choosing, we cannot hope to establish social justice in the United States and we cannot hope to solve the problem of production and employment in the interests of the common good.

Unfortunately, there are still many thousands of American citizens who are opposed to trade unionism on principle and look upon it with a jaundiced eye as nothing more than a selfish pressure group concerned exclusively with the welfare of its own members. They don't see the whole picture. They don't understand the real meaning of democracy. They are living in the past; they are afraid of the future. Sad to say, many of them are the products of our colleges and universities.

I hope that future generations of college and university graduates will have a better understanding of the problems of the day and a greater willingness to recognize the legitimate rights of labor in a society of free men. I am confident that they will and confident, too, that Roosevelt College will always be a leader, as it is today, among those institutions of learning which are striving to bring about a closer and more effective relationship between education and labor—for the good of both and for the common good of our beloved country.

What Road to Labor Peace?
John L. McCaffrey

John L. McCaffrey, president of the International Harvester Company, Chicago, Illinois since 1946, was born in Fayetteville, Ohio in 1892. He was educated in the public schools of Fayetteville and has been with the International Harvester Company since 1909. He was elected vice-president in 1940 and has been a member of the board of directors since 1941.

Mr. McCaffrey spoke before the 54th Annual Congress of American Industry sponsored by the National Association of Manufacturers at the Waldorf-Astoria Hotel in New York on 8 December 1949.

EVER SINCE the mass labor unions appeared in this country, about fifteen years ago, we have been hunting for a sure, quick and easy road to what is called "labor peace."

We have hunted labor peace as men in the Middle Ages sought the philosopher's stone or men in colonial America hunted a Northwest Passage. And we have been just as successful. Tons of paper, years of radio time, and endless hours of discussion and debate have been devoted to labor peace. There is scarcely a politician, a commentator, a lecturer, a professor, or a columnist who has not wrestled a few falls with the topic of labor peace.

And still, as in the old saying, "Gentlemen cry Peace, peace; when there is no peace."

Why have we failed? What has been wrong? After fifteen years of spectacular non-success, can we identify any of the causes of our failure? I think we can. Realizing fully that I may be just as wrong as the other people who have dealt with labor peace, I nevertheless believe there are two major reasons why we have not found it. I also believe there is a way to labor peace but it is not a quick way, nor an easy one nor a simple one. I should like to talk—one at a time—about those subjects.

1. It is my own belief that the first reason we have not found labor peace is because we have sought it by formula. It is probably natural, in a country where so much of what we do and eat and wear depends

upon chemical formulas and engineering equations, that we should try to find a formula or a set system for labor peace. We have tried, all right, but none of our slide rules or our calipers has done us much good. We set up our formula to measure round balls, so to speak, and then the next ball that comes along has a square side and the formula doesn't work.

First off, people embraced the idea that the government could produce labor peace by passing laws. Many people still have that idea.

So we began with the Wagner Act, the announced purpose of which was to remove the causes of industrial strife. And how was this to be done? It was to be done by placing the whole power of the government behind almost anything a union might choose to do. You could summarize the employer's rights under the Wagner Act quite simply: he didn't have any. This theory was about the same as saying that the way to have a properly fed, well-trained child is to give him the keys to a candy store. It worked just about that well.

Next, the government greatly expanded its mediation and conciliation services. The theory was that a government man, sitting in on a dispute, could bring the parties together by using the prestige of the federal or State governments. There was and is something to be said for that approach. Conciliators can often be helpful.

But there is a flaw in this formula too. That flaw is: the conciliator is interested in only one thing, getting the dispute settled. He does not care *how* it is settled. If the settlement is entirely wrong from a moral standpoint or an economic standpoint, that is no concern of the conciliation service. They are interested only in settlements as such, on whatever terms. And the result is that settlement on the wrong basis often makes the next dispute inevitable and even more bitter.

Then, a few years ago, the incumbent President formed the habit of appointing so-called fact-finding boards. The facts were seldom obscure, either to the parties or to any outsider enough interested to inquire. The actual function of such boards was not to find facts but to make recommendations for settlement, in the hope that such recommendations would be accepted by the public as coming from impartial sources.

Their history forcibly reminds me of the story of the Irishman who was told that he must be neutral in a fight that was about to start. And the Irishman said, "Well, all right, but I want to know whose side I'm gonna be neutral on."

I think nearly any unprejudiced observer will agree that the so-called fact-finding boards have seldom been in doubt as to whose side they were neutral on. In practice, they have been devices for helping unions to get things which they otherwise might not have been able to get. As a result, the fact-finding board approach is a discredited one.

No employer in his right mind, no union leader in his right mind, wants to place in the hands of outsiders the power of life and death over his organization. That is what compulsory arbitration does.

Those are the formulas that have been tried. Looking at the record, it is plain that the formulas have failed to produce. Some have limited usefulness; none is a cure. I see no reason to think they will succeed any better in the future.

I do not believe labor peace can be created by force—such as flatly prohibiting strikes. I happen to believe in the right to strike for legitimate ends. I think it should be preserved and I do not believe we should try to purchase labor peace at the price of losing essential freedoms.

To sum up this point, I believe the first reason we have not found labor peace is because we have sought it by quick and easy formulas.

2. The second reason, in my opinion, why we have failed to find labor peace is that we have not been clear as to what labor peace is. Judging by the laws that have been passed and by the written or spoken statements issued, many people seem to believe that labor peace is a negative thing—the mere absence of strikes.

But is it? Does the simple absence of a picket line constitute labor peace? To me, that is like saying that any home is a happy home if only the wife and husband do not heave the china at one another.

What about deliberate slow-downs of production? What about the drumming up of phony grievances to clog grievance and arbitration procedures? What about the technique, so common among the Communist-dominated unions, of stirring up constant small work stoppages or wildcat strikes? What about all those elements of disruption and disharmony which fail to show up in the statistics of the government but which show so clearly in higher costs and lower production and lost earnings for employees?

Certainly a national steel strike or a national coal strike is a dangerous and spectacular event. But merely to prevent or limit such unusual threats is not to achieve labor peace, any more than building a dike against a possible tidal wave constitutes a soil conservation program.

Well, then, if labor peace is not merely the absence of formal strikes or the prevention of national strikes, what is it? Can we describe it? I think we can.

In my opinion labor peace is a relationship between human beings

What Road to Labor Peace?

—which is the prime reason that it cannot be established by formula. Labor peace, I believe, is the condition which exists when management and employees understand one another, feel reasonable confidence in one another, when they share a common fund of information, when they believe in the same economic and political system, when they stop pretending to perfection, when they accept and have regard for their full responsibilities.

I think we shall have true labor peace when—and only when—we are able to establish that kind of relationship between the men who manage a business and the other men who work in it.

3. And that brings me to the third thing I want to talk about—the road to labor peace. How can we achieve it?

Can we do it by government action? I don't believe so. I have already indicated some of the reasons why. The big reason is that good human relationships cannot be created by force.

Can we expect labor peace from a natural and spontaneous improvement in union leadership? I don't believe that either.

We used to be told that the unions were young yet, that they would become responsible and temperate as they grew and matured. Have they? On the whole, I think not.

There are many fine men in the ranks of labor leaders. But in general it seems to me the major union leaders have become more interested in their rivalries with one another, their ambitions for advancement within labor, or their ambitions to become political powers, than in recognizing their responsibilities to the public or the customer or the stockholder. Some are enemies of our business and political systems.

I think we shall have responsible union behavior when—and only when—union members require it from their leaders. A union leader does not care what management thinks of him. He often has little concern for what government officials think of him. He has or pretends to have control of many votes which the public official badly wants. The only way the conduct of union leaders can be influenced is by the opinions and votes of union members. Except in a few dictatorial unions, union leaders *do* respond to that.

If all this is true, and I believe it is, then we can have labor peace only through the long, slow, and painful process of education. Not education by classroom methods necessarily, but education in the sense of the sharing of a common body of knowledge and the acceptance of mutual standards for behavior.

How are we to get those things? Who is to be educated, by whom, and along what lines? Starting with the "Who," if I were selecting the groups most immediately important, I should say certainly the employees; certainly management itself; certainly the high-school and college teachers; certainly the press and radio. And through those groups, of course, the government and the general public.

Is this a job that industry can do? To a large extent, I believe it is but not entirely. I am not talking just about what is usually called "telling industry's story." I agree that we have to do that. But I point out to you that, as far as these other groups are concerned, we cannot expect them to accept what management says as the final word. As matters now stand, industrial management is one party to a controversy and we must expect that the outsider will scrutinize what we say critically. He is entitled to do that.

What kind of education do we need for these groups I have mentioned? Suppose we look at ourselves first, at management. What do we need to learn to do?

I think we must learn to be much franker than we have been in the past, much more candid about all our actions and decisions and ideas. I do not see how we can expect to create trust and confidence and understanding if, in our businesses, we have many doors we will not open. We cannot expect employees to come to the same conclusions we come to unless employees have the same facts we have. We must get over the old idea that all information except the most routine is confidential.

I think also that we will have to distinguish more sharply, and especially in collective bargaining, between genuine questions of principle and matters which are really just questions of advantage. We should not wrap ourselves in a banner of so-called principle when we are really concerned only with economic advantage. And we should be prepared, on questions of genuine principle, to stand firm against the heaviest economic pressure.

What about our employees? Along what lines would we like to see them better educated? First, beyond question, in the economics of our own businesses, what we do, why we do it that way, how it affects them, what plans we have for the future, who our competitors are, what our relative position is, what our profits are, who gets them, what share employees receive from the proceeds of the business, and all the hundreds of other questions that will give them solid knowledge.

Second, I think employees need to know more about capitalism and its merits and demerits and its necessities. I think they can best gain that in terms of the operations of their own company, but I think it must be taught. Finally, I think employees need to know more about how to belong to a union. They need to be taught that the union exists for them and not they for the union leaders, encouraged to state their views, exercise their power, take part in union affairs, steer the union in the direction they want it to go.

Then we have the press and radio group. I believe I have some understanding of the many problems of news gathering and the difficulties of trying to report all phases of human activity. I do not intend to be captious and I hope my editorial friends will excuse me when I say that the reporting of labor-relations matters leaves a great deal to be desired.

It seems to me the labor-relations problem is at least as important to this country as the behavior of the stock market or the results of professional football games. I wish we might more often have in labor news the same wonderful technical competence that is lavished upon sport news. No editor would send a police reporter or political writer to do the main story on the World Series. Yet how many labor stories are treated primarily in the terms appropriate to a political convention or a riot.

Would it be presumptuous to suggest that a man covering labor news should have some knowledge of wage payment systems, of the ordinary provisions of union contracts, of the organization and functioning of manufacturing industry, of the organization and functioning of unions? There are a limited number of such qualified reporters now. I hope there will be many more. Speaking for my own company, if we can assist in their training, we will be most happy to do so.

Finally, I mentioned the teachers, both high school and college. We must especially hope for improvement here, for their teaching will influence labor peace far into the future. I agree that we must make greater efforts to submit to the teachers facts we would like them to know. But even more important, I believe, is that we encourage them to come to us for facts *they* would like to know—and that we open all doors for them when they do come.

Over and beyond that, I solicit the attention of the great university research groups and other research groups and foundations. I ask their attention to a new type of problem. Over the years, the graduate schools and the research groups have done a fine job of collecting information on what is done. If you want to know the details of employee security plans at Standard Oil, they can tell you. If you want to know the status of foreman training at General Motors, they can tell you that. They are marvelous at reporting.

May I suggest to them that they turn a part of their attention, not to what is being done but to what *ought* to be done?

We need a basic philosophy of labor relations, accepted by the public and by all parties, if we are to have labor peace. It can be hammered out by years of trial and error. Perhaps it has to be done that way. On the other hand, perhaps the research groups can speed the process and point to new directions.

They have knowledge. They are genuinely disinterested. They have prestige. They can suggest standards and be free from any suspicion that might attach to such suggestions coming from unions or from industry or from government. May we have the benefits of their creative thinking?

Those are the things I wanted to say to you today. It may be there is no merit in them. Perhaps I have only added to the existing confusion.

The road I think we must follow to labor peace is a long one. It is a difficult one. But I do not believe there is a shorter route. I do not believe the task is impossible. We live in a country which was founded on the belief that the individual human being is important, that he is capable of self-government, that he will accept and exercise responsibility and authority. So whatever is done in the United States must be done by persuading the minds and arousing the consciences of men.

Sooner or later—and I hope sooner—we must set out on this same familiar road if we are to have genuine labor peace.

Business, Government, and Education
Paul G. Hoffman

The occasion of the address below was the Victory Dinner of the Massachusetts Institute of Technology Development Program, held at the Waldorf-Astoria Hotel in New York on 3 May 1951. It was in honor of Mr. Alfred P. Sloan, Jr., Chairman of the Board of the General Motors Corporation. Mr. Hoffman was invited to speak by Dr. Karl Compton and, as he says, he "jumped at the invitation . . . simply because I am one of the millions of Americans who are grateful for M.I.T."

Paul G. Hoffman became president and director of the Ford Foundation after a brilliant success as the administrator of the Marshall Plan. He was born in Chicago on 26 April 1891 and with a year's study at the University of Chicago (1908-09) began as an automobile salesman for the Studebaker Corporation in Los Angeles in 1911. By 1935 he had become president of Studebaker and in April 1948, when President Truman was seeking the best qualified person to head the Economic Coöperation Administration, he selected Mr. Hoffman. He had achieved a considerable reputation as an organizer of the Committee for Economic Development and for his services as chairman of its board of trustees from 1942 to 1948.

When Mr. Hoffman resigned as head of the Economic Recovery Program on 30 September 1950 he declared that the program was defeating Communism in Western Europe and urged that a recovery program there should be continued. His appointment as director of the Ford Foundation, the largest public trust in the world, was announced on 6 November 1950. *Peace Can Be Won,* Mr. Hoffman's book on how "peace can be waged through reconstruction, persuasion, and economic aid in a world divided by cold war," was published in the spring of 1951.

The text printed here is a shorter form of the address as delivered.

A GREAT MANY momentous things have occurred here and abroad during the past generation, and I often think that the sensations and alarms thrust before our eyes almost every day must certainly distract us from many of the really significant developments of our times. These are the slow yet certain forward movements in human affairs that seldom if ever gain the headlines.

I would like to discuss with you this evening one of these basic shifts in the American pattern. It is a shift that already has had a great impact on our way of life, and in my opinion will have an even greater impact in the years ahead. It is also a subject very appropriate for discussion here, because in many ways M.I.T. and the men we are here to honor this evening stand as dynamic symbols of this development.

When the United States of America set up shop in 1776 it was just as highly compartmentalized as a modern department store. Each State insisted upon absolute sovereignty with a vigor that for a time strained the young republic at the seams. This feeling of separatism, naturally enough, ran through the whole society. Religion demanded that it be left severely alone by everybody—particularly by government and competing sects.

Farmers and businessmen put up big "no trespassing" signs over their particular areas of activity. Education was simultaneously erecting its structures in yet another clearly walled-off sector of society.

I am not decrying this period in our history. It is certainly clear to me that it was the one possible way of carrying out, in those times, the firm intention of the founders that government must serve as the people's agent in certain matters, and in those matters alone, and that it shouldn't be allowed to meddle in other areas. Our fathers knew the danger of governmental tyranny. And given the economic and political conditions of the late eighteenth and nineteenth centuries, the extension of this feeling into other parts of the new society was inevitable.

This was an era of insularity, and it lasted a long time. It took a Civil War to bring an end to this political era by driving home to Americans everywhere that political compartmentalization of the various States probably wasn't the best approach to its problems that an expanding nation might take.

The notion that businessmen and farmers and educators and workers also had that they could remain aloof from one another began to give way shortly after the Civil War. In one way or other, each group began to venture forth from its sacrosanct cubbyhole. Farmers began to perceive that businessmen and workers were customers. Educators started to move off their campuses and out into the world of affairs, a move vastly stimulated by land-grant colleges. And the American public decided it was about time for their government to take a hand in regulating those business affairs they thought were getting dangerously big and hard to handle.

The trend began with the Interstate Commerce Commission, and shortly thereafter, in the early years of this century, trust-busting moved from political platform to political fact. Campaign slogans turned into the Sherman Anti-Trust Act, the Clayton Act, and the Federal Trade Commission.

Yet, when we came to the end of the First World War, the myth of insularity among government, business, and education still had a potent hold on the minds of Americans. I have not asked any historians or social scientists about this, but I suspect that this feeling had its roots deep in a conviction that we could only preserve our freedom if we managed somehow to keep business as far as possible out of the hands of government, and government as far as possible out of the hands of business; if we could keep business from meddling in education, and educators from throwing their weight around in government, and so forth.

It is perhaps accurate to say that during the 1920's many of us still believed that the place for educators was in ivory towers, and that businessmen and employees were likely to prove troublesome as soon as they moved out of corporation board rooms and union halls. They certainly still felt that the national interest might be imperiled if government built anything more than a footbridge across the Potomac into either of these other areas. It was only dawning on us slowly that the United States was a whole machine that depended for efficient operation on the smooth meshing together of its various parts.

Parenthetically, I might say here it seems to me very possible that this feeling of insularity extended well over into the field of international relations and found disastrous expression in our failure as a nation to give effective support to the League of Nations.

Then came the national depression. Many of our national myths went into the ashcan, among them the notion that certain major activities could be walled off and left to their own devices. No one can look back on the depression and say that it was a mighty good experience, because it wasn't. In addition to the untold human hardship the depression brought with it, it produced the immediate and astonishing reaction to national insecurity which we promptly dubbed "government planning."

From a nation dedicated to individualism, both the rugged and not-so-rugged varieties, we turned into a nation which appeared to see its sole chance for survival in programs written in Washington.

I do not want to dwell on these sad memories. But I do want to point out here that in going through the agonies of picking up the pieces, we happened upon two related and significant truths: First, we discovered the value of unified effort in the face of common peril. Second, we discovered that a partnership of business, government, and education—a working recognition of interdependence, in short—was not the big bad wolf we had always thought it to be, but that on the contrary, it was an absolute condition for continued progress.

In my opinion, this blending of social forces will, in fifty years, be remarked on by historians as a development of outstanding significance. Because we are so close to the scene, we are probably not as aware as we should be of, first, how this partnership is actually taking form, and, second, its possible meaning for the foreseeable future.

The offices and factories of many of our large corporations today are being used as classrooms by neighboring colleges. Employers and employees seek the coöperation of our great educational institutions in their search for fair answers to hard questions that trouble them. The businessmen of the Committee for Economic Development find more than enthusiastic response among the teachers of the country for its workshop program in the teaching of basic economics—a situation that would have been unthinkable even twenty-five years ago.

Government turns hungrily to both business and education for help and guidance across the whole field of national life. These days it is not unusual for all three elements in our society to join around a single table to work out common problems.

The important phrase here is "common problems." In recognizing mutual problems and objectives, we have come to realize that we are not infringing on the freedoms that are uppermost in our national consciousness, but in fact are taking long steps toward giving them substance and safeguarding them. Freedom without law and order and unity is an empty word.

I have been referring here only to the peacetime forms of this new partnership. There is no need to point out the obvious about its enormous contribution during World War II.

In replacing the walls between the major groups in the United States with windows and doors, we may well have started a reconstruction job which portends far more than any of us can guess. I suggest that it has much more meaning than merely the fact that a great many professors are now on cordial speaking terms with a great many bankers and union representatives, and that businessmen and government officials can get together without blasting the pictures off the wall of the meeting room. Indeed, we may be discovering how to forge the links that will hold our country together at a particularly critical moment in history. We may be discovering that freedom and dignity can be preserved far better by partnership than by compartmentalized action.

And even more important, we may find in it a most useful lesson in the task of bringing free men together in a common front for winning the peace.

For if we have found out that compartmentalization is an outmoded way of life within our own society—in our industries—in our political structure—why can we not say to the rest of the world that it will not work among nations?

The Trustees of the Ford Foundation are so certain that absolute top priority must be given to the question of man's relationship to man and the preservation of free peoples and institutions that they have put the resources of that great enterprise wholly into programs aimed at that single grand target.

The Trustees saw that unless people somehow, some way, found positive means for waging the peace, all other efforts to better the surroundings and the dignity of man would only end up in atomic rubble.

I joined the Ford Foundation because I share that view completely.

I came away from two and one-half years with the Economic Coöperation Administration with twin convictions that I hold with all my mind and heart: First, an enduring peace built on freedom and justice can be won if the free people of the world will dedicate themselves unreservedly to the task. Second, peace can be won only if free people everywhere lock arms so tightly in the common cause that no force can tear them apart.

I have called those two statements personal convictions. I want to go farther and call them facts, hard facts that you must wrap your minds around.

It is horribly strange but also horribly true that while there never seems to be too much difficulty about mobilizing nations for war, mobilizing them for peace is quite a different matter. Many people still seem to be making the error of looking on peace negatively as a mere absence of war. But I say to you that unless we consecrate ourselves as wholly to winning the peace as we have from time to time consecrated ourselves to military victory, the prospects are dim indeed. Peace has to be worked at, not dreamed about and left to someone else.

The reason we have to lock arms is simplicity itself. No single nation has the resources to stand up against an onslaught from the Soviet Union and its satellites—not even the United States, mighty though it is. The free nations can win the peace only if they stand together—work together—and wage the peace together. But if we do lock arms and add the resources of Western Europe to those of North America, we will have a commanding advantage over any possible combination of adversaries.

Almost every day I hear or read something which indicates a feeling that Western Europe can be regarded as a relatively unimportant part of the earth, a weak sister with nothing in particular to contribute. To say that such views dismay me is a masterpiece of understatement.

Western Europe has a population of 275,000,000—men and women of the same stock and outlook and background of most of the fine people in these United States. That's 100,000,000 more people than live in this country and Canada put together.

I don't want to bore you with statistics, but these are a few typical comparisons I think every American should paste firmly in his hat.

The combined coal production of the United States and Western Europe is 965 million metric tons a year. The annual coal production figure for the U.S.S.R. and its satellites is much less than half as much —386 million metric tons. Annual power production in the U.S. and Western Europe together total 612 billion kilowatt hours. The combined Soviet total is 132 billion kilowatt hours.

We and our free neighbors in Western Europe have a crude steel production capacity of 137 million metric tons, against a behind-the-curtain total of 34.8 million metric tons. And there is more than six times more oil production annually on our side than there is on the side of the Soviet's—272 million metric tons against 44 million metric tons.

I suggest that the question comes down to this: Have we any choice except to mobilize these great stockpiles of free traditions and materials into a single giant drive for peace?

Throughout Western Europe and the rest of the free world that question is being asked of the United States, and like the Ancient Mariner's wedding guest, we cannot choose but hear.

But as the free world stands today, mobilization for winning the peace can only be as effective as American leadership and hope will make it.

And a new kind of leadership is called for. . . . In a modern, interdependent world there is no room for dictator nations. American leadership must be that of a leader among equals. It must depend on persuasion rather than coercion, on understanding rather than edicts.

But before we can lead we must unite.

We must unite to make sure we are strong, first of all on the military front. With our free partners in Western Europe, we need military strength of an order which will effectively discourage or defeat aggression. This, may I point out, is military strength quite different from the manpower and firepower needed to conquer a particular country.

We must unite to be strong on the economic front. Our first and greatest obligation is to keep our country strong. And we must keep other free nations strong by helping them to help themselves.

We must unite to be strong on the political front. If we really cherish the dream of a free world, we quite clearly must put all our vigor behind the institutions that are designed to unite honorable nations for the common defense of peace—the United Nations and the Atlantic Pact.

We must unite for strength on the propaganda front. The false promises of Communism across the Voice of Moscow can be heard daily by some 800,000,000 people. The importance of this figure is clear when we learn that at the end of the war only 200,000,000 people were within range of the Kremlin's transmitters.

I say to you that we don't stand a chance of leading the free world to peace unless we can stop quarreling among ourselves and hating one another. The very least we can do for ourselves, the free world, and for our hundreds of thousands of men in Korea is to save our hate for our foes, unite here at home, and knuckle tightly down to the job of winning the peace.

If we really mean what we say about wanting peace, first, last, and always, we have got to have unity—among ourselves and with our friends. And there are some practical tests we can use right at this moment to determine whether unity is lip service or a fact.

The first practical test is the extent to which we back up General Eisenhower in Europe, and the second, General Ridgway in Korea and Japan. Where General Eisenhower is concerned, we all know that we have in him the ideal Supreme Commander for the new European army. He has the power to inspire, the capacity to develop a workable program, and the toughness to see to it that every country carries its fair share of the burden of defense.

And without involving myself in the controversy over General MacArthur, I should like to urge that we stand back of General Ridgway with everything we have got. Any dissension here at home will be marked up on the bitter scoreboard of Korea.

The third test is the intelligence and common sense we display in our support of foreign aid programs to help our free world partners to rearm and in the process to keep their own economies strong and healthy. A withdrawal of all aid could well lead to disunity and even disaster.

The logistics of a successful campaign for peace are not simple. They are fantastically involved. The supply problem covers the world. It includes food, rehabilitation, transportation, measures to strengthen national economies, direct aid to exiles from countries behind the curtain, education, unity of purpose, and hope—to name only a few of the components of enduring peace that must be efficiently mustered.

But if we will only take to heart the lessons of interdependency in our own country, we can handle this fabulously difficult job so well that the last fifty years of the twentieth century may well be the brightest of all time.

Each moment in history is only as great as the challenge of the moment. For that reason alone I think we are living in a privileged period.

I would like to wind up my remarks tonight with the words of a man I revered as much as any American of our day. Arthur Vandenberg not long ago wrote me a letter from his sickbed. Referring to the unpartisan spirit which launched the ECA, he wrote: "This working unity typifies our finest traditions and our greatest safety in the presence of external hazards to all Americans, regardless of party. United, we stand. Divided, we fall. I want America to stand."

CIVIL RIGHTS AND LIBERTIES

The Rough Road Ahead
Roger N. Baldwin

Roger Baldwin describes himself as a political reformer. He was born at Wellesley, Massachusetts in 1884 and educated at Harvard (A.B., 1904; A.M., 1905). From 1906 to 1909 he taught sociology at Washington University in St. Louis. He then served as chief probation officer of the Juvenile Court of St. Louis (1907-10), secretary of the National Probation Association (1908-10), secretary of the St. Louis Civic League (1910-17) and in 1917 became director of the American Civil Liberties Union. He is presently Board Chairman of the International League for the Rights of Man, a UN consultant agency. His writings include *Juvenile Courts and Probation* (1912), *Liberty under the Soviets* (1928), and *Civil Liberties and Industrial Conflict* (1938) and various pamphlets on civil liberties.

This address was broadcast from New York over a CBS radio network on 22 February 1950. The occasion was the 30th Anniversary dinner of the American Civil Liberties Union and Mr. Baldwin was the guest of honor and principal speaker.

The reader is referred to six lectures published under the title, *Civil Liberties Under Attack*, edited by Clair Wilcox (1951). The lecturers are Henry Steele Commager, Zechariah Chafee, Jr., James P. Baxter III, Robert K. Carr, Walter Gellhorn, and Curtis Bok.

DESPITE A not unnatural aversion to accepting as personal recognition what in fact belongs to all of us in the Civil Liberties Union, this thirtieth anniversary is inescapably something of a personal milestone. It marks not a retirement in the usual sense, but rather, may I say, a change of life—not in the usual sense.

I move from the duties of an office handling our many-sided tasks to the special concerns of international civil liberties. I do so both on behalf of the Union on all issues where the United States is involved, and on behalf of the International League for the Rights of Man (which includes the women as well) in the universal struggle for democratic liberties. That League, with which the Union is affiliated, is recognized by the United Nations as a consultant. Its honorary president, Henri Laugier of France, here with us tonight, doubles also as assistant general secretary of the United Nations—an unusual dual personality, official and unofficial.

Despite the confusions of a divided and disordered world, civil liberties stand out for the first time in history as top political issues. Both in our Congress and the United Nations they are the fighting front of democratic expansion. They have split the Democratic Party and thrown more than usual confusion into the Republican. In the not-so-United Nations they split the delegations into those who regard all liberties as the possessions of sovereign peoples and those who regard them as the gracious gifts of governments.

But these splits plainly put into the minority those who reject the common principles both of our Bill of Rights and of the Universal Declaration of Human Rights adopted by the United Nations—with, of course, Soviet and satellite abstentions. Those principles are bound to win out, both in the adoption sooner or later of the civil rights program by Congress and in the international Bill of Rights shortly to be written by the United Nations Commission headed by Mrs. Roosevelt. Already they are embodied in the first convention in history, adopted by the United Nations, for freedom of news and newsreels as between the nations. It will before long come before our Senate for ratification, just as another unprecedented United Nations convention, that on genocide, is now before the Senate.

These efforts may look to some like mere scraps of paper in a world where force still rules. But they mark the beginnings, however feeble and groping, of a system of universal rights in law for all men and women everywhere, on which alone one world can be built when the present two-world tensions subside. Enforcement through a world court and United Nations machinery, now merely sketched, will surely follow. Even the outlines of ultimate world government through them are now visible—to optimists.

It is on that long and not entirely desperate chance that I pit my faith. The practical work for these ends lies for me in the non-governmental agencies of citizens throughout the democratic world. Those popular pressures more than governments, together with the independent press and radio, will largely shape the direction and force of progress.

These democratic forces even in these advanced United States have a formidable task to bring American foreign policy in line with a genuine democratic internationalism. Does our government not too often by-pass the United Nations to buttress its regional interests in cold war strategy? Does it not too often embrace as allies in the containment of Communism those reactionary regimes whose only dubious virtue is their anti-Communism, and whose certain vice is the encouragement of the very Communism they fear? Does our government not too often fail to support abroad those progressive forces and regimes which are not only the most effective opponents of police states of right or left, but the only sure foundations for world democracy?

I presume we all sense in high places the assumption that whatever is good for the United States is good enough for the world, while international morality demands the reverse. Thus in Congress and out we hear democratic socialism confused with police-state Communism because both are opposed to the American system of free private enterprise, and hence, they add, to civil liberties. Could any concept be more disastrous to what we as the strongest democracy profess we desire, an ordered democratic world of free nations—not all in our own image?

But it is possible that our popular forces can democratize by their pressures our foreign policy just as they so largely have democratized our national life these last thirty years. Our country has moved in that time from an era of force and violence in race and labor conflict to an era of reasonably peaceful progress by law. It has moved from the chaos of local controls of our civil liberties to federal controls, and indeed protections—to what Republican leaders call "statism." Our Supreme Court has affirmed in a long series of decisions those rights and liberties recognized only a few years ago in the dissents of Justices Holmes and Brandeis. There are still dissents, but not often on our side. And I might add that the Civil Liberties Union has moved in these years from a position of suspected subversion to one of unexpected respectability. The times have caught up with us; we have not changed.

But the times offer only more challenges to our efforts in this hot climate of cold war. Behind the cold war, I venture to suggest, lies a revolutionary transition toward political world unity, toward an ordered world economy and toward internal democracy. Our rough road at home in this transition to more democracy lies through overcoming first our greatest national failure—inequality in law and opportunity based on race and national origin. We cannot rest content until we have abolished totally the indefensible notion of "separate and equal" accommodations for the races, nor until we have won for every citizen the protections of civil rights in work, housing, education, government, and public accommodations. Until our country does so, its moral authority in international councils will remain, as it is today, questionable.

Another task before us arising from the furor over Communism is to help keep the Communist Party in the open, above ground, instead of driving it into a completely underground conspiracy. Only the maintenance of civil liberties for that party as of all others not guilty of actual violence, squares with our principles. Even J. Edgar Hoover agrees with that—which should, but doesn't, make it unanimous.

It should be accepted as axiomatic that Communism can be defeated only by a democracy so strong in satisfying the demands of progress that Communism will be robbed of its appeal. We have a strong democracy despite its weak spots, despite our present jitters, despite the arms race, despite the contradictions of foreign policy. But it will progress only in the measure that all of us democratic disturbers of the status quo make our pressures insistently effective. As one of the disturbers, the Civil Liberties Union, with its militancy, integrity of purpose, and its not undeserved present respectability, has doubtless another thirty years of useful and tempestuous life ahead.

I shall, I expect, share with you at least some of them.

National Security and Individual Freedom
Francis Biddle, Robert K. Carr, Adlai Stevenson, and Harold C. Urey; Alan Simpson, Moderator

This broadcast, made on 4 February 1951, celebrated the twentieth year of broadcasting by the University of Chicago Round Table.

Francis Biddle was the Attorney General of the United States from 1941 to 1945. During the following two years he was the United States member of the International Military Tribunal. He was born in Paris, France in 1886 and was brought to the United States as a young child. He was graduated from Harvard in 1909 and the Harvard Law School in 1911. During the following year he was private secretary to Justice Oliver Wendell Holmes. He is the author of *Mr. Justice Holmes* (1942), *Democratic Thinking and the War* (1944), and *The Fear of Freedom* (1951).

Robert K. Carr is Parker Professor of Law and Political Science at Dartmouth. In 1947 he was the Executive Secretary of the President's Committee on Civil Rights. Born in Cleveland, Ohio in 1908 he studied at Dartmouth (A.B., 1929) and Harvard (A.M., 1930; Ph.D., 1935). He taught at the University of Oklahoma from 1931 to 1937 before going to Dartmouth. He is the author of *Democracy and the Supreme Court* (1936), *The Supreme Court and Judicial Review* (1942), and *Federal Protection of Civil Rights* (1947).

Adlai Stevenson, the present governor of Illinois, is a Princeton graduate (A.B., 1922). He was born in Los Angeles, California in 1900. During World War II he was Assistant to the Secretary of the Navy. He has also served as Adviser to the Secretary of State (1945), as Adviser to the U.S. Delegation to the San Francisco Conference on International Organization (1945), as U.S. delegate, Preparatory Commission on the United Nations, and as U.S. delegate to the General Assembly in 1946 and 1947.

Harold C. Urey was the winner of the Nobel Prize in Chemistry in 1934. He is now Distinguished Service Professor of Chemistry in the Department of Chemistry and in the Institute for Nuclear Studies at the University of Chicago. Born in Walkerton, Indiana in 1893, he studied at the University of Montana (B.S., 1917) and at the University of California (Ph.D., 1923). He taught at the University of Montana, Johns Hopkins University, and Columbia University before being called to the University of Chicago in 1945. He is the discoverer of the hydrogen atom of atomic weight two and conducted the research for the production of heavy water and for U^{235}, the vital element of the atomic bomb. Professor Urey was a leading member of the chemistry division of the atomic bomb project at the University of Chicago.

MR. SIMPSON: On Sunday morning, February 1, 1931, three professors of the University of Chicago gathered around an old-fashioned carbon microphone to discuss the Wickersham report on prohibition. From that moment there began the first regularly scheduled educational program in the history of radio. It was christened "The Round Table," after a certain well-known table in the dining room of the faculty club of the University. Today is the twentieth anniversary of that Sunday morning.

In establishing the Round Table, the University of Chicago seized upon a new means of fortifying an old ideal. The undertaking was ambitious, but the principles involved were clear:

First, radio was a unique and massive instrument for molding the American mind.

Second, it was the duty of a university to use this instrument as a means of universal education.

Third, its platform should provide a hearing for the best available talent inside and outside the national community. It should seek to unite all the resources of leadership in a joint examination of our problems, our hopes, and our failures.

Fourth, this platform should try to provide a model for every form of purposeful discussion in which free and responsible men engage.

Lastly, acting in the image of the educational ideal, no principles of exclusion should be admitted, except the principle which denies a hearing to passion, dishonesty, and incompetence.

There would be no ax to grind, no censorship, open or concealed.

These principles have never been sacrificed to widen the hearing or to solicit any interest narrower than the best interests of the American people. Yet, the hearing has widened, year after year; and the Round Table has won both the confidence of a national network and the loyalty of the stations which it serves. It is today the most widely heard program of its kind.

The role of American universities in radio, and of radio in American life, has been defined by Robert M. Hutchins as follows: "To formulate, to clarify, to vitalize the ideals which should animate mankind is the heavy burden which rests upon the universities. The task of the Round Table is candid and intrepid thinking about fundamental issues. Free discussion is a necessary condition of a free society. Where men cannot freely convey their thoughts to one another, no freedom is secure. Where freedom of expression exists, the beginnings of a free society and a means for every extension of liberty are already present."

On this anniversary date the Round Table will discuss one of the most vital issues confronting Americans today—the issue of national security and individual freedom.

To introduce our program, we first present, by transcription, the Honorable Adlai Stevenson, governor of Illinois.

GOVERNOR STEVENSON: The topic of today's Round Table, "National Security and Individual Freedom," seems to me most appropriate because this is the twentieth birthday of the Round Table. The University of Chicago has maintained this tradition of free discussion for twenty years of continuous broadcasting. And I wish that I could have participated personally in this Round Table discussion because the appointment this past week by President Truman of the Commission on Internal Security and Individual Rights, headed by Admiral Nimitz, reminds us again that we have failed miserably to find a way to protect ourselves against treason, sabotage, and other subversive acts, on the one hand, without destroying our traditional liberties, on the other.

The enormous, and enormously important, problem which the President has assigned this commission is, in short, to seek the widest balance that can be struck between security and freedom. It is high time—indeed, I think that it is past time—for a reasoned, impartial, objective study of the closely related subjects of national security and individual freedom.

There have been too many wild, irresponsible accusations of disloyalty. The dreadful concept of "guilt by association" has been added to our language. The slanderer is honored. The shadow of suspicion and fear slopes across our land. There is even talk of thought control among Thomas Jefferson's people.

Fear for the integrity of one's good name and the security of one's job has spread like a pall through government, stifling initiative and depriving us of valuable manpower.

On the other hand, this is a national emergency. The world, the free world which we have known, is in danger. Believing as we do in the community of free nations and of free peoples acting peacefully and responsibly through governments freely chosen, we conclude at last that we cannot live in comfortable security with a great imperial power which has seen the barriers to its expansion collapse and is on the move again—taking here, probing there, and pressing relentlessly against the uncommitted, discontented millions of the earth. Capitalizing the old zeal of the Russian people to missionize the world, the leaders of the new Russia, armed with force and the old weapon of fomented revolution, use this seductive new weapon of Communism to soften their victims. But whatever the trappings, the methods, the weapons, the objective is domination—imperialism.

And America, rich, peaceful, and undisciplined, now finds itself face to face with this inscrutable, ruthless conqueror, strong, cunning, and armed with an egalitarian idea which has great appeal for the miserable masses of humanity. No longer is there anyone to protect us. No longer can we sow where and when we are certain to reap. There is no safe investment, no certain harvest, any longer.

So we have concluded, at last, that we must rearm and help all our like-minded friends to rearm. We have concluded that the balance of power in the world must once again be redressed; we have concluded that the free world to continue free must stand fast against aggression and must hastily confront imperial Communism with a preponderance of power.

Against that backdrop of danger a group of sane, responsible men have been assigned the task of diagnosing this national neurosis, the fear of subversive activity within our gates, and to prescribe for an affliction which has been aggravated by the very genuine—indeed, the mortal—danger from without.

The most important goal, as most objective observers agree, is to achieve some sanity and balance in an area of our national thinking which is dangerously out of balance.

MR. SIMPSON: Thank you, Governor Stevenson.

Now, to continue our twentieth anniversary Round Table discussion, we hear Francis Biddle, formerly Attorney General of the United States. To present Mr. Biddle, we take you now to Washington.

MR. BIDDLE: I do not believe that keeping our country internally secure conflicts with the problem of individual freedom. On the contrary, respect for individual freedom is necessary if we are to sustain internal strength and unity. A regimented America, based on the worship of orthodoxy, is not a strong America.

Spies are always a threat, particularly in times like these. We must be eternally vigilant to catch them. But spies are not caught by loyalty oaths and loyalty tests and requirements that Communists register.

Seth Richardson, formerly chairman of the Loyalty Review Board, testified before a Senate committee that the loyalty investigations—and I quote his language—"had not produced one single case of espionage or turned up any evidence directing toward espionage." Spies are caught by patient, quiet, persistent counterespionage. This we have in the Federal Bureau of Investigation.

The men, chiefly politicians, who say that our public institutions are filled with Communists are testifying falsely. Our public institutions are sound; our public servants overwhelmingly are loyal. The constant attack on their loyalty has created an increasing distrust and disunity in the mind of the public.

The obsession increases day by day. Fear of Russia, and of war, has now become fear of liberalism, fear of change, fear of independent thinking, fear, in fact, of being called "Communist." It finds expression in the strange procedures of the Un-American Activities Committee of the House and in similar committees of State legislatures. Teachers are investigated. The American Bar Association would have lawyers take test oaths. Jean Muir is dropped, though later reinstated, from her radio spot on unfounded charges. Pearl Buck and Marquis Childs are not allowed to speak at a public school in the District of Columbia. Attempts are made to smear Anna Rosenberg. McCarthyism, violent and obscurantist, takes hold. The big lies are reiterated until many believe them. Congress, on the eve of an election, hurries through the ill-considered and inept McCarran Law, afraid to resist the spread of thought control.

We seem to have forgotten the hysterical years which followed the first World War—the two thousand sedition trials, the infamous Palmer raids, the application of guilt by association to the five socialists who were ousted from the New York Assembly over the passionate protest of Charles Evans Hughes, later chief justice of the United States Supreme Court. Now there are but few protests, notably, among them,

President Conant of Harvard, Chancellor Hutchins of the University of Chicago, and those scientists who have seen what all this is doing to the free exchange of scientific knowledge, so essential to the growth and to the vitality of our technical equipment.

Our freedom has made us great and strong, but Jefferson's philosophy is forgotten—forgotten his own full tide of successful experiment which has kept us free and firm, as he said, kept us the strongest government on earth. We no longer have that faith in ourselves, in our traditions of freedom.

"Liberty," wrote Walt Whitman, "relies upon itself; invites no one; promises nothing; sits in calmness and light; is positive and composed; and knows no discouragement."

When the laws of the free are grudgingly permitted and laws of informers and spies are sweet to the taste of the people, then only shall the instinct of liberty be discharged from that part of the earth.

MR. SIMPSON: Thank you, Mr. Biddle. You and Governor Stevenson have posed the problem of maintaining our internal security and yet preserving our traditional freedom.

To discuss this problem we now turn to Robert Carr, executive secretary of the President's Committee on Civil Rights and professor of government at Dartmouth College, and to Harold C. Urey, Nobel-Prize winning atomic scientist and professor of chemistry at the University of Chicago.

Mr. Urey, are you worried about our security?

MR. UREY: No. I believe that the United States of America is in a very, very strong position—much stronger than the various people who are discussing this subject would think. I believe that the future belongs to us, not to the totalitarian governments. We are celebrating a twentieth anniversary. I would like to look forward, in discussing this problem, to twenty or even fifty years ahead. The future belongs to the democratic, free way of life, not to the totalitarian way of life.

MR. CARR: Absolutely. I hope that throughout all this discussion of our problem of security we can remember that as a nation we are strong and not weak.

At the same time we must be sure that in winning through over this period of twenty years or more that we do not destroy the very thing which we are fighting to save—our free way of life.

MR. UREY: I agree that it is very well to look far ahead, as I think we should. But I think that it is an excellent idea to remember that we accomplish a long objective only by looking after immediate details, and these immediate details should not be overlooked.

MR. CARR: It might be well, at the very beginning here, to review briefly the present program which is being followed to assure loyalty and security and at the same time to maintain individual freedom.

On the part of government, for example, we have the FBI, which is the detective agency which is seeking to enforce our traditional laws against espionage and sabotage. We have developed, in the last two or three years, an executive loyalty program, which seeks to measure the loyalty of our federal employees. We have on our statute books such things as the Smith and the McCarran acts. We have had various prosecutions of individuals under these investigation laws. We have had several Congressional investigating committees, best known among which, of course, is the House Un-American Activities Committee.

MR. UREY: As Mr. Biddle said, a moment ago, there have been a great many ways in which investigations of various kinds have also gone into our universities. The investigations assume that our universities are honeycombed with disloyal persons—something which has never been true in my experience and, well, I have spent a very large fraction of my life in universities.

We have also had the various "red channels," books which are published purporting to give us a list of all the Communists in the United States and listing among them quite prominent people. Does my memory deceive me? I think that Mrs. Franklin D. Roosevelt was on one of these.

MR. CARR: That is right.

MR. UREY: State-level investigations, as Mr. Biddle said, have also taken place during these last years. The most notable example is the investigation of the University of California by its Board of Regents. We have had the demand for loyalty oaths on the part of universities, State employees, government employees—even county and city employees. All these various things have been tried in recent years.

MR. CARR: And, now, of course, we have the Nimitz Commission—a group of eminent private citizens who have been appointed as a presidential advisory body; and it must consider the basic problem of reconciling our liberty and our authority in the age in which we live.

It must, of course, ask itself certain questions. One of the most important questions which I think it must constantly keep in mind is this: What is the price that we do have to pay for these efforts—governmental and otherwise—to maintain security and to insure loyalty? We are paying a price in a good many different ways.

MR. UREY: Yes, and it is a very high price, from time to time. Might I just mention the price which has been paid, and is being paid, by certain individuals. Many individuals in the United States have been accused of being disloyal. There has been no satisfactory proof which would stand up in a court of law, in most cases, leveled against them. They find themselves with damaged reputations. They find the possibility of securing satisfactory employment much more difficult than they expected. Their whole lives are changed as a result of this.

Of course, we may say that it is true that young men are being killed in Korea, too, and that we should not be too sensitive about a few individuals. However, the boys in Korea are being killed by the enemy. In the United States reputations are being destroyed by people who claim to be the most ardent supporters of the American way of life.

MR. CARR: Then, too, there is the price which we are paying in the area of government. We live in a difficult time. Our government must be strong and vigorous and efficient. We need able personnel in government; and yet it is quite clear that the emphasis which has been put in recent years upon loyalty and security is making it difficult to procure able men for government service. We need, in the government service, men who have imaginations and curiosity, who are tough-minded. Yet loyalty attempts persuade these employees to play things safe, to think no unusual thoughts, to have no dangerous associations, to read no radical books.

The effect, I think, at the level of government personnel, can prove to be very serious, indeed, in these years ahead, as we face these serious problems.

MR. UREY: And also, along exactly a similar line, the whole effect of this loyalty hysteria, which is what I believe it is, is to make people in all walks of life play it safe—think nothing original, nothing new. This is true of our private universities, our State universities. We expect our universities and our colleges to originate new ideas, to train our youth in original thinking and logical thinking; and this, I think, is quite impossible if all the time the professor or the administrative officer has to worry about being accused of being a Communist because he expresses an idea which perhaps is not exactly in agreement with something which someone else in the community thinks.

You see, this thing spreads away from charges of Communism, away from sabotage, away from being a traitor, into being merely different from what someone else would like to have you be. And I think that there has been a very damaging effect upon our universities in the last years because of this hysteria.

MR. CARR: And, above all, it seems to me that we are paying a price in terms of loss of national unity, a sense of strength. We have allowed all this emphasis upon loyalty to persuade us that we are weak when we are actually strong. We have allowed it to persuade us that our government is honeycombed with very dangerous subversive people. We have let one group of the people be stirred up against another group of the people.

MR. UREY: We have lost a faith, is that what you are saying, Carr?

MR. CARR: That is right.

MR. UREY: We have lost a faith in one another, to begin with.

MR. CARR: You know, it has been suggested, again and again, along the way, that in the background of all this loyalty and security program there may really be a full-fledged Communist. It has been suggested that if an international Communist had been given the assignment of somehow sowing seeds of dissension and disunity in the United States, he could not very well have thought up anything more diabolically clever than what has been taking place in view of the loss of faith which you mention, in view of the dissension and the spirit of disunity which has been created.

MR. UREY: Every country such as ours which subscribes to the democratic tradition of Western Europe and the United States needs to have a loyal opposition in government and in public; and the opposition should always be regarded as loyal. It is not that we here plead for a traitorous element. We plead only that those who disagree with the majority should always have the privilege of disagreeing. And it is this fundamental right to disagree with the majority which is threatened by this sort of thing.

I often think that we are going over to a place where we regard anonymous informers as reliable. A police state does not consist of a large number of policemen on the corners; it consists of the police listening to anonymous informers; it is where every citizen of the country is a potential spy on every other citizen of the community; and the police will punish whoever is accused anonymously. This sort of thing, to a certain extent, has been practiced here in recent years, during what I regard as the security hysteria of these recent years.

MR. CARR: We do pay a price; there is no question of that. Now, the Nimitz Commission, it seems to me, must also ask itself the question: To what extent has our security program actually been protecting us?

MR. UREY: Well, scientifically very little, to tell the truth. It is very difficult to tell scientific secrets. It is true that we will have some crooks, some traitors. If you run a large operation, you will have some of these.

You should try to avoid them if you possibly can. But I would like to appeal to our fellow-citizens to realize that it is very, very difficult to sell or to tell scientific facts. It takes a very intelligent person to understand scientific facts. He must be highly trained. And, moreover, scientific matters are, in their nature, very difficult to conceal. If a person is determined to learn some scientific fact, you cannot prevent him from learning it for himself. Thus, the chemistry which takes place in the United States and in the U.S.S.R. is precisely the same. An intelligent person will get exactly the same answers from nature if he wants to ask the same questions. The geology of this country tells the story of the past history of the earth; it also tells it from the rocks in Russia. You cannot prevent the Russians from learning this, and the Russians cannot prevent us from learning it. And the uranium atom behaves just exactly the same on the two sides of the iron curtain. Any intelligent man who asks questions of it will get precisely the same answers. It is difficult, let me repeat, it is *difficult* to tell scientific facts to people, but it is almost impossible to prevent people from learning them, themselves, if they wish to.

MR. CARR: It is also clear, I think, from the evidence which we have accumulated that Congressional investigations and the executive loyalty program cannot provide us with complete security. One of the things that the House Un-American Activities Committee has done, for example, is to build up a file, one million names we are told, of individuals who are regarded as, in some sense, dangerous or potentially dangerous. Yet a short time ago, when the chemist in Philadelphia, Harry Gold, was arrested and charged with espionage, it was discovered that his name was not in that list of one million.

Somewhat later, Representative Nixon, a member of the Un-American Activities Committee, complained, in the House of Representatives, that the existing loyalty program would not have caught Alger Hiss at the time he was a member of the Department of State.

MR. UREY: Not only not catch him, but, as a matter of fact, no loyalty oath would ever make the traitor loyal anyhow, would it?

MR. CARR: That is the point. I cannot see that any possible loyalty program which we might ever devise, however efficient it could be, would find the hidden, true, dangerous subversive espionage agent in the government service.

Now, at the same time I think that we have probably got to concede that in this world in which we live we do need a security program, that we do have a security problem. We just cannot get away from it. But we have to keep in mind that there are certain fundamentals of democracy here which must never be forgotten as we go about the business of devising the satisfactory loyalty program.

For example, we have to recognize the ordinary fact that we can never completely eliminate the possibility of risk. Risk exists in the very nature of the case. We can be as certain as anything can be certain that there are going to be some espionage agents active in the next decade. It seems to me important that we not tear the house down in an attempt to eliminate, finally, all possible risk. That just cannot be done.

MR. UREY: Yes. We should not burn the house down to get a few rats is another way of saying precisely the same thing. We ought to remember that it is important to keep in mind, again, what we are trying to defend—the American way of life, as we often call it: the right to be accused in public of crimes; the right to a fair and open trial; the right to be faced by our accusers; the right to be regarded as innocent until proved guilty; and the belief that unusual and inhuman punishment should not be meted out. These things we must keep in mind while we hunt for a good security program.

MR. CARR: Yes. We have to have that in good security programs. We should also keep in mind that, however much we succeed in perfecting this program, a good loyalty program is necessarily a negative approach to this problem.

We also need to move ahead in terms of trying to maintain our national security in a positive way. Our great basic security here, it seems to me, is our democratic faith, our long-standing tradition of democracy. We must try to perfect our democracy in order to put our best foot forward, to lead from strength and not from weakness. We have come a great way. I would be the last person in the world to minimize the importance of the success which we have achieved in democracy, and yet we do have imperfections in our democratic system. We need to concentrate upon perfecting our democracy, and that should be a positive approach which ought to accompany this negative approach.

MR. UREY: I agree; and I really think that we should leave the security program in the hands of the regular investigating agencies, such as the FBI and the prosecution agencies of the governments and courts. Informers and informants are no good. Laws should be made to punish saboteurs and traitors.

In closing, I should like to say that I would like to repeat what I said at the very beginning. I believe that we are leading from strength in this problem. The future belongs to us; and if we will only remember that we are in an essentially strong position, that we have the correct view of what a government should be, that we have the correct regard for the rights of human beings—if we will only keep to this—our chances of winning out are very strong, indeed.

MR. CARR: Let us overcome this sense of terror that we seem to have picked up in the recent years. We have a problem. I would be the last person to minimize it, but let us remember the great strength of our nation. Let us carry on with our democratic traditions. Let us allow the rest of the world to see what a strong nation we have—what our way of life is like.

RACIAL PROBLEMS

The International Significance of Human Relations

Ralph J. Bunche

Ralph J. Bunche was born in Detroit in 1904. He studied at the University of California (A.B., 1927), Harvard (A.M., 1928; Ph.D., 1934), and has done post-doctoral research at Northwestern University, the London School of Economics, and the University of Cape Town, South Africa. Joining the faculty of Howard University in Washington in 1928, he became head of the department of political science there in 1929. During World War II he served as senior social science analyst in charge of research on Africa and other colonial areas in the British Empire section of the Office of Strategic Services (1941-44). In January 1945 he became chief of the division of dependent area affairs of the Department of State. When Count Folke Bernadotte, the United Nations mediator in Palestine, was assassinated there in 1948, Dr. Bunche took over as his successor. For the past three years he has been Director of the Department of Trusteeship of the United Nations. In September 1951 he assumed a professorship at Harvard.

Following his award of the Nobel Peace Prize in 1950, Dr. Bunche received a number of honorary degrees. In October 1951 he was appointed to the Educational Policies Commission, a joint group of the National Education Association and the American Association of School Administrators.

The address below was given at a Lincoln's birthday dinner in Springfield, Illinois, on 12 February 1951.

I AM DELIGHTED at this first opportunity to visit Springfield. It is particularly gratifying to be here—in a community in which he lived and worked—at this observation of the birthday of a man of rare greatness —the most stalwart figure of our nation's history.

It is not within my feeble capacity, or indeed, within the puny power of words, to do fair honor to Abraham Lincoln. It is not, perhaps, within the power of any of us among the living to do so, except as we may individually dedicate ourselves to the fulfillment of the imperative human objectives which he sought.

Lincoln was a man of great good will. The debt owed to him by our nation is incalculable. The legacy of human values which he bequeathed to us is priceless. Yet, like all of us, Lincoln was mortal, and being mortal, was fallible.

The problems which confronted him challenged to the utmost human wisdom and patience. The decisions he was called upon to make were momentous. A nation was at stake. It is no discredit to him that history records his moments of indecision, his groping, even his bows to political expediency. But in the crucial hours of decision, he found a boundless strength which flowed from his unwavering faith in the "plain people," from the equalitarianism of this great West in which he was reared, from his undecorated belief in the equality and dignity of man.

I have chosen to devote some attention today to the problem of human relations in the precarious world in which we live out our anxious existence. For this would seem to be peculiarly appropriate on this auspicious occasion.

Lincoln, himself, was called upon to save this nation from as great a crisis and conflict in human relations as has ever confronted any nation. And though he met the challenge and saved the nation, even Lincoln could not avert a cruel, tragic, devastating internecine war. Indeed, eighty-six years later, that war is still not fully liquidated, and at times it may seem not entirely clear who actually won it.

Moreover, it must be clear that the greatest danger to mankind today is still to be found in the deplorable human relations which everywhere prevail.

Were Lincoln alive today, I imagine that he could scarcely avoid taking a dark view of the relations among peoples the world over, not, by any means, excluding his own country. It would be understandable if even a quick survey of the current state of world and domestic affairs should induce in him one of those occasional moods of melancholia which some historians have attributed to him.

For what is the situation? The relations among peoples are broadly characterized by dangerous animosities, hatreds, mutual recriminations, suspicions, bigotries, and intolerances. Man has made spectacular progress in science, in transportation and communication, in the arts, in all things material. Yet, it is a matter of colossal and tragic irony that man, in all his genius, having learned to harness nature, to control the relations among the elements and to mold them to his will—even to the point where he now has the means readily at hand for his own virtual self-destruction—has never yet learned how to *live* with himself; he has not mastered the art of human relations. In the realm of human understanding the peoples of the world remain shockingly illiterate. This has always been and today remains man's greatest challenge: how to teach the peoples of the world the elemental lesson of the essential kinship of mankind and man's identity of interest.

We live in a most dangerous age—an age of supersonic airspeeds, of biological warfare, of atomic and hydrogen bombs, and who knows what next. In no exaggerated sense, we all today exist on borrowed time. If we of this generation deserve no better fate, surely our children do. They, certainly, can never understand why we could not do at least as well as the animal kingdom.

We need peace desperately. But the world has always needed peace. Today, however, the question is not the simple one of peace or war, as it has been in the past. The question now is sheer survival—survival of civilization, survival of mankind. And the time is short, frighteningly short.

How is the question to be answered? We may improvise, we may build diplomatic dams, we may pile international pact upon international pact. We may arm to the teeth and to the last ounce of our physical resources. But all this will never be enough so long as deep fears, suspicions, prejudices, and hatreds characterize the relations among the peoples of a now small world.

It is mankind, it is ourselves that we must fear more than the atomic or hydrogen bomb. It is in man's perversities, in his brooding suspicions, in his arrogances and intolerances, in his false self-righteousness and in his apathy that the real danger is to be found. In the final analysis, there is but one road to peace and that is the road of human understanding and fellow feeling, of inflexible determination to achieve peaceful relations among men. That, clearly, is a long, hard road, and today it is too little traveled.

If the relations among men were everywhere, or let us even say *most* everywhere, internationally and domestically, good, there would be little to fear. For then the free peoples of the world would have unassailable strength, and more than that, unwavering confidence in their ability to protect themselves collectively and fully against any maverick who might go on the loose. On the other side of the coin, bad human relations are, indeed, an encouragement and stimulus to the adventures of mavericks. It is on the disunity of peoples that dictators prey.

I am optimistic enough about my fellow beings to believe that it is human *attitudes*, not human nature, that must be feared—and changed. On the international scene, it is these attitudes which have brought the world to the menacing state of affairs of today—the ominous "localized" wars, the "cold war," the maneuverings for power and dominance, the dangerous rivalries, the propaganda battles—cannibalistic struggles in which ethical principles, and moral law are often callously jettisoned. If peoples could not be induced to suspect, to fear, and finally to hate one another, there could be no wars, for governments, from whatever motivations, can only lead peoples into wars—the peoples must fight them. And in these wars, countless numbers of human beings—by nature essentially good, whatever their immediate attitudes—must be sacrificed solely because the peoples of one society or another embark, or permit themselves to be embarked, upon fatal adventures of conquest or domination. On the domestic scene, it is human attitudes, not human nature, which nurture the racial and religious hatreds and bigotries which today permeate many societies, and even in democracies thrive in the fertile soil of complacency.

The picture is foreboding and the immediate future looms ominously. But perhaps there lies the hope. Can man, a thinking animal, capable of both emotion and cool calculation with regard to his self-interest, be brought to his senses in time? Can he see the black doom which awaits him at the end of the path he now follows? I have enough faith in the potentiality of mankind for good to believe that he can save himself. May it be fervently hoped that he will muster the determined will to do so.

Certainly, there is nothing in human nature which renders it impossible for men to live peacefully and harmoniously with one another. Hatred, intolerance, bigotry, chauvinism are never innate—they are the bad lessons taught in society. Despite the fact that in recorded history, mankind has been as much at war as at peace, it cannot be concluded that war is inevitable—a natural state of mankind. Nor do I believe that because hatreds, bigotries, intolerances, and prejudices loom large in the pages of history, these are the natural conditions of man's societal existence on earth.

I think it no exaggeration to say that unfortunately, throughout the ages, organized religion and education have failed miserably in their efforts to save man from himself. Perhaps they have failed because so often they have merely reflected the mean and narrow attitudes of the very peoples they were striving to save.

Human understanding, human brotherhood and solidarity, will be achieved, if at all, only when the peoples of many lands find a common bond through a compelling sense of urgency in achieving common goals. The purposes and principles of the United Nations—with peace and justice and equality as the universal common denominators—afford that bond and the common goals. The implements of modern warfare afford the urgency, if people once understand the frightful implications and elect to survive.

Lincoln, instinctively a true democrat, believed deeply in the essential justice of the plain people, whose better impulses and good will he trusted ultimately to prevail. Given half a chance, I believe that the free peoples of the world today, in their collectivity, will justify Lincoln's faith.

It is not necessary to seek to transform people into saints in order that impending disaster may be averted.

Throughout the world today, thinking and psychology have not kept pace with the times. That people inevitably think in terms of their self-interest is something very little can be done about. But is it not equally tenable that a great deal can be done about influencing people to think and act in terms of their *true* self-interest? In this dangerous international age, notions of exalted and exaggerated nationalism, national egocentrism and isolationism, of chauvinism, of group superiority and master race, of group exclusiveness, of national self-righteousness, of special privilege, are in the interest of neither the world nor of any particular group in it. They are false views of self-interest and carry us all toward the disaster of war. And in the war of tomorrow there can be no true victor; at best there will be only survivors. Our old concepts and values are no longer valid or realistic. The future may well belong to those who first realign their international sights.

I sincerely believe that the generality of peoples throughout the world really long for peace and freedom. There can be no doubt that this is true of the generality of the American people, despite some impatient and ultra-jingoistic hotheads in our midst. If this is true, it is the one great hope for the future. The problem is how to crystallize this longing, how to fashion it into an overpowering instrument for good. The United Nations recognizes acutely the desperate need, but has not yet found the ways and means of mobilizing the peace-loving attitudes of the peoples of the world over the stubborn walls of national egoisms.

Every peace- and freedom-loving nation, every government, every individual, has a most solemn obligation to mankind and the future of mankind in the fateful effort to rescue the world from the morass in which it is now entrapped and to underwrite a future of peace and freedom for all. This is a time of gravest crisis. Constructive, concerted actions and policies—not negativism and recrimination—are called for. There are many motes in many eyes. There is in the world no nation which can stand before the ultimate bar of human history and say: "We have done our utmost to induce peoples to live in peace with one another as brothers."

It must be very clear that what the world needs most desperately today is a crusade for peace and understanding of unparalleled dimension; a universal mobilization of the strong but diffused forces of peace and justice. The collective voice of the free peoples of the world, could be so irresistible as to dwarf into insignificance both A- and H-bombs and to disperse and discourage the warlike and war-minded.

In the existing state of affairs, societies admittedly owe it to themselves to be prepared and protected against any eventuality; they must build up their national defenses. They must do so, incidentally, only because they have not, for reasons of national sovereignty, been willing to give the United Nations the decisive power and means to cope with a powerful act of military aggression. With vigorous measures to ensure national defense, given the present international circumstances, reason and reality could perceive no quarrel. But it would also appear that reason and reality would dictate that since armament can never be an end in itself and must expand itself, if at all, only in war, the only way peace-loving societies might cover their ever-mounting losses from the tremendous expenditures on armaments would be to exert an effort of at least equal magnitude for peace—to the end that the armaments would never have to be used. This, it seems to me, would be at once good economics, good humanitarianism, and good self-interest.

In the final analysis it is peoples who must be won and who alone can win the world-wide struggle for freedom and justice. People can be rallied to ideas. They must be given more than guns and an enemy to shoot at.

And now, if I may take advantage of my nationality and speak for a moment simply as an American citizen rather than an international official, I may ask where do we, as Americans, stand with regard to the challenge of human relations? It is a question, surely, in which Abraham Lincoln would be deeply interested were he with us today.

The United States is in the forefront of international affairs today. The eyes of the world are focused upon us as never before in our history. A great part of the world looks to us for a convincing demonstration of the validity and the virility of the democratic way of life as America exalts it. It would be catastrophic if we should fail to give that demonstration. We cannot afford to fail.

But it is only too apparent that our democratic house is not yet in shipshape order. There are yawning crevices in our human relations; the gap between our democratic profession on the one hand, and our daily practices of racial and religious intolerance on the other, while less wide than formerly, is still very wide.

Race relations is our number one social problem, perhaps our number one problem. It is no mere sectional problem; it is a national—indeed an international—problem. For any problem today which challenges the ability of democracy to function convincingly, which undermines the very foundations of democracy and the faith of people in it, is of concern to the entire peace- and freedom-loving world. Surely, it must be abundantly clear that it is only through the triumph of democracy and the determined support of peoples for it as an imperative way of life that secure foundations for world peace can be laid.

That race relations are gradually improving both in the South and elsewhere in the nation, cannot be doubted. But neither can it be doubted that these relations remain in a dangerous state, that they are a heavy liability to the nation, and constitute a grave weakness in our national democratic armor.

Certainly the costs of anti-racial and anti-religious practices are enormously high. Attitudes of bigotry, when widely prevalent in a society, involve staggering costs in terms of prestige and confidence throughout the rest of the world, not to mention the contamination and degradation resulting from the presence of such psychological disease in the body of the society.

Throughout the nation, in varying degree, the Negro minority—almost a tenth of the population—suffers severe political, economic, and social disabilities, solely because of race. In Washington, the capital of the greatest democracy in human history, Lincoln, the Great Emancipator, sits majestically in his massive armchair behind the marble pillars, and overlooks a city which stubbornly refuses to admit his moral dictum that the Negro is a man; a city in which no Negro can live and work with dignity; a city which, administered by Congress itself, subjects one-fourth of its citizens to segregation, discrimination, and daily humiliation. Washington is our nation's greatest shame precisely because it is governed by Congress and is our capital. Of all American cities, it should symbolize and vitalize our democracy.

In his time, Lincoln saw that slavery had to be abolished not only because as an institution it was contrary to human morality, but also because it was inimical to the interests of the "plain people" of America. By the same token, present-day practices of racial segregation and discrimination should be outlawed as inimical to the interests of all who believe in and derive benefit from democracy, whatever their race or religion.

The vitality of this great country derives from the unity of purpose and the devotion to its democratic ideals of the diversified peoples—by race, religion, and national origin—who make up its population. Disunity and group conflict constantly sap that vitality.

As a nation we have also found great strength in the fact that we have always been able and willing to face our shortcomings frankly and attack them realistically. It is in this spirit and in this knowledge that I, as an American, take occasion to point to our shortcomings. I do not imply, in any sense, that the rest of the world is free of such imperfections, or in given instances, far greater ones.

To enjoy our maximum strength, we need more *applied* democracy. We need to live up to the principles which we believe in and for which we are hailed by the world. We too need a mobilization—a mobilization throughout the country of men and women of good will, of men and women who are determined to see American democracy fulfill its richest promise, and who will ceaselessly exert their efforts toward that end.

Our nation, by its traditional philosophy, by its religious precepts, by its Constitution, stands for freedom and equality, for the brotherhood of man, and for full respect for the rights and dignity of the individual. By giving unqualified expression to these ideals in our daily life we can and will achieve a democratic society here so strong in the hearts and minds of its citizens, so sacred to the individual, that it will be forever invulnerable to any kind of attack.

We cannot eradicate prejudices and bigotries overnight, of course, I seek no miracles. But neither is there anything sacrosanct about the present rate of advance. The pace of progress can be greatly accelerated if a great many of our organizations and institutions—schools, churches, labor unions, industries, and civic organizations—would put a stronger shoulder to the wheel.

I am certain that the majority and more of the American people believe firmly in our democratic way of life and are willing that all our citizens, of whatever color or creed, enjoy it. But on the Negro problem our thinking has become obfuscated by illusions, myths, and shibboleths, and we have been, by and large, complacent about it.

Many of us seek to divorce ourselves from responsibility for this embarrassing contradiction in our democracy by personally deploring race prejudice and practices of discrimination and segregation, and dismissing them as not being representative of the country.

But this is false. So long as such practices widely persist in the society, so long as they are tolerated anywhere in the land, they represent America; they represent you and me. They are part and parcel of the American way. They affect the life and the future of every American, irrespective of color. They betray the faith of the noble man we here honor today.

This may be said of attitudes and practices directed against all American minorities—Negroes, Indians, Spanish-Americans, Orientals—and as well of religious bigotries—anti-Semitism and anti-Catholicism.

The time is past when we may find refuge in rationalizations. The very principles upon which our way of life is based are being dangerously challenged in the world-wide ideological struggle. To the realistic, even cynical, world of today, democratic profession has meaning only in democratic deeds. We cannot, for example, convert the vast masses of Asia and Africa to a democracy qualified by color. But it is vital to the future of human freedom in the world that these peoples, constituting the preponderance of the world's population, be attracted to the democratic way.

We must face the facts honestly. Those who may seek to find comfort in the concept of gradualism on the assumption that time, seen as an inexorable solvent, will eliminate the problem, now find that time has caught up with us. Today, our country needs desperately its maximum strength—its maximum manpower, unity, and moral leadership. But in this very hour, our resources of manpower are squandered in racial strife and racial barriers to employment, our unity is disrupted by racial and religious animosities, and our prestige and moral leadership in the world suffer from the contradictions between the democratic ideals we proudly profess and the domestic practices of which we cannot boast. These contradictions have already cost us prestige, good will and more lives than we have needed to lose on far-off battlefields. In the future these costs in the lives of fine American boys—white, black, brown, yellow, and red—could be far greater, for the same reason.

In this critical period, it appears to me, we have two vital tasks to perform, even while, imperatively, we prepare and man our defenses. We must exert an extraordinary effort to put our interracial house in order. We must strive by our deeds to convince watchful peoples everywhere that we not only profess democracy, but that we deeply believe in it and live it, and that it is applicable to and good for all peoples, whatever their color or creed.

To me, it seems that this is no superhuman or impossible task for my country. It does not require that people of different colors or creeds must begin to clasp each other to their bosoms. It requires no revolution, beyond a psychological one. It does require a substantial change in the attitudes of many of our citizens and our legislators. This is nothing new for America. Within the past century we have seen radical changes in the attitudes of Americans toward many groups in the country—toward the Irish, the Scandinavians, the Polish, the Italians, the Germans, the Chinese, the Latin-Americans, the English, and the American Indians. We have even seen Baptists and Methodists begin to speak to each other.

If I may speak for my own group, all that the American Negro asks is that he be treated like every other citizen—that he be accepted or rejected, not collectively, on the basis of his color, but individually, on the basis of whatever merit he may command. In other words, he asks only the most elemental and fundamental prerogative of citizenship in a democracy—equality of treatment.

What true American can there be, whether from South or North, who would allege that this is too much for any citizen in a democracy to demand; or, indeed, that there could be a democratic society on any other basis?

What kind of a patriot would he be, whether from North or South, who would insist that the nation, in its greatest hour of need, must be denied its full strength solely to ensure that one group of its loyal citizens shall be deprived of equal opportunity, as individuals and on their merits, to rise or fall in the society?

I have great faith in my fellow American citizens. I know that, preponderantly, their consciences are sensitive, their sense of fair play is deep seated, their belief in democracy is genuine and fervent, and that, once they cast off complacency and apathy, once aroused and resolved, their ability to solve problems, to do whatever must be done, is unlimited.

If I may be pardoned for a purely personal reference, I am proud to be an American and I am proud of my origin. I believe in the American way of life, and believing in it, deplore its imperfections. I wish to see my country strong in every way—strong in the nature and practice of its democratic way of life; strong in its world leadership; strong in both its material and spiritual values; strong in the hearts and minds of all of its people, whatever their race, color or religion, and in their unshakable devotion to it. I wish to see an America in which both the fruits and the obligations of democracy are shared by *all* of its citizens on a basis of full equality and without qualification of race or creed.

The United Nations ideal is a world in which peoples would "practice tolerance and live together in peace with one another as good neighbors." If this ideal is far from realization it is only because of the state of mind of mankind. Man's reason and calculated self-interest can be powerful forces for changes in that state of mind. No ideal could be more rewarding. Every individual today has it in his power—in his daily living, in his attitudes and practices—to contribute greatly to the realization of that ideal. We must be strong in our adherence to ideals. We must never lose faith in man's potential power for good.

In this regard, we in America have a historic mission. We are the architects of the greatest design for living yet conceived. We are demonstrating that men of all backgrounds and cultures can be solidly welded together in brotherhood by the powerful force of a noble ideal —individual liberty. To perfect our design for living we need only to demonstrate that democracy is color blind. This we can, and with the support of all men and women of good will, we shall do. Surely, the Great Emancipator had deep faith that we would do so.

The Ideals of American Youth
Harold Taylor

Dr. Harold Taylor, president of Sarah Lawrence College, spoke before the National Student Conference on Human Relations in Higher Education meeting at Earlham College, Richmond, Indiana on 29 March 1951.

Dr. Taylor was born in Toronto in 1914. He studied at the University of Toronto (A.B., 1935; M.A., 1936) and at the University of London (Ph.D., 1938). He came to the United States in 1939 and was naturalized in 1947. Following a period of teaching philosophy at the University of Wisconsin (1939-45) and service in the Office of Scientific Research and Development (1944) he became president of Sarah Lawrence in 1945. Dr. Taylor is the editor of *Essays in Teaching* (1951).

WE ARE here this afternoon to do honor to the ideals of social justice, to the ideals of American youth. We are here because we believe in an idea, the simplest and happiest idea in the world, the most complicated and controversial idea in the world, the most powerful idea in the world—the idea of equality. There are a lot of people who do not realize just how powerful an idea it is. But every little while there is some kind of episode, a little fuss somewhere, and after the fuss is over, a king has been fired, a dictator is thrown out, a government is overthrown, and a large number of people who beforehand weren't treated as equals became equal because they insisted on it. These little episodes have been called by various names; the ones most interesting to us were entitled the French Revolution, and the American Revolution, which were simply arguments about who is equal, and about the fact that some people seemed to be less equal than others.

The truth is that each one of us, in order to live his life fully, must feel the sense of personal worth which can only come from being accepted as an equal by those we meet in our daily lives. It is not that we necessarily demand that people like us and admire us, but only that they do not automatically classify us as somebody not worth knowing and not worth bothering about. We cannot be ourselves, we cannot feel secure, confident, or have a sense of fulfillment unless we are accepted as persons of worth. When we find ourselves faced with those who by their actions and by their words treat us as if we were of no account, as if we had no rights, interests, desires, and aims of our own, we become hostile, anxious, angry, hateful. Before the Revolutionary War, we felt that way about the British when they were stuffy about our rights. Women sometimes feel that way about men. When social justice is not freely granted it is bitterly fought for. We know this from history. If for no other reason than this, for practical reasons of having fewer revolutions, we should all work for the ideal of equality.

But we who came to this conference today have a different, a personal reason. We are not seeking our own advantage. We are enjoying the privilege of working for an ideal. We feel a sense of unity and a sense of companionship because we know that everyone in this room wants to be here as a living symbol of a social ideal. André Gide, one of the greatest literary figures of our age, spoke to all of us here today when he wrote, just before his death two weeks ago, these words:

> At a time when I feel in such peril, so besieged on all sides . . . the fact of knowing that among the young, even if they are few and in no matter what country, there are those who take no rest, who keep intact their moral and intellectual integrity, who protest against all totalitarian commands and undertaking which would subordinate, lower the subject thought or reduce the soul—for it is finally the soul itself which is at stake—it is the fact of knowing that these young people are there, that they exist, it is that which inspires confidence in us, the older folk; it is that fact which keeps me, so old now and so close to leaving this life, from dying without hope.

I think in one way, we who are here today form the most exclusive group there is; we are the worst discriminators. We discriminate against those who hate human beings, and we are so exclusive that we form part of a very small body of men and women throughout the world who care so much about human beings and social justice that we are willing to put our time and energy into achieving it. And you must admit that this world group is certainly much too small and exclusive. We are so exclusive that we enjoy each other's company and do not enjoy the company of those who hate people. We are so exclusive and discriminating that we are trying to remake human nature so that after a while, if the others behave themselves properly, they too can join our group. We too have our bars to membership, our discriminatory clauses. The main clause is that you can't come in unless you want to, unless you are colored, or white, or American, or foreign, or unless you are attached to the human race. We insist, in a subversive sort of way, that you have to be a good human being to be accepted.

All the American travelers who go abroad these days—whether to India, France, England, Indonesia, Indo-China, or Korea—tell us on their return that the first question raised in foreign countries is the question about racial segregation. What can we honestly say about the situation in this country? We can only say that there are a lot of white Americans who are prejudiced and that we have been very slow in correcting the injustices done to Negro citizens. To say anything else would be dishonest. But the next question is, what are we doing about it? The President of the United States and Congress seem unable to legislate it. There are too many politicians who either believe in white supremacy or are afraid to say they don't, too many vested interests in keeping the Negro people in a position of social inequality. But the best answer I know to those who doubt our honesty and our intention is that there are large bodies of private citizens and people of good will, with honest convictions, who are working at the focus of the problem and are doing everything in their power to change the laws and to change the social pattern which has built segregation into the structure of American society. There is a continuing awareness of the problem on the part of the church groups. As Ralph Bunche said the other night, "during the past few years we have seen radical changes in the attitudes of native Americans toward the Irish, the Scandinavians, the Polish, the Italians, the Germans, the Chinese, the Latin-Americans, the English, the American Indians. We have even seen Baptists and Methodists begin to speak to each other."

The Supreme Court of the United States has proven the liberal content of our Constitution by the great decisions it has handed down to us on the issues of segregation. There is no doubt that the public conscience has been touched and that public opinion is aware of the seriousness of the problem and the moral implications it has for American life. A series of moving pictures, each of them successful in making the moral point, a flood of books, magazine articles, broadcasts have brought the discrimination problem into the open. Moral energies which formerly went into other causes are now being poured into the segregation issue. It is even respectable to be active in groups which support the ideals of racial and religious diversity. Even in Mississippi in 1949 we have the astounding phenomenon of a new trial being ordered by the Mississippi Supreme Court in the case of a Negro sentenced to five years in jail for marrying a white woman. The Supreme Court held that the State had failed to prove beyond reasonable doubt that the man was at least one-eighth Negro! In Mississippi, even this can be classified as progress.

We have also made some progress with the armed services. An executive order from the President in 1948 has called for the removal of quotas in recruitment, and removal of discrimination in types of work and promotion. The order affected 100,000 Negroes in uniform and more than 70,000 who work as civilians. This is not only a program to abolish Jim-Crow units but to allow room for promotion for reasons of merit not color. We are on the way to a much more democratic army as a result of new policies.

In the colleges and universities themselves there are devoted persons and groups who are working daily on the discrimination problem and who are making daily progress. We can say that the move towards educational equality for Negroes has tripled in speed during the past ten years, and that we now have a body of educational opinion in the North and the South which will increase the speed of reform still further during the next ten years.

New York State has taken the lead in legislation against educational discrimination by its act of 1948, followed by Massachusetts and New Jersey in 1949. Other States have passed laws against segregation—Indiana, Illinois, Wisconsin, and others to follow. The fears of those who opposed such legislation, the idea that human relations cannot be legislated, and all the other clichés, have been proven wrong. In New York State, before the law was passed, the argument made against it was that no New York State college or university discriminated against Jewish, Negro, or foreign-background students, and, anyway, the colleges themselves were doing everything they could to eliminate it. After this fatuous statement was made, we simply told the opponents, many of whom were college presidents and should have known better, that the law wouldn't affect any college which was behaving decently and would give moral encouragement to those who were behaving badly and claimed they couldn't help it. This has turned out to be true.

We also have the victories of the Sweatt case and the McLaurin case to encourage us, and whereas three years ago there were none, we now have a thousand Negro students in the South working side by side with white students in graduate institutions. Of course, there is always South Carolina, where they have decided that they prefer to shut down the whole school system rather than join America, but perhaps even South Carolina will be unable to hold out very much longer. The important fact, for undergraduate as well as graduate education, for the schools as well as the colleges, is that stated by Chief Justice Vinson when, in his opinion on the McLaurin case, the Chief Justice pointed out that education is not simply a matter of passing courses, reading books, taking credits, but has to do with the personal relation of one human being with another, the psychological effects of working with other human beings in a situation of equality, the psychological and personal damage which is done to the individual who is excluded, segregated, and denied the friendship and association of people of different color and different religion.

It is at this point that education has its greatest chance to help. Suppose we take all these facts together. They add up to a total which shows that America has an answer to the questions raised in other countries about our moral integrity and democratic ideals. At least we have faced the problem, admit the facts, and there are citizens who are devoting their lives to the cure of the disease. The educational system of America is the heart and moral center of the reform of American attitudes. Through it we can actually inspire our young people to carry the ideals of democracy into action. Through it the young people have already inspired many of us to work with them in a common effort. It is in the colleges and universities of the country that the wealth of talent lies for tackling the issues of contemporary society. The college youth of America have always been ahead of the rest of the country in suggesting liberal reforms, in accepting social change, in opening up their lives to new possibilities. The native endowment of the young mind is liberal, spontaneous, open, enquiring, willing to assume the responsibility of leadership. On the question of discrimination the youth have already taken that leadership. At Amherst they defied their elders and broke the fraternity rule against Negro membership. At Minnesota the student council passed a resolution against discriminatory clauses in fraternity rules. Students voted similar action at Rutgers, Harvard, Dartmouth, Swarthmore, Wisconsin, New York University, Brown, Connecticut, and others. A fraternity at Howard University even admitted a white student! The students at the University of North Carolina voted to bring Negro students to their campus.

Everywhere in the country young people are taking the leadership from their elders, are showing the conservatives, the class-conscious ones, the country club set, all those whose natural posture consists of looking down their noses, that they mean business and that they don't intend to have much more nonsense about excluding persons because they don't belong to the right category of *Homo sapiens.*

But what are the educators doing while their students are busy about their reforms? For the most part they are giving lectures and making speeches. They are mimeographing hundreds of course outlines, true-false examinations, curriculum plans, guides to this and that, and surveys of everything. They are dealing with such questions as how many credits of physics or psychology or English or sociology does it take to make a grade-catching sophomore into a credit-ridden junior. While they are answering a series of academic questions which nobody ever asks outside of the academies, the life of American youth is going blithely along, impervious to the tedium of academic classrooms, able to play the game according to the rules, and putting together a series of A's, B's and C's, with an occasional D on the way to graduation.

There are, of course, magnificent exceptions among the educators and teachers—people who are concerned about the total life of each student and the way in which education can help to enrich the moral content of American life. Some of those educators are here today; their very presence here makes it clear that their conception of education is different from the ordinary. I would name others among them—John Dewey, Max Otto, Dean Williamson of Minnesota, and T. R. McConnell of Buffalo—if I thought it would not begin to look like a dangerous organization or a group of people whose only identifying characteristic lay in the fact that they were people I agreed with. But on the whole, the disease of higher education in America is that it is over-organized, dehumanized, and fairly boring. It deals with human problems by turning them into textbook subjects; for dealing with love it gives us courses called Marriage and the Family, which again answer questions which nobody asked; for dealing with people, it gives us psychology 1A or American Institutions; for the white heat of race-relations issues it gives us the statistics of sociological structure; it turns everything which would otherwise be interesting into an academic subject, and lectures at us, examines us, and hopes that by the end of it all we will be democratic, intellectually well-heeled, liberally educated, and kind to everybody.

Liberal education is more than this. It is the way people live together, in college and out of college. The first responsibility of a college in the modern world is to build a community of young men and women who learn in their daily lives the meaning of liberalism and who show to the world by their actions and attitudes what life can be like in a free and kindly society.

This philosophy demands a new design for education which reconstructs the whole of the college where it operates. It demands that the admissions policy be one which deals with individual merit and the personal qualities of each individual who applies. It demands a diversity of students within each college community, with scholarship programs deliberately designed to seek out and welcome those of underprivileged economic and social position. It demands a curriculum which is related to the emotional, social, and intellectual needs of each student, in such a way that each may fulfill the unique powers which lie undiscovered within himself. It demands that the central issues of our age around which the twentieth century is turning should become the central focus of college education. These are issues of human values, of freedom and authority, of Communism and democracy, of capitalism and socialism, of war and peace, of moral and spiritual enrichment. This philosophy demands most of all a community designed to enrich the experience of every person in it.

These are matters which receive too little attention from American education. Yet they are the only things which in the long run really count. Liberal education is designed to change human nature in a liberal direction. I have seen the college communities of America divided into exclusive groups which imitate the worst features of a stratified society; with wealthy, white Gentiles living only with each other while across the road on a less exclusive street live Jewish students in an equally segregated fraternity; in another part of town in boarding houses across the tracks live the "independents," that is, the déclassés, where on tolerance a few Negro students are allowed to live as well. I have seen dormitories where Jewish students have been segregated by floors on the educational grounds that they feel better with their own kind. I have seen young women selecting each other for admission to the sacred environment of a snobbish sorority by estimating the value of fur coats possessed, and by inquiring secretly into the financial position of the victim's family. I know of Gentile sorority rules forbidding members to drink Coca-Cola or dance with Jewish fraternity men. I have seen the whole incredible system supported and condoned by the college authorities themselves, in the North, in the Midwest, on the West coast, all in the name of liberal education. These practices serve only to deepen the prejudices and strengthen the materialistic, antisocial attitudes which liberal education is designed to cure. If we are to develop in America an education worthy of our ideals of human life, each campus must become a place where men and women breathe a moral atmosphere of liberal idealism.

Dr. David Levy, the psychiatrist, has a favorite story about his research in the field of prejudice. He describes his months of research on case studies of prejudice, including the personality patterns of the German Nazi, his careful statistics, his patient efforts, and his final conclusion. He finds, he says, that prejudiced people are narrow-minded. By this Dr. Levy meant that the existence of prejudice towards minority groups on the part of any individual is linked to a whole set of stereotypes and rigid attitudes towards a lot of other things, including women, children, marriage, education, politics, and poor people who want to eat regularly. He points out that one of the deepest effects of prejudice upon the individual is that he gives himself such a bad time. He narrows and constricts his personality to such a point that even when there is nobody else around to hate and condemn, he hates himself and then is unhappy because he is not understood by himself. This way lies schizophrenia.

I suggest therefore that we go the other way, that we hold to the ideals of American youth, with their central concern for equality, not merely because we can then turn to the rest of the world and say, "Look, we're really democratic," although this is a worthy motive, not simply because we can then carry out in practice the ideals we profess, not simply because we would then make America a stronger and healthier society, but because we would then be living a better life. We would live a life which is rich in spiritual satisfaction, which is growing and increasing in the quality of its experience, and is opening to a wider vision of the future of mankind. This is what America really means.

Segregation in the Armed Forces
William L. Dawson

The speech below was given by Representative William L. Dawson of Illinois on the floor of Congress on 12 April 1951. It was a plea to vote for the amendment by Representative Price of Illinois which would require "young inductees to elect, at the time of their induction, whether to serve in segregated or unsegregated units" of the armed forces. At the close of the stirring speech by Mr. Dawson the House, including some Southern Democrats, applauded.

William L. Dawson was born in Albany, Georgia on 26 April 1886. He studied at Fisk University, Nashville, Tennessee (A.B., 1909) and at Chicago-Kent College of Law and Northwestern University School of Law. During World War I he served in the army as a First Lieutenant. Elected to Congress in 1943, he has been chairman of the House committee on Executive expenditures since January 1949.

For the outcome of the Price amendment the following quotation from the *Congressional Record* for Friday, 13 April 1951, gives the details:

CHAIRMAN: The question is on the amendment offered by the gentlemen from Illinois [Mr. Price].

The question was taken; and on a division (demanded by Mr. Powell) there were ayes 107, noes 101.

MR. WILLIAMS OF MISSISSIPPI: Mr. Chairman, I ask for tellers.

Tellers were ordered, and the Chairman appointed as tellers Mr. Price and Mr. Kilday.

The house again divided; and the tellers reported that there were ayes 138, noes 123.

So the amendment was agreed to.

I WAS BORN in the South. I lived there all during the days of my young manhood. When World War I broke out I was above the draft age. I did not have to go, but I believed then as I believe now that it was the duty of every citizen, when the welfare of the nation in which he claims citizenship is at stake, to rally to the call and to give his life, if need be, for the preservation of that nation.

I went to war. I was commissioned William L. Dawson, first lieutenant of infantry. I led Americans in battle—black Americans. This mark you see here on my forehead is the result of German mustard gas. This left shoulder of mine is today a slip joint. I cannot raise this left arm any higher than the shoulder unless I lift it with the other hand. That would have been a good joint, hospitalization would have been available, if I had not been a Negro American.

I served in a segregated outfit as a citizen trying to save this country.

How long, how long, my confreres and gentlemen from the South, will you divide us Americans on account of color? Give me the test that you would apply to make anyone a full-fledged American, and, by the living God, if it means death itself, I will pay it. But give it to me. Why should this body go on record at a time when we are fighting a world war to brand a section of its citizenry as second class?

I have sat in the well of this House and I have seen you gentlemen from the South, and rightly so, stand up and applaud members of other races, nonwhite races, who were darker than I am. I have seen you applaud them, yet you will take me, a citizen of the United States, of your own flesh and blood, and brand me with second-class citizenship.

If there is one place in America where there should not be segregation, that place is in the armed services, among those who fight for this country. Oh, I know how some of you feel, but there is but one God and there is but one race of men all made in the image of God. I did not make myself black any more than you made yourselves white, and God did not curse me when he made me black any more than he cursed you when he made you white.

I would give up this life of mine to preserve this country and every American in it, white or black. Deny to me today, if you will, all that American citizenship stands for; I will still fight to preserve our nation knowing that some day under the Constitution of the United States all of these restrictions will be removed, and that we will move forward before the world as one people, American people, joined in a democracy which shall set the pattern for all the world.

I say to you who claim to love America, in this hour of its stress that the greatest argument the Soviet Union is using among the black peoples of this world to turn them against you is your treatment of me and Americans like me.

No; I do not believe this body means to go off on this tangent, and I believe you who come from the South, if you would look back a little bit, would never, never again take a step to handicap any one of God's children for what they are. I believe that the South is big enough for all of us to live in together in peace and in happiness if we can but have understanding; but we cannot have understanding if you array one against another because of color.

RELIGION

Time Is Running Out
Edward D. Gates

This sermon was delivered by the Reverend Edward D. Gates at the First Presbyterian Church of Peoria, Illinois on 17 September 1950. It was awarded first place in the sermons category of the annual Freedoms Foundation Awards for outstanding contributions to freedom in 1950. The presentation of an honor medal and a sum of $1500 was made by General Omar N. Bradley at Valley Forge, Pa. on 22 February 1951.

Mr. Gates was born in Wauwatosa, Wisconsin in 1921 and was educated at Beloit College. Following his studies in theology at the University of Chicago and the Pacific School of Religion in Berkeley, California, he served as a Chaplain in the United States Navy during World War II with sea duty in the Atlantic.

The First Presbyterian Church of Peoria is 116 years old and, with nearly 2000 members, is among the largest Presbyterian churches in the Middle West. Mr. Gates joined the church as associate minister in 1947 and a year later, at the age of 27, was called as minister. In a remarkably short period some 240 new members joined the church, the church school was doubled in size to 700 members, and a new educational building was erected. Mr. Gates is active in community affairs in Peoria and serves on the Board of Directors of several community-wide organizations. He has been twice chaplain of Peoria Post No. 2, American Legion, the largest post in the state, and also State chaplain of the American Legion, Department of Illinois. He was nominated as one of Peoria's outstanding young men in the year 1950.

I WANT TO tell you about a sermon which I prepared but never delivered. In this sermon I wanted to point out that the crisis the world is now facing is nothing new, that surely things are not as bad as they seem. In my reading I found what I thought to be clever quotations to illustrate my point. For instance, on a recently discovered Syrian tablet nearly 3000 years old were written words to this effect: "Prices and taxes are too high. Parents are neglecting their children and everyone wants to write a book. The world is in a sad state." Or here was Disraeli commenting on conditions of his day: "In industry, commerce, and agriculture there is little hope." Or the Duke of Wellington in 1851, shortly before he died: "I thank God that I may be spared seeing the consummation of the ruin that is gathering about us." And then this arresting paragraph written by Thomas Carlyle just 100 years ago:

> In the days that are passing over us, even fools are arrested to ask the meaning of them; few of the generations of men have seen more impressive days. Days of endless calamity, disruption, dislocation, confusion worse confounded; if they are not days of endless hope, too, then they are days of utter despair. For it is not a small hope that will suffice. These days of universal death must be days of universal new birth if the ruin is not to be total and final.

Here were statements, I believed, that proved my thesis: By its very nature the world must progress. The prophets of yesterday's doom have been proven false. The prophets of today who bring us messages fraught with disturbing news cannot be right. Things are not as bad as they seem.

But I am glad now that I never preached such a sermon. Any minister who preaches a "God's in his heaven, all's right with the world" type of message to his congregation, who thinks that the necessary equipment of a Christian is a set of rose-colored glasses, is doing a great injustice to the people whom he serves. He is certainly neglecting his high office as a spokesman for the church when he refuses to face the cold hard facts of reality. I have one or two such colleagues who still believe that Mr. Vyshinsky and associates are but misunderstood fellows and that the ills of the world would be solved if the sessions of the United Nations were opened with prayer. I believe deeply in prayer, but I also believe that a great deal depends upon who does the praying and with what intention the prayer is given.

No, my friends, this is no time for shallow optimism. Particularly for us who try to be Christians, we must not fall into the false assumption that what we are experiencing today is just another crisis as the world passed through 3000 or even 100 years ago. If you doubt this, listen:

From the year 1900 to 1950 this world of ours has witnessed warfare on a scale that has outslaughtered all previous history. Do you realize that if tonight every man, woman, and child within the continental limits of these United States were suddenly wiped off the earth, their number would be less than the number of human beings who have died in war, or by causes directly resulting from war, during the 50 years, 1900 to 1950! Recent studies by Professor Quincy Wright of the University of Chicago inform us that during the first 30 years of our century European nations alone fought 74 wars, the average war four years long, or wars lasting a total of 297 years. From the eleventh to the twentieth century, during those 900 years, war casualties amounted to about 18 million. But in the first 30 years only of this century, from 1900 to 1930, there were killed by warfare 33⅓% more human beings than in all those previous 900 years! And this does not include five continents and World War II and its immediate prelude.

The Dean of the Harvard Graduate School was correct, I believe, when he said:

> If any human being brought up in the tradition of Western civilization could by some miracle, step outside the familiar pattern of that culture; if history could come to him with the same shock of surprise that a new and stimulating novel brings him; if, in sum, retaining the moral idealism of Western civilization as a standard of measurement, he could yet discover for the first time what has happened to mankind in the last fifty years, such a person would, I think, be overwhelmed by a single tragic conviction: namely, that the history of mankind for the last half century has been a history of deepening horror.[1]

There are many, I suppose, who do not like to be reminded of these facts. And for many of us living in comfortable surroundings when the news of a train wreck killing 30 people takes precedence on the front pages of our newspapers over a report from Korea that only light casualties were suffered—light casualties meaning 200 or 300 men—and when for many the great problem of the day is the length of next year's skirts or the latest escapade of a popular Hollywood star—these facts may indeed seem a bit unreal.

But these are facts and sobering facts. But when you stop and think of it this is a sobering generation. Has it occurred to you that the generation of young men in their thirties or approaching forty years of age has never known what their fathers, or their fathers before them, refer to as "normal times"? Born at the time of World War I, reared during an era of false prosperity, setting out on their own in the face of a devastating depression, for many it was the WPA or the CCC camps; then drafted into World War II; and now many of them are being called back into service for what some consider to be the beginning of World War III.

[1] Jones, H. M., *Education and World Tragedy* (Harvard University Press: 1946), p. 2.

Not since the days of the French Revolution and the Napoleonic era has one generation lived nearly a lifetime in such tumultuous times.

During the month I have been absent from this pulpit it has been my privilege to attend two conferences which were visited by prominent leaders in our industrial, political, and military life. The information given us, much of which does not appear in our daily press, was not encouraging. For instance, we were told on good authority that there are as many Communist meetings in the Los Angeles area as there are church services—perhaps not as many in attendance at these Red meetings, but what is lacking in numbers is made up for in zeal for a cause, a zeal we Christians can envy. All this is not too surprising when we hear of the crowd of 20,000 which gathered at the Los Angeles Airport to bid a cheering farewell to the ten Hollywood writers who were departing to begin their prison terms for contempt of the Congress of the United States for refusing to testify if they were members of the Communist Party. We were reminded of the perilous defenses of our country—that only fifteen bridges span our three great waterways, the Mississippi, the Missouri, the Ohio rivers; that much remains undone as regards the protection of our cities against a possible enemy attack. You who deal in stocks and investments know that business firms and corporations are now listed as regards their "bombing vulnerability." When I returned to Peoria I found on my desk a letter from the Red Cross asking if our church could be used as a first-aid station in event of a bombing attack over Peoria. On reading the request my first thought was one of despair. But on a moment's reflection I was glad and relieved that at last we were facing facts.

For we as Christians must face facts, however terrible and disquieting they may be. We must face the fact, as one writer has put it, that

> We have acquired a unique power, the inverse of all others. We have now become able to blow up this planet, together with mankind and mankind's power of creating power. It is a solemn moment. Until now it could not be said that mankind was the master of its future, for it was still condemned to a future, although each individual could put a bullet through his head any time he liked. Now mankind will have to choose; and it will have to make an heroic effort not to choose the easy way out—suicide. One might say that it begins its maturity from this moment.[2]

[2] Mounier, E., *The Nineteenth Century* (September, 1948), p. 152.

I would not have you think, however, that because I say we must not look at the world through rose-colored glasses, that we must not refuse to face reality however disturbing it may be, that there is no hope. The very fact that this is a time of great crisis should make us all the more resolved to meet it. We, as Christians, should be aware that our religion by its very nature was made to flourish in times of deep distress. As the old Chinese proverb goes: "Better to light one candle than to curse the darkness."

Against this pattern then of enfolding gloom what may we as individuals do? What are the candles that we may light, and keep lighted, in the present darkness of the world? May I this morning suggest at least three:

First, let us, one by one, reaffirm and hold steadfast to our faith in American ideals. Do you realize that from about 400 B.C. until 1776 A.D. no nation of men was ever free—free in the sense that we Americans think of being free; that of all the men and women who have ever walked upon the face of this earth only 3 per cent, only 3 per cent, have been free, and the greater part of that 3 per cent has been Americans! We recognize, of course, that in wartime we must relinquish portions of our individual freedom, but let us relinquish those rights only with the assurance, the clear understanding, and the vigilance that this is a temporary measure.

Now, more than ever before, you and I must understand clearly what American ideals mean, the purpose and function of our government. Contrary to popular notion, it is not our government that gives us our rights to life, liberty, and the pursuit of happiness. The other night over the radio I heard an announcer say that the Constitution is the source of our freedom. However sincere his intentions, he was quite wrong. Our right to life, our right to liberty, our right to pursue happiness, these, according to American doctrine, come not from the Constitution but from God. As the Declaration of Independence puts it: men "are endowed *by their Creator* with certain unalienable rights . . . that to secure these rights, governments are instituted among men" and that "whenever government becomes destructive of those ends it is the right of the people to alter it." On this principle, you see, that government was for the protection of man's right to the individual freedom which God gives to every man, was this nation founded. Indeed, it was the first national government in the history of mankind established specifically for that purpose.

The Founders of this country knew by firsthand experience what all history makes clear: that when protection is not the purpose of government, then government misuses its power, and takes away man's freedom. As my friend, Frederick Overesch, so clearly states it:

> The main purpose of the new American government was to protect every man in his rights to life, liberty, and the pursuit of happiness, so long as he did not interfere with those same rights of any other man. Our American government was founded on the premise that it promised nothing but protection for every man: first, in his right to life, which comes from God—it being up to every man to make his own living; second, his right to liberty, which also comes from God—the government protecting man's right to individual freedom against the misuse of power of other men; third, man's right to pursue happiness, but not guaranteeing or promising happiness.

We know that true happiness can come only from within man himself, and the American government was set up only to protect a man's right to pursue happiness. Never was it the intention or purpose of the founders of our nation that government should provide security beyond the protection of this and these other basic rights.

One by one, we must be on guard against those who do not understand this basic nature of American government and would thus seek to turn our country into a welfare state and thus move the clock centuries back. As Woodrow Wilson has said:

> The history of liberty is a history of the limitation of governmental power, not the increase of it. When we resist, therefore, the concentration of power, we are resisting the processes of death, because a concentration of power is what precedes the destruction of human liberties.

Let us not fall into the trap of believing those who through some other system only promise what the American ideal has already delivered. I said a moment ago that from about 400 B.C. until 1776 A.D. no nation of men was ever free. By the same token, from about 400 B.C. until 1776 A.D. man spent most of his time getting enough food to keep himself alive, keeping a roof over his head, and defending himself. Yet all through this period he had the same natural resources as we have today and the intelligence to use them. But the difference was that he was not free to use his knowledge, free to develop the natural resources. Thus for those 22 centuries nothing much happened to change man's economic life.

But with the birth of the American Republic and up to this year 1950—in just 174 years—we Americans have benefited more economically than any other people in the world, than in any other country where the government set out to plan the pursuit of happiness, where the government promised to provide rather than protect a man in his own God-given rights to life, liberty, and the pursuit of happiness.

In February of this year the Federal Council of Churches sponsored a study Conference on the Church and Economic Life. While the findings of the Conference were not to represent the official views of the Council of Churches, they were to many of us as disturbing as a number of the resolutions passed at the World Council of Churches meeting in Amsterdam late last year. One statement from the Detroit report read this way: "Christians now live in various economic orders: Communist, Socialist, Capitalist, mixed economies and primitive society. No economic order known to man is worthy of the designation 'Christian'." I personally cannot believe that in that statement the Conference is speaking for the majority of American church people. Granted the abuses which the capitalistic system has brought, are we to say that our American system of free enterprise—founded on the belief that government is instituted among men to protect their God-given rights to life, liberty and the pursuit of happiness—is no more Christian than the economic system under which millions of Russians now live in abject slavery?

In these dark and confusing days, let us keep our faith in America strong and steadfast.

And secondly, let us keep faith in ourselves. Not long ago I had lunch with three prominent men of this community. We were discussing current affairs and the deplorable state of the world when one of them turned to me and said: "Ed, the hope of this country and the world rests with you ministers." I told him he need not flatter me simply because I was paying for the lunch. But quite seriously, the other two at the table agreed heartily with what he said. This same sentiment was expressed at a meeting I attended not long ago. A group of clergymen of all denominations were gathered together from all parts of the United States. One after another, laymen of high position in the affairs of this country would stand up to say to us: "It is with you, the moral leaders of the nation, that our hope for a better future must rest."

Now, much as I am impressed by the importance these men attach to my position as a clergyman, I, as a Protestant, object to this sort of thinking. For according to Protestant doctrine every one of us—not only the man in the pulpit—is a minister of God. It is not only the preachers who are preachers. Each person, when he declares him or herself a follower of Jesus, is a moral leader in this community; each one of us, layman or clergyman, is a teacher by example and precept. If it is true that the hope of this country and of the world rests with ministers, then in the deepest and fullest sense it rests with all of us. You, as a business man, are a moral leader of this community, for good or for bad, depending on how you conduct your business. You, as a worker, are a moral leader, for good or for evil, depending on how well and how faithfully you do your work. And you, housewife, teacher, student, farmer, are moral leaders, depending on how honest, how sincere, how trustworthy, how dependable, you are. The future of this country rests with every one of us who is entitled to have an opinion, to read, to write, to think, to pray, and to vote!

But how, someone asks, am I to know what is right and what is wrong? By what criterion am I to judge myself as a moral leader of the community? I know of no more helpful statement in this regard than these words by Montesquieu. In his essay on Personal Morality, he has this to say:

> If I knew something beneficial to myself but harmful to my family, I would drive it out of my mind. If I knew something advantageous to my family, but injurious to my community, I would try to forget it. If I knew something profitable to my community, but detrimental to my country or profitable to my country but detrimental to the human race, I would consider it a crime.

When we go to church we are exercising only a part of our religious life. I want to repeat that: when we go to church we are exercising only a part of our religious life. Sound Christian doctrine asserts that our religious and moral responsibilities do not begin and end at church, but belong with our every waking hour. Let us not lose faith in ourselves to measure up to our high calling as moral leaders.

And finally, let us keep steadfast our faith in God, our belief that right does make might. I want to read to you a paragraph from a newsletter by one of our nation's most respected economists and financial advisors. After reviewing the current situation in Korea and discussing the possibilities of a third World War, this is what he has to say:

> A time of terrific world turmoil is ahead, and perhaps not very far ahead. The United States and all free peoples everywhere should now be girding at top speed, in defense of the one great principle that

is at stake—individual freedom throughout the world. The time is short, and getting shorter day by day. But good has always triumphed in this world, despite agelong setbacks. History so attests. So let us put on the whole armor of God, material and spiritual. Then, dare we doubt the outcome? [3]

My friends, what the ensuing months will bring, none of us, of course, can say. But this we do know: that it will be no easy time for any of us. For some of us our sons and husbands and other loved ones will be off again to war. For many of us there will be increasing privations and more and more of our earnings going to taxes. We will have good reason to curse the darkness. But let us not fail to light a few candles also.

If I had a prayer to offer this morning, as we begin another year at this church, it would be these words of John Holland:

God give us men!
A time like this demands
Strong minds, great hearts, true faith and ready hands.
Men whom the lust of office does not kill;
Men whom the spoils of office cannot buy;
Men who possess opinions and a will;
Men who have honor; men who will not lie.
Men who can stand before a demagogue
And damn his treacherous flatteries without winking;
Tall men, suncrowned, who live above the fog
In public duty and in private thinking.

God give us such men here. And then—and only then—shall we find that not for such men but for their enemies time is running out.

How Can Modern Man Find Faith?
Fulton Oursler, Bishop Austin Pardue, and Irwin Edman; George V. Denny, Jr., Moderator

This discussion was broadcast from New York City on 6 February 1951 by America's Town Meeting of the Air.

Fulton Oursler is perhaps best known for his best seller, *The Greatest Story Ever Told* (1949). He has been a senior editor of *Reader's Di-*

[3] *Babson's Reports,* July 17, 1950, p. 174.

gest since 1944. His famous radio series, "The Greatest Story Ever Told," began in 1947 and he is still co-author of the program. *The Greatest Book Ever Written* (1951) is a retelling of the Old Testament. At present Mr. Oursler is at work on *The Greatest Faith Ever Known,* the story of the Acts of the Apostles and the founding of the Church. Born in Baltimore in 1893, he served as a reporter and critic on the *Baltimore American* (1910-18) and then began his career as a writer of short stories in 1918 and of books and plays in 1923.

Austin Pardue is the Episcopal Bishop of the Diocese of Pittsburgh. From 1938 to 1944 he was Dean of St. Paul's Cathedral in Buffalo, New York. Born in Chicago in 1899, he has studied at Hobart College (1918-20), Nashotah House (1920-22), and the General Theological Seminary (1922-25). Bishop Pardue held rectorships in Chicago, Hibbing, Minnesota, Sioux City, Iowa, and Minneapolis before his call to Buffalo. His books include *Life Out There* and *Prayer Works.*

Irwin Edman is Johnsonian Professor of Philosophy at Columbia University. His better-known books include *Philosopher's Holiday* (1938) *Philosopher's Quest* (1947), and *Under Whatever Sky* (1951). Dr. Edman was born in New York City in 1896. He was graduated from Columbia (B.A., 1917; Ph.D., 1920) and has been a teacher there continuously since 1918. He now serves as Executive Officer of the Department of Philosophy.

MODERATOR DENNY: Good evening, neighbors. Most of you will recall that we asked our audience during the last two weeks to send us their answers to two questions which would be analyzed by Dr. Ernest Dichter, consulting psychologist, in connection with this program. The first question: What worries you most at the present time? The second: What newspaper headline would you like most to see tomorrow morning?

It should be understood that this is not a conventional public opinion poll but represents an analysis of the more than 4,000 replies from Town Meeting listeners from all forty-eight States. As background for this discussion, I'm sure you will be interested in Dr. Dichter's report on your own answers and your own attitudes. This is necessarily a summary of his report. Dr. Dichter.

DR. DICHTER: The one outstanding fact that can be reported as a result of this survey is: "Moral and emotional security are more important to Americans than financial security." This runs directly counter to the stereotype picture of Americans which prevails among many Europeans and other nationals that the American is an individual who is almost exclusively concerned with money.

Almost three times as many Town Meeting listeners indicated that they worried more about the lack of moral and ethical security, lack of leadership and unclear definition of personal and national goals than they do about their own financial future. Sixty-two per cent expressed such moral concern about the present situation. It should be stressed that these answers do not necessarily confirm or deny America's support of the present position of the Administration.

Forty-two per cent of those who wrote state as their main worry: "imminence of war." In this group we tabulated only those answers which had terse statements such as "war," "next war," etc. These percentage figures do not add up to 100 per cent because many respondents gave several answers to one question.

Eighteen per cent worry about economic insecurity. Five per cent worry about the draft, either of themselves, eighteen-year-olds, or a member of the family. Two per cent mention personal worries such as disease, cancer, and special problems. Two per cent are concerned about the growth of "dangerous" political systems and movements. One and one-half per cent mention as their main fear the loss of democratic liberties in the U.S.A. This desire for moral leadership can be considered an expression of the craving of the American people for a firmly established set of moral standards and values.

Second question: What headlines do people want to see? The answers were tabulated again on the basis of their psychological significance. The largest group consisted of those seeking peace through mutual understanding.

Here are the actual figures of these categories: Fifty per cent desired mutual understanding between nations and nonmilitary solutions of world problems. Thirty per cent called peace their greatest anxiety, without further comments. Fifteen per cent suggested passive violent solutions, for example, Stalin assassinated, etc. Twelve per cent mentioned active military solutions—Russia wiped out. Nine per cent mentioned passive peaceful solutions—Russia abolishes iron curtain.

Now concerning this diagnosis, it would seem, at first glance, that Americans lack emotional security and thus lack faith in themselves. It is interesting to note, however, that, actually, the majority of the people who responded felt that the present crisis involves the spiritual and moral backbone of each individual even more than military or diplomatic solutions. This, Mr. Denny, is of course, just a summary of some of our findings.

MODERATOR DENNY: Thank you Dr. Dichter and thanks to all of our Town Meeting listeners who answered these questions. This certainly supplies a fitting background for our discussion this evening on the subject, "How Can Modern Man Find Faith?" We're going to hear from Professor Irwin Edman of Columbia University, Fulton Oursler, author of *The Greatest Story Ever Told,* and Bishop Austin Pardue of Pittsburgh. We'll hear first from Professor Irwin Edman, Johnsonian Professor of Philosophy at Columbia University, author of many books in this field, contributor to the *New York Times,* the *Herald Tribune* and leading American magazines. Professor Edman.

DR. EDMAN: Ladies and gentlemen, my sources have informed me of what the two succeeding speakers may tell you. One of them, I know, is going to give you what he calls "prescription." The other is going to tell you that faith in God is prior and necessary to the love of God. One is a Bishop, Bishop Pardue, the other is a Senior Editor of the *Reader's Digest,* which is a "Bishop of the printed word," and they will correct any false faith I may bring to you.

Ours is generally believed to be an age without faith. It is most disquieting, for many people, that there is nothing left, or seems to be nothing left, to believe in. Our future is, at best, grimly uncertain; our past has betrayed us. There seems nothing in nature or in man that offers security or hope. Freedom has not yet come to a great part of the world; and it has vanished from parts to which it has recently come. The free world is acutely on the defensive, and not all of that world has been freed.

Looking to the larger world of nature and human nature, faith does not seem more plausible. In the eighteenth century, reasonable men could easily believe in the reasonableness of nature and in the progress of mankind through reason. In the nineteenth century, the noblest and the most realistic could believe in the dignity, the nobility of human nature and its fulfillment in democratic institutions. To millions of men and women no such faith any longer seems possible. It is no wonder, therefore, that many have turned, though perhaps not in such large numbers as is generally held, to otherworldly religions.

I have no time to argue what I believe to be the case against the supernatural. I can only state the elements of what may be called a humanistic or secular faith—faith in nature, in man, and in his possible works, rather than in what is conventionally called faith in God. How is man to find once more belief in himself and his own ideals, reliance on that knowledge which he once thought would bring universal happiness, which he now thinks will bring universal destruction? How is man to find belief again in his own ideals?

The first step is to remind ourselves that, bad as our times are, in the long run, knowledge is still power, still moral power, that human beings are still human; that free societies manage somehow to survive and to revive. Knowledge has produced the dreadful instrument of the atomic bomb and worse. Human nature sometimes looks hopeless in an age which has seen a revival of almost universal despotism and violence. But even in our own age science has given us miracles of transport, communication, and medical cure. And human nature by its heroisms and generosities, even in our own time, has revived our faith in human nature. Nature is our home, knowledge is our instrument, man is our ideal, and we can have faith in our own future. That seems to be faith enough.

MODERATOR DENNY: Thank you, Irwin Edman. Fulton Oursler has achieved success in many fields—in newspaper work, detective story writing, and the writing of novels. But he is best known for his religious articles in the *Reader's Digest*—where he's a Senior Editor—his religious novels, *The Greatest Story Ever Told* and *Why I Know There Is a God*, and the radio series he created, "The Greatest Story Ever Told." We welcome your counsel on Town Meeting. Fulton Oursler.

MR. OURSLER: Mr. Chairman and friends. As I listened to the learned discourse, and moving discourse, of Professor Edman and heard him relate me to some kind of bishop and when he told what he believed, I was reminded that sometimes beliefs can be very distorted. It reminded me of a conversation, that I once overheard, by accident, between my young son, Tony, and his pal, Mike Hopkins, the son of the beautiful actress, Miriam Hopkins. They were talking theology, which I'm not going to talk, tonight, and Mike said to Tony, "Do you believe in the devil?" and my Tony said, "No, it's like Santa Claus, it's your father." Beliefs can indeed be distorted.

As I see it the way for modern man to find a true faith is, first, to abandon a false faith, to which he has been passionately devoted and which has now brought him to the edge of destruction.

One of the most hopeful signs is the accelerating collapse of that false faith. We are not, now, as I view our plight, in the midst of a religious revival; we are, instead, in a period of disillusion. Man's worship of himself, the belief that he could stand alone and solve all his problems, solely by his own effort—by intelligence and diligence—was a presumptuous blunder. He gave his worship to materialism; the priests of his fallacious trust were scientists, engineers, and philosophers, whose service to the world is worthwhile only when it is also service to God. Materialism has betrayed us by inventing wonderful gadgets, but finding no discipline by which to insure that they would be used for the general welfare—for progress instead of destruction.

I am asked if psychiatry is not modern man's substitute for God. Like all our other devices, psychiatry is a tool. It's a weapon, although still in its experimental stage. It can never approach its full usefulness until it is employed by men of conscience, men with a sense of moral responsibility, men who love God and want to serve Him. One example of that is that most psychiatrists have a very low percentage of success with alcoholics, but I know practitioners who send hopeless cases to Alcoholics Anonymous—where the percentage of permanently arrested cases is extraordinarily high. Among the first steps of that organization is for the patient to realize that he cannot get well by himself; he must turn his problem over to a higher power. Psychiatry is not a substitute for God; it is one of God's tools, that, when developed and used wisely, can make this a happier world. God is the *only* hope for a happier world.

Jesus once asked the question: "What kind of father is it who if his son asks him for bread will give him a stone? If he asks him for fish will he give him a serpent?" That is the kind of treatment materialism has given its followers.

MODERATOR DENNY: Thank you, Fulton Oursler. Well, there seems to be a sharp difference of opinion there between Fulton Oursler and the philosopher from Columbia University, my friend, Irwin Edman. I wonder if there is such difference between Mr. Oursler and Bishop Pardue. Well, we shall see in a moment. Bishop Austin Pardue, of the Diocese of Pittsburgh, has been active in the Episcopal Church all of his life. Since graduation from Divinity School, he has found time to work a great deal with young people and their problems in Juvenile Court, to sponsor amateur athletics, to write books—the latest being *Prayer Works*—to do a radio series, and maintain a reputation, at the same time, as a very fine administrator. We welcome to Town Meeting, Bishop Austin Pardue.

BISHOP PARDUE: Dr. Edman has stated that he doesn't believe in the supernatural, that he believes in humanism and in the possibilities of man. Mr. Fulton Oursler has said that our accelerating world collapse is due to man's worship of himself in place of God.

My approach to faith would be through the acceptance of Jesus Christ as the divine Son of God, as the Redeemer and the Saviour of mankind. I know that man can find faith by placing his whole trust in Him. How can man know? By the scientific method of experiment. When you are ill you go to a doctor. He does write a prescription and you don't argue with him. Instructions are on the bottle. Perhaps it says, "Shake well before using, try three times a day after meals." And you try it and you probably get well. This is not blind faith. This is faith that is based on experience and on the background of the medical profession.

Throughout the ages the Christian Church has developed innumerable methods of approaching God—through prayer, Bible reading, meditation, worship, service, and the reception of the sacrament—and it has been my experience that, when people are willing to try a method and to try it faithfully and to hold to it, they will find faith and they will find God. Christianity is anything but a debate. It is a way of life.

Communists say that the Christian faith is for the weak, for the people who cannot stand on their own feet. And I agree. It is for the weak. Who is strong? If you scrape all of the false front and the bluff off people, if you know their weaknesses, their lies, their failings, their tempers, their fears, their pasts, how many strong and self-sufficient men do you think you will find? Every man has some god in whom he trusts. It may be money; it may be comfort, personal power, his own intellect, science, physical strength; or else he may be dependent on entertainment, or sleeping pills, or liquor.

A great doctor, here in New York, by the way, told me that over 50 per cent of all the prescriptions written in New York are for sleeping pills or for sedation. And, by the way, I asked an alcoholic friend of mine, one time, why he got drunk and I got a very quick and a very revealing answer. He said, "Because it's the quickest way out of Minneapolis." And Minneapolis is a lovely town.

Every man has some kind of faith. It may be even in the love of his despair, and of his own self-pity. The question is, "In whom do you trust?" I believe with St. Paul that all things less than Jesus Christ shall eventually fail. But He never fails. People ask, "Why should I pray?" or "What should I pray for?" My answer would be to pray for a realization of the presence of God, because where God is, there are all of the virtues and the powers a man will ever need. Pray for forgiveness, so that the short circuits that block His power may be repaired. Pray for healing, for, in the last analysis, only God can heal either a human body or a world. And so I stand with St. Paul, who says, "In Him I live and move and have my being."

MODERATOR DENNY: Thank you very much, Bishop Pardue, and now we are ready for the questions from our interrogators. We have two distinguished interrogators tonight, the minister of the Community Church of New York, Mr. Donald Harrington, and the author of *Watch for the Morning*, Mr. Thomas Sugrue. Mr. Sugrue, may we have your question first, please.

MR. SUGRUE: This one goes to Mr. Oursler or, ricocheting, for Bishop Pardue. On your premise, Mr. Oursler, that modern man has run into a bad place and a false faith and is now being disillusioned and then you also say that the new psychology, psychiatry, psychoanalysis are instruments and tools by which man may, possibly, rediscover himself, but they must be used by men with conscience, why is it, then, that the church, which always has had, as part of its tradition, healing—why doesn't it take over these instruments? Why doesn't it teach its own men and brief them in this new kind of technique for helping man, who finds himself in an extremely complex position with regard to his own problems, nowadays? Left to secular uses, it will gradually decline and fall into the hands of people, perhaps, no less worthy or honest than those charlatans who have always taken advantage of people in trouble.

MR. DENNY: Mr. Oursler?

MR. OURSLER: I quite agree that the church should use every instrument that God has given us. There are some approaches to that, Mr. Sugrue, in a mild way that I am familiar with. Some of them are experimental and I wouldn't want to speak of them here but one very conspicuous evidence is the work being done in the clinic conducted in Marble Collegiate Church by Dr. Norman Vincent Peale, along with Dr. Smiley Blanton, who is a psychiatrist as you know and lecturer at, I think, Vanderbilt University. Certainly, the church has had the idea, I think, at times that they should be able to heal these mental difficulties. But when they face the problem of alcoholism, for example, various priests have said to me, "But why isn't religion enough?" It is enough. If you have enough faith, it is enough. That is true also of cancer or any other disease. I believe that any disease can be cured by a man filled with the faith of God, if it's God's will for him to be healed. But in the meantime we have developed medical techniques and we don't try to heal these things and disregard what medical techniques are available to us. I hope to see an increase of Christian psychiatrists. I know several of them and they are wonderful persons and have wonderful results.

MR. SUGRUE: I just want to ask one quick question, Mr. Oursler. You mention healing—but how are we to heal the man who doesn't know that he is sinning? The man, who murders by killing the ambition of his own son, doesn't believe that he has done wrong. We need someone in the church to help him find out that fact.

MR. OURSLER: Indeed, yes. And there is a wonderful text in the gospels about that. The man who calls his brother a fool is in danger of hell-fire, worse than the others, because calling a man a fool is to rob him of his self-confidence, to destroy his intiative. That is one of the great sins and I wish it were preached more in our churches.

MR. HARRINGTON: I have a question for Bishop Pardue. There is no doubt that modern man has lost his faith to a large extent, and I wonder if organized religion isn't, to a great degree, responsible, in that it has failed, largely, to implement its general principles. I think we would all agree with you, Bishop Pardue, that men could find a way out of their difficulties, if they would follow Jesus, and love God, and love their neighbors as themselves. But what do these general principles, to which we would all agree, mean to a man who has to go out and engage in cutthroat competition in his economic life, who is required to go to war, and kill, and hate, and bomb innocent civilians? Just exactly how do you implement these general principles, to which everybody agrees, into specific programs of action? Isn't it at that point that the church has failed and, therefore, that all people are terribly confused and at war with their own consciences?

BISHOP PARDUE: Well I would not agree that Christianity has failed as you state. Certainly, I agree that many of us in the church have failed, lamentably, to practice the religion of Jesus Christ and to apply it in economic and social and world life. Someone has said that we have been inoculated with a mild form of Christianity which has made us immune to the real thing.

MR. SUGRUE: I'd like Dr. Edman, if he would, to explain to me why his supposedly humanism, or his paganism, sounds so much like Christian mysticism and what the difference is between faith in man, himself, or faith in human nature, and faith in God.

DR. EDMAN: Mr. Sugrue and I share something that heathen or pagan minds have often shared with the most conventionally religious, namely, a deep sense of a certain mystical brotherhood of human beings and a deep sense in the possibilities of man and nature. If my enthusiasm, for those possibilities, seems to make it necessary, according to Mr. Sugrue, to call what I believe in, a belief in divinity, I would gladly agree, except that I might be accused of believing in what organized religion calls a personal God. I'd like just a little semantic distinction on my own. I'm willing to say that I'm as deeply religious as Mr. Sugrue but I would mean something different by the religion I was deeply religious about.

MR. HARRINGTON: I'd like to ask another question of Mr. Edman. I wonder, sir, if it isn't true that what man lacks, today, rather than a lack of faith in God, is a lack of a sufficient faith in himself. I'd like to have you comment on this because it seems to me that the problem, today, is that modern man has lost a sense of his power to participate in the important decisions and problems of our time.

DR. EDMAN: That seems to me, Mr. Harrington, to be a social question. Man feels overpowered by the enormous machinery of social life, the way I felt overpowered, the other day, when I tried to get 96 cents back from the Western Union Telegraph Co. for a telegram that hadn't been delivered—I got the 96 cents back. I think man can revive faith in himself and I think in order to do that, he needs to belittle himself a little less, than some conventional religious leaders counsel him to belittle himself. And just one further observation I want to make concerning the alcoholics who are supposed, apparently, to be the foundation of sound religion because religion works with them. I would appeal to soberer minds.

MR. OURSLER: It is a function of religion to help the weak and God does help the weak in Alcoholics Anonymous.

Is Youth Forgetting Religion?
James Harry Price and Paul Weaver; George V. Denny, Jr., Moderator

This discussion was broadcast as an America's Town Meeting of the Air program over an ABC radio network from Oak Park, Illinois on 31 October 1950. It was held under the auspices of the Oak Park Community Lectures.

The Reverend James Harry Price is rector of the Episcopal Church of St. James the Less in Scarsdale, where he is in charge of one of the largest church schools in the Episcopal Diocese.

Dr. Paul Weaver is Dean of Religious Life and Chairman of the Division of Philosophy and Religion at Stephens College, Columbia, Missouri. During the summer of 1950 he was director of the Inter-University Seminar in Mysore, India where representatives from four continents were in attendance.

MODERATOR DENNY: Good evening, neighbors. We invite you to join us here at Oak Park, Illinois, to discuss a question that vitally concerns every one of us directly or indirectly, "Is Youth Forgetting Religion?"

A generation ago, we called them flaming youth, but today's youth are the sons and daughters of the flaming youth of the jazz age. Flaming youth burned its candles in the speak-easies of the prohibition era. Today's youth—restless, bewildered, and insecure—burns its atomic energy searching in every direction for satisfactions, certainties, and securities.

But has today's youth forgotten religion? According to the Purdue Opinion Panel, recently syndicated by the Chicago *Sun-Times*, 79 per cent of this representative youth group, 4 out of 5, says that it doesn't make any difference what religion you follow, as long as you lead a good life.

In a previous national poll of teen-agers, 22 per cent of them said they felt they were not living up to their religion; 18 per cent wondered what life was all about; and 19 per cent wanted to know how one does set standards of right and wrong.

Religion has been defined as the faith we live by. "Seek and ye shall find," said Jesus Christ. Where is youth seeking for faith and religion today?

To counsel with us tonight, we've invited two experts in the field of religious education, the Reverend James Harry Price of the Episcopal Church of St. James the Less in Scarsdale, New York, which has one of the largest church schools in the country, and Dr. Paul Weaver of Stephens College, who conducts the famous Burrall Class, attended by students of three educational institutions in Columbia, Missouri.

We'll hear first from the Reverend James Harry Price of Scarsdale. Father Price.

FATHER PRICE: Thank you, Mr. Denny. Yes, youth is forgetting religion, just as youth is forgetting American history, spelling, and English grammar, or any other area in which youth is receiving little instruction. The press and the magazines of the country point almost daily to youthful behavior that is scarcely exemplary, which evidence does not do much to sustain Dr. Weaver's side of this argument tonight.

No, Dr. Weaver, the testimony is rather overwhelmingly against you. For instance, J. Edgar Hoover of the FBI says, and I quote, "Approximately one-half of all crimes against property during 1949 were committed by persons under twenty-five years of age."

The special thing about youth is youthfulness, or immaturity. Youth is a part of mankind, and religion is natural to mankind, as sight is natural to the eyes. Like tasting and hearing, religion is in man's nature, because man is a rational being.

The capacity to reason is something man is born with. Reason alone leads man to natural religion, or the seeking of the union of man with God. Ordinarily and outwardly, this consists of doctrines and precepts by which man seeks to bring about this union. Religion is true when its doctrines are in conformity with reason or are revealed by God.

If youth receives no religious instruction, then youth has no religion to forget. If youth knows nothing about violin playing, it is scarcely fair to berate youth for not playing the violin well. For example, I know a young lady in a New England college who is now taking a so-called course in religion, which really is a course in antireligion. It's as if she were taking a course in tennis that taught her that tennis is outmoded and that one really should be playing golf.

Statistics, as we all know, indicate vast increases in juvenile crime, moral irregularity, and youthful restlessness. The president of Wellesley College reports that by and large the girls that come there are essentially ignorant of the religious traditions of their families.

Youth spends most of its time in school, and popular education, if not hostile to religion, is indifferent to it—just leaves it out—and thus leaves out a whole realm of truth and experience. How it has come to pass that so powerful an agency as public education can ignore an area that is so essential to the welfare of the individual child and the future citizenry of our Republic is one of the mysteries of modern education, especially since education, along with religion, consists in developing intelligence, acquiring knowledge, and forming character; and more particularly, since our country is founded upon Christian religious principles clearly set forth in the Declaration of Independence, where we say, "All men are endowed by their Creator"—with a capital C— "with certain unalienable rights."

On our currency, we state, "In God We Trust." On the Great Seal of the United States—it's on the dollar bills in your pockets—the eye over the pyramid symbolizes Divine Providence, and the Latin *Annuit Coeptis* means, "God favors this our undertaking." The triangle in which the eye appears symbolizes God the Father, God the Son, and God the Holy Ghost.

Our armed forces maintain hundreds of chapels and a splendid and heroic corps of devoted chaplains, and church attendance, which is the practice of religion, is required of all students at Annapolis and West Point. Yet this explicitly stated religious faith upon which our Republic is founded is almost as unknown to American youth as is Florentine painting.

Our youth is being denied a big part of its birthright of freedom. Youth is forgetting religion because we are hiding our light under a bushel and acting as though we can't teach them because we don't know ourselves. By the natural law, parents are responsible for education, and teachers are supposed to do what parents would do if they had the technical skill and the time.

MODERATOR DENNY: Thank you, Father Price. Dr. Paul Weaver is Dean of Religious Life and Chairman of the Division of Philosophy and Religion at Stephens College in Columbia, Missouri. He also conducts the famous Burrall Class, which is attended by students of the University of Missouri, Christian College, and Stephens College. We are happy to welcome him back to Town Meeting. Dr. Paul Weaver.

DR. WEAVER: Thank you, Mr. Denny. I agree with Father Price that the religious education of youth has been neglected. I agree with him that our country has been founded upon religious assumptions. I disagree with him, however, when he says that reason alone leads man to religion, or that church attendance is the practice of religion, and I disagree emphatically that youth is forgetting religion.

I could quote a new curriculum in religion at New York University to disprove him, one at Princeton, one at Yale, and the researches of Dr. Shedd which now show that 60 per cent of all our State universities and land-grant colleges are offering courses in religion for academic credit.

George Denny referred to the Burrall Class, which it is my honor to teach. A few weeks ago, well over a thousand young people indicated by poll what they were most interested in. The two leading items were, "Ethics for Our Age" and "How Can I Develop a Mature Religion?" Does that sound as if youth were forgetting the vital matters that religion is about? As a matter of fact, a majority of the youth I know is rather pitiably searching for some sort of foundation for living.

In a philosophy class at my own college recently, students were asked to state what they wanted out of life. Listen to their answers, universally agreed to by every student. "We want more than anything else inner stability and strength. If we can get this, then we will be able to be happy and secure, accept freedom, and grant equality to all other men." Does that sound to you as if youth were forgetting religion, Father Price?

If religion is concerned about the foundation and the direction of people's lives, then how can anyone say that one's attitude toward a creed or a given church has anything to do with whether one is forgetting religion or not?

I will admit that many young people today have the conviction that much of organized religion is not about the quality or the direction of their lives. I fail to see, for example, how church suppers, where people eat poor food at cheaper prices, are religious. Youth is searching for inner stability, for clear ideas about right and wrong—in short, for a faith to live by. What we have done for them falls far short of that.

Young people today look at much of the religion that we offer them like the streetcar conductor in Providence, Rhode Island, looked at a New Haven, Connecticut, token that was given to him one day by mistake. He held it up against the light, he examined it carefully on both sides, and then he said, "What in the world is that?"

During the past summer, I attended an inter-university seminar in

Mysore, India, where we were talking about the role of the university in social development. Overwhelming and staggering was the data of the backward peoples of the world and their needs—millions of people living permanently on the sidewalk, underfed, racked by disease. Said the representatives of these universities, "There's something missing in education today, when the graduate of the university does not care about human needs and does not want to give his life to serve them."

Yes, I think we can agree that there's something missing. And the thing missing is religion. And if by religion we mean anything that Jesus said and did, then it must be clear to us that this religion is more than verbal, more than some rational point of view.

One man came to Jesus and said, "What must I do to be saved?" and He said, "Sell what you have and give to the poor." To another He said, "Drop what you are doing and come after me." The blind came to Him and were made to see, the lame to walk. The modern name of that is medicine. The hungry were made to eat. The modern name of that is economics.

And if we want to follow religion as Jesus showed it to us, then we are going to see that it has to do with integrating human personality around clear purposes that are good and Godlike, and action dedicated to do something about it in the world.

How many of us, for example, can face up to the problems that we see in the world today, the Korean war, the atomic bomb, the threat of a third World War? What is Christian action, and are we taking it? Not at all. We're scared to death. Nor does our Christian teaching save us from this awful problem of the hammer blows of the future.

An undergraduate at Cornell last week said, "I want to learn how to live. Why doesn't the church help me? They always talk about something I don't understand."

Youth demands today a spiritual religion, a religion that will take all the assets of the modern world and make youth stable and strong inside. And youth demands a practical religion, one that will help to solve their problems and one that will help to build a new world of peace, justice, and brotherhood.

I say youth is not forgetting religion. It is religion that has forgotten youth.

MODERATOR DENNY: Thank you, Dr. Weaver. Father Price, I can't believe you don't have a comment or question for Dr. Weaver. Have you, sir?

FATHER PRICE: Yes, thank you, Mr. Denny.

Dr. Weaver has certainly summarized his thinking very cogently in the story of the Providence streetcar conductor. It recalls Alice and the Cheshire cat. "Which way do I go to get out of here?" asked Alice. "That depends on where you want to get to," replied the cat. "It doesn't matter much," said Alice, "so long as I get out of here." "In that case," said the cat, "it doesn't much matter where you go."

Alice couldn't think of any answer to that, and the cat went on, "To the left lives a Mad Hatter, to the right a March Hare. Whichever way you go, you'll go among mad people. I'm mad. You're mad. We're all mad here." "What makes you think I'm mad?" asked Alice with some asperity. "You must be," said the cat, "or you wouldn't be here in the first place."

Dr. Weaver has told us that youth demands a spiritual religion, that we confuse ritual and empty virtues with real religion, and that youth hungers for eternal values, and so on.

I would like to ask Dr. Weaver one simple question phrased in different ways. Can we teach youth science without teaching youth at least one specific science? Can we teach youth sport without teaching some specific sport? Can we teach baseball without balls, bats, and bases?

All that Dr. Weaver has said to us tonight is itself simply another form of religious doctrine and is itself as rigidly dogmatic as what he calls an ideology based on outworn concepts of virtuous duty, which is exactly like saying plane geometry based on outworn concepts of three-sided triangles.

He's offered us a creed which is much less clearly stated than the Apostles' Creed, but a creed, nevertheless. We must beware and remember that he who says, "I shall be free from all creeds," is in those words stating another creed of his own.

To come to my one question to Dr. Weaver. It is, can we teach religion without teaching some doctrine or precepts?

MR. DENNY: Well, Dr. Weaver, he's thrown the ball right in your lap. Will you step up, please?

DR. WEAVER: Well, I'll try to answer that question. I think it's a very good one, and I think it's an important question. Now it may very well be that the position I have taken tonight forces me logically into admitting a creed. If so, I will simply say that my creed is very simple, and is not worked out in terms of a complete set of precepts that are involved with historical quarrels between churches, but I would go back to the Gospels of the New Testament for my creed, and I would quote one who I believe still has a lot of guidance for us, Jesus Himself. He said, "Two things you must do; the first is to love the Lord, your God, with all your heart and mind and spirit and strength, and the second, which is like unto it, is to love your neighbor as yourself." One's a vertical, one's a horizontal; and I think it's important to keep this simple, in order for simple people in the world to find themselves and so live by actual religion.

MR. DENNY: Thank you. And now, Dr. Weaver, have you a question for Father Price?

DR. WEAVER: Yes, I do. Father Price, I'd like to ask you this. If you think that the practice of religion has to do simply with church attendance and is centered in a rational creed, what do you have to say about the tremendous need in the world today, and the example of Jesus, who Himself seemed to be no earnest devotee of a particular church, but who went out into the highways and the byways to serve human need wherever He found it?

FATHER PRICE: I didn't say that ethical conduct or the worship of God in the church was the only thing required of a religious person. It's one of the things. Dr. Weaver's quite wrong in thinking that the Lord spent all of his time on the highways and byways. He was at the wedding feast in Cana of Galilee. He went into the synagogue, as was his custom, and took up the Scripture to read and read from Isaiah, as was his custom. This was religious worship as all Jews have always practiced it.

We must always remember that the first four Commandments are concerned with man's relationship to God, the next six are concerned with ethics. I am not talking about ethics, I'm talking about religion. Ethics is a part of religion and secondary to it. Religion is concerned with the worship and supplication and reconciliation with Almighty God.

The Need for a Spiritual Revival
Swami Nikhilananda

The Reverend Swami Nikhilananda founded the Ramakrishna-Vivekananda Center of New York in 1935 and is at present its spiritual leader. The paper below was presented at the Tenth Conference on Science, Philosophy, and Religion held at the Men's Faculty Club of Columbia University 6-9 September 1949.

Swami Nikhilananda was born at Noakhali, Bengal, India in 1895. After spending four years at the University of Calcutta, he joined the Ramakrishna Order of Monks in 1921 and spent six years at the Himalayan monastery of the Ramakrishna Order at Mayavati. Coming to the United States in 1931 he worked first as As-

The Need for a Spiritual Revival

sistant Minister of the Vadanta Society of Providence, Rhode Island. The center, which he launched two years later, now has headquarters in New York.

The Swami has translated from the Bengali *The Gospel of Sri Ramakrishna* (1942) as well as several of the Hindu scriptures (Sanskrit), including the Bhagavad Gītā (1944) and the first volume of the Upanishads (1949). A second volume of the Upanishads is in preparation.

Professor Nels F. S. Ferre of Vanderbilt University describes the composition of this address as "beautifully written and wise" reflecting "admirably the large-visioned spirit of Hinduism." Dr. Edgar S. Brightman of Boston University adds: "The paper shows a very definite non-Occidental tradition can be the source of universally inspiring ideals which cannot fail to move every openminded reader. Even he who rejects much of the metaphysics of the writer will respect the experience in which it is grounded."

THE HUMAN SITUATION today calls for an intense spiritual revival on a broad humanistic, ethical, and rational basis. The transcendental experiences of religion must breathe a new life and vision into the political, economic, and social affairs of a weary and distracted humanity. The challenge of aggressive evil can be met only by the power of aggressive good. The transformation of human nature—the control of greed, lust for power, and sensuality—is possible only through spiritual disciplines and the knowledge of God, the soul, and the hereafter.

It is said in the Bhagavad Gītā that whenever virtue subsides and vice prevails in the world, the Spirit of God incarnates itself for the vindication of righteousness and the destruction of iniquity. The scene that forms the background of the teachings of the Gītā bears a striking resemblance to the world conditions of our time. A study of these teachings may throw light to guide us out of our present bewilderment.

There reigned in ancient times two royal families in Northern India, the Pāndavas and the Kauravas, who were first cousins. The former represented all the virtues, such as piety, kindness, truthfulness, and unselfishness, whereas the latter, their opposites. Arjuna, the third among the Pāndava brothers, was the personification of the noble knightly qualities. He and his brothers were cheated out of their kingdom and earthly possessions by the evil machinations of their cousins and sent to exile with the promise, however, that they would get back their property after their return. During their absence, the Kauravas consolidated their power and position and ruled the country in the most unrighteous manner. The Pāndavas, after the period of banishment was over, asked back their kingdom but were scornfully refused. All efforts at peaceful negotiation failed, and war became inevitable. The two armies met on the battlefield of Kurukshetra, near modern Delhi, where subsequently India's political fate was decided several times. As the terrible holocaust was about to begin, Arjuna asked his charioteer, Sri Krishna, to take him to the middle of the battlefield, a sort of no man's land, wherefrom he could survey his friends and enemies. Casting his eyes around, he saw, among the belligerents, his brothers, cousins, sons, nephews, uncles, and teachers—people with whom he was intimately related by ties of blood and friendship. The consciousness of the immense responsibility resting on his shoulders as leader of the Pāndavas sent a cold shiver through his spine. He recounted to Krishna, who was also his philosopher and guide, all the evils that resulted from a war, such as economic dislocation, moral disintegration, social anarchy, and the coarsening of man's refined nature. He wanted to run away from the duty of a warrior, who is a defender of justice and righteousness, and live in the forest as a recluse. At that moment of depression, grief, and confusion, he sought Krishna's wise counsel. Krishna's teachings form the background of the Bhagavad Gitā.

Krishna at once diagnosed that Arjuna's malady was a momentary weakness. This malady could not be cured by false platitudes or the expression of foolish sentimentalism. The sunken spirit must be aroused. With stinging words he touched the most sensitive part of the warrior's soul and reproached him for his cowardice, unmanliness, and ignoble dejection of spirit. Krishna knew that Arjuna's depression was the result of his ignorance regarding man's true nature, his duty, his end and means. Out of a sense of false commiseration, Arjuna wanted to give up his dharma, or duty—that of a knight who was pledged to defend righteousness at any cost.

Sri Krishna commenced the teachings of the Gitā with a magnificent discourse on the immortality, the non-duality, and the eternity of the Soul.

> Never was there a time when I did not exist, nor you, nor these kings of men. Never will there be a time hereafter when any of us shall cease to be.
>
> Even as the embodied Self passes, in his body, through the stages of childhood, youth, and old age, so does It pass into another body. Calm souls are not bewildered by this.
>
> Notions of heat and cold, of pain and pleasure, arise, O son of Kunti, only from the contact of the senses with their objects. They come and go; they are impermanent. Endure them, O Bhārata!
>
> That calm man who remains unchanged in pain and pleasure,

whom these cannot disturb, alone is able, O greatest of men, to attain immortality.

The unreal never is. The Real never ceases to be. The conclusion about these two is truly perceived by the seers of Truth.

That by which all this is pervaded, know to be imperishable. None can cause the destruction of That which is immutable.

Only the bodies, of which this eternal, imperishable, incomprehensible Self is the indweller, are said to have an end. Fight, therefore, O Bhārata!

He who looks on the Self as the slayer, and he who looks on the Self as the slain—neither of these apprehend aright. The Self slays not nor is slain.

It is never born, nor does It ever die, nor, having once been, does It again cease to be. Unborn, eternal, permanent, and primeval, It is not slain when the body is slain.

He who knows the Self to be indestructible, eternal, unborn and immutable—how can that man, O son of Pritha, slay or cause another to slay?

Even as a person casts off worn-out clothes and puts on others that are new, so the embodied Self casts off worn-out bodies and enters into others that are new.

Weapons cut It not; fire burns It not; water wets It not; the wind does not wither It.

This Self cannot be cut nor burnt nor wetted nor withered. Eternal, all-pervading, unchanging, immovable, the Self is the same forever.

The root cause of a man's grief and delusion is the identification of the Soul with the body. Fear of death paralyzes him because he is ignorant of the Soul's true nature. The wise perform their duties in the world, cherishing always the knowledge of the Soul's deathlessness. The ignorant man regards himself as the body, endowed with a soul. The illumined sage knows that he is the Soul, possessed of a body. There lies all the difference between the materialistic and the spiritual view of life.

Socrates, rightly called the wisest, the noblest, and the justest man of his time, lived, worked, and died under the spell of immortality. Cheerfully he died, giving a discourse on the Soul's immortal nature.

That the meat of philosophy can sustain a man in his hour of weakness is vividly described in the Book of Job. When that righteous man bemoaned the loss of his property, and the death of his children, and when, suffering from an excruciating physical ailment, he longed for death, the Lord told him about the creation, explained how insignificant a man is as a physical entity, and asked Job to gird up his loins like a real man.

To resume the teachings of the Bhagavad Gitā: In the battlefield, where the grimmest realities of life are faced and fought, where man's very existence hangs by a slim thread and the mind acquires an intense concentration and inwardness, Krishna propounded to Arjuna the science of the Absolute, and showed him the path of liberation from ignorance and attachment. He described at length the nature of God, the Soul, and matter. He explained the meaning of duty and its ultimate purpose. Further, he discussed the various yogas or spiritual disciplines by means of which a man attains to the Highest Goal. They are suited to different temperaments. The active mind pursues the discipline of selfless work. The philosophical mind discriminates between the Real and the unreal, and renounces the unreal. The introspective aspirant practices self-control and analyzes the various states of the mind with a view to ascertaining what lies in the inmost depth of consciousness. The emotional person cultivates an all-absorbing love for God and thereby sublimates his lower passions and desires.

Several conceptions of the Godhead are discussed. God, in His true essence, is Pure Consciousness, incomprehensible to the senses and the mind. Neither being nor non-being, He is described as silence. From the relative standpoint, God is immanent in the universe. He is the Light of lights, within and without all living creatures. Both far and near, He sustains creation by a fragment of His power. In the cosmic mind of the World Soul, all things are foreordained; later on they are accomplished in the concrete universe. The inner controller of men, God walks through all feet, sees through all eyes, hears through all ears, eats through all mouths, thinks through all minds, and feels through all hearts. By Its own inscrutable power the Godhead appears as the Personal God—the Creator, the Preserver, and the Destroyer of the universe, man's Redeemer—and is worshipped as Father-in-Heaven, Jehovah, Allāh, Śiva, Kālī, Vishnu. God further manifests Himself through Divine Incarnations. God becomes man so that man may become God.

Sri Krishna emphasizes in the Gitā the harmony of religions. The different faiths are like so many pearls in a necklace, and God runs through them like the string. God accepts a man's worship, without regard to its form, provided it is whole-souled and sincere. He fulfills everybody's desire, mundane or spiritual. All fulfillments in time and space are transitory. The knowledge of God alone endures from everlasting to everlasting. Man should seek the eternal and immutable Truth where alone is the consummation of all desires.

The special message of the Bhagavad Gitā is that of Karma-Yoga, the discipline of right activity, by which a man can attain to the Highest Good. Karma or work covers all actions of man: physical, verbal, or mental. No embodied soul can live without action, even for a moment. A man's survival demands some sort of action. The illumined sage, who has realized the supreme goal of existence and has nothing to lose or gain in the world, works for the welfare of others and protects the social order. Krishna warns men against non-activity, which results in stagnation and death. But an action can be a fetter or a liberator, depending upon the worker's inner attitude. An egocentric action, performed for a selfish purpose, acts as a chain. It creates attachment to the result and thus binds the worker to the phenomenal world. But the same work acts as a liberator, if performed in a detached spirit for the welfare of others. Man should work as God's instrument, surrendering to Him the results, good or evil, pleasant or painful. This is the secret of right activity. The worker must maintain an inner equanimity, unperturbed by success or failure. He must not come under the sway of love and hate, which are natural for the sense organs in the presence of agreeable and disagreeable things. Slavery is the cause of suffering. It is man's lower nature that is affected by good and evil, and clamors for the results of his actions. But there is a higher Self in every man, who is the witness and not the doer, the spectator and not the actor. Therefore though one part of man must plunge into the duties of life, another part remains the onlooker and surveys the distant horizon of peace by rising above the pairs of opposites. To see non-action in action is the secret of right activity. All actions, if performed in the right spirit, enable one to commune with God. Cloister and laboratory, temple and marketplace, hermit's cell and farmyard, are all fit places of worship. Art, science, philosophy, and religion are all vistas opening on the limitless realm of the Infinite.

The Bhagavad Gitā discusses at length a man's dharma. This really untranslatable Sanskrit word is often rendered in English as duty or religion. The sanction of religion is often derived from an extracosmic God or from scriptural authority. A man's duty is often determined by his education, family tradition, or social position. But dharma belongs to the inner nature of man. It is something within him which points out what is to be done and what is to be avoided. Dharma sustains him in his present state of evolution and shows him the way to further growth. It inspires his thoughts and actions and gives him the stamp of individuality. It is his code of honor and explains his reaction to the world. There is the dharma of the king, the dharma of the philosopher, the dharma of the monk, and also the dharma of the trader. The dictum, "Thou shalt not kill," cannot apply to all men. A man cannot give up his dharma any more than a dreamer can give up his dream.

Hinduism accepts the theory of rebirth and believes that a man's inborn tendencies are created by his past actions. The Soul is immortal, the physical body alone being destroyed at the time of death. A Hindu thinks that the law of karma explains, to a large extent, our inequality at the time of birth. A man's dharma is determined by his own past actions and serves as a sort of blueprint in his present life. He cannot go against his dharma without doing violence to his nature. It shows him the path of least resistance. Hence the Bhagavad Gitā says that a man's own dharma, however imperfect, suits him better than another's dharma which appears to be perfect. One should die following one's own dharma; the dharma of another is fraught with danger. "A worm that is born in filth dies if kept in a pot of rice."

Through the performance of unselfish action, by following the dictates of dharma, a man becomes pure in heart. He is freed from ego, greed, and other baser passions. This is followed by an inwardness of mind which makes contemplation an easy task. In the depth of contemplation, the ultimate Reality is revealed. As a man develops his inner life, actions become fewer. Physical work becomes impossible for him when he is totally absorbed in contemplation. It gradually drops away. Completely transformed by the knowledge of Truth, the enlightened man dedicates himself to the welfare of the world.

The Bhagavad Gitā ends with a striking declaration that where there is complete coöperation between the spiritual power and the kingly power in the world, there one sees glory, success, prosperity, order, and the all-round welfare of man.

The need for a spiritual revival is imperative today to give back to humanity its lost bearings. The rehabilitation of man, after the devastation of two great wars, will not be possible by merely giving food to his empty stomach or by filling his mind with wild ideas. Science and technology may endow him with great power which, if not illumined by deep spiritual truths, will destroy society. What shall it profit a man if he gains the whole world but loses his soul?

Spiritual truths have always shown amazing flexibility in adapting themselves to the changing conditions of time. These eternal verities need a new orientation to suit the present human situation. In this connection the following points may be taken into consideration.

a. Religion is a transcendental experience revealing the eternal relationship between the eternal Soul and its eternal Creator. Its ultimate utility cannot be measured by its effect on the five minute span of human life. One should remember in regard to every material achievement the wise saying of Abraham Lincoln: "Even this shall pass away." The destruction in a few minutes of a city or a monumental building which required the labor and skill of many centuries to build, proves how right Christ was when he warned his followers against laying up their treasures on earth.

b. Though the final religious experience transcends time and space, yet its application lies in the realm of the temporal. "The earth is His footstool." Even the mystic, coming down from his exalted experience, does not explain away the universe. Our life in the world is a manifestation of the life in God. The embodied soul is a mixture of dust and deity. His baser nature cannot be ignored. It is to be transformed into the divine. His cravings for moral perfection, economic security, and sensual enjoyment are legitimate. Through them he ultimately attains to communion with the Infinite.

c. Both meditation and work are effective spiritual disciplines. Through the former, one subdues the restlessness of the mind and acquires inner serenity. Many of our so-called humanitarian activities are inspired by a desire to win name and fame, power and position, or to run away from a guilty conscience or kill the boredom of life. The quality of the work is determined by the thought behind the action. Meditation on God purifies the thought, and the pure in heart can perform truly unselfish action. Again, without work, contemplation may degenerate into laziness and self-deception. The essence of God is Being, but He unfolds Himself in the world process. The One and the many are the two manifestations of the Supreme Reality. Therefore God can be seen both with closed and with open eyes. Intellect, emotion, and meditation, when properly blended, create a balanced life.

d. Twenty-five hundred years ago Buddha said: "Do not believe in what ye have heard; do not believe in traditions because they have been handed down for many generations, do not believe in anything because it is rumored and spoken of by many; do not believe in that as truth to which you have become attached by habit; do not believe in anything on the authority of your teachers and elders. After observation and analysis, when it agrees with reason and is conducive to the good and benefit of all, then accept it and live up to it."

The above is a neat statement revealing the very soul of the scientific method; but it adds something more to the aim of science in that it brings in the factor of human welfare, which some of the scientists in their zeal for the impersonality of science are apt to forget. The Yoga system of Hinduism also insists on arriving at truth through experimentation, observation, and verification. A spiritual truth is valid only when it does not contradict universal reason, one's inner experience, and the experience of other seers of truth.

The divorce of science from religion has been the major tragedy of our times. A statement of the Vedas says that he who worships science alone, enters into a blinding darkness, but into a greater darkness enters he who worships superscience alone. The knowledge of science must be combined with the knowledge of superscience. Through the former one overcomes the physical handicaps of disease and suffering, and through the latter, one attains to immortality.

God reveals Himself in nature as well as through the inner spirit. Science deals with nature, and religion with spirit. Both natural theology and mystical theology bring us the knowledge of God. In future, science will be religious and religion scientific. Which means, religion will not proclaim any truth that will be opposed to reason, and the power released by science will not be exploited for unethical and unspiritual purposes.

e. Spiritual life must be built on the solid foundation of moral laws. Ethics is not a mere device to remove the friction between apparently incompatible human natures. Its validity does not rest on the words of a prophet or a scripture. It must derive its mandate from the universal experience of humanity, irrespective of creed or race or caste. The double standard of ethics often practiced in society has been a potent cause of war. The ultimate sanction of ethics lies in such spiritual perceptions as the divinity of the soul and the unity of existence. We must love our neighbor because he is non-different from ourselves. Further, all living beings are our neighbors. The Bhagavad Gitā says that he who sees himself in all and all in himself does not injure others, because by injuring them he only injures himself. The concept of the oneness of existence must be the basis of all human relationships.

f. Hinduism accepts the doctrine of karma or the law of cause and effect. This applies to the individual life and also to the life of society. Nothing happens without a cause. In the individual life, the present is determined by the past, and the future by the present. Good produces good, and evil produces evil. Likewise, in the life of a nation, the righteous acts of the past are responsible for the present national well-being, and the unrighteous actions for the present misfortune. Neither God nor an inscrutable fate is to be held responsible. The postwar disintegration of moral and economic conditions has been caused by the evil forces that are generally let loose during war. Only right thinking at the present time will bring about a happy future.

g. A religion is kept alive not by learned theologians, but by genuine mystics. Religion has never come into existence by the power of intellect but has been founded on the bedrock of the experiences of prophets. A tall edifice, a big congregation, delectable social activities, and material grandeur are but the trimmings of religion and not its soul. Too much emphasis on organization often kills the spirit. In order to corrupt truth, Satan tempts man to organize it. Every man must be born in a church, but no one should die in it.

h. In the healthy religion of the future there will be no room for bigotry, intolerance, and exclusiveness. There is no such thing as a single scheme of salvation. Salvation is not the monopoly of any church. All paths lead to the hilltop of one and the same God-Consciousness. The different religions are suited to different aspirants in their various stages of progress. All religions are but manifestations in time and space of the Eternal Religion which is a transcendental experience. A man should cherish single-minded devotion to his own faith, and respect for the faith of others.

Man longs for a Universal Religion to which all can subscribe. Where will one find it? Certainly it cannot be an eclectic faith created by gathering the beautiful features of different faiths. That method has been tried but has failed. An eclectic faith, created by man's intellect, may look beautiful, like a bouquet of flowers, but it soon withers away for want of roots. Religion is based upon the experiences of the saints and seers. They preach religious truths by the command of God. Furthermore, a Universal Religion is not created by the sword or money or political power. The major religions of the world—Christianity, Hinduism, Islam, Judaism, and Buddhism—by the test of the survival of the fittest, have demonstrated their usefulness for mankind. They have come to stay; one of them cannot thrive at the expense of another. It should be clearly understood that the salvation of the Christians, Hindus, Moslems, Jews, and Buddhists lies through their respective faiths. It is useless to force Hinduism upon the non-Hindus or Christianity upon the non-Christians. But this does not mean that the different religions cannot be benefited by one another's experience. A genuine religious preacher should try to deepen people's faith in their respective religious traditions.

Where then is the Universal Religion? It is not to be created. It exists and needs to be discovered. It forms the core of all religions. One does not find it in religious myths and rituals, which can never be universal. It lies in the essence, which alone is universal. Rituals and mythologies, which are the concretization of the transcendental truth, are necessary for beginners. They cannot be dispensed with. Through these man prepares himself to realize the ultimate truth.

Variety in unity is the pattern of the universe. John is different from James. But from the standpoint of humanity, they are one. A man is different from an animal. But, as living beings, animals, birds, and plants are all non-different. As Existence Absolute, all things are one. God is the Absolute Existence. In Him the whole universe discovers its unity. This unity exists, it has only to be found out. Let a Christian follow the precepts of his own faith, let a Hindu and a Jew follow theirs. If they strive long enough, they will all ultimately discover God, Who runs like a seam under the crusts of rituals and forms. Or to change the illustration: God is the center and different faiths are the radii which converge in Him. As one moves away from the center, the distance between one radius and another becomes greater. As one comes closer to the center, the distance between the radii is gradually reduced. When one reaches the center, one finds unity with all in God.

Let not a man speak malicious words against another's faith. Let us not destroy or pull down. Iconoclasts never do any good to anybody. Take a man where he stands and from there give him a lift. Deepen by all means his aspiration, but leave him free to follow his path. Ultimately everyone will reach God and attain to perfection.

A healthy religious revival will give man a song to sing in order to reinvigorate his weary body and cheer his distracted spirit. The immensity of the present difficulties need not frighten us. They are a challenge to bring forth the best in man. Great things have been accomplished at times of stress and strife. Hamlet was not written in a time of peace nor the Cathedral of Chartres built when society was normal. As the towers of the Chartres Cathedral stood above the confusion of the eleventh century, so may the spirit of man stand triumphant over the turmoil of the present time.

Religious Philosophy and Intergroup Progress
John LaFarge, S.J.

The Reverend John LaFarge is Associate Editor of *America*. He was born at Newport, Rhode Island in 1880. After obtaining an A.B. at Harvard in 1901 he studied at the University of Innsbruck in Austria and at Woodstock College in Maryland. He was ordained in the priesthood of the Roman Catholic church and entered the Society of Jesus in 1905. Father LaFarge's books include *Jesuits in Modern Times* (1927), *Interracial Justice* (1937), *L'Homme de Couleur* (1938), and *The Race Question and the Negro* (1942). During the spring of 1951 he traveled and lectured in Europe as a representative of the State Department.

This essay was read at the Tenth Conference on Science, Philosophy, and Religion in their Relation to the Democratic Way of Life held at the Men's Faculty Club, Columbia University, in September 1949.

IN THEIR seventh symposium, the members of this Conference considered the problems of power and aggression in Western culture and the methods for the transformation and integration of that culture itself. Naturally enough, this consideration extended to questions of relationships, for good or bad, between the various groups that make up our nation, and to some of the ways by which these relations could be improved.

We now find that the matter of intergroup relationships has made a remarkable advance in certain respects, however little it may have made in others. The *fact* that such relationships form an important object of study and planning—on a community scale, on a national or international plane—is much more familiar to the thinking public than it was three or four years ago. Discussion concerning the President's program of civil rights as well as the issues of recent elections, have helped, as have the detailed debates on human rights in the United Nations, both on the human rights issue as such, and on specific alleged violations of the same. Recent plays, novels, and films have been bringing basic intergroup problems vividly to the public. The repercussions of a story like Alan Paton's *Cry, the Beloved Country,* films like *Gentlemen's Agreement* or *Home of the Brave,* are illustrations.

Again, expert and detailed information on the facts of intergroup life have become more available to the public through various agencies, and such a general coördinating agency as the American Council on Race Relations.

Urgency of the intergroup question is heightened by the new position of world economic leadership our country has assumed (or fallen heir to), symbolized in President Truman's famous "Point Four," for the economic and cultural development of backward world areas. Political and social problems will inevitably follow economic and cultural development. With them, the whole gamut of majority-minority relations, at home and abroad, clamors for our understanding. The effort to integrate newly arrived displaced persons from Europe into our economy and social structure raises a still further set of intergroup queries.

With the problem of intergroup relations moving out of the library into television, as it were, we naturally wonder if the errors of the past will be repeated. It is much to the point to know what our youth are being taught in this respect, so that we can ask ourselves what may be done to improve not only such teaching, but our own way of thinking, if necessary.

A recent report issued by the American Council on Education, entitled *Intergroup Relations in Teaching Materials,* provides information as to what ideas our young people in general are receiving. Through a grant of funds by Milton Biow of New York City, stimulated by the National Conference of Christians and Jews, a representative and unbiased committee, during the years 1944-1946, made a survey and appraisal of 266 textbooks used in schools, twenty-four introductory college texts, and twenty-five college manuals—a total of 315 volumes prepared especially for instructional use.

A study of this report confirms the general increase of interest in the matter of intergroup relations. The growth of interest and of familiarity with the problem is most notable in the texts for college use. Many of these show acquaintance with the bearings and terminology of intergroup discussions. Along with the signs of progress that the textbooks reveal, the survey has catalogued some notable defects.

> The essence of democratic human relations (notes the survey) is respect for individual worth and dignity . . . In the textbooks, however, the individual is usually submerged in the group; there is not adequate attention to the nature and value of personality. (The topic is treated as) one of manners or glamour—how to be polished and urbane (p. 30).
>
> The teaching materials and courses of study fail to tell pupils "what it means to be a human being"; they fail to lay the intellectual foundations for the central ethical principles of the democratic theory (p. 30).

How to capitalize on individual traits forms the keynote of most of the discussion (p. 43).

The ethical issues involved, derived from the basic tenets of the American Creed, are not stressed. Belief in the dignity and worth of the individual is not highlighted (p. 186).

The social derivation of personality is discussed, with the clear implication that group membership affects personality. But the rights and responsibilities of the individual are not considered (p. 190).

Society is seen to be more and more a system of emotionally cold relationships . . . Full and adequate treatment often is lacking of the position of the individual in a democratic social order and of his rights and obligations (p. 183).

Religion is rarely discussed, either as a social phenomenon or as a moral doctrine. In discussions on nationalism or social control, it is sometimes mentioned incidentally, but with the comment that in the last century religion played a more important part in strengthening nationalism than it does today (p. 185).

Emphasis is on processes rather than on policy (p. 181).

The materials in most instances do not make an effort to combat stereotypes and antipathetic attitudes. Usually no attempt is made to present the members of ethnic and racial groups as in-group members, or as potential in-group members, of our society. This may result from the fact that the survey materials often have not been thought through clearly in relation to the stated objectives of the courses.

On the other hand, "excellent factual materials on social groupings in a democracy, on social relationships and on ethnic groups do appear in some of the surveys."

There is little discussion of discrimination as such, but examples are frequently given of the manner in which certain groups are discriminated against in our society. It is doubtful whether merely calling attention to violation of the democratic theory we profess can of itself do much to minimize such practices. There is need for more convincing proof of the technical error committed when group discrimination is practiced as to how its continuance produces undesirable effects upon the community (p. 212).

The concept of diversity in unity is not stressed (p. 200).

The report concludes with the words:

Too often the facts presented are dissociated from the emotional drives which impel action. The writer must be objective about his facts and his descriptions, but he may, and indeed should, feel strongly about his values. Emphatically committed to the American Creed, commitment which he should not conceal, he should present situations dispassionately but interestingly. The will to achieve social change and the techniques of social action must be learned, along with social theory and factual data bearing on ethnic, racial, and religious groups. At present, most college texts are unbalanced because slight attention or no attention at all is given the motivations and techniques of social change; their approach is unnecessarily static (p. 216).

We may hazard a few thoughts as to what bearing this particular inspection may possess toward intergroup relations in general, and to the still wider problem that faces all our symposia.

Features which the authors of the survey have found, for the most part, to be lacking in their material fall largely into two categories.

One of these categories is of an ethical nature: the lack of adequate motivation for intergroup justice and fair play from the standpoint of moral standards and of elementary human rights. There is a tendency to take intergroup maladjustments as merely something "given," and to pass over consideration of the "ought" in favor of merely registering the *status quo*. Significantly, this omission is coupled with lack of consideration for religion.

In pointing to this significance I am not maintaining that religious sentiment, *per se,* is always co-extensive with ethical insistence. As was noted in the Seventh Symposium by Dr. F. Ernest Johnson: "It must not be overlooked that the definitive element in religion has never been ethical agreement but rather a great desire on man's part to come to terms with what he conceives to be ultimate spiritual reality. The impulse to worship seems to be prior to the impulse to obey. A sense of religious dependence is much more pervasive than any ethical discipline." I am simply looking upon religion as a habitual and traditional exponent of ethical doctrine.

In the second category we find the question of idealistic motivation: of a principle or a spiritual passion which will energize what has already been discerned as ethically right. The report complains that the approach to intergroup relations, as shown in the textbooks, is "unnecessarily static." If the approach is static, it must be because some great energizing force has been neglected. Such neglect *is* unnecessary, for the knowledge and use of that force is at the disposal of all, and has long been known under the general title of love.

Love, as applied to the solution of social problems, is as much a tangible reality as are the data of the problems themselves. The social force that will send an Albert Schweitzer into the forests of tropical Africa, or a Vincent de Paul into the slums of seventeenth century Paris, or inspire an Abraham Rubin to effect his intergroup ideals in the world of twentieth century industrialism, is simply not to be explained away as a "dream" or an aberration.

Modern physics has caused us to pay more respect to the substantial reality of energy and dynamics as part of the framework of physical nature. If this holds for the material world, how much more is it verified in the world of human affairs, where love still shows itself as "stronger than death," and as capable of making the individual steadfastly and systematically "surpass himself," to an extent for which no limit has yet appeared.

Implication of the American Council's survey would seem to suggest, therefore, need of a new estimate of the sphere of intergroup relations. Two realms of thought offer themselves for exploration in such a connection.

The first of these realms is that of the relation of the intergroup problem to a determined and organized juridical order. If groups in our country, or in the world at large, are to enjoy security in fundamental human rights, it is difficult to see how they can do so without reference to some greater structure of which they form part. Citizens experience security in civic rights through reference to the fundamental juridical and political structure of the nation. If human beings are to enjoy in their natural rights a security similar to that of the American citizen's civic rights under our Constitution, it would seem that there must be some constitution in the whole framework of humanity's existence to which the individual person or group can appeal.

Individuals do not become equal to one another merely *between themselves* in any conscious or significant way, but through reference to some commonly accepted measure: whether of size, strength, intelligence, goodness, or of conformity to the ultimate measure of all mankind. One of the frequent assertions of minority groups is that they do not feel satisfied, they lack a sense of assurance, as long as the only pledge of their security is the good will of another group. It is difficult to see how any group, no matter how powerful and how benevolent, can convey to another a security which it cannot claim for itself.

Despite all psychological comprehension and all ingenuity of adaptation by social planners, such a relationship is built on sand.

A world concept that can see no ultimate value or significance in anything but pure contingency and complete individual freedom, would seem to be as much a menace to security of intergroup liberties as a totalitarian world concept that denies all liberty to the individual, and looks upon him solely as an expression or instrument of society. It is only when all groups are beholden to a common and superior court or juridical structure of mankind, that either equality or security seems to take on an intelligible meaning.

Such an order of moral law, such a basically juridical structure of human society, finds, in turn, its ultimate justification in the relations of the human race with its Creator. This relation is freed from the realm of mere abstraction, and made a dynamic reality for our daily human existence, precisely through the historical dealings of the same Creator with the human race. "Honor thy father and thy mother," and "Blessed are the merciful," especially when mercy is shown to the stranger and the foreigner, are truths that are as much part of man as his skeleton or blood. It was Sinai and the Sermon on the Mount which were supremely effective in making them an active part of man's historical development.

Here is a still further field of exploration in the first mentioned realm of intergroup justice.

Another area of exploration would be that of the relation of intergroup problems to an adequate and vastly enlarged and deepened concept of social love. By this I mean a love which is not content with mere kindly benevolence, nor restricted to the remedial treatment of human miseries, but one which seeks to find the causes of distress, through organization, science, and education, thereby working toward the creation of a new and better community.

The survey's wording might seem to indicate that the idea of love is now outmoded, judging from the indifference shown to the idea by a certain type of social analysis. The frightening growth of hate and cynicism in the world might scare us into the same conclusion. A careful appraisal, however, may suggest a different outlook. Without minimizing the force of either of these assertions, I suggest that *because* of the devastation wrought by hate, *because* of the growing dissatisfaction with an analysis that harms its own indispensable work by expressing a nervous anxiety about any judgments of value, the modern world is on the eve of a new appraisal of spiritually or religiously motivated love as a social force. Such an appraisal will soberly recognize the *power* of love when spiritually or religiously inspired. It will also demonstrate the wide *scope* such love is capable of attaining, when it is united with real intelligence and expresses itself through the findings of modern sociology and psychology.

Love centered on persons, not on abstractions, works through the operating room and the x-ray, through the social clinic and the scientific organization of the community, with exactly the same reality and power as it did when St. Martin slit his mantle in two in order to shelter the beggar of Amiens from the winter's cold. In fact, a scientifically and sociologically implemented love wakes a new depth of devotion and intelligent selflessness with which its simpler manifestations were not familiar. Grace, to use a theological term, can illumine the mind and fire the heart with new spiritual splendors and more glorious self-surpassings, when it operates under the stress and strain that dedication to genuine social reconstruction requires.

If the idea of law (in the juridical, not the legalistic sense), or if the idea of love is exiled from the area of intergroup relations, it can only be ascribed to an inadequate idea of what is contained beneath these concepts.

A pleasant intellectual Punch and Judy show, suitable for a television set, can be staged by pitting against each other on the one hand the advocates of a bristlingly anti-transcendental type of scientific humanism, in the field of social planning, and on the other a narrow, selfish type of religious sentimentalism. Since the marionettes have been artificially conditioned, they can be made to whack each other merrily over the poll. Why, however, should that be necessary?

The remark made by Paul A. Schilpp in the Eighth Symposium[1] relative to another type of artificially conditioned conflict—that between Eastern mysticism and Western science—is applicable here: "It should be possible to find at least a common ground of meeting by recourse to an intellectual spiritualism which is even today no longer foreign to the world's foremost scientists and which, at the same time, leaves room for the significance and ultimacy of the (at least relatively) free individual moral agent."

Any concept of human relationship that is subject to review and judgment by an ultimate and unchanging authority is obviously open to misinterpretations. An Authority which deals with mankind accord-

[1] *Learning and World Peace*, Lyman Bryson, Louis Finkelstein, R. M. MacIver, editors, Conference on Science, Philosophy, and Religion in Their Relation to the Democratic Way of Life, Inc., New York, 1948, p. 383.

ing to law and covenant can be represented as arbitrary and capricious. The changeless character of an eternal Absolute can be attributed to purely man-made political institutions. Basic natural law can be confounded with mere legalism, while political tyranny can be executed in the name of the sacred and the eternal.

But the fact that a concept is open to abuse is no justification for its abandonment. Rather, it suggests a deeper exploration of the wealth of meaning that it contains. Wrote Rudolf Allers in the Seventh Symposium:[2] "The inability to realize ideal values and to make them the directive forces of life is no reason for not presenting them to the common man. Rather I am convinced that the ability for some kind of higher vision is frequent and greater than is usually assumed. The common man is definitely wronged by the belief that he is unable to live up to an ideal and that his interests will never go beyond the indeed low level on which they stay—or are kept—today. Man, on the whole, is underrated."

If our human relationships are not subject to any higher review, then it is difficult to see why they are not exposed to the mere interplay of contending powers, socially or politically weighted; so that we wake to find we have exchanged the rule of law for the rule of passion. As the American Council report remarks (p. 53): "Unless democratic societies are strong, that is, unless individuals assume their full rights and responsibilities—they may be engulfed in a rising tide of dictatorship, in which a few strong men control, by fair means or foul, the great majority." Our supposed liberation, then, turns out to be merely living on time borrowed from a partly surviving ethical order. It contains within itself the seeds of its own ruin.

The sociologist, on the other hand, can come to recognize that the idea of law and the idea of love are not necessarily a scandal to the purity of the scientific method. As Edgar S. Brightman remarked on another paper by Rudolf Allers:[3] "The essential point of Dr. Allers's paper—that the love of one's neighbor is rational—is in my judgment thoroughly sound . . . It is grounded in the essential nature of persons as persons, while totalitarianism rejects both reason and love."

In my own paper for the Seventh Symposium[4] I expressed the view:

---

[2] *Conflicts of Power in Modern Culture,* Lyman Bryson, Louis Finkelstein, R. M. MacIver, editors, Conference on Science, Philosophy, and Religion in Their Relation to the Democratic Way of Life, Inc., New York, 1947, p. 492.
[3] *Learning and World Peace, op. cit.* p. 295.
[4] *Conflicts of Power in Modern Culture, op. cit.* p. 289.

If we have belief in the past, if we have hope in the future, we shall have love for the person present to us. We shall be strengthened by a continued and immediately present and living bond of loving union between the different groups in our community. And this living bond of love is participation in that ever present love which God communicates to man and which man in his limited manner strives to return to his Creator. Such a bond is the surest confirmation of peaceful and constructive intercultural relations.

Professor Louis Wirth, in the same volume, suggested, in a series of searching questions, how relatively little we know "about the actual potency of ideas and ideals in shaping human destiny." The best way to avoid the mistaken conclusions against which Dr. Wirth warns us is to study the concepts we have been discussing not as lofty abstractions waving a fairy wand over the troubled sea of human existence, but as living realities operating in the daily lives of quite ordinary men.

A powerful drama, *City of Kings,* recently produced at the Blackfriars Theatre in New York, tells the story of a saintly Dominican lay brother, Martin de Porres, who lived and died in Lima, Peru, some 400 years ago. Martin was the son of a partly Negro mother and of a Spanish hidalgo. Among many remarkable things, he was the first person to establish organized hospital management and organized municipal relief work in the New World. He was the victim of gross racial—or as we would say, intergroup—injustice. His complete and crushing triumph over this injustice was achieved precisely through the overwhelming power of his socially and scientifically expressed love for suffering mankind. Why? Because the might and the scope of his love revealed to the smaller community of his religious associates, and to the larger community of his city and nation, his full stature as a spiritual person, measured against the ultimate Measure of all human worth.

It is through the racial groups, their diversity yet unity upon the earth, their mutual tensions yet their boundless constructiveness, that human life progresses, despite all the obstacles that evil places in its way, in a dialectic of law and love. If this is a major element in the meaning of all history, it is peculiarly rich in meaning for our own times. The more deeply we penetrate the full scope of these super-conscious historical forces, and succeed in relating them to the treasures placed at our disposal by the valid elements in modern social analysis, the less likely we would seem to be taken captive by those unconscious forces of history which drag men down to conflict, slavery, and extinction.

Postlude

The Authentic Revolution
Erwin D. Canham

This address was delivered at the Lehigh University Commencement on 19 June 1950. Mr. Canham was awarded the Honor Medal and $1500 for it as the first prize in the Freedoms Foundation judging of college commencement addresses at the ceremonies held at Valley Forge, Pennsylvania on 22 February 1951.

Erwin Dain Canham was born in Auburn, Maine in 1904. He studied at Bates College (B.A., 1925) where he distinguished himself as a debater, and as a Rhodes Scholar at Oxford University (B.A., M.A., 1936). Joining the staff of *The Christian Science Monitor* in 1925 he became its managing editor in 1941 and its editor in 1945. Mr. Canham and several staff members of the *Monitor* are the authors of the book *Awakening: The World at Mid-Century* (1951), the last chapter of which presents a program of individual action.

A. J. Cummings, the columnist of the *London News Chronicle,* has written that this address is "one of the most impressive declarations I have seen for a long time. . . . Without heat, but with devastating force, Mr. Canham elaborates the argument that the true spiritual revolutionaries are the creators of modern Western democracy, and that Communism, with all its large materialistic pretensions is, in theory and practice, black reaction."

LET ME tell you my thesis bluntly at the outset.

It is that the struggle for the salvation of free society in our time will be lost unless we in the West—and particularly we in the United States —awaken to and project the fact that we are the great revolutionaries in world history, and that our revolution is basically a spiritual one which we have already proved in action.

I have returned recently from a month in Western Europe. There I worked on UNESCO Committee in Paris, talked with leaders of the Labor party and of the Conservative opposition in Britain, inspected significant parts of the American occupation in Germany, and conferred in Italy with colleagues from all of Western Europe at a meeting of the International Federation of Newspaper Editors.

All these opportunities to explore the thinking of political, cultural, and informational leadership in Europe have led me straight to my conclusion: that what the world needs most is an awakening to the truly spiritual character of the Western heritage. It is especially necessary that the rest of the world understand the spiritual foundations of America. For we have let most of the world think that the American achievement is primarily materialistic. This is the great gap between ourselves and those who yearn for much more than materialism. And we are the first victims ourselves of the misunderstanding.

The misunderstanding concerning America which is so pervasive in the world today is the key to the future of Western society. For, as Dr. Charles H. E. Malik, Minister of Lebanon to the United States has well said: "To the superficial observer who is unable to penetrate to the core of love and truth which is still at the heart of the West, there is little to choose between the soulless materialism of the West and the militant materialism of the East."

And, as Dr. Charles H. E. Malik of Lebanon further told us in the West: "If your only export in these realms is the silent example of flourishing political institutions and happy human relations, you cannot lead. If your only export is a distant reputation for wealth and prosperity and order, you cannot lead. Nor can you really lead if you send forth to others only expert advice and technical assistance. To be sure to lead and save yourself and others, you must above everything else address your mind and soul. Your tradition, rooted in the glorious Greco-Roman-Hebrew-Christian-Western-European-humane outlook, supplies you with all the necessary presuppositions for leadership. All you have to do is to be the deepest you already are."

There is the challenge of the hour. It is not a challenge requiring the postulating of new fundamentals. It calls for no panaceas. It is a call to awakening and to articulation. The basic need is to understand and to proclaim the truth. The West must find its voice.

Let us, therefore, ask ourselves a few fundamental questions. Let us proclaim the truth on the issues which confront the world. Mankind today is being told that he must choose between revolution and reaction. He is told that Communism represents revolution, and that our system—which is opprobiously called capitalism—represents reaction. In such a confrontation, there would be no choice. Mankind must go forward. But this statement of the issue is an explicit reversal of the truth.

The fact is that Communism—like totalitarianism in any form—represents the blackest of reactions. The fact is that the free system, of which capitalism is only a small and modified part, represents the authentic revolution—not a subversive revolution, but a revolution which sets men free.

We in the Western world are the true standard-bearers of a great and emancipating doctrine. We are the people who ought to be singing the rousing songs and waving banners from the ramparts of the human spirit. Instead, by a tragic reversal, we have allowed ourselves to be thrust into the indefensible position of seeking to protect the status quo. The free system is by no means the same thing as the status quo. Our tradition is not static, but is constantly dynamic. Our tradition strikes off chains. Totalitarianism would put them back on again. The stirring battle cry which ends the Communist Manifesto is itself a delusion. Marx and Engels wrote: "The proletarians have nothing to lose but their chains. They have a world to win." Where, in today's world, are most people in chains? Is it in the United States, where what is perhaps the most enlightened labor contract in history was recently signed by our largest industrial corporation and one of our largest trade unions? Or is it in the world's most extensive Communist state, the Soviet Union, where tragic millions, suffering and dying, are bearing the literal chains of slave labor? Is it in Britain, where labor's own government is in power and is carrying through the most extensive peaceful and gradual social revolution in history? Where are the chains today? Where are the mental chains? Are they in the free universities and the free churches of the Western world? Or are they in the Communist states where man's right to think is now denied on behalf of the omnipotent state, and free science or free religion have ceased to exist?

These are among the facts to which we must awaken.

But let us come at our task in orderly way. Let us first ask ourselves, in the most searching possible fashion, what are the chief claims of Communism, and let us confront these statements with the best truth we know. Then let us examine the two doctrines—Communism and Western democracy—in actual practice, to test their words by their works. And finally, let us chart a plan of campaign in this great battle of truth against falsehood.

First, what are Communism's basic postulates?

The primary claim of Communism—the foundation stone on which it rests—is that of dialectical materialism. It is the assertion that ultimate reality lies in matter, and in matter alone. But the truth as we know it, is that superior to matter in every way is the reality of mind and spirit. In our time an awakening to the metaphysical bankruptcy of materialism is beginning to sweep over thoughtful mankind. The awakening is most striking among the natural scientists. They are finding, in the realm of the very little and of the very large—of the infinitesimal and of the infinite—that old materialistic assumptions are no longer valid. Reality is now by them recognized to be related to consciousness. Time and space are seen to be dependent upon consciousness. Reality is emerging more and more to today's thinker as the basic essence which lies behind and beneath the material manifestation. In short, not the chair of wood and wicker, but the idea of chair existing in consciousness, is seen to come closer to ultimate reality. There is an even more striking and topical proof of the bankruptcy of materialism. Men have wrought the most powerful engines in their experience: from gunpowder and steam and electricity they have progressed to atomic power. And yet they now see that the power to help or harm mankind lies not in the atom itself, not in the uranium or plutonium or tritonium, but in the thinking that motivates the finger which does or does not push the button that does or does not set off these fearful engines of destruction. In the words of a great Yale natural scientist,[1] "Man, not matter, is the chief problem of mankind today."

This awakening of the natural scientists is having a new echo among the theologians. They had been shaken by the materialism of the last century, and, indeed, of the first half of this century. Even they had made altogether too many concessions to the alleged ultimate reality of and through matter. Now they are reverting more confidently to the eternal truths. When enough of the theologians see what powerful allies they have in the scientists of today—when they see how modern cosmological research has proved the unreality of matter—we will be on the threshold of a great spiritual revival.

The second great lie of Communism walks hand in hand with the first. It is that there is no God. Today we have the opportunity of knowing as never before that there is indeed a God, who is the loving Father of all mankind. We do not necessarily have to identify God merely with the single three-letter name: G-o-d. Perhaps it is useful to redefine God as the central Principle of the universe. Perhaps it helps to think of him as eternal Truth and Life and Love. These things cannot be denied. We know the universe is orderly. We know that it works according to established rules and principles, some of which we have been able partially to define. It seems to me to be rationally impossible to recognize the reality of an orderly universe and to deny God. And many of us have constantly the opportunity of turning to God—to Principle—in prayer. During the recent war as so often happens in times of manifest peril, many voices were lifted in humble and receptive prayer. Many regenerative and purifying answers came. But

[1] Dr. Edmund W. Sinnott.

it is important to base prayer upon understanding, rather than on superstition.

Prayer, if I may say so, seems to me to be the process of placing oneself in conformity with divine law. Here, again, truth is profoundly rational and can be accepted and understood in a new vocabulary. It is not necessary to think of prayer as supplication, but rather as an affirmation of man's birthright under the laws of the universe to place himself in harmony with the music of the spheres. Man, not God, has to do his part; God's work—the integrity of an orderly universe—is already done.

Still further to disprove Communist dialectic, take the assertions that there is no objective and eternal truth, and that only the transient and the temporal exist. I am sure that we in the Western world can readily prove to our satisfaction that there is Truth, and that it is transcendent.

Again we can prove it in the working of the laws of the universe. Or we can prove it in the vast and noble reaches of the mind and the heart. There is abundant evidence of the existence of permanent and immanent values. These are accessible to mankind through a humble search for understanding. They come through the path of reason as well as down the road of revelation. They lift humankind out of its own confusions and perversities into the land of eternal truth. They are to be confirmed not only in the religious convictions and teaching of mankind, but in the positive philosophical traditions of Plato and Aristotle, of Hegel and Whitehead.

Finally we come to another great Communist falsehood: that the individual exists for the sake of society and the state. This lie follows logically from the assertion of materialism and the denial of eternal Truth and order. It is the specific doctrine which enslaves mankind. And yet the truth as we know it and prove it in action daily, is that the state and society exist for the sake of the individual. It is this Communist lie which stifles the spirit of man. It is totalitarian. It is contrary to nature and to man.

Again in the eloquent words of Dr. Malik: "That the state, the mere organ of government and order, is the source of every law, every truth, every norm of conduct, every social and economic relationship; that no science, no music, no economic activity, no philosophy, no art, no theology, is to be permitted except if it is state-licensed and state-controlled; all this is so false, so arrogant, so autocratic and tyrannical that no man who has drunk deep from the living waters of the Western

Platonic-Christian tradition can possibly accept it. The state does not come in first place, it comes in tenth or fifteenth place. The university is higher than the state; the tradition of free inquiry is higher than the state; the Church is higher than the state; the family is higher than the state; natural law is higher than the state; God is higher than the state; within limits, free economic activity is higher than the state."

It is good that Dr. Charles H. E. Malik, of Lebanon, who blends in his own culture the best of East and West, should have recognized not only the spiritual importance of Church and university and family, but of free economic activity as well. For this brings us to the crux of our problem today. It is the free economic activity of the West which is most under fire in the contemporary world. It is this free economic activity which is used by those who hate it or misunderstand it to brand the West with the stigma and curse of materialism. The need, therefore, is for an awakening to the spiritual obligation and heritage of the free economic system.

Let us, then, proceed to the second of our main points: an examination of Communism and the free economic system as they reveal themselves in action.

It is not necessary, first of all, to belittle the actual achievements of the Soviet state. Historic objectivity requires us to recall the importance of the transition from czardom, the achievement of partial industrialization in the face of two wars. In a certain narrow framework, the Soviet state has accepted a large obligation to the individuals who make it up. It has gone a long way toward harmonizing the diverse interests of widely separated and scattered racial and cultural groups. In World War II the Red Army under Marshal Stalin helped greatly in resisting and defeating a powerful aggressor.

It is important to recognize also that we have to live with the Russians, and many of the things we find dangerous in the present Soviet state are traits and trends which long antedate Communism. We must find ways of adjusting ourselves to life with an awakened Eurasian continent. It is, perhaps, a blessing for mankind that the awakening and industrialization of this vast area has come about under a system which inevitably handicaps and limits its potential achievement. Sometimes one is appalled at the aggressive possibilities of a Russian Empire organized with the efficiency and power of industrialized Britain in the nineteenth century, or the United States in the twentieth century. A great natural scientist, Dr. Merle Tuve, recently remarked that the greatest single discovery of World War II was the efficiency of the free system. That kind of efficiency coupled with the natural resources and the immense racial dynamism of the people now under the hammer and sickle would make a world force of incalculable potential.

Communism has partly liberated and partly stifled this great capacity. On balance, at the point of the mid-century, there is far more of stifling than there is of liberation. When, as I believe to be inevitable, the Russian peoples are finally and genuinely liberated, we must be ready with a universal system of peace and order. Otherwise, they will be an explosive force against which today's Communism will be a pallid squib. Fortunately, there is also in the Russian people a great and magnificent spiritual and universal yearning. The free Russian soul, in all its exuberance, longs for human brotherhood and bears a heavy burden of anguish for the spiritual failure of humankind. These deep impulses have helped support Communism. They would be far more effective in support of a free system wrought for the benefit of all mankind. The Russian need for religion has partially and temporarily accepted Communism as a religion. When the Russian spirit is ultimately freed, it must find its way fully into the spiritual pastures of the great Western tradition of truth and love. Otherwise, Russia might remain the world's great challenge for long and turbulent years—far more dangerously than in our own time, when Russia is self-curbed by a hopelessly inefficient and inhibiting system. Even under the present limitations, it is unnecessary to add that the Russian achievement is considerable.

But on balance, the system remains one of chains and of slavery. It remains reaction, of the pattern of all the tyrannies that have sought to bind the free spirit of man and to withhold his natural rights down through the millennia. The fact is that Communism in its works is both spiritually and materially sterile. It is fundamentally a failure, because it is unable to utilize more than the merest fraction of the forces which are available. It is the most profligate destroyer of human resources. Its concentration camps and its mass graves are filled with the richest of human talent. Those who survive are denied the immense productive force of free inquiry, of objective experiment, and of full self-analysis.

Against all this, contrast the actual achievement of the free system of the West. The American economy—derided and attacked by its enemies—is today holding the line against world collapse. With all the faults which we know full well lie within our society and in its economic organization, the fact remains that the world today would be in chaos without the stability and productivity of the United States.

I am not here seeking to put a halo around the profit motive; far from it. The first and most important thing to say about the free economic system is that it can survive only to the degree that the individuals and combinations that make it up accept their social obligation.

Moreover, there is a considerable difference between much of the economic organization that passes by the name of capitalism in some parts of the world, and the best of the free economic system which enlightened leadership has brought into being in the United States and elsewhere. In many places, when we defend capitalism, we defend a feudal or a cartelist concept which would appall the thoughtful American business enterpriser. And in general, the economic system which exists in the United States is not quite the system which we have from time to time appeared to be supporting in the Ruhr or in Milan or in Lorraine, or even in Shanghai or Osaka. In some of these places, it is true, a sense of social obligation has dawned. We are not necessarily committed to the task of putting Humpty-Dumpty together again. But it is essential for us to put the importance of social obligation first, and not place ourselves in the position of advocating the return of industrial or financial feudalism.

The free economic system in the United States, and measurably in many other parts of the world—including, particularly, the smaller states where neutrality and/or coöperation have supported much real equality and high standards of living—can be objectively left to stand or fall on its own merits. It stands. It stands because it has given more opportunity to the individual than any other system ever tried. It stands because it is perfectible. It is not dogmatic—or should not be. It should always recognize the imperatives of self-criticism and of change. It should remember the paramountcy of human values. But these are not values of social security alone.

These are serious shortcomings in the idea of security, taken as an ultimate value. No society which enshrined security as an end in itself was able long to continue the march of progress. Dissatisfaction, adversity, risk—these are the imperatives of progress. Furthermore, to enshrine security as an end in itself, and to place its procurement and maintenance in the hands of the state, is to say that the state is above the individual. That is the road of slavery, of social suicide. We must keep the individual and the individual-based forms of organization as our primary values: man and church and school, along with family and free economic activity. The state owes nobody a living. At the same time, it is necessary and effective to organize through the state the many functions which the individual or private organizations cannot accomplish. It goes without saying that insurance barriers against the hazards of the economic system—old age or unemployment—are accepted and legitimate parts of state responsibility. That form of social security can be kept in its proper place.

But the increasing sense of dependency of the individual upon the state is not the obverse of the needful recognition of social obligation. It is, however, often the result of the failure of free enterprise to recognize its social obligation. In an industrial society, dominated by mass production, the individual is peculiarly insecure. He will seek the means of survival through collective action. For the laborer and artisan, protection comes through unions and government. Sometimes it comes through a coöperative relationship with his employer which is best of all. For the employer, protection also comes through collective action, sometimes private and sometimes governmental. But we have made great progress in evolving forms which are consistent both with free enterprise and with the special hazards of an industrial society. And again I must emphasize that these forms work best when they are founded upon a voluntary and perceptive acceptance of social obligation. That is the final and indispensable bulwark of the free system.

The fruits of the system are expressed in material and spiritual terms. Altogether too often, we have remembered only the material rewards. We boast of our standard of living, and when we go abroad the dollars clink in our pockets. We are sometimes obsessed with material gain, and with unrestrained selfishness. We have been our own worst salesmen, for we have convinced most of the rest of the world that we are money-mad materialists. But the greatest fruitage of the free system is spiritual. It lies in the recognition of the essential dignity of man which is implicit in equality of opportunity. It lies in the concept of legitimate service.

Perhaps you will understand me when I say, not too whimsically, that the American filling station is a very good illustration of the triumph of the free system. It is not the mechanical excellence of the filling station which is the chief virtue. It is its spirit. There is an enthusiasm and a self-respect which has infused the filling station, and made it one of the most successful of our various institutions. I do not altogether know why this is so; I merely point out that our free economic system at its best has gone a long way toward the enshrining of human values, and the attainment of a genuinely democratic relationship between server and served. I do not think anyone will deny that this is a spiritual value.

Something of the same achievement was illustrated the other day by the words of a German editor who recently had an opportunity to visit the United States. He was taken to a small Eastern city as the guest of a local newspaper. I asked him how he liked it and what he had learned. He put it in these words: "The best thing was that they introduced me to everybody, and they introduced me to the lift-boy just the same way they introduced me to the Mayor."

Awareness of the individual importance of man is our greatest spiritual achievement. It lies at the heart of the matter. Recognizing the significance of individual man, we have been able to mobilize and utilize the vast and still uncounted and uncountable resources of the human spirit. This is an accomplishment of revolutionary importance. It springs from the circumstances under which Europeans first come to the New World; it is based upon the political and theological roots of our society. It is genuine democracy. Established in the midst of the natural resources of a continent, it has enabled us to become a material and spiritual bastion for the safeguarding of Western civilization.

We have been able to achieve the adequate blending of natural and human resources, and while we have wasted natural resources often in profligate manner, we have come to utilize human resources within enterprising but humane bounds. This is illustrated by our rejection of child labor on the one hand and our increasingly wide opportunities for woman on the other. But I would not gild the lily. There are plenty of dark spots in our human experience, as we have moved toward fuller light. There are dark spots today. They are part of the challenge, part of the incentive, part of the unfinished business without which we would decline and perish.

Once more, quoting Dr. Malik of Lebanon in summary of this reference to the relative achievement of the West: "The only effective answer to Communism is a genuine spiritualized materialism which seeks to remove every trace of social injustice without loss of the higher values which constitute the very soul of the West."

And that brings us to our third point: a plan of campaign in the war of idea. The first necessity is manifestly self-awakening. We must rediscover the ideas by which we live. The ideology of Communism is well known, and widely proclaimed. It is passionately believed by many of those who proclaim it. This awareness and intensity is integrated and guided. There is no comparable intensity or coördination of ideas among those who believe in the free system. There will not be until we look at our heritage in fundamental terms, and arouse ourselves to its revolutionary import today. The obligation of every citizen, of every leader, is to awaken himself and to awaken his fellow man to the significance of today's challenge.

The second necessity, after the awakening, is the voice. Already there are various small voices from the free nations—voices seeking to penetrate the void of human thinking. They must rise to full articulation. We possess today mighty machines for disseminating ideas to every corner of the globe. But we have not yet learned what we have to say. In fact, the message we must say is the same old message of truth down the ages: the significance of man under God, of his brotherhood, of his birthright of freedom. And so let us organize—as American and British officials have recently been seeking to organize in London—a United Voice of Freedom. But as we speak in our united voice, let us not forget the advantages of diversity. The strength of the free system is that it is not regimented. The ideas of freedom must be discovered and proclaimed, orchestrated perhaps, but never stifled and never distorted.

The third necessity, along with the awakening and the voice, is the fuller demonstration of the free system in action. There is contagion in falsehood. Some of the lies of totalitarianism and materialism have penetrated into our own thinking. We must not let them stay there. In this unhealthy atmosphere of no-peace, no-war we have yielded some citadels to the enemy. Some have sought to weaken or destroy the free spirit of inquiry and of teaching in our schools and universities. Happily, enough have seen the truth clearly and have prevented the sabotage of our educational institutions.

In these bewildering times, we have yielded to distrust of human character and the cloud of suspicion—often of slander—hangs heavy over the human spirit. We must learn again to trust character, because free institutions depend upon respect for fellow man. We must spurn the corrosive doubts which do far more harm to our body politic than the dangers to which they pertain. We must, as I have said earlier, manifest social responsibility throughout our economic system. We must make swifter progress toward the removal of racial and religious barriers which prevent true community. These are but a few of our items of unfinished business—of our ways of proving in action the truth by which alone we live.

And finally, let us regain perspective, let us cast off the inferiority complex with which Communism has bemused us, let us reaffirm a consciousness of our birthright.

We stand in human history as the greatest revolutionaries of all time. Not just we Americans—but all of us in the Western world.

We are the guardians of a sacred and dynamic heritage. We have come a long way. We have a long way to go.

We have discovered long since the eternal truth of love and peace and brotherhood. We have discovered and in a measure applied the enormous potency of the free man.

We have lifted part way the heavy burden of toil that has crushed humanity down through the years and more gloriously we have begun to lift the curtain of ignorance which has blanketed the human mind.

We are on the march.

And today we are challenged. For the challenge we may be infinitely grateful. Because our society today faces adversity. There is a hill up which we must climb. We will not decline in slothful and concupiscent ease. We will pit ourselves against the lies which in our time assault the deep foundations of truth. These lies cannot prevail, even to the extent of setting civilization into a relapse, if we are worthy of our heritage.

And we can and will be worthy of that heritage if and as we awaken. The voice of no one of us is powerful enough to awaken all the slumberers in today's world. That is not bad; it is good; for salvation need come through no new Messiah.

It is better that it should come through the people, the little people if you will, as each awakens to the truth about individual man in a society under God—under the divine Principle of order and of harmony. The world that is being reborn can well awaken not through the trumpets of Messiahship but from the inner voice of spiritual consciousness.

But it is our individual and collective duty to think these things through for ourselves, and in our free way to help our brother man to his needful awareness. Let us pass along the message of freedom. One day it will reach critical mass and chain reaction will begin.

Meantime, we must preserve the physical defenses of the Western world by keeping military aggression at bay; we must strengthen the economic sinews and the stability of the free world; we must lead our civilization to higher plateaus of demonstrated freedom and achievement.

And from the valley below, those who have accepted the false doctrines of totalitarianism of the right or the left will one day see the heights which we have ascended, and will join us on the continuous pathway ahead.

The Challenge of Our Time
General of the Army Dwight D. Eisenhower

General Eisenhower delivered this striking address before the English Speaking Union in London on 3 July 1951. He made an eloquent appeal for Winston Churchill's idea of a united Europe. In Paris during the same week representatives of five powers—France, West Germany, Italy, Belgium, and the Netherlands—struggled for agreement on a European army to serve as part of General Eisenhower's command, Allied Powers Europe. The Schuman Plan for the integration of the Continental steel and coal industries, it will be recalled, is designed to give economic unity just as the plan for a European army is to give military unity.

For a sketch of General Eisenhower's career see the note to his speech, "A Report to the Nation," published earlier in this volume.

The editorial page of the *Saturday Review of Literature* for 17 November 1951 is given over to a brilliant report entitled "Eisenhower, Europe & Hope" written from SHAPE Headquarters at Marly, France by William D. Patterson. He informs us: "The Europeans believe that General Eisenhower understands war. That is another reason why he enjoys such universal confidence here. The mention of Senator Robert Taft's isolationism or of General Douglas MacArthur's Far Eastern emphasis for U.S. foreign policy can make Europeans shiver. The triumph of either of these schools of thought would be regarded as a disaster here."

ONE HUNDRED seventy-five years ago, the founding fathers of the American Republic declared their independence of the British Crown. Little could they have known—in the heat and bitterness of the hour—that the severance, accomplished in passion, would through the years flower into an alliance of such fitness and worth that it was never recorded on legal parchment, but in the hearts of our two peoples. The bond that joins us—stronger than blood lines, than common tongue and common law—is the fundamental conviction that man was created to be free, that he can be trusted with freedom, that governments have as a primary function the protection of his freedom.

In the scale of values of the English-speaking people, freedom is the first and most precious right. Without it, no other right can be exercised, and human existence loses all significance. This unity of ours in fundamentals is an international fact. Yet on more than one occasion, it has been obscured in Britain and in my own country by concern with trifles and small disputes, fanned into the flames of senseless antagonisms.

Serious differences in conviction must be beaten out on the anvil of logic and justice. But scarcely need they be dragged into the public forum, in the petty hope of capturing a fleeting local acclaim, at the expense of an absent partner. There are men in this room with whom, in World War II, I had arguments, hotly sustained and of long duration. Had all these been headlined in the press of our two countries, they could have created public bitterness, confusing our peoples in the midst of our joint effort. Decisions were reached without such calamitous results, because those at odds did not find it necessary to seek justification for their personal views in a public hue and cry. Incidentally, a more personal reason for this expression of satisfaction is a later conclusion that my own position in the arguments was not always right. In any case, may we never forget that our common devotion to deep human values and our mutual trust are the bedrock of our joint strength.

In that spirit our countries are joined with the peoples of Western Europe and the North Atlantic to defend the freedoms of Western civilization. Opposed to us—cold and forbidding—is an ideological front that marshals every weapon in the arsenal of dictatorship. Subversion, propaganda, deceit, and the threat of naked force are daily hurled against us and our friends in a globe-encircling, relentless campaign.

We earnestly hope that the call for a truce in Korea marks a change in attitude. If such a welcome development does occur, the brave men on the United Nations forces did much to bring it about. We entered the conflict one year ago, resolved that aggression against free and friendly South Korea would not be tolerated. Certain of the nations furnishing forces had heavy demands elsewhere, including postwar reconstruction at home. Nevertheless, every contingent added evidence of the solidarity and firmness of the free nations in giving an object lesson to aggression. Our success in this difficult and distant operation reflects the fortitude of the Allied troops and the leadership that guided them.

The stand in Korea should serve notice in this area, as well as in the Far East, that we will resist naked aggression with all the force at our command. Our effort to provide security against the possibility of another and even greater emergency which will never be of our making— must go forward with the same resolution and courage that has characterized our Korean forces. The member nations in the North Atlantic Treaty Organization need not fear the future or any Communistic threat —if we are alert, realistic, and resolute. Our community possesses a potential might that far surpasses the sinister forces of slave camp and chained millions. But to achieve the serenity and confidence that our potential can provide, we must press forward with the mobilization of our spiritual and intellectual strength; we must develop promptly the material force that will assure the safety of our friends upon the continent and the security of the free world.

This is the challenge of our times that, until satisfactorily met, establishes priorities in all our thoughts, our work, our sacrifices. The hand of the aggressor is stayed by strength—and strength alone.

Although the security of each of us is bound up in the safety of all of us, the immediate threat is most keenly felt by our partners in Europe. Half the continent is already within the monolithic mass of totalitarianism. The drawn and haunted faces in the docks of the purge courts are grim evidence of what Communistic domination means. It is clearly necessary that we quickly develop maximum strength within free Europe itself. Our own interests demand it.

It is a truism that where, among partners, strength is demanded in its fullness, unity is the first requisite. Without unity, the effort becomes less powerful in application, less decisive in result. This fact has special application in Europe. It would be difficult indeed to overstate the benefits, in these years of stress and tension, that would accrue to NATO if the free nations of Europe were truly a unit.

But in that vital region, history, custom, language, and prejudice have combined to hamper integration. Progress has been and is hobbled by a web of customs barriers interlaced with bilateral agreements, multilateral cartels, local shortages, and economic monstrosities. How tragic. Free men, facing the specter of political bondage, are crippled by artificial bonds that they themselves have forged, and they alone can loosen. Here is a task to challenge the efforts of the wisest statesmen, the best economists, the most brilliant diplomats.

European leaders, seeking a sound and wise solution, are spurred by the vision of a man at this table—a man of inspiring courage in dark hours, of wise counsel in grave decisions. Winston Churchill's plea for a united Europe can yet bear such greatness of fruit that it may well be remembered as the most notable achievement of a career marked by achievement.

The difficulties of integrating Western Europe, of course, appear staggering to those who live by ritual. But great majorities in Europe earnestly want liberty, peace, and the opportunity to pass on to their children the fair lands and the culture of Western Europe. They deserve, at the very least, a fair chance to work together for the common purpose, freed of the costly encumbrances they are now compelled to carry.

Europe cannot attain the towering material stature possible to its people's skills and spirit so long as it is divided by patchwork territorial fences. They foster localized instead of common interest. They pyramid every cost with middlemen, tariffs, taxes, and overheads. Barred, absolutely, are the efficient division of labor and resources and the easy flow of trade. In the political field, these barriers promote distrust and suspicion. They serve vested interests at the expense of peoples and prevent truly concerted action for Europe's own and obvious good.

This is not to say that, as a commander, I have found anything but ready coöperation among the governments of Western Europe. Time and again, I have saluted from my heart the spirit of their armed services— of officers and men alike—from the mountains of Italy to the fjords of Norway, from Normandy to the curtain. Within political circles, I have found statesmen eager to assure the success of their current defense programs. I have no doubt as to the capacity of NATO to surmount even the formidable obstacles imposed upon us by the political facts of present-day Europe.

Yet with the handicaps of enforced division, it is clear that even the minimum essential security effort will seriously strain the resources of Europe. We ignore this danger at our peril since the effects of economic failure would be disastrous upon spiritual and material strength alike. True security never rests upon the shoulders of men denied a decent present and the hope of a better future.

But with unity achieved, Europe could build adequate security and, at the same time, continue the march of human betterment that has characterized Western civilization. Once united, the farms and factories of France and Belgium, the foundries of Germany, the rich farmlands of Holland and Denmark, the skilled labor of Italy, will produce miracles for the common good. In such unity is a secure future for these peoples. It would mean early independence of aid from America and other Atlantic countries. The coffers, mines, and factories of that continent are not inexhaustible. Dependence upon them must be minimized by the maximum in coöperative effort. The establishment of a workable European federation would go far to create confidence among people everywhere that Europe was doing its full and vital share in giving this coöperation.

Any soldier contemplating this problem would be moved to express an opinion that it cannot be attacked successfully by slow infiltration, but only by direct and decisive assault, with all available means.

The project faces the deadly danger of procrastination, timid measures, slow steps, and cautious stages. Granted that the bars of tradition and habit are numerous and stout, the greatest bars to this, as to any human enterprise, lie in the minds of men themselves. The negative is always the easy side, since it holds that nothing should be done. The negative is happy in lethargy, contemplating almost with complacent satisfaction, the difficulties of any other course. But difficulties are often of such slight substance that they fade into nothing at the first sign of success. If obstacles are of greater consequence, they can always be overcome when they must be overcome. And which of these obstacles could be so important as peace, security, and prosperity for Europe's populations? Could we not help? We, the peoples of the British Commonwealth and of the United States, have profited by unity at home. If, with our moral and material assistance, the free European nations could attain a similar integration, our friends would be strengthened, our own economies improved, and the laborious NATO machinery of mutual defense vastly simplified.

A solid, healthy, confident Europe would be the greatest possible boon to the functioning and objectives of the Atlantic Pact.

But granting that we cannot reach maximum security without a united Europe, let us by no means neglect what is within our immediate grasp or deprecate the achievements already attained.

Look back, I ask you, over a space of two years only. Consider the dangerous level to which morale and defensive strength had descended, the despairing counsel of neutralism, appeasement, and defeatism that then existed. Against such a backdrop, the accomplishments of the North Atlantic Treaty Organization are magnificently manifest. We are joined together in purpose and growing determination; we know the danger, we have defined our goals. Each day we make headway. The basic economies of European nations are on the upswing; the chaos and floundering of the postwar years are definitely behind. The international forces for Atlantic defense are no longer merely figures on paper; the international organization is no longer a headquarters without troops. The forces—ground, naval, and air—are assembling. They are training together and the spirit of mutual respect and coöperation that marks their joint maneuvers is heartening and encouraging. Still far too few in numbers and short of equipment, their ranks are filling; machines and weapons reach them in a steady stream.

The military and political leaders of the participating nations no longer slowly feel their way forward in an endeavor without guiding precedent. Caution that is inescapable in a new and unique enterprise has been replaced by confidence born out of obstacles overcome. The

Allied Powers in Europe are constituting a team for defense; one capable of assuring a lasting and secure peace.

The winning of freedom is not to be compared to the winning of a game—with the victory recorded forever in history. Freedom has its life in the hearts, the actions, the spirit of men and so it must be daily earned and refreshed—else, like a flower cut from its life-giving roots, it will wither and die.

All of us have pledged our word, one to the other, that this shall not be. We have cut the pattern for our effort—we are devoting to it available resources for its realization. We fight not only our own battle—we are defending for all mankind those things that allow personal dignity to the least of us—those things that permit each to believe himself important in the eyes of God. We are preserving opportunity for men to lift up their hearts and minds to the highest places—there must be no stragglers in such a conflict.

The road ahead may be long—it is certain to be marked by critical and difficult passages. But if we march together, endure together, share together, we shall succeed—we shall gloriously succeed together.

Appendix

THE PRELUDE

Questions

1. Are people living in the twentieth century any happier than those living in the Middle Ages, or any other period?
2. What are the enduring gains of the period 1900-1950?
3. What are the failures or shortcomings of the period 1900-1950?
4. Can "the problem of world production yielding at least a minimum living to the whole population" be solved? By what means?
5. Has man "so destroyed the resources of the world that he may be doomed to die of starvation"?
6. Is it commonly agreed that "air mastery is today the supreme expression of military power"?
7. What answers may be given to Mr. Churchill's question about the Soviet government: "Why have they deliberately acted for three long years so as to unite the free world against them?"?
8. Do you agree with Mr. Churchill's answer today: "It is because they fear the friendship of the West more than its hostility"?
9. Do you believe that "Europe would have been communized like Czechoslovakia, and London under bombardment some time ago but for the deterrent of the atomic bomb in the hands of the United States"?
10. Give your own views on Mr. Churchill's belief that war is not inevitable. What evidence can you use?

Topics for Speeches, Essays, and Discussions

A review of Churchill's memoirs. Churchill as a literary stylist. Churchill as an orator. The Conservative party. The Labour party. British general elections. The 1946 speech at Fulton, Missouri reëxamined now. The "Old Churchillians." How to get along with the Russians. Why Mr. Churchill visited the United States in January 1952. Reactions and results of the visit. The effects of his address to the Congress. The Churchill plan for a federated Europe. Mr. Churchill as he appears in the war memoirs of Generals Eisenhower and Bradley, Admiral Leahy, Cordell Hull, Henry L. Stimson, James F. Byrnes, and others. The prospects of the Conservative party in Britain. The possibility of dissension in the Labour party. Roosevelt, Churchill, and Stalin. The conference at Yalta.

THE WORLD OUTLOOK IN THE ATOMIC AGE

Questions

1. Do you concur in Mr. Hutchins' dictum: "The educational system of a country is a reflection of what the country thinks it wants"?
2. Why must the people of this country "rediscover the ends of human life and of organized society"?
3. Was it wise to use the atomic bomb against Japan? Why not use it in Korea?
4. Can we look forward to more leisure as a result of atomic energy?

What comment can you make on each of the following four statements?

5. "If the great issues of power politics are not to be settled by war they can be settled only by diplomacy and in no other way at all, since there is no other way."
6. "The only rational purpose of foreign policy is the protection and promotion of national interests, not the propagation and vindication of moral principles."
7. "Collective security as a means of keeping the peace is an illusion."
8. "The security of Western Europe cannot be achieved by military means but only by diplomatic means."
9. Do you agree with Dr. Bush that "we cannot count indefinitely upon strategic bombing as a sole means of averting war"?
10. What does Professor Einstein mean when he says that "the idea of achieving security through national armament is, at the present state of military technique, a disastrous illusion"?
11. Do you agree with him that "in the end, there beckons more and more clearly general annihilation"?
12. What evidence supports Trygve Lie's contention that "there has been a steadily growing tendency to relegate the United Nations to a secondary position in international affairs and to give first priority instead to the old familiar expedients of arms and alliances"?

Topics for Speeches, Essays, and Discussions

The career of Robert M. Hutchins. The contributions of the University of Chicago to atomic energy. Why the atomic bomb has been bad (or

Appendix

good) for the world. The internationalism of science. The abolition of war. The mission of America—to transform the world, not to dominate it. The implications of appeasement. The services of Vannevar Bush in World War II. Under what conditions should we again use the atomic bomb? The role of the tank in modern warfare. Has World War III begun? Einstein's contribution to the Atomic Age. The theory of relativity. Nuclear physics. The responsibilities of scientists. How the Russians broke the secret of the atomic bomb. The Manhattan project. The possibilities of the hydrogen bomb. Should the United Nations control the development of atomic energy? The Baruch plan. The Smyth report. The peacetime uses of atomic energy. Enrico Fermi. Harold C. Urey. Niels Bohr. J. Robert Oppenheimer. James B. Conant. Vannevar Bush. The National Science Foundation. Mr. Lie's Ten Points.

THE UNITED STATES AND FOREIGN AFFAIRS

General

Questions

1. Does Dr. Toynbee really mean that "the domestic politics of the United States have now become the government of the Western World as a whole"?
2. Why is "a union of the democratic Western nations around the United States . . . a paramount necessity for all of us"?
3. What are the possibilities of a "common political constitution" which Toynbee advocates?
4. Do you agree with Ambassador Kennan that "a study of the great decisions of national policy in the past leaves the historian impressed with the difficulty of analyzing the future clearly enough to be able to make really reliable calculations of the consequences of national action"?
5. What is meant by the statement that "we would do well to think of the conduct of foreign affairs as a problem of style even more than of purpose"?
6. "There is no uglier tendency in American nature than the quickness to moral indignation and to wild suspicions of bad faith which many of us display when other people do not think as we

Appendix

do." Can you give examples at the level of national policy and conduct?
7. Do you agree with Secretary Acheson that "it does not follow . . . that the two systems, theirs and ours [U.S.S.R. and U.S.A.] cannot exist concurrently in the whole great realm of human life"?
8. Do you accept the seven areas of difference with the Russians listed by Mr. Acheson?
9. In his 1952 State of the Union message President Truman lists some ten items on the credit side of the 1951 ledger and five on the debit side. Do you think this is an accurate accounting?
10. Reviewing the President's actual efforts to "weed out" and "punish" corrupt government employees, what do you think of this part of the address? Why should Congress apply "rigorous standards of moral integrity in its own operations"?

Topics for Speeches, Essays, and Discussions

Arnold Toynbee as historian. *A Study of History*. The United States as a world leader. The decline of British prestige. The role of the President in world affairs. Mr. Kennan's article in *Foreign Affairs* on "The Sources of Soviet Conduct." His training for an ambassadorship. Why the Russians opposed Mr. Kennan's appointment in *Pravda*. Dean Acheson as Secretary of State. Why Senator McCarthy opposes the State Department. Mr. Acheson's testimony at the investigation of General MacArthur. The Politburo. The Russians in the United Nations. Marxist doctrine and Soviet policy. A review of *The Pattern of Responsibility:* Edited by McGeorge Bundy from the Record of Secretary of State Dean Acheson. Dean Acheson and Alger Hiss. President Truman's 1951 and 1952 State of the Union messages compared. Editorial comment on the 1952 message. Mr. Truman as a speaker. How the President prepares his speeches. A rhetorical criticism of the 1952 State of the Union message. "A Fair Deal for All Americans."

The War in Korea

Questions

1. Did the United States Military government fail in the occupation of South Korea?
2. How much did the United States do to help the people of Korea toward democracy and land reform? Should we have attempted to impose our ways?

Appendix

3. What role did the United Nations play in Korea immediately preceding the June 25 attack—and afterwards?
4. "American imperialism is hostile to all liberation struggles of Asian peoples, and is particularly hostile to the great victory of the Chinese people." Can you argue against this statement by General Wu?
5. Is it true that the United States government has already begun to use Japan "as a means to launch aggressive wars against a series of Asian countries"?
6. What comment can you make to Colonel Limb's charges: "You have known full well that the so-called 'government' in northern Korea was merely a puppet regime established in complete violation of the will of the Korean people by the Soviet Union to serve its own purposes, etc."?
7. How would you answer General Ridgway's two questions: "Why are we here?" and "What are we fighting for?"?
8. Was President Truman justified in relieving General MacArthur?
9. Do you approve of the way he handled the problem?
10. Was General MacArthur within his command prerogatives in his conduct of the Korean war?
11. Should he have attempted as he did on 24 March 1951 to confer with the enemy for a truce?
12. Do you approve of General MacArthur's plan for a speedy victory in Korea?

Topics for Speeches, Essays, and Discussions

The geography and resources of Korea. Dr. Syngman Rhee and what he stands for. General Hodge in Korea. The land reform program. How the thirty-eighth parallel decision was made. The phases of the United Nations military campaign in Korea. The Inchon landing. The invasion of the Chinese Communist army. The problem of supply in Korea. The cease-fire talks beginning in June 1951. The military lessons of the Korean campaign. The Senate hearing on General MacArthur. The political implications of General MacArthur's recall. The role of Great Britain, France, Turkey, and other countries in the Korean war. New weapons development in Korea. The capture of General Dean. The charges and countercharges about atrocities. The exchange of prisoners. Casualty losses in Korea. The role of the Medical Corps in Korea. Blood for the wounded. The training of combat leaders. Air support. The navy and the marine corps. Rotation policies. American artillery. ROK soldiers. Jet warfare. Psychological warfare leaflets. The United States

Appendix

Eighth Army. What would have happened if the United Nations had not intervened.

The Far East

Questions

1. How is United States Far Eastern foreign policy made?
2. What part does public opinion play in the process?
3. What part does the Department of Defense play in the process?
4. Do you agree with Secretary Acheson that in China "the Communists won by default, not by what they offered"?
5. What is novel about Dean Rusk's address on Chinese-American friendship?
6. Do you agree with Mr. Rusk when he says that "the Chinese are being pressed to aggressive action in other areas—all calculated to divert the attention and energies of China away from the encroachments of Soviet imperialism upon China itself"?
7. What does Justice Douglas mean by the statement: "The revolutions which are brewing are not, however, Communist in origin nor will they end even if Soviet Russia is crushed through war"?
8. What comments can you make on the catalogue of specific complaints Justice Douglas enumerates: absence of medical care, lack of schools, desire for land-ownership, and desire to learn to farm the modern way? Would the Point Four program help?
9. What are the essential characteristics of the Japanese peace treaty according to Mr. Dulles?
10. What is the reaction of the Japanese people to the terms of the treaty signed at San Francisco in September 1951?

Topics for Speeches, Essays, and Discussions

Dean Acheson's qualifications as Secretary of State. How the State Department makes policy. The work of the Senate Foreign Relations committee. The operation of the Joint Chiefs of Staff. The White House and foreign affairs. Career diplomats. The role of General Marshall in China. General Wedemeyer's report. The charges of General Stilwell in his memoirs. The beginnings of Chinese-American friendship. American missionaries in China. The Standard Oil Company in China. What Justice Douglas reports in his book. The tactics of the Russian delegation at the Japanese Peace Conference. What Ambassador Dulles had

Appendix

to do with the draft of the Japanese peace treaty. Mr. Acheson's chairmanship. How the treaty was debated in the Senate.

Russia and Communism

Questions

1. What do you believe was the purpose of Premier Stalin's interview?
2. How do you react to Stalin's answer to the question: "Do you consider a new world war inevitable?"
3. What comment can be made to Congressman Velde's charge that "our relief program and our foreign policy have been wrong"?
4. How can we Americans "show by our good deeds that we believe in the dignity of man, whether he is white, yellow, or brown"?
5. Are you impressed with Mr. Gitlow's explanation of how Communists make converts?
6. Do you believe he is right about Communists and Communism in our colleges and universities?
7. What is involved in Mr. Fischer's belief that "the real issue in our struggle against Communism is to win the majority of mankind to our side"?
8. How do you appraise the work of the House Un-American Activities Committee?
9. What inferences can you draw from General Osborn's remarks about the Russian amendments before the Atomic Energy Commission?
10. How do you explain the tactics of antagonizing everybody at the conferences they attend?

Topics for Speeches, Essays, and Discussions

The life of Joseph Stalin. Stalin as recalled by Churchill in his memoirs. Impressions of General Walter Bedell Smith in *My Three Years in Moscow*. The career of Benjamin Gitlow. The Communist *Daily Worker*. Why the party line changes. The Psychological Strategy Board in Washington. Harold Stassen's interview with Stalin. What General Mark Clark learned about dealing with the Russians (as found in *Calculated Risk*). The Russian mind. Maxim Litvinov. The Russians at social functions. John Fischer's explanation in *Why They Behave Like Russians*. Russia's contribution to the United Nations. Russian literature —past and present. The trial of the Communist leaders in Judge

Appendix

Medina's court. Earl Browder's rise and fall. Whittaker Chambers. Judith Coplon. Klaus Fuchs. Elizabeth Bentley. The trial of Cardinal Mindszenty. The Vogeler case. The Oatis case. Alger Hiss. Owen Lattimore. The Loyalty Review Board and Mr. Service. The *Amerasia* affair. Russian techniques of psychological warfare. The Russian budget for propaganda. The annual Russian youth congress in Berlin. The explanations of Morris Ernst about why Americans become Communists (*New York Herald Tribune* Forum volume for 1951). What the Russian peasant has gained in the past thirty years. John D. Littlepage's book, *In Search of Soviet Gold*. Senator Vandenberg's famous question: "What is Russia up to?"

The Defense of Europe

Questions

1. What are the stated purposes of the North Atlantic Treaty Organization?
2. What is the estimated military strength of Russia?
3. What is the estimated military strength of the Allied Powers?
4. What are some of the obstacles to the establishment of a European army?
5. Should there be a limit to the number of American divisions we send to Europe?
6. Should the West Germans be allowed to form an army—in divisions or in regimental combat teams?
7. Do you agree with General Marshall that the "greatest factor in the creation of military strength for Western Europe . . . is the build-up of morale—of the will to defend—the determination to fight if that be necessary"?
8. How do you react to M. Auriol's statement: "In that case, the national armies must be progressively replaced by a United Nations army as provided by the common charter"?
9. What is the purpose of the "25 highly armed Russian divisions" in Eastern Germany as mentioned by Dr. Adenauer?
10. Is not the policy of the integration of Europe likely to lead to war with the Soviet Union?

Topics for Speeches, Essays, and Discussions

The career of General Dwight D. Eisenhower. The role of General Marshall in World War II. The cost of maintaining six divisions in Europe.

General Thomas T. Handy's command. The Seventh United States Army and General Manton S. Eddy. The contribution of France to the defense of Europe. The British and the Schuman plan. The problem of standardization of arms. Yugoslavia and Turkey in Western defense. The problem of Spain. The work of the Mutual Security Agency. The role of propaganda in the defense of Europe. The Voice of America. Radio Free Europe. Should our government have paid the $120,000 to Hungary for the release of the four American airmen in December 1951? Were our retaliatory measures strong enough? What should be the American policy toward General Franco? Should there be an organization similar to NATO for the countries of the Middle East? The Communist party in France. In Italy. The role of the U.S. Strategic Air Force in the defense of Europe. General Lauris Norstad. General Curtis E. LeMay. The role of General Gruenther as Chief of Staff of SHAPE. Field Marshal Montgomery's duties as Deputy Commander. The German generals. The Rhine river. The Iberian peninsula. Strategic airfields. Coal and steel in Western Europe. What the Marshall Plan accomplished. What Mutual Security is supposed to do. The headquarters at Marly, France. The defense of the Mediterranean. How long can the United States support the rest of the world with arms? René Pleven in France. The modernization of the French army. The Russian air force. Russian generalship. Could Russia be occupied? The prospect of revolution in Russia.

THE UNITED STATES AND HOME AFFAIRS

Problems of Mobilization and Manpower

Questions

1. Mr. Harriman states that: "During the war it was the hope of our government that the nations united in war to destroy the Axis would remain united in the common purpose of maintaining the peace." Why has this not come about?
2. Is it true that "the strength of our moral position today rests upon the fact that we made every effort to reach an understanding with the Soviet Union"?
3. What is meant by General Lanham's statement that "an Army de-

Appendix

rives its moral strength from the people it defends—from their confidence, their affection, their institutions, their beliefs"?
4. Do you agree with General Lanham "that three key groups in our country are under ceaseless attacks—our representatives in Congress, our business, our military leaders"?
5. "Why has the Soviet Union not extended its power to the English channel since the close of World War II?"
6. Can you illustrate Dr. Conant's dictum that "what determines the course of history is the estimate of man in control of national destinies as to the chances of success in a future year"?
7. In the light of the Korean truce talks begun in the summer of 1951 what value do you attach to General Clark's statement: "We must be on guard against phony peace proposals. We must not permit ourselves to be lulled again into a false sense of security"?
8. Do you agree "that the one indispensable element in the winning of wars is the doughboy with plenty of guts, a stout and courageous heart, and his rifle and bayonet"?
9. Should college students who maintain high scholastic standards be deferred or exempted from military service?
10. Should the government subsidize the graduate training of students in the sciences, engineering, and medicine?

Topics for Speeches, Essays, and Discussions

The career of W. Averell Harriman. His contribution to the American Assembly at Columbia University. His duties as Mutual Security Administrator. The information and education program of the armed services. Do our soldiers, sailors, marines, and airmen in Korea know what they are fighting for? Will UMT accomplish what it proposes to do? The role of American colleges and universities in the present defense effort. The military budget. Is it wise to continue to train land armies in an atomic age? Why have the United Nations forces been unable to win a decisive victory in Korea? What does Dr. Arthur S. Flemming predict for the nation's manpower in the next ten years? (*U.S. News and World Report* for 4 January 1952). General Marshall's prediction of a Garrison State for the next ten to twenty years. The Committee on the Present Danger. The military potential of our country which the President inaugurated in January 1953 will inherit. Is it time to decrease our defense efforts? Mobilization and inflation. Women in World War II and in the present defense effort. Waste in the military program. The national debt. What would happen if we did not mobilize? Is the United

Appendix

States furnishing more than its share in manpower in the program for mobilization? Who pays the bill?

Control of Production and Prices

Questions

1. Can you comment on Senator Taft's fear "that we do not get in the state of being a perpetual military mind—that we do not make ourselves into a great imperialist nation, as many nations have in the past"?
2. Which of Mr. Weil's proposals do you prefer: "a longer work week, whatever the week may be, forty-four hours, forty-six hours, and at whatever pay *or* the other sacrifices . . . in shortages of goods which are not produced if they do not work longer"?
3. What do you think of Mr. Weil's idea "to consider a program of a certain portion of that tax being refundable to the individuals who paid the tax at some considerably later date when the inflationary dangers were substantially less"?
4. "What can we do now to come back to normal when the emergency is over?"
5. How do you react to Mr. Wilson's statement: "If while I am talking here tonight a firm truce were to be signed, I say to you that we must not deflect by one whit from our inflexible determination to become strong, and remain strong"?
6. What does Mr. Wilson mean when he says "the next eight months [November 1951 through June 1952] will test our national character in the crucible of an historic emergency"?
7. Do you agree with Mr. Reuther that "the recent so-called control order is a fraud upon the American people"?
8. Can Mr. Newsom's assertion that "farm families buy more things on the average than the family living in town" be substantiated?
9. Mr. Newsom asserts: "We must, if necessary to control inflation, control wages, prices, and profits." Do you agree?
10. Will the two-dollar bill of 1952 buy as much as the one-dollar bill of 1940?

Topics for Speeches, Essays, and Discussions

Was price control a success in World War II? What is the effect of the law of supply and demand in the present economy? Can we prepare for

Appendix

war and produce for a peacetime economy at the same time? The career of Robert A. Taft. His book on foreign policy. His ability as a speaker. The strategy of his campaign for the 1952 presidential nomination. The merchandising policies of Mr. Weil's company—Macy's. The qualifications of Charles E. Wilson for his present position. The career of Michael V. DiSalle. The role of the farmers in our present mobilization program. The role of labor in the program. The role of investors in the program. The value of the dollar in 1936, 1940, and 1952. Has Mr. DiSalle's program been successful? Have housewives succeeded in buyers' strikes? Prices and white-collar workers. Fringe benefits. Take-home pay for auto workers. Unemployment in Detroit during changeovers. Rising taxes. Government bonds. How to hedge against inflation. When should controls end? Was it wise to remove them in 1946? The cost of control enforcement and regulation.

Science and Research

Questions

1. Do you agree with Dr. Compton when he says "that science and technology are largely responsible for much that we find good in the world, and are capable of being the common denominator of many things we seek to accomplish in the decades ahead"?
2. What does Whitehead mean when he says that the greatest invention of the nineteenth century was the method of invention?
3. What is the significance of Dr. Millikan's evaluation that "Maxwell's book has created the present age of electricity in much the same way that Newton's *Principia* created, a hundred years earlier, the mechanical age in which we are still living"?
4. Can you analyze Dr. Ridenour's sentence: "We must expect that our ideas of weapons and strategy based on World War II are likely to be incomplete or misleading as guides to the future of armed maneuver and of warfare"? Is the war in Korea a new departure?
5. Do you agree that "American supremacy over possible enemies must be qualitative, not quantitative, in nature"?
6. Why is it unwise for us to mobilize all our resources for a short-term war when a long one is in prospect?
7. How do you react to Dr. Smyth's proposal for "a student scientific corps with enrollment beginning in the freshman year and continuing through graduate training"?

Appendix

8. What are the major advantages and disadvantages of nuclear fires and chemical fires?
9. What does Dr. Weinberg mean when he says "it is much too early to say that nuclear-energy extraction will always be expensive, will never find a place in our power economy comparable to the present practice of chemical energy"?
10. Can you comment on Dr. Weinberg's sentence: "For the atom to fulfill its latent promise to man, we scientists must of course show technically that there is in the atom such promise; but we must also bring the world out of its present chaos so that the way of the atom can indeed be the way of peace."

Topics for Speeches, Essays, and Discussions

The career of Dr. Karl T. Compton. The accomplishments of science at mid-century. The inadequacies of science. Scientific method. Science and superstition. The state of the social sciences. The role of the humanities in the advance of science. The function of research in the universities. The nationalizing of scientific research. The growth of private research. The training of scientists. Publication and research. Pure versus applied science. Science versus technology. Have the twentieth century discoveries of science made man happier? The contributions of European scientists. The prospects for the second half of the twentieth century.

Health and Medicine

Questions

1. What is the significance of Dr. Selye's hope that ACTH and cortisone "will give us sufficient tools with which to study adaptation—the adjustment of our bodies to any change such as disease, or cold, or heat, changes which we might encounter in everyday life, including even nervous and psychic distress."?
2. Can you comment on the sentence: "Although ACTH and cortisone probably do not act to cure these diseases [rheumatoid arthritis, rheumatic fever, and many allergies] they do change their course in a dramatic way"?
3. Do you agree with Dr. Henderson that "within the next three years . . . 90 million persons will be enrolled with the voluntary prepaid medical plans—and when that number has been reached, the prob-

Appendix 548

lem [of national health insurance] will have been largely resolved"?
4. Why is the American Medical Association opposed to national health insurance (the Ewing Plan)?
5. Do you agree with Dr. McKay that the doctor of the present day "is a bungling novice in the art of human relations with his patients, who are, after all, his greatest assets and medicine's stock in trade"?
6. Can you comment on the statement of the article in the *Reader's Digest* for December 1947 which reports "the shocking fact that many of the 9 million surgical operations performed annually in America are unnecessary"?
7. What does Dr. McKay mean when he says, "The doctor who has a license to practice medicine and joins a county medical society is usually fixed for life"?
8. What examples can you cite to illustrate Mr. Ewing's contention that "in America today, there is a barrier between the doctor and the patient"?
9. How would national health insurance differ from the present relationship between doctor and patient?
10. Can you comment on Dr. Hawley's observation that "too much of the opposition to the Ewing Plan ignored the existence of some rather obvious problems in the field of medical care, and offered no constructive suggestions as to their solution"?

Topics for Speeches, Essays, and Discussions

What is required to educate a physician in the United States today? Do we have enough doctors? Do we have enough medical schools? Is present-day medical education adequate? General practice *versus* specialization. Mental illness. The findings of Selective Service about national health. Medical care in the armed forces. Psychosomatic medicine. The achievements of American medicine. Medical advances in the Korean war. Euthanasia or mercy-killing. The statistics of Blue Cross and Blue Shield. The statistics of the Ewing Plan. The statistics of hospital care. The value of antibiotics. Medical service and hospitals during an atomic attack. The importance of national health in the defense effort.

Education

Questions

1. What has been done to improve salary conditions for teachers since Mr. Hutchins spoke? Is it adequate?
2. What has been done to alleviate the shortage of teachers? Is it adequate?
3. Do you agree with Mr. Hutchins when he says that "the American people, whatever their professions, do not take education very seriously"?
4. Do you agree with the statement that "the belief that education can in some way contribute to vocational and social success, has done more than most things to disrupt American education"?
5. What has academic freedom to do with Quincy Wright's two great problems of the world—war and poverty?
6. What does Mr. Griswold mean by the sentiment: "War and the preparation for war are not conducive to the reflective life that produces great teaching and great scholarship"?
7. What are the implications of the statistics: "By 1960 our school population is expected to increase to 37,000,000 (from 29,000,000 in 1950) and our college to 4,600,000 (from 2,500,000)"?
8. How do you react to Dean McIntosh's statement: "Our first goal must, therefore, be to impart to young people the freshness of intellectual excitement, the opportunity for independent and creative activity, the delight in discussion and discovery that form an essential part of true education"?
9. Do you agree that "graduate schools and colleges which glorify research and publication at the expense of the art of teaching are guilty of a grave and perhaps irreparable sin against civilization"?
10. What is the implication of Mr. Thomas' statement, "Spectacular as has been our American progress, in contrast with that of other peoples of the earth, we have merely scratched the surface of the possibilities offered by those great human principles of liberty and dignity"?

Topics for Speeches, Essays, and Discussions

What is the purpose of college? The Great Books Program. The curriculum for the A.B. degree. Standards for graduation. Private versus publicly supported institutions. The case for the small liberal arts college. College fraternities and sororities. Intercollegiate football. Subsidizing of athletics. The meaning of academic freedom. The future of American universities. The effect of UMT on the colleges. Progressive education. The value of graduate study. The function of the university. The recommendations of the President's Commission on Higher Education. The program of the American Council on Education. The National Education Association. The American Association of University Professors. The Association of Land Grant Colleges. Federal aid to equalize opportunity in education. The Fulbright program. The policy of the National Association of Manufacturers towards education. The financing of higher education. Loyalty oaths. Negroes in southern graduate schools.

Philosophy, Literature, and the Arts

Questions

1. What does Professor Overstreet mean when he says that "philosophy, therefore, has not only the urgent task of helping man to become a productive rather than a destructive member of his kind, but it now has at its command scientific data that bear directly upon the problem of man's social ineptitude"?
2. What is meant by "psychological maturing"?
3. Do you agree that "It seems wholly reasonable to say that the basic job of education should, first and foremost, be to help young people to grow up into a genuine intellectual, emotional, and social maturity (and to help adults to keep growing up)"?
4. "What should religion be except the invitation for man to grow up into the full maturity of his emotional and spiritual powers?"
5. Do you agree with Mr. Faulkner that "the young man or woman writing today has forgotten the problems of the human heart in conflict with itself which alone can make good writing because only that is worth writing about, worth the agony and the sweat"?
6. Do Mr. Faulkner's own career and his own writing exemplify the ideas he presents in his acceptance address?
7. Why was the Nobel award made to William Faulkner?
8. What lessons can be drawn from Hitler's attempts to control artists and their arts?
9. Can art and music prosper under the rule of Soviet Russia?
10. What is the function of art in a democratic society?

Topics for Speeches, Essays, and Discussions

The role of the philosopher in a democratic society. Professor Overstreet's book, *Influencing Human Behavior*. The career of William

Faulkner. The history of the Nobel awards. American philosophy today. William James. John Dewey. Charles Peirce. George Santayana. Alfred North Whitehead. "Recent Trends in Philosophy." The short stories of William Faulkner. The effects of television on literature and reading. The chief distinctive characteristics of recent American literature. The effects of American literature in Europe. The American motion picture as an art form. Television and the theater. The Federal government and art. The fellowships program of the Rockefeller, Guggenheim, and Ford Foundations. The rising cost of books. The national taste in literature. American literature in the colleges. *The Literary History of the United States*. The influence of the comics on children. The readership of the *Reader's Digest, Life,* and *Time*. The recognition of American artists.

Labor and Industry

Questions

1. Do you agree with Matthew Woll that "our country, with its economy based on private enterprise and personal adventure, represents today an economy with a growing sense of social responsibility, and with a growing recognition of labor's rights and responsibilities in the life of the nation"?
2. What is the status of the trade-union movement in Russia?
3. Should the United States have recognized Soviet Russia in the first instance?
4. What is the place of Samuel Gompers in the American labor movement?
5. Is it true as Mr. Murray says "that it was the working people of America who built the innumerable educational institutions which are now the glory of our country"?
6. Is it true that "until very recently our institutions of higher learning for the most part were either unfriendly to the cause of organized labor, or if not unfriendly, somewhat apathetic and aloof"?
7. Or is the opposite of this statement more likely true?
8. How can we best achieve "the road to labor peace"?
9. Do you agree that "the labor relations problem is at least as important to this country as the behavior of the stock market or the results of professional football games"?
10. Can you comment on the sentence of Paul Hoffman: "The Trustees of the Ford Foundation are so certain that absolute top priority must be given to the question of man's relationship to man and

Appendix

the preservation of free peoples and institutions that they have put the resources of that great enterprise wholly into programs aimed at that single grand target"?

Topics for Speeches, Essays, and Discussions

The career of Matthew Woll. The tactics of John L. Lewis. Why labor "talks tough." The role of education departments in labor unions. Conciliation techniques in labor controversies. The American Arbitration Association. The summer workshop programs of labor unions. The career of Paul G. Hoffman. The National Association of Manufacturers. The Chamber of Commerce of the United States. The U.S. Department of Labor. The Bureau of Labor Statistics. The role of labor unions in political campaigns. The "escalator clause" in the General Motors-UAW contract. The type of government official we need. Can educators "teach" character? The Taft-Hartley Act. Should it be amended to legalize maritime hiring halls as proposed in Senate Bill 1044? Can federal aid to education be financed by revenue from tidelands oil? Communists in labor unions.

Civil Rights and Liberties

Questions

1. Can you explain Mr. Baldwin's statement "that the Civil Liberties Union has moved in these years from a position of suspected subversion to one of unexpected respectability."
2. Do you believe that the Communist Party in the U.S. should be kept above ground?
3. What does the Civil Liberties Union stand for?
4. Do you agree with Governor Stevenson that "we have failed miserably to find a way to protect ourselves against treason, sabotage, and other subversive acts, on the one hand, without destroying our traditional liberties, on the other."
5. Can you comment on the words of Walt Whitman: "Liberty relies upon itself; invites no one; promises nothing; sits in calmness and light; is positive and composed; and knows no discouragement"?
6. Can you comment on the sentence of Mr. Biddle: "Spies are not caught by loyalty oaths and loyalty tests and requirements that Communists register"?
7. Should the McCarran Internal Security Act be amended to allow more freedom for students and others to enter the country?

Appendix

8. What advantages would there be to setting up a Civil Rights section in the Department of Justice with power to check on all violations of civil rights?

Topics for Speeches, Essays, and Discussions

The meaning of Civil Liberties. The guaranties of our Constitution. The report of the President's Commission on Civil Rights. The role of the Federal Bureau of Investigation. Recent Supreme Court cases dealing with civil rights. The great dissenters of the Supreme Court—Justices Brandeis and Holmes—on civil rights. The features of the Tydings Act, the Fair Trade law, and the Robinson-Patman Act as they relate to civil rights.

Racial Problems

Questions

1. Do you agree with Dr. Bunche that man "has never yet learned how to *live* with himself; he has not mastered the art of human relations"?
2. What does Dr. Bunche mean when he says that "in no exaggerated sense, we all today exist on borrowed time"?
3. What can we honestly say about racial segregation in our country today?
4. What progress has been made in admitting Negroes to colleges and universities throughout the country?
5. Should Negroes be denied admission to hotels, restaurants, and theaters? Are they?
6. Should colored persons be discriminated against, other qualifications being equal, in consideration for employment?
7. What should be the policy toward Negroes in the armed forces?
8. What progress has been made in really allowing Negroes to go to the polls and vote?
9. Where do the churches stand on the problem of racial tolerance and acceptance?

Topics for Speeches, Essays, and Discussions

Why Communists play up American racial problems. The case of Paul Robeson. The career of Dr. Ralph Bunche. The Emancipation Proclamation. The attitude of Abraham Lincoln towards Negroes as expressed in his writings and speeches. The role of Negroes in the Civil War. How

Appendix

does racial discrimination begin? The migration of Negroes as shown in the 1950 census. The Mexican problem—wetbacks. The Hollywood treatment of racial problems. Racial intermarriage. Racial prejudice. The statistics of "minorities" in the United States. The National Association for the Advancement of Colored People. Booker T. Washington. W. E. Burghardt DuBois. Should quotas for minorities be set up for admission to colleges and universities? Negroes in the District of Columbia. In Georgia. "Crossing the Color Line."

Religion

Questions

1. What is the main theme of the Reverend Mr. Gates's sermon, "Time Is Running Out"?
2. "What worries you most at the present time?"
3. "What newspaper headline would you like most to see tomorrow morning?"
4. Can you comment on Dr. Edman's humanistic or secular faith?
5. Do you agree with Fulton Oursler that "the way for modern man to find a true faith is, first, to abandon a false faith to which he has been passionately devoted and has now brought him to the edge of destruction"?
6. What does Bishop Pardue mean when he says: "Christianity is anything but a debate. It is a way of life"?
7. "Can we teach youth science without teaching youth at least one specific science? Can we teach youth sport without teaching some specific sport? Can we teach baseball without balls, bats, and bases?"
8. How would you comment on Dr. Weaver's statement about what Stephens College students want out of life: "We want more than anything else inner stability and strength. If we can get them, then we will be able to be happy and secure, accept freedom, and grant equality to all other men"?
9. Do you agree with Swami Nikhilananda that "the root cause of man's grief and delusion is the identification of the soul with the body"?
10. How do you think intergroup relations can be improved?

Topics for Speeches, Essays, and Discussions

College students and religion. Is the power of the church declining? The education of ministers. The beliefs of various denominations. Christian

Appendix

Science. The Catholic Church. Religious literature. Religion and radio/television. What the Jews believe. Jewish holidays. The commercialization of Christmas and Easter. Should religious worship take place in the schools? How can modern man find faith? Should Protestant denominations merge? The rise of the Community Church. What should preachers discuss in sermons? The role of music in religious worship. The Washington Cathedral. The Cathedral of St. John the Divine. "Enthusiasm" and religion. The power of church hymns. The place of chapel services in the college. Compulsory chapel attendance. The reading of the Bible. Recent translations of the Bible. Is there a need for spiritual revival? Billy Graham. Religion in the schools.

POSTLUDE
Questions

1. Do you agree with Erwin Canham's thesis?
2. How do you comment on his statement "that what the world needs most is an awakening to the truly spiritual character of the Western heritage"?
3. Can you explain: "The fact is that Communism—like totalitarianism in any form—represents the blackest of reactions. The fact is that the free system, of which capitalism is only a small and modified part, represents the authentic revolution—not a subversive revolution, but a revolution which sets men free"?
4. What does Dr. Edmund W. Sinnot of Yale mean when he says: "Man, not matter, is the chief problem of mankind today"?
5. Do you agree that the free economic system "can survive only to the degree that the individuals and combinations that make it up accept their social obligation"?
6. What was the main purpose of General Eisenhower's speech to the English Speaking Union?
7. Why has European integration failed in the past?
8. What has been the success of the administration of the zones of Germany occupied by the French, British, and Americans?
9. What is General Eisenhower's staff preparing for at SHAPE?
10. Would it not be better to make SHAPE a United Nations command like that of General Ridgway?

Topics for Speeches, Essays, and Discussions

The career of Erwin D. Canham. Charles H. E. Malik. The great revolutions of history. Does the individual exist for the sake of society and

Appendix

the state? Or vice versa? The work of Mr. Canham on UNESCO. The main theme of his book, *Awakening*. The career of General Dwight D. Eisenhower since 1945. His World War II assignments. General Eisenhower as president of Columbia University. The American Assembly topic for May 1952: Inflation. The English Speaking Union. The Mutual Security Agency. Why Europeans admire (or dislike) the United States. General Eisenhower as a political candidate. The attitude of the Russians towards General Eisenhower now. The proposals for disarmament. Agenda for another conference of Stalin, Churchill, and Truman.

Methods for Stimulating Discussion

A. Analytical

1. What was the purpose of the speech (a) for the immediate audience, (b) for the remote radio or television audience?
2. Considering such factors as the particular time the speech was delivered, the speaker's objectives, the known or inferred capabilities of the speaker, what was the task to be accomplished?
3. Identify the principal parts of the address—the Introduction, the Discussion or Body, and the Conclusion.
4. State the central idea and the main or supporting ideas. Make a short sentence outline.
5. What principal devices for maintaining attention and interest are used by the speaker?
6. What appears to be deliberately omitted from the speech?
7. What evidences are there of the speaker's adaptation of his ideas to the particular audience?
8. What special devices of ethical or personal appeal (the speaker's cultivation of his own reputation, character, integrity, and special qualifications) does the speech possess?
9. What special devices of logical appeal (syllogisms, enthymemes, examples, revelation of soundness or defect of major premises, minor premises, or conclusions) are used?
10. What special devices of emotional appeal (reference to man's fundamental or impelling motives, play upon anger, fear, etc.) are evident?

B. Critical

1. Is this the actual text spoken or one edited after the delivery?
2. Do you consider the speech well adapted to the age, intelligence

Appendix

level, state of knowledge of the subject, divisions of interest, and partisanship of the audience?
3. What good features of style (e.g., choice of words, structure of sentences, paragraphs, order of ideas, clarity and comprehension, originality, unity, coherence, emphasis, use of figures, general organization, does the address possess? What doubtful ones?
4. What good understandings of the task of the speaker are revealed?
5. May the speech be interpreted in different ways by persons of different allegiances and interests? Is this good or bad?
6. As far as can now be ascertained (e.g., by newspaper accounts, editorials, remarks of radio commentators, "experts," ordinary citizens, later speakers, votes, known changes of public opinion, formal actions, refusals to act, indifference, etc.) what was the effect of the speech?
7. Is the speech better than or below the usual standard of accomplishment of the speaker?
8. Does the speech reveal use of or neglect of good rhetorical (persuasive) principles?
9. Does the speech possess any special literary qualities? Any that may make it worth reading years hence?
10. In what specific ways could the speech be improved?

C. Historical
1. What significant events relating to the subject preceded the speech?
2. What actions, motives, or demands may have prompted the speech?
3. To what principal events does the speaker either refer in his speech or assume a knowledge of by his hearers?
4. Does the speaker seem to state accurately causes and effects?
5. Was the speaker a participant in the policy he prescribes? Does he have a special interest?
6. Does the speaker give an objective account of the events he describes? Or does he "color" or "slant" them to his needs?
7. Who are the principal opponents of the views the speaker expresses? What do they say? What are the true facts?
8. Did the speaker add to or subtract from his reputation by this speech?
9. Does the immediate audience help to explain the way the speaker develops his main ideas?
10. Do the medium of publication and the readership of the speech enhance its acceptance now?

Appendix

D. Editorial

These directions for practice in revision are based upon a student's assignment to rewrite, condense, vivify, and generally improve where possible portions or the whole of the printed text.

1. Read through the speech cutting out unnecessary words, sentences, paragraphs.
2. Reduce the length of sentences over twenty words wherever you can justify it.
3. Reduce the number of sentences in a paragraph when the speaker's meaning will not suffer.
4. Replace with simpler words all words you think would be difficult for a college sophomore to understand.
5. Improve upon the verbs using more specific ones wherever possible.
6. Strike out uncontributing and overworked adjectives.
7. Improve the attention power of the first few sentences.
8. Repair the bridges between main ideas. Get better transitional phrases and sentences.
9. Increase the use of dialogue and direct quotation wherever possible.
10. Increase the frequency of the use of words like "you" and "we" and "our" if the sense permits.
11. Make the examples stand out. Improve the writing after expressions like "for instance," "to cite a specific case," and so forth.
12. Reduce new ideas into familiar examples and familiar terms.
13. When you quote a person make sure your reader knows why he is worth quoting. Identify him and his qualification on the particular subject.
14. Simplify the statistics by comparison if possible.
15. Make good use of restatement for emphasis and clarity.
16. Make sure the reader will know what the speaker wants him to understand, to believe, or to do—in the final paragraphs.
17. Make a final check of punctuation to see that it aids understanding rather than promotes confusion.
18. Are the usual rules of grammar, syntax, and good usage followed?
19. Write a précis of the speech reducing it to one fourth of the original.
20. On what grounds can you justify the changes you have made in the speech either as being better stylistically or more effective rhetorically than the original?

Index of Speakers and Addresses

Acheson, Dean, 85, 154
Ackerman, Edward, 109
Address to the Congress, 146
Address to the Security Council of the United Nations, An, 126
Adenauer, Konrad, 237
America and the Atomic Age, 19
American Medical Association Presidential Inaugural Address, An, 337
Auriol, Vincent, 230
Authentic Revolution, The, 517

Background of Korea, 109
Baldwin, Roger N., 437
Biddle, Francis, 440
Blough, Roy, 271
Bond, Niles, 109
Bunce, Arthur C., 109
Bunche, Ralph J., 452
Bush, Vannevar, 54
Business, Government, and Education, 429

Canham, Erwin D., 517
Carr, Robert, 440
Challenge of Our Time, The, 529
Chang, John M., 109
Chinese-American Friendship, 165
Churchill, Winston S., 3
Citizen's Stake in Academic Freedom, The, 369
Clark, Mark W., 265
Compton, Karl T., 294
Conant, James B., 256
Conn, Jerome, 328

Dawson, William L., 469
Defense of the Free World, The, 54
DiSalle, Michael V., 285

Dorfman, Albert, 328
Douglas, William O., 169
Dulles, John Foster, 175

Edman, Irwin, 480
Einstein, Albert, 58
Eisenhower, Dwight D., 220, 529
Ewing, Oscar R., 350

Faulkner, William, 397
Fischer, Louis, 196
Frank and Candid Light, The, 118
Fulcrum of Western Civilization, The, 77

Gates, Edward D., 472
Gitlow, Benjamin, 202
Goals of Education Are Not Sufficient Today, The, 382
Griswold, A. Whitney, 376
Gustavson, Reuben, 19

Harriman, W. Averell, 245
Hawley, Paul R., 355
Henderson, Elmer L., 337
High School Commencement Address, A, 386
Hoffman, Paul G., 429
How Can Modern Man Find Faith? 480
How Can We Stop Rising Prices? 285
How Communists Make Converts, 202
Hsiu-Chuan, Wu, 126
Hutchins, Robert M., 19, 359

Ideals of American Youth, The, 462
Integration of Europe, The, 237
International Significance of Human Relations, The, 452

559

Index

Interview with a Pravda Correspondent, An, 191
Is Youth Forgetting Religion? 489

Kennan, George F., 80

Labor's Role in Higher Education, 419
LaFarge, John, 506
Lanham, Charles T., 249
Let Us Make Peace, 175
Lie, Trygve, 61
Limb, Ben C., 118

MacArthur, Douglas, 146
Man Thinking, 376
Marshall, George C., 225
McCaffrey, John L., 423
McIntosh, Millicent C., 382
McKay, Hamilton W., 343
Mobilizing America's Strength for World Security, 245
Mobilizing and Training a Citizen Army, 265
Mobilizing for Defense, 281
Moral Core of Military Strength, The, 249
Murray, Philip, 419

National Interest of the United States, The, 80
National Security and Individual Freedom, 440
Need for a Spiritual Revival, The, 495
New Problems, New Philosophers, 391
Newsom, Herschel D., 285
Nikhilananda, Swami, 495
Nuclear Energy Development and Military Technology, 321

Ogburn, William F., 19
On Accepting the Nobel Award, 397
On Assuming Command of the Eighth Army, 138
Organized Labor and Current International Developments, 410

Osborn, Frederick, 211
Oursler, Fulton, 480
Overstreet, Harry A., 391

Pach, Walter, 398
Pardue, Austin, 480
Peace in the Atomic Era, 58
Peace Without Appeasement, 40
Prepayment Plans, 355
Present Crisis and the American Economy, The, 271
Present Danger, The, 256
Preventing a New World War, 140
Price, James Harry, 489

Redfield, Robert, 19
Religious Philosophy and Intergroup Progress, 506
Report from the President of France, A, 230
Report to the Nation, A, 220
Reuther, Walter P., 285
Ridenour, Louis N., 312
Ridgway, Matthew B., 138
Road to Peace, The, 61
Rough Road Ahead, The, 437
Rusk, Dean, 165

Schuman, Frederick L., 40
Science, Technology, and National Security, 312
Scientific Manpower, 317
Segregation in the Armed Forces, 469
Selye, Hans, 328
Smyth, Henry D., 317
Stake of the Arts in the Democratic Way of Life, The, 398
Stalin, Joseph, 191
Statement before the Senate Armed Services Committee and the Senate Foreign Relations Committee, A, 225
State of Science, The, 294
State of the Union, The (1952), 95

Index

Stevenson, Adlai, 440
Stress and Disease, 328

Taft, Robert A., 271
Taylor, Harold, 462
Tensions Between the United States and the Soviet Union, 85
Thomas, E. J., 386
Time Is Running Out, 472
Toynbee, Arnold, 77
Truman, Harry S., 95, 140
Twentieth Century, The—Its Promise and Its Realization, 3

United States Policy Toward Asia, 154
United States, Russia, and the Atomic Bomb, The, 211
Urey, Harold, 440

Velde, Harold H., 196

Weaver, Paul, 489
Weighed in the Balance, 343
Weil, Richard, Jr., 271
Weinberg, Alvin M., 321
What Are the Real Issues in Our Fight Against Communism? 196
What Health Insurance Would Mean to You, 350
What Road to Labor Peace? 423
Where Do We Go from Here in Education? 359
Wilson, Charles E., 281
Woll, Matthew, 410
World in Revolution, A, 169
Wright, Quincy, 369

THE EDITOR of this book, Harold F. Harding, has been a member of the Department of Speech at Ohio State University since 1946. Prior to that time he taught at Iowa State College, Harvard University, Cornell University, and George Washington University. He is a member of the Executive Council of the Speech Association of America and was until recently editor of the *Quarterly Journal of Speech*.

In 1949 he was an adviser to the Student Conference on United States Affairs at West Point. In 1950 he was a member of the Seminar on United States Foreign Policy conducted by the Brookings Institution at Denver. He has been a lecturer at the Army War College and, since 1948, has been a consultant to the Command and General Staff College at Fort Leavenworth, Kansas.